THE OECD CONVENTION ON BRIBERY

The OECD Convention is the first major international treaty specifically to address 'supply-side bribery' by sanctioning the briber. The OECD Convention establishes an international standard for compliance with anti-corruption rules by 36 countries, including the 30 OECD members and six non-member countries, with the leading OECD exporting countries receiving particular attention. This book is an article-by-article commentary which gives particular attention to the results of the OECD monitoring process as applied to state implementation.

Companies in particular are at ever greater risk of legal and 'reputational' damage resulting from failure to comply with the anti-corruption standards, set inter alia, by the OECD Convention. This book provides them with comprehensive guidance on the OECD standards.

The commentary also constitutes a significant work of comparative criminal law. It is written and edited by persons who include experts involved in development of the Convention standards as well as academics and legal practitioners.

MARK PIETH is Professor of Criminal Law at Basel University, chairman of the OECD Working Group on Bribery in International Business Transactions, and member of the Swiss Federal Gaming Commission, chairman of the board of the Basel Institute on Governance and member of the UN Independent Inquiry Committee into the Iraq Oil-for-Food Programme. He was formerly member of Financial Action Task Force (FATF) and head of section of Economic and Organised Crime at the Swiss Ministry of Justice and Police, member of the Chemical Action Task Force on Precursor Chemicals and chairman of the UN Intergovernmental Expert Group Commission to determine the extent of illicit trafficking in drugs. He has published in the fields of economic and organised crime, money laundering, corruption, sentencing and criminal procedure.

LUCINDA A. LOW is a partner at Steptoe & Johnson LLP, Washington DC, with a practice focusing on US and international anti-corruption laws and assisting US and foreign companies with compliance with international business laws and regulations. She is a widely recognised authority on the Foreign Corrupt Practices Act and related international conventions from the OECD, OAS, United Nations, and European Union. In addition to her legal practice in these fields, she has published widely on anti-corruption laws. Ms Low is also a member of the US Secretary of State's Advisory Committee on International Law and a member of the Board of Directors of Transparency International-USA.

PETER J. CULLEN is head of section for European public and criminal law at the Academy of European Law in Trier, Germany. He qualified as a solicitor in Scotland in 1990. From 1990 to 1999, he held the position of Jean Monnet Lecturer in European Community Law at the University of Edinburgh. He has previously published on EU law and German constitutional law.

The OECD Convention on Bribery

A COMMENTARY

A Commentary on the Convention on Combating Bribery of Foreign Public Officials in International Business Transactions of 21 November 1997

Edited by
MARK PIETH, LUCINDA A. LOW AND PETER J. CULLEN

CAMBRIDGE
UNIVERSITY PRESS

CAMBRIDGE UNIVERSITY PRESS
Cambridge, New York, Melbourne, Madrid, Cape Town, Singapore, São Paulo

Cambridge University Press
The Edinburgh Building, Cambridge CB2 8RU, UK

Published in the United States of America by
Cambridge University Press, New York

www.cambridge.org
Information on this title: www.cambridge.org/9780521868174

First published 2007

Printed in the United Kingdom at the University Press, Cambridge

A catalogue record for this publication is available from the British Library

ISBN 978-0-521-86817-4 hardback

CONTENTS

NOTES ON CONTRIBUTORS

AKITA N. ADKINS is an associate at Foley & Lardner LLP, Washington, DC. She is a member of the firm's litigation department and its securities litigation, enforcement and regulation, general commercial litigation and white collar and corporate compliance practice groups. She has experience in anti-bribery investigations under the FCPA. Ms Adkins graduated from the University of Pennsylvania School of Law.

NICOLA BONUCCI is Director for Legal Affairs at the OECD. He advises the Secretary-General of the OECD and the member countries on all legal issues related to the operations of the OECD. Since 1997, Mr Bonucci has been closely involved in the monitoring and follow-up of the OECD anti-bribery Convention. In particular, he has been associated with a number of Phase 1 and Phase 2 evaluations, including the on-site visit of the USA which took place in 2002.

GREGORY S. BRUCH is a partner and chair of the securities litigation, enforcement and regulation practice group at Foley & Lardner LLP, Washington, DC. Mr Bruch also practises with the white collar defense and corporate compliance practice group. Mr Bruch spent twelve years with the Securities and Exchange Commission division of enforcement in Washington, DC. He served as staff attorney, senior counsel, branch chief and, from 1995 to 2001, assistant Director. In that capacity he was involved in prosecution of cases involving the Foreign Corrupt Practices Act. Mr Bruch is also adjunct professor at Georgetown University Law Center.

PETER J. CULLEN is head of section for European public and criminal law at the Academy of European Law in Trier, Germany. He qualified as a solicitor in Scotland in 1990. From 1990 to 1999, he held the position of Jean Monnet Lecturer in European Community Law at the University of Edinburgh. He has previously published on EU law and German constitutional law.

MAURICE HARARI is a partner with the law firm Lachat Harari & Associés in Geneva. Mr Harari also lectures at the University of Fribourg and serves as a Substitute Judge on the Geneva *Cour de Cassation pénale.* He frequently sits as expert on federal and cantonal commissions, most recently on the expert commission which drafted the Swiss law on sharing of the confiscated proceeds of crime. Mr Harari graduated from the Law Faculty of the University of Lausanne and completed his legal education at New York University and Harvard University.

ANNE VALÉRIE JULEN BERTHOD is a Swiss attorney and associate in the Geneva office of Bär & Karrer LLP. She is a member of the firm's litigation department. Ms Julen Berthod graduated with an LLM. from New York University School of Law in 2005. She has worked as a clerk at the Highest Court of the State of Geneva. Her legal experience includes the fields of contract law, white collar crime and international co-operation in criminal matters.

LUCINDA A. LOW is a partner at Steptoe & Johnson LLP, Washington DC, with a practice focusing on US and international anti-corruption laws and assisting US and foreign companies with compliance with international business laws and regulations. She is a widely recognised authority on the Foreign Corrupt Practices Act and related international conventions from the OECD, OAS, United Nations, and European Union. In addition to her legal practice in these fields, she has published widely on anti-corruption laws. Ms Low is also a member of the US Secretary of State's Advisory Committee on International Law and a member of the Board of Directors of Transparency International-USA.

MARK PIETH is Professor of Criminal Law at Basel University, Chairman of the OECD Working Group on Bribery in International Business Transactions, and member of the Swiss Federal Gaming Commission, chairman of the board of the Basel Institute on Governance and member of the UN Independent Inquiry Committee into the Iraq Oil-for-Food Programme. He was formerly member of the Financial Action Task Force (FATF) and head of the Section of Economic and Organised Crime at the Swiss Ministry of Justice and Police, member of the Chemical Action Task Force on Precursor Chemicals and chairman of the UN Intergovernmental Expert Group Commission to determine the extent of illicit trafficking in drugs. He has published in the fields of economic and organised crime, money laundering, corruption, sentencing, and criminal procedure.

INGEBORG ZERBES is Assistant Professor of Criminal Law at the Faculty of Law of the University of Vienna. She co-operates with the Max Planck Institute of Foreign and International Law in Freiburg im Breisgau (section Austria and Switzerland). Dr Zerbes is also grantee of a research award from the Austrian Academy of Science. Her main research concerns European and International criminal law and undercover policing. Dr Zerbes is a graduate of the University of Vienna.

PREFACE

In recent years there has finally been a global awakening to the need to fight corruption in order to promote development and preserve respect for public institutions.

I watched from side-stage when the problem of international corruption first broke in the mid-1970s. I was a practicing lawyer in Canada representing Lockheed Aircraft Corporation in what was then the largest military procurement in Canadian history. Suddenly Lockheed was caught up in scandals related to bribery of foreign public officials in several jurisdictions outside Canada. These scandals gave rise to the U.S. Foreign Corrupt Practices Act, a pioneering effort to curb international bribery and severely penalise the senior management of corporations who engaged in it. (As it turned out, Lockheed was the first to be exposed, but many more followed.)

I am proud that OECD and other countries joined this battle in 1997 with the negotiation of the Convention on Fighting Bribery of Foreign Public Officials in International Business Transactions. This binding treaty obliges signatories to take responsibility for corrupt practices of the companies operating from their territory – wherever in the world they may bribe.

What changed to enable the OECD to draft and conclude a convention against bribery in the late 1990s? The answer is globalisation. In the 1970s, countries still saw themselves as competing with each other, promoting the interests of their companies abroad. Globalisation changed the perception. It was clear that companies, not governments, were the competitors – and they needed a level playing field. During the same period several major bribery scandals in the OECD countries roused public indignation and led to the formation of non-governmental groups like Transparency International which pressed for cleaner government. Since it came into force in 1999, a hallmark of the Convention has been rigorous monitoring of its implementation in law and its enforcement. This has been absolutely necessary since the stakes are so high. The monitoring has demonstrated that the Convention has indeed inspired many positive changes in the legal and law enforcement capacities of the Parties to the Convention. But the monitoring has also shown that many Parties still fall short of fully implementing the Convention and fulfilling their commitment to stop international bribery.

The battle against corruption will last many years. We must not diminish our efforts. I hope that the present book will increase public awareness of the Convention and of what should be expected of the countries that signed it.

MR. DONALD J. JOHNSON, P.C. Q.C.

Secretary General of the OECD (until Spring 2006)

ACKNOWLEDGEMENTS

It has been a great satisfaction after sixteen years as Chairman of the OECD Working Group on Bribery to see through this book on the core piece of our efforts, the OECD 1997 Convention on Corruption.

All contributors, including those such as Nicola Bonucci who have played a central role in the development of OECD anti-corruption standards are, however, intervening in a personal capacity.

These preliminary remarks give me a welcome opportunity to mention that this project would not have been possible without the generous funding of the Swiss National Fund (SNF) and the Freiwillige Akademische Gesellschaft (FAG) in Basel. Furthermore I would like to thank all who have made this critical analysis possible.

First, I would like to thank the authors of the chapters. I am confident that we have been able to strike a fair geographic balance by inviting contributions from the United States (Gregory Bruch, Akita Atkins, and Lucinda Low), the United Kingdom (Peter Cullen) and continental Europe (here again the French and Italian speakers Nicola Bonucci, Maurice Harari, and Anne Valérie Julen Berthod) and the German speakers (Ingeborg Zerbes and Mark Pieth). A further attempt to balance the contributions between academics (Ingeborg Zerbes, Peter Cullen, Mark Pieth) practitioners (Gregory Bruch/ Akita Atkins, Maurice Harari/Anne Valérie Julen Berthod, Lucinda Low) and representatives of institutions (Nicola Bonucci) has proved rather successful.

Second, I would like to thank my co-editors for their support, especially Peter Cullen for donating a sabbatical year from the Academy of European Law (ERA) in Trier for an intensive year on this project. The Academy's Director, Wolfgang Heusel, kindly agreed to Peter's release for this period.

Furthermore, I would like to express my appreciation to all who supported the authors with their preparatory work, namely Christoph

Bloch, Stephanie Eymann, Rebekka Gigon, André Kanyar, Daniel Küpfer, and Giovanna Lanza.

I owe a very special thank you to Denise Berger and the team of proof-readers and correctors, namely, Katrin Aegler, Rebekka Gigon, and Isabelle Gonçalves, who spent at least three months in a final marathon to enable the completion of the text.

Finally, I would like to thank the staff of Cambridge University Press for their professional support.

MARK PIETH
Co-ordinating Editor

OECD texts, national laws and cases have been included in this book up to 31 December 2005.

ABBREVIATIONS

General abbreviations

ADB	Asian Development Bank
AI	Amnesty International
ASEAN	Association of South-East Asian Nations
APG	Asia/Pacific Group on Money Laundering (OECD)
ASIL	American Society of International Law
BCBS	Basel Committee on Banking Supervision
BG	Bundesgericht (Federal Court, Switzerland)
BGE	Bundesgerichtsentscheid (Federal Court Decision, Switzerland)
BGH	Bundesgerichtshof (Federal High Court, Germany)
BIAC	Business Advisory Committee (OECD)
BIS	Bank for International Settlements
BVerfG	Bundesverfassungsgericht (Federal Constitutional Court, Germany)
BVerfGE	Bundesverfassungsgerichtsentscheid (Federal Constitutional Court Decision, Germany)
CATF	Caribbean Action Task Force
CBCA	Canada Business Corporations Act
CDU	Christlich Demokratische Union (Christian Democratic Union) (Germany)
CDD	Customer Due Diligence
CEO	Chief Executive Officer
CFA	Committee on Fiscal Affairs (OECD)
CFO	Chief Financial Officer

CIHEAM	Centre International de Hautes Études Agronomiques Mediterranéennes (International Centre for Advanced Mediterranean Agronomic Studies)
CIME	Committee on Investment and Multinational Enterprises (OECD)
COE	Council of Europe
COSO	Committee of Sponsoring Organizations of the Treadway Committee
CPS	Code for Crown Prosecutors (England and Wales) (see List of Selected Documentation)
DAC	Development Assistance Committee (OECD)
DAFFE	Directorate for Financial, Fiscal, and Enterprise Affairs (OECD)
EC	European Communities
ECGD	Export Credit Guarantee Department (UK)
ECG	Export Credits Group (OECD)
ECOSOC	Economic and Social Council (UN)
ERA	Europäische Rechtsakademie Trier (Academy of European Law Trier)
ESAAMLG	Eastern and Southern African Anti-Money Laundering Group
EU	European Union
FATF	Financial Action Task Force
FCPA	Foreign Corrupt Practices Act (USA)
FIFA	Féderation Internationale de Football Association
FINTRAC	Financial Transactions Reports Analysis Centre of Canada
FIU	Financial Intelligence Unit
FSF	Financial Stability Forum
GAFISUD	Grupo de Acción Financiera Internacional Sudamericano (South American Financial Action Task Force)
GATT	General Agreement on Tariffs and Trade (WTO)
GCA	Global Coalition for Africa
GRECO	Group of States Against Corruption
HRW	Human Rights Watch
IACC	International Anti-Corruption Conference
IBC	International Business Corporation
IAP	International Association of Prosecutors
IAPAC	International Auditing Practices Committee (International Federation of Accountants)
IAS	International Accounting Standards

IBT	International Business Transactions
ICC	International Chamber of Commerce
ICFTU	International Confederation of Free Trade Unions
ICRC	International Committee of the Red Cross
IDRC	International Development Research Centre
IGO	Intergovernmental Organisation
IIC-OFFP	Independent Inquiry Committee into the United Nations Oil-for-Food Programme
ILA	International Law Association
ILC	International Law Commission
IMAC	(Federal Act on) International Mutual Assistance in Criminal Matters (Switzerland)
IMF	International Monetary Fund
IOC	International Olympic Committee
IOSCO	International Organisation of Securities Commissions
IPU	Interparliamentary Union
ISO	International Organization for Standardization
MDB	Multilateral Development Banks
MDP	Ministry of Defence Police (UK)
MENAFATF	Middle East and North Africa Financial Action Task Force
MLA	Mutual Legal Assistance
MLLA	Mutual Legal Assistance Agreements
MLAT	Mutual Legal Assistance Treaties
MNE	Multinational Enterprise
NATO	North Atlantic Treaty Organization
NEPAD	New Partnership for Africa's Development
OAS	Organization of American States
OECD	Organization for Economic Co-operation and Development
OFC	Off-Shore Centre
OI	Oxfam International
OSCE	Organisation for Security and Cooperation in Europe
PACI	Partnering Against Corruption Initiative (WEF)
PEP	Politically Exposed Person
POCA	Proceeds of Crime Act (UK)
POLISARIO	Frente Popular de Liberación de Seguía el Hamra y Río de Oro (Polisario Font)
PUMA	Public Management Group (OECD)
Rn.	Randnummer (marginal number)
SEC	Securities and Exchange Commission (US)
SFO	Serious Fraud Office (UK)

SIDA	Swedish International Development Cooperation Committee
SIGMA	Support for Improvement in Governance and Management
SME	Small and Medium-Sized Enterprise
SPAI	Stability Pact for South-Eastern Europe
TI	Transparency International
TRACE	Transparent Agents and Contraction Entities
TRACFIN	Traitement du Renseignement et Action Contre les Circuits Financiers Clandestins (France)
TRNC	Turkish Republic of Northern Cyprus
TUAC	Trade Union Advisory Committee (OECD)
UN	United Nations
UNESCO	United Nations Educational, Scientific and Cultural Organization
UN ODCCP	United Nations Office for Drug Control and Crime Prevention
UNICORN	Global Unions Anti-Corruption Network
US GAAP	US Generally Accepted Accounting Principles
WCL	World Confederation of Labour
WEF	World Economic Forum
WGB	Working Group on Bribery (OECD)
WTO	World Trade Organisation

Country abbreviations[1]

AR	Argentina
AU	Australia
AT	Austria
BE	Belgium
BG	Bulgaria
BR	Brazil
CA	Canada
CH	Switzerland
CL	Chile
CZ	Czech Republic
DE	Germany
DK	Denmark

[1] Based on the list of the International Organization for Standardization (ISO).

EE	Estonia
ES	Spain
FI	Finland
FR	France
GR	Greece
HU	Hungary
IE	Ireland
IS	Iceland
IT	Italy
JP	Japan
KR	Korea, Republic of
LU	Luxembourg
MX	Mexico
NL	Netherlands
NO	Norway
NZ	New Zealand
PL	Poland
PT	Portugal
SE	Sweden
SI	Slovenia
SK	Slovakia
TR	Turkey
UK	United Kingdom
US	United States

CONVENTION ON COMBATING BRIBERY OF FOREIGN PUBLIC OFFICIALS IN INTERNATIONAL BUSINESS TRANSACTIONS

Adopted by the Negotiating Conference on 21 November 1997

Preamble

The Parties,

Considering that bribery is a widespread phenomenon in international business transactions, including trade and investment, which raises serious moral and political concerns, undermines good governance and economic development, and distorts international competitive conditions;

Considering that all countries share a responsibility to combat bribery in international business transactions;

Having regard to the Revised Recommendation on Combating Bribery in International Business Transactions, adopted by the Council of the Organisation for Economic Co-operation and Development (OECD) on 23 May 1997, C(97)123/FINAL, which, *inter alia*, called for effective measures to deter, prevent and combat the bribery of foreign public officials in connection with international business transactions, in particular the prompt criminalisation of such bribery in an effective and co-ordinated manner and in conformity with the agreed common elements set out in that Recommendation and with the jurisdictional and other basic legal principles of each country;

Welcoming other recent developments which further advance international understanding and co-operation in combating bribery of public officials, including actions of the United Nations, the World Bank, the International Monetary Fund, the World Trade Organisation, the Organisation of American States, the Council of Europe and the European Union;

Welcoming the efforts of companies, business organisations and trade unions as well as other non-governmental organisations to combat bribery;

Recognising the role of governments in the prevention of solicitation of bribes from individuals and enterprises in international business transactions;

Recognising that achieving progress in this field requires not only efforts on a national level but also multilateral co-operation, monitoring and follow-up;

Recognising that achieving equivalence among the measures to be taken by the Parties is an essential object and purpose of the Convention, which requires that the Convention be ratified without derogations affecting this equivalence;

Have agreed as follows:

Article 1
The Offence of Bribery of Foreign Public Officials

1. Each Party shall take such measures as may be necessary to establish that it is a criminal offence under its law for any person intentionally to offer, promise or give any undue pecuniary or other advantage, whether directly or through intermediaries, to a foreign public official, for that official or for a third party, in order that the official act or refrain from acting in relation to the performance of official duties, in order to obtain or retain business or other improper advantage in the conduct of international business.

2. Each Party shall take any measures necessary to establish that complicity in, including incitement, aiding and abetting, or authorisation of an act of bribery of a foreign public official shall be a criminal offence. Attempt and conspiracy to bribe a foreign public official shall be criminal offences to the same extent as attempt and conspiracy to bribe a public official of that Party.

3. The offences set out in paragraphs 1 and 2 above are hereinafter referred to as "bribery of a foreign public official".

4. For the purpose of this Convention:

   a. "foreign public official" means any person holding a legislative, administrative or judicial office of a foreign country, whether appointed or elected; any person exercising a public function for a foreign country, including for a public agency or public enterprise; and any official or agent of a public international organisation;
   b. "foreign country" includes all levels and subdivisions of government, from national to local;
   c. "act or refrain from acting in relation to the performance of official duties" includes any use of the public official's position, whether or not within the official's authorised competence.

Article 2
Responsibility of Legal Persons

Each Party shall take such measures as may be necessary, in accordance with its legal principles, to establish the liability of legal persons for the bribery of a foreign public official.

Article 3
Sanctions

1. The bribery of a foreign public official shall be punishable by effective, proportionate and dissuasive criminal penalties. The range of penalties shall be comparable to that applicable to the bribery of the Party's own public officials and shall, in the case of natural persons, include deprivation of liberty sufficient to enable effective mutual legal assistance and extradition.

2. In the event that, under the legal system of a Party, criminal responsibility is not applicable to legal persons, that Party shall ensure that legal persons shall be subject to effective, proportionate and dissuasive non-criminal sanctions, including monetary sanctions, for bribery of foreign public officials.

3. Each Party shall take such measures as may be necessary to provide that the bribe and the proceeds of the bribery of a foreign public official, or property the value of which corresponds to that of such proceeds, are subject to seizure and confiscation or that monetary sanctions of comparable effect are applicable.

4. Each Party shall consider the imposition of additional civil or administrative sanctions upon a person subject to sanctions for the bribery of a foreign public official.

Article 4
Jurisdiction

1. Each Party shall take such measures as may be necessary to establish its jurisdiction over the bribery of a foreign public official when the offence is committed in whole or in part in its territory.

2. Each Party which has jurisdiction to prosecute its nationals for offences committed abroad shall take such measures as may be necessary to establish its jurisdiction to do so in respect of the bribery of a foreign public official, according to the same principles.

3. When more than one Party has jurisdiction over an alleged offence described in this Convention, the Parties involved shall, at the request of one of them, consult with a view to determining the most appropriate jurisdiction for prosecution.

4. Each Party shall review whether its current basis for jurisdiction is effective in the fight against the bribery of foreign public officials and, if it is not, shall take remedial steps.

Article 5
Enforcement

Investigation and prosecution of the bribery of a foreign public official shall be subject to the applicable rules and principles of each Party. They shall not be influenced by considerations of national economic interest, the potential effect upon relations with another State or the identity of the natural or legal persons involved.

Article 6
Statute of Limitations

Any statute of limitations applicable to the offence of bribery of a foreign public official shall allow an adequate period of time for the investigation and prosecution of this offence.

Article 7
Money Laundering

Each Party which has made bribery of its own public official a predicate offence for the purpose of the application of its money laundering legislation shall do so on the same terms for the bribery of a foreign public official, without regard to the place where the bribery occurred.

Article 8
Accounting

1. In order to combat bribery of foreign public officials effectively, each Party shall take such measures as may be necessary, within the framework of its laws and regulations regarding the maintenance of books and records, financial statement disclosures, and accounting and auditing standards, to prohibit the establishment of off-the-books accounts, the making of off-the-books or inadequately identified transactions, the recording of non-existent expenditures, the entry of liabilities with incorrect identification of their object, as well as the use of false documents, by companies subject to those laws and regulations, for the purpose of bribing foreign public officials or of hiding such bribery.

2. Each Party shall provide effective, proportionate and dissuasive civil, administrative or criminal penalties for such omissions and falsifications in respect of the books, records, accounts and financial statements of such companies.

Article 9
Mutual Legal Assistance

1. Each Party shall, to the fullest extent possible under its laws and relevant treaties and arrangements, provide prompt and effective legal assistance to

another Party for the purpose of criminal investigations and proceedings brought by a Party concerning offences within the scope of this Convention and for non-criminal proceedings within the scope of this Convention brought by a Party against a legal person. The requested Party shall inform the requesting Party, without delay, of any additional information or documents needed to support the request for assistance and, where requested, of the status and outcome of the request for assistance.

2. Where a Party makes mutual legal assistance conditional upon the existence of dual criminality, dual criminality shall be deemed to exist if the offence for which the assistance is sought is within the scope of this Convention.

3. A Party shall not decline to render mutual legal assistance for criminal matters within the scope of this Convention on the ground of bank secrecy.

Article 10
Extradition

1. Bribery of a foreign public official shall be deemed to be included as an extraditable offence under the laws of the Parties and the extradition treaties between them.

2. If a Party which makes extradition conditional on the existence of an extradition treaty receives a request for extradition from another Party with which it has no extradition treaty, it may consider this Convention to be the legal basis for extradition in respect of the offence of bribery of a foreign public official.

3. Each Party shall take any measures necessary to assure either that it can extradite its nationals or that it can prosecute its nationals for the offence of bribery of a foreign public official. A Party which declines a request to extradite a person for bribery of a foreign public official solely on the ground that the person is its national shall submit the case to its competent authorities for the purpose of prosecution.

4. Extradition for bribery of a foreign public official is subject to the conditions set out in the domestic law and applicable treaties and arrangements of each Party. Where a Party makes extradition conditional upon the existence of dual criminality, that condition shall be deemed to be fulfilled if the offence for which extradition is sought is within the scope of Article 1 of this Convention.

Article 11
Responsible Authorities

For the purposes of Article 4, paragraph 3, on consultation, Article 9, on mutual legal assistance and Article 10, on extradition, each Party shall notify to the Secretary-General of the OECD an authority or authorities responsible for making and receiving requests, which shall serve as channel of communication for these matters for that Party, without prejudice to other arrangements between Parties.

Article 12
Monitoring and Follow-up

The Parties shall co-operate in carrying out a programme of systematic follow-up to monitor and promote the full implementation of this Convention. Unless otherwise decided by consensus of the Parties, this shall be done in the framework of the OECD Working Group on Bribery in International Business Transactions and according to its terms of reference, or within the framework and terms of reference of any successor to its functions, and Parties shall bear the costs of the programme in accordance with the rules applicable to that body.

Article 13
Signature and Accession

1. Until its entry into force, this Convention shall be open for signature by OECD members and by non-members which have been invited to become full participants in its Working Group on Bribery in International Business Transactions.

2. Subsequent to its entry into force, this Convention shall be open to accession by any non-signatory which is a member of the OECD or has become a full participant in the Working Group on Bribery in International Business Transactions or any successor to its functions. For each such non-signatory, the Convention shall enter into force on the sixtieth day following the date of deposit of its instrument of accession.

Article 14
Ratification and Depositary

1. This Convention is subject to acceptance, approval or ratification by the Signatories, in accordance with their respective laws.

2. Instruments of acceptance, approval, ratification or accession shall be deposited with the Secretary-General of the OECD, who shall serve as Depositary of this Convention.

Article 15
Entry into Force

1. This Convention shall enter into force on the sixtieth day following the date upon which five of the ten countries which have the ten largest export shares set out in DAFFE/IME/BR(97)18/FINAL (annexed), and which represent by themselves at least sixty per cent of the combined total exports of those ten

countries, have deposited their instruments of acceptance, approval, or ratification. For each signatory depositing its instrument after such entry into force, the Convention shall enter into force on the sixtieth day after deposit of its instrument.

2. If, after 31 December 1998, the Convention has not entered into force under paragraph 1 above, any signatory which has deposited its instrument of acceptance, approval or ratification may declare in writing to the Depositary its readiness to accept entry into force of this Convention under this paragraph 2. The Convention shall enter into force for such a signatory on the sixtieth day following the date upon which such declarations have been deposited by at least two signatories. For each signatory depositing its declaration after such entry into force, the Convention shall enter into force on the sixtieth day following the date of deposit.

Article 16
Amendment

Any Party may propose the amendment of this Convention. A proposed amendment shall be submitted to the Depositary which shall communicate it to the other Parties at least sixty days before convening a meeting of the Parties to consider the proposed amendment. An amendment adopted by consensus of the Parties, or by such other means as the Parties may determine by consensus, shall enter into force sixty days after the deposit of an instrument of ratification, acceptance or approval by all of the Parties, or in such other circumstances as may be specified by the Parties at the time of adoption of the amendment.

Article 17
Withdrawal

A Party may withdraw from this Convention by submitting written notification to the Depositary. Such withdrawal shall be effective one year after the date of the receipt of the notification. After withdrawal, co-operation shall continue between the Parties and the Party which has withdrawn on all requests for assistance or extradition made before the effective date of withdrawal which remain pending.

Annex
Statistics on OECD Exports

	OECD EXPORTS		
	1990–1996 US$ million	1990–1996 % Of Total OECD	1990–1996 % Of 10 largest
United States	287 118	15,9%	19,7%
Germany	254 746	14,1%	17,5%
Japan	212 665	11,8%	14,6%
France	138 471	7,7%	9,5%
United Kingdom	121 258	6,7%	8,3%
Italy	112 449	6,2%	7,7%
Canada	91 215	5,1%	6,3%
Korea (1)	81 364	4,5%	5,6%
Netherlands	81 264	4,5%	5,6%
Belgium-Luxembourg	78 598	4,4%	5,4%
Total 10 largest	**1 459 148**	**81,0%**	**100%**
Spain	42 469	2,4%	
Switzerland	40 395	2,2%	
Sweden	36 710	2,0%	
Mexico (1)	34 233	1,9%	
Australia	27 194	1,5%	
Denmark	24 145	1,3%	
Austria*	22 432	1,2%	
Norway	21 666	1,2%	
Ireland	19 217	1,1%	
Finland	17 296	1,0%	
Poland (1)**	12 652	0,7%	
Portugal	10 801	0,6%	
Turkey*	8 027	0,4%	
Hungary**	6 795	0,4%	
New Zealand	6 663	0,4%	
Czech Republic***	6 263	0,3%	
Greece*	4 606	0,3%	
Iceland	949	0,1%	
Total OECD	**1 801 661**	**100%**	

Note: *1990–1995; **1991–1996; ***1993–1996

Source: OECD, (1) IMF

Concerning Belgium-Luxembourg: Trade statistics for Belgium and Luxembourg are available only on a combined basis for the two countries. For purposes of Article 15, paragraph 1 of the Convention, if either Belgium or Luxembourg deposits its instrument of acceptance, approval or ratification, or if both Belgium and Luxembourg deposit their instruments of acceptance, approval, or ratification, it shall be considered that one of the countries which have the ten largest exports shares has deposited its instrument and the joint exports of both countries will be counted towards the 60 percent of combined total exports of those ten countries, which is required for entry into force under this provision.

COMMENTARIES ON THE CONVENTION ON COMBATING BRIBERY OF FOREIGN PUBLIC OFFICIALS IN INTERNATIONAL BUSINESS TRANSACTIONS

Adopted by the Negotiating Conference on 21 November 1997

General:

1. This Convention deals with what, in the law of some countries, is called "active corruption" or "active bribery", meaning the offence committed by the person who promises or gives the bribe, as contrasted with "passive bribery", the offence committed by the official who receives the bribe. The Convention does not utilise the term "active bribery" simply to avoid it being misread by the non-technical reader as implying that the briber has taken the initiative and the recipient is a passive victim. In fact, in a number of situations, the recipient will have induced or pressured the briber and will have been, in that sense, the more active.

2. This Convention seeks to assure a functional equivalence among the measures taken by the Parties to sanction bribery of foreign public officials, without requiring uniformity or changes in fundamental principles of a Party's legal system.

Article 1. The Offence of Bribery of Foreign Public Officials:

Re paragraph 1:

3. Article 1 establishes a standard to be met by Parties, but does not require them to utilise its precise terms in defining the offence under their domestic laws. A Party may use various approaches to fulfil its obligations, provided that conviction of a person for the offence does not require proof of elements beyond those which would be required to be proved if the offence were defined as in this paragraph. For example, a statute prohibiting the bribery of agents generally which does not specifically address bribery of a foreign public official, and a statute specifically limited to this case, could both comply with this Article.

Similarly, a statute which defined the offence in terms of payments "to induce a breach of the official's duty" could meet the standard provided that it was understood that every public official had a duty to exercise judgement or discretion impartially and this was an "autonomous" definition not requiring proof of the law of the particular official's country.

4. It is an offence within the meaning of paragraph 1 to bribe to obtain or retain business or other improper advantage whether or not the company concerned was the best qualified bidder or was otherwise a company which could properly have been awarded the business.

5. "Other improper advantage" refers to something to which the company concerned was not clearly entitled, for example, an operating permit for a factory which fails to meet the statutory requirements.

6. The conduct described in paragraph 1 is an offence whether the offer or promise is made or the pecuniary or other advantage is given on that person's own behalf or on behalf of any other natural person or legal entity.

7. It is also an offence irrespective of, inter alia, the value of the advantage, its results, perceptions of local custom, the tolerance of such payments by local authorities, or the alleged necessity of the payment in order to obtain or retain business or other improper advantage.

8. It is not an offence, however, if the advantage was permitted or required by the written law or regulation of the foreign public official's country, including case law.

9. Small "facilitation" payments do not constitute payments made "to obtain or retain business or other improper advantage" within the meaning of paragraph 1 and, accordingly, are also not an offence. Such payments, which, in some countries, are made to induce public officials to perform their functions, such as issuing licenses or permits, are generally illegal in the foreign country concerned. Other countries can and should address this corrosive phenomenon by such means as support for programmes of good governance. However, criminalisation by other countries does not seem a practical or effective complementary action.

10. Under the legal system of some countries, an advantage promised or given to any person, in anticipation of his or her becoming a foreign public official, falls within the scope of the offences described in Article 1, paragraph 1 or 2. Under the legal system of many countries, it is considered technically distinct from the offences covered by the present Convention. However, there is a commonly shared concern and intent to address this phenomenon through further work.

Re paragraph 2:

11. The offences set out in paragraph 2 are understood in terms of their normal content in national legal systems. Accordingly, if authorisation, incitement, or one of the other listed acts, which does not lead to further action, is not itself punishable under a Party's legal system, then the Party would not be required to make it punishable with respect to bribery of a foreign public official.

Re paragraph 4:

12. "Public function" includes any activity in the public interest, delegated by a foreign country, such as the performance of a task delegated by it in connection with public procurement.

13. A "public agency" is an entity constituted under public law to carry out specific tasks in the public interest.

14. A "public enterprise" is any enterprise, regardless of its legal form, over which a government, or governments, may, directly or indirectly, exercise a dominant influence. This is deemed to be the case, inter alia, when the government or governments hold the majority of the enterprise's subscribed capital, control the majority of votes attaching to shares issued by the enterprise or can appoint a majority of the members of the enterprise's administrative or managerial body or supervisory board.

15. An official of a public enterprise shall be deemed to perform a public function unless the enterprise operates on a normal commercial basis in the relevant market, i.e., on a basis which is substantially equivalent to that of a private enterprise, without preferential subsidies or other privileges.

16. In special circumstances, public authority may in fact be held by persons (e.g., political party officials in single party states) not formally designated as public officials. Such persons, through their de facto performance of a public function, may, under the legal principles of some countries, be considered to be foreign public officials.

17. "Public international organisation" includes any international organisation formed by states, governments, or other public international organisations, whatever the form of organisation and scope of competence, including, for example, a regional economic integration organisation such as the European Communities.

18. "Foreign country" is not limited to states, but includes any organised foreign area or entity, such as an autonomous territory or a separate customs territory.

19. One case of bribery which has been contemplated under the definition in paragraph 4.c is where an executive of a company gives a bribe to a senior official of a government, in order that this official use his office – though acting outside his competence – to make another official award a contract to that company.

Article 2. Responsibility of Legal Persons:

20. In the event that, under the legal system of a Party, criminal responsibility is not applicable to legal persons, that Party shall not be required to establish such criminal responsibility.

Article 3. Sanctions:

Re paragraph 3:

21. The "proceeds" of bribery are the profits or other benefits derived by the briber from the transaction or other improper advantage obtained or retained through bribery.

22. The term "confiscation" includes forfeiture where applicable and means the permanent deprivation of property by order of a court or other competent authority. This paragraph is without prejudice to rights of victims.

23. Paragraph 3 does not preclude setting appropriate limits to monetary sanctions.

Re paragraph 4:

24. Among the civil or administrative sanctions, other than non-criminal fines, which might be imposed upon legal persons for an act of bribery of a foreign public official are: exclusion from entitlement to public benefits or aid; temporary or permanent disqualification from participation in public procurement or from the practice of other commercial activities; placing under judicial supervision; and a judicial winding-up order.

Article 4. Jurisdiction:

Re paragraph 1:

25. The territorial basis for jurisdiction should be interpreted broadly so that an extensive physical connection to the bribery act is not required.

Re paragraph 2:

26. Nationality jurisdiction is to be established according to the general principles and conditions in the legal system of each Party. These principles deal with such matters as dual criminality. However, the requirement of dual criminality should be deemed to be met if the act is unlawful where it occurred, even if under a different criminal statute. For countries which apply nationality jurisdiction only to certain types of offences, the reference to "principles" includes the principles upon which such selection is based.

Article 5. Enforcement:

27. Article 5 recognises the fundamental nature of national regimes of prosecutorial discretion. It recognises as well that, in order to protect the independence of prosecution, such discretion is to be exercised on the basis of professional motives and is not to be subject to improper influence by concerns of a political nature. Article 5 is complemented by paragraph 6 of the Annex to the 1997 OECD Revised Recommendation on Combating Bribery in International Business Transactions, C(97)123/FINAL (hereinafter, "1997 OECD Recommendation"), which recommends, inter alia, that complaints of bribery of foreign public officials should be seriously investigated by competent authorities and that adequate resources should be provided by national governments to permit effective prosecution of such bribery. Parties will have accepted this Recommendation, including its monitoring and follow-up arrangements.

Article 7. Money Laundering:

28. In Article 7, "bribery of its own public official" is intended broadly, so that bribery of a foreign public official is to be made a predicate offence for money laundering legislation on the same terms, when a Party has made either active or passive bribery of its own public official such an offence. When a Party has made only passive bribery of its own public officials a predicate offence for money laundering purposes, this article requires that the laundering of the bribe payment be subject to money laundering legislation.

Article 8. Accounting:

29. Article 8 is related to section V of the 1997 OECD Recommendation, which all Parties will have accepted and which is subject to follow-up in the OECD Working Group on Bribery in International Business Transactions. This paragraph contains a series of recommendations concerning accounting requirements, independent external audit and internal company controls the implementation of which will be important to the overall effectiveness of the fight against bribery in international business. However, one immediate consequence of the implementation of this Convention by the Parties will be that companies which are required to issue financial statements disclosing their material contingent liabilities will need to take into account the full potential liabilities under this Convention, in particular its Articles 3 and 8, as well as other losses which might flow from conviction of the company or its agents for bribery. This also has implications for the execution of professional responsibilities of auditors regarding indications of bribery of foreign public officials. In addition, the accounting offences referred to in Article 8 will generally occur in the company's home country, when the bribery offence itself may have been committed in another country, and this can fill gaps in the effective reach of the Convention.

Article 9. Mutual Legal Assistance:

30. Parties will have also accepted, through paragraph 8 of the Agreed Common Elements annexed to the 1997 OECD Recommendation, to explore and undertake means to improve the efficiency of mutual legal assistance.

Re paragraph 1:

31. Within the framework of paragraph 1 of Article 9, Parties should, upon request, facilitate or encourage the presence or availability of persons, including persons in custody, who consent to assist in investigations or participate in proceedings. Parties should take measures to be able, in appropriate cases, to transfer temporarily such a person in custody to a Party requesting it and to credit time in custody in the requesting Party to the transferred person's sentence in the requested Party. The Parties wishing to use this mechanism should also take

measures to be able, as a requesting Party, to keep a transferred person in custody and return this person without necessity of extradition proceedings.

Re paragraph 2:

32. Paragraph 2 addresses the issue of identity of norms in the concept of dual criminality. Parties with statutes as diverse as a statute prohibiting the bribery of agents generally and a statute directed specifically at bribery of foreign public officials should be able to co-operate fully regarding cases whose facts fall within the scope of the offences described in this Convention.

Article 10. Extradition:

Re paragraph 2:

33. A Party may consider this Convention to be a legal basis for extradition if, for one or more categories of cases falling within this Convention, it requires an extradition treaty. For example, a country may consider it a basis for extradition of its nationals if it requires an extradition treaty for that category but does not require one for extradition of non-nationals.

Article 12. Monitoring and Follow-up:

34. The current terms of reference of the OECD Working Group on Bribery which are relevant to monitoring and follow-up are set out in Section VIII of the 1997 OECD Recommendation. They provide for:

i) receipt of notifications and other information submitted to it by the [participating] countries;

ii) regular reviews of steps taken by [participating] countries to implement the Recommendation and to make proposals, as appropriate, to assist [participating] countries in its implementation; these reviews will be based on the following complementary systems:
   - a system of self evaluation, where [participating] countries' responses on the basis of a questionnaire will provide a basis for assessing the implementation of the Recommendation;
   - a system of mutual evaluation, where each [participating] country will be examined in turn by the Working Group on Bribery, on the basis of a report which will provide an objective assessment of the progress of the [participating] country in implementing the Recommendation.

iii) examination of specific issues relating to bribery in international business transactions;

iv) . . .

v) provision of regular information to the public on its work and activities and on implementation of the Recommendation.

35. The costs of monitoring and follow-up will, for OECD Members, be handled through the normal OECD budget process. For non-members of the OECD, the

current rules create an equivalent system of cost sharing, which is described in the Resolution of the Council Concerning Fees for Regular Observer Countries and Non-Member Full Participants in OECD Subsidiary Bodies, C(96)223/FINAL.

36. The follow-up of any aspect of the Convention which is not also follow-up of the 1997 OECD Recommendation or any other instrument accepted by all the participants in the OECD Working Group on Bribery will be carried out by the Parties to the Convention and, as appropriate, the participants party to another, corresponding instrument.

Article 13. Signature and Accession:

37. The Convention will be open to non-members which become full participants in the OECD Working Group on Bribery in International Business Transactions. Full participation by non-members in this Working Group is encouraged and arranged under simple procedures. Accordingly, the requirement of full participation in the Working Group, which follows from the relationship of the Convention to other aspects of the fight against bribery in international business, should not be seen as an obstacle by countries wishing to participate in that fight. The Council of the OECD has appealed to non-members to adhere to the 1997 OECD Recommendation and to participate in any institutional follow-up or implementation mechanism, i.e., in the Working Group. The current procedures regarding full participation by non-members in the Working Group may be found in the Resolution of the Council concerning the Participation of Non-Member Economies in the Work of Subsidiary Bodies of the Organisation, C(96)64/REV1/FINAL. In addition to accepting the Revised Recommendation of the Council on Combating Bribery, a full participant also accepts the Recommendation on the Tax Deductibility of Bribes of Foreign Public Officials, adopted on 11 April 1996, C(96)27/FINAL.

REVISED RECOMMENDATION OF THE COUNCIL ON COMBATING BRIBERY IN INTERNATIONAL BUSINESS TRANSACTIONS

Adopted by the Council on 23 May 1997

THE COUNCIL,

Having regard to Articles 3, 5a) and 5 b) of the Convention on the Organisation for Economic Co-operation and Development of 14 December 1960;

Considering that bribery is a widespread phenomenon in international business transactions, including trade and investment, raising serious moral and political concerns and distorting international competitive conditions;

Considering that all countries share a responsibility to combat bribery in international business transactions;

Considering that enterprises should refrain from bribery of public servants and holders of public office, as stated in the OECD Guidelines for Multinational Enterprises;

Considering the progress which has been made in the implementation of the initial Recommendation of the Council on Bribery in International Business Transactions adopted on 27 May 1994, C(94)75/FINAL and the related Recommendation on the tax deductibility of bribes of foreign public officials adopted on 11 April 1996, C(96)27/FINAL; as well as the Recommendation concerning Anti-corruption Proposals for Bilateral Aid Procurement, endorsed by the High Level Meeting of the Development Assistance Committee on 7 May 1996;

Welcoming other recent developments which further advance international understanding and co-operation regarding bribery in business transactions, including actions of the United Nations, the Council of Europe, the European Union and the Organisation of American States;

Having regard to the commitment made at the meeting of the Council at Ministerial level in May 1996, to criminalise the bribery of foreign public officials in an effective and co-ordinated manner;

Noting that an international convention in conformity with the agreed common elements set forth in the Annex, is an appropriate instrument to attain such criminalisation rapidly.

Considering the consensus which has developed on the measures which should be taken to implement the 1994 Recommendation, in particular, with respect to the modalities and international instruments to facilitate criminalisation of bribery of foreign public officials; tax deductibility of bribes to foreign public officials; accounting requirements, external audit and internal company controls; and rules and regulations on public procurement;

Recognising that achieving progress in this field requires not only efforts by individual countries but multilateral co-operation, monitoring and follow-up;

General

I. **RECOMMENDS** that Member countries take effective measures to deter, prevent and combat the bribery of foreign public officials in connection with international business transactions.

II. **RECOMMENDS** that each Member country examine the following areas and, in conformity with its jurisdictional and other basic legal principles, take concrete and meaningful steps to meet this goal:

i) criminal laws and their application, in accordance with section III and the Annex to this Recommendation;
ii) tax legislation, regulations and practice, to eliminate any indirect support of bribery, in accordance with section IV;
iii) company and business accounting, external audit and internal control requirements and practices, in accordance with section V;
iv) banking, financial and other relevant provisions, to ensure that adequate records would be kept and made available for inspection and investigation;
v) public subsidies, licences, government procurement contracts, or other public advantages, so that advantages could be denied as a sanction for bribery in appropriate cases, and in accordance with section VI for procurement contracts and aid procurement;
vi) civil, commercial, and administrative laws and regulations, so that such bribery would be illegal;
vii) international co-operation in investigations and other legal proceedings, in accordance with section VII.

Criminalisation of Bribery of Foreign Public Officials

III. **RECOMMENDS** that Member countries should criminalise the bribery of foreign public officials in an effective and co-ordinated manner by submitting proposals to their legislative bodies by 1 April 1998, in conformity with the agreed common elements set forth in the Annex, and seeking their enactment by the end of 1998.

DECIDES, to this end, to open negotiations promptly on an international convention to criminalise bribery in conformity with the agreed common elements, the treaty to be open for signature by the end of 1997, with a view to its entry into force twelve months thereafter.

Tax Deductibility

IV. **URGES** the prompt implementation by Member countries of the 1996 Recommendation which reads as follows: "that those Member countries which do not disallow the deductibility of bribes to foreign public officials re-examine such treatment with the intention of denying this deductibility. Such action may be facilitated by the trend to treat bribes to foreign officials as illegal."

Accounting Requirements, External Audit and Internal Company Controls

V. **RECOMMENDS** that Member countries take the steps necessary so that laws, rules and practices with respect to accounting requirements, external audit and internal company controls are in line with the following principles and are fully used in order to prevent and detect bribery of foreign public officials in international business.

A. Adequate accounting requirements
   i) Member countries should require companies to maintain adequate records of the sums of money received and expended by the company, identifying the matters in respect of which the receipt and expenditure takes place. Companies should be prohibited from making off-the-books transactions or keeping off-the-books accounts.
   ii) Member countries should require companies to disclose in their financial statements the full range of material contingent liabilities.
   iii) Member countries should adequately sanction accounting omissions, falsifications and fraud.

B. Independent External Audit
   i) Member countries should consider whether requirements to submit to external audit are adequate.
   ii) Member countries and professional associations should maintain adequate standards to ensure the independence of external auditors which permits them to provide an objective assessment of company accounts, financial statements and internal controls.
   iii) Member countries should require the auditor who discovers indications of a possible illegal act of bribery to report this discovery to management and, as appropriate, to corporate monitoring bodies.

iv) Member countries should consider requiring the auditor to report indications of a possible illegal act of bribery to competent authorities.

C. Internal company controls

i) Member countries should encourage the development and adoption of adequate internal company controls, including standards of conduct.

ii) Member countries should encourage company management to make statements in their annual reports about their internal control mechanisms, including those which contribute to preventing bribery.

iii) Member countries should encourage the creation of monitoring bodies, independent of management, such as audit committees of boards of directors or of supervisory boards.

iv) Member countries should encourage companies to provide channels for communication by, and protection for, persons not willing to violate professional standards or ethics under instructions or pressure from hierarchical superiors.

Public procurement

VI. RECOMMENDS:

i) Member countries should support the efforts in the World Trade Organisation to pursue an agreement on transparency in government procurement;

ii) Member countries' laws and regulations should permit authorities to suspend from competition for public contracts enterprises determined to have bribed foreign public officials in contravention of that Member's national laws and, to the extent a Member applies procurement sanctions to enterprises that are determined to have bribed domestic public officials, such sanctions should be applied equally in case of bribery of foreign public officials.[1]

iii) In accordance with the Recommendation of the Development Assistance Committee, Member countries should require anti-corruption provisions in bilateral aid-funded procurement, promote the proper implementation of anti-corruption provisions in international development institutions, and work closely with development partners to combat corruption in all development co-operation efforts.[2]

[1] Member countries' systems for applying sanctions for bribery of domestic officials differ as to whether the determination of bribery is based on a criminal conviction, indictment, or administrative procedure, but in all cases it is based on substantial evidence.

[2] This paragraph summarises the DAC recommendation, which is addressed to DAC members only, and addresses it to all OECD Members and eventually non-member countries which adhere to the Recommendation.

International Co-operation

VII. RECOMMENDS that Member countries, in order to combat bribery in international business transactions, in conformity with their jurisdictional and other basic legal principles, take the following actions:

i) consult and otherwise co-operate with appropriate authorities in other countries in investigations and other legal proceedings concerning specific cases of such bribery through such means as sharing of information (spontaneously or upon request), provision of evidence and extradition;
ii) make full use of existing agreements and arrangements for mutual international legal assistance and where necessary, enter into new agreements or arrangements for this purpose;
iii) ensure that their national laws afford an adequate basis for this co-operation and, in particular, in accordance with paragraph 8 of the Annex.

Follow-up and institutional arrangements

VIII. INSTRUCTS the Committee on International Investment and Multinational Enterprises, through its Working Group on Bribery in International Business Transactions, to carry out a programme of systematic follow-up to monitor and promote the full implementation of this Recommendation, in co-operation with the Committee for Fiscal Affairs, the Development Assistance Committee and other OECD bodies, as appropriate. This follow-up will include, in particular:

i) receipt of notifications and other information submitted to it by the Member countries;
ii) regular reviews of steps taken by Member countries to implement the Recommendation and to make proposals, as appropriate, to assist Member countries in its implementation; these reviews will be based on the following complementary systems:
   - a system of self-evaluation, where Member countries' responses on the basis of a questionnaire will provide a basis for assessing the implementation of the Recommendation;
   - a system of mutual evaluation, where each Member country will be examined in turn by the Working Group on Bribery, on the basis of a report which will provide an objective assessment of the progress of the Member country in implementing the Recommendation.
iii) examination of specific issues relating to bribery in international business transactions;
iv) examination of the feasibility of broadening the scope of the work of the OECD to combat international bribery to include private sector bribery

and bribery of foreign officials for reasons other than to obtain or retain business;

v) provision of regular information to the public on its work and activities and on implementation of the Recommendation.

IX. NOTES the obligation of Member countries to co-operate closely in this follow-up programme, pursuant to Article 3 of the OECD Convention.

X. INSTRUCTS the Committee on International Investment and Multinational Enterprises to review the implementation of Sections III and, in co-operation with the Committee on Fiscal Affairs, Section IV of this Recommendation and report to Ministers in Spring 1998, to report to the Council after the first regular review and as appropriate there after, and to review this Revised Recommendation within three years after its adoption.

Co-operation with non members

XI. APPEALS to non-member countries to adhere to the Recommendation and participate in any institutional follow-up or implementation mechanism.

XII. INSTRUCTS the Committee on International Investment and Multinational Enterprises through its Working Group on Bribery, to provide a forum for consultations with countries which have not yet adhered, in order to promote wider participation in the Recommendation and its follow-up.

Relations with international governmental and non-governmental organisations

XIII. INVITES the Committee on International Investment and Multinational Enterprises through its Working Group on Bribery, to consult and co-operate with the international organisations and international financial institutions active in the combat against bribery in international business transactions and consult regularly with the non-governmental organisations and representatives of the business community active in this field.

Annex

Agreed Common Elements of Criminal Legislation and Related Action

(1) *Elements of the offence of active bribery*

i) *Bribery* is understood as the promise or giving of any undue payment or other advantages, whether directly or through intermediaries to a public official, for himself or for a third party, to influence the official to act or refrain from acting in the performance of his or her official duties in order to obtain or retain business.

ii) *Foreign public official means* any person holding a legislative, administrative or judicial office of a foreign country or in an international organisation, whether appointed or elected or, any person exercising a public function or task in a foreign country.

iii) *The offeror is any person*, on his own behalf or on the behalf of any other natural person or legal entity.

(2) *Ancillary elements or offences*

The general criminal law concepts of attempt, complicity and/or conspiracy of the law of the prosecuting state are recognised as applicable to the offence of bribery of a foreign public official.

(3) *Excuses and defences*

Bribery of foreign public officials in order to obtain or retain business is an offence irrespective of the value or the outcome of the bribe, of perceptions of local custom or of the tolerance of bribery by local authorities.

(4) *Jurisdiction*

Jurisdiction over the offence of bribery of foreign public officials should in any case be established when the offence is committed in whole or in part in the prosecuting State's territory. The territorial basis for jurisdiction should be interpreted broadly so that an extensive physical connection to the bribery act is not required.

States which prosecute their nationals for offences committed abroad should do so in respect of the bribery of foreign public officials according to the same principles.

States which do not prosecute on the basis of the nationality principle should be prepared to extradite their nationals in respect of the bribery of foreign public officials.

All countries should review whether their current basis for jurisdiction is effective in the fight against bribery of foreign public officials and, if not, should take appropriate remedial steps.

(5) *Sanctions*

The offence of bribery of foreign public officials should be sanctioned/punishable by effective, proportionate and dissuasive criminal penalties, sufficient to secure effective mutual legal assistance and extradition, comparable to those applicable to the bribers in cases of corruption of domestic public officials.

Monetary or other civil, administrative or criminal penalties on any legal person involved, should be provided, taking into account the amounts of the bribe and of the profits derived from the transaction obtained through the bribe.

Forfeiture or confiscation of instrumentalities and of the bribe benefits and the profits derived from the transactions obtained through the bribe should be provided, or comparable fines or damages imposed.

(6) *Enforcement*

In view of the seriousness of the offence of bribery of foreign public officials, public prosecutors should exercise their discretion independently, based on professional motives. They should not be influenced by considerations of national economic interest, fostering good political relations or the identity of the victim.

Complaints of victims should be seriously investigated by the competent authorities.

The statute of limitations should allow adequate time to address this complex offence.

National governments should provide adequate resources to prosecuting authorities so as to permit effective prosecution of bribery of foreign public officials.

(7) *Connected provisions (criminal and non-criminal)*

- Accounting, recordkeeping and disclosure requirements
  In order to combat bribery of foreign public officials effectively, states should also adequately sanction accounting omissions, falsifications, and fraud.
- Money laundering
  The bribery of foreign public officials should be made a predicate offence for purposes of money laundering legislation where bribery of a domestic public official is a money laundering predicate offence, without regard to the place where the bribery occurs.

(8) *International co-operation*

Effective mutual legal assistance is critical to be able to investigate and obtain evidence in order to prosecute cases of bribery of foreign public officials.

Adoption of laws criminalising the bribery of foreign public officials would remove obstacles to mutual legal assistance created by dual criminality requirements.

Countries should tailor their laws on mutual legal assistance to permit co-operation with countries investigating cases of bribery of foreign public officials even including third countries (country of the offeror; country where the act occurred) and countries applying different types of criminalisation legislation to reach such cases.

Means should be explored and undertaken to improve the efficiency of mutual legal assistance.

RECOMMENDATION OF THE COUNCIL ON THE TAX DEDUCTIBILITY OF BRIBES TO FOREIGN PUBLIC OFFICIALS

Adopted by the Council on 11 April 1996

THE COUNCIL,

Having regard to Article 5 b) of the Convention on the Organisation for Economic Co-operation and Development of 14th December 1960;

Having regard to the OECD Council Recommendation on Bribery in International Business Transactions [C(94)75/FINAL];

Considering that bribery is a widespread phenomenon in international business transactions, including trade and investment, raising serious moral and political concerns and distorting international competitive conditions;

Considering that the Council Recommendation on Bribery called on Member countries to take concrete and meaningful steps to combat bribery in international business transactions, including examining tax measures which may indirectly favour bribery;

On the proposal of the Committee on Fiscal Affairs and the Committee on International Investment and Multinational Enterprises:

I. RECOMMENDS that those Member countries which do not disallow the deductibility of bribes to foreign public officials re-examine such treatment with the intention of denying this deductibility. Such action may be facilitated by the trend to treat bribes to foreign public officials as illegal.

II. INSTRUCTS the Committee on Fiscal Affairs, in cooperation with the Committee on International Investment and Multinational Enterprises, to monitor the implementation of this Recommendation, to promote the Recommendation in the context of contacts with non-Member countries and to report to the Council as appropriate.

PART I

Introduction

Introduction

MARK PIETH

Preamble to the OECD Convention

The Parties,

Considering that bribery is a widespread phenomenon in international business transactions, including trade and investment, which raises serious moral and political concerns, undermines good governance and economic development, and distorts international competitive conditions;

Considering that all countries share a responsibility to combat bribery in international business transactions;

Having regard to the Revised Recommendation on Combating Bribery in International Business Transactions, adopted by the Council of the Organisation for Economic Co-operation and Development (OECD) on 23 May 1997, C(97)123/FINAL, which, inter alia, called for effective measures to deter, prevent and combat the bribery of foreign public officials in connection with international business transactions, in particular the prompt criminalisation of such bribery in an effective and co-ordinated manner and in conformity with the agreed common elements set out in that Recommendation and with the jurisdictional and other basic legal principles of each country;

Welcoming other recent developments which further advance international understanding and co-operation in combating bribery of public officials, including actions of the United Nations, the World Bank, the International Monetary Fund, the World Trade Organisation, the Organisation of American States, the Council of Europe and the European Union;

Welcoming the efforts of companies, business organisations and trade unions as well as other non-governmental organisations to combat bribery;

Recognising the role of governments in the prevention of solicitation of bribes from individuals and enterprises in international business transactions;

Recognising that achieving progress in this field requires not only efforts on a national level but also multilateral co-operation, monitoring and follow-up;

Recognising that achieving equivalence among the measures to be taken by the Parties is an essential object and purpose of the Convention, which

requires that the Convention be ratified without derogations affecting this equivalence;

Have agreed as follows: ...

Chapter contents

I. History and development of the legal framework

1. Why attempt to combat corruption now?

Corruption is by no means a new phenomenon. It is as old as human nature itself; however, political and economic corruption has taken on a specific meaning during the latter half of the twentieth century. With decolonisation, former colonial states, but also newcomers amongst exporting nations, tried to maintain or establish their power basis with the emerging elites in the southern hemisphere by buying allegiances. Whereas the motivation to bribe will have been primarily economic, to a large extent corruption was also used as a political means in the struggles of the Cold War to secure influence across the world. If therefore the East-West *détente* has not immediately brought a substantial reduction in political and economic bribery, the opening of the East and the growing pace of globalisation are essential conditions for a process towards openly addressing corruption as a serious impediment to worldwide development.[1] It is no coincidence that, since 1990, a dramatic change in public attitudes regarding corruption has taken place. This development can be identified both in the northern and southern hemispheres. There are commentators who maintain that the rampant bribery in industrialised centres of, for instance, Italy, could be attacked by law enforcement only following the East-West *détente*, since the highly corrupt former political structures were until then perceived as necessary bulwarks against Soviet influence. In a similar way, it became possible to criticise persons holding high political or legal office in other European states, such as Germany, France, and Belgium, for their lack of sensitivity to conflicts of interest.[2]

This is not to say that political change or globalisation as such have led to a reduction of bribery. In fact, in an initial period the contrary may have been the case.[3] Whereas the extent of 'graft' by political exponents in potentially rich countries in the South (e.g. Angola, Brazil, Nigeria or the Philippines) is now common knowledge,[4] we still need to develop a clear understanding of the full dimensions of commercial bribery. So far, we are getting used to dramatic headlines about payments worth hundreds of millions of dollars, or euros, in order to acquire contracts, obtain exploitation rights or permits to build pipelines, etc.[5] Reliable analyses of the dimensions of the problem are, however, still rare,[6] and we are only just beginning to understand some of the reasons for the persistence of the problems.[7]

Legislative action against transnational commercial bribery in fact began well before these geopolitical changes, for reasons primarily linked to the local political agenda of the United States. The enactment of the Foreign Corrupt Practices Act (FCPA) in 1977 marked the first important step.

[1] Crutchfield George, Lacey and Birmele 1999, 9; Pieth 1997a, 119 et seq.

[2] Belgium: *Neue Zürcher Zeitung*, 9 December 1994, 1; France: *Neue Zürcher Zeitung*, 13 November 2003, 5, *New York Times*, 14 November 2003, 9, *Guardian*, 13 November 2003 (online edn); Germany: BBC News, 29 June 2000 (online edn), Focus, 11/2004, 18 et seq.

[3] Even the preamble of the OECD Revised Recommendation of 1997 (henceforth cited as OECD 1997a) suggests that 'bribery is a widespread phenomenon in international business transactions' (2nd indent); see also the Official Documents at the beginning of this book.

[4] Angola: Global Witness Report, March 2004, 36; Brazil: Neue Zürcher Zeitung, 26 July 2005, 5, *Financial Times*, 22 July 2005, 11; Nigeria: *Basler Zeitung*, 21 October 2002, 44, BBC News, 20 October 2000 (online edn), *Neue Zürcher Zeitung*, 4 October 2000, 25; Philippines: BBC News, 1 February 2002 (online edn), *Neue Zürcher Zeitung*, 22 April 1998, 7.

[5] Acres: M2 Pressure, 23 July 2004; World Bank List of Debarred Firms, available at: http://www.worldbank.org >projects&operations>procurement; Giffen: *Neue Zürcher Zeitung*, 2 April 2003, *Financial Times*, 30 May 2003, 4; Halliburton: Financial Times, 30 March 2004, 6, *Nene Zürcher Zeitung*, 14/15 February 2004; Siemens-Enelpower: *Süddeutsche Zeitung*, 20 August 2004 (online edn).

[6] Mauro 1995, 681 et seq. [7] Cartier-Bresson 2000, 11; Rose-Ackerman 1999, 40.

2. The US initiatives against 'Foreign Corrupt Practices'

2.1. Early legislative activities[8]

2.1.1. SEC disclosure programme and enactment of the FCPA

In the mid 1970s media reports revealed that US companies were acquiring business at home and abroad through clandestine payments to foreign public officials. Such questionable practices were exposed in particular by the Watergate Special Prosecutor examining questionable contributions to President Nixon's re-election campaign.[9] Following a public outcry, the US Securities and Exchange Commission (SEC) created a voluntary disclosure programme and announced an amnesty for companies under the condition that they disclosed past payments to foreign public officials and introduced internal anti-bribery compliance procedures.[10] Shocked by the extent of the revelations,[11] the administration of President Ford suggested legislation requiring US companies to disclose bribes. The draft of 1976, however, failed to pass the Democratic-dominated Congress. The administration of President Carter shortly afterwards pushed for legislation criminalising the bribery of foreign public officials and demanded the definition of additional accounting and auditing requirements and 'in-control standards' to be supervised and, if necessary, sanctioned by the SEC. The new law entered into force in December 1977.[12]

2.1.2. Interpreting the developments

Scholars have taken the enactment of the FCPA more or less for granted; few discuss the reasons for such an unusual step in the 1970s. It is true that an international debate about the behaviour of large Multinational Enterprises (MNEs) had already reached a critical stage. The fact that the OECD enacted its first version of an 'OECD Guideline for Multinational Enterprises' in 1976 was an expression of the need perceived by governments to contain public discontent with the role of MNEs. On the other hand, there must have been strong domestic reasons for the US

[8] Corr and Lawler 1999, 1255; Low 2003a, 3; Schoenlaub 1999, A-1057.

[9] Hines 1995, 3 et seq.; Tarullo 2004, 673.

[10] Hearings on Activities of American Multinational Corporations Abroad Before the Subcommittee on International Economics Policy of the House Committee on International Relations, 94th Cong. 57, 63 et seq. (1975). For the findings of the SEC cf. the Report of the Comptroller General of the United States to Congress in 1981.

[11] More than 400 companies, over 100 of them amongst the 500 largest in the world, owned up to having paid substantial bribes in the recent past.

[12] FCPA 1977 (Pub. L. No. 95-213, 91 Stat. 1494 (1977)).

legislator to take this step unilaterally, reasons going beyond the general sympathy of the Carter administration for business ethics.[13] Case law and legislative materials suggest that the US legislator believed it was acting to protect the free market system against the erosion of public confidence. On a more concrete level it had an interest in preventing US companies from becoming dependent upon such behaviour and thereby losing their competitive edge over others. Additionally, it was feared that businesses with an ethical track record would cave in under the pressure of competition and lower their standards. Still, it remains interesting that the United States acted unilaterally without prior consultation with major trading partners. This may be explained with reference to the size and nature of some of the cases revealed. Notably, the Tanaka-Lockheed scandal, involving Japan's Prime Minister and one of the largest defence contractors in the United States, was highly embarrassing for US foreign policy. Defence industry insiders of that time offer additional explanations: lobbyists in Washington apparently feared that the defence industries could attempt to open up new markets, including with the help of illicit means, especially in the Middle-East, if transnational bribery was tolerated. Even if this additional explanation cannot be corroborated, together with the other theories it indicates that enacting the FCPA was probably not only an effort to protect the US image abroad, but a very straightforward and fundamentally utilitarian step to keep the private sector from interfering with US foreign policy and national security interests, as defined by the Government.[14]

2.2. Efforts to internationalise the FCPA

It rapidly became evident to the US business sector that the FCPA (at least seen from a short-term perspective) placed it at a competitive disadvantage compared to its foreign competitors.[15] It was therefore quite an obvious step to support the drafting of an anti-corruption Convention in the context of the Economic and Social Council (ECOSOC) of the United Nations (UN). In fact, the UN made great efforts to negotiate such a Treaty in the late 1970s; due to North-South and also East-West differences the efforts ended without success and had to be abandoned in 1979.[16]

[13] Tarullo 2004, 673.

[14] Pieth, 1999b, 1; Schoenlaub 1999, A-1057 with reference to US court decisions (e.g. *U.S.* v. *Donald Castle* 1925 F. 2d 831 [5th Circ. 1991]).

[15] Langer and Pelzmann 2001, 3; Tarullo 2004, 676 (note 31): reference to Warren Christopher, Deputy Attorney-General when the FCPA was passed.

[16] Cf. the work of, first, the ECOSOC's Commission on Transnational Corporations, and later of its Committee on an International Agreement on Illicit Payments; Pieth 1999c, A-1039.

Similarly, the rules of conduct developed by the International Chamber of Commerce (ICC) in parallel to the UN negotiations, and aiming to supplement an international public standard, were finalised. They too remained, however, a more or less dead letter without the public backing of the Convention, until new efforts in the 1990s proved more successful.[17]

2.3. What did work?

Towards the late 1980s, pressure mounted within the US business sector to either tone down or even abolish the FCPA or to encourage major competitors to follow suit. Successive publications of the US Department of Commerce, based on complaints by the private sector and frequently adding references to intelligence sources, presented figures showing lost business due to foreign bribery by foreign competitors.[18]

2.3.1. FCPA 1988

In 1988, the FCPA was reformulated.[19] Documents of the time raise the question whether the intention was 'clarification' or 'evisceration'.[20] Some of the amendments, e.g. the shift from the 'knowledge standard' for indirect bribery and the widening of the exceptions, seemed to weaken the law.[21] Essential for the future, however, was the President's obligation under the new law to pursue negotiations with major competitors to conclude an international agreement against foreign bribery. This provided the domestic legal justification for the US request to the OECD in 1989 to initiate work on an instrument on combating bribery of foreign public officials.[22] There was to be debate then and later within various US administrations about the choice of an organisation to pursue the issue. As a consequence of the traditional US distrust of the UN, it was obvious that this organisation was not considered. However, the GATT would have been an option.[23] In 1989

[17] For the history of the ICC Rules of Conduct, cf. Heimann 2003, 13 et seq.

[18] The carping became more than ever explicit: cf. Hines 1995, 19 et seq., with reference to the US Department of Commerce, Unclassified Summary of Foreign Competition, October 1995 (pre 1994: 100 cases, amounting to \$45 billion, and 1994–98: 239 cases amounting to \$108 billion); Kantor 1996, in Sacerdoti 2003, 43; *Wall Street Journal*, 23 February 1999 (calling OECD members the worst offenders); Gareis 1999, A-1013; cf. also Schoenlaub 1999, A-1058.

[19] FCPA Act 1988 (Pub. L. No. 100-418, 102 Stat. 1107 (1988)); Tarullo 2004, 674.

[20] Bliss and Spak 1989, note 16.

[21] Crutchfield George, Lacey and Birmele 1999, note 109; Hines 1995, 21; Low 2003a, 1; Tarullo 2004, 679.

[22] OECD 1999, F-1005.

[23] An option suggested even as late as 1997 by the US Trade Representative, M. Kantor.

the G-7 had just taken a similar decision in a related area – following on from the 1988 UN Convention Against Illicit Traffic in Narcotic Drugs and Psychotropic Substances it had created the Financial Action Task Force on Money Laundering (FATF). And it asked the OECD to supply secretariat services, in particular because it was hoping to make use of the OECD's well-established 'peer review' and 'soft law' procedures.[24] Moreover, the OECD, as the organisation of the major exporting and investing nations, seemed to be best suited to develop international rules on foreign commercial bribery.[25]

2.3.2. Initiative in the OECD

The Paris-based Organisation for Economic Co-operation and Development (OECD) was created in 1960 and had a crucial role in the post-war reconstruction of Europe. It was created to facilitate the implementation of the US European Recovery Program or Marshall Plan. Together with the Bretton Woods institutions, the OECD managed to implant into European politics a shift of paradigm from aggressive mercantilism to economic co-operation.[26] The 1960 OECD Treaty stated its main goal as follows: to enable its state Parties to consult and co-operate in order 'to use more effectively their capacities and potentialities so as to promote the highest sustainable growth of their economies and improve the economic and social well-being of their people'.[27]

Over the post-war period, the OECD has evolved into the pre-eminent organisation of the industrialised nations for international economic research. The OECD has a key role in economic analysis; on a policy level, securing free market access is still the paramount concern of its members. After the fall of communism and the opening of East European markets, bribery is more than ever perceived as a non-tariff trade barrier to European and global trade. The issue therefore blends well into the OECD's work programme of promoting exports and foreign investment.

Within the some 120 committees and subgroups of the OECD consensus politics has become well established.[28] Peer review has become an accepted method of securing compliance by state Parties with their

[24] Financial Action Task Force on Money Laundering, Reports, Paris, February 1990.
[25] Cf. the reference to the mandate of the OECD as an organisation in OECD 1997a, preamble: see also note 3 and OECD 1999, F-1005.
[26] Guilmette 2004a, 28. [27] OECD 1960, 7th recital. [28] Guilmette 2004a, 44.

Treaty obligations.[29] Its subtlety commends itself to states, and its effectiveness can be enhanced by the exercise of peer pressure, depending on the topic.

3. The OECD initiatives against corruption

3.1. 1989–1994

3.1.1. The first tentative steps

The idea that, in 1989, the topic of corruption was new in a forum dealing with international business would be wrong. Just as the private sector, through the ICC, had worked on the issue between 1975 and 1977 (Shawcross Committee).[30] So the OECD, as early as 1976, had itself already addressed corruption – even if in a still rather general manner – in its 'Guidelines for Multinational Enterprises'.[31] However, the political context of the 1970s was quite different from that of the 1990s. Beyond the issue of unfair competition, the Guidelines had aimed to come to terms with the general discontent and criticism pertaining to the behaviour of MNEs in the 1970s; they were widely condemned for basing their action entirely on profit-maximisation. Moreover, it must be added that these early instruments did little to change endemic corrupt practices around the world.

The nature of the discussions concerning commercial bribery in the 'Ad Hoc Group on Illicit Payments'[32] at the OECD, which began its work in 1989, was thus entirely different from what it is today.[33] Even though the efforts were being undertaken in parallel to the work of high-powered task forces like the FATF and Carribean Action Task Force (CATF), the issue was treated with distrust by the state Parties. The representation was rather on the low-level (including the US delegation) and the work rhythm slow in the beginning.[34] The OECD Council insisted on cautiously worded mandates on an annual basis, first requesting a comparative review of national legislation, then a series of feasibility studies of possible substantive actions and procedural approaches. Only after several years of preliminary work was it possible to envisage proposing a Recommendation on specific actions to be taken by the state Parties.[35]

[29] OECD 2003a. [30] Heimann 2003, 13. [31] Para. VI OECD 2000b.

[32] A Working Group which was created by the Committee on International Investment and Multinational Enterprises of the OECD (CIME): cf. OECD 1999, F-1005.

[33] OECD 1999, F-1005 et seq.; Pieth 2000a, 54 et seq.; Sacerdoti 2003, 72 et seq.

[34] Tarullo 2004, 675, 677.

[35] Council Decisions of March 1989 C(89)49; of June 1990 C(90)87; of February 1992 C(92)16; Ministerial Communiqué of 2 June 1998 (CES(93)22).

There was no NGO support at the time, no other international organisations were as yet addressing the topic, and the private sector was quite uninterested in these discussions. In fact, this general scepticism went along with double standards at home. Even though in all OECD state Parties corruption was prohibited domestically, countries did not feel responsible for what their companies did vis-à-vis foreign officials, be it on their own territory or abroad. Furthermore, the vast majority of state Parties still allowed tax deductibility of bribes,[36] thereby indirectly condoning such practices. Frequently, politicians and economic leaders saw bribery as a means of supporting domestic industrial or business interests.[37]

Whereas the Republican administration of George Bush senior (1988–1992) would probably have been ready to accept a 'no' by major competitors such as Japan, if only in order to further weaken or even abolish the FCPA, the Clinton administration (elected in 1992) had no choice but to aggressively pursue the internationalisation of the FCPA. They followed in the footsteps of the Carter administration in this respect: from 1993 Secretary of State, Warren Christopher, who had been involved in the drafting of the FCPA under Carter in 1977, dramatically intensified the efforts to promote an OECD instrument.[38] At home, US companies were convinced by a sequence of high-profile cases prosecuted by the Department of Justice, leading to rather high sanctions, that there was no way back from the FCPA: see the cases against Goodyear decided in 1989, General Electric in 1994 and Lockheed Corporation in 1995.[39] Meanwhile, major competitors in Europe and Asia, who were not really interested in the abolition of the FCPA, agreed that the international community needed at least to consider action against transnational bribery. This change of attitude led to the 1994 Recommendation.

3.1.2. The Recommendation of 1994

The Recommendation of 1994[40] itself makes rather unspectacular reading. It starts with the general Recommendation to state Parties of the OECD to 'take effective measures to deter, prevent and combat the bribery of foreign public officials in connection with international business transactions'

[36] Sacerdoti 2003, 71. [37] Pletscher 1999, 275, 279. [38] Tarullo 2004, 675.

[39] *U.S.* v. *Goodyear International Corp.*, 2 FCPA Rep. 698.1601 (D.D.C. 1989); *U.S.* v. *Steindler*, 3 FCPA Rep. 699.131 (S.D. Ohio 1994); *U.S.* v. *Lockheed Corp.* 3 FCPA Rep. 699.175 (N.D. Ca. 1995).

[40] OECD 1994; also OECD 1999, F-1106.

(para. I). It goes on to give a tentative 'shopping list' of issues which it invites each member to examine (para. II). If in hindsight this does not seem much of an achievement, it needs to be pointed out that this was the first international document in which states publicly promised to 'take concrete and meaningful steps to meet this goal' and agreed to monitor implementation and follow up this Recommendation (para. VIII), in particular 'to carry out regular reviews of steps taken by Member countries to implement the Recommendation and to make proposals, as appropriate, to assist Member countries in its implementation'.

Even if this Recommendation was not legally binding, its value lay in its political impact.[41] Its real significance has been to generate confidence within the OECD and within other organisations and NGOs that bribery could be overcome, provided states, the private sector, and civil society all co-operated. Both the Council of Europe (COE) and Transparency International (TI) picked up their work on corruption shortly after the adoption of the 1994 Recommendation.[42] For the future evolution of the OECD initiative, the passage on follow-up and on monitoring was crucial: it introduced a peer process which was to allow this initiative to develop into one of the most dynamic instruments of international law.[43]

Summing up, on an abstract level, a shift of attitude towards commercial bribery was made possible by geopolitical and global economic change (East-West *détente* and expanding globalisation). On a more concrete level, an institution like the OECD, backed by strong political will, was needed to create a real anti-corruption drive. Instrumental too was the effective lobbying of the US business sector, being sensitive to trade disadvantages allegedly suffered since the enactment of the FCPA in 1977. The process nevertheless remained arduous because in 1994 Governments continued to be largely ambivalent and the private sector outside the United States sceptical. They still needed to be convinced that strictly enforced harmonisation over a limited period would genuinely lead to a reduction of bribery without endangering their competitive position.

3.2. 1994–1997

The ensuing years involved the participants in a detailed examination of the items contained in the 'shopping list' and marked the transition from

[41] OECD 1999, F-1006; Guilmette 2004a, 77.
[42] Aiolfi and Pieth 2002, 350; Pieth 2000a, 52; Sacerdoti 1999, 214.
[43] For further details see part III. of this ch.

unilateral to collective action.[44] Once again, state Parties' laws were analysed (1995). Priority was given to criminalisation, since it became evident that it was crucial for all other aspects to draw a clear line between permitted and forbidden behaviour. An essential step in this process was taken when, in 1996, the Council agreed with the Working Group on Bribery (WGB) that it was 'necessary to criminalise the bribery of foreign public officials in an effective and co-ordinated manner'.[45] The WGB was the renamed expert committee in charge of developing the rules. Ministers asked it, through the CIME, to 'further examine the modalities and the appropriate international instruments to facilitate criminalisation'.[46] With this mandate the WGB would develop, on the one hand, a substantive standard, i.e., the 'Agreed Common Elements',[47] which would be the blueprint for the Convention; and on the other hand, it would once more engage in discussions about the adequate legal form (Recommendation or Convention?). Before getting there, however, over the next three years the WGB picked up a series of other key issues from the 'shopping list', studied them, and developed language for the revision of the Recommendation in 1997.[48] In so doing, it applied the 'interactive process' for which the OECD has become famous.[49]

In the same period the WGB's sister entities within the OECD structure, partly in co-operation with the WGB, developed Recommendations on some of the issues contained in the 1994 Recommendation: the Committee on Fiscal Affairs (CFA) continued its work on banning tax deductibility of bribes[50] and the Development Assistance Committee (DAC) on anti-corruption provisions in bilateral aid-funded procurement and related matters.[51] Independently of the efforts of the WGB, a series of other OECD sub-committees have since raised issues relating to combating corruption (PUMA, SIGMA, etc.).[52]

The text of the Revised Recommendation of 23 May 1997[53] pulled together the analytical work done on the items of the 'shopping list' and transformed

[44] Aiolfi and Pieth 2002, 351; Pieth 2000a, 54; Sacerdoti 1999, 214 et seq.; ibid. 2003, 72 et seq.
[45] OECD 1999, F-1008, 1011. [46] See previous note 45.
[47] Cf. Annex in OECD 1997a and see the Official Documents at the beginning of this book.
[48] Cf. the detailed texts contained in OECD 1999, F-1003–1128: accounting requirements, external audit and internal company controls, the use of access to public procurement to counter-corruption, etc.
[49] Progressing from fact-finding, brainstorming, and Recommendations to more precise language and eventually to very specific requirements. Cf. Guilmette 2004a, 94.
[50] OECD 1999, F-1041. [51] OECD 1999, F-1092, 1101, 1116.
[52] OECD: Public Management Group (PUMA); Support for Improvement in Governance and Management (SIGMA); see also I.3.4.4. below.
[53] OECD 1997a.

the 1994 Recommendation into a far more meaningful document, specifying commitments of state Parties in a series of areas. Like the earlier text, it contains procedures for follow-up and for review of the Recommendation in the future (section VIII.). The Revised Recommendation defines the actions to be taken by state Parties in such a concrete manner that some members felt the most sensitive topics (criminal law and book-keeping rules) needed to be carried over into a legally binding instrument.[54]

3.3. From the Revised Recommendation to the Convention of 1997

Since 1993, when the decision was taken to opt for a Recommendation, the WGB had worked under the assumption that in such diverging legal systems 'soft law' was the quickest and most subtle way to harmonise rules on transnational bribery. The Revised Recommendation continued to pursue this approach by defining, inter alia, a template of criminal rules to be implemented by state Parties, namely the 'Agreed Common Elements of Criminal Legislation and Related Action' (ACE) appended to the Recommendation.[55]

In the final round of negotiations on the Recommendations, some countries, led by France and Germany, suggested that criminalisation required a more binding legal form. In order to promote this approach, they proposed a draft Convention, largely drawing upon texts recently agreed in the COE or European Union (EU) frameworks.[56] Whereas Germany suggested the UN as the best forum to negotiate such a Treaty, France favoured the WTO. In opposition to the 'collective unilateralism' so far embraced by the WGB,[57] France and Germany also sought to follow a traditional inter partes approach. The heated debates about the best way to bring about a binding instrument allowing for a rapid change of law in all key jurisdictions provoked the WGB into action. Between June and August 1997 a first draft of the Convention was developed on the basis of contributions by France, Germany, Italy, the United States, and the Secretariat; the draft was further refined at an informal meeting in Lugano in August 1997 under the 'Friends of the Chairman' format ('Lugano I Conference'). In two following negotiation conferences (October and November)[58] the text was finalised. It was signed by Ministers on 17 December 1997 in Paris.[59]

[54] Pieth 2000a, 54; Sacerdoti 2003, 32.
[55] Reproduced for readers at the beginning of this book along with the Recommendation itself.
[56] See II.2.2. below. [57] See II.1. below.
[58] Working Documents DAFFE/IME/BR(97)12 and 16.
[59] Pieth 2000a, 55; Sacerdoti 2003, 73. See the full text of the Convention at the beginning of this book.

The extraordinary speed with which this process was concluded was facilitated by a compromise of May 1997, which is reflected in section III.(1) of the Revised Recommendation:

> 'Member countries should criminalise the bribery of foreign public officials in an effective and co-ordinated manner by submitting proposals to their legislative bodies by 1 April 1998, in conformity with the agreed common elements set forth in the Annex, and seeking their enactment by the end of 1998.'

In the next paragraph (section III.(2)) the Council took the binding procedural 'Decision':

> 'to open negotiations promptly on an international Convention to criminalise bribery in conformity with the agreed common elements, the Treaty to be open for signature by the end of 1997, with a view to its entry into force twelve months thereafter.'

Under normal circumstances this ambitious calendar would have simply been unrealistic. However, due to the intense political pressure[60] exerted by more than one country, the envisaged deadline for entry into force was missed by only a few months, with the Convention entering into force on 15 February 1999. The negotiating situation was very much inspired by what economists call the prisoner's dilemma.[61] From the moment the decision to go ahead was taken by G-7 countries, notably Canada, Germany, Japan, the United Kingdom, and the United States, who all ratified in 1998, the Convention was a done deal. The negotiations behind the scenes and the extent of the peer pressure necessary to convince state Parties are not discussed here. Of course, in this phase of the emergence of international rules, the contribution of the private sector and of the NGOs was crucial. In particular, the NGO TI helped convince sceptical business leaders and politicians in some key countries that the time was ripe to commit themselves to combating transnational economic bribery.[62]

Even though the Convention has received far more publicity, the Revised Recommendation is still in force and remains the basic 'politically binding' text, embodying the overall consensus on how best to combat the bribery of

[60] Cf. the detailed inside story by the US 'sherpa': Tarullo 2004, 675.

[61] Guilmette 2004a, 59; Tarullo 2004, 668.

[62] From 1995 onwards, the WGB held regular meetings with representatives of the private sector, trade unions, and Non Government Organisations (NGOs): Business and Industry Advisory Committee to the OECD (BIAC), Trade Union Advisory Committee to the OECD (TUAC), International Chamber of Commerce (ICC) and TI. In the final stage of the negotiations, TI's intervention proved to be instrumental: it drafted a helpful letter signed by Chief Executive Officers (CEOs) of large international companies.

foreign public officials in business transactions, including the entire preventive concept and the basic rules on follow-up and co-operation.

3.4. Ratifying and implementing the Convention

3.4.1. Ratification

In comparison to traditional criminalisation Treaties, it is remarkable not only how quickly the OECD Convention entered into force; it has also been ratified and implemented by the entirety of its constituency in an exceptionally short space of time. Whereas all state Parties adopted implementing legislation, one country needed longer to ratify for technical reasons.[63] In the meantime all countries have ratified (See table).

OECD Bribery Convention Ratification Status as of 24 November 2005

Country	Deposit of instrument of ratification/ acceptance	Entry into force of the Convention	Entry into force of implementing legislation
Argentina	8 February 2001	9 April 2001	10 November 1999
Australia	18 October 1999	17 December 1999	17 December 1999
Austria	20 May 1999	19 July 1999	1 October 1998
Belgium	27 July 1999	25 September 1999	3 April 1999
Brazil	24 August 2000	23 October 2000	11 June 2002
Bulgaria	22 December 1998	20 February 1999	29 January 1999
Canada	17 December 1998	15 February 1999	14 February 1999
Chile	18 April 2001	17 June 2001	8 October 2002
Czech Republic	21 January 2000	21 March 2000	9 June 1999
Denmark	5 September 2000	4 November 2000	1 May 2000
Estonia	23 November 2004 (accession instrument)	22 January 2005	1 July 2004
Finland	10 December 1998	15 February 1999	1 January 1999
France	31 July 2000	29 September 2000	29 September 2000
Germany	10 November 1998	15 February 1999	15 February 1999
Greece	5 February 1999	6 April 1999	1 December 1998
Hungary	4 December 1998	15 February 1999	1 March 1999
Iceland	17 August 1998	15 February 1999	30 December 1998
Ireland	22 September 2003	21 November 2003	26 November 2001
Italy	15 December 2000	13 February 2001	26 October 2000
Japan	13 October 1998	15 February 1999	15 February 1999
Korea	4 January 1999	5 March 1999	15 February 1999
Luxembourg	21 March 2001	20 May 2001	11 February 2001
Mexico	27 May 1999	26 July 1999	18 May 1999

[63] Ireland.

Country	Deposit of instrument of ratification/ acceptance	Entry into force of the Convention	Entry into force of implementing legislation
Netherlands	12 January 2001	13 March 2001	1 February 2001
New Zealand	25 June 2001	24 August 2001	3 May 2001
Norway	18 December 1998	16 February 1999	1 January 1999
Poland	8 September 2000	7 November 2000	4 February 2001
Portugal	23 November 2000	22 January 2001	9 June 2001
Slovak Republic	24 September 1999	23 November 1999	1 November 1999
Slovenia	6 September 2001 (accession instrument)	5 November 2001	23 January 1999
Spain	4 January 2000	4 March 2000	2 February 2000
Sweden	8 June 1999	7 August 1999	1 July 1999
Switzerland	31 May 2000	30 July 2000	1 May 2000
Turkey	26 July 2000	24 September 2000	11 January 2003
United Kingdom	14 December 1998	15 February 1999	14 February 2002
United States	8 December 1998	15 February 1999	10 November 1998

3.4.2. Securing implementation and application

The rapid pace of implementation is mainly attributable to sustained peer pressure, which is directed to the various forms of follow-up addressed by the Revised Recommendation and the Convention. As we will see, one approach focuses on the formal steps towards implementation (*Tour de Table*); another evaluates the abstract substantive implementation ('Phase 1 monitoring'), with a re-evaluation of laws after they have been amended to meet the critical comments of the WGB ('Phase 1bis monitoring'); and finally, there is the most ambitious procedure yet, focusing on effective application ('Phase 2 monitoring'[64]). The procedures of this Phase 2 are the prerequisite for one of the most effective harmonisation efforts in international law of the past years.[65]

3.4.3. Accession and further substantive work

Apart from monitoring, the WGB pursues two other lines of work. On the one hand, it is struggling to define an adequate way of growing, inviting further countries to join in order to allow the peer process to maintain its bite.[66] On the other hand, the WGB has the mandate to continue work on substance.

[64] Discussed in detail in part III. of this ch. [65] More sceptical Tarullo 2004, 680 et seq.

[66] Accession to the Convention is governed by its Art. 13 (see discussion in ch. on Article 13 below).

In the area of criminal law, five issues were already identified for further deliberation during the negotiations of the Convention. In December 1997, therefore, the Council invited the WGB to further explore:

- extension of the Convention to cover party officials and political parties;
- extension of the Convention to cover candidates for political office;
- dealing with bribery through Offshore Centres (OFCs);
- giving closer attention to money laundering related to bribery; and
- ensuring that the use of foreign subsidiaries for bribery does not result in a substantial loophole in the rules of the Convention.[67]

Since 1997, a number of further issues has been targeted: some are already contained in the 'shopping list' of the 1994 Recommendation, like the use of subsidies, export credit conditions, etc., to prevent companies from bribing; others are based on more recent, but nevertheless serious requests for further action, especially the initiative by the ICC to examine the possibility of creating an additional instrument on 'private to private bribery'.[68]

3.4.4. Becoming part of an anti-corruption 'system'

Encouraged by the adoption of the Convention other sub-groups within the OECD structure have extended their focus to preventing corruption. The CFA,[69] PUMA,[70] DAC,[71] ECG,[72] SIGMA,[73] and CIME for the Guidelines for Multinational Enterprises[74] and the Working Group on Corporate Governance[75] are all contributing to an 'anti-corruption system' within the OECD.

These efforts can be said to form part of a wider anti-corruption movement, going beyond the 'supply side' to cover the 'demand side'[76] and also embracing the role of financial centres[77] in organising bribery. They include other Intergovernmental Organisations (IGOs) and the Multilateral Development Banks (MDBs),[78] civil society in a wider sense (private sector,[79] NGOs,[80]

[67] OECD 1997c. [68] Heine, Huber and Rose 2003. [69] OECD: Committee on Fiscal Affairs.
[70] OECD: Public Management Group; see also note 52.
[71] OECD: Development Assistance Committee. [72] OECD: Export Credits Group.
[73] Support for Improvement in Governance and Management (cf. for SIGMA programme: http://www.sigmaweb.org); see also note 52.
[74] See also note 32. [75] OECD 2004b.
[76] COE, EU, UN, Organisation of American States (OAS), Stability Pact for South-Eastern Europe (SPAI), Asian Development Bank (ADB), Global Coalition for Africa (GCA), New Partnership for Africa's Development (NEPAD).
[77] FATF in general and the UN in repatriation of assets (UN Convention Against Corruption, ch. IV).
[78] Especially the World Bank and the regional development banks.
[79] Vincke and Heimann 2003.
[80] TI; Global Witness; Accountability International; TRACE, etc.

academia,[81] and the media).[82] Bi-annual conferences (organised, for example, by the International Anti-Corruption Conference (IACC[83]) and the Global Forum Against Corruption)[84] serve as important platforms for the development of this wider movement. TI acts as its secretariat.

The international agreements adopted over the last decade, in particular, have helped to create a sense of political urgency in dealing with issues of corruption.

On a regional level the OAS came first, with its Inter-American Convention Against Corruption of 29 March 1996, a very broad instrument fostering above all mutual legal assistance. The EU adopted its 'Protocol to the Convention on the Protection of the European Communities' Financial Interests on 27 September 1996 and the Convention on the Fight Against Corruption on 26 May 1997; the COE also adopted two anti-corruption Treaties: the Criminal Law Convention of 27 January 1999 and the Civil Law Convention of 4 November 1999. These Treaties have already been implemented by many states. Most recently the UN adopted a comprehensive global anti-corruption Convention, covering criminal law, preventive measures, development co-operation and the repatriation of assets.[85]

Whereas the UN Treaty has not yet been supplemented by a real follow-up instrument, the COE has developed what is probably the most sophisticated instrument of mutual evaluation.[86] The OAS has more recently started its own evaluation programme.[87]

This plethora of activities should not, however, create the illusion that the goal of effectively combating bribery in international business transactions is close at hand. There are serious problems of coordination within this movement, and it is sometimes hard to distinguish the political and rhetorical 'progress' from practically meaningful efforts.

II. The approach: 'collective unilateralism' to tackle the 'supply side' of corruption

1. A focused ambition

The OECD initiative against transnational commercial bribery has, from the very beginning, deliberately restricted its scope to reducing the 'supply',

[81] E.g. Basel Institute on Governance. [82] Coeurdray 2003, 54 et seq.
[83] A biennial conference devoted to civil society action against corruption.
[84] Intergovernmental conference organised back-to-back with IACC.
[85] These international instruments are further discussed in II.2.2. below.
[86] Group of States Against Corruption (GRECO): cf. GRECO 1999, establishing this Group.
[87] OAS anti-corruption follow-up mechanism: cf. http://www.oas.org >sectors>corruption.

i.e., the influx of corrupt funds, especially into economies of the southern hemisphere.[88] The idea here is that it is easier to tackle potential bribe-payers, especially if they are commercial operators, because of their vulnerability. At the same time, if all major competitors refused to pay, even after tenacious solicitation by officials and their middlemen, bribes would become much harder to come by. Reducing the influx of bribe money would ultimately benefit the competitors by 'levelling the playing field' for them; it would also favour the population administered by the officials, since corrupt officials would lose their ability to buy allegiances.[89] Of course, this logic depends upon an even application of the anti-bribery rules to all potential bribe-payers. An anti-bribery system must therefore ensure that those continuing to bribe will be sanctioned and ultimately disbarred from business.

2. A narrow definition of corruption

The focused approach finds its expression in a narrow concept of corruption pursued, however, with all available means.

2.1. International business transactions

Consistent with the role of the OECD as the leading economic organisation of industrialised states, representing roughly 70% of the world's exports and over 90% of the Foreign Direct Investment (FDI), the Convention is restricted to bribery 'in international business transactions'.[90]

Not all countries will adopt this narrow approach, all the more, since some have implemented the OECD Treaty in conjunction with other regional instruments such as the COE or EU Treaties. The OECD cannot, however, overstep its mandate as an organisation for economic development. On the other hand, the OECD has to make sure that 'international business' is not given too narrow a meaning.[91]

2.2. Active bribery

Since companies domiciled in OECD countries are the world's major exporters and investors, they are most exposed to solicitation and to

[88] OECD 1999, F-1005; Aiolfi and Pieth 2002, 349; Pieth 2000a, 52; Sacerdoti 2003; Tarullo 2004, 681.
[89] Cf. the double rationale in the preamble to the Convention, first recital.
[90] See preamble to the Convention and ch. on Article 1 below.
[91] See ch. on Article 1 below.

the temptation to pay bribes in order to secure business. Focusing on the source of corrupt payments, the OECD, therefore, follows the approach chosen by the FCPA[92] and limits itself to criminalising the offering and the payment of bribes, so-called active bribery.

In comparison, according to regional European instruments the recipient is also subject to criminal sanctions. From a EU perspective the recipient's responsibility is just as much a concern as the donor's action is. EU action in the anti-corruption field should be analysed against the background of the process of economic and political 'integration' to which the Union is subject. The Communities on which the Union is based were founded with the main economic goal of establishing and maintaining a single market for goods, persons, services, and capital; achieving this goal required the creation of a body of legislation common to all state Parties. European laws are enacted and interpreted at a 'supranational' level. In fighting fraud against the budget of the Communities, the Union protects first and foremost a common economic interest.[93] The Protocol to the Convention on Protection of the Communities' Financial Interests[94] indeed aims at protecting the Communities' budget being based on provisions which entered into force with the Maastricht Treaty of 1992. This Treaty made criminal justice co-operation part of the remit of the EU: the EU's Convention on the Fight Against Corruption of 26 May 1997[95] is also an instrument of this policy which aims at the improvement of judicial co-operation in the fight against corruption. It frees itself, however, from the link to the Community's financial interests, making corruption of or by public officials – be they national or Community officials – a matter of Union-wide concern.

Equally, the COE[96] does not limit its sphere of influence to the pursuit of the briber only. The Council's definition of corruption results from its mandate: the facilitation of transnational co-operation in criminal matters. Mutual legal assistance, extradition, and confiscation of the proceeds of crime form the core of this remit. By promoting a broad definition of corruption, including all kinds of corrupt behaviour, the Council primarily aims at creating a legal 'platform' on the basis of which judicial co-operation can be pursued across the borders of the state Parties. The ultimate goal of all this is to create a harmonised economic criminal law for the whole of Europe.

[92] Attempts by the US Department of Justice to broaden the scope of the FCPA by indicting the official for conspiracy have so far failed (cf. *U.S.* v. *Eagle Bus Mfg.*, 2 FCPA 698.6910 (S.D. Tex. 1990).

[93] Pieth 1999a, 346. [94] Art. 2 EU 1996b. [95] EU 1997a. [96] COE 1999a.

The UN Convention of 2003[97] closely follows this approach by requiring legislators to criminalise not only active and passive domestic bribery, whether public or private, but also active and passive transnational commercial bribery (see Arts. 15–19 and 21–22). The Convention does not, however, even attempt to resolve the inherent conflict: whereas Article 16(1) deals with the active bribery of foreign public officials in a similar way the OECD's autonomous approach does, Article 16(2), albeit worded less strictly ('shall consider adopting'), seems to adopt the same definition of 'official' as in Art. 16(1). It is excluded, however, that a foreign country, running the case against the recipient of the bribe from abroad, should define the 'public official' independently of the 'victim country'. Exactly this problem has led the OECD to refrain from criminalising the recipient.[98] This extension could indicate a careful move towards creating a ius gentium against corruption.

2.3. Public officials

So far, the Convention concerns only advantages offered to public officials. There have been various attempts to enlarge the scope, be it to politicians, to private bribery in general, or, more specifically, to sports organisations.[99] However, the OECD system has restricted itself to public bribery. One of the issues still being studied is the topic of private bribery, which equally distorts competition. With growing privatisation, a substantial part of the problem is being shifted into the private sector.[100]

2.4. Foreign officials

Furthermore, the OECD's interest is focused on transnational bribery, i.e., the bribery of foreign officials. Domestic bribery is regarded as a local issue to be left to other organisations dealing with the mandate of harmonising law in general.

Concerning this aspect, again, the Convention of the COE and other European instruments go a step further, in accordance with their mission of integration. They outlaw bribery inside the common economic area, including cases which take place in one country only. The Inter-American Convention does not limit its application to transnational cases either. We have discussed the UN Convention above.

[97] UN 2003. [98] See ch. on Article 1 below. [99] See previous note 98.
[100] Heine, Huber and Rose 2003: foreword by Maria Livanos Cattaui.

2.5. Exclusion of facilitation payments

The Convention is also directed at serious cases of 'genuine' or 'grand' corruption. Even if 'petty corruption',[101] when endemic, can seriously hamper public life and endanger the trust in public institutions, it was the view of the state Parties to the Convention that it would be very difficult to tackle all forms of 'grease money' and gratuities with a kind of 'long arm jurisdiction'. In order to restrict itself to actual bribery the OECD Convention offers two concepts:

– The Convention leaves room for state Parties to restrict the criminalisation of petty 'grease payment'. Official Commentary 9[102] puts it this way:

> 'Small facilitation payments do not constitute payments made 'to obtain or retain business or other improper advantage' within the meaning of paragraph 1 and, accordingly, are not an offence. Such payments, which, in such countries, are made to induce public officials to perform their functions, such as issuing licences or permits, are generally illegal in the foreign country concerned.'

Such undisputedly harmful actions need not be criminalised by state Parties, notwithstanding their incongruence with the Convention's ideals. Official Commentary 9 goes on to point out that in this respect programmes on 'good governance' are more effective than criminalisation:

> 'Other countries can and should address this corrosive phenomenon by such means as support for programmes of good governance. However, criminalisation by other countries does not seem a practical or effective complementary action.'

– The Convention leaves it to state Parties whether to punish bribery intended to bring about a non-illegal act or omission by the official. Therefore it is up to the state Parties whether they choose to restrict the offence to a 'breach of duty' concept[103] – an alternative approach to creating an exception for 'facilitation payments'.

3. With a broad geographic reach

Unlike a traditional Treaty, the OECD Convention not only has effects inter partes. Since state Parties seek to enforce correct behaviour within

[101] For the distinction between 'grand' and 'petty' corruption, cf. Moody-Stuart, 1997.
[102] See note 110 for the legal nature of the Official Commentaries in OECD 1997b.
[103] See ch. on Article 1 below.

the entire reach of their jurisdiction (territorially or extraterritorially), the effects of the Convention are meant to be deployed erga omnes: even bribing the official of a country not a party to the Convention is therefore to be regarded as an offence. This was also the approach chosen by the FCPA. Thus, 'unilateralism' has been substituted by a 'collective unilateralism': among themselves the state Parties agreed no longer to tolerate bribery of any foreign public official worldwide. Even though the primary reason for this attitude may be to further the states' own business interests, the approach also contains an essential element of taking responsibility towards the countries afflicted by corruption.[104]

4. Further specifics of the OECD instruments

The anti-corruption system to which members of the WGB have agreed is therefore made up of two international instruments: the Revised Recommendation of 23 May 1997 and the Convention of 21 November 1997. Even though international lawyers consider only the Convention legally binding, the monitoring system[105] has its roots in the implementation and application of the Recommendation. Therefore the evaluation texts contain both legal and political observations: first, the identification of legal flaws compared to the binding standard, and second, a note of political considerations suggesting further action in areas regulated by 'soft law'.

We should also note that the Convention is primarily a 'criminalisation Treaty'. Nevertheless, it also contains non-criminal provisions. On the one hand, it allows state Parties to use non-penal measures as substitutes in certain areas (e.g. Article 2: Corporate Liability); on the other hand, the accounting and auditing provisions of Article 8 go beyond criminal law.[106]

The Convention was deliberately drafted so as to necessitate implementing legislation in state Parties; it is not self-executing. The rules are in general too open to be directly applied; they must be integrated into domestic law. One of the consequences of this is that the WGB will thoroughly screen even legislation which simply copies the formulations of the Convention into national law, because the wording could obtain a different meaning in the domestic context.[107]

[104] Cf. OECD 1997b, preamble. [105] See III.3. below. [106] Sacerdoti 2003, 74 et seq.
[107] E.g. GR-Ph1, 17.

Furthermore, the 'Negotiating Conference' formulated a series of *Official Commentaries*[108] to supplement the Convention. The background was as follows: some issues seemed too specific to be introduced into the Convention; other topics needed exemplification (e.g. the definition and treatment of public enterprises); in further areas disputed issues could be treated in a more subtle way (e.g. exceptions and defences). The notes were originally conceived as footnotes; only later on in the process were they shifted into a separate document with the title of 'Commentaries on the Convention on Combating Bribery of Foreign Public Officials in International Business Transactions'. As indicated in the text, they were adopted by the Negotiating Conference on 21 November 1997 alongside the Convention in exactly the same procedure (unanimous decision). It is therefore correct to treat them as *Travaux Préparatoires* in the sense of Article 32 of the Vienna Convention on the Law of Treaties of 1969.[109] Even though they have not been ratified by the state Parties, because of the manner of their adoption, we may nevertheless regard them as an 'authentic interpretation' of the Convention.[110]

III. Methodology: going new ways in international law

1. Respecting basic national legal principles

The WGB had to address a very challenging goal: the harmonisation of rules across a range of widely divergent legal traditions in a very limited space of time. As we have seen, the original method chosen was to develop 'soft law' Recommendations to state Parties and to follow them up in 'peer reviews'. This approach has a long history within the organisation.[111] The imposition of a legally binding criminalisation requirement, as the centrepiece of the anti-corruption initiative, created a new challenge. In the mere six months between the adoption of the Revised Recommendation and the signing ceremony of the Convention it was certainly out of the question to attempt any kind of legal unification,[112] not least since some of the differences were of a fundamental kind (different concepts of criminal

[108] These (numbered) Official Commentaries, adopted by the Negotiating Conference at the same time as the Convention (OECD 1997b) are reproduced at the beginning of this book.

[109] Vienna Convention 1969.

[110] Cf. Sacerdoti 2003, 74, who would, however, not go quite as far as the authors of this commentary.

[111] Guilmette 2004a; OECD 2003a.

[112] For discussion of legal 'unification', cf. Delmas-Marty 1998, 107 et seq.

procedure and evidence, liability of legal persons, etc.). If, therefore, the standard expression of respect for the state Parties' 'jurisdictional and other basic legal principles', contained in section II. of the Revised Recommendation, were not to impede significant harmonisation, a flexible yet meaningful approach needed to be chosen. Not unlike the method applied by the EU legislation in the form of 'Directives', the OECD chose to define goals rather than means: the method termed 'functional equivalence' was applied to compliance with the Convention obligations.

2. 'Functional equivalence'

2.1. The principle

The method used by the Negotiating Conference is termed 'functional equivalence'. The Convention borrowed this concept from the methodology of comparative law and developed it further.[113] The approach assumes that every legal system has its own logic, which is not necessarily determined by legal texts alone. Only the holistic appraisal of the law in operation, including informal rules and practices as well as functions assumed by other legal institutions, will allow to assess whether the overall legal effects produced by a country's legal system adequately meet the requirements of the Convention. The crucial advantage over the more formal methods of comparison of law is that the functional approach goes beyond comparing individual institutions. Even if it is a challenging methodology, it is especially well suited for the purposes of the peer evaluation envisaged by the OECD anti-bribery system.

The concept was first introduced into the OECD instruments by the preamble to the Convention:

> '[r]ecognising that achieving equivalence among the measures to be taken by the Parties is an essential object and purpose of the Convention, which requires that the Convention be ratified without derogations effecting this equivalence;'[114]

and then, more specifically, in Official Commentary 2:

> 'This Convention seeks to assure a functional equivalence among the measures taken by the Parties to sanction bribery of foreign public officials without requiring uniformity or changes in fundamental principles of the Party's legal system.'

In a number of ways the *Travaux Préparatoires*, the Official Commentaries or even the Convention itself indicate options or leeway for alternative

[113] Pieth 2000a, 56 et seq.; Pieth 2000b, 477 et seq. [114] OECD 1997b, preamble: final recital.

approaches. How the principle of functional equivalence can be applied in practice is finally revealed only in the course of the evaluation of countries' legislation and practice. We shall now give a few examples of how the methodology has so far been understood.

2.2. Examples

2.2.1. Integration in national legal systems

A fundamental question not explicitly answered by either Convention or Official Commentary is the way in which criminalisation of bribery of foreign public officials should be introduced into the legal system(s) of a state Party. The *Travaux Préparatoires*[115] recount that the WGB envisaged four methods of criminalisation:

- explicit and specific criminalisation of bribery of foreign public officials (following the model of the FCPA);
- making use of a general bribery statute broad enough to encompass the obligations of the Convention (perceived at the time to be the UK approach);
- amending existing domestic bribery statutes to include foreign bribery (called 'assimilation', an approach chosen by many state Parties); or
- introducing the rule into specific unfair competition legislation.

It emerged from this analysis, inter alia, that the WGB would accept the Japanese or Polish[116] choice to include the offence in a specialised statute outside the traditional criminal code, even if it were focused on unfair competition. The proviso added in the discussion by the WGB, however, was that regular prosecutors and judges rather than competition authorities or other agencies of an economic character should deal with infringements.

2.2.2. Definition of the criminal act

The definition of the criminal act[117] in Article 1(1) of the Convention is based on a quid pro quo concept of bribery, whereby the pro quo (the goal of the briber) is defined in a rather open manner (following the French, British, and US approaches): 'in order that the official act or refrain from

[115] OECD 1999, esp. F-1037–1040; Sacerdoti 2000, 36.
[116] JP-Ph1, 1, 26 (in general); PL-Ph1, 32 (regarding corporate liability).
[117] Pieth 2000a, 57.

acting in relation to the performance of official duties'. In order to put at ease those countries whose definition of corruption refers to breach of duty, Official Commentary 3 reiterates and exemplifies the concept of functional equivalence as follows:

> 'Article 1 establishes a standard to be met by Parties, but does not require them to utilise its precise terms in defining the offence under their domestic laws. A Party may use various approaches to fulfil its obligation, provided that conviction of a person for the offence does not require proof of elements beyond those which would be required to be proved if the offence were defined as in this paragraph...Similarly, a statute which defines the offence in terms of payment 'to induce a breach of the official's duty' could meet the standard, provided that it was understood that every public official had a duty to exercise judgement or discretion impartially and this was an 'autonomous' definition, not requiring proof of the law of the particular official's country.'

It will be noted that the concept of functional equivalence is not simply a formula to accept all domestic variations; it insists on certain minimum requirements.

2.2.3. Corporate liability

Whereas in the above example the Official Commentary gives options in defining corporate liability,[118] far more leeway is left to the appreciation of the WGB during the evaluation process. Article 2 and Article 3(2) merely provide the wider framework; the Convention allows countries to choose whether they wish to introduce a criminal or an equivalent civil or administrative concept of liability, as long as the sanctions are 'effective, proportionate, and dissuasive'. The chapter on Article 2 of this commentary[119] will show how the WGB is building up a body of rules to fill even this very open standard with meaning.[120]

2.2.4. Confiscation

In a further example of functional equivalence, the Convention itself provides alternatives in Article 3(3) when requiring confiscation of the proceeds of bribery[121] or the application of 'monetary sanctions of comparable effect'. From a strictly legal perspective confiscation and fines are two quite different concepts. Rightly, lawyers would dispute their

[118] Pieth 2000a, 58. [119] See ch. on Article 2 below.
[120] Cf. especially the discussion in the Phase 2 report on Germany: DE-Ph2, 28 et seq.
[121] Pieth 2000a, 57.

comparability: fines are calibrated according to the degree of culpability, whereas confiscation depends upon the proof of provenance of the proceeds of crime. Nevertheless, the OECD system against corruption is less concerned with the abstract rationale than with the concrete likelihood of ill-gotten gains being siphoned off. Therefore the WGB did not object when the United States and Korea opted for confiscatory fines.[122]

2.3. *A gradual* rapprochement *expected*

What functional equivalence means can be fully understood only in the context of the Phase 2 evaluations,[123] in which the WGB focuses particularly on the effectiveness of national implementing legislation. It is obvious that these methods allow countries to adopt different approaches when implementing the agreed standards.[124] It is, however, to be expected that there will be a *rapprochement* among countries as the monitoring process continues. The amount of detailed information gathered under the now established Phase 2 evaluation procedure is proving to be considerable, and discussions are becoming more and more fine-tuned.

3. Monitoring

The peer process developed during the 'soft law' phase and maintained even after the drafting of a binding law made it possible to achieve ratification and implementation of the OECD Treaty in such a short time by all state Parties. However, monitoring in this sense is neither a dispute settlement procedure by state Parties nor supervision of implementation by an independent court. It is, rather, the assessment by a group of peers of the effectiveness of implementation and application. Inevitably, this will result in a mixed technical and political procedure: in particular, for this reason it is essential that clear rules are followed.

IV. Legal basis and characteristics of OECD monitoring

The legal basis for the monitoring procedure is contained, firstly, in section VIII of the Revised Recommendation, in which the Council instructs the CIME through the WGB 'to carry out a programme of systematic follow-up to monitor and promote the full implementation of the Recommendation'.

[122] KR-Ph1, 22; US-Ph1, 22; see our commentary on Article 3(3) below.
[123] See part IV. of this ch. and our commentary on Article 12 below.
[124] Critical: Low 2003a, 36; Aiolfi and Pieth 2002, 352.

The obligations are further specified in Article 12 of the Convention and in Official Commentary 34.[125] These rules oblige state Parties to the Convention both to submit to the evaluation and to participate as evaluators. The procedures are left open, except that they provide for both 'vertical' analyses of implementation in each country and for 'horizontal' analyses, examining specific issues across the board.

The WGB has developed an elaborate sequence of monitoring procedures, drawing upon the experience of OECD subcommittees and the organisation's accession procedures,[126] and on human rights audits by the UN and other fora. It also made use of recent experiences with peer evaluation within the FATF. Similar monitoring mechanisms have been introduced in other organisations dealing with corruption, especially in the COE[127] and the Organisation of American States.[128]

There are, however, marked differences between the OECD system and other such procedures. First, the theory (at least) is that the OECD monitoring is state Party-driven and not Secretariat-driven. The so-called 'lead examiners' are responsible for the draft report submitted to the WGB, even if the Secretariat has a role in securing that equal standards are applied: in the WGB, unlike the FATF, the peer evaluation is conducted by peer states rather than individual experts. Furthermore, there is a very active role for the private sector and civil society in this process, and finally, the reports are always fully published and made available on Internet. These last two points also serve to distinguish the OECD system from others.

1. Four monitoring mechanisms

The four types of monitoring procedures developed by the OECD's WGB serve different purposes.

1.1. Tour de Table

In the *Tour de Table*, conducted at least four times a year by the WGB, countries report on the legislative progress in implementation and, more recently, on the steps taken to react to WGB critique. This information is published periodically on the Internet.[129] The procedures of the *Tour de Table*[130] allow the state Parties also to raise questions about concrete cases

[125] For full details see ch. on Article 12 below. [126] OECD 2003a.
[127] Notably in GRECO: see note 86. [128] See notes 76 and 87. [129] OECD 2004c.
[130] Procedural order, 'Outline for a Revised Tour de Table' of 12 February 2004, adopted by the WGB.

of transnational commercial bribery which have come to their attention or have been reported publicly. This part of the exchanges remains confidential. The arrangement makes the *Tour de Table* both a valuable means of keeping track of formal change and a very useful informal sounding board for issues of practical application.

1.2. 'Phase 1 monitoring'

'Phase 1',[131] now approaching conclusion, has proved a rapid way to assess the abstract legal compliance of implementing laws with the agreed standards of the Convention and the Revised Recommendation. Even though it did not raise issues of application, it developed into a very useful tool and the WGB did not shy away from harsh critique. Basically, three types of deficiencies were identified:

- major issues in need of immediate action;
- issues requiring observation in the application phase, to be pursued further in the context of Phase 2;
- other minor shortcomings, to be ironed out as and when the opportunity lends itself.

Major deficiencies demanding immediate legislative action were identified in about one-third of the evaluated countries.

1.3. 'Phase 1 plus' or 'Phase 1bis' monitoring

'Phase 1 plus' is a follow-up procedure to Phase 1: once the state Parties have reacted to the critique of the Group and supplemented or modified their laws, the new legislation will be formally re-evaluated. The report is then appended to the Phase 1 reports and published in the same manner.[132]

1.4. 'Phase 2 monitoring'

'Phase 2 monitoring'[133] concentrates on the application in practice of the Convention and of the Recommendation: this involves looking at the

[131] Procedural order published at: http://www.oecd.org >browse by topic: Corruption> Convention> Procedure of self- and mutual evaluation Phase 1.

[132] Cf. so far 'Phase 1 plus' evaluations for Bulgaria, Czech Republic, Iceland, Italy, Japan, and United Kingdom.

[133] Procedural order for Phase 2: DAFFE/IME/BR(99)33, published at: http://www.oecd.org > browse by topic: Corruption>Convention>Procedure of self- and mutual evaluation Phase 2.

structures established both to prevent and to prosecute cases of bribery. Resource levels, training, etc. are discussed both with public agencies and selected private sector operators (either MNEs[134] or Small and Medium Sized Enterprises (SMEs)).[135] Phase 2 monitoring follows the basic structures of the Phase 1 evaluation, but is more resource intensive, because of the nature of the issues involved, because of the on-site visit to the country, and because of the multitude of interlocutors (up to one hundred in a full Phase 2 evaluation!). The WGB has since developed an oral and a written follow-up to the Phase 2 monitoring.[136]

2. WGB evaluation procedures

WGB evaluations for the OECD follow the procedures set out below.

2.1. Preparatory stage

The first stage is preparatory, involving the evaluated country filling in a detailed questionnaire.[137] The Secretariat and the lead examiners (chosen by the Chair in consultation with the Management Group of the WGB, on the suggestion of the Secretariat) will raise concrete questions in need of further detailed treatment.

In Phase 2 a more specialised follow-up questionnaire and on-site visit follow.

In all procedures a draft report is prepared by the Secretariat and discussed with lead examiners and with the country examined. The country is entitled to present its observations; if at all possible, these will be included. The texts are presented to the WGB.

2.2. Hearings and finalisation of report

The hearings start with an informal consultation between examiners, representatives of the country examined, and the Secretariat in order to clarify misunderstandings and, if possible, minimise disagreement.

[134] See I.2.1.2. above.

[135] Cf. the standardised profile adopted in Phase 2 evaluations published at: http://www.oecd.org>browse by topic: Corruption>Convention>Country Reports>Phase 2 Country Reports.

[136] See IV.3. below.

[137] Both standardised Phase 1 and Phase 2 questionnaires published at: http://www.oecd.org >browse by topic: Corruption>Convention>Procedure of self- and mutual evaluation> Phase 1 and Phase 2.

The first reading of the report in the plenary sessions of the WGB allows the examiners to make their case, the country examined to respond, and the other members of the WGB to give their opinion, ask questions and raise further issues.

In the case of Phase 1 evaluations, the examiners draft a short evaluative text to be appended to the descriptive text; in the case of Phase 2 evaluations, Recommendations on the country evaluated are drafted. The draft concerned is immediately submitted to the examined country for informal comment on the evening of the first day of hearings.

The following day a second hearing concentrates on the evaluative text or Recommendations, on which the WGB will give a value judgement; the second hearing must result in an agreed text, to be adopted verbatim. There is, however, the possibility for the examined country to include a dissenting opinion in the report (see below).

After the meeting the OECD Secretariat used to send a revised report reflecting the Group's discussion and including the agreed evaluation. This report was sent to the delegates for approval via a written procedure. After difficulties of interpretation arose since the process is gradually getting tougher, it was decided to hold a third reading, still within the same meeting, and adopt the full report, an executive summary, and a brief press release by the WGB.

Two general comments should be added at this point: First, the *private sector* and *civil society* both play an essential role in the procedures of the WGB. Whereas, in Phase 1, their contributions are introduced in writing and distributed to the WGB as 'room documents', an elaborate system of hearings during the on-site-visits allows all opinions to be heard by the examiners.

Second, the whole evaluation process is based on the concept of *unanimity*, the general working principle of the OECD as an organisation. The country evaluated is, however, expected to abstain from blocking consensus within the group; it will nevertheless be given ample time to represent its case and can even introduce a dissenting opinion into the published text. The Working Group may then indicate whether it shares this opinion; a rejection will clarify to the wider public that the country stands alone with its interpretation. Finally, under the conditions of unanimity, if the country finds an ally, the consensus of the Group can be blocked and the text will be modified. This last observation may raise the concern that in an intergovernmental process with decisions taken ultimately in camera, countries with similar shortcomings might collude to prevent critical comments.[138] This is, however, unlikely as, on the one hand, the Secretariat and Chair have assumed the roles of neutral observers: they have repeatedly raised questions of substance and consistency quite independently of the evaluators. On the other hand, the competitive pressure on state Parties in the area dealt with by the WGB is so strong, that it would be economically and politically unwise to give any participant preferential treatment.

2.3. Publication

Following the completion of the written procedure, the OECD Secretariat arranges for publication of the final report on the website: whereas the Phase 1 evaluations are submitted to the Council once a year, Phase 2 evaluations are published on the OECD website immediately upon adoption.[139] The country evaluated may choose to organise a media event to mark this publication, to which representatives of the OECD may be invited.

3. Follow-up to 'Phase 2 monitoring'

When it became clear that a full round of Phase 2 monitoring was going to take close to seven years, state Parties saw the need to introduce a follow-up mechanism to the Recommendations made by the WGB in Phase 2.[140] In a recent revision of the Guidelines for Monitoring,[141] the WGB therefore created an elaborate follow-up mechanism. It distinguishes an ordinary procedure for all Parties and extraordinary measures to be taken in the case of persistent lack of adequate implementation.

3.1. Ordinary follow-up

One year after the Phase 2 hearing, countries are invited to present an **oral report** on the steps taken to react to the Recommendations made by the WGB. A brief discussion within the group is summarised by the Secretariat and included in the summary record of the meeting. It remains an internal document of the group. Two years after the Phase 2 evaluation countries are expected to produce a **written report** on their efforts to react

[138] Cf. the concern articulated by Low 2003a, 47 that 'mutual back scratching' could impede effective monitoring by the WGB.

[139] See note 137. [140] See ch. on Article 12 below. [141] OECD 2005.

to the WGB Recommendations. A more intensive discussion within the group, led by 'intervenants' (typically the former lead examiners), is held; and a short summary, adopted by the WGB plenary, is published as an annex to the Phase 2 report on the OECD website.

3.2. Extraordinary measures

In order to make the peer process more effective, the WGB has identified a series of graded measures in case implementation remains insufficient. On the soft end of the scale it could, for instance, request written reports. As a more intense follow-up measure, a second on-site visit could be requested by the WGB – be it already in the Phase 2 report[142] or after persistent non-compliance with the Convention. Other measures, like official letters to governments, high-level political missions to state Parties or formal public statements and press releases, are within the discretion of the WGB.

3.3. A 'Phase 3 monitoring'?

Currently discussions have been initiated within the OECD on the future of monitoring after Phase 2. No decision has been taken so far. The general tendency is, however, to look for a lean option of continued follow-ups whilst maintaining the pressure to implement and apply the rules. Obviously, intensified co-ordination with other monitoring efforts is a key issue.

4. Critical assessment

Commentators, of course, ask the question whether the OECD Convention is really working. Whereas some see it as an 'unambiguous success story',[143] others just as flatly declare its 'ineffectiveness'.[144] This difference of opinion can be explained partly by the divergence of focus: whereas nearly all commentators agree that concluding the Convention was a success, they disagree on its application record. While considerations of public diplomacy may indeed motivate countries to adopt texts rather than apply rules,[145] it may also be difficult for an outside observer of the OECD process to assess the full impact of the instruments, including the monitoring mechanisms applied. Several indicators in fact point towards the instruments having more impact than the critics would allow.

[142] JP-Ph2, 57; and optional LU-Ph2, 46. [143] Guilmette 2004a, 146.
[144] Tarullo 2004, 680 et seq. [145] Tarullo 2004, 687.

It is often repeated that OECD countries are slow in generating prosecutions for bribery. Correctly, Tarullo[146] assumes that the lack of prosecutions is probably not a reliable indicator of general compliance. Certainly, domestic prosecutors and law enforcement agencies need time to become accustomed to their new role: they need training, resources, and know-how to run an international case, and all of these may still be in short supply. They must link up with their counterparts abroad; many large international bribery cases are complex, because they involve the co-operation of several jurisdictions (those where acts were committed, effects were felt, actors located, and funds prepared and/or laundered). Nevertheless, in the course of Phase 2 evaluations several first convictions have been notified.[147] Furthermore, several dozens of cases in total are currently under investigation in state Parties.[148]

As the following example illustrates, there is indirect evidence that the risk of being taken to court on charges of transnational bribery is taken very seriously by shareholders worldwide.

When it was reported in the Norwegian Press that Statoil had entered a \$15.2 million contract with Horton Investments Ltd., a small consulting company based in the Turks and Caicos, for advice on securing oil concessions in Iran, the mere suspicion of possible bribery led to a drop in share prices of over \$1 billion in little more than a week. Shortly afterwards, before an inquiry could even get under way, three senior officials had to step down: the Chairman, the Chief Executive Officer, and the Director of Exploration and Production. The degree of nervousness that this case generated on the stock markets across the globe demonstrates how serious the issue of transnational bribery by a public company is taken nowadays (Statoil is listed on the New York Stock Exchange, and inquiries and investigations have been opened both in Norway and in the United States). The case shows that executives are facing increasing risks.[149]

V. The role and responsibilities of enterprises

The OECD instruments against bribery are addressed to state Parties.[150] They should implement and secure the application of the standards

[146] Tarullo 2004, 684 et seq.

[147] Apart from the United States, cf. especially Canada (1), Korea (2) and Switzerland (1).

[148] Analysing media reports of investigations and data on prosecutions supplied by state Parties, a figure of 47 current cases is estimated. These cases diverge considerably in size, and several of them will probably not lead to charges, let alone convictions.

[149] NO-Ph2, 4, 39 (para. 102), 45 (para. 145); *Payvand's Iran News*, 3 July 2004; *Oekocrim*, 12 September 2003 (press release); *Daily Telegraph* (UK), 24 September 2003 (online edn).

[150] Cf. the exceptions relating to rules on accounting, 'in-control' and auditing, which (partly) address the private sector (Rec. para. V and Art. 8 of the Convention).

concerned. The ultimate goal, however, is not the criminalisation of as many bribers as possible. The system seeks rather to deter corporate entities which may be prone to indulge in significant commercial bribery: they should be convinced that by taking such action they would risk serious material and reputational damage. The indirect goal is thus to raise material and reputational risk for corporate entities, by threat of legal (criminal) sanction. This risk should induce them to introduce meaningful compliance programmes. This means more than just writing a company code, even though a clear statement by the Chief Executive Officer or President is crucial.[151] It means organising training, offering help in uncertain situations (internal helplines), supervision, and, ultimately, in-house discipline.[152] It also means applying particular care when dealing with non-employees acting on behalf of the company (third parties like agents, sales representatives, etc.) and developing 'due diligence' procedures, clear contractual relationships,[153] adequate remuneration, and safe remuneration agreements,[154] as well as effective supervisory and auditing procedures.

Smaller companies, in particular, may be helped by following model codes developed by representatives of the private sector[155] or by NGOs;[156] larger corporations will most likely introduce their own approach, adapted to their management concepts. The action of intergovernmental organisations and governments will not go beyond the development of the basic legal framework to counteract transnational commercial bribery. Law enforcement practice will take time to make an impact. It may therefore be crucial for key business sectors to implement standards more quickly or to fill gaps in the system.[157] Already in a series of sectors, leading businesses are creating their own industry-wide standards to prevent bribery and related issues. So far, sector-specific standards in the financial sector[158] and in Engineering and Construction[159] have been published. According to reports, similar efforts are under way in the Energy Sector, in Power Systems, in the Defence Industry, and in the Pharmaceutical Industry.[160] The World Economic Forum (WEF), together with the NGO TI and the Research Centre 'Basel Institute

[151] Art. 7 ICC 2005; Vincke and Heimann 2003, 30 et seq.
[152] Vincke and Heimann 2003, 34 et seq.; Corr and Lawler 1999, 1331 et seq.
[153] Corr and Lawler 1999, 1333 et seq.; Davies 2003, 57 et seq. [154] Art. 3 ICC 2005.
[155] The leading role of the ICC Rules of Conduct (ICC 2005).
[156] Business Principles 2003. [157] Aiolfi and Pieth 2002, 356 et seq.
[158] Wolfsberg 2002c; also Pieth and Aiolfi 2003a, 267 et seq.
[159] Business Principles for Countering Bribery in Engineering and Construction Industry, an Initiative of the WEF, TI and the Basel Institute on Governance of January 2004. Cf. more recently: PACI 2005.
[160] *The Economist*, 2 March 2002, 11 and 67 et seq.

on Governance' in collaboration with the Global Compact of the UN, is working on the overall architecture of these standards.

These industry-related groups can serve to unite the key competitors in developing a common approach to the definition of the grey area between legal and illegal behaviour; the reduction of facilitation payments may be one beneficial result. The groups can also provide concerted action in relation to third parties (agents, joint venture partners and, in particular, foreign subsidiaries).

General codes, industry-specific agreements, and company compliance programmes can all contribute greatly to the efficacy of the public standards against commercial bribery. Indeed, they are a necessary complement to these standards.[161]

References

For documentation see the consolidated bibliography at the end of this book.

Aiolfi, G. and M. Pieth (2002), 'How to Make a Convention Work: The Organisation for Economic Co-operation and Development Recommendation and Convention on Bribery as an Example of a New Horizon in International Law' in C. Fijnaut and L. Huberts (eds.), *Corruption, Integrity and Law Enforcement*, Leiden, Boston, 349.

Bliss, J.C. and G.J. Spak (1989), 'The Foreign Corrupt Practices Act of 1988: Clarification or Evisceration?', *Law & Policy in International Business* **20**, 441.

Cartier-Bresson, J. (2000), 'The Causes and Consequences of Corruption: Economic Analyses and Lessons Learnt' in OECD (ed.), *No Longer Business as Usual*, Paris, 11.

Coeurdray, M. (2003), *Du dévoilement médiatique de la 'corruption' à la gestion déontologique des affaires* (dissertation/thesis), Paris.

Corr, C.F. and J. Lawler (1999), 'Damned If You Do, Damned If You Don't? The OECD Convention and the Globalization of Anti-Bribery Measures', *Vanderbilt Journal of Transnational Law* **32**, 1252.

Crutchfield George, B., K.A. Lacey and J. Birmele (1999), 'On the Threshold of the Adoption of Global Anti-Bribery Legislation: A Critical Analysis of Current Domestic and International Efforts Toward the Reduction of Business Corruption', *Vanderbilt Journal of Transnational Law* **32**, 1.

Davies, M.N. (2003), 'The Role of Agents and Sales Representatives' in F. Vincke and F. Heimann (eds.), *Fighting Corruption*, Paris, 57.

Delmas-Marty, M. (1998), *Trois défis pour un droit mondial*, Paris.

Gareis, R.J. (1999), 'The 1998 Amendments to the US Foreign Corrupt Practices Act: A Comparative and Pragmatic Analysis of, and with, the OECD Convention on Combating Bribery of Foreign Officials', *International Trade Corruption Monitor (ITCM)*, A-1013.

Global Witness Report (2004), *Time for Transparency: Coming Clean on Oil, Mining and Gas Revenues*, Washington.

[161] Vincke and Heimann 2003, 24 et seq.

Guilmette, J.-H. (2004) [cited Guilmette 2004a], *The Power of Peer Pressure – Development Co-operation Among Nations Using OECD and IDRC Network Approach* (unpublished manuscript).

Heimann, F. (2003), 'The ICC Rules of Conduct and the OECD Convention' in F. Vincke and F. Heimann (eds.), *Fighting Corruption*, Paris, 13.

Heine, G., B. Huber, and T.O. Rose (2003), *Private Commercial Bribery – A Comparison of National and Supranational Legal Structures*, Freiburg i. Br.

Hines, J.R. (1995), *Forbidden Payment: Foreign Bribery and American Business after 1977* (National Bureau of Economic Research, Working Paper 5266, available at: http://www.nber.org > Publications > Working Papers).

Langer, S.H. and J. Pelzman (2001), 'An Analysis of the OECD Convention on Combating Bribery of Foreign Officials' in K. Fatemi (ed.), *International Public Policy and Regionalism at the Turn of the Century*, Amsterdam, New York, 60.

Low, L.A. (2003) [cited Low 2003a], 'The Global Legal Framework: The OECD, OAS and Council of Europe Antibribery Conventions: New International Standards and National Anti-Corruption Laws: Challenges for Effective Implementation and Enforcement' (unpublished paper, prepared for a Conference in Paris, April 2003).

Low, L.A. and M.L. Burton (2000), 'The OECD, OAS and Council of Europe Antibribery Conventions – A Comparison with the Corrupt Practices Act: New International Standards and their Implications', *The California International Practitioner*, Vol. **10**, No. 2, 1.

Mauro, P. (1995), 'Corruption and Growth', *Quarterly Journal of Economics* **110**, 681.

Moody-Stuart, G. (1997), *Grand Corruption*, 3rd edn, Oxford.

OECD (2003) [cited OECD 2003a], *Peer Review: A Tool for Co-operation and Change*, Paris.

Pieth, M. (1997) [cited Pieth 1997a], 'International Cooperation to Combat Corruption' in K.A. Elliott (ed.), *Corruption and the Global Economy*, Washington, 119.

Pieth, M. (1999) [cited Pieth 1999a], 'Die Strafbarkeit der aktiven Bestechung ausländischer Beamter' in M. Pieth and P. Eigen (Hrsg.), *Korruption im internationalen Geschäftsverkehr: Bestandesaufnahme, Bekämpfung, Prävention*, Neuwied, Kriftel, Basel, Frankfurt a. M., 341.

Pieth, M. (1999) [cited Pieth 1999b], 'International Efforts to Combat Corruption' in American Bar Association (ed.), *The Foreign Corrupt Practices Act: How to Comply under the New Amendments and the OECD Convention*, Chicago, E-1.

Pieth, M. (1999) [cited Pieth 1999c], 'International Efforts to Combat Corruption', *International Trade Corruption Monitor (ITCM)*, A-1038.

Pieth, M. (2000) [cited Pieth 2000a], 'From Ideal to Reality: Making the New Global Standard Stick' in OECD (ed.), *No Longer Business as Usual*, Paris, 51.

Pieth, M. (2000) [cited Pieth 2000b], "Funktionale Äquivalenz" Praktische Rechtsvergleichung und internationale Harmonisierung von Wirtschaftsstrafrecht', *Zeitschrift für Schweizerisches Recht* **119**, 477.

Pieth, M. and G. Aiolfi (2003) [cited Pieth and Aiolfi 2003a], 'The Private Sector Becomes Active: The Wolfsberg Process' in A. Clark, and P. Burell (eds.), *A Practitioner's Guide to International Money Laundering Law and Regulation*, Surrey, 267.

Pletscher, T. (1999), 'Wie halten wir uns sauber? – Bekämpfung der Korruption aus Sicht der Wirtschaft' in M. Pieth and P. Eigen (Hrsg.), *Korruption im internationalen Geschäftsverkehr: Bestandesaufnahme, Bekämpfung, Prävention*, Neuwied, Kriftel, Basel, Frankfurt a. M., 275.

Rose-Ackermann, S. (1999), 'Globale Wirtschaft und Korruption' in M. Pieth and P. Eigen (Hrsg.), *Korruption im internationalen Geschäftsverkehr: Bestandesaufnahme, Bekämpfung, Prävention*, Neuwied, Kriftel, Basel, Frankfurt a. M., 40.

Sacerdoti, G. (1999), 'Das OECD-Übereinkommen 1997 über die Bekämpfung der Bestechung ausländischer Amtsträger im internationalen Geschäftsverkehr' in M. Pieth and P. Eigen (Hrsg.), *Korruption im internationalen Geschäftsverkehr: Bestandesaufnahme, Bekämpfung, Prävention*, Neuwied, Kriftel, Basel, Frankfurt a. M., 212.

Sacerdoti, G. (2000), 'To Bribe or not to Bribe?' in OECD (ed.), *No Longer Business as Usual*, Paris, 29.

Sacerdoti, G. (2003), *Responsabilità d'impresa e strumenti internazionali anticorruzione*, Milano.

Schoenlaub, F.E. (1999), 'International Bribery, Corruption and Fair Competition: Part 1', *International Trade Corruption Monitor (ITCM)*, A-1056.

Tarullo, D.K. (2004), 'The Limits of Institutional Design: Implementing the OECD Anti-Bribery Convention', *Vanderbilt Journal of International Law* **44**, 665.

Vincke, F. and F. Heimann (2003), *Fighting Corruption*, Paris.

PART II

Commentary

Article 1. The Offence of Bribery of Foreign Public Officials

INGEBORG ZERBES[1]

Article 1 – The Offence of Bribery of Foreign Public Officials:

1. Each Party shall take such measures as may be necessary to establish that it is a criminal offence under its law for any person intentionally to offer, promise or give any undue pecuniary or other advantage, whether directly or through intermediaries, to a foreign public official, for that official or for a third party, in order that the official act or refrain from acting in relation to the performance of official duties, in order to obtain or retain business or other improper advantage in the conduct of international business.

2. Each Party shall take any measures necessary to establish that complicity in, including incitement, aiding and abetting, or authorisation of an act of bribery of a foreign public official shall be a criminal offence. Attempt and conspiracy to bribe a foreign public official shall be criminal offences to the same extent as attempt and conspiracy to bribe a public official of that Party.

3. The offences set out in paragraphs 1 and 2 above are hereinafter referred to as 'bribery of a foreign public official'.

4. For the purpose of this Convention:

a. 'foreign public official' means any person holding a legislative, administrative, or judicial office of a foreign country, whether appointed or elected; any person exercising a public function for a foreign country, including for a public agency or public enterprise; and any official or agent of a public international organisation;

b. 'foreign country' includes all levels and subdivisions of government, from national to local;

c. 'act or refrain from acting in relation to the performance of official duties' includes any use of the public official's position, whether or not within the official's authorised competence.

[1] Translated from the German by Peter J. Cullen.

Official Commentary

Article 1. – The Offence of Bribery of Foreign Public Officials:

Re paragraph 1:

3. Article 1 establishes a standard to be met by Parties, but does not require them to utilise its precise terms in defining the offence under their domestic laws. A Party may use various approaches to fulfil its obligations, provided that conviction of a person for the offence does not require proof of elements beyond those which would be required to be proved if the offence were defined as in this paragraph. For example, a statute prohibiting the bribery of agents generally which does not specifically address bribery of a foreign public official, and a statute specifically limited to this case, could both comply with this Article. Similarly, a statute which defined the offence in terms of payments 'to induce a breach of the official's duty' could meet the standard provided that it was understood that every public official had a duty to exercise judgement or discretion impartially and this was an 'autonomous' definition not requiring proof of the law of the particular official's country.

4. It is an offence within the meaning of paragraph 1 to bribe to obtain or retain business or other improper advantage whether or not the company concerned was the best qualified bidder or was otherwise a company which could properly have been awarded the business.

5. 'Other improper advantage' refers to something to which the company concerned was not clearly entitled, for example, an operating permit for a factory which fails to meet the statutory requirements.

6. The conduct described in paragraph 1 is an offence whether the offer or promise is made or the pecuniary or other advantage is given on that person's own behalf or on behalf of any other natural person or legal entity.

7. It is also an offence irrespective of, inter alia, the value of the advantage, its results, perceptions of local custom, the tolerance of such payments by local authorities, or the alleged necessity of the payment in order to obtain or retain business or other improper advantage.

8. It is not an offence, however, if the advantage was permitted or required by the written law or regulation of the foreign public official's country, including case law.

9. Small 'facilitation' payments do not constitute payments made 'to obtain or retain business or other improper advantage' within the meaning of paragraph 1 and, accordingly, are also not an offence. Such payments, which, in some countries, are made to induce public officials to perform their functions, such as issuing licenses or permits, are generally illegal in the foreign country concerned. Other countries can and should address this corrosive phenomenon by such means as support for programmes of good governance. However, criminalisation by other countries does not seem a practical or effective complementary action.

10. Under the legal system of some countries, an advantage promised or given to any person, in anticipation of his or her becoming a foreign public official, falls within the scope of the offences described in Article 1, paragraph 1 or 2. Under the legal system of many countries, it is considered technically distinct from the offences covered by the present Convention. However, there is a commonly shared concern and intent to address this phenomenon through further work.

Re paragraph 2:

11. The offences set out in paragraph 2 are understood in terms of their normal content in national legal systems. Accordingly, if authorisation, incitement, or one of the other listed acts, which does not lead to further action, is not itself punishable under a Party's legal system, then the Party would not be required to make it punishable with respect to bribery of a foreign public official.

Re paragraph 4:

12. 'Public function' includes any activity in the public interest, delegated by a foreign country, such as the performance of a task delegated by it in connection with public procurement.

13. A 'public agency' is an entity constituted under public law to carry out specific tasks in the public interest.

14. A 'public enterprise' is any enterprise, regardless of its legal form, over which a government, or governments, may, directly or indirectly, exercise a dominant influence. This is deemed to be the case, inter alia, when the government or governments hold the majority of the enterprise's subscribed capital, control the majority of votes attaching to shares issued by the enterprise or can appoint a majority of the members of the enterprise's administrative or managerial body or supervisory board.

15. An official of a public enterprise shall be deemed to perform a public function unless the enterprise operates on a normal commercial basis in the relevant market, i.e., on a basis which is substantially equivalent to that of a private enterprise, without preferential subsidies or other privileges.

16. In special circumstances, public authority may in fact be held by persons (e.g., political party officials in single party states) not formally designated as public officials. Such persons, through their de facto performance of a public function, may, under the legal principles of some countries, be considered to be foreign public officials.

17. 'Public international organisation' includes any international organisation formed by states, governments, or other public international organisations, whatever the form of organisation and scope of competence, including, for example, a regional economic integration organisation such as the European Communities.

18. 'Foreign country' is not limited to states, but includes any organised foreign area or entity, such as an autonomous territory or a separate customs territory.

19. One case of bribery which has been contemplated under the definition in paragraph 4.c is where an executive of a company gives a bribe to a senior official of a government, in order that this official use his office – though acting outside his competence – to make another official award a contract to that company.

Chapter contents

5.1.1. The aim
5.1.2. Negotiation stage: 'offering' and 'promising' an advantage
5.1.3. Completed offence: 'giving' an advantage
5.1.4. Late rewards
5.2. The limits of criminal defences
5.3. Point of completion
5.4. Horizontal comparison
5.4.1. Explicit reference to all phases of the crime
5.4.2. Broadening of the offence
5.4.3. Danger of limiting scope of offence
5.4.4. Defences or excuses not foreseen by the Convention
6. Indirect bribery
6.1. The basis of criminal responsibility for the acts of others
6.1.1. The practical need to extend responsibility
6.1.2. Liability for third party action: legal conditions
6.2. Responsibility for bribery by independent agents
6.3. Liability in respect of bribery by subsidiaries
6.4. Horizontal comparison
7. Consideration for the bribe: 'acting in relation to the performance of official duties'
7.1. Taking advantage of a public function
7.2. Possible limits
7.2.1. General limitation to breach of duties
7.2.2. Exception of small facilitation payments
7.3. Horizontal comparison
7.3.1. No limitation to sphere of competence of public official
7.3.2. Breach of duties concepts in domestic law
7.3.3. Wide definition of official action with tolerance of small facilitation payments
7.3.4. Broad concepts without provision for exceptions
8. Objective of bribery: improper advantage in the conduct of international business
8.1. Limitation to business advantage
8.2. Improper advantages
8.3. Horizontal comparison
8.3.1. Extension to other walks of life
8.3.2. Limitation to transnational business
8.3.3. The 'obtaining or retaining business' concept of the FCPA
8.3.4. Improper nature of the advantage

III. MENS REA

1. Dolus eventualis
2. Horizontal comparison

IV. EXTENSION OF CRIMINAL RESPONSIBILITY

1. Inclusion of transnational bribery in the existing criminal justice system

I. Preliminary remarks

1. Scope of application

Article 1 of the Convention specifies the conduct which constitutes the offence of bribery of foreign public officials. The offence is more limited in substantive terms, but has wider geographic application, than offences defined by other international instruments dealing with transnational bribery. This can be explained by the specific mandate of the OECD, which is an *economic organisation* of the world's leading industrial nations, whose members control the bulk of international trade.[2] The object of the OECD is to promote trade relations on the basis of a 'level playing field of commerce'.[3] The 1997 Convention is to be seen in this context: it seeks to eliminate bribery in international transactions first and foremost because it distorts fair competition.[4]

Before the Convention, bribery of foreign public officials had been criminalised only in the United States, namely since enactment of the US Foreign Corrupt Practices Act of 1977 (FCPA 1977). This situation led to an immense competitive disadvantage for US companies. While US investors faced (criminal) sanctions for engaging in bribery, their foreign competitors could bribe with impunity, and do so to win contracts at the Americans' expense. This 'lost business',[5] i.e. economic considerations, led the OECD to push for anti-corruption measures 'levelling the playing field' again.[6] Everyone in the marketplace should be bound by the same restraints.[7]

[2] The Convention has been signed by thirty-six countries, whose global trade makes up about 70% of world exports and around 90% of foreign investments: see Introduction of this commentary.
[3] Pieth 1999a, 344. [4] Preamble, first recital. [5] Gareis 1999, A-1013.
[6] Gareis 1999, A-1013.
[7] For a detailed discussion of the history of the Convention see I.2.3. in the Introduction of this commentary.

The criminal law provisions of the Convention reflect this regulatory objective vis-à-vis global trade:[8]

- The subject-matter of the Convention is limited to *business transactions.*

  Of the other international instruments addressing this subject, only the Convention of the United Nations (UN) Against Corruption of 2003 is similarly limited to business transactions.

- Multinational companies based in the world's leading industrial nations dominate the global market in their role as investors and exporters. Where bribery features in international transactions, it is they who usually pay the bribe in order to win contracts against competitors. Bribes are paid, in particular, to officials of developing countries. Accordingly, the OECD's anti-corruption strategy is supply-side driven, focusing on the source of corrupt payments: the bribes should be cut off at source to eliminate their impact on global trade (with developing countries in particular). The Convention follows the FCPA approach by combating only *active bribery.*[9] The sanctioning of the foreign public official, on the other hand, is no concern of the OECD; this is left to the state which is 'victim' of the corruption in question.[10] It is for this state, not a foreign state, to remedy the breach of public trust in official conduct which the official's acceptance of the bribe represents: that is the traditional approach of international criminal policy, to which the Convention adheres. Regional instruments, such as those of the European Union (EU), the Council of Europe (COE) and the Organisation of American States (OAS), and the UN Convention call for penalisation of both parties to the transaction, i.e. the giver and the recipient of the bribe.

  The approach of EC/EU law derives from the special nature of the EU as a supranational organisation committed to advancing 'integration' among its Members by means of creating a unified legal space for the operation of certain common 'Community' or 'Union' policies.[11] These policies reflect shared interests of the Member States and are partially financed by a common budget. The Protocol of 27 September 1996 to the Convention on the protection of the European Communities' financial interests[12] is linked to the protection of this budget, whereas the EU Convention of 26 May 1997 on the fight against corruption[13] has a broader remit and frees itself from the link to

[8] For further details cf. Pieth 1999b, A-1041 et seq.; and see part II in the Introduction of this commentary.
[9] 15 U.S.C. §§ 78dd-1, -2 und -3 FCPA 1977; Low 2003a, 4. [10] Pieth 1999a, 346.
[11] Pieth 1999a, 343. [12] EU 1996b. [13] EU 1997a.

the Community's financial interests. The Convention makes corruption of or by public officials – be they national or Community officials – a matter of Union-wide concern; it obliges the Member States to criminalise and to sanction both active and passive bribery involving such officials.

The COE's Criminal Law Convention on Corruption of 27 January 1999[14] and its Additional Protocol of 15 May 2003[15] are, likewise, not limited to the criminalisation of supply-side bribery; they also cover the passive corruption of the recipient. The broader definition of corruption by COE anti-bribery instruments aims to advance the organisation's goal of improving judicial co-operation among its members – mutual legal assistance, extradition, confiscation. The aim of these instruments is not so much to create a body of uniform criminal law relating to corruption as to establish a minimum degree of approximation of the offences concerned, sufficient to facilitate all forms of judicial co-operation.

The OAS Convention of 1996 also covers active and passive bribery, but only in relation to national public officials. For transnational bribery it focuses only on criminalisation of the briber – like the OECD Convention it does not address the responsibility of the bribe-taker, the foreign public official.[16]

The solution of the UN Convention of 2003 is similar. While the criminalisation provisions of chapter 3 of the Convention encompass active and passive bribery in relation to national public officials, there is no obligation upon Parties to the UN Convention to bring a foreign public official to book for his or her acceptance of a bribe. Article 16(2) states merely that 'each state party shall consider' adopting measures to criminalise such conduct.

- To date, the Convention applies only to pecuniary or other advantages conferred upon *public officials*. No agreement could be reached on a prohibition of corruption in the private sector; private actors are not bound by the same objective standards as state bodies. Nevertheless, the 'level playing of commerce' can equally be disturbed by action in the private sphere, distorting, as it does, the conditions of fair competition. Thus, the OECD also has the long-term aim of adopting measures in this field. The amendment of the Convention to cover private corruption is envisaged.[17]

The EU Framework Decision of 22 July 2003 on combating corruption in the private sector[18] and the COE's Criminal Law Convention on Corruption of 27 January 1999[19] have already gone down this path by calling upon Member Parties to criminalise active and passive corruption.

By contrast, American states chose in their OAS Convention to restrict the fight against corruption to the public sphere.

Finally, the UN's Convention on Corruption has private as well as public corruption in its sights. It calls for each state party to 'consider adopting'

[14] COE 1999a. [15] COE 2003. [16] For details cf. Low 2003a, 20 et seq.

[17] The International Chamber of Commerce (ICC) continues to request action on private corruption; the OECD's Working Group on Bribery (WGB) is considering how to respond.

[18] EU 2003a, building on Art. 2 EU 1998b. [19] Arts. 7 and 8 COE 1999a.

measures to make active and passive bribery criminal offences. But there is no obligation to do so.

- The Convention applies only to cases of *transnational* bribery. It is unilateral in the sense of applying to officials both of contracting parties and non-contracting parties, but it remains silent concerning domestic corruption. OECD measures aim to protect the market for cross-border trade, but do not purport to influence the functioning of the domestic market. How the state Parties to the Convention criminalise bribery of or by their own public officials remains a matter for them alone. The treaties of the EU, COE, OAS, and UN go further by criminalising domestic bribery too, whether active or passive in nature.

The EU's Convention on the fight against corruption requires Member States to criminalise active and passive bribery involving:

- officials of other EU Member States;
- their own public officials; and also
- Community officials.

This approach reflects the EU's integration goal referred to above. Bribery involving officials of third states (i.e. non-EU states) or of other international organisations is not, on the other hand, a matter for the EU Convention. The COE's Criminal Law Convention goes much further. It does not limit the definition of 'foreign public official' to officials of another COE state. Like the OECD Convention, it aspires to unilateral coverage: the bribery offence should be prosecuted, whether the official involved is from a contracting party or not. And it goes one step further than the OECD by calling for criminal measures against the foreign official concerned.

The OAS Convention also adopts this global approach. While confined to active bribery, the criminalisation intended by the Convention should apply to officials of all foreign states. There is, however, one caveat here in the form of an 'escape clause':[20] contracting parties are obliged to criminalise transnational bribery only to the extent that this is consistent with 'its Constitution and the fundamental principles of its legal system'.[21]

The active bribery offence provided for in the UN Convention on Corruption replicates that contained in Article 1(1) of the OECD Convention. However, 'each state party shall consider' also the criminalisation of the conduct of the foreign public official in accepting the bribe.[22]

- The Convention applies to cases of 'serious and 'genuine' corruption in international business. It draws certain limits to criminalisation:

  - It does not necessarily apply to the small facilitation payments, which are commonplace in certain countries and thought necessary in order to induce the performance of official duty. Such payments are recognised by the

[20] Low 2003a, 22. [21] Art. VIII OAS 1996. [22] Art. 16(2) UN 2003.

Convention as harmful,[23] but need not be criminalised as bribes within the meaning of the Convention.[24]

- The Convention usually leaves it to the criminal policy of the state Parties whether they will also criminalise the giving of bribes in order to achieve the performance of professional duties; state Parties may instead choose to limit criminalisation to breach of duties.[25]
- If an undue payment within the meaning of the Convention is paid to a foreign public official, but that payment is in fact permitted under the law of the foreign state, then it does not fall under the Article 1 prohibition.[26]
- General defences available under national criminal law are left untouched by the Convention. Grounds of justification or excuse available in national systems may, therefore, also be applied in this context to deny or reduce criminal liability.[27]

2. Functional equivalence

The principle of 'functional equivalence' is explained in Official Commentary 3 as follows:[28]

> 'Article 1 establishes a standard to be met by state Parties, but does not require them to utilise its precise terms in defining the offence under their domestic laws. A Party may use various approaches to fulfil its obligations, provided that conviction of a person for the offence does not require proof of elements beyond those which would be required to be proved if the offence were defined as in this paragraph. For example, a statute prohibiting the bribery of agents generally which does not specifically address bribery of a foreign public official, and a statute specifically limited to this case, could both comply with this Article.'

State Parties may therefore use whatever means they regard as appropriate to fulfil the terms of Article 1; the criminalisation of active bribery of foreign public officials need not be achieved in identical ways. The criminalisation of foreign bribery in general terms is just as acceptable as the extension of an existing offence applicable to bribery of domestic officials to foreign officials.[29] What is important is that the objective standard of the Convention be met, though 'functional equivalence' of different legal instruments or measures is not easily obtained.[30]

State Parties may not add conditions to the Article 1 offence, which would limit its scope of application. It would not be permissible, for example, to

[23] These are indeed the subject of numerous anti-bribery initiatives of civil society and the economy. Their codes of conduct prohibit facilitation payments. Cf., for example, the World Economic Forum Partnership Against Corruption (PACI) of 2005 (http://www.weforum.org).
[24] See further II.7.2.2. below. [25] See II.7.2.1. below. [26] See II.4.2. below.
[27] See II.5.2. below. [28] See also III.2 in the Introduction of this commentary.
[29] Sacerdoti 2000, 36.
[30] Low 2003a: 'this equivalence...remains a distant vision' (36).

allow criminal liability for foreign bribery to apply only as from a certain minimum level of bribe, or to make criminalisation of bribery dependent on the existence of a prior agreement or 'pact' to pay the amounts in question.[31] Even implementing legislation which precisely reproduces the wording of the Convention may not be acceptable, if the terms used are capable of being construed, in the light of national law, in a way which departs from the Convention or is imprecise. National interpretations should not lead to gaps in the criminalisation of foreign bribery.[32]

If the foreign bribery offence is laid down by accessory criminal law (*Nebenstrafrecht*), a state Party must ensure that an independent judicial body enjoys jurisdiction over the offence. The process of adjudication of liability must be free from instructions.[33]

II. Objective elements of the offence

1. The offender: 'any person'

The 'Agreed Common Elements' appended to the Revised Recommendation of 1997, on the basis of which the Convention was drafted, already established that the offeror of a bribe, i.e. the offender, could be 'any person'. Two consequences flow from this: the first is that bribery is not a 'special offence', capable of being committed only by a certain category of persons, for example, a company's directors. The pool of potential offenders is unlimited. The FCPA used to limit the persons covered to 'issuers'[34] and to 'domestic concerns'.[35] These restrictions contained in the FCPA[36] were lifted in order to comply with the Convention. The application of the Act now extends to 'any person'.[37]

The second consequence is that liability for acts of foreign bribery may also rest with *legal persons*, not only natural persons. This is made explicit by Article 2 of the Convention. Those countries whose laws limit

[31] The French requirement of precisely such a prior 'bribery pact' between the offeror and the bribe-taker is problematic here: cf. FR-Ph1, 5.

[32] This issue was raised in the context of Greek legislation: cf. GR-Ph1, 17.

[33] See ch. on Article 5 below.

[34] These are all foreign and domestic companies, whose shares are registered with the US Securities and Exchange Commission (SEC): 15 U.S.C. § 78dd-1 FCPA 1977.

[35] Any citizen, national or resident, of the United States or any corporation etc. which has its principal place of business in the United States, or which is organised under US laws: 15 U.S.C. § 78dd-2 FCPA 1977.

[36] Cf. with regard to the (still problematic) 'interstate nexus requirement': US-Ph2, 31.

[37] 15 U.S.C. § 78dd-3 FCPA 1977: 'other than issuers or domestic concerns'; cf. Low 2003a, 6 et seq.

liability to natural persons will find themselves in breach of the Convention.[38]

The application of the Article 1 offence to 'any person' means that, in principle, no one is immune from prosecution. The conferral of immunity on holders of public office, such as Parliamentarians or Members of the government, or on Heads of State, such as monarchs, does not breach this aspect of the Convention.[39] Such immunity may, however, prove problematic if conferred in absolute terms. As a rule, however, national laws foresee the possibility of lifting such immunity in the case of criminal conduct by the office-holder concerned. Various procedures may be provided for, ranging from prosecution only after removal from office[40] to the lifting of the immunity in the particular case by the institution concerned (e.g. Parliamentary decision in respect of one of its Members)[41] or to a decision by the Parliament in respect of a Head of State.[42]

The long-established immunities of monarchs are a special case; their immunity may not be impugned. With regard, for example, to the British monarch – in the United Kingdom justice is still done in the name of 'the Crown' – or to the Swedish monarch or Luxembourg's Grand-Duc, tradition dictates that they may not be prosecuted in their own courts. There is no will in the international community to challenge these constitutional safeguards applying to the position of the Head of State.[43] The wording of Article 1 should in this respect be narrowly construed. The topic of immunity is indeed hardly addressed in the OECD context; it receives very little attention compared to the process of the COE in the Group of States Against Corruption (GRECO). It is not convincing to explain this on the basis of the Convention's concentration on active bribery. Holders of high public office may not only find themselves in the role of recipients of bribes. They may well exhibit expansive tendencies of 'foreign investment' themselves.

[38] Argentina (AR-Ph1, 3). The same applies to Italy at the time of its first evaluation. There was at that time only a proposal to create corporate liability for bribery; only natural persons could commit the crime: cf. IT-Ph1, 4 et seq., 34. In the meantime, namely since 2 May 2001, this loophole has essentially been filled; the new situation nevertheless leaves open the legal question whether state-owned or state-controlled companies may also be criminally liable. Cf., therefore, the criticism in IT-Ph2, 39.

[39] This topic is discussed in AR-Ph1, 3, but no specific conclusion is drawn.

[40] Arts. 53, 59, 60, and 66 of the Constitution of Argentina.

[41] For example, Art. 57 Austrian Constitution.

[42] For example, Art. 63 Austrian Constitution.

[43] The subject of immunity of the sovereign or Head of State was raised in respect of Luxembourg (LU-Ph1, 3) and New Zealand (NZ-Ph1, 4). In these cases the traditional privileges were not put into question. The special position of the Sovereign was, likewise, not challenged during the COE's GRECO process.

2. Recipient: foreign public official

2.1. Autonomous definition

According to Article 1 of the Convention, a foreign public official is at the receiving end of the bribe. Each state, however, has its own idea about who is to be regarded as a public official. How should a multilateral Convention regulate the matter? The crucial consideration here is that OECD instruments should serve global economic interests. The fight against corruption therefore demands that countries adopt a definition of foreign public official which is as uniform as possible.[44]

It was in this spirit that the OECD succeeded in agreeing upon an autonomous definition. All players in the global market are, accordingly, faced with a common prohibition, which reduces the risk of distortion of competition caused by divergent laws. The Convention's common definition removes the 'national law variable'; punishment will not depend on the vagaries of national law of the 'victim state' but on the application of a uniform (high) OECD standard (Article 1(4)(a) of the Convention). In this respect, the OECD Convention is comparable to the OAS and UN Conventions, which also aspire to global coverage with their definition of the foreign public official. These international instruments go further than their European (EU or COE) counterparts.

> The EU instruments are characterised by the fact that they pertain to a supranational organisation which lacks a (direct) competence to enact criminal law. EU law envisages instead minimum approximation of national criminal law in certain fields. Its definition comprises national and Community officials. The former are defined by the domestic law of the Member State in question, the latter by EC law. There is no need for an overarching common definition.
>
> The Criminal Law Convention on Corruption of the COE is, first and foremost, an instrument for promoting effective mutual legal assistance, extradition and confiscation of the proceeds of crime.[45] The object of the exercise here is to establish legal conditions enabling the 'dual criminality' requirement, which traditionally underlies such judicial assistance, to be met. Thus, it suffices to allow the definition of 'public official' to be determined by national law.

Given the decision to impose an autonomous definition, the *domestic law* of the victim state applies only to determine the *actual field of activity* of the official, e.g. it determines whether the person is a Member of Parliament or judge, within the national system. Whether that field of activity brings the person within the *definition of 'foreign public official'* under the Convention's

[44] Pieth 1999a, 347; and see part II.3 in the Introduction of this commentary.
[45] Pieth 1999b, A-1044.

system is a matter to be determined exclusively in the light of the *Convention's criteria* (as contained in Article 1). It would be contrary to Article 1 and to the goal of homogeneous application of the Convention for the definition of 'public official' to be left to the law of his or her home state (victim state).[46]

The adoption by national legislation of a special definition of foreign public official, in line with that of the Convention, would serve the interests of legal clarity and certainty. Such a definition would be preferable to the integration of Article 1, even *verbatim*, into general national bribery law. It would also be desirable for such a special definition to be adopted even where the national constitution requires that domestic law be interpreted in the light of international obligations. Those obligations might in some cases imply a standard lower than that of the OECD Convention.[47] National law should, preferably, only dispense with an independent definition of foreign public official, if its definition of national public official itself contains all the necessary elements to satisfy the terms of Article 1(4)(a) or goes beyond this.[48] A narrower definition of domestic official clearly should not be used.

In relation to Common Law systems, we must pose the question whether the definition of foreign public official must be laid down by *statute*. The question whether,[49] or the extent to which, foreign public officials – within the meaning of the Convention – would be caught by national law which did not refer to them explicitly, should not depend on future case law.

2.2. Structure and principle underlying the definition

The Convention combats bribery in the context of a private-public relationship. The situation envisaged by the Convention is that of a private person or company facing a contracting party which has *higher legal authority* deriving from its status as a public body (either the state itself or manifestation of the state).[50] The Convention definition therefore focuses on those public bodies which may exercise such special powers:

- From an institutional perspective,[51] what is important is the allocation to one of the three branches of government[52] – legislative, executive (i.e. administration of government) or judicial: '"foreign

[46] Belgian and Mexican implementing legislations was for this reason considered inadequate in the respective Phase 1 enquiries: BE-Ph1, 20; MX-Ph1, 3, 23.

[47] Cf. also the discussion of Spanish legislation: ES-Ph1, 4, 24 et seq.

[48] Cf., for example, how Norway has implemented the Convention: NO-Ph1, 2 et seq., 14.

[49] Cf. UK-Ph1, 25, raising this issue in the light of UK law, and referring inter alia to the risk that judicial law-making of this kind might contravene the prohibition on retroactive penal legislation contained in Art. 7 COE 1950.

[50] See II.2.5. below. [51] See II.2.4. below. [52] See II.2.5.1. below.

public official" means any person holding a legislative, administrative or judicial office of a foreign country' (Article 1(4)(a), part I).

- If it is not possible to allocate the person concerned to one of these branches of government, what then counts is the nature of the official's function or role. This reflects the intended functional understanding.[53] According to this approach, one's status as foreign public official derives from the content of the activity concerned: '"foreign public official" means. . .any person exercising a public function for a foreign country' (Article 1(4)(a), part II).
- Finally, public international organisations also exercise sovereign powers, insofar as states have transferred these to them by treaty.[54] The decisions of international organisations must also, therefore, be objectively based, and any bribery committed by their officials should likewise be subject to criminal sanction: '"Foreign public official" means. . .any official or agent of a public international organisation' (Article 1(4)(a), part III).

The functional understanding is the basic principle here and may be summarised as follows: a foreign public official is anyone who *carries out a public function for another country or for an international organisation.* His or her allocation to a state body is an indication, rather than conclusive proof, of this status. One may be a foreign public official without belonging to one of the three branches referred to; not all persons working for these state bodies are necessarily performing a public function: distinctions will need to be drawn in the light of the activities in question.

2.3. Functional classification

2.3.1. The term 'public function'

The functional understanding of 'public official' is expressed in the phrase 'exercising a public function for a foreign country' (Article 1(4)(a), part II). What determines this status is not allocation, of an informal or formal nature, to the legislative, executive, or judicial organs of government, but simply the exercise of a public function for another country. The functional understanding of this status is independent of any particular form of organisation, and the activity in question does not require a specific legal basis. Official Commentary 12 expands upon the definition of the

[53] See II.2.3. below. [54] See II.2.5.2. below.

Convention as follows: '"[p]ublic function" includes any activity in the public interest, delegated by a foreign country'. This, therefore, implies two elements: first, the act of delegation by the foreign country concerned and, second, the linkage between the delegated activity and the public interest. The leading example which can be given of this form of delegation by a foreign country, is 'the performance of a task delegated by it in connection with public procurement' (Official Commentary 12).

A government which submits a contract for tender usually delegates a number of diverse functions. All the persons engaged by it to assist with the tender procedure should be regarded as public officials in the functional sense. A range of specialist functions would be covered – from the technical workers, such as engineers, to the financial experts, IT-specialists, experts on weaponry (in case of contracts for the supply of arms), down to the rapporteurs commenting on the tenders received. A further example would be persons such as the Chief Executive Officer (CEO) of a company who organises the conduct of public procurement proceedings.[55]

Delegation is carried out by a foreign state.[56] The act of delegation need not take any particular form. The person concerned may be engaged under the authority of public law or private law; he or she may have the status of an employee or act as a contractor only for the specific contract in question.

Official Commentaries 13–16 make clear that an activity will always be in the *public interest* where the overarching authority of the state stands behind it.[57] A person representing the state occupies a position of authority deriving from his delegated powers; this position of power distinguishes him or her from the ordinary citizen, who is his or her contractual counterpart. The person concerned may not carry out acts of state as such – this would bring them within the scope of 'public official' from an institutional perspective[58] – but they will exercise state authority when carrying out the delegated activity. The term 'public service' is not therefore to be understood as implying any judgment about the desirability of the activity in question from the point of view of social welfare or other ethical considerations, as might be supposed from a first cursory reading. Rather, the Convention simply covers all forms of state behaviour elicited by offer or payment of a bribe. Moreover, the potential nature or field of (delegated) activity encompassed by the definition of the Convention is unlimited.

It is not only delegation in the context of public procurement which Article 1 intends to cover. Every other activity carried out following delegation

[55] See e.g. the *Acres-Lesotho* case, which is discussed in II.6.2. below.
[56] See II.5.2. below. [57] See further II.2.3.2. et seq. below. [58] See II.2.4. below.

of state powers by a foreign country infers the exercise of a public function within the meaning of the Convention. So, a historian charged by an administrative agency to carry out a report on an old building in order to judge its suitability for protection as part of national heritage would qualify as a public official, as would a doctor entrusted with the giving of an opinion on the admission of a particular medicine to the market under public authorisation procedures. Equally, a lawyer who comments on a legislative proposal for a Ministry of Justice would qualify as a public official.

An activity in the public interest delegated by a foreign state may be carried out:

- by bodies enjoying a status conferred by public or administrative law – 'exercising a public function. . .including for a public agency' (Article 1(4)(a));[59]
- under private law provisions, in particular by a public enterprise – 'exercising a public function. . .including for. . .a public enterprise' (Article 1(4)(a));[60]
- without a specific legal authorisation but in exercise of de facto state powers – 'public authority may in fact be held by persons. . .not formally designated as public officials' (Official Commentary 16).[61]

A flexible national definition such as 'all kinds of public employees in foreign states' would satisfy the Convention, if 'employee' were broadly understood to include persons in private and public forms of employment.[62]

2.3.2. Exercise of a public function within a 'public agency'

Official Commentary 13 defines a public agency as 'an entity constituted under public law to carry out specific tasks in the public interest'. Under this definition, the public official belongs to an institution governed by public law. The body which employs him or her will be controlled by the national administration. It will in effect be an arm of the national civil or public service. National public law will determine the scope of control by the administration of the public agency's activities, the instruments used to exercise this control, and the precise extent of such control. These matters need not be specifically provided for; the allocation of the agency to the remit of national public law suffices. In some countries, this is the case

[59] See II.2.3.2. below. [60] See II.2.3.3. below. [61] See II.2.3.4. below.
[62] As in the Swedish anti-corruption law: cf. SE-Ph1, 4 et seq., 23.

for representative bodies of employees and employers, for universities or for certain religious communities, where they are organised not as private entities but as bodies subject to public law which are (co-)controlled by the government. Persons exercising official functions within such institutions – be they trade union officials, University professors or representatives of the established Church – are then also equally public officials.

2.3.3. Exercise of a public function within a 'public enterprise'

Public tasks may also be carried out under private law by undertakings. *Formally*, undertakings such as companies fall outside the sphere of application of public law: their conduct is governed by private law (especially company and commercial law). If, however, the state really controls the company or its activities, then *in substance* the undertaking is performing *a public, not a private, function.* If its employees are bribed, this amounts in fact to 'purchase' of state decision-making, just as if the individual concerned was part of the national public or civil service. Employees of a public enterprise, through which a state chooses to carry out public tasks, must therefore be regarded as falling within the scope of the Convention and be treated as public officials.

In this context we must, however, first ask how a company subject to private law can come to be regarded as a public enterprise within the meaning of the Convention. What criteria determine the answer to this question? The overriding criterion is 'dominant influence' of the undertaking in question by the government. Official Commentary 14 states that 'A "public enterprise" is any enterprise, regardless of its legal form, over which a government, or governments, may, directly or indirectly, exercise a dominant influence.' The fact that the vehicle in respect of which that influence is exercised may be subject to private law is immaterial. It is not the legal form of the object of state influence which is important, but the fact of such influence. The state's influence over the undertaking may be direct or indirect in nature, have a clear legal basis or be de facto.[63] So long as that influence, however expressed, is dominant in the sense of controlling the main corporate decisions, the state will be acting within a public enterprise. The possible means of such control are many:

- The state can take measures to control *ownership* of an enterprise. Depending on the legal form of the body concerned, this may

[63] US-Ph2, 32 (para. 109).

mean owning the subscribed capital or taking a certain number of shares in the company. Official Commentary 14 explains: '[the dominant influence] is deemed to be the case, inter alia, when the government or governments hold the majority of the enterprise's subscribed capital, control the majority of votes attaching to shares issued by the enterprise'.

- The state may also seek to gain dominant control of the *personnel* of the company, meaning the senior management who direct its affairs. The state may appoint the majority of managers to the relevant company bodies. Official Commentary 14 states: 'or [the government or governments] can appoint a majority of the members of the enterprise's administrative or managerial body or supervisory board'.
- Dominance over the enterprise can also be achieved by intervening in *company policy and decision-making.* This may, for example, take the form of issuing binding instructions to the directors of the enterprise. The behaviour of the company may also be determined by intense supervision by state authorities of its activities, going far beyond the state's general supervision obligations. What the company does may also be prescribed in advance by legislation.
- Dominance may be achieved even in the absence of a legal foundation for the exercise of state influence. *Unofficial influence* can be enough. For example, an air transport company controlled by members of the family of government ministers would be classed as a public enterprise.

Assuming it can be shown, on the basis of the above, that a public enterprise operates on the market, we move to the next question which is to determine whether it is in fact performing a *public function.* The authors of the Convention assume that this is the case. Official Commentary 15 begins as follows: '[a]n official of a public enterprise shall be deemed to perform a public function'.

This will not be the case only in the exceptional circumstance where the enterprise concerned has to operate on the market without any particular *state aid or assistance.* If the undertaking enjoys no monopoly, if it must face the competition on the market in the same way as other undertakings, and does not receive any special subsidies or any other preferential treatment from the state, then we cannot say that the state is acting through it to achieve the performance of one of its public functions. In this sense, Official Commentary 15, part II continues as follows: 'unless the enterprise operates on a normal commercial basis in the relevant market, i.e. on a basis which is substantially equivalent to that of a private enterprise, without preferential subsidies or other privileges'.

On this view, the state may be acting on the marketplace through the enterprise concerned, but will be doing so on the same level and subject to the same conditions as other economic actors. If the public enterprise behaves like any other company on the market, the state is choosing not to exercise its special 'sovereign powers' and itself becomes an ordinary competitor for business. The enterprise concerned is not protected by the state and is, therefore, exposed to the full force of competition, winning or losing according to its ability to face the challenges of the marketplace without external state support. In such a situation bribery committed against officials of the enterprise will amount to private corruption, which does not fall within the scope of the Convention.

On the other hand, a public enterprise will be deemed to be performing a public function, if any of the following considerations apply:

- if the state *shelters* the enterprise from competition;
- if the public authorities *favour* the enterprise over others without objective justification;
- if it receives preference in the grant of *state subsidies*;
- if it obtains *trading licences or other permissions* more easily than other enterprises;
- if the enterprise wins *contracts* containing *state guarantees* against the occurrence of certain eventualities (e.g. commitment to purchase).

It is not enough for the enterprise occasionally to receive a subsidy or periodically to win in a tender procedure for its activities to fall within the scope of the Convention. Only clear and systematic state support for the activities of an undertaking will bring it within these terms; such intervention indicates that the state is not prepared to play the competitive game but is rather using its sovereign powers to overcome the effects of the free play of competition. Compared to the other actors on the market, the public enterprise thus benefits from a special authority conferred by public powers.

> A special position within the domestic economy will suffice. To take again the example of airline companies, they would be deemed to fulfil a public function so long as they enjoy a state-guaranteed monopoly position at home, even if they have to compete like any other airline on the international market.

The persons employed by the state to do its bidding, as it were, in such enterprises are, functionally, public officials: they communicate the authority of the state to other contracting parties. Whoever 'buys' their decision by bribing them also buys a decision which is subject to an objective standard, like all state decisions. This is conduct which contravenes the Convention.

It is the *de facto influence or control* exercised by the state, in one or more of the ways described above, which lends the activities of the public enterprise the quality of 'public function'. From the perspective of the Convention, the content of those activities is, on the other hand, irrelevant. The Convention simply does not take a position on what should be seen as a public task. This enables the OECD to avoid being caught up in the complex ideological debates about the appropriate extent of public involvement (and especially public financial investment) in fundamental policy areas of national importance, such as the running of the utilities (gas, electricity, water, telecommunications, etc.) and also health, education, and transport services (e.g. rail travel). Different constitutional traditions and the distinctive history of industrial and socio-economic development in particular countries have produced sometimes markedly different conceptions of the best 'social economic model', and of the extent to which that model should be protected by state protection or intervention. A more liberal 'Anglo-Saxon model' is currently presented as threatening the European social model by setting the economy free from 'excessive' public regulation. For the anti-bribery Convention, what counts is neither a (neo-)liberal nor a welfare state policy orientation. What counts is the nature of the power exercised by the enterprise pursuing the activity in question: if the dominant source of this power is the state, i.e. *Staatsmacht*, the activity will be deemed to be public in nature, regardless of ideology or politics.

Liberalising economic trends in certain countries have resulted in large-scale privatisation of some of the industries referred to above. The utilities, in particular, but also, for example, the airline and railway industries, have been denationalised and put in the hands of private operators. But it is only where the state withdraws completely from its controlling position that persons employed by such enterprises lose their position as public officials and become private actors. If the state continues to exercise dominant control over an undertaking after privatisation, the status as public official and as public enterprise is not lost.

The same principle applies to the reverse situation, in which state-run or state-controlled undertakings become engaged in spheres of industry traditionally reserved for private enterprise, and in which social welfare considerations play a limited role. We can mention here the examples of the banking sector, and the oil and automobile industries. The state may well become involved in the services provided by these undertakings, whose staff may then be treated as public officials under the Convention. They will have this status, however, only if the affairs of the enterprise concerned are controlled by the state to a degree such as to shield it from real competition.

As we already pointed out, it may well be argued on grounds of social welfare that certain economic activities, industries or services of national importance should be placed under national public control: the utilities, health, education, and transport may fall into this category. This ideology, or the opposing (neo-)liberal one – namely that on grounds of economic efficiency and quality of service these areas should be removed from public monopoly – is not part of the Convention equation.

This ideological abstinence is necessary and indeed represents a significant achievement of the Convention. The autonomous definition of foreign public official would not work if the Convention had to take account of the sometimes widely divergent not to say incompatible views of the state Parties on the appropriate deployment of state power in modern industrial economies. It would not be possible to reconcile all these divergences. Confronted by this situation, the Convention has found its own independent, apolitical criteria with which to guide the process of uniform interpretation and application.

2.3.4. De facto exercise of a public function

The Convention aims to protect every exercise of public power carried out under foreign state authority from exposure to bribery. This protection is extended to foreign state authority exercised without a specific legal basis, i.e. the de facto exercise of such authority. Here we are concerned with situations in which state authorities sponsor, support, or at least stand behind certain persons, without formally engaging them and without their becoming part of a public enterprise. A person exercising only such de facto authority may, therefore, also be classified as a foreign public official. So the Convention also turns its attention to those persons to whom the state may clearly allocate certain tasks, but without conferring official authority or public status of any kind on them (within a public enterprise) and even without entering into a formal contracting relationship. The relevant Official Commentary 16 reads as follows: '[i]n special circumstances, public authority may in fact be held by persons (e.g. political party officials in single party states) not formally designated as public officials. Such persons, through their de facto performance of a public function, may, under the legal principles of some countries, be considered to be foreign public officials'. Somewhat reservedly, viz. only 'in special circumstances', and subject to whether its 'legal principles' so permit, the Convention thus provides that persons who exercise state authority *informally* may be regarded as falling under the functional classification of the Convention's foreign public official. Their de facto position as such means that, if they are offered bribes, the Convention is breached.

There is no strict obligation here: as the Official Commentary makes clear, the Convention is permissive, not mandatory, on this point. Activities which may be regarded, by tradition, as of a private nature need not artificially be construed as public in character (public functions) just because of their proximity to the foreign state. According to the requirement of the Convention, persons who have just *some kind of influence* on foreign public officials may not – as a consequence thereof – be defined as foreign public officials themselves. Buying such influence – 'trading in influence' – is criminalised by certain state Parties.[64] The COE Criminal Law Convention on Corruption (Article 12 COE 1999a) and UN Convention Against Corruption (Article 18 UN 2003) follow a similar path. The OECD Convention is narrower. Apart from one special case,[65] it does not foresee such criminalisation – either explicitly or by an expansive interpretation of the notion of public official.

Perhaps a little surprisingly, persons who apply for office within the civil or public service, candidates for political office or candidates for positions as officials of political parties are not regarded as, de facto, carrying out public functions. This is the case notwithstanding the obvious public profile of such offices and their proximity to the state.

> Both the candidature for political office and party activity itself are undertaken with the goal of shaping state activity. Ministerial hopefuls, at least, can play on their prospects of future public office by 'selling' their future position of power to prospective buyers. Higher political offices (at least) are usually obtained only after progress within the party machine, and those who obtain such office will continue to adhere to the party line. Thus, party officials who do not themselves hold public office may well influence state policy by means of pressure exerted behind the scenes. And they may well themselves obtain unfairly preferential treatment through these links.

[64] Art. 433–1 French Code of Criminal Procedure; discussion of this in FR-Ph2; Art. 222bis, s. III Mexican Code of Criminal Procedure; Art. 308 Austrian Code of Criminal Procedure; since 2003 also s. 276c Norwegian Criminal Code.

[65] See II.7.1. below for a discussion of Official Commentary 19.

Candidates for political office are at best camped on the foothills of power. They are only on the threshold of obtaining public office. And party officials are, indeed, behind the curtains of power. So, notwithstanding a certain proximity to the exercise of state authority, their position is clearly different from the actual holders of such authority. Given this state of affairs, OECD members have, thus far,[66] not adopted the general US approach of criminalising bribery of parliamentary candidates, party members or party officials.[67] Accordingly, the Convention remains open on this point, stating in Official Commentary 10 as follows with regard to candidates for public office:

> 'Under the legal system of some countries, an advantage promised or given to any person, in anticipation of his or her becoming a foreign public official, falls within the scope of the offences described in Article 1, paragraph 1 or 2. Under the legal system of many countries, it is considered technically distinct from the offences covered by the present Convention. However, there is a commonly shared concern and intent to address this phenomenon through further work.'

The involvement of citizens as party activists or campaigners on behalf of political parties is, in essence, a private activity protected by the fundamental right of free political association; in free societies, this activity may not be controlled by the state. Members of political parties are clearly not ex officio or per se public officials within the meaning of the Convention.

There is only one exception to this, namely where one is a party official in a *one-party state.* In such societies, such as China or Vietnam, the party is the state and dictates the terms of all political activity. Party politics are state politics, party decisions synonymous with state decisions, party offices are state or public offices. At least therefore from a certain position within the party hierarchy, the party official concerned may be regarded as exercising state authority – and his function can be regarded as a 'public function'. Official Commentary 16 of the Convention clearly recognises this possibility, but leaves it to the state Parties, in accordance with their national legal principles, to determine whether and to what extent such de facto authority can be regarded as falling within the definitions of the Convention.

Of course, even in free societies, which imply multi-party democracies, party political activity is subject to anti-corruption legislation. Their proximity to political power indeed makes party officials particularly susceptible to financial abuses or other intrigue, as recent examples illustrate. They are at risk

[66] This is, however, one of the 'five issues' currently under discussion. See Introduction of this commentary.

[67] According to the FCPA 1977 it is a crime to bribe 'any candidate for foreign political office' or 'any foreign political party or official thereof'.

of exploiting their links to politicians or of being exploited. A separate category of *indirect bribery* is therefore recognised by the Convention: this applies when a party member is used as an agent to bribe the public official.[68] Party officials or candidates for political office may be regarded as third party beneficiaries, if the bribe flows into party coffers or accrues to them as individuals.[69]

2.4. Institutional classification

Looking at the Convention's definition from an institutional angle, a public official is anyone 'holding a legislative, administrative or judicial office' (Article 1(4)(a), part I). This means any person belonging to a legislative, executive, or judicial organ. How the person comes to join the institution is immaterial. According to the Convention they may either be elected or appointed to any of these branches of government; it is not, however, necessary for the national implementing legislation to distinguish between election and appointment, provided that any general definition used by national law is sufficiently broad to cover both possibilities.[70] 'Public officials' in this institutional sense include government ministers, civil or public servants working in ministries, police, and customs officers and officials with responsibility for maintaining commercial or company registers. Professional and lay judges, and likewise jurors in Common Law systems, fall within the definition, as do prosecutors. All other manner of court officials are also subsumed by the Convention's institutional interpretation, including, for example, court registrars or stenographers. Security staff allocated to the service of the courts would also be covered. It is also plain that Members of Parliament are public officials: they are part of the legislative branch of government and so covered by the institutional definition.[71]

We must also, however, make certain distinctions within these institutional categories according to the nature of the *function* carried out for the institution concerned. What is important to qualify someone as falling within the institutional definition is the exercise, be it extensive or minimal, of state authority (sovereign power). That must be distinguished from ordinary tasks, which do not imply the exercise of special powers or authority, such as a cleaner's job or other routine tasks of

[68] See II.6.2. below. [69] See II.3. below.
[70] Cf., for example, the Phase 1 report on Austria: AT-Ph1, 24.
[71] German anti-corruption law had to be amended in order to conform to this. In the United Kingdom too, it was necessary to clarify this. See II.2.6.2. below for our horizontal comparison.

building maintenance. Such cleaning and maintenance work is essential, but those persons are not public officials: their labour lacks any substantive link to the institution's policy or mandate. So, if one chooses to bribe a cleaner working in such an institution in order to gain access to papers or to interfere with documentation, then one does not bribe a public official.

Only persons who have some substantive association with the policy or mandate of the institution are covered in this institutional sense. They need not themselves be directly concerned in the decision-making process. Employees occupying a rather low position in the institutional hierarchy, without an independent area of responsibility, and who simply carry out the orders of their superiors, may yet be covered as a result of their contribution to institutional output. Assistants or clerks in the registry of a court, and also court interns in training, all of whom are likely to be dealing only in a very routine way with the preparation of court documents or procedures, are part of the institution, even if they do not share in its decisions – the same applies to other persons who assist in the administrative work lying behind judicial, legislative and executive decisions, or who otherwise aid such decisions, such as members of expert working groups assisting in the drafting of a law or in the development of plans for certain public projects. The rapporteur preparing the reports on tender applications for the institution concerned would, for this purpose, be classed as part of the institution.

To sum up, it is not necessary for the finding that one holds public office to show that one is responsible for the decision in question (or accountable for it). What is required is that one should have some influence on the decision concerned. This may be minimal influence, but in cases of minimal influence the dividing line is probably a thin one: it would be difficult to say that a secretary who simply types what is put in front of him or her, or a clerk who is responsible only for photocopying and shredding documents, really exercises substantive influence of any kind on institutional outcomes. Such borderline cases would be left for national law to determine in the light of general penal policy.

2.5. 'State' authority

2.5.1. Foreign country

'Public officials' in the sense of the Convention are persons who exercise 'sovereign authority'. The question to be examined here is: what kind of entities can engender such authority and bestow it on the official?

According to Article 1(4)(a), the answer is first, *foreign countries*, and second, *international organisations.*[72]

Official Commentary 18 defines 'foreign country' expressly as 'not limited to states'; it also 'includes any organised foreign area or entity such as an autonomous territory or a separate customs territory'. *States* bestow public authority on the official; this status and the accompanying authority can also be conferred by *quasi-state entities*, including certain regions.

The 'foreign' quality of the country is defined globally in accordance with the overall Convention scheme. 'Foreign' in this sense is not only any state Party other than the offender's country of nationality but any other nation or appropriately organised entity. The Convention criminalises the offence of bribing a foreign public official in this global sense. The briber must, of course, originate from one of the OECD Convention signatory countries, but the foreign official may appertain to any other state, thus clearly including non-OECD states as well as OECD members and Convention signatories.

a. States

The generally accepted indicia of statehood have passed into customary law and may be defined as first, a permanent population, second, a defined territory, and third, a government whose authority (sovereignty) applies to this population and territory.[73] A state comes into existence as soon as these three elements are present. Recognition by other states has in principle no constitutive effect.[74] On the other hand, following recognition,[75] the state may enter into diplomatic relations with other states.[76] Not only that: after being recognised, it may also conclude treaties and take part in international organisations. In particular, following revolutionary events involving the overthrow of a previous regime, recognition provides an important factual indication that the three elements constitutive of state authority have been established.[77]

At present there are 193 states: the 191 Members of the UN, plus Taiwan and the Vatican. While the decision-making power of some states is limited by a form of *international administration*, this does not affect their statehood. For example, East Timor (Timor-Leste) is a state,

[72] See II.2.5.2. below regarding international organisations.
[73] Cf., for example, American Law Institute 1987, Restatement of the law, third: 'Foreign Relations Law of the United States', Vol. **1**, § 201 ('State Defines').
[74] Warbrick 2003, 236; Seidl-Hohenveldern and Hummer 2004, 135.
[75] Brownlie 2003, 88 et seq. points out the ambiguity in the concept of recognition.
[76] Seidl-Hohenveldern and Hummer 2004, 154.
[77] Warbrick 2003, 236; Doehring 2003, 70; Frowein 1968, 13.

notwithstanding the fact that the *UN Mission of Support in East Timor*[78] retains certain competences to act for it in security matters. A similar situation pertains in Bosnia-Herzegovina: its statehood is not questioned, even though the High Representative appointed under the Dayton Agreement may enact laws or take decisions which contravene the will of the elected Parliament.

b. Organised areas or entities

The definition of public official in the Convention is not bound to statehood in the narrow sense. The offence of bribery also applies to officials acting in the name of an 'organised area or entity'. This term is meant to catch all bodies which, although they do not possess complete sovereignty over territory and population, have established de facto governmental authority, in terms of their territorial and/or personal rule. The first example given by Official Commentary 18 of this kind of rule is the rather vague term 'autonomous territory'. The rulers of such a territory are in occupation of and subject to a certain degree of control by a (fully sovereign) state. Nevertheless, it is clear that they too exercise sovereignty autonomously – in some cases comprehensively. The office-holders in such a territory must therefore be regarded as public officials and are 'foreign' also vis-à-vis the state to whose (partial) control they are subject.

This doctrine also applies to the *British Crown Dependencies*, i.e. the Isle of Man, Jersey, and Guernsey (the smaller islands of Alderney and Sark are part of the Bailiwick of Guernsey). These islands are not part of the United Kingdom. They have a special relationship with the United Kingdom expressed in particular by the fact that the Crown (the Queen as represented by Her Majesty's Government) retains certain prerogative powers in respect of the islands. Notwithstanding the fact that the islands are self-governing, with their own governments, parliaments, courts, and legal systems, the United Kingdom is responsible for the islands' international relations and for their defence. Comparable constitutional arrangements pertain to Britain's *Overseas Territories* (of which there are fourteen, including the British Virgin Islands, Bermuda, Turks and Caicos and the Falkland Islands). In the absence of 'external sovereignty', these territories cannot be regarded as fully fledged states. As they enjoy full 'internal sovereignty', their public officials do, however, enjoy and may exercise sovereign authority. Even British nationals who bribe officials of such territories would therefore make themselves culpable under the Convention.

[78] Established according to UN 2002.

Similar considerations apply with regard to Greenland and the Faroe Islands which are subject ultimately to Danish sovereignty. And the French *départements d'outre-mer* (for example, Corsica), *territoires d'outre-mer* und *collectivités territoriales*, and the Dutch territories of Aruba und the Antilles (Curacao, Bonaire, Saba, Sint Eustatius, Sint Maarten) also fall into this category.

It is possible for there to be an *organised area or entity* within the meaning of the Convention where the question of sovereignty over the area in question is disputed. The status as public official is, however, judged with respect to the real situation of control on the ground, which means that the Convention avoids taking a position on the legal niceties. In particular, a *stabilised de facto regime*[79] is capable of conferring the status of public official on its servants. Such a regime can be said to exist where one of the state Parties disputing sovereignty succeeds in establishing an effective autonomous government in a region, even if that region cannot take full part in the international community owing to the lack of recognition. For example, *Northern Cyprus* is regarded only by Turkey as an independent state. It is, however, uncontestable that an autonomous government operates there, *in fact*. Northern Cyprus thus represents a stabilised de facto regime, and its public officials are therefore covered by the Convention definition.

The anti-bribery rules of the Convention go a step further. They regard an *organised area or entity* as established in circumstances where a state was able to maintain territorial sovereignty but is still confronted by an opposing entity which has itself established partial sovereignty. *Palestine* provides an example of this, being neither a state nor a de facto regime.[80] Israel continues to exercise territorial sovereignty in respect of the Palestinian 'Autonomous Territories': there is no evidence of an effective and independent Palestinian state notwithstanding the Autonomy Agreement and despite recognition by a good two-thirds of all states.[81] There is, nevertheless, a Palestinian government in the shape of the 'Palestinian National Authority', a Palestinian Parliament known at the 'Palestinian National Council' and a separate judiciary. Moreover, there is international representation as a result of observer status at the UN.[82] From all this it is clear that the persons who exercise a public function for Palestine fall to be regarded as public officials within the meaning of Article 1(4)(a) of the Convention.

[79] Frowein 1968, 5 et seq.
[80] 'State in statu nascendi' according to wording of Brownlie 2003, 77.
[81] Epping 2004, 62; Dahm, Delbrück and Wolfrum 1989, 130; Seidl-Hohenveldern and Hummer 2004, 151.
[82] UN 1974.

The situation of the *Democratic Arab Republic of Sahara (Western Sahara)* is similar in this respect. Morocco exercises de facto control over the disputed territory. Active bribery of officials of the members of the government-in-exile (currently in Algeria), or of the *Frente Popular de Liberación de Seguía el Hamra y Río de Oro* (POLISARIO) as the representatives of the Western Sahara to the outside world, would still have to be regarded as a breach of the Convention. Another example is *Kosovo.* Kosovo is part of Serbia but it is currently under a provisional UN regime and it is also exercising a certain degree of self-administration.[83] All members of the governmental apparatus are therefore public officials.

By contrast, the decision-makers of rebel or terrorist groups such as the Guerilla Fighters of Sierra Leone or of Columbia, the Darfur rebels or the Basque separatist fighters, are not public officials. While such groups may be fighting for supremacy of the disputed territories and while they may already enjoy considerable powers there, they do not control the area to the degree necessary to establish a stable de facto regime or partial autonomy. In these circumstances, they are not subjects of international law and any authority enjoyed by their officials is not sovereign authority.

Finally, Official Commentary 18 also subsumes 'separate customs territory' within the definition of *organised areas or entities.* This encompasses all areas of a country regarded as foreign territory solely for customs or foreign exchange purposes, or in the context of the regulation of external trade: customs-free warehouses or larger customs-free areas, such as Helgoland in Germany or Samnaun in Switzerland as well as the customs-free zones of airports would be counted in this category. The goods concerned are brought into these zones, stored and sold, as the case may be, without attracting customs duty. The customs authorities who administer these zones do so as foreign public officials; as far as these duties are concerned, they are also 'foreign' to the states within whose political jurisdiction they fall.

c. Coverage of all governmental entities

Article 1(4)(b) states that "foreign Country" includes all levels and subdivisions of government, from national to local'. By 'government' is meant every type of organisational entity exercising sovereign authority. The phrase 'levels and subdivisions. . .from national to local' seeks to encompass all authorities exercising power within a federal systems and every local authority. By 'country' is therefore meant every institution of a legislative,

[83] UN 1999b.

administrative, or judicial nature pertaining to the national level or to the level of provincial or local government.

2.5.2. International organisation

Not only countries but also associations of countries may confer public office. Article 1 uses the expression 'international organisation'. The principal application of this expression is to an association of states. But it goes further than this: '"Public international organisation" includes any international organisation formed by states, governments, or other public international organisations, whatever the form of organisation and scope of competence, including, for example, a regional economic integration organisation such as the European Communities' (Official Commentary 17). This definition takes account of the existence of associations of other non-state entities, including dependent states with limited legal capacity,[84] of local governments or other international organisations possessing a certain amount of sovereign authority. All these non-state bodies nevertheless possess sufficient international capacity to form international organisations in which they collectively exercise certain common powers, for the achievement of common objectives. An international organisation can therefore be defined as an association of entities possessing either full or partial sovereign authority under international law, which pursues certain common goals by means of common institutions and by means of an international treaty: it will be 'established and based upon a treaty, which pursues common aims and which has its own special organs to fulfil particular functions within the organisation'.[85]

Neither the form of the organisation nor its area of responsibility is material. Nor is the fact that it may have a regional rather than a global remit. The specific policy orientation of the organisation is likewise irrelevant. All of the following types of organisations would be covered by the terms of the Convention:

- the UN as an organisation to promote peaceful international relations, world economic and social development, environmental protection, culture, and educational exchanges between nations;
- all the institutions and agencies of the UN (including ECOSOC, UNESCO, etc.);
- the NATO and OSCE as organisations with a security or defence policy remit;

[84] 'Gliedstaaten': cf. Bindschedler 1995, 1291.
[85] Bindschedler 1995, 1289; cf. also Hailbronner 2004, 171.

- the COE as an institution promoting liberal politics and fundamental rights throughout Europe since 1950;
- the EU and OECD and other economic associations of states (though they each also have political goals);
- all the institutions and agencies of the EU (notably Council, Commission, European Parliament, European Court of Justice, and Court of Auditors);
- other regional groupings of states such as the Arab League, OAS, ASEAN, etc;
- all other regional or global international organisations with economic, development, social, environmental of cultural objectives;
- organisations to promote global or regional inter-state communications (e.g. Universal Postal Union).

Whether a person is to be regarded as an *official* of such an organisation depends on his or her function within it. The meaning of 'official. . .of an international organisation' is to be understood in the context of the definition of 'foreign public official' in Article 1(4)(a).[86] Some international organisations replicate the decision-making structures of states, regarding the basic division of their responsibilities into legislative, executive, and judicial powers. If staff members of these organisations exercise any of the decision-making power of the organisation in the legislative, executive, or judicial sense, then they will be deemed to be foreign public officials in the same way as if they were exercising those powers on behalf of the state. This applies regardless of the formal (legal) basis for their action.

Membership of the staff of an international organisation will establish one as a foreign public official in an *institutional* sense, but the *functional* qualification we noted above in relation to public officials of foreign states, also applies to the staff of international organisations.[87] We discussed above the different forms of 'output' in relation to states and concluded that anyone who substantively contributes to any of these outputs would be regarded as a public official. The performance of routine tasks like cleaning, or the provision of technical support by IT specialists, or the services of chauffeurs, gardeners, etc., which may be very essential tasks in terms of maintenance of buildings or support for technical infrastructure, are all carried out in a private activity without a substantive link to the decision-making output of the institution. The bribery of those persons would

[86] The Swedish interpretation does not therefore suffice: cf. SE-Ph2, 39.
[87] See II.2.4. above.

amount to private corruption, but would not fall foul of Article 1 of the Convention. Such action may be punishable under other criminal law provisions. There may again, however, be borderline cases where it is difficult to decide whether the person is really contributing to the output of the organisation or not. Very low-level clerical or secretarial staff would probably fall outside the Convention's remit.

The decisions of international organisations are 'corporate' in nature; that is to say they are decisions of the organisation, not its individual members. This applies no matter how the decisions were reached, by majority or by unanimity. Every person working within the organisation who is engaged in the decision-making process is regarded as a public official of this organisation: if he or she is bribed, then the 'victim' is the organisation itself, not a foreign state. Thus, the 'foreign' element of the definition is met in every case, regardless of whether the bribe-giver and the bribe-taker are of the same nationality and independently of the location of the organisation's headquarters or the place of the criminal act.

Applying what we have said, all members of staff of the organisation who carry out activities related to its decision-making functions would be regarded as foreign public officials; persons carrying out merely technical or service support tasks are not. Therefore, all the international civil or public servants working for the international organisations or their sub-agencies listed above, i.e. UN, OECD, EU, etc., would be covered by the definition, ranging from the very high officials to the more lowly administrators. Temporary agents employed by them or project-based workers are included. Persons delegated to serve in certain decision-making capacities for these institutions, such as ambassadors, or even delegates to one particular meeting, would also fall under the remit of the Convention. Members of the armed services would be included. Experts or consultants working in sub-groups of the agencies or institutions concerned likewise fall under Convention jurisdiction, even if they are working independently, i.e. even if they are not bound to follow the instructions of the international organisation concerned. And individuals allocated to work for an international organisation in an independent enquiry would also be covered by the definition.

2.5.3. Coverage of non-governmental organisations?

The Convention does not, in principle, cover the activities of non-governmental organisations (NGOs). NGOs are, however, increasingly making their voice and presence felt in areas of international concern.

They are composed of private persons or associations of persons who have banded together in some common cause. NGOs are established to lobby, campaign and demonstrate in the public sphere for the achievement of their goals. They are financed by members' contributions or donations from private benefactors.

The work of NGOs is increasingly international in nature, reacting to globalisation. International concerns addressed by them include:

- legal or constitutional questions related to 'good governance' (e.g. Transparency International (TI), International Law Association (ILA), Inter-Parliamentary Union (IPU));
- the protection of human rights (e.g. International Committee of the Red Cross (ICRC), Amnesty International (AI), Human Rights Watch (HRW));
- economic and employment policy (e.g. International Chamber of Commerce (ICC));
- environmental policy (e.g. Greenpeace, Friends of the Earth);
- certain international sports associations, notably the International Olympic Committee (IOC) and the Féderation Internationale de Football Association (FIFA);
- organisations promoting social rights, employment opportunities and also gender equality (e.g. International Confederation of Free Trade Unions (ICFTU), World Confederation of Labour (WCL) – both are global confederations of regional organisations);
- world development policy (e.g. Oxfam International (OI)).

The founders and members of NGOs are private persons. Individuals are not in general subjects of international law, so they cannot transfer legal personality to these organisations. NGOs are therefore subject to the domestic laws of the states in which they are situated or in which they conduct their activities. Their office-holders are not public officials and do not perform any public function,[88] the fairness of which the OECD Convention would strive to protect.

Exceptionally, international law does confer upon an NGO a limited degree of international legal personality. This is the case for the ICRC,[89] whose humanitarian services may be called upon by the parties to international armed conflicts (in particular its power to visit and check prison camps in which prisoners of war are detained). NGOs now make hugely important contributions to many programmes developed by

[88] Doehring 2004, 85. [89] Art. 5(4) Geneva 1977.

international organisations, including crisis recovery programmes; their role in crisis regions, after periods of armed conflict or natural disasters, has been particularly prominent in recent years. They may help in the rebuilding of public administration in such regions, or provide social assistance. They may also be involved in developing health or social services, in conjunction with the local authorities. NGO representatives may also attend at elections in certain countries as observers representing the international community. In all of these scenarios, they are helping deliver what are in effect public services. They are in many cases simultaneously implementing the will of the international community, for example, as expressed in the mandate of the UN or another international organisation. In reality therefore NGOs may well be exercising a form of state authority. We should also observe that international sporting associations, in particular, may enjoy enormous advantages or privileges in their host countries. Members of the IOC and FIFA, for example, receive significant tax benefits and may even enjoy 'diplomatic' immunity in many of the countries in which they have offices.

The 'functional concept' which is at the heart of the definition of foreign public official in statal terms should also be applied to actors working in an international organisation or in bodies closely associated with the performance by the latter of (global) public functions. The staff of NGOs who participate in the sovereign tasks of states or of international organisations may be compared to experts of a working group who assist the Ministry of Justice in preparation of laws or with an expert appointed by a court to give an expert opinion to inform its decision in a particular case. On this analogy, NGO representatives should be included in the Convention's definition of persons regarded as foreign public officials, the bribery of whom it criminalises, in as much as they can be called upon to perform public functions.[90] The IOC has itself approached the OECD in this regard, stating that it wishes 'to be governed by the Convention';[91] its functionaries would then be better protected against offers of bribes.

This thesis is not, however, generally accepted among commentators or by the WGB. At present, therefore, it is not possible to say that the Convention mandates such an interpretation.

[90] Accordingly, German criminal law now applies to bribery of functionaries of NGOs when they implement a programme established by a governmental body: see II.2.6.2. below. Norwegian criminal law also criminalises the bribery of employees and contractors of NGOs: cf. NO-Ph2, 30.

[91] Letter from the IOC to the Secretary General of the OECD, DAFFE/IME/BR/WD(99)20.

2.6. Horizontal comparison

2.6.1. Approaches aligned with the definitions of Article 1(4) of the Convention

The definitions contained in Australian, Canadian, New Zealand, and US law, those of the Asian legal systems applying the Convention, and the definitions of Austrian, Finnish, Norwegian, Portuguese, and Swiss law, and of certain central and eastern European countries,[92] follow the approach of the Convention in so far as they embrace both a *formal* interpretation of (foreign) public official, on the one hand, and a definition based on the *substance* of their activities, on the other hand. Their laws present the following options, side by side:[93]

- An *institutional* classification, according to the official's affiliation to one of the branches of government; see, for example, the FCPA's approach in this regard: 'any officer or employee of a foreign government or any department thereof'.
- A *functional* classification, in the light of the public nature of the official's role ('any person acting in an official capacity'); persons falling within this definition would include, in particular, those working for a *public agency.* Employees of a *public enterprise* would also be covered, depending on their functions. To take again the example of the FCPA, we can refer in this respect to its category 'any officer or employee of. . .any department, agency, or instrumentality thereof [of a foreign government]. . .or any person acting in an official capacity for or on behalf of any such government or department, agency, or instrumentality'.

  In the *Syncor case,*[94] hospitals owned by the Taiwanese state were regarded as 'instrumentalities' of the state – and therefore bribery of the doctors employed there was seen as corruption of public officials within the meaning of the FCPA. The *InVision case,*[95] on the other hand, concerned inter alia the assessment of state-owned or state-run airports.

- Finally, the carrying out of a public function in or on behalf of an international organisation: 'any officer or employee. . .or a person acting in an official capacity. . .for or on behalf of any. . .international organisation', as the FCPA definition would have it.[96]

[92] Cf., for example, Bulgaria: BG-Ph1, 4; Czech Republic: CZ-Ph1, 4; Slovakia: SK-Ph1, 4 et seq.
[93] For the US provisions quoted in this regard, cf. 15 U.S.C. § 78dd-1(f)(1) FCPA 1977.
[94] *SEC* v. *Synor International Cooperation,* Litigation Release No. 17887, December 10, 2002.
[95] See II.6.1.2. below. [96] 15 U.S.C. § 78dd-1(f)(1) FCPA 1977.

The terminology used in the legislation of the state Parties is, quite obviously, different; it varies in its degree of precision. Australia, for example,[97] fulfils its Convention obligations by means of a broad definition of 'foreign government body': this definition comprises not only every 'authority of the government' but also 'a part of the government' – and this in turn embraces *public agencies* and *public enterprises.* All persons fulfilling functions in those bodies, whether of a contractual, statutory, or customary law nature, are to be regarded as foreign public officials.

The WGB has noted the risk of losing some of the substance of the Convention in its translation into an Asian language.[98] However, both Korean and Japanese legal systems follow an approach to definition of the foreign public official,[99] which fundamentally runs parallel to the Convention. To take the example of Japan, its definitions of public official are as follows (five-fold):

- first of all, the *institutional* category: 'any person who engages in public service for a...foreign government' (cf. Article l(4)(a), first sub-clause of the Convention);
- second, *functional* in the sense of Article 1(4)(a), second sub-clause, namely 'any person who exercises a public function, which belongs to the authorised competence of a...foreign government or an international organisation and is delegated by them';
- third, another *functional* definition, namely 'any person who engages in public service for an entity constituted under foreign special laws to carry out specific tasks in the public interest': this catches activities carried out for a *public agency* (cf. Article 1(4)(a), sub-clause 2);
- fourth, again a *functional* definition: 'any person who engages in service for an enterprise' – this is designed to cover holders of office in a *public enterprise* (cf. again Article 1(4)(a), sub-clause 2 of the Convention);[100]
- fifth and finally, the holder of public office in an *international organisation*: 'any person who engages in public service for an international organisation' (cf. Article 1(4)(a), sub-clause 3 of the Convention).

[97] S. 70(1) Australian Criminal Code.
[98] Cf., for example, KR-Ph1, 4: it is not possible easily to distinguish 'business' from 'tasks'.
[99] Art. 2 Korean Act on Preventing Bribery of Foreign Public Officials in International Business Transactions; Art. 10bis(2) Japanese Unfair Competition Prevention Law.
[100] See, however, directly below.

The major structural flaw of the otherwise commendable incorporation of the definitions of the Convention in (South-) Korean law is the failure to treat North Korean public officials either as domestic or foreign public officials – with the consequence that bribery of such officials would not be prosecuted under South Korean law.[101]

Whereas there are relatively clear and comprehensive rules in the above-mentioned countries concerning the official's (institutional or functional) connection to an organisation, a key question has emerged regarding the categorisation of an *undertaking or enterprise* as public in nature: the question is asked under what circumstances such a basically private entity can be regarded as acting as a representative of the state. The precise criteria determining this question are not necessarily laid out in legislation. Such a gap may, however, be filled by recognition of the functional definition in diverse non-statutory materials which predate the Convention – for example, case law or academic commentary or other authoritative interpretative materials. This applies to the United States, for example: the Department of Justice has issued a number of interpretative opinions,[102] setting out the criteria relevant to a finding that an enterprise is public in nature. These are: first, state ownership; second, state control; third, the object or purpose of the company; and fourth, the categorisation of the undertaking as public by the national law of its home state. These criteria serve to clarify further – and in a sufficiently broad sense – the rather vague phraseology of the FCPA 'instrumentalities [of a foreign government]', which is intended to capture inter alia public enterprises.[103] As far as Europe is concerned, we can point to the examples of Austria and Switzerland as countries in which preparatory statutory materials and legal doctrine (academic commentary) authoritatively interpret state control over an enterprise – rather than the more random question of its legal form – to be the factor determining public status.[104] Such state control can be evidenced by majority state participation in the enterprise (ownership criterion), statutory specification of its activities, or state supervision.[105]

[101] KR-Ph2, 33 et seq.

[102] FCPA 1977, Review Procedure Release 04/29-10-1980 on the Saudi airline owned by the Saudi government; Release 02/26-07-1983 on expenses of a general manager of a foreign government-owned and -controlled government; Release 01/20-04-1993 on a quasi-commercial entity owned and supervised by a foreign government.

[103] The Phase 2 report on the US nevertheless indicates some continuing 'potential uncertainty' (US-Ph2, 32).

[104] Arts. 110(4) and 322^{octies}(3) Swiss Criminal Code; s. 74(4c) Austrian Criminal Code.

[105] Regarding Austria, the explanatory notes to the Government Bill 1230 BlgNR XX. GP on s. 74(4c) provide an interpretation consistent with Official Commentaries 14 and 15. For Switzerland cf. Botschaft, Bundesblatt 1999 VI 5497, 5539; Balmelli, 1996, 121 et seq.

Legislation on this question in Asia is abstract in its terms. The approach of Korean legislation is two-fold: first, reference is made to *control of the capital or shares* of the enterprise, i.e. where the foreign government holds over 50% of the subscribed capital/the shares, second, we can note, more abstractly, the inclusion of all other forms of *de facto control* – 'substantial controlling power'.[106] The law does not, therefore, limit the notion of state control to the exercise of formal methods alone: that would indeed be insufficient in terms of the Convention requirements. Thus, Japan is censured by the WGB for failing to apply its legislation (notwithstanding recent amendments)[107] to forms of state dominance that do not extend to majority control of shares or of capital, for example, the 'golden share' scenario.[108]

Japanese law, namely, defines a public enterprise exclusively in the following terms:

- in terms of state control of a majority of share capital with voting rights;
- in terms of state control of subscribed capital;
- in terms of the right of the state to appoint more than half of the management team of the company.[109]

In fact, the three criteria of this law stress state ownership, precisely in terms of Official Commentary 14.

Australian law addresses the subject of public undertakings with considerable precision. Its law indicates the circumstances under which an enterprise will be regarded as subject to de facto state control.

This will, in particular, be the case where the (foreign) state controls over 50% of the capital or of the votes attached to the share capital of the undertaking, appoints more than half of the body's board of directors, or where, formally or informally, the board carries out state instructions. The state may also place itself in a position of dominance by other means such as 'trusts, agreements, arrangements, understandings, and practices'.[110] It is irrelevant whether there is a legal basis for such control or whether there are legal means of enforcing such influence.

106 Art. 2(2)(c) Korean Act on Preventing Bribery of Foreign Public Officials in International Business Transactions. The WGB is not, however, satisfied that this formulation sufficiently corresponds to the wording of Official Commentary 14 (KR-Ph2, 32 et seq.). This seems somewhat harsh, given the fact that some countries lack any kind of legislative specification.

107 Amendments to the Unfair Competition Prevention Law, December 25, 2001; government ordinance in accordance with Art. $10^{bis}(2)(iii)$ of this law.

108 JP-Ph1^{bis}, 30 and JP-Ph2, 4 (concerns of the WGB still present).

109 Art. $10^{bis}(2)(iii)$ Unfair Competition Prevention Law.

110 S. 70.1 Australian Criminal Code.

Furthermore, control may be established on the basis that the undertaking enjoys *special legal preferment by the state*, i.e. benefits in terms of 'special legal rights or a special legal status. . .special benefits or privileges'.[111]

The FCPA contains a limitation where international organisations are concerned. The US statute confines its application to international organisations which have been formally designated as such, for example, under the International Organizations Immunities Act,[112] or as a result of formal recognition by the US President.[113] Thus, it seems that the process of US recognition of international organisations has to date extended to all organisations to which Article 1(4)(a) of the Convention is applicable.

2.6.2. Definitions with a markedly autonomous structure

We can identify a group of countries whose legislative scheme and structures (including the terminology used) diverge significantly from the approach of the Convention. The United Kingdom and Ireland, as Common Law countries,[114] form part of this group, as do the legal jurisdictions of the following Continental European states: Belgium, France, Germany, Italy, Poland, Slovenia, and Sweden. Among South American countries, Brazil may be counted as part of this group. The explanation for the distinctive structures of these countries may lie in the fact that they adapted to the Convention simply by applying their pre-existing national definitions of the bribery offence to commission of the crime in a transnational situation. Following this line, the definition of *foreign public official* was approached via the traditional interpretation of *domestic official*. This approach can, however, only be consistent with the autonomous approach of the Convention, if the position of the domestic official is also seen by national law in functional terms, regardless of the legal form in which his or her public function is clothed. The greater the extent of divergence by the traditional definitions of national law from the Convention's approach, then obviously the greater the degree of adaptation required.

We will now survey the positions taken by certain specific countries, first of all Norway: Norwegian criminal law[115] defines foreign public official not in

[111] S. 70.1 Australian Criminal Code; cf. AU-Ph1, 5. [112] 22 U.S.C. § 288.

[113] The EU and Europol, for example, have been designated by the President by the Executive Order 13259, March 19, 2002.

[114] Cf. the special position of Scotland within the United Kingdom: it has a legal system distinct from that of England and Wales, with different origins and its own rules on matters of criminal law and procedure. Cf. generally Gordon 2000.

[115] Comprehensively reformed as a result of Act 79/2003.

terms of institutions, activities or functions, but in relation to different types of contractual affiliation: according to their 'connection with a post, office or commission...in a foreign country'.[116] None of these terms is defined more specifically by legislation; only the comprehensive preparatory legislative materials (*Travaux Préparatoires*), 'which have important weight in the Norwegian legal tradition'[117] provide further information. These materials specify, first of all, that one must understand 'foreign countries' to include not only states but also international organisations, including NGOs. Secondly, the three categories of public officials are described in greater detail:

- the term 'post' is used in a catch-all sense to refer to all basic or ordinary forms of employment ('ordinary service and employment');[118]
- the term 'office' is used in order to describe persons who hold a leading position in a state institution or in an enterprise. The implication here is that an 'office'-holder is someone who occupies a position of trust in the public sphere: Members of Parliament, judges, arbitrators and Members of government are examples of the persons who should be placed in this category;
- the term 'commission' is intended to encompass the work carried out in the public interest on any other basis, notably on a contractual basis, however short-term that may be. This group of contracted persons comprises all public officials in a functional sense who do not hold 'office' within the meaning of the second alternative referred to above: experts, lawyers, or trustees, in so far as they act for an undertaking, organisation or authority would be covered by this branch of the definition.[119]

In the absence of jurisprudence, it is extremely difficult to judge whether these rather complex definitions of Norwegian law would be sufficient to cover the ground intended by the Convention: there is, to date, no evidence of their application in decided cases.[120]

If we look at Sweden, we discover that there are as many as nine categories of public official set out in the Criminal Code,[121] which may be summarised as follows:

- first, we find a list of individual positions indicating an *institutional affiliation* as public official;

[116] S. 276a Norwegian Criminal Code. [117] NO-Ph2, 24, 32. [118] NO-Ph2, 30.
[119] NO-Ph2, 30. [120] NO-Ph2, 32.
[121] Ch. 20, s. 2 Swedish Criminal Code (version in revised form in force since 1 July 2004).

- second, we find two *functional* clauses pertaining to 'a person who. . .exercises public authority' and to whom 'a position of trust' has been given to perform a specific public task;
- third, we find that officials and agents of international organisations are also classified as persons 'who by reason of a position of trust have been given certain tasks' which are deemed to be public in nature; bribery of such persons is a criminal offence. Swedish law, however, falls short of the requirements of the Convention by restricting the application of its bribery law to international organisations of which Sweden itself is a member.[122]

This restriction contained in Swedish legislation is replicated by Irish law, namely by the Corruption (Amendment) Act 2001.[123] The term 'agent'[124] is central to the Irish definition of public official: it is elaborated upon by means of a list of legislative, judicial, and administrative offices. The WGB concluded that the interpretation of this term by Irish law fulfils the functional elements of the definition of foreign public official, at least in principle,[125] as well as the institutional definition. But like its Swedish counterpart, the legislation concerned falls short of the Convention requirements by limiting the international organisations to which it applies to 'any body established under an international agreement *to which the state is a party*'.

Regarding UK law, a more fundamental problem than that relating to the appropriateness of the national definition of foreign public official was revealed by the first Phase of WGB evaluations, viz. whether UK law in fact applied at all to the foreign public official. Neither *statutory law* – in the shape of the surely outdated Acts of 1889, 1906, and 1916 – nor *Common Law*, guaranteed an adequate legal basis for the prosecution or other legal follow-up of transnational corruption.[126]

> The key term 'agent' was used in the Act 1906[127] to mean persons 'serving under the Crown' or for a 'public body': the latter was further defined by the Act 1916 as 'local and public authorities of all descriptions'.[128] The Act 1889[129] expressly excluded from its application 'any public body. . .existing elsewhere than in the United Kingdom'.

It is clear that these UK rules failed to implement the Convention. The Anti-Terrorism, Crime and Security Act 2001[130] remedied the situation by making

[122] SE-Ph2, 39. [123] No. 27 Corruption (Amendment) Act 2001.
[124] Para. 2(5)(c) Corruption (Amendment) Act 2001.
[125] IE-Ph1, 9. [126] UK-Ph1, 5.
[127] S. 1(3) Prevention of Corruption Act 1906.
[128] Sub-ss. 4(2) and (3) Prevention of Corruption Act 1916.
[129] S. 7 Public Bodies Corrupt Practices Act 1889.
[130] In force since 12 February 2002.

clear that foreign public officials were also covered by the bribery offence: from the entry into force of the Act, 'it is immaterial if the functions of the [bribed] person. . .have no connection with the United Kingdom and are carried out in a country or territory outside the United Kingdom'.[131] Thus, the meaning both of the term 'agents'[132] and of the 'public body'[133] served by the agent, have been extended to territories outside the United Kingdom.

Notwithstanding this reform, the legal situation remains 'characterised by complexity and uncertainty'.[134] The 2001 Act merely took over the previous definitions and added a foreign element. It fails to offer a modern definition. Although the definitions used in the 2001 Act broadly cover the categories of public official contained in Article 1(4) of the Convention,[135] the important question whether, or to what extent, judges and Members of Parliament are covered remains open.

> Even if Members of Parliament and of the judiciary are in principle embraced by the term 'agents', only actions taken outside their public duties should be covered ('if they were not acting in their official capacity').[136] Such an interpretation, however, runs contrary not only to Convention requirements but also to the wording of the Act 1906, which refers to 'any act in relation to his [the agent's] principal affairs or business'[137] – and which necessarily establishes a link to parliamentary or judicial activities.[138]

The Common Law fails fully to close this loophole. Although judges are regarded under Common Law as public officials,[139] the position with Parliamentarians remains in doubt. According to a narrow interpretation, they do not hold 'office'.[140] This narrow view may be defensible, but a more recent judicial authority[141] argues for a broader definition of the notion of public official, which would also cover Members of Parliament. A clarification of UK anti-corruption legislation was promised by the introduction into Parliament in 2003 of the Corruption Bill, but Parliamentary time to proceed with this legislation had not been found, at the time of writing, suggesting a lack of political urgency to amend the law.[142]

[131] S. 108(1) Anti-Terrorism, Crime and Security Act 2001.
[132] S. 1(4) Prevention of Corruption Act 1906 (as amended by The Anti-Terrorism, Crime and Security Act 2001).
[133] As defined in s. 7 Act 1889, and extended by s. 4(2) Act 1916.
[134] UK-Ph2, 58. [135] As determined in UK-Ph1, 6 and UK-Ph2, 60.
[136] S. 1(1) Act 1906. [137] S. 1(1) Act 1906. [138] UK-Ph1, 6.
[139] Law Commission 1998, 19.
[140] UK-Ph1, 6 and cf. the continuing concerns about this in UK-Ph2, 59.
[141] This is in fact the only half-way clear judicial pronouncement on the matter: *Greenway and others*, Central Criminal Court, June 1992 (UK-Ph2, 59). The case did not, however, proceed to full trial.
[142] UK-Ph2, 9.

As regards Germany, the Criminal Code maintains the established definition of public official.[143] This structure is transposed, with some extension, to the international dimension.[144] The German definition of public official for the purposes of transnational bribery comprises the following categories:

- judge of a foreign state;
- public official of a foreign state; this category comprises both the institutional and functional dimensions already discussed: there is a general 'functional' clause in German legislation which captures activities carried out for a public authority or public enterprise, or in any other context;
- 'public official and other member of staff' of an international organisation: in this context, German law goes further than the Convention strictly requires[145] by extending the scope of 'corruptible' persons to members of NGOs working on a programme founded by an international organisation; the implementation of such a programme brings the NGO concerned within the protection of the criminal law: for example, it would be a crime under German law to bribe election observers in the former Yugoslavia;
- a special provision extends the definition to foreign Parliamentarians: without such a provision, it would, namely, not be possible to ensure that the bribery of foreign members of Parliament was criminalised, as the Convention unmistakably requires; this is because German Members of Parliament are not regarded as holders of public office: the offence of bribery is applicable to them only in connection with the buying of votes at general elections or at elections to the European Parliament;
- a further special provision also applies to members of the armed services, in the context of transnational bribery.

French law (whose example has been followed by Luxembourg) divides non-EU[146] foreign public officials into the following categories:

- 'persons entrusted with public authority': by this is meant all functions carried out in exercise of administrative, judicial, or

[143] S. 11(1)(2) German Criminal Code.
[144] Ss. 1 and 2(1) German Act on Combating Bribery of Foreign Public Officials in International Business Transactions; s. 1 German Act on Combating Bribery of Public Officials of Member States of the European Union and of Community Officials.
[145] This extension should be viewed positively, as we have argued above: see II.2.5.3. above.
[146] See on this issue II.2.6.3. below.

military power, independently of any formal status of the person concerned;

- 'persons charged with a public service mission': this is intended to cover those persons who carry out public service tasks at a lower level, i.e. persons 'not entrusted with public authority';
- 'persons holding an elected office': this category, comprising Parliamentarians etc. thus receives separate consideration;
- 'persons holding a judicial office': a special category.

In this way all eventualities of the Convention's Article 1 definition should be covered.[147]

Italian legislation, at first sight, appears to present difficulties or uncertainties as it fails to respect the autonomous approach of the Convention. Apart from EU officials, Italian law defines foreign public official in the light of its domestic public officials: someone is only regarded as a foreign public official, if their activities would qualify them as an Italian public official, were they carried out for Italy and not a foreign power. The problem is not, however, a serious one, as the various categories of Italian national official, taken together, are sufficiently broad to cover all the intended categories of the Convention.[148]

The Polish situation appears somewhat similar to the Italian one, with the national terminology having simply been extended to cover the transnational dimension and a foreign public official being defined as a 'person performing a public function in a foreign state or an international organisation'. 'Public function' is not further defined by statute, so it will be necessary for this to be given a sufficiently broad meaning as case law and practice develops. A limitation of the notion of 'public official' to specific public posts, in the context of commission of offences associated with those offices, would be too narrow, failing, for example, to cover employees of public enterprises. In interpreting the phrase 'public function' in relation to the national public official, case law to date does in fact appear to offer sufficient breadth.[149]

Slovenia's new[150] anti-bribery legislation provides a further example of a legal system whose approach is based upon traditional notions of who is a public official. It refers first of all to existing national categories,[151] before

[147] At least this was the assessment by the French delegation (FR-Ph1, 9). The point has, however, yet to be tested in practice (FR-Ph2, 40).

[148] Art. 322bis(2) read together with Arts. 357 und 358 Italian Criminal Code (IT-Ph1, 7 et seq.).

[149] PL-Ph1, 5 et seq.; Supreme Court, judgement of October 10, 1991, case *IKZP* 21.91.

[150] Slovenian Official Gazette 40/04.

[151] This in fact creates the problem of dependence on the national law of the 'victim state', but we will consider this point only later (see II.2.6.6. below).

referring to three specific types of foreign entities with which the foreign official may be affiliated:[152]

- first, a 'foreign country'; this phraseology is, however, unduly narrow as it refers only to 'countries' and not to territories within countries which may be organised on a quasi-state basis. It fails, for example, to capture 'autonomous territories' or 'separate customs territories';[153]
- second, a 'public international organisation';
- third, an 'international court or tribunal'.

Apart from the omission of public enterprises from this list,[154] it is also evident that, as far as the military are concerned, only members of the Slovenian armed forces are mentioned as being subject to the criminal law on bribery; this omission suggests that the bribery of foreign soldiers, etc. would escape punishment, contrary to the Convention.[155] Furthermore, Slovenian law does not cover the de facto exercise of state authority by non-state entities.

Finally, in Brazil,[156] a 'foreign public official' is a person holding a 'position, a job, or a public function' in one of the following bodies of a foreign country:

- in 'state bodies';
- in 'diplomatic representations';
- in 'an organisation or enterprise directly or indirectly controlled by the public authorities'; or
- in 'international public organisations'.

On the face of it, this list would appear to go quite far. It is not, however, completely convincing, when looked at in the light of the definition of the domestic, i.e. Brazilian, public official.[157] The domestic official is defined in functional terms, not by reference to a list of institutions with which he or she may be associated. The divergence in these approaches left the WGB questioning whether a court, in interpreting who is covered by the term foreign public official, 'might exclude certain categories of foreign public official'[158] embraced by the domestic definition.

[152] Art. 126 Slovenian Criminal Code.
[153] See II.2.5.1. above. [154] See on this question II.2.6.6. below. [155] SI-Ph1, 7.
[156] Art. 337-D Brazilian Criminal Code. [157] Art. 327 Brazilian Criminal Code.
[158] BR-Ph1, 6 (the fear being that categories of 'foreign public official' not specifically named would be excluded).

2.6.3. Alignment with obligations under EC/EU law

Members of the European Union who are also signatories to the OECD's anti-bribery Convention must somehow reconcile their twin sets of obligations under the respective legal instruments. In this connection, we can notice that the laws of Austria, Belgium, Finland, France, Ireland, Luxembourg, and Italy all make special provision relating to Community officials. France went so far as to establish a special offence for Community officials and for officials from EU Member States and Germany even a special law,[159] but in compliance with the Convention these provisons apply the same penalty to bribery of non-EU officials or officials of other international organisations. There is nothing in the Convention which prevents state Parties from distinguishing between different categories of officials in this way, provided that two conditions are fulfilled: first, that the EU- or EC-related offence comprises all the necessary type of actions which could contravene the Convention; second, that where the specific definition of Community official or the specific offence does not apply, the more general definition or general offence can come into play, to ensure compliance with the obligations of the Convention. It is permissible only to sub-divide (or sub-define) a group of persons already established as being subject to the protection of the Convention as possible recipients of bribes.

Denmark[160] offers a counterpoint to the very detailed stipulations of certain other EU Member States in its concise definition, under the Criminal Code,[161] of the 'foreign public office or function'. Without further ado, this phraseology is sufficient to cover officials of all EU Member States, non-EU countries and all Community officials – the latter expression also embracing EU Commissioners, Members of the European Parliament, the European Court of Justice and the European Court of Auditors.[162]

2.6.4. The use of non-specific or general language

Some state Parties do not employ the specific terminology of Article 1(4) of the Convention in their implementing legislation but satisfy themselves with overarching definitions couched in general language. This approach is acceptable so long as the common Convention standard is then guaranteed as a result of interpretation by the courts (case law) or otherwise de facto

[159] 435–2 French Criminal Code; German Act on Combating Bribery of Public Officials of Member States of the European Union and of Community Officials.
[160] Compare II.2.6.4. below. [161] S. 122 Danish Criminal Code. [162] DK-Ph1, 5.

binding legal sources.[163] But there is a caveat to the latter point: where the basic principles of the law in this area are themselves dependent on (post-Convention) jurisprudence, the necessary certainty is lacking. Whether reliance can be placed on the courts or on legal practice interpreting general or open legal language 'correctly' – here in the sense of being consistent with international legal instruments such as the Convention – is a matter for each legal culture to decide for itself. There may be a predisposition in certain legal cultures – including some Nordic Union countries – for the legislature to employ general catch-all terminology,[164] and not to go into specifics: 'the law does not regulate everything in detail'.[165] German law (and systems based upon or related to it) follows a much stricter approach, tending to try and cover all eventualities with very specific language: this is justified by considerations of legal certainty. In such systems, we can therefore readily anticipate a more detailed set of definitions of corrupt behaviour. In the light of these considerations, we will now consider the findings of the WGB in respect of the general or open approach to legislating. We should bear in mind that in this area, as in others, the Convention seeks only a functional equivalence of state Parties' laws, not any more precise harmonisation.

Not all countries adopt the distinction between *appointed* and *elected* persons. For example, Australia and Canada and the European countries Austria,[166] Bulgaria,[167] Denmark,[168] Hungary,[169] Norway,[170] and Slovakia[171] all refrain from such a distinction. According to the legal terminology used in these countries, it is customary to regard elected posts as also falling within the definition 'public official'.

It is not a mandatory requirement of the Convention specifically to include the phrase 'foreign country', which appears in Article 1(4)(b), in implementing legislation. The inclusion within the scope of the Convention of *all levels of statehood*, including those of a regional nature, and of quasi-state authorities, may be secured by interpretative methods – in particular by application in practice but also by virtue of preparatory legislative materials. It is possible, for this reason, to declare sufficient the use of the general wording 'foreign state', by Bulgaria,[172] the Czech Republic,[173]

[163] For example, in Denmark, Iceland, and Norway the legislative *Travaux Préparatoires* are in general accorded considerable importance as a source of interpretation: cf. for Denmark: DK-Ph1, 1, 5 in the context of 'public official'); for Norway and Iceland: cf. NO-Ph2, 24, 32 and IS-Ph2, 23.

[164] NO-Ph2, 24. [165] Cf., for example, the case of Denmark (DK-Ph1, 1).

[166] S. 74(4c) Austrian Criminal Code. [167] Art. 93(15c) Bulgarian Criminal Code.

[168] S. 122 Danish Criminal Code. [169] Art. 137(3) Hungarian Criminal Code.

[170] S. 276a Norwegian Criminal Code. [171] S. 89(10) Slovak Criminal Code.

[172] Art. 93(15c) Bulgarian Criminal Code. [173] S. 162a(2) Czech Criminal Code.

Germany,[174] France,[175] and Hungary.[176] Similarly, the Canadian approach, which is to use the phrase 'country other than Canada'[177] and the Danish formulation 'foreign or international public office'[178] would suffice. The Japanese use of 'foreign government' is also acceptable.[179] In the United States, parallel legislation to the FCPA provides the necessary interpretative guidance.[180]

The Nordic countries Denmark, Finland, and Norway also manage to cover themselves as far as the application of their anti-bribery legislation to *public agencies* and *public enterprises* is concerned; notwithstanding the lack of specific reference to these entities, persons working for them (in a functional sense) would be caught as a result of the interpretation of general legislative formulations: 'any person who performs a public duty for a foreign state',[181] 'a person exercising a...foreign public function'[182] or 'anyone in connection with a post, office or commission...in a foreign country'.[183]

On the other hand, the WGB was less convinced by the Turkish legislator's general formulation 'officials...carrying out a legislative, administrative, or judicial function in a foreign country or exercising a public function in international business transactions'.[184] This seemed not to guarantee that Turkey would be in a position to prosecute persons who go about bribing officials of international organisations.[185]

Some countries are conspicuous by their complete *failure* – for a variety of reasons – to provide *for a statutory definition* of foreign public officials. Again, even this approach may be consistent with the Convention, provided that the necessary interpretation can be supplied by other reliable and binding sources, such as is the case with Denmark. With regard to other countries, the position is as follows: Greek anti-corruption legislation, instead of providing its own definition, refers directly to the text of the Convention. This method of implementation may be described as 'incorporation by reference': a foreign public official is quite simply 'a foreign public official in the meaning of the OECD Convention ratified in Article 1 of the present law'.[186]

[174] Ss. 1 and 2 German Act on Combating Bribery of Foreign Public Officials in International Business Transactions.

[175] Art. 435-3 French Criminal Code. Neither in this case, nor in that of Germany, was the WGB completely convinced by the wording selected: cf. FR-Ph2, 40 and DE-Ph2, 40.

[176] Art. 137(3) Hungarian Criminal Code.

[177] S. 2 Canadian Corruption of Public Officials Act.

[178] S. 122 Danish Criminal Code.

[179] Art. 10bis(2)(i) Japanese Unfair Competition Prevention Law 1999.

[180] Foreign Agent Registration Act 1938.

[181] S. 20(3) Finish Criminal Code.

[182] S. 122 Danish Criminal Code.

[183] S. 276a Norwegian Criminal Code.

[184] Art. 211(3) Turkish Criminal Code.

[185] TR-Ph1, 6, 26.

[186] Art. 2(1) Greek Law 2656/1998 (in the amended version introduced by Law 3090/2002).

> Based on the argument that the whole text of the Convention, by virtue of its ratification, had become binding law in Greece, the legislature first of all dispensed with *any* reference to the definition of foreign public official. As a result, it was unclear whether the definition of the domestic public official might not be used – either instead of or in addition to the text of the Convention itself – in such a way as to limit the scope of the term.[187] This problem was eradicated by the introduction of an express reference to the Convention.[188]

Spain provides another example of a state signatory which fails to provide a statutory definition, justifying this approach by reference to the self-executing nature of the Convention definition. As in the Greek case, following ratification the Convention meaning would take direct legal effect in the country, and Spanish judges would be obliged to apply Article 1(4) of the Convention directly. The problem in such a case, however, lies in the possibility of conflict with other international instruments dealing with the same subject matter. Without a clear demarcation of precedence, it would not be obvious that the OECD Convention standard would prevail.[189] Similar considerations apply in the case of Argentina. Equally, there is no legislative definition of who is a 'public official from another state':[190] the Argentinian delegation to the WGB justifies this open approach by saying that reliance would be placed on the interpretatative commentaries of the Convention (the Official Commentaries). But, again, there is a risk that the standard of the OECD Convention would not necessarily be followed by the criminal courts, given that Argentina also subscribes to the OAS Convention, whose definition of foreign public official is more restricted.

A similar line is taken by the Netherlands. There is no detailed legislative definition. Reliance is placed on the general wording 'person in the public service'. It is, however, maintained that a sufficiently broad definition is supplied by practice (based on consistent case law authority); in particular, the Convention itself is relied upon as the authoritative source of interpretation as provided for in the *Travaux Préparatoires* of the Dutch legislation.[191] Dutch implementation, nevertheless, also poses the question whether the courts can really be trusted to provide the correct interpretation of the Convention.

Last of all, we can refer to the almost corruption-free island paradise of Iceland. The Icelandic case is slightly more convincing, perhaps, in terms of compliance, than the other examples we have looked at. Although, like them,

[187] GR-Ph1, 17. [188] GR-Ph2, 27. [189] ES-Ph1, 4.
[190] Art. 258bis Argentine Criminal Code.
[191] Cf. the official opinion of the Dutch government referred to in the Phase 1 report (NL-Ph1, 7 et seq.).

lacking any further elaboration of 'foreign public official' in its legislation, the explanatory notes issued in respect of its legislation do in fact offer interpretative guidance which is close to the Convention meaning. They contain the phrase 'any person engaged in public administration, commissioned, or otherwise lawfully instituted in office': this is sufficiently wide to comprise all persons carrying out activities on behalf of the state, independently of their institutional affiliation.[192] In the light of the fact that, in the Icelandic legal system, the explanatory notes form the authoritative source of statutory interpretation, an adequate application of the Convention's autonomous interpretation of the phrase 'foreign public official' would seem to be guaranteed.[193]

2.6.5. Inadequate implementation: definition based on foreign law

Whether a 'foreign public official' has been bribed is a matter for the OECD Convention to determine, autonomously. There is no room for another legal source to decide the matter, whether that be the law of the state served by the foreign public official or the rules of the international organisation by which he or she may be employed.

Belgian law provides that, outside the EU, the legal status of foreign public official is to be decided according to the law of the foreign state or the statute of the international organisation concerned.[194] This approach is clearly in breach of the Convention, failing as it does to ensure that the criteria of Article 1(4) are respected. Hungary, on the other hand, has now rectified the non-autonomous approach it allowed to slip into its 2001 legislation.[195] Mexico has also adopted similar corrective measures: the relevant legislation of 2005 has removed the reference to foreign law.[196]

Difficulties are also presented by Slovenian legislation, whose approach to the definition of foreign public official requires not only conformity with the definition of Slovenian officials but also with the domestic foreign definition: the WGB stated in its recent Phase 1 report that Slovenian legislation thus fails to accord with the Convention.[197]

[192] IS-Ph1, 3.

[193] The WGB's Phase 2 report on Iceland nevertheless expresses some disquiet concerning the lack of specificity of the statutory language (IS-Ph2, 23).

[194] Arts. 250(2) and 251(2) Belgian Criminal Code; the WGB condemned this state of affairs already in the Phase 1 report: cf. BE-Ph1, 20. Nevertheless, Belgium has to date not altered its law on this point: cf. BE-Ph2, 36.

[195] Art. 137(3)(a) Hungarian Criminal Code (version in force since March 2004). A previous version of the Code, based on Act CXXI 2001, corrected some of the deficiencies in Hungarian legislation detected in the Phase 1 evaluation: cf. HU-Ph1^{bis}, 17 et seq., 19.

[196] Art. 222bis Mexican Criminal Code (version in force since 2005); for the WGB's concerns regarding the previous version of the Mexican law: cf. MX-Ph1, 3 and MX-Ph2, 11.

[197] SI-Ph1, 6 et seq. and 38 et seq.

Portuguese law also shows some weaknesses arising from its distinction between 'foreign public official'[198] and 'foreign political official'.[199] It only defines the former in the light of the Convention's autonomous approach, leaving the latter to be determined by reference to the foreign legislation concerned. As we have seen, the 'foreign political official' is not in fact subject to the jurisdiction of the Convention; nevertheless, the non-autonomous approach of Portuguese law to such officials creates certain risks of incomplete application of the Convention. Such risks could be avoided, if Portuguese law's definition of 'foreign public official' was sufficiently watertight to comprise all conceivable categories of persons performing public functions. This is not, however, the case, as it is not certain that members of a foreign legislature would be included.[200]

2.6.6. Extension of definition to persons on fringe or threshold of public office

We have already noted that the FCPA definition extends to persons operating on the threshold or the fringes of public office. US law, namely, threatens criminal punishment for bribery of candidates, political parties and party officials of foreign states. This approach is likely to persuade other countries to treat such cases as further examples of transnational bribery under their laws, but so far only Belgium and Portugal have followed suit.

In Belgium, the law extends the provisions on bribery to persons who are applicants for a public function, who lead others to believe that they will exercise such a function or who, by misrepresenting themselves, mislead others into believing that they exercise such a function.[201] Here, therefore, there is also a notion of 'fictitious' public officials. And finally, as we saw in the previous section with regard to Portugal, bribery of 'foreign political officials'[202] can fall within the prohibitions of the Convention.

3. Third party beneficiaries

3.1. Compelling the use of false motives for official action

The public official need not himself be the person to enjoy the advantage given to influence his official behaviour. He may also be minded to confer an

[198] Art. 41-A(2) Portuguese Decree Law 28 1984.
[199] Art. 41-A(3) Portuguese Decree Law 28 1984.
[200] PT-Ph1, 6. [201] Art. 246(3) Criminal Code; and cf. BE-Ph1, 4.
[202] Art. 41-A(3) Portuguese Decree Law 28 1984.

advantage on a third party; this will likewise constitute a false or illegitimate motive for exercise of his public powers. Thus, a businessman bribes a public official not only in the case where he pays the latter a bribe directly. He also does so when he arranges a scholarship or place at University or College for the official's son, when he gives the official's wife a fur coat, if he makes a contribution to the political party to which the official may be affiliated or contributes to the coffers of the undertaking for which the official works. All these situations are to be regarded as bribery within the terms of Article 1 of the Convention. It makes no difference whether the official himself or a third person associated with him gains the advantage. A legal provision limiting the advantage accruing from the bribe to the official himself – 'for that official' – will therefore fall short of the Convention standard.[203]

3.2. The circle of third party beneficiaries

The scope of the offence provided for by Article 1 is quite clear: it covers all cases in which the public official receives an offer or a promise of an advantage or benefit for a third party. The third party's benefit – for whatever motives – is the basis on which the *public official is interested or is deemed to be interested* in the advantage in question (the bribe) and in respect of which his decision is to be bought.

It is not sufficient to provide that the third parties are persons with whom the public official has a *special empathy* or relationship. A public official is not necessarily only interested in supporting persons in a close personal or professional relationship to him. Just as he may wish to support his family, friends, his party, or the enterprise or undertaking for which he works, so might he also wish to confer a benefit upon a trades union, association, a particular newspaper, specific research project, NGO, or other person or body.

> The *Shering-Plough Corporation* case of 2004 concerned an NGO as third party beneficiary.[204] The president of a charitable foundation, the *Chudow Castle Foundation*, was at the same time Director of a public health authority – and in this capacity responsible for deciding in public procurement proceedings about the purchase of pharmaceutical products. In knowledge of this state of affairs, the Polish subsidiary of the US Schering-Plough Corporation made payments to the *Chudow Castle Foundation* to the tune of $75 000. These 'contributions' were in fact bribes: they aimed to influence the decision-making of the President in the public procurement procedure.

[203] This was the wording of s. 116b of the Slovak Criminal Code that was found to be wanting in the evaluation of Slovakia (SK-Ph1, 5 et seq.).

[204] SEC Administrative Proceeding Filing No. 3-11517, June 9, 2004.

The relationship of the public official to the beneficiary, and why he might be seeking to benefit them, is not of interest. An offence will therefore be drawn too narrowly, if the legislation requires a particular type of connection between public official and third party beneficiary; equally, the law should not limit the offence to cases where the public official acts out of particular motives or provable motives.

There is only one person who may not be considered as third party beneficiary within the meaning of the Convention, and that is *the state itself*. If the state is enriched, then there can be no injured state as a result of the abuse of public office. If a payment is made into a public fund or pot, in order to influence the official, then that can be regarded as corruption in a broadly understood sense, given the obvious manipulation of state authority by illegitimate means. Whoever draws on those funds – for example, by means of 'kickbacks' – commits a fraud or breach of trust. But such behaviour would not breach Article 1 of the Convention – even when it is obvious that persons in power have helped themselves to the boosted public funds in question, in a criminal manner.

> It is therefore imprecise to refer to 'corruption' when describing the abuses of office allegedly committed in relation to the operation of the UN's 'Oil-for-Food Programme', established in the 1990s to allow humanitarian relief to reach Iraq, whose oil supplies were then embargoed. It is more correct to refer to the surcharges on oil prices and kickbacks in relation to humanitarian aid as breaches of UN Security Council Resolution 661/1990.[205]

The Convention does not aim at detection or correction of the absence of transparency regarding the exercise of state powers, a lack of control of state expenditure, or the illegitimate distribution of state funds in foreign countries. Anti-bribery laws are not the appropriate instrument for dealing with support for illegal regimes. For that, they are too narrow. The appropriate instrument is rather legislation implementing an internationally agreed embargo.

The criminal liability of the donor of the bribe is not altered by the fact that the third party beneficiary may not have been involved in the bribery compact or deal. Whether he was or he was not is irrelevant, as is the question whether the bribe was paid to the official or directly to the third party. Direct payments must also be covered by the legislation.[206]

[205] For the details of the events concerned and an analysis of what occurred cf. the final report of the Independent Inquiry into the United Nations Oil-for-Food Programme, September 7 and October 27, 2005 (http://www.iic-offp.org).

[206] Cf. this point as borne out in the country reports for Denmark (DK-Ph1,35), Italy (IT-Ph1, 33), the Netherlands (NL-Ph1, 35), and Slovenia (SI-Ph1, 9). While their laws were all satisfactory in this regard, Argentinian law was not, but Art. 258bis, the offending provision, was amended in 2003 (AR-Ph1, 5).

3.3. Horizontal comparison

3.3.1. Explicit rule for third party beneficiaries

Among European countries, Austria,[207] Finland,[208] Germany,[209] Greece,[210] Hungary,[211] Iceland,[212] Portugal,[213] the Slovak Republic,[214] Spain,[215] Sweden,[216] and Switzerland[217] all extend the offence of bribery of a foreign public official to benefits conferred on 'another person'. Among South American countries, the laws of Argentina,[218] Brazil,[219] and Chile[220] are similar.

Canada's Corruption of Foreign Public Officials Act also refers explicitly to payments 'to any person' – if only those 'for the benefit of a foreign public official'. The latter is not intended, however, as a limitation. The formulation originates from the Criminal Code of 1985 and is sufficiently broad in application: it implies the power of the foreign public official, in the words of the Phase 1 report, to 'direct or confer such a benefit on a third party'; this is sufficient to cover what the Convention intends by 'favourable publicity'.[221]

3.3.2. The effectiveness of open-textured language

What if the offence is phrased in open-textured language? Several states fail explicitly to mention advantages conferred on third parties. This is not necessarily a breach of the Convention, provided that a sufficiently broad interpretation is guaranteed. It should, namely, be evident from any of a number of surrounding sources – the general rules of criminal law, structural or systemic considerations,[222] explanatory reports to legislation (*Travaux Préparatoires*), jurisprudence and academic writing[223] – that every agreement to trade 'benefit for public act' is punishable, regardless of whoever derives the benefit or advantage.

With regard to Australia, the law states that the beneficiary of the bribery 'may' only be the public official himself.[224] Neither UK statute

[207] S. 307 Austrian Criminal Code. [208] S. 13(2) Finnish Criminal Code.

[209] S. 334 German Criminal Code.

[210] Art. 2(1) Greek Act Ratifying the Convention on Combating Bribery of Foreign Public Officials in International Business Transactions (Act 2656/1998).

[211] Art. 258B(1) Hungarian Criminal Code.

[212] S. 2(1)(b) Icelandic Prevention of Corruption (Amendment) Act 2001.

[213] Art. 44-A Portuguese Decree Law 28 1984.

[214] S. 116b Slovak Criminal Code (in version enacted 2001).

[215] Art. 445bis Spanish Criminal Code. [216] Ch. 17(7) Swedish Criminal Code.

[217] Art. 322^{septies} Swiss Criminal Code.

[218] Art. 258bis Argentine Criminal Code (in version enacted 2003): cf. Art. 2 OECD 2005.

[219] Art. 337-B Brazilian Criminal Code. [220] Art. 250bis-A Chilean Criminal Code.

[221] CA-Ph1, 5. [222] For example, as in Italy. [223] Cf., for example, Denmark: DK-Ph1, 6.

[224] Ss. 70.2(1)(a) and (c) Australian Criminal Code.

nor Common Law explicitly refers to third parties.[225] Other legal systems applying open-textured definitions of the offence are: Belgium,[226] Bulgaria,[227] Denmark,[228] France,[229] Hungary,[230] Iceland,[231] Italy,[232] the Netherlands,[233] New Zealand,[234] Norway,[235] the United States,[236] and most recently Poland.[237] The definitions used by their legal systems are all regarded as being broad enough to extend to third party beneficiaries.

> In Italy, the criminalisation of active bribery, in case of benefit to third parties, is achieved by extrapolation from the passive offence: an Italian public official also commits a crime when the advantage goes to a third party.[238] Apparently, this link between passive and active offences is made in a clear and convincing way only there.[239] In Bulgaria, the same result pertains in theory, but it is regarded as uncertain whether the Bulgarian criminal courts will follow this line of argument; thus far, there is no jurisprudence, even regarding internal cases, to go on.[240] Finally on this point, we may mention the terms of Icelandic law, which refers to third party benefit only in the context of passive bribery. In such a case, the WGB fears that the converse conclusion will be drawn, and has called for explicit clarification.[241]

According to the Turkish solution, the unspecific formulation 'directly or indirectly'[242] is designed to capture both the bribe donor, as intermediary, and also the level of the recipient, including third party benefit. There is a restriction, however, in the law which requires a 'relationship' between the public official and the third party: this, as we have seen, is contrary to the Convention.[243]

[225] UK-Ph1, 6 et seq. [226] Art. 246(2) Belgian Criminal Code.
[227] Art. 304 Bulgarian Criminal Code. [228] S. 122 Danish Criminal Code.
[229] Arts. 435-2, 435-3, 435-4 French Criminal Code; strengthened by case law (Cass. Crim., 7 February 2001).
[230] Art. 258B Hungarian Criminal Code.
[231] S. 109 Icelandic Criminal Code. In this case it is not possible to have unqualified confidence in the open-textured language of the Criminal Code, given the more explicit definition employed by the Icelandic Tax Act (75/1981): cf. IS-Ph2, 25.
[232] Art. 322bis read together with Arts. 318 and 319 Italian Criminal Code.
[233] The corresponding passive bribery offence is also interpreted in this broad sense: cf. the notes on the Dutch Ratification Bill, 19 mentioned in NL-Ph1, 9.
[234] S. 105C New Zealand's Crimes Amendment Act 2001.
[235] S. 276 Norwegian Criminal Code; notwithstanding the very broad wording of the legislation the WGB continues to express doubts in its Phase 2 report for Norway (NO-Ph2, 26).
[236] Discussion was opened on this question in US-Ph2, 32.
[237] Polish law has recently filled the gap in its anti-bribery legislation previously caused by the limitation of third party benefits to 'material benefit': this had resulted in immaterial benefit accruing to the third party as a result of the bribe not being taken into account. Cf. OECD June 2005, 58.
[238] IT-Ph1, 8.
[239] The line of argument held up even in the context of the more critical Phase 2 investigations.
[240] BG-Ph2, 29 et seq. [241] IS-Ph2, 24. [242] Art. 211/3 Turkish Criminal Code.
[243] TR-Ph1, 7.

The Convention's two Asian signatories, Japan[244] and Korea,[245] likewise fail to make explicit the punishability of transnational bribery, when committed for the benefit of third parties. In both countries, however, the offence of bribery of domestic officials is broader and does extend explicitly to such cases.[246] In the evaluation of these countries,[247] the question was therefore asked whether the case law applicable to national offences could also be applied to the transnational offence. There is some risk that judicial practice would limit transnational bribery conversely and that consequently only such cases in which payments flow directly to the official would be defined as criminal.

> An additional point of interest arises from the Japanese case law reviewed by the WGB and this is the requirement, with regard to domestic bribery, of a benefit 'in substance' to the public official.[248] Such a benefit was found to exist in the case of payment of the salary of a secretary for a Councillor.[249] This type of scenario does not, however, fall within the definition of third party benefit, because in such a case it is the public official himself who derives the benefit. He has obtained the services of a paid employee, without himself having to pay anything. The limitation of the criminal offence to such situations would be inadequate to meet the more far-reaching goal of the Convention. It is only when an advantage for the public official is seen in the very power to direct who will be the ultimate beneficiary that such an approach is acceptable.[250]

The same question was raised – and seems to have been solved – with regard to Mexico: in the case of third party beneficiaries only the bribery of domestic,[251] not foreign officials[252] had been criminalised explicitly. As a consequence of the WGB's criticism,[253] Mexico finally adopted a Bill containing a reference to a third party beneficiary determined by the bribed public official.

After this analysis of the evaluations of the WGB – particularly the Phase 2 reports – we can say that open-textured legislation is regarded as rather dubious. The offence should be defined as precisely as possible. The doubts can, however, be dispelled, but only where case law shows that the necessary broad interpretation has been adopted.

[244] Art. 10bis Japanese Unfair Competition Prevention Law. [245] KR-Ph1, 4 et seq., 22.

[246] Art. 197(2) read together with Art. 198 Japanese Criminal Code; Art. 130 Korean Criminal Code.

[247] JP-Ph2, 44; KR-Ph2, 33 et seq., 45. [248] JP-Ph1, 5, 28; JP-Ph2, 44.

[249] Cf. the *KSD* case: Tokyo District Court, 26 March 2005, cited in JP-Ph2, 44.

[250] This wider approach was officially put forward by the Japanese delegation: cf. JP-Ph1, 5. In the second Phase 2 report the WGB recommended that Japanese law be clarified.

[251] Art. 222 Mexican Federal Criminal Code.

[252] Previous version of Art. 222bis Mexican Federal Criminal Code.

[253] MX-Ph2, 11, 57.

4. The bribe: any undue pecuniary or other advantage

4.1. Factual nature

4.1.1. Advantage of any kind

The bribe payment usually takes the form of a bank deposit or transfer or the payment of cash. A bribe may also take the shape of the transfer of other assets, for example, property. The WGB has, however, recognised the danger in limiting benefits to those of a *material nature:* restricting the scope of bribery prohibited by the Convention to 'material benefit(s)' alone[254] would risk allowing a substantial amount of corruption to go scot-free. It is for this reason that the phrase 'pecuniary or other advantage' appearing in Article 1(1) of the Convention goes further, extending also to *immaterial benefits* which are not expressed in money terms. Examples of the latter would include obtaining a school place for the official's child,[255] support for society/social or business opportunities,[256] or a helping hand up the career ladder. The arrangement of all kinds of personal favours for the official, whether related to his career or his private life, is covered. Other examples might include access to an exclusive club,[257] or contacts to a VIP.[258] The advantage may also take the shape of certain information and/or advice which is valuable to the official.

In order to guarantee objectivity in the criminal law, it is necessary to evaluate the advantage. Without any kind of *measurement*, it would not be possible to say that an 'advantage' had occurred. This does not mean that the category of bribe objects is thereby limited to material ones, as it is quite possible to give a monetary value to an immaterial benefit. For instance, every promotion, a larger office, more leisure time, and other forms of professional advancement can be measured in salary terms. The improvement of professional opportunities can also be valued.[259] If the bribe in question consists of new contacts, of a personal or also sexual nature, there is a market for these, enabling the price to be (approximately) calculated.[260] On the other hand, mere polite approaches or simple ingratiation will not, without more, be capable of valuation and cannot therefore be objectively defined: the criminal law is not concerned with them as they are not true bribes.

It would not be contrary to the Convention for the criminal law relating to corruption to insist that the bribe be capable of being converted into a monetary value. Provided that what stands behind the law is that an

[254] Cf. the former provisions of the Bulgarian Criminal Code criticised by the WGB in BG-Ph1, 18 and since amended.

[255] Cf., for example, SI-Ph1, 5; NO-Ph2, 28. [256] Cf., for example, KR-Ph1, 2.

[257] FI-Ph2, 32; NO-Ph2, 28. [258] PL-Ph1, 4. [259] For an example cf. SK-Ph1, 4.

[260] Cramer 2001, 2575 et seq. (Rn. 19); Balmelli 1996, 138 et seq.; TR-Ph1, 6; NO-Ph2, 28.

advantage must be objectively identifiable – with monetary value being the reference point – there is no necessary limitation to material advantages in the sense of *tangible benefits*.[261]

4.1.2. Horizontal comparison

The requirements of the Convention concerning the nature of benefits etc. regarded as criminal have been largely implemented by contracting parties. Virtually without exception, the legal systems subject to the Convention deem advantages of all kinds to fall within the offence. Monetary payments, other material goods, personal services, private or professional advantages, or perks of all kinds are covered.[262] The national provisions in question fall into one of three categories:

- First, provisions referring to immaterial benefits with precision and in an explicit way:

  Into the first category fall the definitions of Argentina ('any object of pecuniary value, or other benefits such as gifts, favours, promises or advantages'[263]), Australia ('any advantage...not limited to property'[264]), Canada ('loan, reward, advantage or benefit of any kind'[265]), Mexico ('money or any other advantage, whether in assets or services'[266]) and New Zealand ('any money, valuable consideration, office, or employment, or any benefit'[267]). Where Europe is concerned, further examples come from Bulgaria ('gifts or any other kind of advantage'[268]), Denmark ('gift or other privilege' – although it is not clear there, however, whether 'favourable publicity'[269] can also incur a criminal penalty), Iceland ('gift or other advantage'[270]), Italy ('money or other advantages'[271]), the Netherlands ('a gift or a promise...or...a service'[272]) and the United Kingdom ('any gift or consideration' and 'any undue award'[273]). Finally, we may refer to the case of Japan as a further example of a country with a precise legislative definition of an advantage ('any pecuniary or other advantage'[274]).

[261] Balmelli 1996, 138 et seq.
[262] The latest country to come into line with Convention requirements was Bulgaria, which has corrected the former deficit in its law. The amending legislation was passed by Parliament in 2002 (BG-Ph2, 28 et seq.).
[263] Art. 258bis Argentine Criminal Code. [264] S. 70.1 Australian Criminal Code.
[265] Art. 3(1) Canadian Corruption of Foreign Public Officials Act 1998.
[266] Art. 222bis Mexican Federal Criminal Code. [267] S. 105C(1) New Zealand Criminal Code.
[268] Art. 304 Bulgarian Criminal Code. [269] DK-Ph1, 3.
[270] S. 109 Icelandic Criminal Code. It should, however, be noted that case law on national bribery cases indicates that there may be a limitation to physical assets, so that the wide interpretation required by the Convention is not necessarily guaranteed: cf. IS-Ph2, 21 et seq.
[271] Art. 332bis Italian Criminal Code. [272] Arts. 177, 177a, 178 Dutch Criminal Code.
[273] The first phrase comes from s. 1(1) Act 1906 (see note 126). It is the Common Law which refers to 'any undue award'.
[274] Art 10^bis(1) Japanese Unfair Competition Prevention Law.

- Second, provisions using catch-all, overarching phraseology:

Here we may cite the example 'advantages of any kind' used by Belgium,[275] France,[276] Luxembourg;[277] Spain ('presents, gifts, offers or promises'[278]), and among non-European states the United States ('anything of value'[279]).

- Third, provisions which are extremely imprecise, but an extensive interpretation of which is guaranteed by surrounding legal sources.

Norway and Switzerland each use the imprecise phrase 'advantage', but the *Travaux Préparatoires* indicate that a wide interpretation would be favoured, even if there are no clear indications yet in practice.[280] Korea's vague use of the term 'bribe' is expanded upon by the explanatory manual of the Korean Ministry of Justice and by the jurisprudence of the highest courts, in such a way as to fulfil the Convention's requirements.[281]

In certain cases, the WGB's evaluations revealed that immaterial benefits were treated as illegal bribes only if they could be converted into a monetary value. Such an approach is not, however, contrary to the Convention, as monetary value is taken simply as an objective indicator of the advantage conferred.

Mexico, for example, refers to civil law principles in its limitation of immaterial benefits to those 'that can be converted to money or tangible property'.[282] The same applies in the Austrian and Belgian legal systems: case law decided to date on the subject of domestic bribery refers exclusively to benefits expressed in monetary terms.[283]

Only Chile, apparently, still employs wording which is clearly too narrow, by limiting the application of anti-corruption legislation to 'economic advantage'.[284]

4.2. Legal nature

4.2.1. Permission to pay official: factual determination

According to Article 1(1), it is only an 'undue...advantage' to the public official which is subject to criminal punishment. The advantage will be regarded as undue, if it is *not foreseen by a binding legal provision* (usually a statutory norm). If the public task in question is, however, carried out by law

[275] Art. 246(2) Belgian Criminal Code. [276] Arts. 435-2, 435-3, 435-5 French Criminal Code.
[277] Art. 247 Luxembourg Criminal Code. [278] Art. 445bis Spanish Criminal Code.
[279] 15 U.S.C. § 78dd-1 FCPA 1977.
[280] S. 276a Norwegian Criminal Code; NO-Ph2; Art. 322^{septies} Swiss Criminal Code.
[281] Art. 3(1) Korean Act on Preventing Bribery of Foreign Public Officials in International Business Transactions; cf. on the interpretation of this Act: KR-Ph1, 2; KR-Ph2, 29 and the decision of the Supreme Court 95 Do 1269, September 25, 1995 cited there.
[282] MX-Ph, 3. [283] AT-Ph1, 2; BE-Ph1, 4.
[284] Art. 250^{bis}A Chilean Criminal Code: cf. CL-Ph1, 29.

for a standard fee or tariff, and the person receiving the service does not pay the fee into a general public fund but rather directly to the public official, then the payment given was due and obviously not criminal in any way. In some countries, notarial acts may be carried out in the service of the state and the notary concerned will receive payment directly from the client.

The question whether the benefit was in fact due is a matter for the law of the victim foreign state to determine. This is expressed by Official Commentary 8: '[i]t is not an offence, however, if the advantage was permitted or required by the written law or regulation of the foreign public official's country, including case law'. By relying on foreign law, the Convention here seems to make an exception to the 'autonomous interpretation' approach. But the foreign law determines only the *question of fact*. So it is only at first sight that this matter appears to be regulated exclusively by the various laws of the countries whose officials are corrupted. As we shall now see, the Convention – autonomously – supplies the *legal* parameters within which those laws fall to be interpreted.

4.2.2. Level of legal authority required for permission

It is clearly insufficient for the authorities to rely simply on *local practice* or *tolerance* ('turning a blind eye') with regard to payments to their public officials in connection with the carrying out of their tasks. Official Commentary 8, as we have seen, refers expressly to 'written law or regulation', and Official Commentary 7 provides further elaboration: '[i]t is also an offence irrespective of, inter alia, the value of the advantage, its results, perceptions of local custom, the tolerance of such payments by local authorities'. Only a *clearly binding legal norm* of the foreign state – embedded in legislation or case law – is an adequate legal basis for permitting an advantage. It is only *express permission* of the advantage, not simply the failure to outlaw it, which allows the benefit to be conferred.[285] In so far as corruption is prohibited by law in the state concerned – and this is the case now, on paper, on virtually a worldwide basis – then it is doubly clear that the exceptional permission of a payment must also be established on the same binding legal level.

4.2.3. Scope of statutory permission

The consideration for a due advantage can never be an illegal action of the public official. There can be no explicit or *implicit statutory permission* for a

[285] Hence the existing doubts concerning the Australian understanding of the matter: cf. AU-Ph1, 4, 23; the point is also mentioned in AR-Ph1, 4.

benefit or advantage designed to generate an *impermissible* official act or indeed to influence the exercise of official discretion in an unreasonable (non-objective) way.

It therefore follows that a fee can be paid only for an official act which was *clearly legal.* By defining the scope of the offence in terms of 'undue advantages', Article 1 and Official Commentary 8 are fully within the scheme or principle of the Convention as expressed in Commentaries 3 and 4, namely that any attempt to buy acts contrary to official duty or in breach of proper discretion is criminal; only payments, etc. which are specifically authorised by law should not be criminalised.

4.2.4. Horizontal comparison

Most of the signatory states have indeed implemented the Convention to the effect that payments or other benefits which are made in conformity with a strict legal basis are not criminalised: such advantages may take the form of a *legal entitlement or legal claim*, for example, payments to a notary, who may in some countries, and in some circumstances, take fees for a duty performed in the public interest. The criminal law of the signatory states will either exclude such legal advantages altogether from its definition of the offence, or will make them part of a legitimate defence. The laws concerned, of course, vary as to their degree of strictness and/or precision, as the following examples should illustrate.

France adheres strictly to the line set out in Official Commentaries 7 and 8, namely that the criminal law should target advantages 'without legal basis' ('*sans droit*'). To escape from punishment, the donor in question must be able to show that he has acted on the basis of a clear statutory provision. The French example is followed by Luxembourg.[286] Similar approaches are followed by Greece,[287] and by Italy.[288] Here too, permission can be conferred only on an express legal basis. Among central and eastern European countries, the Czech Republic[289] and Hungary provide further examples of this line. Hungarian criminal law was altered to refer to 'undue favour', ruling out in the process the possibility of justification according to customary practice.[290]

Canada expands on the notion of undue advantage by referring not only to the permission granted by a state's laws but also to that mentioned by the

[286] Art. 435-3 French Criminal Code: cf. FR-Ph2, 41; Art. 247 Luxembourg Criminal Code: cf. LU-Ph2, 33.

[287] Art. 235, 236 Greek Criminal Code read together with Art. 2 Greek Law 2656/1998.

[288] IT-Ph1, 6. [289] S. 162a(1) Czech Criminal Code.

[290] Art. 258B Hungarian Criminal Code: cf. HU-Ph2, 39; regarding the previous legal position: cf. HU-Ph1, 4.

statutes of an international organisation.[291] Regarding the United States, we may refer to the defence mentioned by the FCPA, which appears exemplary: it refers to an advantage which is 'lawful under the written laws and regulations of the foreign official's country'.[292] In fact, the defence appears to have been of little practical impact, mainly because it would be very difficult to determine what kind of payments, apparently bribes, were in fact 'lawful'.

The Korean solution[293] follows the Convention very closely, on the one hand, by making clear that even a very minor advantage can be justified only as far as it is 'permitted by the law of the foreign public official's country'.[294] Korea's general criminal law, however, muddies the waters somewhat by suggesting that conduct 'in pursuance of accepted business practices, or...which does not violate the social rules'[295] should not be punished. Were this rule to be applied to cases of active bribery of foreign public officials, this would be a breach of the Convention.[296]

Some countries are rather more generous than the requirement of clear statutory permission would allow, by tolerating gifts of an insignificant amount without such a basis, on the ground that they do not constitute any kind of danger. It is not, however, possible to regard such peccadilloes as permitted under the perspective of 'due advantage' (Official Commentaries 7 and 8). They may, however, be qualified as 'small facilitation payments' (Official Commentary 9),[297] provided that no gifts, etc. may be given in return for illegal official acts. Where the consideration for the payment, gift, etc. of this kind is unclear, that does not necessarily mean that an otherwise complete criminalisation strategy is endangered – the uncovering of major corruption cases is not jeopardised. Risks of abuse would, however, remain.

Such risks become apparent if we consider the case of Slovakia, which has also now defined the term 'undue'.[298] It follows Official Commentary 8 by excluding from this definition benefits, etc. paid in accordance with a legal basis. At the same time, the law also applies a de minimis threshold of acceptable 'minimum gifts of very small value'. Persons who give 'socially acceptable gifts' such as 'a bunch of flowers or a pen' and hand them

[291] S. 3(3)(a) Canadian Corruption of Foreign Public Officials Act.

[292] 15 U.S.C. §§ 78dd-1(c)(1), 78dd-2(c)(1), 78dd-3(c)(1) FCPA 1977.

[293] Art. 3(2) Korean Act on Preventing Bribery of Foreign Public Officials in International Business Transactions.

[294] Cf. at least the translation cited in KR-Ph1, 2 and note the wording on the OECD homepage: http://www.oecd.org.

[295] Art. 20 Korean Criminal Law Act, which applies to criminal law generally and therefore also to crimes of bribery.

[296] The WGB therefore recommends that the explanatory manual of the Korean Ministry of Justice should be amended in order to clarify the position: cf. KR-Ph2, 28.

[297] See further discussion in II.7.2.2. below.

[298] S. 89(12) Slovak Criminal Code.

over in the context of the foreign official's actions, are not punishable. This tolerance may only, however, be exercised when the gifts are of a really insignificant character and in the appropriate 'social context'.[299]

Danish law provides a further example of a legal system which does not base its approach in this regard exclusively on written law. The point of interpretation relates to the phrase 'unjustified grants'.[300] Local custom or usual practice is allowed to play a role here. The criminal law will not intervene in the case of 'usual gifts' given on anniversaries, retirements, or similar occasions. Nor would it apply to small rewards not agreed in advance or to the 'gratuities' customary in the country.[301] The latter may even be allowed to pass muster with the prosecution authorities, if they are paid in order to induce the public official to commit a breach of duty.[302]

Referring now to Norway, the meaning of the term 'improper'[303] is plainly unclear. As in other cases, one must point to the *Travaux Préparatoires* for assistance. The criteria used vary, however, according to the type of case and it is therefore not easy to predict on which side of the fence the criminal law would fall. The WGB has recommended that the position be clarified by means of general guidelines issued by the highest state prosecutor.[304]

The 'tolerance zone' in Australia goes too far.[305] On the one hand, 'customary' and other 'officially tolerated benefits' are – rightly – regarded as 'undue' independently of their level.[306] But all benefits, even substantial ones, which are merely not forbidden in the state of the bribed official, escape punishment as part of a legal defence.[307]

In Austria, Germany, and Switzerland a 'bribe' committed in consideration for correct performance of the foreign official's tasks is not, in fact, a bribe – it is not a crime.[308] This means that there is no need for them to accommodate a 'due advantage' exception. The defence is only applicable in the case of a legitimate act of the official, but if such an act is not in any case capable of giving rise to criminal liability, any defence is otiose.

> The due advantage exception foreseen by Swiss law for 'advantages authorised by departmental regulations'[309] is therefore applicable only to

[299] SK-Ph1, 4. [300] Art. 122 Danish Criminal Code.
[301] One can see this from the *Travaux Préparatoires* relating to Act 228 (implementing legislation) of 4 April 2000 and the official reports or statements (both sources are cited in DK-Ph1, 3).
[302] It would, therefore, be difficult to allow them to fall under the definition of 'small facilitation payments' in the sense of Commentary 9. Cf. the WGB's doubts related to Official Commentaries 7 and 8 in DK-Ph1, 4, 25.
[303] S. 276a Norwegian Criminal Code. [304] Note the critical comments in NO-Ph2, 28 et seq.
[305] AU-Ph1, 4, 23. [306] S. 70.2(2) Australian Criminal Code.
[307] S. 70.3 Australian Criminal Code. [308] See II.7.3.2. below.
[309] Art. 322^{octies}(2) Swiss Criminal Code.

cases of domestic bribery, in relation to which acts done in performance of duty may give rise to criminal liability; such domestic cases do not raise any kind of issue under the Convention.

Other national legislation – that of Argentina and Japan, for example, or in Europe the laws of Belgium, Finland, Iceland, and the Netherlands – appears to offer no mercy at all: even payments or benefits foreseen by legislation can give rise, in principle, to criminal liability. This approach is, however, likely to be moderated in practice, as a result of interpretation, or given certain procedural conditions.

Argentina,[310] Norway (under legal principles)[311] and the Netherlands – Dutch law regulates the matter by use of prosecutorial discretion ('opportunity principle'),[312] – all moderate the situation expressly. Icelandic law leaves the question open. Finland intends to criminalise 'due advantages' where the payment is made with an intention to influence official behaviour.[313] Finnish law also imposes a form of aggravated criminal liability for 'considerable' bribe payments.

5. Actus reus: to offer, promise or give

5.1. The Phases of the bribery agreement

5.1.1. The aim

The Convention targets every act which is disposed to influence a foreign public official to take a corrupt decision (the quid pro quo).[314] The danger commences when the public official can reckon with or counts on an advantage and (still) exists when that advantage is indeed available. Whoever creates such a situation is subject to criminal sanction. The three methods of committing the offence – offer, promise, and giving of the advantage – therefore capture every kind of pressure or compulsion implied by the agreement, and also its fulfilment.

5.1.2. Negotiation stage: 'offering' and 'promising' an advantage

An offer is a declaration by the bribe-giver, on his own initiative, indicating his *readiness to pay* for the official act in question. By promising to do so, he makes a *definitive commitment.* The promise is given either of his own motion – then it is at the same time an offer – or he is prompted to make it by the public official. The offer and the promise can be made tacitly; they need not be explicit. In what circumstances such a tacit act can be said to

[310] AR-Ph1, 4. [311] NO-Ph1, 2. [312] NL-Ph1, 7. [313] FI-Ph1, 3. [314] Pieth 1999a, 348.

have occurred is not, however, susceptible to objective general criteria. It rather depends on the social customs or habits of the locality.

Neither offer nor promise requires an answer. The offence is complete as soon as it would be theoretically *possible* for the official *to perceive* that he or she is being offered or promised something in return for carrying out a specific official act, even if there were no such perception in fact.[315]

5.1.3. Completed offence: 'giving' an advantage

By 'giving' is meant transferring an advantage to the control of another person. How that process takes place depends on the nature of the advantage. A physical object will obviously require the handing over of possession; funds will be electronically transferred to a bank account; a place in University or College will be guaranteed by enabling registration to take place. The transfer will finally be effected when the object of the bribe is in a position in which it can be controlled, i.e. by taking up possession, drawing on the bank account, or taking up the place at University, etc. Whether the official ever actually takes control is not important: the act of giving does not depend on the act of receiving.

To limit the offence to the act of transfer of the bribe itself would not, however, be sufficient to meet the terms of the Convention. Prior agreements and other acts preparatory to the transfer must also be included by national legislation as criminal conduct.[316] Conversely, an act of bribery committed on the spur of the moment, without prior agreement, must also be regarded as an offence; otherwise spontaneous gifts etc. such as cash pushed under the table, which are also obviously bribes, would escape punishment.

Giving is an independent manifestation of the bribery act. The offence must therefore also be capable of being committed by the carrying out of a bribery agreement entered into by someone other than the donor of the bribe. Bribe donors are as guilty as those who may have concluded the previous (illegal) agreement, or made the (illegal) promise to the foreign public official. They are not excused from criminal liability, simply because the bribe agreement was entered into by somebody else. It could be that an agent or subsidiary undertaking made the first 'contract to bribe' or it may be that the bribe donor himself took that step. In either case, the preliminary acts can be distinguished from the quite independent offence of transferring the bribe.

[315] See II.5.3. below.

[316] Bulgaria was therefore criticised in the Phase 1 report for limitation to the act of transfer: cf. BG-Ph1, 18. It has since extended its legislation as required: cf. BG-Ph2, 28.

Looking then at the 'chain of offences' involved in the bribery of a foreign public official, the end of the chain is reached only when the transfer of the bribe is effected. This is important from the point of view of the application of state Parties' implementing legislation. Acts of bribery of a foreign public official are punishable under such legislation in so far as they were committed after its entry into force; this would cover bribes which had already been agreed before then, but which were completed only thereafter. Two or more different periods of prescription will apply, based on the preliminary acts or on the completion of the bribe by giving; the prescription of the former must not prevent prosecution of the latter separate offence.

5.1.4. Late rewards

What about the case of a foreign public official accepting a later payment for a favourable decision, the payment being one not previously announced? In such a case, it is not possible to say with any certainty that the official acted under the influence of the payment or other benefit. The Convention therefore leaves it open to the state Parties whether to criminalise the payment of late (ex post facto) rewards for acts of foreign public officials.

We should, however, signal our doubts about such rewards. The possibility that the official acted out of expectation of a later reward cannot be ruled out. Such suspicions can easily be hardened, if there is evidence that a practice of these rewards has become established within a business relationship. If late payments, presents, or other benefits to reward favourable decisions are *de rigueur* in the business relations between the foreign public official and his 'clients', then we have a situation of bribery. In so far as any advantage is conferred in anticipation of favourable action *in the future* – even if it is disguised as a late benefit or reward – the conditions of the offence will be fulfilled. A person who accustoms 'his' public sector official partners to expect rewards for their favourable decisions may therefore be deemed to make an implicit promise or offer. The size of the amount involved is decisive. A large amount will hardly be capable of being classified as a minor present or reward which is not linked to prior favourable performance of the official act.

5.2. The limits of criminal defences

The Convention and its Official Commentaries foresee no circumstances under which an act of bribery may be committed with impunity. Correct implementation therefore means that there should be no *special grounds of defence or excuse* for the bribery of a foreign public official.[317]

It should therefore make no difference from whom the *initiative* to commit the bribe originated. It is not a defence to bribery, if the proposal to bribe came from the public official himself, even if the latter demanded a bribe and made this demand from a position of considerable power or authority that does not offer a justification for the briber. The exercise of other forms of pressure, including provocation and even compulsion, by the public official or anyone else, should likewise not constitute an obstacle to prosecution of the briber. Nor, finally, is there a defence that one was merely following orders of one's boss, who gave the instruction to bribe.

There are countries in which *corruption is a tradition.* In others, success in business cannot be ensured without use of bribery and in others still, bribery is simply tolerated and no action is taken by prosecutors.[318] None of these approaches should, however, be tolerated by a country applying the Convention. Otherwise, the whole goal of the Convention would be undermined. Official Commentary 7 therefore states: 'It is also an offence irrespective of, inter alia,. . .the alleged necessity of the payment in order to obtain or retain business or other improper advantage.'

On the other hand, every criminal justice system applies certain *general defences and excuses* for criminal behaviour. In particular, criminal behaviour induced by emergency situations, such as cases of self-defence, is usually regarded as justified. The offender may also benefit from certain excuses, if he makes amends for his behaviour (effective repentance) or fails to follow through his criminal attempt. The Convention respects the choices of national systems of criminal justice in such matters; it certainly does not seek to overturn them. The Convention standard requires only that the briber receive no better treatment than other offenders who might seek to invoke these defences or excuses. All usual defences and excuses should pertain to the bribery offence, as they would to others. It is, however, rather doubtful that these would find much practical application in bribery cases. To give an example: using bribery to win a contract, in order to stave off insolvency, is unlikely to be justifiable, as most legal systems will not treat economic duress in the same way as physical duress.

[317] Apart from the issue of 'facilitation payments' discussed in II.7.2.2. below.

[318] The French courts do not accept any of these factors as justification for bribery. Cf., for example, the judgments issued in connection with the *ELF* scandal (Cass. Crim, 3 February 1992; Cass. Crim. 30 May 2001): these and other decisions of the French courts are cited in FR-Ph2, 40. Pressure from abroad can be a ground for reduction of sentence only (NO-Ph2, 25).

An instruction to bribe, issued by a superior of the briber, will itself be an offence. Errors as to the law or as to facts will not justify or excuse criminal behaviour unless they cannot be attributed to the offender. Usually, the latter will be responsible, if he has not informed himself of the legal situation, despite being engaged in business relations which would make such enquiries routine. Equally, a person should pay attention to 'red flags'[319] of a factual nature. The offender in a leading position in a company, who has failed to provide transparent systems which would reveal illegal payments, cannot complain of lack of knowledge or error.

5.3. Point of completion

Bribery is completed as soon as the object of the bribe, i.e. the public official, has perceived the existence of an offer or promise to bribe or as soon as it is *possible* for him *to obtain access* to the bribe. It is not important what he actually notices or does; the official does not have to perceive the advantage or obtain the benefit.

It can, of course, happen that blockages in transmission or receipt may occur. For example, an employee may forget to send the letter that contains the offer of a bribe; a bank may decide not to make a transfer in the absence of funds in the account, or because it suspects something is awry; or the email expressing the promise will not be sent to the correct address or might be deleted as spam. In such cases, notification to the would-be addressee of the letter, e-mail, or bank transfer is blocked: there is *no possibility* of his obtaining knowledge of it, or of receiving the advantage. One cannot, in these circumstances, speak of a completed promise or offer; there is no offering, promising, or giving, what we have is merely an attempt to bribe the public official.

We must again distinguish these cases of *frustrated bribe offers*, etc. from what we might call 'frustrated success', meaning where the public official does have potential access to communication of the bribe, or to the bribe itself, but access is in fact blocked at the receiving end. This may occur for a number of reasons: failure to pass on mail within the public official's office, failure to withdraw money from a bank account, failure to open an e-mail, etc. Here, offer or promise or transfer of the bribe has occurred, but these actions have not achieved the intended result: the public official has failed to receive anything and his decision is therefore not subject to influence by the bribe. But success is not necessary for commission of the offence. The act of bribery has already occurred.

[319] See detailed discussion in II.6.2. below.

Where the attempt to bribe is subject to the same penalty as the completed act of bribery, this differentiation will make no difference. Where a reduced penalty is foreseen for the former, or where it is not punishable, then, of course, the distinction is important. The Convention leaves it to the state Parties to apply their own general rules relating to criminal attempts.

5.4. Horizontal comparison

5.4.1. Explicit reference to all phases of the crime

A large number of state Parties follows the Convention more or less to the word.

> Austria, Bulgaria, Denmark, Finland, Germany, Greece, Iceland, Italy, Japan, Korea, Mexico, Slovakia, Switzerland and Sweden all refer to *offering, promising* and *giving.*

State Parties may also, however, legitimately choose to employ their own wording.

> One can cite the following examples of acceptable compliance with the Convention standard, by use of independent wording: Argentina ('offers or gives...any object...or other benefits...as promises'[320]); Hungary ('gives or promises'[321]), Luxembourg ('proposing or giving...offers, promises, gifts or advantages'[322]); Netherlands ('makes a gift or promise...or renders or offers...a service'[323]); Norway ('gives or offers'[324]); Poland ('provides...or promises to provide'[325]); and Spain ('through presents, gifts, offers or promises'[326]). The Dutch wording was regarded as somewhat ambiguous owing to the use of the word 'service' in conjunction with 'renders or offers' but not with 'make a gift or promise'. Case law has, however, clearly dispelled any doubts about the law being too limited in its application.[327]
>
> Canada and New Zealand also use wording which is sufficiently broad, in its own way, to meet the Convention standard: the Canadian legislation reads as 'gives, offers, or agrees to give or offer'[328] and New Zealand legislation is almost identical.[329] In the United Kingdom, the statutory wording 'gives or agrees to give or offers'[330] sits alongside the Common Law wording 'offering'[331]. Finally, the Australian legislator, besides using the words 'providing, promising and offering' also cleverly included the indirect offence of causing to do any of these acts.[332]

US legislation adopts a distinctive structure: central to the definition of the offence is the phrase 'in furtherance of an offer, payment, promise...or

[320] Art. 258bis Argentine Criminal Code. [321] Art. 258/B Hungarian Criminal Code.
[322] Arts. 247, 249, 250 Luxembourg Criminal Code.
[323] Arts. 177(1) and 177a(1) Dutch Criminal Code.
[324] S. 276a Norwegian Criminal Code. [325] Art. 229(1) Polish Criminal Code.
[326] Art. 445bis Spain Criminal Code. [327] NL-Ph1, 6.
[328] Art. 3(1) Canadian Corruption of Foreign Public Officials Act.
[329] S. 105C(2) New Zealand Criminal Code.
[330] S. 1(1) Prevention of Corruption Act 1906. [331] UK-Ph1, 5.
[332] Ss. 70.2.(1)(a)(ii) and 70.2.(1)(a)(iv) Australian Criminal Code.

authorisation of the payment [etc.]'.[333] In deciding what conduct falls under this definition, one must ask whether the act took place inside or outside the United States and who was the offender – 'US companies and nationals' or 'foreign companies and nationals'. In our context, what is important is that there are no limitations of the kind applicable to 'US interstate' business where transnational transactions are concerned. 'Transnational' in the latter sense refers both to cases where foreign business people commit bribes within the United States and where US business people commit bribery abroad.[334]

5.4.2. Broadening of the offence

In practice, it may sometimes be difficult to prove that the offer, etc. to bribe was related to a specific act of the public official. In some countries, these evidential problems are resolved by decoupling these elements: it does not require to be proved that the bribery was committed in anticipation or expectation of a concretely pending official decision.

Germany – but only in relation to public officials of other EU states and to Community officials[335] – Bulgaria,[336] Greece,[337] Luxembourg,[338] Poland,[339] and Switzerland[340] all extend their criminal law provisions beyond the scope strictly required by the Convention to include 'bribery ex post', i.e. they extend it to the payment of rewards for official acts which have already been taken. Behind this approach is the assumption that there will have been a prior (ex ante) bribery agreement: indeed in these countries there is an irrefutable legal presumption that this is the case.

In Poland, there is a rule that the giving of presents also falls under the definition of bribery where they are given not in order to exact a concrete official act but in order to engender a positive atmosphere: 'where a person bribes a public official for the purpose of obtaining a 'general positive attitude of the official'.[341] In such cases, the offender is seeking political support or privileges of some kind which are not manifested in a particular decision. This solution avoids the difficult task of distinguishing between coaxing of public officials and actual corruption.

[333] 15 U.S.C. §§ 78dd-1(a), 78dd-1(a), 78dd-2(a) and 78dd-3(a) FCPA 1977.
[334] US-Ph1, 3.
[335] S. 334 German Criminal Code when read with s. 1 Act on Combating Bribery of Member States of the European Union and of Community Officials.
[336] Art. 304(1) Bulgarian Criminal Code: cf. Ph2, 28. [337] Art. 2 Greek Act 2656/1998.
[338] Art. 249 Luxembourg Criminal Code. [339] Art. 229(3) Polish Criminal Code.
[340] Art. $322^{septies}$ Swiss Criminal Code: cf. CH-Ph2, 32.
[341] Cf. PL-Ph1, 7, which discusses Art. 229 Polish Criminal Code.

5.4.3. Danger of limiting scope of offence

The offence of bribery of foreign public officials must not be limited either to criminalising only the last parts of the chain of offences or only the prior agreement. Bulgarian law, which penalised initially only the *transfer* of the bribe but not any preparatory acts, required to be extended.[342]

It would also, however, contravene Article 1 of the Convention were commission of the offence of bribery in its later stages to depend on the existence of a bribery *agreement.* The legal situation in France and Belgium, where it is not very clear from the legislative provisions that the mere transfer of the payment or benefit is punishable, is therefore problematic. In interpreting the words 'the act of proposing,...offers, promises, gifts, presents or advantages',[343] the French courts have so far required the existence of at least some form of understanding between the bribe donor and the recipient of the bribe; it must at least be clear to the official that he is being rewarded for a particular official decision.[344] This approach would appear to be too limited, in particular where indirect bribery is concerned: it is not clear that, where a bribe agreement with an agent fails, the person pulling the strings could also be found guilty.[345]

The wording of Belgian law – 'proposing...an offer, promise or advantage' would also seem to be unacceptably ambiguous or limited.[346] It is true that it is no longer required that an agreement between the active and passive state Parties should succeed. But is it clear that Belgian anti-bribery law would extend to the actions of person A, who merely passes on to the public official the bribe which has been promised to him by person B? In principle, the answer is 'yes': A would be regarded as an accessory to B's act of bribery. But it is possible that, for A to be convicted, Belgian law would require full proof of B's act. It is therefore not at all clear that the law in either France or Belgium is in conformity with the Convention in this respect.

The position in Luxembourg is that the offence of bribery is characterised by the existence of a form of 'corruption pact'.[347] There should, in other words, be an underlying bribery agreement between the active and passive sides of the bargain. Luxembourg law nevertheless regards the offence as

[342] Now, Art. 304 Bulgarian Criminal Code correctly refers to 'offering, promising, and giving'.
[343] Arts. 435-2, 435-3, 435-4 French Criminal Code.
[344] FR-Ph1, 5.
[345] As revealed by the following decision: Cass. Crim., 30 June 1999 (cited in FR-Ph2, 41).
[346] Art. 246(2) Belgian Criminal Code: cf. BE-Ph2, 34 et seq.
[347] LU-Ph1, 4; LU-Ph2, 32.

completed where a proposal of the kind suggested is rejected by the public official or is not in fact perceived by him.[348] But practitioners still see a problem with the need to prove corruption pacts: this is indeed 'the most serious problem in establishing the offence of corruption' and a relaxation of the law has been recommended.[349]

The underlying concept of Italian anti-corruption law is similar to that of the other legal systems just referred to: the offence of bribery can be committed only when the offender has entered into an agreement with the public official.[350] There is, however, a special offence of '*istigatione*' for situations in which the foreign public official received the offer, but subsequently ignored or rejected it.[351] Where the official did not even perceive the bribe, the crime is one of attempted bribery. Italian law thus seems to cover all eventualities foreseen by the Convention. There is nevertheless one problem with Italian law as it stands, relating to the need to show that the offer or promise was of a suitable or appropriate character. According to the Italian courts, this appropriateness is proved in particular by reference to the financial means of the recipient of the bribe and in the light of the sum proposed as bribe. This means that Italian law links the commission of the offence to the 'value of the advantage', an approach which is inconsistent with Official Commentary 7.[352]

The Mexican legal definition of the act of bribery is clear and is not interpreted restrictively. Nonetheless there is a certain risk of a wrong approach being taken in practice. It seems that the time of commission of the act is identified with the first act in the chain of bribery offences. This approach is derived from the practice employed with regard to passive bribery. It means that the offence of bribery would already be committed by virtue of the giving of an offer or promise to the foreign public official: this is consistent with the Convention. The later fulfilment of the offer or promise would not, however, be punished, given that it does not constitute a further attempt to influence the official. Such an approach would raise difficult questions. First, if the preliminary agreement to bribe had been concluded before the entry into force of the 1999 Mexican implementing legislation, would the carrying out of this agreement in 2000 be punishable? Second, if the offer of the bribe had been made by a non-Mexican national in a foreign state, could the Mexican authorities prosecute in respect of the later transfer of the bribe

[348] Arts. 247, 249, 250 Luxembourg Criminal Code (version of 15 January 2001).
[349] LU-Ph2, 33.
[350] Cf. s. on corruption of foreign public officials contained in Art. 322bis Italian Criminal Code.
[351] Art. 322 Italian Criminal Code.
[352] IT-Ph2, 31 et seq. (with references to case law), 52.

money, etc. in Mexico? Third, if the offer was so far back in time as to have already prescribed, could the authorities nevertheless take action in respect of the later transfer?[353]

The French insistence on the existence of a prior bribery agreement raises similar questions concerning the time of commission of bribery in the context of a multiple-stage bribery process. The law's reference to the 'act of proposing'[354] suggests that this is the defining action in that process. If the offer was made before the implementing legislation took effect, it could then be argued that any transfer of the bribe money, etc. based on that previous decision would have to be tolerated. In the view of France, the latter approach could be justified by reference to the principle of non-retroactivity of criminal penalties.[355]

5.4.4. Defences or excuses not foreseen by the Convention

Some countries foresee special defences or excuses for the offence of bribery. This means that they have not implemented the Convention properly. The Convention only permits defences or excuses to apply in cases where the public official has performed an act strictly in fulfilment of his duties, as previously pointed out.[356] In addition, the Convention accepts without question the general approach of national criminal law to minor offences or hardship cases; these cases may well not be subject to the full rigour of criminal law or to any penalty. What is not, however, permitted is to give the briber *greater* scope to escape criminal liability than other offenders. The WGB's reaction was always consistent: never to permit special grounds of defence or excuse. All special exceptions are to be disallowed.

This approach applies particularly to concepts which would allow the offender to provide a justification on the basis of the behaviour of the public official. Italian criminal law, for example, enables the briber to escape criminal liability by referring to '*concussione*' of the public official.[357] By this is meant situations in which the public official abuses his position: he blackmails the offender, who can only avoid damage to himself by agreeing to the illegal arrangement.[358] In Bulgaria, if blackmail by the public official is proved, this can lead to the acquittal of the briber but only where he (the official) has

[353] MX-Ph2, 14. [354] Arts. 435-2, 435-3, 435-4 French Criminal Code.

[355] The WGB has criticised this approach: cf. FR-Ph1, 5, 30. The subject was not taken up again in the Phase 2 evaluation.

[356] See II.5.2. above. [357] Art. 317 Italian Criminal Code.

[358] Cf. the somewhat intricate debate regarding concussion as a defence to bribery in the Phase 2 report for Italy: IT-Ph2, 33 et seq., 52. The WGB recommends that Italian law does not follow this approach.

expressed 'effective repentance' by voluntarily informing the public authority of his act, without delay.[359] The defence of *provocation* by the public official, which went further, was removed from the legislation, following the criticism levelled at Bulgaria in the Phase 1 report.[360]

The notion of *duress* is used by Hungarian legislation to describe the defence or excuse based on compulsion. The duress ground may be invoked generally in all cases, not only in corruption cases, and is therefore less objectionable than the Italian or Bulgarian solutions. Hungarian law was, however, amended in 2001 to remove the defence based on the initiative of the public official – this was a particularly objectionable clause, seen from the viewpoint of the Convention.[361]

The Czech Republic and Slovakia have introduced a defence of *effective repentance* for the crime of bribery.[362] According to these systems, the offender must be acting further to a demand of the public official and he must voluntarily inform the public authority concerned as soon as possible after his act. Under Greek law, a reduction in sentence or even full acquittal may be granted to persons who report their offence to the authorities before they can begin an investigation.[363]

Legal systems which allow effective repentance to be used as a defence or excuse do so for criminal policy reasons which are basically sound: it is just one possible way of dealing with types of offending. It is not for the Convention to challenge such policy choices. In so far as the defence is employed exclusively in bribery cases, however, it favours the briber over other offenders and is therefore questionable.

6. Indirect bribery

6.1. The basis of criminal responsibility for the acts of others

6.1.1. The practical need to extend responsibility

Undertakings operating on a transnational basis clearly not only do business through company staff travelling from headquarters. For their

[359] Art. 306 Bulgarian Criminal Code, which was criticised in the Phase 2 report: cf. BG-Ph2, 30.

[360] BG-Ph1, 19.

[361] Cf. Act CXXI 2001 (the amending legislation) and on this point HU-Ph1^{bis}, 4.

[362] S. 163 Czech Criminal Code: for a critical view of this provision, cf. CZ-Ph1, 21. And cf. s. 163 Slovak Criminal Code: note adverse comments in SK-Ph1, 22. The WGB seems increasingly critical in SK-Ph2, 33 et. seq.

[363] Art. 236 Greek Criminal Code refers to the bribery of Greek public officials but applies by analogy to transnational cases: cf. the criticism contained in GR-Ph2, 29.

transactions upstream and downstream they also make use of their – sometimes extensive – network of branches; they also employ agents or consultancy firms for particular projects; and they use distributors. Contact with foreign public officials is thus usually handled by external intermediaries acting exclusively in the interests and under the direction of the company headquarters. If the latter are the beneficiaries of the contracts concluded overseas, or if they are in fact controlling the deals, then they must also take responsibility for their conclusion in accordance with the law. If we apply this thinking to the anti-bribery law envisaged by the Convention, it means that indirect as well as direct bribery of foreign public officials should be covered, and indeed Article 1(1) says as much: the offence may also be committed 'through intermediaries'. Where agents, consulting firms, distributors, or foreign-based branches use bribes to achieve contracts, the company employing the agents or the parent company risks criminal action on the ground of indirect bribery. The same applies to their senior management. Neither legal nor natural persons can evade liability by 'delegating' bribery to others.

Moreover, we should add that the agent, consultant, distributor, and subsidiary will themselves be committing an offence. For the purposes of Article 1, it does not matter whether the bribery is committed in one's own name or if the briber himself enjoys the fruits of the bribe (i.e. the favourable act or advantage conferred in exchange for it). Official Commentary 6 therefore also refers to the responsibility of the intermediary: 'The conduct described in paragraph 1 is an offence whether the offer or promise is made or the pecuniary advantage is given on that person's own behalf or on behalf of any other natural person or legal entity.' The criminal prosecution of intermediaries pursuant to the Convention standard will, however, often falter owing to lack of jurisdiction of the courts in the OECD countries. The intermediary will usually have acted in the foreign public official's own country and will frequently himself be a citizen of this state. Article 4 of the Convention does not, however, foresee an extension of jurisdiction beyond the principles of 'territoriality' and 'active personality' to capture the conduct of agents and subsidiaries in general.[364]

Indirect bribery overlaps substantially with *complicity* in the act of bribing a foreign public official, which is referred to in paragraph 2 of Article 1: both categories infer responsibility for payments or negotiation of deals made indirectly by another. The Convention made special provision for indirect bribery *through intermediaries* as part of the offence in order not to

[364] See ch. on Article 4 below.

be dependent on the widely varying definitions of complicity contained in national law. Anyone entering a foreign market by means of intermediaries should be made (jointly) responsible for their actions in accordance with criteria which are autonomous in the sense of not being linked to national definitions. The reference in Article 1 is also important, because it places indirect bribery on the same level as the direct form: it makes clear both are equally reprehensible. Complicity à la Article 1(2) is meant to provide the added guarantee that lower level categories of aiding commission of the main offence are criminalised.

It is of no further importance that the line between complicity and indirect bribery is a fuzzy one. The drawing of this line is left to the state Parties. Insofar as a state opts for a very broad definition of complicity, it may not be necessary for its criminal law to provide expressly for commission of bribery through intermediaries.

6.1.2. Liability for third party action: legal conditions

Criminal liability of the undertaking itself or its senior executives may not be founded solely on the basis that the company profited from the act of bribery of its go-betweens or its subsidiaries. Criminal law theory contains the fundamental principle that a person can be liable for the acts of another, *objectively* speaking, only if he is *able to control* these acts and is also *legally obliged to control* them. The concrete nature of the control possibilities and obligations depends on the relationship to the intermediary. The position will vary according to whether independent intermediaries[365] are appointed to act in the name of the company or whether the situation is that of contracts concluded by a subsidiary,[366] for which the parent concern is formally responsible.

With regard to *subjective responsibility*, this always requires the existence of a certain level of awareness of the commission of the offence, i.e. a certain *intention* or *mens rea.* Article 1 of the Convention requires a certain intention, whether the bribery is of a direct or indirect character. Notwithstanding the individual differences between national concepts, there is a certain amount of common ground between them: intention will be inferred wherever someone knows or has serious grounds to believe that his agent is committing bribery but does nothing to prevent it. The FCPA, for example, sets out the requirement for indirect bribery of *knowledge:* 'knowing'[367] of the illegal act is

[365] See II.6.2. below. [366] See II.6.3. below.
[367] 15 U.S.C. §§ 78dd-1(a)(3), 78dd-2(a)(3), 78dd-3(a)(3) FCPA 1977.

required, which is defined as a 'state of mind' in which 'such person is aware...or...has the firm belief'.[368]

This is, however, not all that is to be said about intention. It is not possible for management to escape responsibility by deliberately closing their eyes to the facts of bribery by their agents or subsidiaries that are before them. The FCPA deals with cases of *wilful ignorance* of this kind by elaborating on its concept of 'knowing' as follows: 'knowledge of the existence of a particular circumstance...is established if a person is aware of a high probability of the existence of such circumstance'.[369] This passage has been interpreted to mean that no manager may be excused the tactics of 'wilful blindness', 'conscious disregard', 'deliberate avoidance of knowledge', or other 'head in the sand' techniques.[370]

> The original version of the FCPA of 1977 described the subjective element of the offence of indirect bribery as 'knowing' or having 'reason to know'. The latter variant was, however, repeatedly criticised for its vagueness: it seemed to stretch too far. The law was amended in 1988 in order to remove the possibility that liability could be established on the basis of 'simple negligence' or 'mere foolishness'.[371] Nevertheless, the dividing line between negligence and wilful blindness is not altogether clear.

Deliberate aversion of one's gaze from certain business deals may certainly be regarded as indicating awareness of the high probability that bribery is taking place. This line has been followed by the SEC in its action against the US oil firm *Baker Hughes Incorporated (BH)*, which it accused of making payments to agents in India and Brazil, without bothering to verify that the payments were legitimate.

> The facts of these cases were as follows:
>
> In 1998, acquired Western Atlas Corporation and as a result of this also an Indian subsidiary, *Western Geophysical.* This Indian subsidiary recruited an agent, in order to obtain certain shipping permits. Having been successful in one case, the agent put in a bill of $15 000 for his services. When the subsidiary asked *BH* management in the US for its permission to pay the agent, this was granted without further ado.
>
> In 1995, BH wanted to restructure its network of Brazilian subsidiaries. Speed was of the essence, in order to profit from certain tax breaks. A Brazilian agent of the subsidiary saw his chance to approach the local tax authorities and demanded a fee of $10 000 in order to achieve the

[368] 15 U.S.C. §§ 78dd-1(f)(2)(A), 78dd-2(h)(4)(A), 78dd-3(h)(4)(A) FCPA 1977, in the version of the 1988 amendments.

[369] 15 U.S.C. §§ 78dd-1(f)(2)(B), 78dd-2(h)(4)(B), 78dd-3(h)(4)(B) FCPA 1977, in the version of the 1988 amendments.

[370] These quotes are taken from the House Conference Report 100-560 on The Omnibus Trade and Competitiveness Act 1988, 920 et seq.; cf. also Brown 1999, F-7, F-8.

[371] Brown 1999, F-8.

restructuring within just one week. BH again authorised payment of the desired amount to its subsidiary with no questions asked.

In both cases, the SEC's position on liability was that *Baker Hughes* had made payments to an agent 'without making an adequate enquiry to ensure that the amount would not be paid to a foreign government official in violation of the FCPA.'[372] It was not, however, proved that bribe money had in fact passed, but the concern should have ruled out this possibility, as made clear under the FCPA Accounting Provisions.

Another set of facts was revealed by the case against *Baker Hughes.*[373] This concerned a tax statement of the Indonesian Finance Ministry, which indicated that the tax due by an Indonesian subsidiary controlled by *Baker Hughes* amounted to over $3.2 million. According to the SEC's administrative release, the Chief Financial Officer (CFO) and the Financial Controller of *BH* authorised the subsidiary to make a payment of $143 000 to their tax consultants *KPMG.* On this occasion, research by the SEC left no doubt of the illegal intentions behind this payment. The agency also alleged that Baker Hughes' CFO and Controller knew or were aware of a high probability that *KPMG* intended to use $75 000 of the $143 000 to pay an Indonesian government tax official, who in return would reduce the tax payable by the Indonesian subsidiary to only $270 000. The SEC did not, however, impose a fine; it issued a declaration that *BH* was in breach of the FCPA and made an order to desist from further infringements.[374]

Another clear finding of intention in a case of indirect bribery was made in *InVision.* The company *InVision Technologies* produced detection devices for finding explosives, designed for airports. It was accused by the SEC of paying a total of $792 000 to agents or distributors to enable them to bribe public officials in China, the Philippines, and Thailand. The bribery had a similar structure in all three countries. It consisted of the agent in each region informing first the regional sales manager of *InVision* and then also the company's senior executive of his intention to bribe the public official of the state-run airport authority in question. These approaches were not, however, rebuffed. Rather, the management either made the payment requested directly or authorised the transaction to continue. The SEC

[372] SEC Securities Exchange Act of 1934 Release No. 44784, Accounting and Auditing Enforcement Release No. 1444, Findings and Order in the matter of *Baker Hughes Incorporated*, September 12, 2001: Facts C and D.

[373] SEC Securities Exchange Act of 1934 Release No. 44784, Accounting and Auditing Enforcement Release No. 1444, Findings and Order in the matter of *Baker Hughes Incorporated*, September 12, 2001: Facts B.

[374] The civil proceedings brought by the SEC against the directors were terminated at second instance on July 14, 2004 (5th Circuit Court of Appeals). Cf. SEC Litigation Release No. 18863, Accounting and Auditing Enforcement Release No. 2092, September 1, 2004.

therefore concluded: *InVision* was aware of a high probability that its foreign sales agents or distributors paid or offered to pay something of value to government officials in order to obtain or retain business for *InVision*; despite this, *InVision* authorised improper payments to the agents or distributors, or allowed them to proceed with transactions on *InVision's* behalf, in violation of the FCPA.[375]

> The civil claim of the SEC resulted in a settlement. *InVision* had been fully taken over by *General Electrics (GE)* before the SEC decision and there had been an agreement between *GE* and the US Department of Justice that the former would not inherit any of the outstanding liabilities of of *InVision* in respect of its illegal transactions. The SEC nevertheless fined *GE* to the tune of $1 million, precisely on the basis of legal succession.[376]

6.2. Responsibility for bribery by independent agents

Negotiations in international business transactions are frequently conducted by agents, consultancies, or distributors. The function of these intermediaries is to represent the interests of the foreign undertaking in countries in which they themselves are not present, and to act on their behalf. Such action may take the form of market analysis, winning of customers and contracts, looking after existing customers, and the negotiation and conclusion of contracts. The advantage of the agent lies first and foremost in his or her personal connection to the territory concerned and in his ability to win business for their principal in that region. The agent will speak the local language, know the customs, and should also have knowledge of the local legal system. Given the key role they can play in international business, the recruitment of agents or advisors, consultants, etc. has become at the same time unavoidable and not without risk.[377] This risk arises from the fact that agents become involved precisely in the crucial phase of business: in the winning or conclusion of contracts, in business start-up procedures, in organisation of production, etc. These are precisely the moments when decisions by the foreign public official are called for.

The risk element to which we refer arises in the first instance from the fact that the intermediaries are not a part of the undertaking, and are therefore *not bound* by internal guidelines or procedures. In many cases, indeed, they are completely ignorant of company rules. A second risk aspect would be the insistence on *high commissions* for provision of their

[375] SEC Securities Exchange Act of 1934 Release No. 51199, Accounting and Auditing Enforcement Release No. 2186, *In Vision* Settlement, February 14, 2005.
[376] SEC Litigation Release No. 19078, Accounting and Auditing Enforcement Release No. 2187, *In Vision* Settlement, February 14, 2005.
[377] Heimann and Mohn 1999, 541.

service: these high commissions would comprise a bribe factor, i.e. part of the commission would be destined for the pockets of the foreign public official or his associates, in order to induce a favourable decision.[378]

Intermediaries work *independently*; they are self-employed and therefore not bound by the guidance or instructions issued by the company to its employees. Can or must the principal company or person control its or his agent in these circumstances? The answer has to be 'yes'. The duty which arises from the Convention is derived from the principle that anyone who creates a *situation of risk* or danger is obliged to take the appropriate precautionary measures, to *protect* against the occurrence of harm. This clearly applies in our scenario, where the risk is present as a consequence of the use of independent agents to do business in a foreign country.

> The harm in question arises already from the agent's offer of a bribe. The harmful effects of corruption do not depend on damage caused to a particular person or to specific legal interests.

There clearly are genuine *control opportunities*. The methods used to exercise such control can and do vary from one branch to another. We can offer this concise summary:

- the agency contract may contain specific *rules of conduct*, which the agent is obliged to respect, if he wishes to be recruited;
- there can be provision *to dismiss* the agent on suspicion of corruption (the possible grounds for suspicion will be mentioned below);
- one can introduce *transparent accounting rules* and insist, in particular, on reasonable billing for services, to exclude the possibility of expense claims being used for bribe money.

The undertaking can escape liability for bribery of a foreign public official committed by its agent only in circumstances where all possible precautionary measures have been used in order to avoid damage occurring. How is it possible for the company using the agent to find out that he has been involved in corrupt deals, so that it may take counter-measures? The answer to this question has been worked out on the basis of the experience of multinational enterprises: criteria have been developed so that one can speak of the existence of certain 'red flags' which should alert the company to the likelihood of misdeeds.[379] These include the following:

- the company acting as agent has neither its seat in the country in which it provides its service, nor does it carry out any other business in this country;

[378] Davies 2003, 59. [379] Davies 2003, 65 et seq.

- the agent company demands payment of its commission before it has concluded the contract in question;
- the accounts or bills for services rendered fail to specify in any detail either the content of the negotiations done or when they were carried out. Instead they refer only in a general way to 'services' and 'expenses';
- the key factor[380] is whether the commission fee which is demanded is a reasonable one, i.e. one which is proportionate to the job in question. The expenses claim should also be related to actual expenses incurred. An exorbitant commission or expenses claim will be a clear indicator of corrupt practices;
- the agent company demands payment via a third party or in a different country than the one in which it is situated;
- the agent company offers its services without being approached by the principal and does so shortly before conclusion of a contract or after unsuccessful negotiations by the principal;
- the agent company emphasises that it alone can secure the conclusion of the contract, because only it knows the right people;
- the company structure and financial organisation of the agent company is lacking in transparency; it appears to have hardly any staff;
- the agents are not bound to any particular codes of conduct;
- the competence of the agents working in the field is suspect;
- there are personal connections between the agents and the decision-makers of the foreign state.

That these red flags may be indicators of corruption – while not, of course, proving its existence – is common knowledge among undertakings. A businessman who allows an agent to work for him or his company notwithstanding such indicators, cannot then plead ignorance when corruption occurs. On the basis of the presence of these red flags in the context of an agent – principal relationship, it is possible to presume the intention of the principal to commit bribery through his agent. It will not assist a manager to avoid looking into the business records, as we have seen that *wilful blindness* also amounts to a case of 'knowing'.

This thinking was the basis underlying the decision of the French courts in the case concerning the development of the harbour of Bonifacio: the assertion of lack of knowledge of a payment by its intermediaries of

[380] Heimann and Mohn 1999, 541.

€10 000 to members of the Corsican administration was deemed not to relieve the accused of liability.[381]

The *Statoil* case[382] also dealt with bribery by an agent company. The Norwegian firm *Statoil* recruited the British-based *Horton Investments* (Turks and Caicos Islands) as go-between for a big oil deal. Statoil used the company as a conduit for no less than 115 million Norwegian Kroner of bribes destined for the son of the then Iranian President Rafsanjani. These bribes were dressed up as payment for 'consultancy' by the latter. According to media reports,[383] *Statoil* was ordered to pay a fine equivalent to €24 million. Proceedings in relation to this case remain pending in the United States, before the SEC.

The *Acres-Lesotho* case provides a further example of a case in which the bribes were paid to a foreign public official via an agent. Over the period 1991 and 1999, the Canadian engineering company *Acres International Limited* paid a total of $500 000 into Swiss accounts held in the name of Mr and Mrs Bam, their agents in Lesotho. More than half of this amount was destined to land on another Swiss accounts, namely that of Mustapha E. Sole, the CEO of *Lesotho Highland Water Projects* (*LHWP*). The transfer was designed to secure the rights of *Acres* to carry out a project for which it had made an offer in the procurement procedure. The *LHWP* was financed to the tune of $110 million by the World Bank, for the purpose of dam construction. A number or dams were planned; water would thereafter be channelled from the Maluti hills into the centre of Lesotho to the benefit of South Africa.

> What is interesting about this case are not so much the facts of the criminal behaviour as what happened afterwards. This proved to be the first case in which a multinational enterprise situated in a developing country was prosecuted in criminal proceedings – and then fined $2 million.[384] The judgment had immediate and significant ramifications upon the World Bank, which resumed its suspended investigations and, following one of it most extensive debarment proceedings ever, decided to remove *Acres* from any financing for a period of three years.[385]

The most expensive case in FCPA history, from the point of view of the accused, concerned a producer of military equipment, namely *Titan Corporation*, from San Diego.[386] In order to assist its conduct of business in Benin, *Titan* decided to employ an agent who was close to the country's President, or at least close to his circle of power. In the course of only three

[381] Cass. Crim., January 8, 1998, cited in FR-Ph2, 39.
[382] Oekokrim, September 12, 2003 (press Release).
[383] BBC News, 29 June 2004 (http://www.news.bbc.co.uk).
[384] Lesotho High Court Appellate Decision, August 21, 2003 (http://www.odiousdebts.org).
[385] World Bank's News Release 2005/33/S, July 23, 2004. [386] Low 2005, 23.

years, more than $5 million flowed via this agent into the pockets of Benin's highest public officials. In particular, the agent also supported the President's election campaign. On pleading guilty, *Titan* was fined $28.5 million, pursuant to a plea agreement.[387] To add insult to injury, the planned takeover of the concern by *Lockheed Martin Corporation* foundered.

> The following facts were revealed by the case:
>
> According to the SEC, *Titan* began, in part by using its *Titan* Wireless subsidiary, to invest in a project for development of Benin's telecommunications network in 1999. On the same day as the main contract was concluded, *Titan* recruited an adviser of the President of Benin as its agent. This agent was paid in excess of $3.5 million between 1999 and 2001. The payments were arranged either on the direct say-so of *Titan's* senior management in San Diego or by *Titan* Africa, one of its wholly owned subsidiaries. Although *Titan* was aware of the proximity of their agent to the country's President, no proper enquiries were undertaken as to his suitability for the post: his background, qualifications and work experience were not examined, and his bills were paid without checking the work performed. And yet there were red flags galore which should have warned off *Titan*. For example, the bills for his services were extravagantly high, and the billing had taken place only a few days after the conclusion of the Consulting Agreement – what could the agent possibly have achieved, within a matter of only six days, to deserve payment of $400 000? Numerous sub-agents and further consultants were mentioned on the bills; there was even reference to payment into a relation's account. In the course of the period when the bills were being paid, *Titan* won all the important contracts relating to the telecommunications project.
>
> *Titan* used the same agent and friend of the Benin President in order to support the President's electoral campaign, to the tune of $2 million. In return it received an even greater stake in the projects in question. The *Titan* management not only organised the illegal payments; it also massaged the figures in the final accounting to make them appear as genuine fees for a consultancy.
>
> From 1999 to 2003, payments were also made to agents in various countries by Datron World Communication (DWN), which was acquired by Titan in 2001. These payments amounted to some 50% of annual profits, yet no meaningful due diligence was conducted prior to their authorisation.

It is also possible for *political parties and candidates* for political office to act as intermediaries. The parties or their candidates are not yet public officials themselves[388] but they may clearly be capable of exerting influence on public officials, as we have discussed, and can therefore lend

[387] Plea Agreement: *U.S.* v. *Titan Corporation*, S.D. Ca., Case No. 05CR0314-BEN, March 1, 2005; SEC, Litigation Release No. 19107, Accounting and Auditing Enforcement, Release No. 2204, *Titan* Settlement, March 1, 2005. A detailed discussion of the case is contained in the Complaint of the *SEC* v. *Titan Corporation*, D.D.C., Civil Action No. 05–0411 (JR), March 1, 2005. For an analysis of the case, cf. also Low 2005, 22 and Cadwalader, Wickersham & Taft, Newsletter on the FCPA 1977, March 2005 (http://www.cadwalader.com).

[388] See discussion of this in II.2.3.4. above.

themselves rather well as go-betweens. It is perhaps not surprising, then, that contributions to party funds may amount in reality to bribes aimed at public officials.

> According to media reports, donations to the German Christian Democrats (CDU) in the 1990s ended up being turned into bribes to high German public officials, uncovered as part of the *ELF* scandal.[389]

Party political donations are now regarded as a fundamentally dangerous way for an enterprise to establish a political foothold.[390]

The final point to make in this section is that the Convention makes no distinction between agents who are oblivious to the illicit nature of the deal that they are making on behalf of their principal, and those who are colluding with them. The liability of the facilitator will be the same; after all, someone who employs an innocent third party to do his dirty work for him is willing the whole transaction and is in control of it.

6.3. Liability in respect of bribery by subsidiaries

The Convention does not fully resolve the question of the liability of undertakings based in a Convention country for bribery carried out by a foreign subsidiary. Discussions are in progress at international level with the aim of establishing such liability: The role of subsidiaries in bribery transactions is one of the *five issues* on which the WGB has issued a negotiating mandate.

There is already a clear risk that enterprises active in international business will face such liability, though this currently depends on national legislation. Certain Convention countries do envisage the parent company being made responsible for the acts of bribery of its subsidiaries, even where no domestic court in the country where the bribery took place would enjoy jurisdiction. Most of the judgments on this question have been made by US courts, whereas the courts of the United Kingdom and Germany, for example, have been noticeably more reticent.[391] The national approaches to this question indeed show significant differences, but can nevertheless provide pointers to the possible interpretation of international law. Given the trend in national law toward liability for acts of bribery by subsidiaries, it would not seem unreasonable to interpret the Convention as inferring liability of the parent company. The condition for such liability is, however, that the subsidiary is so close to its parent that it really does act as its *intermediary.*

[389] Cf. among other references *Der Spiegel*: http://www.spiegel.de. There is also some discussion of this case in ch. on Article 5 below.

[390] Heimann and Mohn 1999, 540.

[391] Cf., for example, on this issue Miller's study of 1998.

The relationship fulfils this proximity criterion when the subsidiary operates without independence, as a mere *branch* of the parent headquarters. In such a scenario, the management function rests entirely with the parent, with all decisions being taken directly there. If, in such circumstances, bribery is committed by the staff of the subsidiary, the parent is equally responsible for their acts.[392]

We may contrast this scenario with the type of case where the subsidiary is *formally independent* of its parent, i.e. self-sufficient in terms of its day-to-day functioning. US sources refer to a 'general rule of corporate separateness', in the context of such a relationship.[393] If it has not given any explicit instruction to make an illegal payment, one cannot presume that the parent wished to use its subsidiary as its intermediary in a bribery case. For liability of the parent to be inferred, the *objective* requirement would be a hierarchical relationship between parent and subsidiary, the *subjective* one that the parent must have known, at least potentially, about the bribery.

On this view, the parent would be liable for acts of bribery committed by its subsidiary, if the following (cumulative) conditions are fulfilled:

- first, the parent controls the expenditure of the subsidiary or is at least under a legal obligation to do so;
- second, the exercise of such control reveals that this expenditure (or a portion of it) is indeed destined for the benefit of a foreign public official.

The conditions are fulfilled where the parent company so *dominates* the subsidiary, by whatever legal construction, as to make it almost its *alter ego.* The latter then enjoys no real independence: its formal status as an independent entity exists only on paper. In US parlance, one would say that in such cases, we have *piercing of the corporate veil*, to reveal the real power behind the subsidiary undertaking.

A foreign subsidiary may also act as intermediary of its parent undertaking in the capacity of *agent* or *distributor.* A so-called 'trading house' may often play this role: the trading house is formally independent but contractually embedded in the structure of its parent company. The same rules would apply to such intermediary companies as apply to the use of agents.[394] In other words, the parent company giving the instructions

[392] See ch. on Article 2 below for a discussion of the vicarious responsibility of the undertaking for acts of its employees.
[393] Brown 1999, F-4 refers to various US Common Law sources.
[394] See II.6.2. above.

would be liable for allowing false accounting to occur without carrying out proper checks.

In some states, the parent company is subject to certain *statutory duties* of supervision or due diligence which may offer an additional possibility to hold the parent company responsible for acts committed by its subsidiary. With regard to the accounts of its subsidiary, there may, for example, be a duty to check and approve the accounts 'in reasonable detail, accurately, and fairly'.[395] The subsidiary would be bound, in addition, to comply with internal accounting controls. In the United States, issuers whose shares are quoted on the Stock Exchange have to comply with FCPA accounting provisions. As soon as an issuer controls more than 50% of another undertaking's securities with voting rights, it assumes responsibility, at the level indicated in the FCPA, for the company books and for record-keeping, including the tracking of expenditure.[396]

In order to fulfil its duties of control, the parent company must give particularly close attention to the subsidiary company's books. If properly kept books are presented to the parent, they will reveal the occurrence of any illegal spending. It is from the moment of submission of these books that an intention to corrupt may manifest itself in the shape of knowing or presuming or wilfully ignoring the facts as presented. It is from this point onwards that the undertaking must take steps to halt further illegality. If it fails to do so, under some circumstances its inertia may be interpreted as an admission which can lead at least to civil liability for illegal payments made by its subsidiary.[397]

If, on the other hand, the books presented to the parent company are incomplete or if they are not well presented, they may be rejected. The parent company is obliged to seek further explanation for accounts which do not reveal, for example, why an immense commission or fee is being demanded, without clear justification. Failure by the parent to follow up such gaps in accounts will be attributed to wilful blindness on its part. If a bribe is actually paid by the subsidiary to the foreign public official in such a case, and received by him, the parent company will be regarded as liable for the bribery. If, however, the payments which were not correctly (truly)

[395] Cf. the formulation contained in 15 U.S.C. § 78m(b)(2)(A) FCPA 1977.

[396] This follows from the fact that, according to 15 U.S.C. § 78m(b)(6) FCPA 1977, issuers with minority status need only make an attempt 'in good faith' to maintain the internal accounting controls: cf. Low 2005, 11.

[397] Cf., for example, the SEC's position applying to the *ABB* case: SEC Litigation Release No. 18775, Accounting and Auditing Enforcement Release No. 2049, *ABB* Settlement, July 6, 2004.

or fully recorded are not in fact made, the parent will be liable only for failure to check the accounts.

In the *Baker Hughes* case, it could not be proved that bribes had actually been received by the public officials in India and Brazil. The SEC was therefore not able to maintain an allegation of bribery against the company, and had to be satisfied instead with the charge of failure to observe FCPA accounting provisions.[398]

A subsidiary may decide to falsify the accounts, disguising the illegal expenditure as something legitimate. In that case, the parent company cannot be held responsible for the bribery committed by its subsidiary. These were the facts in the *IBM* case. According to the settlement, bribery by *IBM*'s wholly owned subsidiary *IBM-Argentina* was uncovered.

> *IBM-Argentina* won a contract from the National Bank of Argentina (*Banca Nacion Argentina, BNA*) to set up a new computer system. It then entered into a sub-contract with an Argentinean firm to carry out this work, paying it some \$22 million to do so – \$4.5 million alone was finally paid to public officials employed by the BNA.

The senior management of *IBM-Argentina* deceived the parent undertaking about these arrangements. Not only did it conceal the illegal payments by means of a false entry in the accounts, it also falsified documents. *IBM* Headquarters knew nothing of the bribery by its subsidiary and had no access to facts that it might be said to have wilfully ignored; it therefore lacked intention. As soon as the parent company's management discovered the deception, it acted without delay. The persons responsible were sacked, control procedures stepped up, and all illegal payments to the sub-contractor stopped. Finally, the alleged failure to provide for effective book-keeping by *IBM-Argentina* led to a settlement.[399]

In a contrasting case, the Swiss concern *ABB* (a power and automation technology company), quoted on the US Stock Exchange, was accused of having offended against the books and records provisions and also of neglecting its duty to control the activities of its various foreign subsidiaries. In the absence of such controls, *ABB* settled upon the allegation of indirect bribery; a number of *ABB* subsidiaries were shown to have paid bribes amounting to \$1.1 million to government officials of Nigeria, Angola, and Kazakhstan between 1998 and 2003. The SEC Release points out that while

[398] See II.6.1.2. above.

[399] SEC Securities Exchange Act of 1934 Release No. 43761, Accounting and Auditing Enforcement, Release No. 1355, Findings and Order in the matter of *IBM Corporation*, December 21, 2000; SEC Litigation Release No. 16839, *IBM* Settlement, December 21, 2000.

this was going on, the *ABB* parent concern 'lacked any meaningful internal controls to prevent such illicit payments'.[400]

> The public officials of the countries concerned received bribes in a number of forms: 'pay' in respect of fictitious consultancy contracts, cash, cars, electricity generators, membership of clubs, entertainment expenses, the payment of their mobile telephone bills and financing of shopping expeditions while in the United States. In return for these bribes, they granted projects to the various *ABB*-subsidiaries, revealed business secrets relating to competitors of *ABB* while giving *ABB* bids favourable consideration.
>
> The civil claim made by the SEC against the *ABB* ended in being settled. The civil penalty of $10.5 million and the $5.9 confiscation of profits represent the highest financial sanction ever imposed by the SEC against a non-US undertaking.

The notion that responsibility for bribery can be derived directly from failure to exercise proper control (of a subsidiary) results in effect in liability for negligence. The commission of bribery, however, requires more than negligence, meaning that the failure of control must be classified as a particular type of deficit or lack of supervision. According to the FCPA, a concern can therefore be regarded as 'knowing'[401] of bribery of a foreign public official, only if it in fact knew of it or if it deliberately avoided knowledge of the incriminating facts (inter alia by ignoring the red flags referred to above). Nevertheless, the SEC, which in the context of its civil enforcement alleged a violation of anti-bribery provisions by *ABB*,[402] did not discuss the knowledge of the parent company.

In its proceedings against the *Diagnostics Products Corporation (DPC)*, the SEC also failed to carry out an analysis of the knowledge requirement of the FCPA.[403] The company in question was accused by the SEC – again in the context of civil enforcement – of being responsible for the bribery carried out by a subsidiary, and of failing to control that subsidiary in a number of respects and of breaking book-keeping rules. Yet in the case papers which have been made public, the SEC does not establish the basis for its bribery allegation. It bases the deficits of control on the sole fact that the illegal

[400] SEC Litigation Release No 18775, Accounting and Auditing Enforcement Release No. 2049, *ABB* Settlement, July 6, 2004. For a detailed discussion cf. the Complaint of the *SEC* v. *ABB Ltd.*, D.D.C., Civil Action No. 1:04CV01141 (RBW); and on the separate prosecution of the US and UK subsidiaries cf. *U.S.* v. *Vetco Gray, Inc. and ABB Vetco Gray UK Ltd.*, S.D. Tex., Case No. 04-CR-279–01, July 6, 2004.

[401] For issuers: 15 U.S.C. § 78dd-1(a)(3) und (f) FCPA 1977.

[402] SEC Litigation Release No. 18775, Accounting and Auditing Enforcement Release No. 2049, *ABB* Settlement, July 6, 2004.

[403] SEC Securities Exchange Act of 1934 Release No. 51724, Accounting and Auditing Enforcement, Release No. 2249, Findings and Order in the matter of *DPC Corporation*, May 20, 2005.

behaviour of its subsidiary lay undetected by *DPC* for a long time. The SEC should have sought, rather, to classify the nature of the parent company's failure of control and in this way reached conclusions about the level or nature of its 'knowing'; any reference by the SEC to wilful ignorance of the risk of bribery was, however, absent from the accusation.

The facts of the *DPC* case are described in the SEC Release as follows: *DPC*, a manufacturer of medical equipment, organised its sales in the Chinese market through its Chinese subsidiary, *DePu*. The latter was at first 90% owned by *DPC*, then wholly owned by it, with its profits being shown on its parent company's balance sheet. *DPC* only realised, however, in 2002 that since its foundation in 1991, *DePu* had regularly won its contracts by bribing Chinese public officials. This case also resulted in a settlement.

> *DePu* had paid been paying 3% to 10% commission to the laboratory workers and doctors responsible for the purchase of medical equipment, so that they would order same from *DePu*. A total of around $1.6 million had been paid in cash over a period of eleven years and been wrongly recorded in the accounts. These details were known only to the *DePu* management, not to *DPC*.

The case resembles the *IBM* case in so far as *DPC* terminated the illegal payments as soon as they became apparent. But by contrast to the *IBM* case, *DPC* was not deceived by falsification of documents, but rather by incorrect accounting entries. The SEC's decision nevertheless to treat the parent company as responsible for the bribery carried out by its subsidiary may be partly linked to the fact that *DPC* swallowed up more than $2 million worth of the profits made as a result of the illegally obtained contracts.[404]

6.4. Horizontal comparison

The following countries provide explicitly for the offence of indirect bribery of foreign public officials, in the context of international business: Australia,[405] France,[406] Luxembourg,[407] Mexico,[408] Portugal,[409] Slovakia,[410] Spain,[411] and the United States.[412] Such an approach is not, however,

[404] Cf. Cadwalader, Wickersham & Taft, Newsletter on the FCPA 1977, June 2005: http://www.cadwalader.com.

[405] Ss. 70.2(1)(ii) und (iv) Australian Criminal Code: 'a person is guilty. . .if the person causes a benefit'.

[406] Arts. 435-2, 435-3, 435-4 French Criminal Code.

[407] Art. 247 Luxembourg Criminal Code.

[408] Art. 222bis Mexican Criminal Code.

[409] Art. 41-A Portuguese Decree Law 28 1984.

[410] S. 161b Slovak Criminal Code.

[411] Art. 445bis Spanish Criminal Code.

[412] 15 U.S.C. §§ 78dd-1(a)(3), 78dd-2(a)(3), 78dd-3(a)(3) FCPA 1977; for a more detailed discussion of the US legal position, see II.6.2. above.

mandatory, so long as a general rule (which may relate to complicity) exists which criminalises indirect bribery in the same way as direct bribery.

General rules of this kind exist in a number of Convention states, including Germany,[413] Italy,[414] the Netherlands,[415] and several central and eastern European[416] and Nordic[417] countries. In the absence of express legislative provision, case law has played a role here in defining the liability of the man pulling the strings behind the scenes for bribery carried out by his puppet, the agent. New Zealand law provides a further example of a legal system which can afford not to have an explicit rule on liability for indirect bribery, given that the phrase 'to a person' in its legislation includes offers, promises, and payments to intermediaries – for passing on.

The laws of the United Kingdom[418] and Belgium[419] are, in principle, similar in that they also hold liable the person who directs another to bribe. The way in which their laws deal with the responsibility of an undertaking for foreign subsidiaries does not, however, reach the Convention standard. It is only where the bribery committed by the subsidiary has been subject to 'direction or authorisation by a directing mind' that liability of the parent undertaking can be established. This principle is applied even in the case of wholly owned subsidiaries.[420]

The Hungarian rule presents a slightly different problem. Indirect bribery is supposed to be captured by the phrase 'with regard to him/her to another person'. This is concerned primarily with the situation where an advantage has been given to the intermediary to confer on the foreign public official, but it must also be clear that the foreign bribery offence also applies to the case where an intermediary does not receive such an advantage, but where the latter has communicated an offer or promise to the foreign public official.[421] In Portuguese law, the offence requires that the intermediary has acted with the 'consent or ratification'[422] of his principal. This restriction is reasonable so long as a failure of the management to act can be interpreted as tacit consent.

[413] S. 25 German Criminal Code. [414] IT-Ph1, 6 et seq.; IT-Ph2, 32 et seq.

[415] Supreme Court, judgement of 21 October 1918, NJ 1918, 1128 (cited in NL-Ph1, 7).

[416] Cf., for example, Art. 20 Bulgarian Criminal Code and Art. 18(1) Polish Criminal Code; for the Czech Republic: cf. CZ-Ph1, 4.

[417] For example, note in this regard the *Travaux Préparatoires* of the relevant Norwegian legislation, i.e. Art. 276a(2) Norwegian Criminal Code, confirmed in the *Statoil* case (discussed in II.6.2. above): cf. NO-Ph2, 26; concerning Finland: cf. FI-Ph2, 17.

[418] UK-Ph2, 60. [419] BE-Ph2, 39.

[420] UK-Ph2, 65. One can find a similar point of view among the directors of Icelandic companies in relation to their anti-bribery legislation (IS-Ph2, 36).

[421] Cf. the reference in HU-Ph1, 4 to Art. 258B(1) Hungarian Criminal Code.

[422] Art. 41-A Portuguese Decree Law 28 1984.

In the Japanese and Korean legal orders, bribery by intermediaries is punishable, whereas mere attempts to bribe are not.[423] The latter is acceptable, from a Convention point of view, in principle, though on the other hand it creates the problem that where an agent fails to pass on an offer, promise, or gift from his principal, the latter will not be sanctioned.[424]

7. Consideration for the bribe: 'acting in relation to the performance of official duties'

7.1. Taking advantage of a public function

From the point of view of the briber, the foreign public official owes him 'consideration' for his offer, etc. This consideration should take the form of the direction of his public office to the goal intended by the bribe. By official act, in this sense, is meant not only those acts performed squarely within the official's own realm of competence, but also decisions which he takes 'in relation to' his duties. The latter may extend to actions outside his sphere of duties, as the next example shows.

Official Commentary 19 provides the example of use of one's official position outside the normal legal scope of one's duties: 'One case of bribery which has been contemplated under the definition in paragraph 4.c is where an executive of a company gives a bribe to a senior official of a government, in order that this official use his office – though acting outside his competence – to make another official award a contract to that company.' This situation is known as 'trading in influence': the bribe is paid to the public official not for his official act, but for the procurement of action by a fellow official. The first official can still be said to be acting 'in relation to' his own duties but the colleague's decision clearly falls outside his competence.

Decisions by the official which do not come within the purview of the Convention are therefore only those made without reference to the official's duties. In such cases, the public official does not exercise his official powers at all; he does not act in an official capacity but merely uses the *practical advantages* of his office to carry out a certain activity. To give two examples: the behaviour of the judge who takes personal possession of seized goods, then sells them and pockets the proceeds, or the conduct of the police

[423] Art. 10bis(1) Japanese Unfair Competition Prevention Law; as far as Korea is concerned, the explanatory manual of the Ministry of Justice provides the corresponding broad interpretation of Art. 3(1) Korean Act on Preventing Bribery of Foreign Public Officials.
[424] Cf. therefore the criticism contained in KR-Ph2, 32.

officer who allows friends to use his police car for private purposes (holiday, etc.) does not fall under Article 1 of the Convention. In neither example just given is there a substantive connection to the judicial or police function; they have each used the practical advantages offered by their offices (be it the key to store or access to police parking pool) to enable them to commit other property offences. They have not, however, acted in an official capacity.[425] State Parties may, of course, decide to extend the reach of the Convention to such cases, if they wish.[426]

Whether the official in fact takes the decision expected of him by the briber is immaterial. He does not even need to be aware that he has been offered such an advantage with this aim in mind. The act is completed when the briber carries out his intention.

7.2. Possible limits

In order to implement the Convention properly, national criminal law must ensure, at least, that 'grand corruption' is prohibited: by this is meant bribery which prompts the official to act illegally. In principle, therefore, state Parties may limit the offence to bribery which aims to induce a *breach of duties*; advantages conferred on the public official in return for the performance of his duties need not, on the other hand, be criminalised (Official Commentaries 3 and 4).[427]

It would, however, be more in keeping with both the spirit and the wording of the Convention, if the level of discretion or tolerance afforded to state Parties were limited according to certain criteria. Article 1(1) of the Convention contains a legal limit or criterion in so far as the offence refers to 'undue advantage'. As a consequence, only those advantages can be excluded from the scope of the offence which are clearly authorised and foreseen by legislation.[428] Official Commentary 9 envisages a quantitative limit for bribes which do not fall under Article 1, namely 'small facilitation payments', understood to mean minor 'greasing of the palms' which do not exceed a kind of socially acceptable maximum.[429]

It remains open to the state Parties, of course, not to adopt either of these limits and to insist upon the criminalisation of all forms of corrupting influence upon public officials, whether the consideration is breach of

[425] The same dividing line is drawn for the statutory bribery offence under the UK's Prevention of Corruption Act 1906: cf. Law Commission 1998, 55 et seq.

[426] As, for example, in French criminal law, which captures acts merely 'facilitated' by the public function.

[427] See II.7.2.1. below. [428] See II.4.2. above. [429] See further in II.7.2.2. below.

duties or their correct performance. From a pragmatic point of view, indeed, the broader offence is preferable, being easier to prove.[430]

7.2.1. General limitation to breach of duties

Article 1 will have been implemented correctly, if someone is punished only for inducing the foreign official to commit an illegal act. According to this concept, payments – naturally including just small facilitation payments – which are made only to encourage performance of duties will not be punished. Official Commentary 3 makes this clear: 'Similarly, a statute which defined the offence in terms of payments, "to induce a breach of the official's duty" could meet the standard'.

The notion of breach of duties is defined by the Convention autonomously in so far as the concept of impartiality is concerned: this is the foreign official's primary and inalienable obligation, to act impartially. The duty is not subject to alteration by national legislation. We can refer here again, firstly, to Official Commentary 3, for support: 'provided that it was understood that every public official had a duty to exercise judgement or discretion impartially and this was an 'autonomous' definition not requiring proof of the law of the particular official's country.' Official Commentary 4 contains this further specification in relation to the particular case of public procurement: 'It is an offence within the meaning of paragraph 1 to bribe to obtain or retain business or other improper advantage whether or not the company concerned was the best qualified bidder or was otherwise a company which could properly have been awarded the business.'

The duty of impartiality thus clearly applies without exception. From this, it follows that the exercise of official discretion must fall within the remit of the possible offence. If public officials are bribed while exercising their discretion, the consideration being sought by the bribery must be regarded in any case as the breach of duties. Behind this approach lies a general suspicion. The authors of the Convention were influenced by their conviction that an advantage offered to the foreign public official is bound to influence how he uses his discretion. The person offering such an advantage is, on this view, speculating on the abuse of this discretion for a corrupt purpose, and should be punished. This is the case even though, objectively speaking, the official's decision may seem to be a perfectly justifiable and reasonable one. It would not be feasible, especially in

[430] Pieth 1999c, A-1047.

complex cases, to require the courts to revisit the issue whether the official might have decided differently had the advantage not been offered.

If, therefore, a state Party does decide to limit its law to cases of inducement of breach of public duties, it must also ensure that discretionary decisions are, as such, covered by the definition. The Convention standard would not be achieved were the law to refer only to *illegal* acts (contrary to legislation or case law),[431] as this would not necessarily cover conduct within official discretion, but influenced by improper motives. Thus, implementing legislation should refer to action *contrary to duties.*

7.2.2. Exception of small facilitation payments

Official Commentary 9 opens to state Parties the possibility of adopting a more restricted limitation, by excluding only *small* facilitation payments from the scope of their Article 1 offence. The condition must be that these transfers really are of a *minor nature not exceeding the social norm* pertaining to them in the society in question: 'Small "facilitation" payments do not constitute payments made 'to obtain or retain business or other improper advantage" within the meaning of paragraph 1 and, accordingly, are also not an offence. Such payments, which, in some countries, are made to induce public officials to perform their functions, such as issuing licenses or permits, are generally illegal in the foreign country concerned.' This approach encourages concerns and their branches to resolve the 'problem' of such payments outside the realm of the criminal law, notably through good governance practices: 'Other countries can and should address this corrosive phenomenon by such means as support for programmes of good governance. However, criminalisation by other countries does not seem a practical or effective complementary action.'

Although it is not necessary to set an explicit maximum amount, any model which excludes small facilitation payments must set *certain criteria* as to what might be regarded as *tolerable.* The Convention does not stipulate a particular figure but there should be a *qualitative criterion.* National law would have to make clear that these payments cannot be used either to induce a breach of duties ('no risk of inciting public officials to behave in a manner inconsistent with their duties'[432]) or as a basis for a discretionary decision. Small facilitation payments may be used only for inducement of lawful decisions of the public official, where no discretion is involved.

[431] Cf. the definition of the offence in Spanish law (ES-Ph1, 5 et seq., 24).
[432] CH-Ph1, 22.

Applying Official Commentary 7 to the Convention, it would be contrary to the Convention standard for state Parties to allow their local customs or practices to determine what level of payment would be tolerable. That would offend also against the idea of autonomous definition. Commentary 7 states: '[i]t is also an offence irrespective of ...[the advantage's] perceptions of local custom, the tolerance of such payments by local authorities'. Some state Parties distinguish structurally between *exceptions for facilitation* payments and *affirmative defences.*[433] Both issues concern payments which are not made to induce the public official to a breach of his duties. Thus, for the purposes of an international commentary of the OECD provisions, a collective treatment is appropriate.

We must also consider, in this context, to what extent the affirmative defence of *expenditure for the promotion and advertisement* of products can be regarded as legitimate. In order to bring products onto the market, it is frequently necessary to obtain an official authorisation of some kind. Increasingly, it has become common for the producer or promoter of the product to organise events at which the new invention etc. is first demonstrated or illustrated to the officials concerned. The promoter will often decide that his purposes are best served by covering the costs incurred by the officials concerned in attending the event: their travel and accommodation costs (in expensive hotels) will be covered, plus entertainment expenses and the costs of gifts, etc. They will receive test or pilot versions of the new products. In addition, the costs of bringing their partners or families to the event may be covered.

This form of corporate entertainment (but for officials) is obviously designed to influence the official to make a decision in favour of authorisation of the product. The practice is particularly widespread in the US, and has spread to Canada. Both countries have decided to allow these costs, to a certain extent, but have imposed limits on what may be regarded as fair and tolerable expenditure. A certain level of investment in both marketing and advertising will be tolerated, but it is decided on a case-by-case basis what the limit might be.

The reports and opinions of the US Department of Justice have established certain standards or rules-of-thumb, for example, that pilot or test versions of products may be distributed to foreign officials, precisely to enable them to test the products themselves, not for their personal use.[434]

> The case in question concerned officials of the then Soviet ministry of trade, whose government incidentally also had to be informed about the matter.

[433] E.g. US law: cf. Deming 2005, 15 et seq. [434] Release 02/11-12-1981.

Another release of the Department of Justice suggests that it can be legitimate (i.e. not bribery) to invite the general manager of a foreign state undertaking (public sector body) to go on a 'promotional tour' of the US, with his wife.[435]

In this context, it is especially important for transparency to be guaranteed. The costs of any such promotional tour must, the Department Release emphasises, be charged and recorded in the relevant company books and the expenses paid directly to the service providers and not the general manager.

7.3. Horizontal comparison

7.3.1. No limitation to sphere of competence of public official

The notion of official action intended by Article 1 of the Convention should not be limited to conduct within the sphere of authorised competence of the public official.

Italian and Korean legislation conform to this interpretation. As far as Italy is concerned, case law extends official action to action by the official which is merely facilitated in a practical sense by his position.[436] This case law has been decided in domestic cases but is equally applicable to transnational bribery. Regarding Korea, the courts have also made up for the lack of clarity in legislation by clarifying that the official who leaves his sphere of competence does not thereby escape the realm of criminal responsibility for bribery.[437]

A number of countries employ overarching or catch-all terminology in their legislation in order to capture action outside the official's own public role: 'anything in relation to his official duties'[438] (Denmark); 'judicial or official act' or 'in connection with [the Member of Parliament's] mandate or functions'[439] (Germany); 'an action related to his official duty'[440] (Iceland); 'in connection with a post, office or commission'[441] (Norway); 'for the exercise of official duties'[442] (Sweden); 'any act in relation to [the] official activity'[443] (Switzerland).

With regard to the German version, some doubts were expressed about the rather narrow wording used, but these have been put to rest by indicating

[435] Release 02/26-07-1983. [436] IT-Ph1, 9. [437] KR-Ph1, 5.
[438] S. 122 Danish Criminal Code.
[439] Ss. 1 und 2(1) Act on Combating Bribery of Foreign Public Officials in International Business Transactions.
[440] S. 109 Icelandic Criminal Code – the version applying before the new law (147/1998) was limited to breach of duties.
[441] S. 276a Norwegian Criminal Code. [442] Ch. 17(7) Swedish Criminal Code.
[443] Art. 322^{septies} Swiss Criminal Code.

> that the German courts would rely on Article 1(4)(c) of the Convention,[444] and by the fact that the German language version appears broader.

Japanese and Mexican legislation regulates this matter in greater detail, distinguishing between these two types of official action as follows: 'acting in relation to the performance of official duties' is juxtaposed with the mere 'using his [the official's] position'.[445] French and Luxembourg legislation follows a similar approach by providing a reference to official action going beyond the competence of the official: 'or in a manner facilitated by his [the official's] function'.[446]

> In any case, the first part of the French and the Luxembourg legislation would satisfy the requirements of Article 1(1) as the wording used – 'in accordance with his function' – encompasses more than the duties to which the official is subject.[447]

In similar fashion, the Common Law countries Australia and New Zealand have gone for broad formulations: 'whether or not. . .within the scope of the official's authority'[448] and 'in the exercise of the official's duties', but with a sufficiently broad concept of 'duty'[449] in the Australian case. Argentina now possesses a definition of exemplary character, i.e. 'whether or not within the official's authorised competence', having amended its previously limited legislation.[450]

United Kingdom law is also sufficiently flexible in this respect, even if the wording used differs significantly from the text of the Convention. The statutory definition is 'any act in relation to his [the agent's] principal's affairs or business'[451], whereas the Common Law reads 'to fail to act in accordance with his [the official's] duties'.[452]

A yet different approach can be found in US legislation, namely in an amended general clause of the FCPA.

The FCPA differentiates[453] among the following sought-for forms of response by the public official to (an offer or promise of) bribery:

- action (of all kinds) within the official's sphere of competence ('in his [the official's] capacity');
- action 'in violation of the lawful duty of such official';
- action influencing the official 'to use his influence with a foreign government or instrumentality thereof'.

444 DE-Ph1, 18; DE-Ph2, 40. 445 Art. 10bis(1) Japanese Unfair Competition Prevention Law.
446 Arts. 435-2, 435-3, 435-4 French Criminal Code; Arts. 247, 250 Luxembourg Criminal Code.
447 FR-Ph1, 10. 448 S. 105C(2) New Zealand's Crimes Amendment Act 2001.
449 AU-Ph1, 6. 450 Art. 258bis Argentine Criminal Code.
451 S. 1(1) Prevention of Corruption Act 1906. 452 UK-Ph1, 7.
453 15 U.S.C. §§ 78dd-1(a)(1), 78dd-2(a)(1), 78dd-3(a)(1) FCPA 1977.

In the final analysis, however, every (paid) objective 'to secure any improper advantage' is punishable, without restriction to a particular category of official action.

With regard to central and eastern European states, we can refer to the examples of Poland and Slovakia, both of which also use sufficiently broad wording: 'in connection with the performance of this [the public official's] function'[454] and 'in relation to the performance of official duties'.[455]

> There is, however, a further qualification in Slovak law, which may cause some difficulties. There is specific provision for bribery of Members of Parliament or of any other 'public assembly' and for bribery of judges.[456] In these cases, the reference to official action is to 'performing his function'. In contrast to the position regarding public officials in general, this provision might be understood too narrowly.

Hungarian law now refers to all actions 'in connection with the functioning of a foreign official person'. The former legal limitation to actions 'to the detriment of the public interest' has been dropped.[457]

The definitions in Belgium, Finland, and the Netherlands, on the other hand, are problematic, because they appear to limit the offence to actions of the public official *within* his area of competence.

Starting with the Finnish definition, we find only a vague reference to the aim of the inducement ('for his [the public official's] action in service'[458]); regarding Dutch law, we find a three-way differentiation between the sought-for actions ('acts or omissions in breach of a public servant's official duties',[459] 'acts or omissions without breaching his/her official duties'[460] and 'influence over a judge with respect to a decision in a case'[461]); finally with regard to Belgium, the most problematic case of the three, we find the following reference to public action, also differentiated in three respects: 'to engage in an improper acts while carrying out official duties', 'to perform a proper but unpaid official act' and 'to commit a criminal offence or misdemeanour in the course of official duties'.[462] It is possible that in these three countries the legislation could be interpreted so as not to cover acts having a mere factual connection to the public official's position.[463]

> This certainly seems to be the case in Belgium. There, when the public official acts in a way which exceeds his competence, the offence concerned cannot be bribery, and it is only *possible* that such conduct could be criminalised under

[454] Art. 229, s. 1 Polish Criminal Code. [455] S. 161b Slovak Criminal Code.
[456] S. 161c Slovak Criminal Code. [457] S. 258B(1) Hungarian Criminal Code; HU-Ph1[bis], 15.
[458] Ss. 13 and 14 Finnish Criminal Code. [459] Art. 177.1(1) Dutch Criminal Code.
[460] Art. 177a.1(1) Dutch Criminal Code. [461] Art. 178.1 Dutch Criminal Code.
[462] Art. 247 Belgian Criminal Code.
[463] Cf. therefore the criticism of the 'exact power' theory contained in FI-Ph1, 3.

> another heading, if the act performed was illegal.[464] This gap in Belgian legislation is not closed by virtue of the fact that the 'official act' is also deemed to include preparatory acts. The offence of *trading in influence* will, however, be committed in some cases where the official has acted outside his official duties. This is covered by the Belgian Criminal Code, namely bribery that is 'aimed at inducing a person exercising a public function to use the. . .influence he possesses because of his function to induce a public authority or administration to perform or restrain from an act'.[465]

Greek law shows some similarities to the Belgian position, with its apparently open wording being interpreted restrictively.[466]

However national laws are framed, from the viewpoint of the Convention it is imperative that they should be given a broader rather than a narrower reading, in order that payment for actions outside the sphere of competence of the official are treated either as bribery or as trading in influence.

7.3.2. Breach of duties concepts in domestic law

Austrian,[467] German[468] and Swiss[469] law share the characteristic that they punish as bribery only those payments etc. which seek to sway the official to commit an act in *breach of his official duties* or a *discretionary act.* They do not punish 'bribery' for fulfilment of these duties: that, on this minimalist view of their international obligations, does not in fact constitute bribery.[470] All three countries do, however, criminalise payments to domestic officials in return for performance of duties.

The limitation to bribery for breach of duties in transnational cases renders less extensive forms of tolerance superfluous. The exception for *small* facilitation payments therefore has no role to play in this context.[471]

> This applies also to the Swiss situation, in which the conferment of 'advantages of minor value in conformity with socially accepted practices' on public officials does not incur a criminal penalty.[472] According to the Swiss, such 'social acceptability' can be present only in respect of payments made to induce action in conformity with official duties.[473] Freedom from criminal responsibility can therefore apply only in relation to payments etc. to domestic officials.

[464] BE-Ph1, 5 et seq. [465] Art. 247(4) Belgian Criminal Code.
[466] GR-Ph1, 4; GR-Ph2, 27, 45. [467] S. 307(1)(6) Austrian Criminal Code.
[468] Art. 334(1) and (3) German Criminal Code; ss. 1 und 2 Act on Combating Bribery of Foreign Public Officials in International Business Transactions.
[469] Art. 322^{septies} Swiss Criminal Code.
[470] Whereas Germany and Switzerland fulfil their minimum international obligations by express provision in their legislation, in Austria it is the preparatory legislative materials (*Travaux Préparatoires*), jurisprudence, and doctrine, which together secure an interpretation consistent with the Convention: explanatory notes to the 'revision draft parliament protocols' (1230 BlgNR XX. GP on s. 307 Austrian Criminal Code: cf. AT-Ph1, 7).
[471] Compare DE-Ph1, 2. [472] Art. 322^{octies} Swiss Criminal Code. [473] CH-Ph1, 3.

In formal terms, this model is in perfect conformity with the Convention: see Official Commentaries 3 and 4. Nowadays, however, the WGB adopts a stricter line in this regard, questioning compliance with the Convention where there is no upper limit on the amount of the advantage conferred on the official in return for performance of his duties.[474] In fact, the problem is not as serious as it seems, because the amounts handed over in such circumstances are generally very small – in reality, therefore, the *breach of duties model* comes down to roughly the same as a tolerance of *small facilitation payments.*

The Spanish model attracts the criticism of the WGB at an earlier point, namely in relation to the very definition of breach of duties. Here, the legislator has adopted too narrow a line, by failing to include discretionary decisions.[475] The definition refers only to *criminal acts* committed by the official or all other *'unjust' actions or omissions.*[476]

7.3.3. Wide definition of official action with tolerance of small facilitation payments

A number of state Parties have opted to exclude from the definition of bribery not all payments, benefits, etc. conferred in respect of performance of official duties but only the *trivial, bagatelle-type cases* implied by the Convention's terminology 'small facilitation payments'. Of the Nordic countries, Denmark, Iceland, and Sweden (but not Finland and Norway), have opted for this approach: among Common Law countries, Australia, Canada, New Zealand, and the United States. Korea has also gone down this road. The common denominator of all these systems is that the person who merely 'greases the palm' of the public official in order to prompt him to perform his duties, i.e. to carry out a quite legal act, will not be liable to a criminal penalty. The precise method of implementation of this approach varies considerably from one state to the next, and they also differ in relation to the limits of what is permissible (their reliability in terms of the Convention can also vary accordingly).

Denmark[477] and Sweden[478] take the view that a person who extracts a legitimate public act by means of a small payment does not achieve an

[474] CH-Ph2, 33; cf. also CH-Ph1, 22. The WGB has not, on the other hand, (yet) indulged in any criticism vis-à-vis Austria or Germany concerning their limitation of criminal responsibility to inducing the breach of duties.

[475] ES-Ph1, 5 et seq.

[476] Art. 445bis read together with Arts. 419, 420, 421 Spanish Criminal Code.

[477] Cf. the Danish *Travaux Préparatoires.*

[478] Ch. 17(7) Swedish Criminal Code, SE-Ph1, 3 et seq.

'improper' advantage. It is problematic, however, that in both countries local custom (in the country of the recipient) can be used as the basis for justifying this approach.[479] This is contrary to Official Commentary 7. Additionally, it is not clear whether facilitation payments may also be used to induce discretionary decisions: if this were the case, the standard implied by Official Commentary 3 would be breached.[480] The law in Iceland[481] follows a slightly different approach: it does not explicitly rule out the possibility of small facilitation payments, but the law on such matters is interpreted rather strictly.[482]

With regard to Canada and the United States, it is possible to defend a charge of bribery on the basis that the benefit to the public official was in fact in the form of a gift in the context of product promotion or presentation.[483] All 'reasonable and bona fide expenditure, such as travel and lodging expenses'[484] or 'reasonable expenses incurred in good faith'[485] are covered by this *affirmative defence*. Such expenses must be connected with or arise in the framework of:

- the 'promotion, demonstration, or explanation of products or services' belonging or pertaining to the payer of the 'bribe'; or
- the 'execution or performance of a contract with a foreign government or agency'.[486]

These exceptions are problematic, because their boundaries are unclear and because they offer the potential for abuse, leading to impunity for acts which should really incur a criminal penalty.[487] The danger they represent is, however, at least moderated by the fact that the burden of proof in relation to exculpatory circumstances, rests, in general, with the accused person.

A further category of exceptions or defences arises under the FCPA and under Canadian law, and likewise in the Australian and New Zealand legal systems. They make an *exception* for minor payments, whose principal or

[479] SE-Ph1, 4, though the WGB does not in fact repeat in that report the criticism voiced in respect of Denmark: DK-Ph1, 4, 25.
[480] Cf. the mention of this in DK-Ph1, 4. [481] S. 109 Icelandic Criminal Code.
[482] IS-Ph1, 2.
[483] For a discussion of the general importance of this as a possible ground of criminal defence, see II.7.2.2. above.
[484] 15 U.S.C. §§ 78dd-1(c)(2), 78dd-2(c)(2), 78dd-3(c)(2) FCPA 1977.
[485] S. 3(3)(b) Canadian Corruption of Foreign Public Officials Act.
[486] This is the wording of the FCPA 1977.
[487] US-Ph1, 21, 25; US-Ph2, 34 et seq., 38; CA-Ph1, 23; CA Ph2, 28 et seq.

primary purpose is to accelerate or implement 'routine governmental actions'.[488] The position here may be summarised as follows:

- A bribe given to induce an official to act outside his authorised competence cannot be classified as an innocent attempt to accelerate routine governmental action.
- Bribes to induce official action in breach of duties or discretionary decisions are not permitted – irrespective of whether those actions may be defensible as such, they would be in breach of the Convention standard, as pointed out by Official Commentary 3. Given this standard, a number of deficits of national legislation may be identified. The FCPA fails explicitly to rule out discretionary decisions. The exclusionary approach adopted by New Zealand leaves it in essence to the courts to decide whether certain types of advantages not mentioned in this list, which the Convention would clearly regard as illegal, would be excluded under its law as being routine governmental action: unfair tax breaks, favourable foreign exchange rates[489] or business licences, for example. Similar doubts arise in relation to the Australian definition, in so far as it appears to leave open the possibility that decisions which are partially discretionary could be regarded as routine governmental actions, for example, 'processing a visa or work permit'.[490]
- Official acts concerning the conclusion and continuation of business relations and the conditions of such relations may not in any case be interpreted as 'routine'.[491] One may not use 'small benefits' to public officials in order to promote one's business: local tolerance of such practices is not permitted.
- One may also not invoke the routine governmental actions defence on the basis that the main purpose of the bribe is to induce such actions: this will not be deemed to excuse payments or other advantages conferred before then in return for illegal conduct by the public official.
- The notion of routine governmental actions is conceptually broader than that of small facilitation payments. The WGB insists, however, that they should be subject to a numerical limit, at least

[488] 15 U.S.C. §§ 78dd-1(b), 78dd-2(b), 78dd-3(b) FCPA 1977; cf. the definitions in 15 U.S.C. §§ 78dd-1(f)(3), 78dd-2(h)(4), 78dd-3(f)(4) FPCA 1977; ss. 105C(a) and (b) New Zealand's Crimes Amendment Act 2001; ss. 70.4(1) und (2) Australian Criminal Code; ss. 3(4) and (5) Canadian Corruption of Foreign Public Officials Act.

[489] NZ-Ph1, 8. [490] S. 70.4(2)(b)(ii) Australian Criminal Code.

[491] See II.8. below.

> 'where the size...is inappropriate'.[492] A payment of $50 000 for a government approval would, for example, be regarded as going 'far beyond any kind of acceptable payment'.[493]

Our conclusion is that the routine governmental actions exception creates serious problems, whichever version we may mention: Australian, Canadian, New Zealand, or the United States. The WGB sees this matter as 'an area of risk and open to misuse'[494]: the practices in question threaten to break the walls erected by the Convention in order to contain corruption. It is particularly disturbing in this context to note that such an exception does not apply to domestic bribery.[495]

Australia combines its tolerance of *de minimis* bribery of this kind with the embracing of transparency. Under this model, the 'briber' who wishes to rely on his affirmative defence must confess his actions immediately. He must also record what he has done and state clearly in the relevant note or entry that what was paid over was only a 'genuine facilitation payment to secure or expedite non-discretionary[496] routine governmental action of a minor nature'.[497]

We find that Korea too circumscribes its tolerance of bribery of a minor character by allowing only 'small pecuniary or other advantage' in order to secure the 'ordinary and routine' work of a public official.[498] This approach is, in principle, acceptable in scope. The difficulty here lies in the absence of any upper limit for the amounts in question. The courts have so far failed to set such a limit and none exists in legislation, meaning there is no certainty as to the permissible level of advantage which may be conferred.[499] There is thus a risk that criminal sanctions will not be imposed in appropriate cases.

7.3.4. Broad concepts without provision for exceptions

Some countries employ neither form of exception allowed by the Convention. They go beyond what is strictly required of them under the

[492] US-Ph1, 8. [493] US-Ph1, 8 (note 23). [494] US-Ph2, 34.
[495] US-Ph2, 34, 38; CA-Ph2, 26.
[496] This approach thus enables the possible gap in the law to be filled by ensuring that payments in respect of discretionary decisions are not taken outside the scope of the Convention.
[497] AU-Ph1, 7.
[498] Art. 3(2) Korean Act on Preventing Bribery of Foreign Public Officials in International Business Transactions.
[499] KR-Ph1, 2 et seq., 21 et seq.; the WGB has accordingly recommended that the matter be followed up: cf. KR-Ph2, 29.

Convention and punish bribery without exception, even minor transgressions in respect of legitimate acts of the public official. This stricter approach is evident in certain Latin American countries[500] and in Japan,[501] at least on the basis of the wording of the legislation.

> The legal position in Japan is in fact rather unclear. There is some discussion there of certain minor bribery – 'greasing' or 'lubricating' payments – being tolerable but the conditions for this have not been clarified, or are disputed. The limits of tolerance are in any case fuzzy. The local customs of the official's country, i.e. the victim state, would seem to determine whether a criminal penalty would be appropriate: this is problematic from a Convention standpoint, as we have seen. The WGB is rightly concerned at the situation. An exception for small facilitation payments demands clear regulation, and may not depend on the variable of local customs.[502]

Among European countries, both France and Luxembourg are in the vanguard of the 'hardliners' camp' – they do not allow facilitation payments of any kind, not even 'petty gifts'.[503]

If we look at other European states, we find that for Bulgaria,[504] Italy,[505] the Netherlands,[506] and Poland,[507] bribery aimed at inducing breach of duties is just one of the offences targeted by national legislation. These countries do, however, tend to classify 'breach of duties bribery' as bribery of a more aggravated form. Among the Nordic countries, Finland and Norway punish even minor 'greasing' or 'lubricating' payments.[508] Bribes aimed at inducing breach of duties are not, however, in general subject to higher penalties than those aimed at other acts, unless the case is a particularly serious one.

In Finland, the advantage conferred on the public official or the expected benefit expected in return must be 'considerable' for it to qualify as aggravated.[509] Opinions seem to differ quite starkly as to what is regarded as 'considerable' in this sense, with the police and prosecutors, in particular, offering radically divergent views (difference of factor of five). Nor are the non-financial criteria relevant to the assessment of the advantage apparent. There is a lack of clarity in Finnish criminal policy and sentencing in this area.[510]

[500] AR-Ph1, 6; MX-Ph1, 3.
[501] Art. $10^{bis}(1)$ Japanese Unfair Competition Prevention Law; JP-Ph1^{bis}, 3.
[502] JP-Ph2, 39 et seq. [503] LU-Ph1, 5; FR-Ph1, 6. [504] Art. 304(3) Bulgarian Criminal Code.
[505] Art. 322bis Italian Criminal Code; for further qualifying conditions: cf. IT-Ph1, 3 et seq.
[506] Art. 177a Dutch Criminal Code. [507] Art. 229 Polish Criminal Code.
[508] S. 13 Finish Criminal Code; s. 276a Norwegian Criminal Code; NO-Ph2, 28.
[509] Aggravated Bribery, s. 14 Finish Criminal Code.
[510] The WGB has therefore called for clarification; FI-Ph2, 16 et seq.; see ch. on Article 3 below.

The Norwegian case leaves even more questions unanswered, where aggravated bribery – so-called 'Gross Corruption'[511] – is concerned. This is said to pertain where:

- the official has breached the special trust placed in the exercise of his functions;
- where a 'considerable economic advantage' has transpired as a result of the bribery;
- when serious economic or social damage was risked by the bribe transaction;
- where papers or balance sheets were falsified.

Greek practice reveals certain similarities to these Nordic countries.[512] United Kingdom legislation is also, in principle, all-encompassing. A concentration of resources on the prosecution and investigation of serious cases is, however, very likely in practice.[513] Similarly, Dutch law offers a broad enough basis to pursue every act of bribery, no matter how small it may be; the reality, however, is that the prosecutor will use his discretion to decide whether to prosecute cases of small facilitation payments. He should be guided by general instructions. It should be clear that these instructions may not offer impunity to those who would try and facilitate the taking of discretionary decisions by the offer of a bribe.

8. Objective of bribery: improper advantage in the conduct of international business

8.1. Limitation to business advantage

The essence of the Convention is to prevent bribery being used as a means of advancing one's *economic interests* on the global market. Corruption should not be part of 'business as usual'. Article 1 of the Convention is limited to the use of bribery to gain advantages in *international business.*

Business obtained or retained through bribery will *always* be regarded as an 'improper' advantage. This approach requires that all would-be bidders for a contract should be punished for bribery, even the bidder who might

[511] S. 276b Norwegian Criminal Code; the WGB regards the qualifications as somewhat opaque: cf. NO-Ph2, 31 et seq.

[512] For example, some exceptions to criminal liability are allowed with regard to small payments for port officials to induce them to perform their functions: cf. Athens Court of Appeal 159/1982.

[513] UK-Ph2, 52 et seq.; see also ch. on Article 5 below.

have won without resorting to illegal methods, i.e. the best bidder as well as those less qualified. Official Commentary 4 spells this out: 'It is an offence within the meaning of paragraph 1 to bribe to obtain or retain business or other improper advantage whether or not the company concerned was the best qualified bidder or was otherwise a company which could properly have been awarded the business.' It is therefore neither the economic viability or feasibility of the bid which is tested nor the economic advantage which may accrue to the state concerned, from a viable contract. It would not be reasonable to expect a judge to test the (insufficient) quality of a bid or to prove a negative. It is very important to emphasise that it is always bribery under the Convention for a foreign public official to be paid in return for the granting of business, without regard to the economic benefit which the transaction might bring to the foreign state concerned.

Article 1 is not restricted to obtaining or retaining of business but covers every 'other improper advantage' which Official Commentary 5 defines as follows: '"Other improper advantage" refers to something to which the company concerned was not clearly entitled, for example, an operating permit for a factory which fails to meet the statutory requirements.' Such other business-related advantages could derive from official decisions relating more to the day-to-day operation of the business than to the retaining of contracts. Apart from official authorisations of all kinds, one could mention the possible grant of subsidies or grants relating to business operations, the relaxing of certain environmental or other regulatory standards, tax breaks, accelerated approval procedures for company products or for business premises, the reduction or avoidance of contractual penalties, etc.

> The case of the US Californian firm *InVision* concerned a contractual penalty. They were doing their business in China (2002–2003) through an intermediary. *InVision* ran into trouble with its delivery deadlines vis-à-vis its Chinese partner, a state airline company; it faced contractual penalties. According to the SEC Release, its management thereupon decided to use its intermediary to bribe the airline company, in order to avoid these penalties.[514]

The FCPA contains a potential loophole in that it remains limited to payments made 'in order to assist...in obtaining or retaining for or with, or directing business to, any person'.[515] This wording alone does not appear sufficient to guarantee that, in addition to obtaining and retaining business, other business advantages, indeed business advantages of all kinds, would be covered.[516]

[514] For a discussion of the structure of the case, see II.6.1.2. above.
[515] 15 U.S.C. § 78dd-1(a) FCPA 1977.
[516] See, however, the discussion of the *Kay* case in II.8.3.3. below.

8.2. Improper advantages

An advantage is 'improper' where an undertaking is not entitled to nor has any claim upon it. Whether, in a particular case, a business advantage can be regarded as legitimate, and therefore as proper, can be determined only in the context of the underlying official act from which it emanates or accrues. That advantage represents the outcome, the intended outcome, of the official decision induced by the bribe. A *legitimate* business advantage must therefore have its roots in a *legitimate* official decision, meaning one taken in conformity with official duties. Insofar as a state Party wishes to remove the 'purchase' of proper business advantages from the scope of criminalisation, it must do the same in respect of the underlying official decision, either on a general basis[517] or under the 'small facilitation payments' model referred to above.[518] The scope which the Convention allows in respect of excuses or defences for bribes aimed at inducing performance of duties also determines the question of what business advantages may be tolerated. E contrario, the circumstances which point to a business advantage being regarded as 'improper' will also imply that the underlying official decision is flawed.

Under a system of criminal law which also applies the Article 1 offence to bribes aimed at extracting the performance of official duties, it is not possible to envisage a result or outcome in respect of which the beneficiary would not be punished. One may not promise, offer, or give a bribe in return for an advantage to which the briber would anyway have been entitled, even when this leads to a 'proper' advantage.

8.3. Horizontal comparison

8.3.1. Extension to other walks of life

The Convention concerns only economic matters. The state Parties are, however, free to extend the application of their criminal law concerning corruption to other walks of life. Indeed, more than a few of them do not limit their laws to bribery aimed at business matters. The Benelux countries, Hungary, Poland, Switzerland, and several Nordic countries[519] fall into this category. Similarly, the United Kingdom does not stipulate in the 1906 Act or in Common Law a particular area in which the briber should be active, in order to fall under the scope of criminal law: purchase of any official act

[517] See II.7.2.1. above. [518] See II.7.2.2. above.

[519] Ch. 17(7) Swedish Criminal Code; s. 276a Norwegian Criminal Code; s. 13 Finnish Criminal Code.

is criminal.[520] A similar line is taken by the Council of Europe's Criminal Law Convention on Corruption.[521]

Austria, France, Germany, and Italy all make a distinction in this matter, based on their obligations under EU law on the one hand and the OECD Convention, on the other. They prohibit in a general way bribery aimed at public officials of other Member States of the Union or at Community officials, whatever the context.[522] They also implement the OECD Convention strictly, limiting the scope of implementing legislation to the corruption of public officials from non-EU states in economic matters.[523]

8.3.2. Limitation to transnational business

A narrower approach is taken by other states: among European countries, Bulgaria,[524] Greece,[525] Iceland,[526] Slovakia,[527] and Spain[528] all follow the line that only advantages obtained in intenational business are subject to criminal sanction. Japan,[529] Korea,[530] Mexico,[531] New Zealand,[532] and the United States[533] also sing from this hymn sheet. The legislation of Argentina[534] and Australia[535] likewise invokes only economic interest as the target of bribery, though there is no limitation to transnational transactions.

The Canadian legislation implementing the Convention applies to 'advantage in the course of business' only, with 'business' in this context being understood to mean only those activities undertaken for profit.[536] This is possibly too narrow. Many bodies from the non-profit sector outgrow their tennis club-type origins and begin to operate with similar means as business concerns.[537]

[520] UK-Ph1, 7. [521] COE 1999a.

[522] S. 1 German Act on Combating Bribery of Public Officials of Member States of the European Union and of Community Officials; s. 307(1)(1) Austrian Criminal Code; Art. 322bis(1)(1) Italian Criminal Code; Art. 435-2 French Criminal Code.

[523] Ss. 1 und 2(1) German Act on Combating Bribery of Foreign Public Officials; s. 307(1)(6) Austrian Criminal Code; Art. 322bis(2)(2) Italian Criminal Code; Arts. 435-3, 435-4 French Criminal Code.

[524] Art. 304(2) Bulgarian Criminal Code. [525] Art. 2 Greek Act 2656/1998.

[526] S. 109 Icelandic Criminal Code (the text of the Convention was adopted word for word).

[527] S. 161b Slovak Criminal Code. [528] Art. 445bis Spanish Criminal Code.

[529] Art. 10bis(1) Japanese Unfair Competition Prevention Law.

[530] Art. 3(1) Korean Act on Preventing Bribery of Foreign Public Officials in International Business Transactions.

[531] Art. 222bis Mexican Federal Criminal Code.

[532] Art. 105C(2) New Zealand's Crimes Amendment Act 2001.

[533] 15 U.S.C. §§ 78dd-1(a), 78dd-2(a), 78dd-3(a) FCPA 1977.

[534] Art. 258bis Argentine Criminal Code: cf. AR-Ph1, 6.

[535] S. 70.2(1) Australian Criminal Code.

[536] Ss. 2 und 3(1) Canadian Corruption of Foreign Public Officials Act.

[537] Cf. the WGB's critical comments in CA-Ph2, 28.

Japan demonstrates a similar preoccupation with profit-making entities, but the legal basis is not entirely clear. In the absence of clear lines, it is not, for example, evident whether every concrete transaction in the course of business requires to be profitable.[538]

Japan's 'main office exception' has, however, been dropped, having been found to contravene the Convention.[539] According to this construction, business done in a foreign country would no longer be regarded as 'international' as soon as the Japanese company concerned had set up its 'main office' there. One could therefore bribe the officials of the country with impunity. The employees of a foreign subsidiary of a Japanese concern could also escape punishment for bribery in their place of operation, provided that a foreign branch had a main office there, even if it was in all respects dependent on the parent concern. The law has now been repealed, but instead of the main office exception, the wording 'in an international commercial transaction' was integrated in the offence. Thus, some concerns remain about the amending legislation.[540]

8.3.3. The 'obtaining or retaining business' concept of the FCPA

The FCPA limits US anti-corruption law to payments or other advantages made 'in order to assist...in obtaining or retaining for or with, or directing business to, any person'.[541] This wording renders it difficult to capture all types of bribery-induced advantages intended to be captured by the Convention, particularly those which go further than 'obtaining' new business or 'retaining' existing business ties. These, as we have seen, can include various forms of relief from onerous business or regulatory burdens which might affect business operations but may not be directly linked to concrete contracts.

> There was discussion in 1977, 1988 and most recently 1998 of an amendment being introduced to the FCPA in order to deal with this apparent gap. It would have extended the scope of the offence as follows: 'or other action in seeking more favorable treatment by a foreign government'[542] but was turned down by legislators.

[538] JP-Ph2, 42 et seq.

[539] JP-Ph1, 24; Art. 10bis(3) Japanese Unfair Competition Prevention Law was repealed in its entirety.

[540] JP-Ph2, 9, 41 et seq.

[541] 15 U.S.C. § 78dd-1(a) FCPA 1977.

[542] House, H.R. Conference Report No. 100–576, at 918 (1988), reprinted in 1998 U.S.C.C.A.N. 1547, 1951.

The issue came to a head in the context of tax breaks.[543] Reduction or relaxation of taxes or fees does not lead directly to the obtaining of business. In practice, the narrow terms of the legislation have been extended in order to cover preferences or advantages which *indirectly* lead to the obtaining or retaining of business.

The leading decision is *U.S. v. Kay*. The CEO and the Vice-President of *American Rice (ARI)* paid bribes to customs and tax officials in Haiti in order to obtain a reduction of import duties and taxes. At first instance, the US courts adopted the traditional narrow reading of the statute and acquitted those charged.[544] The Court of Appeals overturned this verdict in deciding that the advantage accruing from the reduction in duties would indeed 'assist in obtaining or retaining business', thus adopting a broader interpretation of this wording. Not every such relief, however, may fall under the FCPA; there had to be a 'business nexus'. Those responsible were sentenced to thirty-seven and sixty-three months' imprisonment, respectively.[545] In the light of this decision, the appeal in the similar case of *Mattson and Harris* was eagerly awaited; the District Court had rejected the SEC's civil claim at first instance, relying on the first instance decision in *Kay*.[546] The SEC has in fact in the meantime withdrawn its complaint and appeal proceedings have been terminated.[547]

Doubts remain about how other cases might be resolved. How other types of tax breaks or relief will be treated after *Kay* is just one question. What about official decisions to pass building inspections or surveys? If the (early) use of the building is urgently required in order to seal a business deal or maintain business, then payment to a foreign public official for this could easily be subsumed under the formula 'payment intended to

[543] A detailed discussion of the legal questions arising did not, however, take place in the major cases, which arose in the 1990s, because they were settled out of court: *U.S.* v. *Vitusa Corporation*, Cr. 94-253 (MTB) D.N.J., 1994, 3 FCPA Reporter at 699.169 and *U.S.* v. *Herzberg*, Cr. 94-254 (MTB) D.N.J., 1994, 3 FCPA Reporter at 699.165 ended with plea agreements being made; an agreement was also reached in the civil action *SEC* v. *Triton Energy Corporation*, D.D.C., Civil Action No. 1:97CV00401, February 27, 1997.

[544] *U.S.* v. *Kay and Murphy*, S.D. Tex., Case No. H-01-914, April 16, 2002.

[545] *U.S.* v. *Kay*, United States Court of Appeals (5th Circuit), 359 F.3d 738, February 4, 2004. Cf. the useful analysis contained in Cadwalader, Wickersham & Taft, Newsletter on the FCPA 1977, July 2005: http://www.cadwalader.com.

[546] Cf. Weinstein and Trambley 2003 for a discussion of the first instance decisions in both cases.

[547] For further discussion of this cf. *Baker Hughes* case in II.6.1.2. above; on civil action cf. *SEC* v. *Mattson and Harris*, Memorandum and Order, CV-H01–3106, S.D. Tex., September 9, 2002; for the dismission by the United States Court of Appeals (5th Circuit) on July 14, 2004 cf. SEC Litigation Release No. 18863, Accounting and Auditing Enforcement Release No. 2092, September 1, 2004.

assist...indirectly in obtaining or retaining business'.[548] If, however, an illicit deal is done to release an unfinished building from inspection regulations in order to meet certain obligations to a partner, then it is less clear that this could be subsumed under the notion of indirect assistance to the obtaining or retention of business. In such a case, the FCPA concept may really be too restricted.

8.3.4. Improper nature of the advantage

The conditions under which a business advantage will be regarded as proper depend upon the extent to which the payment of bribes is decriminalised in the country concerned.

In those countries – Austria, Germany and Switzerland and also (to an excessive degree) Spain[549] – in which the anti-bribery legislation applies only in respect of payments, etc. for breach of duties, a business advantage stemming from an act done in exercise of official duties will not be punishable. In so far as it is only the donor of small facilitation payments who remains free of sanction, the legitimacy of any business advantage will operate in his favour only if he has invested a small amount to obtain it. Most countries have adopted the latter option, including Australia, Canada, Denmark, Iceland, Korea, New Zealand, Sweden, and the United States.[550] In these legal systems, the law strictly requires that a contract may not in any circumstances be bought by bribery, even where the public official may have acted completely correctly:

- US law has drawn the line in relation to *routine governmental actions*[551] accordingly: decisions of public authorities concerning the continuation of a business relationship or the terms of business may not be classified as routine in this sense. It is therefore not permitted to use small payments in order to win or retain business.
- In legal systems in which one distinguishes in an abstract way between clearly illegal acts of public officials, clearly proper or legitimate acts (based on clear rules) and discretionary acts, decisions relating to the opening of business relations, their conduct and terms, are generally a matter for discretionary decision-making. As we have seen, discretionary decisions of the public official fall clearly within the scope of the Article 1 prohibition.[552]

[548] *U.S.* v. *Kay*, United States Court of Appeals (5th Circuit), 359 F.3d 738, February 4, 2004.
[549] See II.7.3.2. above. [550] See II.7.3.3. above. [551] See II.7.3.3. above.
[552] Spanish legislation is therefore inadequate in this regard (see II.7.3.2. above).

In those state Parties to the Convention which apply their bribery legislation to *all* forms of official action, including correct action in accordance with duties, the bribing undertaking also finally risks being punished, if it pays for a business benefit to which it is entitled: this is the position under a large number of legal systems, both European and non-European, notably Argentina, Bulgaria, Finland, France, Greece, Japan (extensive model), Luxembourg, Mexico, the Netherlands, Poland, Norway, and the United Kingdom.

III. Mens rea

1. Dolus eventualis

The word 'intentionally' is used by Article 1 to indicate the subjective element of the offence of active bribery of foreign officials (*mens rea*). State Parties are obliged to punish only those acts committed with intention. What precisely falls under 'intentionally' in this context, and what other mental elements may be included in the definition of the offence, are not laid down by the Convention or are laid down only in a very general fashion.

The respective legal traditions of the state Parties will determine the concrete elements of the Convention standard of intentional corruption. In Common Law systems, the term *mens rea* is used to describe the 'mental' elements required for a particular crime. English law and systems derived from or related to it use this term to cover the various types of mental requirements for the commission of a crime. *Mens rea* may consist in intention or knowledge, in recklessness, or in negligence.[553] According to most Continental legal systems, a distinction is also made between intention on the one hand and negligence and recklessness on the other. Intention conveys the idea of a certain degree of volition, distinguishing it clearly from negligence and recklessness.

Within the various definitions of intention which one can find in national legal systems, two elements can usually be found: first, a certain degree of *volition* or *conscious choice*, at least an acceptance of the crime (element of volition), and secondly a certain degree of *knowledge*, at least the serious supposition of the existence of the various elements of the offence (knowledge element), going beyond inattentiveness or

[553] Gordon 2000, 250 et seq.: 'crimes are often referred to as crimes of intent, crimes of recklessness, or crimes of negligence' (para. 7.11).

carelessness.[554] If it is obvious that the offender was aware of the main facts, the necessary degree of volition is assumed: he cannot then convincingly argue that he did not intend the damaging consequences of his action.

Under the Convention system, the *mens rea* required is intention at least in the form of *dolus eventualis* as just described: this is the form of intention implied by the word 'intentionally', which emerges from the Convention's Article 1. Whoever is involved in a transaction in which he only as much as seriously *supposes* that bribery is involved, has the necessary *mens rea.*

> The COE Convention on Corruption[555] goes further on the question of responsibility of legal persons. Bribery which is the result of an undertaking's 'lack of supervision or control' can also lead to its criminal responsibility.

It would not be consistent with the Convention standard for a state Party to set a higher standard of intention (e.g. actual knowledge or malice) than dolus eventualis as its *starting point* for criminal responsibility. *Stricter* forms of intention will, of course, be caught by the more moderate form, and the Convention leaves it to the state Parties whether to include other mental elements such as recklessness or negligence in their definitions (they are not part of the Convention standard). Where a state party chooses to include negligent commission in its definition of the offence, it will be for it to decide what it means, in the light of its traditions, and also to decide how concepts such as 'conscious negligence'[556] might be defined.

It is relatively easy to establish intention in relation to an offender who has himself arranged the bribe or paid it over. Other cases are much more difficult to judge, especially those in which an undertaking or its management should be held responsible for acts of bribery carried out by their employees, agents or subsidiaries. Responsibility in such cases cannot be avoided merely by maintaining ignorance of the corrupt methods of one's staff. Guilt will depend on access to the information in question. If, on checking the books, a reasonably astute businessman would have discovered the illegal expenditure in question – on the basis perhaps of the red flags to which reference was made above[557] –, then this knowledge can also be attributed to the undertaking in question; a failure to take corrective action in the face of such knowledge then presumes acceptance of the corrupt behaviour. If, on the other hand, the management failed to get to know of the situation, simply because it did not carry out any checks, this displays wilful ignorance and can also go to showing the necessary intention.

[554] Jescheck and Weigend 1996, 297 et seq. [555] Art. 18(2) COE 1999a.
[556] This is not the same as 'wilful neglect': cf. Gordon 2000, 269 (para. 7.34).
[557] See II.6.2. above.

Someone commits a crime of intent when they act intentionally with respect to *all* the factors or elements making up the offence. If the accused erred as to one of these elements, it cannot be said that the act was fully willed by him when he made his promise or offered his gift. How state Parties precisely resolve this dogmatic issue – of error as to the elements of the offence – is a matter for them, in the light of the principles of their criminal justice systems. The Convention does not dictate a particular approach; it rather seeks to respect the established general rules of national criminal law. A further example can be found here of functional equivalence in action.

It is not permitted to limit the commission of the offence to intent with knowledge: this would leave too much room for abuse, as lack of knowledge is not easily disproved.

2. Horizontal comparison

Intention is the mental element or *mens rea* demanded by most legal orders in the absence of an explicit *mens rea* requirement for the offence in question. In Civil Law countries, intention is frequently defined by reference to both of the elements we discussed above, namely knowledge and volition. To act *knowingly*, the offender must have been aware that he was committing bribery himself or through another person, as the case may be; he must at least have reckoned with it. To act *willingly*, the offender must have resolved to commit the crime, or have reckoned with the occurrence of corruption under his management. A person has intention when he seriously believes it possible to fulfil the objective elements of the offence and acts accordingly to carry them out. He does not, however, have to know that what he is doing is actually criminal. This concept is defined partly in legislative texts or *Travaux Préparatoires*, partly by case law or academic writings. The elements of knowledge and consent must apply to all the objective elements of the offence.

The Australian Criminal Code[558] derives from a quite different legal culture, yet it is similar in several respects to the Civil Law tradition. It also starts from the proposition that the offender 'means to engage in that conduct' and that he is aware of the crucial facts ('he/she believes [a circumstance]...exists or will exist) and that he wills the outcome or at least reckons with it (he/she [wishes] to bring [a result] about or is aware that it will occur in the ordinary course of events').[559]

[558] See II.6.1.2. above

[559] These are the quotations contained in AU-Ph1, 3.

Otherwise, the Common Law countries lack such a formal definition of intention. The statute law of the United Kingdom, for example, fails to include any clear indication of the level of knowledge required by the offender of the relevant facts for him to intend to bribe. There is only the rather vague term 'corruptly',[560] to limit the mental element required for the commission of the offence to intention. The offender will act corruptly by making an offer by which he intends to influence the recipient, regardless of how the public official would have acted in the absence of this offer.[561] Proof of such influence will depend on the 'nature and the circumstances'[562] of the offer, in particular how high it is. English Common Law also focuses on the intention of the offender to influence the foreign public official to act 'contrary to the known rules of honesty and integrity'.[563]

> In the UK's Corruption Bill, presented to Parliament in 2003, a legislative definition of 'corruptly' was written into the legislation, based on the one hand on the volition of the offender, on his will to influence the recipient to perform a certain act and presuming on the other hand belief on his part that the latter was in fact influenced.[564] Framing the concept in this way would meet the Convention standard.[565]

Under New Zealand law, the domestic offence of bribery requires that a person is punished for bribery committed 'corruptly'; this also applies to transnational bribery. The Common Law understanding of this concept is that the offender must have acted in awareness that he was doing wrong (committing a crime): 'corruptly implies that the actor is aware that the act is improper'.[566] What is required is 'deliberately knowing that the act is one which the law forbids'.[567] The risk of this formulation of intention is that it may – contrary to Official Commentary 7 – leave the way open to excuse the offender on the ground that corrupt practices are customary in the country concerned or are tolerated by the local authorities. That possibility should be ruled out in practice. This consideration led to revision of Australian criminal law: the legislator decided to drop the term 'corruptly' and also removed the defence of 'custom'.

Using the term 'corruptly' would be reasonable if it were designed to exclude those cases where the offender had been duped or deceived into believing that the payment he was making was in fact required under the law of the foreign state. It would be difficult to maintain credibility on this point where high sums are concerned.

[560] S. 1(1) Prevention of Corruption Act 1906. [561] US-Ph1, 2.
[562] UK-Ph1, 4. [563] UK-Ph1, 4.
[564] Ss. 5(1)(a) und (b) Corruption Bill (drafted, presented to Parliament in 2003).
[565] Cf. the evidence of Pieth given to the Joint Committee on The Draft Corruption Bill, June 2, 2003: answer to Question 348.
[566] NZ-Ph1, 33. [567] NZ-Ph1, 4.

The FCPA describes the intention of the individual offender in an equally vague fashion.[568] The specially formulated offence of indirect bribery, however, demands a more exacting definition, and this has to some extent been provided. The legislation refers to the offender acting 'while knowing that...will be offered, given or promised'.[569] *Knowing* in this context means not only actual knowledge – 'if such person is aware'[570] – but also a strong conviction: 'if such person has a firm belief'.[571] A higher level of awareness is obviously needed than is required for simply negligence, but 'deliberate disregard or wilful blindness'[572] are encompassed by the definition. A person thus also has knowledge if he simply ignores the facts revealed by the illegal methods of his intermediary.

IV. Extension of criminal responsibility

1. Inclusion of transnational bribery in the existing criminal justice system

The state Parties have the task of extending their existing national criminal law on bribery to include the transnational variant. They are not thereby obliged to give it any special status. First, as we have seen,[573] all valid grounds of defence to or exception from criminal liability may be used. Second, the Convention leaves it to national law to decide how criminal responsibility is extended beyond the simple offence as such.

All legal systems probably extend responsibility, in the first instance, to persons beyond the immediate offender who does everything himself to:

- the person who participates as an accomplice in the offence;[574]
- the person who merely attempts to commit the crime;[575]
- the person who enters into a conspiracy with others to commit the crime.[576]

There may be other ways of extending criminal responsibility but it is these three which are developed by the Convention, in Article 1(2): 'complicity in...an act of bribery of a foreign public official shall be a criminal offence. Attempt and conspiracy to bribe a foreign public

[568] 15 U.S.C. §§ 78dd-1(a), 78dd-1(b), 78dd-1(c) FCPA 1977.
[569] 15 U.S.C. §§ 78dd-1(a)(3), 78dd-2(a)(3), 78dd-3(a)(3) FCPA 1977.
[570] 15 U.S.C. §§ 78dd-1(f)(2)(A)(i), 78dd-2(h)(2)(A)(i), 78dd-3(h)(2)(A)(i) FCPA 1977.
[571] 15 U.S.C. §§ 78dd-1(f)(2)(A)(ii), 78dd-2(h)(2)(A)(ii), 78dd-3(h)(2)(A)(ii) FCPA 1977.
[572] Cf. US-Ph1, 5 discussing 15 U.S.C. §§ 78dd-1(f)(2)(B), 78dd-2(h)(2)(Bi) and 78dd-3(h)(2)(B) FCPA 1977; compare II.6.2. above.
[573] See II.2.5.2. above. [574] See II.2. below. [575] See II.3. below. [576] See II.4. below.

official shall be criminal offences to the same extent as attempt and conspiracy to bribe a public official of that Party'. The concepts of national law should be applied to transnational bribery as they would to the equivalent domestic offence; they should not be construed or evaluated differently: 'the offences set out in paragraph 2 are understood in terms of their normal content in national legal systems' (Official Commentary 11).

2. Complicity

2.1. Convention legal framework

According to Article 1(2), every form of 'complicity' in bribery must be punished, 'including

- incitement;
- aiding and abetting; or
- authorisation'.

The Convention does not, however, determine, at the international level, exactly what type of conduct falls under these options relating to complicity. Again, the evaluation is left to the national systems of criminal justice themselves. Official Commentary 11 therefore accepts the possibility that a form of complicity which is frustrated, i.e. leads to nothing, will not incur a criminal penalty: '[a]ccordingly, if authorisation, incitement, or one of the other listed acts, which does not lead to further action, is not itself punishable under a Party's legal system, then the Party would not be required to make it punishable with respect to bribery of a foreign public official'. If, according to one of its general rules, a state does not punish an offender whose contribution to the crime is not in fact used, then in a bribery case it will not be required to punish the accomplice who made the bribe money available, if that money is not put to use.

In more complex bribery cases, one will have a complicity scenario of a different nature: the persons who concluded the bribery deal or transaction will not be the same as those who seek to implement it. The true contracting party – the concern, which would like to obtain the contract – will transfer as a bribe to the officials of the foreign government the amount agreed by their intermediary. The transfer may also be effected indirectly, again via the agent. For such a scenario, the Convention has developed the following rules or principles governing the complicity and criminal responsibility of those involved.

In the first instance, we have the position of the agent. He makes a promise, which is itself unlawful. Here, the agent is criminally responsible for that promise, even if it is not accepted and regardless of any profit or other business advantage which may accrue to his or her undertaking (the one pulling the strings). It is also not relevant to the agent's guilt, in these circumstances, whether the undertaking demanded, or merely favoured or approved the promise, or even whether it knew at all about it.

The management of the concern will be criminally liable for their agent's illegal deal. Their action will come under the rubric of indirect bribery 'through intermediaries', in so far as they were aware of the agent's illegal activity and approved it. It may, however, be difficult here for the prosecution to prove intention.[577] In addition, another act of bribery is committed where the bribe that has been negotiated is finally paid out. The commission of the offence this time consists in the actual transfer of the advantage (money, gift, etc.), with intention being presumed.

Where an agent is used, we can therefore see that both parties are offenders, the concern and the agent alike, because they both fulfil the terms of Article 1. They will commit the crime of bribery as accomplices, in the narrow sense of the word, when the agent is used explicitly as the bribery intermediary, and as independent actors when the arrangements between the principal and the agent are less concrete in nature, in other words where there was no co-ordinated implementation of a common plan. According to this model, there is no place for application of the rules concerning incitement or assistance.

The role of the banks in bribery transactions is another matter. Banks may function as a conduit for bribe monies, arranging for the transfer in question, on the instructions of their customer who is in this case acting illegally. They perform a technical role in making the practical arrangements. Seen objectively, they therefore do play a part in the whole scheme of bribery. But it will be difficult to prove the necessary intention. Their participation will in general be unwitting and innocent, but it may be possible to infer an intention on the basis of failures relating to banking supervision. The international norms in question relating to this matter, and binding on the bank, would have to be studied – be they of a self-regulatory or state-inspired nature.[578] If it can be demonstrated that the bank in question respected these norms, by taking all the required measures to check the legality of large transactions, in particular, it will hardly be

[577] See II.6.1.2. and III.1. above.

[578] Regarding the due diligence rules of banks cf. in particular Wolfsberg 2000, updated in 2002.

possible to assume knowledge and from that knowledge to infer intention to support the bribery carried out by its customer. On the other hand, a sufficiently serious lack of care could lead to an assumption of criminal responsibility on the basis of wilful blindness.

2.2. Horizontal comparison

In bribery cases, complicity questions are posed mainly in the context of indirect bribery. State Parties may therefore also seek to resolve them under that heading.

> In Norway, the role of the accessory is also defined within the crime of bribery itself, and this role is given equivalent weighting to other manifestations of offending.[579]

Most Civil Law countries deal with questions of participation in the offence in the general parts of their Criminal Codes which are applicable to all crimes. They usually distinguish between the following types of participation: perpetration itself, which can be direct or indirect, incitement, and other forms of assistance. This is the approach taken in German-speaking jurisdictions (Austria,[580] Germany,[581] and Switzerland[582]), in Latin America and in Japan and Korea. Other European countries following this line are Bulgaria,[583] Finland,[584] Hungary,[585] Iceland,[586] the Netherlands,[587] Poland[588] (here there are some slight differences), Portugal,[589] Slovakia,[590] and Spain.[591]

> Regarding the Netherlands, incitement is applicable to all crimes, whereas the role of accessory is applicable only with regard to serious crimes. This distinction does not, however, matter for our purposes as bribery is always regarded as serious.

The application of Italian law[592] achieves the same result, though its scheme follows suit with Denmark[593] by not making an explicit distinction between the types of complicity but punishing them all equally. Belgium follows a somewhat different line: contributions which help cause the crime or are even essential for its commission[594] – such as the instruction to bribe in the first place or the grant of a loan for this purpose – are distinguished from lesser

[579] S. 276a Norwegian Criminal Code. [580] Ss. 12, 13, 14 Austrian Criminal Code.
[581] Ss. 25, 26, 27 German Criminal Code. [582] Arts. 24 und 25 Swiss Criminal Code.
[583] Arts. 20, 21, 22 Bulgarian Criminal Code. [584] Ch. 5 Finnish Criminal Code.
[585] S. 21 Hungarian Criminal Code. [586] S. 22 Icelandic Criminal Code.
[587] Arts. 47.1 and 48 Dutch Criminal Code. [588] Arts. 18.1, 18.2, 18.3 Polish Criminal Code.
[589] Art. 26 Portuguese Criminal Code. [590] Ss. 9(2) and 10(1) Slovak Criminal Code.
[591] Art. 27 Spanish Criminal Code. [592] Art. 110 Italian Criminal Code.
[593] S. 23 Danish Criminal Code. [594] Art. 66 Belgian Criminal Code.

forms of participation in the offence, which are more 'facilitative' in nature, for example, advice or providing information on contacts, etc.[595]

Australia too has such a rule in its Criminal Code.[596] In the United Kingdom, there is also an established Common Law scheme relating to the guilt of accessories, in the form of aiding and abetting (sometimes also referred to as 'acting in concert', or in Scotland as 'art and part' guilt).[597] The principles of English legislation are still to be found in the Accessories and Abettors Act 1861. According to this legislation, those assisting the principal in whatever capacity in his commission of the crime in question will be prosecuted with equal vigour: section 8 of the legislation refers to 'aid, abet, counsel, procure, or incite'.

All these systems include the forms of participation encompassed by Article 1 of the Convention. The person who 'directs' the bribery, even if not by his own hand, is guilty, as is the person who instigates it, whoever assists in the transaction, whether by advice, information, joint planning or organisational support or by paving the way for negotiations or by providing the finances. For this reason, participation in a mere conspiracy to bribe also represents participation in the crime itself, even if only one member of the conspiracy in fact does the bribing – this is because, no matter whether a frustrated conspiracy is punishable or not, the participation in the deal or bribery agreement assists the commission of the later act of bribery.

> The sanctions issue is ultimately dealt with in a comparable way by the state Parties, though they may approach it differently. In German-speaking jurisdictions, Nordic countries, central and Eastern European states and in France and Italy, the full sanctions tariff is applied, in principle, to all forms of complicity; low-level manifestations may, however, end up attracting a lower sentence and higher penalties have been known for those playing the leading part in the crime. Argentina,[598] the Benelux countries, Korea[599] and Spain,[600] on the other hand, already make this abstract distinction in their legislation, with the full penalty being applicable only to the main forms of co-operation and a lower sanction attaching to those playing the role of facilitators.[601]

Official Commentary 11 indicates that the Convention accepts those systems which do not punish an act of participation 'which does not lead to further action'. Such systems include Austria, Germany, Switzerland, and the Benelux countries. Here, the principle is that where the assistance serves no final purpose, because the main actor does not even attempt the crime,

[595] Art. 67 Belgian Criminal Code. [596] S. 11.1(1) Australian Criminal Code.
[597] Gordon 2000, 158 et seq. [598] Arts. 45, 46 Argentine Criminal Code.
[599] Arts. 31(1), 32 Korean Criminal Code. [600] Arts. 27, 63 Spanish Criminal Code.
[601] See ch. on Article 3 below.

no criminal responsibility should attach to that 'helper' or abettor. Transferring this principle to a case of bribery, we can conclude that a lender who finances another's intended bribery will not be criminally liable, if the borrower uses the loan for a proper purpose and does not even attempt to offer it to the public official as a bribe. Such an approach is not at all inconsistent with Article 1 of the Convention.

3. Attempt

3.1. Assimilation of rules to transnational bribery

Criminal responsibility for transnational bribery should begin at the same point of commission of the offence as it does for domestic bribery. As Article 1(2) of the Convention puts it: '[a]ttempt...to bribe a foreign public official shall be [a] criminal offence...to the same extent as attempt...to bribe a public official of that Party'. So when the attempt to commit domestic bribery is punished, the same rule should apply to the attempt to bribe a foreign public official.

Equally, if a frustrated attempt, which does not cause any damage, is not punishable under the legal order of one of the state Parties, the unsuccessful attempt to bribe a foreign public official may escape punishment also. This is expressed by Official Commentary 11: '[a]ccordingly, if...one of the...listed acts [including attempt], which does not lead to further action, is not itself punishable under a Party's legal system, then the Party would not be required to make it punishable with respect to bribery of a foreign public official'. There may also be systems which do not impose punishment at all for criminal attempts: this approach too is respected by the Convention.

Given the approach of the Convention to the commission of bribery it is, however, rather difficult to envisage many cases of attempted bribery, as opposed to the completed act. As we have seen,[602] a mere offer to bribe is sufficient to complete the offence, even before any harmful events have ensued. The maker of the offer faces punishment for the completed offence, even if the chosen foreign public official has not registered its existence, for example, because the written offer went missing in the post or because an agent failed to pass it on – or rejected it.[603] There is certainly no requirement that the desired official act should be carried out. What alone is decisive is the objective of the briber in making his offer, not that it either

[602] See II.5.3. above. [603] Compare FR-Ph1, 5, 11; PL-Ph1, 8.

be accepted or received: 'neither a completed payment nor a successful result is a requirement'.[604] Liability in respect of the full offence may not therefore be made dependent upon the actual occurrence of the intended bribe or upon the damage it represents. Such liability must apply to the 'danger' represented by the offer itself, i.e. to the 'threat' of harm.

It can be seen that the room left by the Convention for the non-punishability of non-threatening attempts is really rather small. Some cases are conceivable: for example, a test transfer of bribe money to a special account or the making available of funds for the bribe may be classified as attempts.

The withdrawal from execution of an offence such as bribery may result in mitigation of sentence or in the person escaping punishment entirely, in some states.[605] These rules, in their different forms, are consistent with the Convention. For example, a letter which has already been posted can be retrieved or a bank transfer cancelled, but as soon as the recipient has become aware of an offer, the offence is complete. If the maker of the offer only takes it back at this stage, there can be no effective legal withdrawal, though in some state Parties he may be able to invoke the law relating to 'effective repentance'.[606]

3.2. Horizontal comparison

3.2.1. Distinction between attempts and mere preparatory acts

State Parties to the Convention do not punish mere preparatory acts; they are not (yet) classified as attempts to commit the crime of transnational bribery. Their definitions of attempt focus on the threat of damage which such actions represent. To put it in simplified fashion, the attempt is punishable because it leads to damage, without the offender having to pass any further thresholds. Germanic legal systems apply the dogma that the phase of attempt commences with the act which immediately precedes the execution of the full offence. This is the approach taken by Germany,[607] Switzerland, and Slovakia, but also France.[608] The approach of the Criminal Attempts Act 1981, which applies to England and Wales, is less abstract, describing an attempt simply as something 'more than merely preparatory'.[609]

[604] US-Ph1, 9.

[605] For example, Art. 43 Argentine Criminal Code; s. 24 German Criminal Code, etc.

[606] See II.5.4.4. above. [607] S. 22 German Criminal Code.

[608] 'Manifestée par un commencement d'exécution': Art. 121(3) French Criminal Code.

[609] S. 1 Criminal Attempts Act 1981.

3.2.2. Distinction between attempts and completion of the crime

Those countries which accept bribery as occurring independently of the promise or offer reaching the public official are in full conformity with the Convention's perspective of the very early occurrence of the full offence. A mere attempt to commit bribery is not envisaged by the FCPA, nor by Belgian, Finnish, French, Hungarian, or Spanish law, given the fact that they all regard the full offence as having been committed when someone seeks to induce a public servant.[610] In Italy too, the briber has completed the offence when he has done all in his power to communicate an offer, even when his communication has failed to reach the intended recipient.

> According to Italian case law, the crime can in some circumstances be completed by a person even before he targets a *specific* public official and before he fixes the amount of the bribe, or even before he has decided on the precise nature of his demands.[611]

Given their very broad approach to completion of the offence in relation even to unsuccessful offers or promises, the Swedish solution of having no law of attempted bribery is perfectly acceptable. The law of attempt applies there only with regard to certain specific crimes.[612] And it should be noted in any case that the penalty for the full crime is only available as maximum sanction for attempts. The WGB also tolerates the approach of Japan[613] and Korea[614] to limit their law of criminal attempts to special crimes which do not include the offence of bribery.

Greater scope for the law of attempt is allowed by the legal systems of Argentina, Bulgaria, Denmark, Germany, Mexico, Poland, and Switzerland. Correctly, all these systems punish as the full offence an offer which was duly made by the briber but rejected by the public official. But there is only an attempt to bribe where the offer has not yet been registered by the official.

> According to the more refined approach of Argentine law,[615] the act is already completed where an offer has been delivered to the official but he has not registered its arrival, i.e. he is not yet aware of it. It is on the other hand only an attempt to bribe when the offer has been stopped or blocked on its way to the official, for example, an e-mail which does not get through.
>
> Luxembourg has a very particular approach here, which says that the offer to bribe the official will remain as an attempt as long as the official has not yet accepted or rejected it. During this period, the maker of the offer should be able to withdraw it, without fear of penalty. The approach of the Convention is, however, stricter: bribery is completed before the official's reaction.[616]

[610] E.g. FI-Ph1, 5; HU-Ph1, 7. [611] IT-Ph1, 6. [612] Ch. 23(1) Swedish Criminal Code.
[613] Art. 60 Japanese Criminal Code. [614] Art. 29 Korean Criminal Code. [615] AR-Ph1, 7.
[616] The stance of Luxembourg was not, however, further criticised by the WGB: cf. LU-Ph1, 11.

As we have seen, UK law does not offer much in the way of abstract formulation of attempt, noting only that it amounts to more than preparation.[617]

There is little in the way of case law concerning the transition between the attempt and the completed crime. The issue is probably not so very important, because in most countries the same punishment is proposed for both: this is the case in Australia,[618] Austria,[619] Denmark,[620] Germany,[621] Iceland,[622] and Poland,[623] for example, even where the attempt does not have any damaging effects. Moreover, the Convention respects the choices of the state Parties in this matter. It therefore accepts the position of other states which may choose lower sanctions for attempts, either as a general rule or as an option. Nor does the Convention put into question the rule applying, inter alia, in Austria and Germany, that attempts which have no prospect of success ('impossible attempts') will not be punished.

4. Conspiracy

4.1. Assimilation of conspiracy to the international dimension

The preparation of a criminal act is in general not punishable except where the preparations themselves constitute a particular danger. A conspiracy with others to commit a crime is reckoned to be considerably more dangerous than an individual offender acting alone. Many international Conventions now exist which call for criminal law measures to be taken against the dangers emanating from organised groups. The Convention does not take a position on this issue. The state Parties are free to decide whether they should criminalise the common planning of a bribery offence, for example, where a group of conspirators decide to set up a fictitious company.

What the Convention aims at in Article 1(2), as in other Articles, is assimilation of the treatment of transnational bribery with domestic bribery. If conspiracy to bribe is prosecuted in the domestic context, the same should happen in relation to its transnational manifestation: 'conspiracy to bribe a foreign public official shall be criminal offence. . .to the same extent as. . .conspiracy to bribe a public official of that Party'.

[617] Cf. s. 1 Criminal Attempts Act 1981, which applies to England and Wales.
[618] S. 11.1(1) Australian Criminal Code. [619] S. 15 Austrian Criminal Code.
[620] S. 21(2) Danish Criminal Code. [621] S. 23 German Criminal code.
[622] S. 20 Icelandic Criminal Code. [623] PL-Ph1, 8.

4.2. Horizontal comparison

In most states, the crime of conspiracy or of participation in a criminal organisation is applied only to the most serious offences, in particular to crimes of violence and crimes against the state. This is the position broadly adopted by the following countries: Austria, France, Germany, Japan, Korea, Luxembourg, Spain, Slovakia, Sweden, and Switzerland. They all punish conspiracy to commit specified serious offences, excluding bribery. French law, for example, punishes those who conspire to commit crimes which would undermine the state or which are aimed against the national territory.[624] In Germany, conspiracy is limited to crimes defined as *Verbrechen* (serious criminal offences): bribery does not fall into this category, because the minimum sentence for the offence is less than one year.[625]

Equally, these states do not punish conspiracy to commit transnational bribery. The existence of a common criminal plan may serve, however, to increase the sentence in some cases.[626] The behaviour in question may also be sufficient to constitute the formation of an illegal criminal organisation, at least in those states which do not strictly limit such cases to the most serious (violent) crimes.[627] Mexico is about to introduce a more repressive law on bribery which will include an offence of conspiracy.[628]

In Common Law countries, anti-bribery legislation clearly targets the conspiracy to bribe. The law bites at the earliest stage of the process of common planning. In the United States, conspirators face the full force of the FCPA. A separate crime of conspiracy applies in England and Wales and in Scotland, with the crime consisting in the agreement to effect any criminal purpose (i.e. to commit any Common Law or statutory offence).[629] The crime of conspiracy to commit foreign bribery is, however, committed only when 'the agreement is carried out in accordance with their [the conspiring parties'] intention'.[630] Australia follows a similar line: conspiracy to commit bribery is punishable in the same way as the crime itself.[631]

In Argentina, Belgium, Italy, the Netherlands, Poland, and most of the Nordic countries, it is, on the other hand, only those forms of conspiracy

[624] Art. 412–2 French Criminal Code. [625] Art. 30(2), s. 12 German Criminal Code.
[626] Cf., for example, Art. 335(3) German Criminal Code.
[627] Cf., for example, Art. 129 Dutch Criminal Code; 260ter Swiss Criminal Code.
[628] Arts. 12bis and 222ter Mexican Federal Criminal Code in its draft version: cf. MX-Ph2, 12.
[629] Cf. for England and Wales: s. 1(1) Criminal Law Act 1977. As Gordon 2000, 228 points out: '[t]he crime consists in the agreement though in most cases overt acts done in pursuance of the offence are available to prove the crime' (para. 6.57).
[630] S. 1(1) Criminal Law Act 1977. [631] S. 11.5(1) Australian Criminal Code.

which lead to the creation of a criminal organisation which are punishable; conspiracy as such is not.

References

For documentation see the consolidated bibliography at the end of this book.

Balmelli, M. (1996), *Die Bestechungstatbestände des schweizerischen Strafgesetzbuches*, Bern.

Bindschedler, R. L. (1995), 'International Organisations, General Aspects' in R. Bernhardt (ed.), *Encyclopedia of Public International Law*, Vol. **2**, Amsterdam, 1289.

Brown, H. L. (1999), 'Parent-Subsidiary Liability under the Foreign Corrupt Practices Act' in American Bar Association (ed.), *The Foreign Corrupt Practices Act: How to Comply under the New Amendments and the OECD Convention*, Chicago, F 1-51.

Brownlie, I. (2003), *Principles of Public International Law*, 6th edn, Oxford.

Cadwalader, Wickersham and Taft (2005), FCPA Newsletter, March, June and July edns (available at: http://www.cadwalder.com).

Cramer, P. (2001), commentary of § 331 in A. Schönke and H. Schröder (Hrsg.), *Strafgesetzbuch*, 26th edn, Munich, 2570.

Dahm, G., J. Delbrück, and R. Wolfrum (1989), *Völkerrecht*, 2nd edn, Berlin, New York.

Davies, M. N. (2003), 'The Role of Agents and Sales Representatives' in F. Vincke and F. Heimann (eds.), *Fighting Corruption*, Paris, 57.

Deming, St. H. (2005), *The Foreign Corrupt Practices Act and the New International Norms*, Chicago.

Doehring, K. (2004), *Völkerrecht*, 2nd edn, Heidelberg.

Epping, V. (2004), 'Völkerrechtssubjekte' in K. Ipsen, *Völkerrecht*, 4th edn, München, 55.

Frowein, J. A. (1968), *Das de facto Regime im Völkerrecht*, Köln, Berlin.

Gareis, R. J. (1999), 'The 1998 Amendments to the US Foreign Corrupt Practices Act: A Comparative and Pragmatic Analysis of, and with, the OECD Convention Combating Bribery of Foreign Officials', *International Trade Corruption Monitor (ITCM)*, A-1013.

Gordon, G. (2000), *The Criminal Law of Scotland*, 3rd edn, Edinburgh.

Hailbronner, K. (2004), 'Der Staat und der Einzelne als Völkerrechtssubjekte' in W. Vitzthum (ed.), *Völkerrecht*, 3rd edn, Berlin, New York, 149.

Heimann, F. and C. Mohn (1999), 'Die Rolle der Privatwirtschaft bei der Bekämpfung der Korruption' in M. Pieth and P. Eigen (Hrsg.), *Korruption im internationalen Geschäftsverkehr: Bestandesaufnahme, Bekämpfung, Prävention*, Neuwied, Kriftel, Basel, Frankfurt a. M., 531.

Jescheck, H. H. and T. Weigend (1996), *Lehrbuch des Strafrechts: Allgemeiner Teil*, 5th edn, Berlin.

Low, L. A. (2003) [cited Low 2003a], 'The Global Legal Framework: The OECD, OAS and Council of Europe Antibribery Conventions: New International Standards and National Anti-Corruption Laws: Challenges for Effective Implementation and Enforcement' (unpublished paper, prepared for a Conference in Paris, April 2003).

Low, L. A. (2005), 'Enforcement of the FCPA in the United States: Trends and the Effects of International Standards' (presentation at the 3rd Annual Conference of the International Bar Association, International Chamber of Commerce, and Organization for Economic Co-operation and Development, *The Awakening Giant of Anti-Corruption Enforcement* in Paris, 4–6 May 2005).

Miller, S. K. (1998), 'Piercing the Corporate Veil Among Affiliated Companies in the European Community and in the U.S.: A Comparative Analysis of U.S., German, and U.K. Veil-Piercing Approaches', *American Business Law Journal* 36, 73.

Pieth, M. (1999) [cited Pieth 1999a], 'Die Strafbarkeit der aktiven Bestechung ausländischer Beamter' in M. Pieth and P. Eigen (Hrsg.), *Korruption im internationalen Geschäftsverkehr: Bestandesaufnahme, Bekämpfung, Prävention*, Neuwied, Kriftel, Basel, Frankfurt a. M., 341.

Pieth, M. (1999) [cited Pieth 1999b], 'International Efforts to Combat Corruption' in American Bar Association (ed.), *The Foreign Corrupt Practices Act: How to Comply under the New Amendments and the OECD Convention*, Chicago, E-1.

Pieth, M. (1999) [cited Pieth 1999c], 'International Efforts to Combat Corruption', *International Trade Corruption Monitor (ITCM)*, A-1038.

Sacerdoti, G. (2000), 'To Bribe or not to Bribe?' in OECD (ed.), *No Longer Business as Usual*, Paris, 29.

Seidl-Hohenveldern, I. and W. Hummer (2004), 'Die Staaten' in H. Neuhold, W. Hummer, and Ch. Schreuer (Hrsg.), *Österreichisches Handbuch des Völkerrechts*, Vol. **1**, 4th edn, Wien, 135.

Warbrick, C. (2003), 'States and Recognition in International Law' in M. D. Evans (ed.), *International Law*, Oxford, 205.

Weinstein, M. J. and C. A. Trambley (2003), 'Obtaining or Retaining Business under the Foreign Corrupt Practices Act: The Implication of U.S. v. Kay and SEC v. Maltson' (presentation at the 2nd Annual Conference of the International Bar Association, International Chamber of Commerce, and Organization for Economic Co-operation and Development, *The Awakening Giant of Anti-Corruption Enforcement* in Paris, 24–25 April 2003).

Article 2. The Responsibility of Legal Persons

MARK PIETH

Article 2 – Responsibility of Legal Persons

Each Party shall take such measures as may be necessary, in accordance with its legal principles, to establish the liability of legal persons for the bribery of a foreign public official.

Article 3 – Sanctions

1. The bribery of a foreign public official shall be punishable by effective, proportionate, and dissuasive criminal penalties. The range of penalties shall be comparable to that applicable to the bribery of the Party's own public officials and shall, in the case of natural persons, include deprivation of liberty sufficient to enable effective mutual legal assistance and extradition.

2. In the event that, under the legal system of a Party, criminal responsibility is not applicable to legal persons, that Party shall ensure that legal persons shall be subject to effective, proportionate and dissuasive non-criminal sanctions, including monetary sanctions, for bribery of foreign public officials.

3. Each Party shall take such measures as may be necessary to provide that the bribe and the proceeds of the bribery of a foreign public official, or property the value of which corresponds to that of such proceeds, are subject to seizure and confiscation or that monetary sanctions of comparable effect are applicable.

4. Each Party shall consider the imposition of additional civil or administrative sanctions upon a person subject to sanctions for the bribery of a foreign public official.

Official Commentaries

Article 2 – Responsibility of Legal Persons

20. In the event that, under the legal system of a Party, criminal responsibility is not applicable to legal persons, that Party shall not be required to establish such criminal responsibility.

Article 3 – Sanctions

Re paragraph 4:

24. Among the civil or administrative sanctions, other than non-criminal fines, which might be imposed upon legal persons for an act of bribery of a foreign public official are: exclusion from entitlement to public benefits or aid; temporary or permanent disqualification from participation in public procurement or from the practice of other commercial activities; placing under judicial supervision; and a judicial winding-up order.

Chapter contents

I. The significance of corporate liability in combating bribery

Considering that criminal law traditionally focuses on personal guilt, we can suppose that a criminalisation convention would concentrate in the first place on the conditions of *individual* responsibility. However, the *Travaux Préparatoires* to the Convention make clear that the topic of corporate liability was addressed from the very beginning of the drafting process, recognising the fact that corporate responsibility is crucially important in the context of combating transnational commercial bribery.[1]

Large multinational corporate structures, in particular, have become increasingly decentralised. In practice, their activities involve complicated decision-making procedures and it is frequently difficult, if not impossible, to find an individual responsible for a decision to bribe.[2] It may happen that an individual employee resorts to illegal practices in order to boost his personal sales performance; alternatively the occasional rogue employees will be caught colluding with criminal officials to defraud company and state authority alike.[3] It is, however, overall not uncommon for companies to become involved in bribery quite deliberately, and in a premeditated fashion. On the other hand, the instances in which a clear management decision to bribe will be on record are bound to be very rare and these will probably not be the serious cases envisioned by the OECD Convention. Typically, managers will leave it to front-line operators to take the actual decisions. They might, however, tolerate corrupt behaviour more or less

[1] OECD 1999, F-1031. [2] DE-Ph2, 31; BG-Ph2, 26 et seq.
[3] Cf. the case *U.S.* v. *Steindler*, 3 FCPA Rep. 699.131 (S.D. Ohio 1994).

implicitly, supply the necessary means, or at least create the corporate climate that condones such illegal behaviour. Frequently euphemisms like 'business as usual'[4] are used in-house to describe what may be considered inevitable according to corporate culture. Under these circumstances the fairness of prosecuting individual low-level decision-makers alone, rendering them exclusively responsible, is highly questionable.[5]

Beyond individual wrongdoing, it is exactly this devious corporate culture that needs to be tackled, if the Convention wants to change attitudes in its centre of gravity, if, that is, it really wants to reduce 'grand corruption'[6] or the 'supply side' of corporate bribery.[7] It is therefore no coincidence that most modern international instruments against bribery include provisions on corporate liability.[8] The OECD text can in fact be seen as a forerunner of a worldwide harmonisation effort.[9]

Academics, frequently referring to the US experience, claim that corporate liability has a particularly high deterrent effect, since it raises legal and 'reputational' risks for corporations as such.[10] Whereas 'general deterrence' has remained a heavily disputed theory when referring to the effects of criminalisation on individuals, it seems that the *homo oeconomicus*, to whom the liberal thinkers of enlightenment (Beccaria, Smith, Bentham) alluded, is a far more realistic perspective in the corporate world. The simplicity of shareholder value concepts corroborates the claims of the 'law and economics' scholars.[11]

In the materials developed by the OECD's Working Group on Bribery (WGB) additional technical reasons were given for insisting on corporate liability, especially in relation to reluctant state Parties: in the Phase 2 evaluation of Bulgaria, for example, examiners held that 'corporate entities' were 'frequent vehicles for the payment of bribes', and went on to say that 'the use of elaborate financial structures and accounting techniques to conceal the nature of transactions is commonplace'.[12] On the closely related issue of confiscation – another key instrument to raise the stake in cases of bribery – the WGB has repeatedly warned that the absence of liability

[4] Cf. the OECD publication with this title: OECD 2000a.
[5] DE-Ph2, 31; on individual responsibility in relation to corporate responsibility: cf. Wells 2001, 160 et seq.
[6] Moody-Stuart 1997.
[7] Low 2003a, 13; Pieth 2000a, 52; Sacerdoti 2003, 71 et seq.
[8] Cf. Arts. 2 and 3(2) OECD 1997b; Arts. 18 and 19 COE 1999a; Arts. 3 and 4 EU 1997b; Art. 26 UN 2003.
[9] Möhrenschlager 1999, 102; Tarullo 2004, 665 et seq.
[10] Coffee 1999, 28 et seq.
[11] Posner 1994; Arlen and Kraakman 1997, 687 et seq.; Cohen 1996, 399 et seq.
[12] BG-Ph2, 26.

of legal persons severely undermines the ability to confiscate in cases of foreign bribery.[13]

Whereas the regional anti-corruption instruments deal with more or less related legal systems, the OECD Convention has to span a far wider universe. Its concepts apply to Common Law, Civil Law, Eastern European and Far Eastern legal systems and must also be embraced by possible newcomers like China, India, Russia, and South Africa. Since corporate liability is a matter where concepts diverge considerably across the world, and since it is a legal construct very much in development,[14] the OECD negotiators opted for a very broad common denominator indeed. Above all, the OECD refuses to become involved in the debate on criminal versus non-criminal corporate liability: the Convention deliberately allows both approaches, even if the international trend points towards criminal responsibility.[15] The bottom line is, however, defined in Article 3(1) and (2): whatever kind of sanctions are imposed, they must be 'effective, proportionate, and dissuasive'. The Convention merely adds two elements: first, non-criminal as well as criminal sanctions have to include as a minimum 'monetary sanctions'; second, Article 3(4) requests state Parties to consider the imposition of additional civil or administrative sanctions upon a person, even where the Party has chosen criminal liability for companies (the solution also chosen by the European Union (EU), whereas the Council of Europe (COE) Convention is silent on this issue).

It should already be evident that the Convention's approach is rather 'basic' and that in order to define 'functional equivalence'[16] in this area, further 'horizontal analyses' will be necessary.[17]

In the following discussion of Article 2 the most frequent models of corporate liability will be outlined (part II.); then the requirements of the Convention will be discussed in detail, with reference also to other international treaties (part III.), and certain conclusions will be drawn in part IV.

II. The variety of models available

Academics proffer several concepts to describe the various approaches to corporate liability. The following overview will outline the most common

[13] BG-Ph2, 27; CH-Ph1, 23. [14] Low 2003a, 44.

[15] Art. 3(2); Official Commentary 20; whereas more recent international instruments, especially the Revised 40 Recommendations of FATF 2003, contain a primary obligation to create a criminal corporate responsibility: cf. Rec. 2b FATF 40/2003: 'Criminal liability and, where that is not possible, civil or administrative liability should apply to legal persons.'

[16] Official Commentary 2; Pieth 2000a, 56 et seq.

[17] E.g. MX-Ph1, 24.

models of corporate criminal liability (section 1.) and give an account of the furthest developed non-criminal concepts (section 2.).

1. Models of corporate criminal liability

From a historical perspective there are essentially two major approaches. The development started, both in the Anglo-Saxon world and later in Civil Law countries, with traditional 'anthropomorphic' models,[18] namely by imputing individual misbehaviour of agents to companies. This is quite a logical development, replicating the legal emancipation of corporate personality in civil law. Two sub-concepts (the 'identification model' and 'vicarious liability') will have to be distinguished. Furthermore, some legal systems chose a simple and radical variation of vicarious liability, namely 'strict' or 'absolute' liability, blocking all excuses or defences of the master for acts of his servant: this approach was believed to be at the same time more dissuasive and more easily manageable, especially in a jury trial system.

Both in Common Law and in Civil Law countries, a more recent development has seen a shift towards a fundamentally different, more autonomous objective concept of corporate liability, the emergence of genuine 'corporate fault', or even 'the deficient company'.

1.1. Imputation theories

The negative effects of industrialisation, both in the United States and the United Kingdom, led legislators and courts to develop two early forms of corporate liability. They have their 'anthropomorphic' basis in common.

1.1.1. 'Vicarious liability' ('*respondeat superior*')

In the United States[19] the development started from the civil responsibility of the master for his servant ('*respondeat superior*') and developed, especially in federal law, into the theory of vicarious criminal liability, allowing the imputation to the corporation of the misbehaviour of employees acting within their responsibilities and for the intended benefit of the company. The theory was first developed on the basis of specific statutes, but it was rapidly generalised. In US federal law the approach was construed as a form

[18] Heine 2000, 5.
[19] Coffee 1999, 14 et seq.; DiMento and Geis 2005, 159 et seq.; Wells 2000, 4.

of strict liability. This concept also applies to the Foreign Corrupt Practices Act (FCPA).[20] It is therefore not possible to exonerate the company simply by prohibiting illegal behaviour in company by-laws or even by elaborate compliance concepts. Sentencing Guidelines,[21] however, provide for considerable mitigation of sentences for sound compliance plans.

Critics[22] of the vicarious liability approach in general consider it at the same time too broad – blaming the company whenever the individual employee was at fault, even where the company itself was faultless – and too narrow (liability still needs to be triggered by the fault of an individual related to the company). Critical voices from the defence counsel community on the other hand regard its application to the FCPA as excessive, since it goes far beyond international requirements.[23]

1.1.2. 'Identification theory' ('alter ego')

Beginning in the 1940s, an alternative model emerged in the United Kingdom, allowing corporate liability to be extended beyond statutory offences in general to the most serious crimes implying intent or recklessness ('true crimes', especially '*mens rea* offences'). The traditional 'nominalist'[24] perspective of incorporation in the United Kingdom disputed the existence of a corporation beyond the collectivity of individuals. Based on this view, courts held the corporation exclusively responsible for acts of its '*directing mind*':[25] In an analogy to the human body Lord Denning and others[26] distinguished between the 'hand' and the 'brain' of the company. This approach was formulated most explicitly in *Tesco* v. *Nattrass*[27] by the House of Lords.

This 'identification' or 'alter ego' approach has had a significant influence on the development of corporate liability around the world,[28] even if it became evident that it is too narrowly focused on the involvement of the most senior company officials. The theory was hardly adequate for the

[20] Acquaviva 2003, 172; Coffee 1999, 28 et seq.; Wells 2001, 132.
[21] Coffee 1999, 27, 37; US-Ph2, 16; Sentencing Guidelines 1991: ch. 8; for practical experience: cf. e.g. *U.S.* v. *Goodyear International Corp.*, 2 FCPA Rep. 698.1601 (D.D.C. 1989).
[22] Wells 2000, 4; 1993, 109 et seq.; Heine 2000, 4.
[23] Cf. Low 2003a, 1, 44; for a more fundamental critique cf. Parker 1996, 381 et seq.
[24] Wells 2000, 2; cf. also C. Wells 1999, 120 et seq.
[25] Viscount Haldane, in *Lennard's Carrying Co.* v. *Asiatic Petroleum* [1915] A.C. 713.
[26] Lord Denning in *Bolton (Engineering) Co.* v. *T. J. Graham & Sons Ltd.*, 1 Q.B. 159, 172 (C.A. 1956).
[27] *Tesco Supermarkets, Ltd.* v. *Nattrass* [1972] Appeal Cases 153.
[28] Cf. its influence in Canada, New Zealand and US state law; but also the French systems of corporate liability.

modern decentralised structures of large multinational corporations.[29] Whereas the development in the United Kingdom itself was rather slow, the concept was extended dynamically in the Commonwealth.[30] Canada in particular gave the concept of the 'directing mind' a broader meaning.[31]

In *Civil Law countries* these ideas have been picked up and concepts have been generated based either on vicarious liability or on an identification approach.[32] They generally adopted imputation models which hold companies responsible for the acts and omissions of their leading persons.[33] Both the COE and the EU in its Second Protocol have used identical formulae to define these leading persons:

> 'Article 18, Council of Europe Convention – Corporate Liability
>
> 1. Each Party shall adopt such legislative and other measures as may be necessary to ensure that legal persons can be held liable for the criminal offences of active bribery, trading in influence and money laundering established in accordance with this Convention, committed for their benefit by any natural person, acting either individually or as part of an organ of the legal person, who has a leading position within the legal person, based on:
>
> • a power of representation of the legal person; or
> • an authority to take decisions on behalf of the legal person; or
> • an authority to exercise control within the legal person;
>
> as well as for involvement of such a natural person as accessory or instigator in the above mentioned offences.'[34]

They have, however, gone beyond the traditional 'identification theory' by adding a second paragraph, according to which state Parties engage to:

> 'ensure that a legal person can be held liable where the lack of supervision or control by a natural person referred to in paragraph 1 has made possible the commission of the criminal offences mentioned in paragraph 1 for the benefit of that legal person by a natural person under its authority.'[35]

Even with this addition the approach remains an imputation concept, since it still implies a personalised lack of control by one of the leading persons mentioned above. By indirectly holding the corporation responsible for

[29] Critical: Coffee 1999, 30; Ferguson 1999, 155 et seq.; Heine 2000, 4; C. Wells 1999, 121.

[30] C. Wells 1999, 119 et seq., 222 with reference to Meridian (*Meridian Global Funds Management Asia Ltd.* v. *Securities Commission* (1995) All England Reports 918; cf. also Wells 2001, 112.

[31] Coffee 1999, 19; Ferguson 1999, 170 et seq. (with reference to *Canadian Dredge & Dock Co. Ltd.* v. *The Queen* (1985), 19 C.C.C. (3d) 1 (S.C.C.); CA-Ph1, 8 et seq.

[32] For France cf. Delmas-Marty 1994, 305 et seq.

[33] Austria: § 2(1) Verbandsverantwortlichkeitsgesetz.

[34] Art. 18(1) COE 1999a; cf. also Art. 3(1) EU 1997b.

[35] Art. 18(2) COE 1999a; cf. also Art. 3(2) EU 1997b.

mistakes of ordinary employees or even agents it moves, however, towards a wider concept of 'corporate fault'.

1.2 Objective theories

Concurrently, not only in the realm of Common Law or Civil Law, but also in other legal jurisdictions, including South-East Asian law, a move towards a more objective focus on the fault of the corporation itself[36] has taken place, under the influence of changing corporate structures. This has been felt particularly during the last decade.[37]

Among Common Law jurisdictions the Australian approach probably provides the best example:

> The provisions of the new Australian Criminal Code Act 1995[38] hold the corporation responsible for acts by an agent, employee or officer to the corporation (section 12.2). In addition, for *mens rea* crimes (intention, knowledge or recklessness) the *'fault element must be attributed to a body corporate that expressly, tacitly or impliedly authorised or permitted the commission of the offence'* (section 12.3). Authorisation or permission can be fulfilled in three ways: the first approach reproduces the traditional identification liability (misconduct by leading officer); the second extends the imputation to acts and omissions of 'high managerial agents' (and thereby replicates the Canadian approach); and the third indent refers to a 'corporate culture' which *'directed, encouraged, tolerated or led to non-compliance with the relevant provisions'.* The Act goes as far as to address *tacit authorisation* or even (in a fourth indent) the *failure to create* a culture of compliance.[39]

Similar 'holistic approaches' are now to be found in several modern laws and in practice.[40] In effect, they shift the focus of corporate responsibility from misbehaviour of a leading person to a deficiency of the company, which could be quite independent of individual failure: the deficiency could even predate the arrival at the company of the current managers.

The new Swiss law on corporate criminal liability entered into force on 1 October 2003; it relies entirely on objective criteria when introducing a primary corporate liability for serious economic crime (corruption, money laundering, financing of terrorism)[41] committed by any employee or representative. Regarding corruption, the text requires: first, an (intentional) act of bribery by an employee or agent; second, that this act was in

[36] Coffee 1999, 30; Heine 2000, 4; Wells 2000, 6.
[37] Cf. esp. Fisse and Braithwaite 1988, 468.
[38] Part 2.5, s. 12(2) et seq. Australian Criminal Code Act 1995.
[39] Coffee 1999, 20; Wells 2000, 8; ibid. 1999. [40] Heine 1995, 248 et seq.
[41] CH-Ph1, 7 et seq.; Pieth 2001; Heine 2003.

the potential interest of the company; and third, that it was an expression of the *'lack of reasonable organisational measures'*.[42]

Both Japanese and Korean[43] corporate criminal liability are construed according to this model of organisational deficiency: the fact that a crime was committed by a company representative (including agents) in relation to its business, creates a reputable presumption that there has been a lack of due diligence in the corporation. Although the legislation offers a defence, under both laws the burden of proof is on the defendant.

Such objective standard models come rather close to strict liability combined with mitigation of sanctions for convincing compliance concepts.[44]

2. Non-criminal corporate liability

Most laws know some civil or administrative sanctions against serious misbehaviour of corporations, but only a few[45] have reorganised these rules in such a way as to meet the standards set by the most recent international instruments against corruption. The German and the Italian laws may be among these few.

The standards of liability in these systems are construed similarly to the approach taken with regard to corporate criminal liability: they address the same issues, defining the entities covered, the persons triggering liability by their acts, the link to the corporate goal, and the issue of lack of adequate supervision.

As the Convention does not rule out a non-criminal solution, the question whether a model is 'sufficient' for the purposes of the Convention depends on the effectiveness of its application, as measured in the Phase 2 evaluation.

When carrying out its evaluations, the WGB places great emphasis on the 'functional equivalence' of criminal and non-criminal corporate liability. Both, in the cases of the new Italian law[46] and the German *Ordnungswidrigkeitengesetz*,[47] it has been noted that administrative sanctions were determined by criminal courts responsible for trying bribery by natural

[42] Art. 100^{quater} Swiss Criminal Code; Heine 2003, 24 et seq.; Pieth 2001, 1 et seq.; ibid. 2003, 353 et seq.; ibid. 2004, 597 et seq.; CH-Ph1, 7 et seq.; CH-Ph2, 37 et seq.
[43] For Japan: JP-Ph1, 7 et seq. and Shibahara 1999, 39 et seq.; for Korea: KR-Ph1, 7 et seq.
[44] See III.4.5.2. below.
[45] In the eyes of the WGB the laws in, inter alia, Brazil, Bulgaria, Czech Republic, Hungary, Slovenia, and possibly also in Poland are inadequate.
[46] IT-Ph1, 13, 34; Sacerdoti 2003.
[47] DE-Ph1, 5 et seq., 18 et seq.; DE-Ph2, 28.

persons. In both cases, establishing the liability of a natural person is not a condition for a finding of corporate liability.[48] Additionally, it is considered a crucial indicator of equivalence that for the purposes of mutual legal assistance, corporate liability may be treated as 'criminal'.[49]

The Phase 2 evaluation of Germany nevertheless raised serious questions as to whether prosecution practice, which seemed to diverge considerably within the country, took the issue of corporate liability seriously enough. Doubts were raised in particular when prosecutors based in some of Germany's leading economic centres stated that they were not fully aware of their responsibilities regarding companies. This may be a reflection of the ancillary and non-criminal nature of the fines.[50] The insistence with which the WGB interviewed prosecutors may serve as an indicator that a general policy shift on an international level towards criminal responsibility and against administrative liability of legal persons is currently taking place.[51]

The treatment of Italian and German administrative corporate liability contrasts clearly with the Polish solution, which was met with far more reservations by the WGB. Polish procedure is genuinely 'administrative' in that it presupposes a final judgement or other final decision in criminal proceedings against a natural person. Based on the judgement, the President of a special agency (The Office for Protection of Competition and Consumers) may, under certain circumstances, institute proceedings against the enterprise.[52] The WGB expressed doubts whether the standard of effective, proportionate, and dissuasive sanctions was fully met and recommended re-examination in Phase 2.[53] This very cautious formula is clearly a consequence of the lack of a horizontal evaluation of corporate liability standards within the OECD framework. Considering the heightened scrutiny the WGB gave the German model, it seems highly doubtful that the Polish arrangement will pass the test in the Phase 2 evaluation.

III. Setting standards for corporate liability: the requirements of the OECD Convention

1. General remarks

Despite the insistence that responsibility of legal persons is particularly crucial in preventing bribery in international business transactions, the

[48] IT-Ph1, 13; critical however IT-Ph2, 40.
[49] IT-Ph1, 29; DE-Ph1, 15 et seq.; DE-Ph2, 31.
[50] DE-Ph2, 30. [51] See note 15. [52] PL-Ph1, 11 et seq., 15. [53] PL-Ph1, 32 et seq.

texts of Articles 2 and 3 of the Convention are not very articulate when it comes to defining the minimum standard to be implemented by state Parties.

Article 2 merely obliges state Parties 'to establish the liability of legal persons for the bribery of foreign public officials'. The clause inserted, 'in accordance with its legal principles', does not add anything new: it simply recalls the overarching principle under which the Convention has been drafted, i.e. 'functional equivalence' (Official Commentary 2). When compared with the far more eloquent clauses in the Convention of the COE on Corruption of 27 January 1999 (Article 18) and the Second Protocol to the EU Convention on the protection of the European Communities' financial interests of 19 June 1997 (Article 3), Article 2 of the OECD Convention indicates just how mindful the drafters were of national particularities. Article 26 of the more recent UN Convention Against Corruption follows the model of the OECD.

The interpretation of the Convention therefore has to respect such differences. Nevertheless, within the process of evaluation the WGB is forced to develop standards. The anchor point for 'benchmarking' is contained in Article 3. First, Article 3(1) makes clear that 'the bribery of a foreign public official shall be punishable by effective, proportionate and dissuasive criminal penalties'. The second paragraph of the text adds:

> 'In the event that under the legal systems of a Party, criminal responsibility is not applicable to legal persons, that Party shall ensure that legal persons shall be subject to effective, proportionate and dissuasive non-criminal sanctions, including monetary sanctions, for bribery of foreign public officials.'

In the context of evaluating the functional equivalence of corporate liability, the formula 'effective, proportionate, and dissuasive' addresses the adequacy of the entire approach for the whole concept of corporate liability. It goes well beyond mere sanctioning. Based on the models discussed above[54], but also by reference to treaties covering similar terrain (EU and COE) the WGB attempts to develop standards in its evaluation practice by addressing four sets of issues:

- the definition of legal entities covered;
- standards of liability;
- sanctions;
- enforcement.

[54] See part II. of this ch.

2. Defining the legal entities covered

2.1. Legal person v. business entity

The term 'legal person' is not defined in the OECD Convention. The understanding is that this term refers back to the law of the state Parties. This is the solution chosen by the COE and EU instruments.[55]

First, it must be mentioned that not all state Parties limit themselves to 'legal persons' when dealing with corporate liability. Some address the responsibility of 'enterprises', 'corporations', or 'business entities'.[56] Other state Parties try to achieve a similar result by expanding the scope of traditional legal persons (usually a definition to be found in their civil code or company law[57]) to all entities 'entitled to rights'[58] or 'capable of doing business'. In various state Parties mere partnerships are now included in the list of legal entities covered.[59] Some state Parties explicitly include single-owner businesses, at least beyond a certain size.[60] With a few exceptions, the older concepts of corporate liability, are defined more narrowly, especially in Common Law jurisdictions,[61] even though a tendency to expand the definition has been recorded.[62]

So far, the WGB intervened on this point only where a Party fell below the standard set by its own law. In the case of Greece[63] not all legal persons – according to the Greek definition of this term – were covered by the scope of the anti-corruption law: foundations and associations were not included at the time of the Phase 1 examination. Considering the possibilities of hiding 'slush funds' behind such corporate structures, this point was rightly criticised by the OECD.

2.2. Public entities?

The question arises whether the state itself or departments of state and also international organisations may be exempted from the scope of regulation by anti-corruption legislation. In some countries it may be the case that at

[55] Cf. the definition provision of each instrument referred to above: COE 1999a; Art. 1(f) EU 1997b.
[56] E.g. Poland, Sweden, Switzerland.
[57] For Common Law cf. Wells 2001, 81 et seq. [58] Iceland.
[59] Belgium, Germany, Italy, Netherlands, New Zealand, Norway.
[60] Denmark, Switzerland. [61] Australia, Canada, United Kingdom.
[62] The United States gave up the limitations to 'issuers' and 'domestic concerns' in the 1998 Amendment to the FCPA.
[63] GR-Ph1, 17.

least the central government of the state cannot be taken to court by the state itself.[64] It is another question whether agencies of local government may fall under the remit of legislation covering corporations.[65] Certainly, where the state has endowed entities with powers to engage in contracts on its behalf, these bodies should not be allowed to escape regulation. The nature of 'state-owned' or 'state-controlled' enterprises differs from one state to the next, but the WGB has insisted that such bodies be covered by the state Parties' definitions of 'legal persons'.[66] Nowadays, most state Parties simply subject state-owned or state-controlled enterprises to the general law, though others distinguish them according to the social goal[67] of the enterprises. This issue is examined in greater depth in the chapter on Article 1 of the Convention.

3. Substantive liability

Based on the national systems and the other international instruments, standards of liability must address the following issues:

- crimes covered by corporate liability;
- benefit to the legal person;
- level of person engaging corporate responsibility;
- relationship between procedure against natural and legal persons;
- standard of liability (strict liability?, corporate negligence?).

3.1 Crimes covered

The corporate liability provisions of the OECD Convention must apply to all forms of corruption under Article 1. The way state Parties achieve this goal does not matter for the purposes of the Convention: they may introduce a generally applicable concept of corporate liability,[68] by listing specific crimes for which corporate liability would be applicable, including transnational bribery,[69] or by addressing the issue of transnational bribery in a specific code.[70]

[64] E.g. Germany; according to Austrian law (§ 1(3) Verbandsverantwortlichkeitsgesetz) not even local public entities are criminally accountable.
[65] France. [66] Cf. the comments directed at the Mexican law: MX-Ph1, 24.
[67] Commercial or public; e.g. Denmark, Finland.
[68] United Kingdom. [69] France, Switzerland.
[70] United States.

3.2. Benefit to the legal person

3.2.1 Company interest

All concepts of corporate liability seek to make a distinction between crimes serving purely private goals of the perpetrator and bribery intended to further the interests of the corporation.[71] The delimitation of the field of corporate responsibility for acts of company employees is far from uniform. Frequently the formulae refer to acts 'on behalf of', 'in the name of', 'in the interest of' or 'for the benefit of' the legal person.

One can distinguish between at least three levels of 'connection' between the act concerned and the company interest, ranging from a rather loose connection to a very 'intense' relationship: the closer the connection required, the more exclusive is the approach to corporate liability.

A first group of countries merely requests that the bribery has been committed 'in relation to' or 'in connection with' the business of the legal person, or simply 'in the course of its operations'.[72] According to a second group of countries, a 'general interest test' is required: 'on behalf of', 'in the name of', 'in furtherance of the interest of', 'for the gain of', etc. These are the standard formulations adopted by most Party states.[73] From the point of view of effective, proportionate, and dissuasive corporate liability provisions, it seems excessive to require evidence that the corporation has actually *benefited* from the crime. It is therefore questionable whether a country would meet the standard of the Convention, if the issue was addressed by the formula that the company has 'accepted the act or the benefit'.[74] Finally, some countries attempt to exclude crimes for mere personal interest by an explicit exception clause.[75] Rather original is the Swedish solution to relax the supervisory duties where the link to the company activities becomes weak.[76]

3.2.2. Within the scope of corporate duties

Additional qualifiers need to be distinguished from the interest test that may be found in some laws, such as that the employee in question acts

[71] For a historical perspective cf. Ferguson 1999, 161 et seq.
[72] Iceland, Japan, Korea, United Kingdom.
[73] Belgium, Canada, Finland, France, Germany, Italy, Mexico, Norway, Portugal, Switzerland, United States.
[74] Coffee 1999, 21: with reference to Art. 51 Dutch Criminal Code.
[75] Canada (except where company becomes a victim), Denmark, Italy.
[76] SE-Ph1, 7.

within the field assigned to him/her or within his/her duties.[77] This requirement should not be confused with the question whether he or she has acted contrary to instructions: the latter question should be addressed in terms of fulfilment of the standard of liability.[78]

3.3. Level of person engaging corporate responsibility

For the purpose of benchmarking, the most relevant requirement is probably the so-called 'leading person criterion'. As highlighted in our overview of models,[79] the more traditional approaches made corporations liable only for the acts of senior company officials. This had a theoretical basis in the *'alter ego'* concept and a practical grounding in the then prevailing patriarchal leadership model.[80] In the light of modern, decentralised decision-making, these approaches are coming under pressure.

A rough overview of existing laws (not necessarily reflecting all the intricacies of modern case law and ongoing discussions in law committees) allows us to distinguish between four groups of Party states:

- The United Kingdom's definition of *'directing mind'*, even after the more recent case law[81] and the Law Commission's Report,[82] still seems to be the most demanding of the laws discussed here.
- Canada applies a somewhat broader definition of *'directing mind'* (including all employees with *'decision-making authority on matters of corporate policy'*)[83] and is apparently planning to include cases where these senior company officers were aware of or wilfully blind to criminal behaviour of their subordinates. New Zealand seems to have relaxed the elitist standards of Common Law in a slightly different direction by focusing on the real (factual) control over related activities.[84]
- According to a further category, made up mostly of Continental European countries and in line with the approach of the COE and EU, two separate criteria are cumulated: first, beyond acts

[77] Canada, United Kingdom, United States; for the usual conditions of the 'identification doctrine' cf. Wells 2001, 85 et seq.

[78] See 3.5. below. [79] See part II. of this ch.

[80] For an early example cf. *Lennard* case (see reference in note 25).

[81] Cf. the *Meridian* case of 1995 (see reference in note 30).

[82] Law Commission 1996; C. Wells 1999, 121 et seq.; Wells 2005, 154 et seq.

[83] CA-Ph1, 8; CA-Ph2, 29; Ferguson 1999, 171 et seq., referring to the *Canadian Dredge & Dock* case (see reference in note 31).

[84] NZ-Ph1, 12.

committed or condoned by senior management, personalised management failure is included; second, the company will additionally be held responsible for *'culpa in eligendo, instruendo et custodiendo'* of senior managers ('lack of supervision rule').[85]

- The largest group of countries has decided to impute misbehaviour of 'any employee' to the company.[86] Some countries explicitly include agents and other third parties engaged in the company's interest in their texts or explanatory reports.[87] Among these the United States follows a strict liability rule;[88] others demand an objective corporate fault;[89] Japan and Korea have shifted the balance of proof for the absence of negligence onto the corporation.[90]

Even though this criterion is crucial for the effectiveness of corporate liability, the WGB has so far been hesitant to pronounce itself on a minimum standard relating to the level of the person required to engage responsibility. Discussions were held in 2000 and 2002 whether the European standard contained in COE and EU instruments (see Article 18(2) of the COE Convention and Article 3 of the EU Second Protocol) should be adopted by the OECD as a kind of compromise solution. So far, no decision has been taken. It nevertheless seems that in Phase 2 pressure on the first group of countries to widen the range of persons triggering corporate liability will grow. Similarly, in relation to the third group of countries referred to above, the WGB has already criticised those which have not yet established the 'lack of supervision' rule.[91]

3.4. The relationship between procedures against natural and legal persons

The relevant provisions of both EU and COE instruments emphasise that proceedings against legal persons[92] should not exclude action against natural persons. For an established concept of corporate liability the reverse

[85] Art. 3(2) EU 1997b; Art. 18(2) COE 1999a; Austria, Finland, France, Germany, Greece, Italy, Japan, Sweden.

[86] Belgium, Denmark, Iceland, Korea, Mexico, Netherlands, Norway, Switzerland, United States.

[87] Denmark, Iceland, Korea, Switzerland, United States.

[88] United States.

[89] Finland, Japan, Korea, Sweden, Switzerland.

[90] Japan, Korea; for details see III.3.5. below.

[91] FR-Ph1, 12, 30; however, academic writing and practice suggest this concern may be unfounded in the case of France: cf. Delmas-Marty 1994, 308 and further comments in III.3.6. below.

[92] Cf. more recently Art. 26(3) UN 2003.

situation should also apply: the fact that an individual has been prosecuted should not automatically exclude corporate liability.[93] Even though the text of the OECD Convention is silent 'in both directions', it may be assumed that for an *'effective, proportionate and dissuasive'* concept of corporate liability there should be no categorical exclusion of the prosecution either of natural or legal persons.[94]

It is a different matter whether an individual offender must be identified and convicted or even sanctioned before corporate liability can be engaged. This question has however stirred an unnecessary debate: bribery is a mens rea crime, requiring intent or at least knowledge. Therefore someone in the company must fulfil these requirements.[95] However, there are cases in which, due to complex decision-making procedures, the information is scattered over several officers and only its combination brings full knowledge. Furthermore, it could be that within a group of decision-makers it remains unclear whether they all have participated in the decision. For such situations modern legislation in some states, or current jurisprudence, is satisfied, if one person in the relevant circle can be shown to have had knowledge, intent, or to have violated his or her supervisory duties.[96] Other jurisdictions have explicitly repudiated such concepts of *'aggregate knowledge'*.[97]

In two cases the WGB expressed doubts whether a country met its obligations according to international law, since the state Parties' laws require the conviction of an individual as a prerequisite even to begin proceedings against a corporation.[98]

3.5. Standard of liability

Classic imputation theories ('identification theory' and 'vicarious liability') have held the corporation responsible for the misconduct of its officers.[99] Under all systems even the best of compliance models will not be able to shield the corporation from liability, if the *'directing mind'* him- or herself authorised or even ordered the illegal conduct. As far as such systems

[93] Cf. the discussions in Switzerland: Pieth 2001, 10; ibid. 2003, 358; Heine 2001, 307 et seq.; ibid. 2003, 27 et seq.

[94] On this issue from a perspective of national law: Cohen 1996, 399 et seq.; Fisse 1991, 255 et seq.; Wells 2001, 160 et seq.

[95] Cf. explicitly: Denmark.

[96] DE-Ph2, 32, § 120; IS-Ph1, 6; FR-Ph1, 12; NO-Ph1, 4 et seq.; United States: for 'collective knowledge' doctrine: Wells 2001, 134.

[97] Cf. United Kingdom: *Bingham J.* in the case against *P. & O. Ferries* in the aftermath of the disaster of Zeebrugge: Wells 2001, 108 et seq.

[98] MX-Ph1, 24; PL-Ph1, 11, 32. [99] See II.1.1. above.

impute the behaviour of junior staff to the organisation, they either apply an absolute (strict) liability[100] or a duty-based approach. The European development of the 'identification theory', especially on the Continent, has seen the evolution of a personalised 'lack of supervision' approach, promoting and following the COE and EU instruments:[101] thus, the corporation will be held liable for mismanagement in selecting, instructing and supervising junior staff.

So-called 'objective' or 'holistic' theories[102] move away from personal blame for the lack of supervision by employees or managers in order to define organisational blame[103] or *'corporate fault'*.[104] Based on experience with environmental disasters, explosions, rail crashes, maritime disasters, etc., this theory implies that creating a complex corporate structure may in itself be hazardous. This risk needs to be counterbalanced by adequate organisational concepts, an appropriate corporate culture, and credible compliance efforts, the lack of which will entail corporate responsibility independently of individual management failure.[105] As Celia Wells puts it, this *'model locates corporate blame in the procedures, operating systems, or culture of a company'*.[106]

Under these systems, in contrast to a system of strict liability, the prosecution would have to prove the insufficiency of compliance concepts. Alternatively, the corporation could be granted a 'due diligence defence'.[107] One of the reasons for the choice of strict liability seems to be that this task can be formidable, especially in the context of a jury trial.[108] Practical reasons may therefore dictate shifting the discussion of adequate compliance plans into the sentencing phase, governed by a professional judge. Whereas some of the European countries, with a far more inquisitorial trial system, are confident that the adequacy of corporate organizational arrangements can be discussed in court,[109] some countries have, however, chosen – as an intermediary solution – a due diligence approach with reversal of the burden of proof. In Australia, Japan, and Korea the law offers an exception to the responsibility of the corporation, under the condition that it has fulfilled its organisational and supervisory obligations. The corporation itself bears the burden of proof for this assertion.[110]

[100] E.g. United States.
[101] Cf. especially Austria, France, Germany, and Italy.
[102] Wells 2001, 85 et seq. and see II.1.2. above.
[103] Heine 2000, 4; Coffee 1999, 30. [104] C. Wells 1999, 119 et seq.
[105] Australia, Denmark, Finland, Japan, Korea, Sweden, Switzerland.
[106] Wells 2001, 85. [107] Gobert 1998, 14. [108] Coffee 1999, 31.
[109] Heine 2003, 36 et seq., 38 et seq.; Pieth 2001, 14 et seq.; ibid. 2004, 604 et seq.
[110] Cf. for a similar approach: Law Commission 1996 (see note 82); Wells 2001, 120 et seq.

3.6. Defining the 'bottom line' of substantive liability of corporations according to the OECD Convention

3.6.1. Corporate criminal liability

It is not just sanctions and sanctioning practice, but also the choice of attribution model, which need to pass the test of *'effectiveness, proportionality and dissuasiveness'*.

From the point of view of 'dissuasive power' strict vicarious liability seems to come out on top.[111] Additionally, this approach has the advantage of being simple to manage. So simple that even laymen, including members of a jury, can apply the concept. As we have seen, critics[112] have, however, maintained that the system oversimplifies: it holds the company responsible even where it has done all it could to prevent the crime (although it may receive a mitigated sentence for a sound compliance programme). In our view, there is not and should not be a requirement in international law to adopt strict liability of legal persons for corruption cases.

The identification model, the second and most significant school of thought in corporate criminal liability, with practical examples both in Common Law countries (Canada, New Zealand, UK, and US state law) and Civil Law states (France, Belgium), equally depends upon the wrongdoing of an individual imputed to the company. But our preceding analysis has shown that some of the applications of this approach focus narrowly on crime committed either by the most senior company representatives only[113] or by those concerned with business policy decisions.[114] This would exclude liability of the company for the wrongdoing of less senior staff, even where they carried major responsibilities on a technical level.[115] Moreover, in some constituencies the 'elitist' character of this approach is reinforced when constructions like the 'aggregate' or 'collective' knowledge of the 'directing mind' are repudiated.[116]

Critics have raised doubts whether this approach meets the requirements of national[117] and international law.[118] We believe that the test of 'effectiveness, proportionality, and dissuasiveness' can be met only if this

[111] Coffee 1999, 28 et seq. [112] See II.1.1.1. above.
[113] For United Kingdom: *Tesco* or *Meridian* case (see references in notes 27 and 30).
[114] For Canada: *Canadian Dredge & Dock* case (see reference in note 31).
[115] Ferguson 1999, 176 et seq.
[116] For United Kingdom: see III.3.4. above; critical Wells 2001, 156.
[117] Aiolfi and Pieth 2005, 401 et seq.; Gobert 1998, 13 et seq.; Ferguson 1999, 13 et seq.; Wells 2001, 152; Wells 2005, 154 et seq.
[118] Ferguson 1999, 176 et seq.; Wells 2001, 143. Still cautious at the time in the light of so many other deficiencies: UK-Ph1, 8 et seq.; now more forcefully: UK-Ph 2, 59 et seq.

approach deems management failure to include the lack of due diligence in hiring, the absence of education and instruction, and a failure of supervision and control. Those laws which comply with the requirements of Article 18(2) of the COE Convention or with the similar terms of Article 3(2) of the Second Protocol of the EU can therefore also be regarded as consistent with the requirements of the OECD Convention regarding corporate liability.[119]

From an effectiveness perspective, many academics are moving towards an 'autonomous approach'.[120] For a 'mens rea crime' this approach, of course, also requires an offence to have been committed by an individual, employee, or agent of the company; this person does not, however, have to be a 'directing mind'. Rather, responsibility of the corporation is triggered by lack of organisation, a breakdown of management procedures, or where management allows a deviant corporate culture to develop. Applying this model and going beyond the above-mentioned enlarged identification model, mere disorganisation on the level of management – not attributable to individual managers – would suffice for corporate liability.[121] This approach has the advantage of placing due diligence and compliance 'centre stage'. Gobert rightly points out that offering a 'due diligence defence', rather than creating strict liability, is more subtle and more motivating to companies: it uses the 'carrot' rather than the 'stick'.[122] On the other hand, it is equally true that 'due diligence' and 'compliance' are not simple concepts and that a jury might well be at a loss to apply them. The challenges to professional judges do not, however, diverge substantially from other offences committed as a result of lack of diligence (e.g. cases of professional negligence by architects, surgeons, mountain-guides etc.).[123]

3.6.2. Non-criminal liability

The classic international instruments against corruption all allow for the alternatives of '*criminal or non-criminal sanctions*'.[124] It is equally true that the instruments attach these sanctions to the commission of 'criminal' offences (explicitly in Article 19(1) of the COE Convention. It is therefore

[119] Cf. the examples of France: III.3.3. above (see note 85); Austria, § 3, s. 2.
[120] Coffee 1999, 33; Fisse 1991; Gobert 1998; Heine 1995, 319 et seq.; Pieth 2001, 1 et seq.; ibid. 2003, 353 et seq.; ibid. 2004, 597 et seq.; Wells 2001, 85, 156 et seq.
[121] For example, Australia, Korea, and Switzerland: see II.1.2. above.
[122] Gobert 1998, 12 et seq. [123] Pieth 2004, 604 et seq.
[124] Art. 26(4) UN 2003; Arts. 18 and 19(2) COE 1999a; Art. 3 EU 1997b; Art. 3(2) OECD 1997b.

obvious that the negotiators of anti-corruption treaties did not intend that corporate responsibility should be transferred fully into the domain of traditional civil or administrative law.

Indeed, more recent international legal sources are increasingly moving towards a primary requirement of corporate criminal liability. See for example the Revised Forty Recommendations of the FATF, which merely allow for administrative corporate liability on a secondary level.[125] Furthermore, evaluation task forces give those countries favouring non-criminal liability a far more thorough screening, mainly because corporate liability might not be pursued with the same rigour as in criminal law.[126] It may be assumed, therefore, that the pressure towards criminal liability in public international law will only grow further in the years ahead.[127]

4. Sanctions

4.1. Sanctions against corporations

The objectives of corporate sanctions are contested.[128] Some systems, especially those based exclusively on corporate fines, are directed at general deterrence. The approaches which mix fines and forfeiture are primarily interested in siphoning off illegal profits (forfeiture, confiscation). Finally, the restrictions on corporate behaviour or 'freedom', such as orders, conditions, prohibitions, etc., pursue a more preventive or rehabilitative goal (especially in the case of nomination of a trustee).[129] In sum, the regulation of sanctions for corporations reflects a very diverse range of attitudes to corporate control in the state Parties: given this situation, the imposition of an international standard becomes all the more difficult.

4.2. The international standard

At first sight the standards of the international treaties show considerable differences.

[125] Rec. 2b FATF 40/2003 (see note 15).
[126] This was a concern first raised in the OECD Phase 2 evaluation of Germany, cf. DE-Ph2, 30 and see II.2. above.
[127] Bundesministerium für Justiz (Austria) 2004, 15 et seq.
[128] Coffee 1981, 397 et seq.; Heine 1999, 237 et seq.
[129] Gobert 1998, 9 et seq.

Article 4(1) of the EU's Second Protocol contains the following provision on sanctions for legal persons:

> 'Each Member State shall take the necessary measures to ensure that a legal person. . .is punishable by effective, proportionate and dissuasive sanctions, which shall include criminal or non-criminal fines and may include other sanctions such as:
>
> (a) exclusion from entitlement to public benefits or aid;
> (b) temporary or permanent disqualification from the practice of commercial activities;
> (c) placing under judicial supervision;
> (d) a judicial winding-up order.'

This first paragraph applies to crimes authorised by leading company officials. The enumeration of sanctions restricting corporate freedoms is taken from a COE Recommendation of 1988[130] and is also inspired by French law.

Interestingly enough, with regard to the second paragraph, the EU text diverges from the COE approach and restricts itself to requesting effective, proportionate, and dissuasive sanctions or measures in the case of lack of adequate supervision.

Clearly, the formula *'effective, proportionate and dissuasive sanctions, including. . .fines'* inspired the OECD in its drafting efforts of 1997. The OECD has, however, simplified the overall approach.

Article 3(1) of the OECD Convention, which sets the standard for criminal sanctions, applies to natural and legal persons alike. Article 3(2) then allows for non-criminal sanctions against corporations, but subject to the same standard. Article 3(3), again addressing natural and legal persons alike, provides for seizure and confiscation of bribe money or requires 'monetary sanctions of comparable effect'. Finally, Article 3(4) asks state Parties to consider *'the imposition of additional civil or administrative sanctions'* upon natural or legal persons: in this regard, Official Commentary 24 embraces the EU list of optional additional sanctions beyond fines.

In the preceding sections the analysis of binding sanctioning requirements under the OECD Convention must distinguish between financial and non-financial sanctions. Furthermore, the principles of sanctioning must also be discussed. This overview should then allow us to define a standard in order to judge overall effectiveness.[131]

[130] COE 1988. [131] See III.4.3.–III.4.6. below.

4.3. Financial sanctions

Under the heading of financial sanctions, the WGB evaluates whether:

- they are provided for at all;
- they are comparable to sanctions for domestic bribery or other serious domestic crime (e.g. fraud, theft etc.);
- forfeiture is precluded by fines or vice versa.

4.4. Other sanctions

4.4.1. Criminal sanctions

Common Law countries have maintained a broad range of sanctions for companies, going beyond fines and ranging from remedial orders, sometimes linked to probation, to Community service orders, to adverse publicity orders or restraint-oriented sanctions.[132] Furthermore, one has to consider the sanctions as elements in a graded approach, including into the equation also civil sanctions.[133]

In Continental Europe, following the Recommendation of the COE of 1988, some Mediterranean countries in particular have gone well beyond mere monetary sanctions. France, for example, has developed an elaborate system of restraint orders. French law provides for the:

- disallowance of the performance of specific professional or social activities;
- prohibition of public appeals for funds;
- issuance of cheques, using payment orders;
- placement under supervision;
- closure of one or more establishments;
- exclusion from public procurement.

Italy and Portugal have introduced similar sanctioning systems (even if the Italian approach is only quasi-criminal in nature).

Official Commentary 24 mentions such restraint-orientated sanctions as illustrations of the additional 'civil or administrative sanctions' referred to in Article 3(4) of the OECD Convention, thereby overlooking the fact that in some countries these non-financial sanctions are really penal sanctions.

[132] Clough 2002; Gobert 1998, 6 et seq.; Préfontaine 1999, 277 et seq.; Wells 2001, 31 et seq.
[133] Fisse 1993, 255 et seq.

4.4.2. Additional civil or administrative sanctions

Many countries have indeed followed up Article 3(4) by introducing further civil or administrative sanctions against legal persons. Measures introduced include civil fines,[134] exclusion from public procurement[135] or public subsidies[136] and from certain business operations. Civil liability for corporate wrongdoing is foreseen in general terms by all countries and general civil and/or company law also regulates the dissolution of the companies (a general Civil Law sanction for legal persons pursuing an illegal goal).

4.5. Sanctioning principles

Sanctioning principles are closely linked to the sanctioning rationale.[137] Depending on whether deterrence, prevention, or restitution is in the foreground systems will give different emphasis to:

- crime-related factors;
- corporate culpability ('personal' dimension);
- the situation of the company and 'post-offence' issues.

Some countries, notably the United States, have codified these factors, specifically for corporate liability, in their Sentencing Guidelines;[138] others refer to the general rules of sanctioning.

4.5.1. Crime-related factors

The starting point of most sanctioning procedures is the gravity of the fault. Here the dimensions of illegal gain or savings or, alternatively, the damage inflicted on victims is relevant.[139]

4.5.2. Corporate culpability

This criterion of corporate culpability attempts to capture all references to the level of deliberateness, recklessness, or negligence in hiring, instructing, and supervising personnel. In the context of so-called 'objective models',

[134] United States.
[135] Austria, Belgium, Brazil, France, Germany (partially), Hungary, Italy, Poland, Portugal, Spain, Switzerland, United States.
[136] Italy, Portugal, and United States. [137] See III.4.1. above.
[138] Sentencing Guidelines 1991, ch. 8.
[139] Denmark, Finland, France, Germany, Greece, Mexico, United States.

the degree of the 'disorganisation' of the company – independently of the extent of the culpability of individual managers – would be taken into account.[140] The absence of a sufficient corporate compliance programme would be considered an essential element of culpability.[141]

4.5.3. Situation of the company and post-offence development

a. Economic situation of the company

Many sentencing systems for corporations admonish judges to take into consideration the economic potential of the company to be sentenced.[142] On the one hand, sanctions (especially fines) need to have a sufficient deterrent effect. On the other hand, they should not suffocate all incentive to do business. Additionally, sentencers need to be aware of undesirable spill-over effects[143] which may affect third parties, particularly employees of the enterprise concerned.

In the case of Poland sentencing is made directly dependent on the previous year's tax returns, thus potentially excluding weak earners and new companies from sanctions.[144] The OECD's WGB has criticised this approach, since new companies and bad earners could elude sanctions entirely. A more subtle way of taking the economic situation of a company into account is by the application of a 'day fine system' (first developed for natural persons) to companies.[145] With regard to small companies the fact that managers and major stockholders may have already been personally sanctioned for the bribery in question could also be considered under this heading and lead to a dramatic reduction of the sanction.

b. Restitution and rehabilitation

Some countries apply the general sentencing principle that the imposition of fines should not get in the way of restitution of damage caused.[146] In its new law on corporate liability, Italy offers a considerable 'rebate' of up to ⅓ or ½ of the fines for credible rehabilitative efforts within the corporation.[147] The concept of restitution depends on the notion of 'victim'. Sometimes corruption is described as a 'victimless crime'. But this perspective is too narrow. Both, the state whose public official is being corrupted as well as

[140] Sweden and Switzerland. [141] United States. [142] E.g. Denmark and Italy.
[143] Gobert 1998, 2 et seq. [144] PL-Ph1, 15 et seq., 32 et seq.
[145] Cf. the examples of Denmark and Portugal.
[146] Cf. the case of The Netherlands, whereas other countries insist that fines should pass a deterrent message beyond mandatory restitution or forfeiture (United States).
[147] Magrini 2003, 120.

corporate competitors, will suffer as a result of the crime. On the other hand, it is true that the extent of damage caused is rather difficult to assess.

Thus it would appear that 'symbolic restitution' (e.g. Community service of some kind or payments to charities) and the siphoning off of profits would be the most adequate response.

4.6. *Judging effectiveness*

In general, the OECD WGB has been hesitant to give directions on which sanctions it considers 'effective, proportionate and dissuasive' in the abstract. The occasional statement in the context of the Phase 1 evaluations appears to be rather ad hoc and uncoordinated.

Where there is a clear gap in a country's law, the task of criticism is easier: see the evaluative reports criticising certain countries for the complete absence of corporate liability.[148] Apart from these cases, the strongest verdict on sanctions can be found in the evaluation of Japan:

> 'The WGB does not consider the sanctions available for legal persons to be sufficiently effective, proportionate and dissuasive in view of the large size of many of its corporations, particularly since seizure and confiscation (as noted below) are not available under Japanese legislation.'[149]

By virtue of this finding, the WGB established two principles: first, that sanctions against corporations must be sufficiently 'tough' to have an impact on large multinational corporations; second, that according to the concept of functional equivalence a trade-off is possible between two theoretically quite different instruments, i.e. the corporate fine and the forfeiture/confiscation of illicit profits (Article 3(3) of the Convention).

On the basis of these principles, judging effectiveness of sanctions involves a three-step procedure:

- In a first step, the scope of sanctions needs to be tested against domestic law in each country. Article 3(1) mentions the primary concept: '*The range of penalties shall be comparable to that applicable to the bribery of the Party's own public officials*'. Since bribery is considered a serious offence, the WGB has repeatedly compared the scope of sanctions for domestic and foreign bribery with the sanctioning options for serious economic crime in general (theft, fraud, embezzlement etc.). Under these rules some maximum fines

[148] In Phase 1: Argentina, Austria, Brazil, Bulgaria, Czech Republic, Luxemburg, Poland, Slovak Republic, Spain, Switzerland.

[149] JP-Ph1, 28 et seq.

are allowed to be low, as long as the national threshold for corporate sanctions is low overall.

- In a second step, the sanction that is in tune with domestic sanctioning principles will be compared on an international level. Here the desire to secure a level playing field of commerce and prevent 'regulatory arbitrage' by imposing sufficiently high sanctions is at the forefront of considerations. The WGB has considered 300 million yen (approx. $/€2.7 million) to be insufficient.[150] This raises the question how maximum sanctions of $/€1 million contained in the legislation of most countries could ever pass muster with the OECD.
- On a third level, an answer could be given by including quasi-corporate fines in the equation. The US maximum of $2 million dollars did not convince the WGB, especially since forfeiture and confiscation of profits is only available in exceptional circumstances (in cases of money laundering). The United States nevertheless satisfied the OECD on this point, both in Phase 1 and Phase 2, because it was able to prove that under their '*alternative fine provisions*'[151] they could go well beyond the statutory maximum of the FCPA. In practice, heavy monetary sanctions have been imposed.[152]

One should not, however, accept forfeiture as a complete substitute for corporate sanctions. Article 3(3) of the Convention proposes the introduction of unlimited forfeiture of the proceeds of transnational bribery separately from and in addition to '*effective, proportionate and dissuasive sanctions*'.[153]

Under Article 3(2) of the Convention, the WGB has so far not gone beyond requesting financial sanctions. Only under the additional requirement of Article 3(4) has the topic of non-financial sanctions been raised in the context of additional administrative or civil sanctions.

5. Application

The definition of the adequate procedure for the application of corporate liability is left to the Party states. One issue, however, needs to be addressed

[150] JP-Ph1, 28 et seq. [151] US-Ph1, 11 et seq.; US-Ph2, 15.

[152] As in the cases of *U.S.* v. *Crawford Enterprise* (1982) a fine of $3.45 million; for *U.S.* v. *National Airmotive Corp.* (1994) a criminal sanction of $1.25 million and civil forfeiture of $1.75 million; for *U.S.* v. *Lockheed Corp.* (1994) a fine of $21.1 millions; cf. Annex to US-Ph2, 41 et seq.

[153] For a critical assessment see part. VIII. in ch. on Article 3(3) below.

under this heading, namely, how wide is the discretion of prosecuting agencies when it comes to open a case against a legal person?

5.1. Prosecutorial discretion

The issue of prosecutorial discretion will be discussed in its wider context in the chapter on Article 5.[154] In this chapter the issue of possibly diverging practices in the treatment of natural and legal persons is in point. When prosecuting natural persons seventeen OECD state Parties are bound by the rule of mandatory prosecution ('principle of legality'), whereas fourteen allow discretion ('principle of opportunity'). Regarding the prosecution of legal entities figures are rather different: eighteen of the twenty-four countries who have to date introduced either criminal or non-criminal corporate liability follow the discretionary approach. Even some of the strongest believers in mandatory prosecution of natural persons have converted to discretion when it comes to companies.[155] During its Phase 1 evaluation the WGB has observed that several countries lacked rules on how to apply prosecutorial discretion relating to corporate liability.[156] It was left to the Phase 2 evaluations to assess whether the principle of discretion undermines the effectiveness of corporate liability. So far, the results appear rather ambiguous.

In one group of countries which has known the concept of corporate responsibility for some time, no cases of domestic or international bribery have been run against companies so far.[157]

In a second group some cases are now appearing in which companies are involved as defendants.[158] It is, however, difficult to tell on what basis this prosecutorial decision has been taken.

In the United States twenty-one companies and twenty-six individuals have been convicted for criminal violations of the FCPA in the years 1997–2001.[159] Critics observe that, while in the early days FCPA liability and corporate liability in particular appear to have been invoked sparingly, a dramatic increase is now being recorded.[160]

[154] See ch. on Article 5 below.
[155] Finland, Germany, and Iceland; in the case of Germany this is a consequence of its administrative approach to the sanctioning of companies (DE-Ph2, 32).
[156] Canada, Denmark, Germany, Iceland, New Zealand, Poland.
[157] FI-Ph2, 18; IS-Ph2, 27 et seq.
[158] For Canada no conviction of a company for foreign bribery has been reported to date; however, a first company is being prosecuted (CA-Ph2, 16); in Korea, so far two companies have been tried for foreign bribery (KR-Ph2, 8 et seq.).
[159] US-Ph2, 16. [160] Tarullo 2004, 674.

In the evaluation of Germany – a country maintaining strict mandatory prosecution for individuals but allowing discretion for companies – practitioners reported interesting regional differences: whereas in Frankfurt and Berlin corporate liability was 'rarely' applied to (domestic) corruption, in Munich far more prosecutions against companies have been launched in corruption and related cases.[161]

Overall, it emerges that the perseverance with which corporations are prosecuted for either domestic or foreign corruption is very much a matter of prosecution policy. This aspect must therefore form part of our criteria when the effectiveness of the system is evaluated.[162]

IV. Corporate liability and sanctions: conclusions

1. Corporate liability

One of the major deficits identified in mutual evaluations is a widespread failure to implement Article 2. So far only twenty-four of the thirty-six Party states have introduced corporate criminal liability. Most other countries maintain that they are planning to introduce it in the near future; typically, however, such reform would depend on wider criminal reform projects.[163]

With respect to those countries which have implemented corporate criminal liability, the application of a mere identification model, imputing only offences of the most senior management to corporations and also frequently refusing a concept of 'aggregate knowledge', would in our view fail to meet the requirements of 'effective, proportionate and dissuasive sanctions'.[164]

On the other hand, the terms of Articles 2 and 3 of the Convention would be met by countries whose liability concept includes lack of due diligence by senior management, allowing junior agents to engage in bribery (cf. also Article 18(2) of the COE Convention).[165]

Acting pursuant to Article 3(2) of the Convention, some countries have chosen to introduce a non-criminal corporate liability for legal persons.[166] Manifestations of this approach are, however, very thoroughly screened by the WGB in the application phase, as it is well known that prosecutors are

[161] DE-Ph2, 28 et seq. [162] See ch. on Article 5 below.
[163] Cf. Argentina, Austria, Chile, Czech Republic, Luxembourg, Poland, Slovak Republic, Turkey.
[164] See III.3.6.1. above. [165] See previous note 164.
[166] In particular, Germany, Italy, and Spain.

inclined to treat non-criminal liability less seriously than traditional criminal sanctions imposed on individuals.[167] We must, however, distinguish between Article 3(2) implementation and the imposition of additional non-criminal sanctions (of a civil or an administrative nature) suggested by Article 3(4) of the Convention. These are two entirely different matters.

2. Sanctions

Discussions of sanctioning requirements have, quite rightly, revolved around the imposition of 'monetary sanctions' (Article 3(2) of the Convention).

Some countries already find it difficult to pass the 'internal coherence test' (meaning coherence with the national treatment of domestic bribery or other serious crimes according to Article 3(1)). For example, Nordic countries generally apply low maximum penalties; certainly, the Danish maximum of sixty-day fines[168] would be too low in comparison with sanctions for other serious crimes.

On the second level of evaluation[169] (testing against the international standard), three groups of countries need to be distinguished:

- Older manifestations of corporate liability generally adopt relatively low maximum fines,[170] well below \$/€500 000. This appears particularly unsuited and inadequate to sanction corrupt conduct by a multinational enterprise.
- A second group of countries, some of which have only recently enacted laws on corporate liability, foresees maximum penalties of around \$/€1 million.[171] If the critique levelled against Japan is taken seriously,[172] it must apply also to this group, unless special rules apply to aggravated cases.
- Several jurisdictions know no upper limits in serious cases or raise the sanction level well above the \$/€1 million threshold.[173] Alternatively, the aggregate of civil and criminal sanctions together with forfeiture has been considered sufficient.[174]

[167] See III.3.6.2. above. [168] DK-Ph1, 10. [169] See III.4.6. above.
[170] Australia, Denmark, Sweden, The Netherlands.
[171] Austria, Belgium, Finland, France, Germany, Italy, United States.
[172] JP-Ph1, 28 et seq. and see III.4.6. above.
[173] Canada, Germany, Greece, Hungary, Iceland, Ireland, Korea, New Zealand, Norway, Portugal, Switzerland, United Kingdom
[174] United States: see critique in III.4.6. *in fine* above.

References

For documentation see the consolidated bibliography at the end of this book.

Acquaviva, G. (2003), 'Il Foreign Corrupt Practices Act statunitense e il dilemma della lotta alla corruzione internazionale: azione unilaterale o cooperazione multilaterale?' in G. Sacerdoti, *Responsabilità d'impresa e strumenti internazionali anticorruzione*, Milano, 167.

Aiolfi, G. and M. Pieth (2005), 'International Aspects of Corporate Liability and Corruption' in S. Tully (ed.), *Research Handbook on Corporate Legal Responsibility*, Cheltenham (UK), Northhampton (USA), 689.

Arlen, J. and R. Kraakman (1997), 'Controlling Corporate Misconduct: An Analysis of Corporate Liability Regimes', *New York University Law Review* **72**, 687.

Clough, J. (2002), 'Sentencing the Corporate Offender: The Neglected Dimension of Corporate Criminal Liability' in J. Clough and C. Mulhern (eds.), *The Prosecution of Corporations*, Melbourne.

Coffee, J. C. (1981), 'No Soul To Damn: No Body To Kick: An Unscandalised Inquiry into the Problem of Corporate Punishment', *Michigan Law Review* **79**, 386.

Coffee, J. C. (1999), 'Corporate Criminal Liability: An Introduction and Comparative Survey' in A. Eser, G. Heine and B. Huber (eds.), *Criminal Responsibility of Legal and Collective Entities*, Freiburg i. Br., 9.

Cohen, M. A. (1996), 'Theories of Punishment and Empirical Trends in Corporate Criminal Sanctions', *Managerial and Decision Economics* **17**, 399.

Delmas-Marty, M. (1994), 'Die Strafbarkeit juristischer Personen nach dem neuen französischen Code Pénal' in B. Schünemann and C. S. González (Hrsg.), *Bausteine des europäischen Wirtschaftsstrafrechts, Madrid-Symposium für Klaus Tiedemann*, Köln, Berlin, Bonn, München, 305.

DiMento, J. F. C. and G. Geis (2005), 'Corporate Criminal Liability in the United States' in S. Tully (ed.), *Research Handbook on Corporate Legal Responsibility*, Cheltenham (UK), Northhampton (USA), 159.

Eser, A., G. Heine and B. Huber (eds.) (1999), *Criminal Responsibility of Legal and Collective Entities*, Freiburg i. Br.

Ferguson, J. (1999), 'The Basis for Criminal Responsibility of Collective Entities in Canada' in A. Eser, G. Heine and B. Huber (eds.), *Criminal Responsibility of Legal and Collective Entities*, Freiburg i. Br., 153.

Fisse, B. (1991), 'The Attribution of Criminal Liability to Corporations: A Statutory Model', *Sydney Law Review* **13**, 277.

Fisse, B. (1993), 'Rethinking Criminal Responsibility in a Corporate Society: An Accountability Model' in P. Grabosky and J. Braithwaite (eds.), *Business Regulation and Australia's Future*, Canberra, ch. 18.

Fisse, B. and J. Braithwaite (1988), 'The Allocation of Responsibility for Corporate Crime: Individualism, Collectivism and Accountability', *Sydney Law Review* **11**, 468.

Gobert, J. (1998), 'Controlling Corporate Criminality: Penal Sanctions and Beyond', *Webjournal of Current Legal Issues* **2**.

Heine, G. (1995), *Die strafrechtliche Verantwortlichkeit von Unternehmen*, Baden-Baden.

Heine, G. (1999), 'Sanctions in the Field of Corporate Criminal Liability' in A. Eser, G. Heine and B. Huber (eds.), *Criminal Responsibility of Legal and Collective Entities*, Freiburg i. Br., 237.

Heine, G. (2000), 'Corporate Liability Rules in Civil Law Jurisdictions' (OECD Room Document (DAFFE/IME/BR(2000)23, Paris).

Heine, G. (2001), 'Europäische Entwicklungen bei der strafrechtlichen Verantwortlichkeit von Wirtschaftsunternehmen und deren Führungskräften', *Schweizerische Zeitschrift für Strafrecht* **119**, 22.

Heine, G. (2003), 'Das kommende Unternehmensstrafrecht (Art. 100^{quater} et seq.)', *Schweizerische Zeitschrift für Strafrecht* **121**, 24.

Low, L. A. (2003) [cited Low 2003a], 'The Global Legal Framework: The OECD, OAS, and Council of Europe Antibribery Conventions: New International Standards and National Anti-Corruption Laws: Challenges for Effective Implementation and Enforcement' (unpublished paper, prepared for a Conference in Paris, April 2003).

Magrini, P. (2003), 'L'attuazione della Convenzione OCSE contro la corruzione negli Stati membri: il quadro comparato' in G. Sacerdoti (ed.), *Responsabilità d'impresa e strumenti internazionali anticorruzione*, Milano, 95.

Möhrenschlager, M. (1999), 'Developments on the International Level' in A. Eser, G.Heine and B. Huber (eds.), *Criminal Responsibility of Legal and Collective Entities*, Freiburg i. Br., 89.

Moody-Stuart, G. (1997), *Grand Corruption*, 3rd edn, Oxford.

OECD (ed.) (2000) [cited OECD 2000a], *No Longer Business as Usual: Fighting Bribery and Corruption*, Paris.

Parker, J. S. (1996), 'Doctrine for Destruction: The Case of Corporate Criminal Liability', *Managerial and Decision Economics* **17**, 381.

Pieth, M. (2000) cited Pieth 2000a, 'From Ideal to Reality: Making the New Global Standard Stick' in OECD (ed.), *No Longer Business as Usual*, Paris, 51.

Pieth, M. (2001), 'Internationale Anstösse zur Einführung einer strafrechtlichen Unternehmenshaftung in der Schweiz', *Schweizerische Zeitschrift für Strafrecht* **119**, 1.

Pieth, M. (2003), 'Die strafrechtliche Verantwortung des Unternehmens', *Schweizerische Zeitschrift für Strafrecht* **121**, 353.

Pieth, M. (2004), 'Risikomanagement und Strafrecht: Organisationsversagen als Voraussetzung der Unternehmenshaftung, Risiko und Recht' in Festgabe *zum Schweizerischen Juristentag 2004*, Basel, Bern, 597.

Posner, R. A. (1994), *The Economics of Justice*, Cambridge (USA).

Préfontaine, D. (1999), 'Effective Criminal Sanctions against Corporate Entities: Canada' in A. Eser, G. Heine and B. Huber (eds.), *Criminal Responsibility of Legal and Collective Entities*, Freiburg i. Br., 277.

Sacerdoti, G. (2003), *Responsabilità d'impresa e strumenti internazionali anticorruzione*, Milano.

Shibahara, K. (1999), 'Le droit japonais de la responsabilité pénale, en particulier la responsabilité pénale de la personne morale' in A. Eser, G. Heine and B. Huber (eds.), *Criminal Responsibility of Legal and Collective Entities*, Freiburg i. Br., 39.

Tarullo, D. K. (2004), 'The Limits of Institutional Design: Implementing the OECD Anti-Bribery-Convention', *Vanderbilt Journal of International Law* **44**, 665.

Tully, S. (ed.) (2005), *Research Handbook on Corporate Legal Responsibility*, Cheltenham (UK), Northhampton (USA).

Wells, C. (1999), 'Developments in Corporate Liability in England and Wales and a New Offence of Corporate Killing – the English Law Commission's Proposals' in A. Eser, G. Heine, and B. Huber (eds.), *Criminal Responsibility of Legal and Collective Entities*, Freiburg i. Br., 119, 217.

Wells, C. (2000), 'Criminal Responsibility of Legal Persons in Common Law Jurisdictions' (OECD Room Document DAFFE/IME/BR(2000)22, Paris).

Wells, C. (2001), *Corporations and Criminal Responsibility*, 2nd edn, Oxford.

Wells, C. (2005), 'Corporate Criminal Responsibility' in S. Tully (ed.), *Research Handbook on Corporate Legal Responsibility*, Cheltenham (UK), Northhampton (USA), 147.

Article 3. Sanctions

PETER J. CULLEN

Article 3 – Sanctions

1. The bribery of a foreign public official shall be punishable by effective, proportionate and dissuasive criminal penalties. The range of penalties shall be comparable to that applicable to the bribery of the Party's own public officials and shall, in the case of natural persons, include deprivation of liberty sufficient to enable effective mutual legal assistance and extradition.

2. In the event that, under the legal system of a Party, criminal responsibility is not applicable to legal persons, that Party shall ensure that legal persons shall be subject to effective, proportionate and dissuasive non-criminal sanctions, including monetary sanctions, for bribery of foreign public officials.

3. Each Party shall take such measures as may be necessary to provide that the bribe and the proceeds of the bribery of a foreign public official, or property the value of which corresponds to that of such proceeds, are subject to seizure and confiscation or that monetary sanctions of comparable effect are applicable.

4. Each Party shall consider the imposition of additional civil or administrative sanctions upon a person subject to sanctions for the bribery of a foreign public official.

Official Commentary

Article 3 – Sanctions

Re paragraph 3:

21. The 'proceeds' of bribery are the profits or other benefits derived by the briber from the transaction or other improper advantage obtained or retained through bribery.

22. The term 'confiscation' includes forfeiture where applicable and means the permanent deprivation of property by order of a court or other competent authority. This paragraph is without prejudice to rights of victims.

23. Paragraph 3 does not preclude setting appropriate limits to monetary sanctions.

Re paragraph 4:

24. Among the civil or administrative sanctions, other than non-criminal fines, which might be imposed upon legal persons for an act of bribery of a foreign public official are: exclusion from entitlement to public benefits or aid; temporary or permanent disqualification from participation in public procurement or from the practice of other commercial activities; placing under judicial supervision; and a judicial winding-up order.

Chapter contents

I. Introduction: The goals of Article 3

This chapter is divided into three main parts: the first, this short introduction to the objectives of Article 3; the second, a discussion of the origin of the standard 'effective, proportionate, and dissuasive' sanctions, with particular reference to EC/EU law; and the third, a detailed analysis of the sanctioning standard of the OECD's anti-bribery Convention and the particular requirements it imposes on state Parties.

The OECD Table appended to this commentary indicates, in summary, how the national laws of the state Parties to the Convention in fact sanction the bribery of foreign officials.[1]

Article 3 of the Convention establishes a common minimum standard for the sanctioning of the bribery of foreign public officials. The OECD Convention requires that those found guilty of corrupting a foreign public official be punishable by 'effective, proportionate, and dissuasive criminal penalties'.

Additional requirements of Article 3 are that the 'range of penalties' by which foreign bribery is punishable should be comparable to that applied in cases of domestic bribery and that the sanctions available against natural persons 'shall. . .include deprivation of liberty sufficient to enable mutual legal assistance and extradition.' Sanctions applicable to *legal persons* need not be of a criminal nature, if the legal system of a Party does not allow it, but the alternatives must, like any criminal sanctions, meet the 'effective, proportionate, and dissuasive' test, and must include monetary sanctions.[2]

Paragraph 3 of the Article requires seizure and confiscation of the bribe or proceeds of the bribe, 'or monetary sanctions of comparable effect'. This chapter will not discuss Article 3(3) of the Convention, concerning confiscation. This will be the subject of a separate chapter.[3]

[1] See Annex A of this commentary.
[2] Sanctions against legal persons are discussed in detail in the ch. on Article 2 (III.4.) above.
[3] See ch. on Article 3(3) below.

Paragraph 4 requests state Parties to consider the imposition of additional 'civil or administrative sanctions'.

The clear thinking behind Article 3 is that the criminalisation of foreign bribery will not be effective without some guarantee that 'companies [will] face *substantially similar...penalties* for international bribery, no matter what their country of origin' (italics added).[4] In the 'Agreed Common Elements of Criminal Legislation and Related Action' attached to the 1997 Recommendation,[5] the basic 'plan of attack' of the OECD relating to the harmonisation of criminal sanctions was already outlined:

> 'The offence of bribery of foreign public officials should be sanctioned/punishable by effective, proportionate and dissuasive criminal penalties, sufficient to secure effective mutual legal assistance and extradition, comparable to those applicable to the bribers in cases of corruption of domestic public officials.'

The Convention, which was drafted on the basis of these Common Elements, does not therefore establish its own sanctioning regime; it pursues instead a minimum degree of harmonisation based upon this rather general standard. As we shall see, the standard was imported from European Community law.

The Convention as a whole is based on a concept of harmonisation of laws which refers to the achievement of 'functional equivalence' regarding the implementing measures to be taken by the state Parties. This principle is stated in Official Commentary 2:

> 'The Convention seeks to assure a functional equivalence among the measures taken by the Parties to sanction bribery of foreign public officials, without requiring uniformity or changes in fundamental principles of a Party's legal system.'

Compared to European Community (EC) or European Union (EU) law,[6] this appears, on the face of it, to be a less exacting harmonisation strategy. Certainly, the standard imported from EC or EU law instruments falls to be applied very much in the OECD's own 'harmonisation context'.

[4] Cf. OECD 1999, F-1001, F-1008. As Pieth points out, the *Travaux Préparatoires* were in fact the 'preparatory materials for the discussions held in the Working Group before drafting the Recommendation of 1997' (OECD 1997a). Cf. also OECD 1999: Introduction, F-1003.

[5] See OECD 1997a and the Agreed Common Elements of Criminal Legislation and Related Action in the Documentary Appendix of this commentary.

[6] Since the creation of the European Union (EU) in 1993, as distinct from the European Communities (EC), it has been necessary to distinguish between EC law, which derives from the founding Community Treaties, and the new body of EU law, which derives from the provisions of the Treaty on EU concerning 'intergovernmental' co-operation (notably, for our purposes, Title VI of the latter, concerning criminal justice co-operation). But the term 'EU law' is also sometimes used, rather confusingly, to embrace both sets of legal provisions and the legal instruments deriving from them. (On the EC and EU distinction, cf. Arnull, Dashwood, Ross and Wyatt, 2000, 15 et seq. and ch. 8.)

The basic orientation of the OECD Convention is towards the national systems of criminal justice:[7] the requirements of the Convention should be met with full respect for their autonomy, traditions and special substantive or procedural features, which may not be overridden but rather should be accommodated within the scope of compliance with criminalisation and effective sanctioning of foreign bribery.[8] What this precisely means, in terms of the level of adjustment required by national systems, will become clear only when we look at the practice of the Working Group on Bribery (WGB) in their monitoring of state Parties' implementation. It is apparent, however, from the text of the Convention, from previous instruments, and from the *Travaux Préparatoires* of the Convention[9] that a significant 'margin of appreciation' should be left to national systems, in the achievement of the intended goals.

The medium-term goals of the OECD's anti-bribery Convention could be more clearly stated. The 'Mid-Term Study' of implementation of the Convention currently being undertaken by the OECD may throw some light on the extent of harmonisation expected by the WGB and the OECD Secretariat.[10] As for the United States, which can also claim a large measure of 'paternity' or 'maternity' of the Convention, the 2004 Department of Commerce review emphasises the practical impact of the Convention on bribery in international transactions, and is not so much interested in the degree of harmonisation of criminal laws required to achieve this. What is wanted by the United States is implementation such that the number of contracts won by competitors of US firms after bribing foreign public officials is significantly reduced.[11]

On the legal level the Convention appears to offer the OECD and its WGB only a limited mandate with regard to the harmonisation of national criminal law: it may direct a national criminal justice system to deploy its resources to combat foreign bribery, but it leaves the manner of such deployment in the hands of the national authorities, according to the usual

[7] Pieth 2006: '[d]em Text von Art. 3(1) ist zu entnehmen, dass sich der Strafrahmen im Sinne der funktionalen Äquivalenz am lokalen Sanktionsniveau orientieren soll. Damit werden erhebliche Differenzen in Kauf genommen. . .Die WGB hat dieses Prinzip der landesinternen Kohärenz weiterverfolgt'.

[8] Aiolfi and Pieth 2002, 351 et seq.

[9] 'The objective was to develop a high standard for national actions which would be the basis for an effective effort. At the same time, Members recognised that it is necessary to accommodate the fundamental principles of each country's legal and administrative systems.' (OECD 1999, F-1008).

[10] See ch. on Article 12 below.

[11] Department of Commerce 2004, 52 (reporting a measure of success in this respect).

national rules, provided that the minimum standards of the Convention are met. What precisely those minimum standards are, with regard to sanctions, is the purpose of enquiry in this chapter.

II. Origin of the standard 'effective, proportionate and dissuasive' sanctions

1. Pre-Convention discussions

The choice of the standard 'effective, proportionate and dissuasive' was one of a number of possible options considered by the WGB when preparing the Revised Recommendation of 1997 and the later Convention.[12] It appealed because of its general nature, being preferred to a numerical definition of an average penalty to which the Parties should aspire. The average penalty for bribery of domestic officials was estimated by the *Travaux Préparatoires* at between three and five years and in aggravated cases up to ten years.[13] Article 3 is perhaps referring to these levels implicitly when it talks of adhering to the 'range' of penalties applicable to the bribery of the Party's own public officials. The Convention does not purport to equalise state Parties' penalties: that would run counter to the idea of limited harmonisation. It does, however, seek to achieve a certain 'evening out', to facilitate functional equivalence.

The formula 'effective, proportionate, and dissuasive' is as far as the Convention gets to a common standard. The *Travaux Préparatoires* clearly indicate that this EC standard was being considered as one of the options[14] and the drafts of Article 3 indicate that the OECD Secretariat, the US, and the European (Franco-German) delegations all favoured its adoption.[15] Opinions differed on how far the penalty of deprivation of liberty sufficient to give rise to extradition should be specified, i.e. whether it should be limited to certain cases.[16]

The fact that this EC-inspired standard – which has also now been taken on by Council of Europe[17] and UN Conventions[18] – was in the

[12] OECD 1999, F-1030–1031. [13] OECD 1999, F-1030–1031.

[14] OECD 1999, F-1030. The OECD 1999 draw the formula from Art. 5 of the EU 1996b. The EU 1997b establishes a similar standard for legal persons (see II.2.4. below).

[15] Cf. preparatory document DAFFE/IME/BR(97)11, 9.

[16] Preparatory document DAFFE/IME/BR(97)11, 9: France and Germany proposed that deprivation of liberty in this sense should be limited to 'serious cases'.

[17] Art. 19 COE 1999a. [18] Art. 26 UN 2003.

course of being fleshed out by the jurisprudence of the European Court of Justice may have escaped the attention of the WGB, or been ignored, perhaps because they saw the standard developing differently in the OECD context. Nevertheless, for the purposes of this commentary, we regard it as instructive to compare how the EC institutions have developed their standard; some aspects of the EC (and now also EU) approach may lend themselves, now or in the future, to adoption by the OECD.

2. Application of the standard in EC and EU law

2.1. Basic approach of EC law

In the absence of an EC programme of harmonisation of penalties, except in a limited number of sectors of policy, breaches of Community legislation are sanctioned according to national law, be it national criminal law or civil or administrative law. Leaving sanctions to national law is consistent with the idea of administrative partnership between Community and national organs: legislation is enacted at the central (EC/EU) level but implemented at the national level. Such an approach promotes respect for 'national institutional autonomy'.[19]

The Community, moreover, denied itself any criminal competence per se. In principle, criminal law remained outside EC legislative jurisdiction,[20] a position which has only altered recently.[21]

The founding EC Treaties did provide for economic (i.e. non-penal) sanctions in certain areas, notably in the field of competition policy, which is policed by the European Commission. Undertakings face increasingly heavy fines for breach of EC anti-cartel laws.[22] These fines are, however, expressly declared to be 'not...of a criminal nature'.[23] The 'penal policy' of the

[19] 'Respect for Community law is principally organized through and should be guaranteed through national rules. It falls upon national rules to provide the competent authorities, the competent jurisdictions and the procedural and substantive rules.' (Boch 2000, 103).

[20] Cf. Case 203/80 *Casati* [1981] ECR 2595 (cf. Boch, 2000, ch. 9 for other cases).

[21] Note the decision of the European Court of Justice that criminal penalties may be required by EC legislation where necessary to enforce certain Community policies: Case 176/03 *Commission* v. *Council*, 13 September 2005 (not yet published in European Case Reports, but cf. OJ 2005 No. C315, 10 December 2005, 2). See also II.2.3. below.

[22] Geradin and Henry 2005.

[23] Cf. Art. 23(5) of the EC Regulation governing anti-cartel investigations and fine procedures: EU 2002d, 1.

Commission in competition matters is now directed by a form of 'Sentencing Guidelines'.[24] Moreover, EU Member States may also, since treaty reforms of the 1990s, incur substantial monetary penalties for failure to observe judgements of the European Court of Justice.[25]

Notwithstanding these important developments, it is national law, not Community law, which predominantly sanctions the breach of EC Treaty provisions, regulations, directives, or other legislation. This is the case even for areas of policy subject to considerable substantive regulation, such as fraud against the Community budget, environmental policy, or EU sex discrimination legislation. As the scope of Community law in these and other policy areas expanded, it became more difficult to justify significant divergences in the matter of remedies and penalties.

Lacking a clear legislative jurisdiction to approximate remedies and penalties, differences in national law were not ironed out by legislation of the Commission or Council. It was thus left to the European Court of Justice to develop a standard that would push the Member States towards a more common approach to the sanctioning of breaches of Community law, while still leaving the procedures for their imposition or application to national judges or other authorities.

The 'effective, proportionate, and dissuasive' standard was the European Court of Justice's answer to this dilemma. The introduction of this sanctioning standard was at first closely linked to the principle of 'assimilation'. Effectiveness meant, at the least, that national authorities would take measures to penalise breaches of Community law which were as stringent as those directed at similar breaches of national law. After case law from the European Court of Justice,[26] this principle was inserted into the EC Treaty by the Maastricht Treaty, in the context of the fight against fraud on the Community budget.[27]

[24] EU 1998a, 3.

[25] Art. 228 EC Treaty. And cf. Case C-387/97 *Commission* v. *Greece* [2000] ECR I-5047. These sanctions are discussed by Douglas-Scott 2002, 419 et seq.

[26] Case 68/88 *Commission* v. *Greece* [1989] ECR 2965. The principle had already been stated, in similar terms, in relation to civil law remedies, in Case 33/76 *Rewe-Zentral Finanz eG and Rewe-Zentral AG* v. *Landwirtschaftskammer für das Saarland* [1976] ECR 1989, para. 5: 'It is for the domestic legal system of each Member State to designate the courts having jurisdiction and to determine the procedural conditions governing actions at law intended to ensure the protection of the rights which citizens have from the direct effect of Community law, it being understood that such conditions cannot be less favourable than those relating to similar actions of a domestic nature.'

[27] Art. 209a (ex Art. 280) EU 2002a, introduced by the Maastricht Treaty on EU, states: 'Member States shall take the same measures to counter fraud affecting the financial interests of the Community as they take to counter fraud affecting their own financial interests.'

2.2. A broader concept of 'effectiveness' in EC law

The assimilation principle remains a valid means of securing a certain basic degree of compliance with Community rules, but it has been supplemented by a wider notion of 'effectiveness' which has led the European Court to prescribe in more detail how national courts or other authorities should sanction breaches of Community law.[28] One result of this approach has been the Court's support for the criminalisation of conduct which is seriously detrimental to a fundamental Community interest.[29] On the other hand, the Court has deployed the 'proportionality' principle to moderate the 'negative' impact of national criminal law on the exercise of Community rights: national sanctions may be overridden by Community law, if they prove 'too onerous' in terms of their effect on Community rights or freedoms, and they must not be used in a discriminatory manner against persons from other Member States.[30]

The 'effectiveness' and 'proportionality' elements of this standard have been interpreted very much on a case-by-case basis,[31] in a flexible way, and with due regard to the discretion of the sanctioning authority, which is allowed a certain 'margin of appreciation'.[32] In terms of 'dissuasion', the lack of a European penal policy, as such, has meant that the EU has not taken a position on how exactly sanctions may impact on criminal behaviour. Reliance was, however, placed on the 'dissuasive' effect of national criminal law in relation to public order offences which led to interruption of Community trade.[33] And, in the context of competition policy, the 'quasi-criminal' penalties which may be imposed on companies clearly reflect a belief in the capacity of heavy monetary sanctions to deter repeated breaches of the Community's anti-trust rules.[34]

2.3. The Amsterdam Treaty and the EU's Green Paper on sanctions

Recently, the EU has begun to address matters of penal policy, and in particular criminal sanctions, more directly and more deeply. The 2004

[28] Craufurd Smith 1999, esp. 300 et seq.

[29] Case C-265/95 *Commission* v. *France* [1997] ECR I-6959.

[30] Case C-348/96 Criminal Proceedings against *Donatella Calfa* [1999] ECR I-11.

[31] This is also the conclusion of Tobler 2005, 17.

[32] The discretion given to Community institutions is greater than that afforded to the Member States: compare Case C-301/97 *Netherlands* v. *Council* [2001] ECR I-885 or Case C-331/88 *The Queen* v. *Ministry of Agriculture, Fisheries and Food and Secretary of State for Health ex parte FEDESA and others* [1990] ECR I-4023 – dealing with sanctions in the context of the Common Agricultural Policy – with *Commission* v. *France* (see note 29), *Calfa* (see note 30) or Case 157/79 *R.* v. *Pieck* [1980] ECR 2171, which concern Member State sanctions.

[33] Case C-265/95 *Commission* v. *France* [1997] ECR I-6959.

[34] Commission Guidelines (see note 24).

Green Paper of the European Commission on sanctions is the first EU policy paper systematically to address the subject of approximation of national criminal penalties and their enforcement, including sentencing policy.[35] This paper should be seen against the background of the creation under the Amsterdam Treaty of an EU competence to 'approximate' or harmonise certain aspects of national crimes, including penalties for those crimes. The Amsterdam Treaty has led to a veritable flurry of new EU legislation, in the shape of 'Framework Decisions', proposed by the European Commission or the Member States, and then adopted by the EU's Council of Ministers.

These Framework Decisions may harmonise 'minimum rules relating to the constituent elements of criminal acts and to penalties in the fields of organised crime, terrorism and illicit drug trafficking'.[36] In the Framework Decisions adopted to date,[37] the EU Member States have begun to adopt a new approach to the harmonisation of national sanctions, based on the stipulation of so-called 'minimum-maximum' penalties, according to the following four-level scale:

- level 1: penalties of a maximum of at least between one and three years of imprisonment;
- level 2: penalties of a maximum of at least between two and five years of imprisonment;
- level 3: penalties of a maximum of at least between five and ten years of imprisonment;
- level 4: penalties of a maximum of at least ten years of imprisonment.

As the Green Paper on sanctions points out,[38] this means that the lower end of each scale is the starting point for the maximum penalties for the offence. One or other scale will be chosen, depending on the subject matter concerned and on the consensus as to which scale would be appropriate. The Framework Decision on combating corruption in the private sector, for example, provides that certain offences be punishable by a maximum penalty of at least one to three years.[39] A special scale may be applied to particularly heinous crimes such as terrorism: the Framework Decision on the combating of terrorism, for example, sets the 'minimum-maximum' penalty at eight years of imprisonment for the participation in a terrorist group, and fifteen years for directing such a group.[40]

[35] EU 2004a. [36] Art. 31(e) Treaty on European Union.
[37] Cf. list in EU 2004a, 15–17 (note that they range over wider fields than those expressly referred to in Art. 31(e)).
[38] EU 2004a, 17. [39] Art. 4(2) EU 2003a, 54. [40] EU 2002b, 3.

The degree of approximation of sanctions implied by this approach is in fact quite limited. Moreover, as the Green Paper points out, there is no legislation of the Union laying down minimum sanctions.[41] Equally, there is no Union legislation bearing upon the enforcement of custodial penalties. And, in contrast to the Community legislation governing competition policy, there has, to date, been no provision by Framework Decisions for financial penalties. A recent Commission proposal relating to strengthening the criminal law framework for the enforcement of the law against ship-source pollution would, however, introduce fines, rather than imprisonment, for such pollution-related offences.[42]

2.4. EU law concerning corporate criminal liability

Regarding sanctions for legal persons, the Second Protocol of the Convention on the protection of the EC's financial interests (referred to throughout this commentary as 'the Second Protocol'), which was adopted under the earlier Maastricht Treaty version of Title VI of the Treaty on EU, set the tone for future legislation of the Union. Article 3 requires Member States to make legal persons liable for fraud, active corruption and money laundering; and Article 4 of the Second Protocol requires them to make those offences 'punishable by effective, proportionate, and dissuasive sanctions'.[43]

The provisions of the Second Protocol have been repeated in numerous Framework Decisions adopted since the entry into force of the Amsterdam Treaty. We see from these Framework Decisions that the approach of the Union, like that of the OECD, is to promote but not to require corporate criminal liability. The EU's 'effective, proportionate, and dissuasive' standard is applicable both to criminal and non-criminal sanctions. For example, Article 6 of the Council Framework Decision on combating corruption in the private sector states that: '[e]ach Member State shall take the necessary measures to ensure that a legal person…is punishable by effective, proportionate, and dissuasive penalties, which shall include criminal or non-criminal fines'.

In addition, other possible penalties are listed: '(a) exclusion from entitlement to public benefits or aid; (b) temporary or permanent disqualification from the practice of commercial activities; (c) placing under judicial supervision; or (d) a judicial winding-up order'.[44] These additional

[41] EU 2004a, 17. [42] EU 2003c. [43] EU 1997b, 12 and EU 1997c, 8.
[44] Cf. Art. 6 of the Framework Decision.

alternative civil or administrative penalties are also endorsed by the OECD, for legal persons.[45]

The EU has put figures on what it means by 'dissuasive fines' in competition cases: undertakings found in breach are now at the receiving end of rather draconian fines, though their actual dissuasive effects are not proved.[46] As we saw, these competition law fines are expressly deemed to be of a non-penal nature.[47]

2.5. Impact of EC and EU law on national sanctions: an assessment

We may summarise the approach of EC/EU law to sanctions in the following ten points:

First, the standard 'effective, proportionate and dissuasive' was developed by the European Court of Justice as a rather soft standard for approximation of national sanctions.

Second, the 'effectiveness' criterion would be satisfied in most cases by the assimilation of sanctioning for 'analogous' breaches of national and Community law, whether for crimes against property or persons.

Third, EC case law clearly supports the criminalisation of conduct threatening essential Community interests, on the basis of a somewhat wider concept of effectiveness than assimilation.

Fourth, the 'minimum-maximum' method of approximation of imprisonment sanctions has, despite the absence of empirical evidence of its likely effects, become the norm for European Commission proposals under Title VI of the Treaty on EU.

Fifth, this new method certainly goes beyond the 'effective, proportionate and dissuasive' formula, even if the formula is usually still retained as a back-up.

Sixth, like the OECD Convention, several Framework Decisions also add the requirement that the custodial penalties imposed must be of a level sufficient to enable extradition to occur.

Seventh, what is a 'proportionate' fine or penalty is in most cases left very much to the discretion of the sanctioning authority. The Court of Justice has, however, made it very clear that EC law can override national criminal law on this basis, including sentences deemed by the Court to be excessively

[45] Cf. Official Commentary 24 and see III.3.3.3. below. Official Commentary 24 expands slightly the second penalty listed in the EU documents, referring also to temporary or permanent disqualification from public procurement.

[46] Cf. Geradin and Henry 2005.

[47] See note 23.

'restrictive' of fundamental Community policies. Putting figures on what this means for fines imposed under national law is difficult. Deprivation of liberty may now be mandated by EU legislation, but imprisonment under national law of EU nationals exercising Treaty rights is subject to very close scrutiny, on proportionality grounds, by the Courts in Luxembourg.

Eighth, EU law clearly embraces corporate liability and endorses criminal liability and criminal fines for undertakings, though non-criminal forms of corporate liability are also accepted. Sanctions for legal persons are in any case subject to the general standard 'effective, proportionate, and dissuasive'. The sanctions foreseen for legal persons in EU instruments include civil and administrative orders. The EU standard is thus enforced vis-à-vis companies, though it risks being undermined by the exceptionally slow implementation of the EU instruments concerned. The Second Protocol and the EU Convention on Corruption are still not in force, more than seven years after their adoption.

Ninth, we should note that EC and EU instruments fail, currently, to lay down uniform penalties for transnational corruption or other forms of organised crime. Uniformity of penalties is currently no more a goal of EU policy for transnational crime, than it is a goal of the OECD Convention. In this respect, neither the EU nor the OECD goes down the road recommended by several academic studies of 'unification' of criminal penalties in certain fields.[48] Sanctions in the field of competition policy and certain other sectors such as fishing and agriculture have, on the other hand, been gradually harmonised under Community policies, but they are of a non-criminal nature.

Finally, it remains to be seen whether the loose EU sanctioning standards introduced pursuant to the Treaty on European Union will actually have any impact on the sentencing practice of the EU Member States, when seeking to deter these transnational crimes. In general, the EU standard lacks the hard cutting edge that would be required to make significant inroads into national sentencing practice. European case law on sanctions will have some impact on national court practice in particular cases, but only legislation is likely to make a real difference. Evaluation of Framework Decisions is, however, only just beginning. What has been achieved by the EU to date appears largely symbolic: the Framework Decisions signal to the Member States how seriously the Union regards certain types of criminality,

[48] Cf. the report of the 'Corpus Juris' study, which recommended fixed penalties for fraud against the Community budget as part of a uniform Community code. The report also recommends certain sentencing principles. Cf. Arts. 14–17 of the draft agreed in Florence in 2000 (published in Delmas-Marty and Vervaele 2000, 189 et seq.).

and encourage a common effort to combat them, without fundamentally altering national sentencing policy.

III. Establishing minimum standards for sanctions: approach of the OECD convention and the WGB

Sanctions against legal persons are discussed in detail above in our chapter on Article 2 of the Convention, although we will also deal with some aspects of corporate offending in this chapter, when discussing deterrence.[49] The main focus of this chapter is, however, the sanctions applied to natural persons.

1. Interpreting the Convention standard: background issues

What exactly does the Convention's goal of 'functional equivalence' mean, when we study the measures taken by the Parties to sanction foreign bribery?

To answer this question we will look not only at the terms of the Convention itself (and its Official Commentaries), but also at the practice of the OECD's WGB. The latter's role is a seminal one, as it is the body which interprets what is meant by the standard 'effective, proportionate, and dissuasive' and which then transmits its opinion to the Parties on whether the standard is met. This standard is not defined by the Convention, which means that the WGB enjoys a degree of leeway in its interpretation.

The work of the WGB is, however, subject to certain innate limits. First, it is not a Court whose decisions, like those of the European Court of Justice, bind the state Parties. Its recommendations can appear peremptory, where there is a clear failure to reach the Convention standard, but they are more often couched in persuasive diplomatic language, than in mandatory legal terms. Second, the WGB is bound by the general aims of the Convention, notably by the overriding goal of criminalisation of foreign bribery.[50] Criminalisation, however, does not imply uniformity of penalties: the harmonisation goal is a limited one, as we have already noted. The 'effective, proportionate, and dissuasive' standard must, therefore, be understood and applied against this background. The WGB might well lose credibility and support if it went beyond these parameters, and demanded excessive uniformity of sanctions.

[49] See III.3.4. below.

[50] The general parameters of the Convention are reflected not only in the express terms of the instrument itself, but also in its preamble, in the Official Commentaries to the Convention and in preceding instruments such as the OECD 1997a. The work of the WGB is also informed by the *Travaux Préparatoires*, which were drafted during the preparatory work on that Recommendation (OECD 1999; and see note 4).

The standard 'effective, proportionate, and dissuasive' is the overarching standard for sanctioning of foreign bribery under the Convention. The Convention could have made this even clearer by stating that this standard should be ensured 'in any event', as in the formulation of the standard by the European Court of Justice.[51] As it is, the standard appears as the first sentence of Article 3(1), without any linguistic linkage to the more specific parameters which follow. Despite this, it is clear that the effectiveness standard is always the final measure of compliance by the Parties with Article 3 of the Convention. The evaluations and recommendations of the WGB contained in the monitoring reports (especially in the Phase 2 reports), invariably cite the standard as their final benchmark.

The following specific parameters relating to sanctions are outlined in Article 3(1):

- first, that 'the range of penalties shall be comparable to that applicable to the bribery of the Party's own public officials';
- second, that, 'in the case of natural persons', the range of penalties shall 'include deprivation of liberty sufficient to enable effective mutual legal assistance and extradition'.

In line with the approach of the WGB, we will first consider these more specific sanctioning parameters, as related to natural persons, before studying the interpretation and impact of the OECD Convention's overarching 'effectiveness, proportionality, and dissuasion' standard.

2. Article 3(1) – specific parameters for the sanctioning of corruption by natural persons

2.1. The 'assimilation' standard

2.1.1. Assimilation with domestic bribery offences

Ensuring that the Parties treat active bribery of foreign officials as severely[52] as domestic bribery requires, as a first step, that the same penalties must be

[51] According to the European Court of Justice in Case 68/88 *Commission* v. *Greece* [1989] ECR 2965, while Member States may, in the absence of harmonised EU-wide penalties, choose the type of penalties (e.g. administrative or criminal) by which they sanction transgressions of Community law, 'they must ensure in particular that infringements of Community law are penalized under conditions, both procedural and substantive, which are analogous to those applicable to infringements of national law of a similar nature and importance and which, in any event, make the penalty effective, proportionate, and dissuasive'.

[52] Indeed the comparative test is framed by the WGB in terms of similar standards of severity, rather than similar 'mildness', in keeping with its general preference for heavier rather than lighter sanctions for bribery: see III.3.4.1. below.

available, in principle, to sanction each type of offence. Whether judges would actually treat the two types of cases equally severely in practice is quite another matter. National judges might in fact be expected to sanction corruption of national officials more sternly because of the more obvious, direct impact on national administration. Be that as it may, the WGB is bound by the terms of the Convention to establish whether foreign bribery is punishable by a similar 'range' of penalties.

The requirement in the Convention's Article 3 is a relatively explicit one, and should therefore not have been difficult for the legislator implementing the Convention to meet. And indeed, the Phase 1 reviews of implementation by state Parties have revealed that the latter have, almost invariably, simply taken the penalties applicable in laws prohibiting domestic corruption, and applied them in identical terms to the bribery of foreign public officials.

In the rare cases where either the implementing legislation or another legal source, applied to foreign bribery sanctions *lower* than those applied to the domestic variety,[53] the WGB has called for realignment. In Slovakia, the non-aggravated form of bribery was punishable by a maximum penalty of two years imprisonment in case of foreign bribery, but by a maximum of three years for bribery of domestic officials. The WGB's response was clear:

> 'punishability is therefore more severe in case of bribery of a domestic official than with regard to foreign public officials. This does not meet the requirements of the Convention calling for comparable penalties.'[54]

A considerably larger difference in penalties existing under US law – five years maximum for foreign bribery compared to fifteen years maximum for bribery of domestic officials – also led the WGB to recommend an alignment.[55] The fact that the US authorities in practice sanction foreign bribery as seriously[56] as its domestic counterpart did not justify the discrepancy being maintained on paper; the maintenance of two significantly different ranges of penalties failed to satisfy the requirements of the Convention. Looking at paper differences in Argentina did not, by contrast, lead the WGB to recommend an alignment of sanctions for aggravated bribery; the Argentinean authorities explained that the foreign bribery offence was subject to tighter conditions of enforcement than the heavier

[53] The US FCPA 1977 was in force before the Convention, though it has been amended since, in the light of Convention requirements: see Low 2005 and her ch. in this commentary.
[54] SK-Ph1, 9. [55] US-Ph2, 15, 40.
[56] Or as leniently: the WGB Phase 2 report on US application indicates concerns about 'rather moderate' penalties being imposed in practice (US-Ph2, 16).

imprisonment sanction for the domestic offence.[57] Equally, in the case of Chile, the sanctions for aggravated domestic bribery offences are, in rather restricted circumstances,[58] higher than those for equivalent foreign offences. The WGB was prepared to overlook this difference as the domestic and foreign offences were, in all other cases, subject to comparable sanctions.[59]

The Convention does not, therefore, require *absolute equivalence*, in terms of the punishability of domestic and foreign bribery. What the WGB will not tolerate is any *significant divergence* in the range of penalties, which is likely to result in practice in the imposition of less severe sanctions for the bribery of a foreign official.

In the context of assimilation, we should note that sentencing guidelines must also apply in a comparable way to cases of foreign and domestic bribery. Any factors which would suggest greater weight being given to the penalisation of the domestic offence should not be considered.[60]

What if foreign bribery is punishable more harshly than domestic bribery? This is the case under the laws of a few of the Parties to the OECD Convention.[61] The WGB would appear to have nothing adverse to say about this state of affairs: implicitly, it seems to find it a good thing that foreign bribery might in some cases receive harsher treatment than the bribery of domestic officials. The likelihood of such harsher penalties being imposed in practice may, however, not be great. This is a matter to be followed up in Phase 2 reviews, or thereafter (there is currently little, if any, case law on which to work). Where a more onerous sanction attaches to foreign bribery, the WGB has expressed concern that, in the case of overlapping domestic and foreign offences, the national court might apply the domestic offence in favour of the defendant, 'thus resulting in discriminatory punishments'.[62]

One can question whether the WGB's approach to more onerous penalties being imposed for the foreign offence is really 'proportionate'. If it would regard the penalty for the domestic offence as adequate, why go along with a higher offence for foreign bribery? The answer lies in the basic

[57] AR-Ph1, 9 et seq.

[58] These concern certain discrepancies relating to the range of penalties applicable to the aggravated offence: CL-Ph1, 9 et seq.

[59] CL-Ph1, 9 et seq., 30.

[60] Cf. the Portuguese case: PT-Ph1, 11 et seq. (discussing sentencing guidelines in relation to fines in lieu of imprisonment).

[61] Cf., regarding imprisonment, Australia, and in some circumstances, also Portuguese law. In Japan, fines for natural persons are higher in the case of foreign bribery than for the domestic offence (JP-Ph1, 10).

[62] PT-Ph1, 13.

policy of the WGB. As we shall see, the WGB has consistently welcomed the increases in sanctions which have followed from implementation of the Convention in national law; it has explicitly called for such increases in its monitoring reports, indicating its desire to push Parties towards relatively severe sanctions for a phenomenon which hitherto went (and still largely goes) unpunished, even if states are increasingly tackling domestic corruption.

Thus it should not be surprising that the WGB finds higher penalties for foreign corruption unobjectionable. Later in this chapter, we will have more to say about WGB policy on the effectiveness of sanctions; we will see that the latter has interpreted the Convention standard to the effect that relatively low sanctions may be accepted (subject to certain qualifications) where this is consistent with the culture of the criminal justice system concerned.

2.1.2. Assimilation with other forms of economic crime

The WGB has taken assimilation a step beyond the express terms of the Convention by introducing into its evaluation of sanctions for the offence of active bribery of foreign public officials a comparison with other forms of economic crime, notably theft, fraud, and embezzlement. WGB country reports contain observations on whether the penalties for these offences and foreign bribery offences are in a broadly similar range. Minimum[63] and maximum[64] penalties may be compared, and the comparison is not necessarily limited to these three specific offences. The comparisons are carried out systematically by the WGB in every case, but the comprehensiveness or intensity of the analysis depends on the amount of information provided by the country concerned.

If it finds that other economic crimes such as embezzlement are much more severely penalised, the WGB will make an observation to this effect in its report.[65] Such a finding could, in a serious case, persuade the WGB to question whether foreign bribery is being tackled with sufficient 'effectiveness'.[66]

[63] Cf. MX-Ph1, 9.

[64] For example, Netherlands (NL-Ph1, 15) and New Zealand (NZ-Ph1, 13).

[65] Cf. the report on Austria which points to the higher penalties for offences against property (AT-Ph1, 9, 25). Note also the case of the Czech Republic, which imposes considerably higher tariffs for larceny, embezzlement, and fraud, if the offender causes 'significant or major damage', but not for bribery (CZ-Ph1, 8). Chile has also been criticised for its much higher penalties for embezzlement compared to bribery (CL-Ph1, 11).

[66] Cf. the findings in the Danish report, for example: after noting that penalties for other similar offences include a maximum of eight years for fraud in aggravated circumstances, and a maximum of four years for tax fraud, whereas the maximum for active bribery is only three years, the WGB expressed its 'particular concern' about this apparent failure to meet the Convention's standard (DK-Ph1, 26). Cf. also CL-Ph1, 11.

A comparison of sanctions for these different forms of economic crime may serve the interests of both 'parties' to the evaluation process: the WGB will be anxious to establish that foreign bribery is penalised at least as heavily as these comparable offences; on the other hand, the state Party subject to the evaluation may 'defend' apparently rather low penalties by indicating that this is the usual level for offences of an economic nature.[67] Comparatively low penalties for economic crime, including the foreign bribery offence, have been justified by some Parties to the Convention by distinguishing them from offences against the person, which are said to merit a much tougher response.[68]

In its Phase 2 reports on application of the Convention standard, the WGB's review is often confronted by a lack of prosecutions for the offence of foreign bribery. It is therefore often forced to rely on statistics for bribery of *domestic officials*, in order to gather an impression of how bribery offences as such are sanctioned.[69] The Phase 2 examination may then draw on comparisons between sanctions imposed for domestic bribery, on the one hand, and for 'similar economic crimes such as theft and embezzlement',[70] on the other hand.

2.2. Deprivation of liberty sufficient to enable effective mutual legal assistance and extradition

One of the goals of the Convention is to facilitate improved judicial co-operation between Parties in relation to the offence of active foreign bribery. Articles 9 and 10 of the Convention link the criminalisation of the bribery offence under the Convention with the provision of effective mutual legal assistance and extradition.[71] Criminalisation alone, however, without a minimum level of sanction, would not necessarily be sufficient to allow Parties to co-operate.

As far as extradition is concerned, the minimum sentencing threshold is usually set at one year's deprivation of liberty. This is the standard required by the Council of Europe Convention on Extradition, to which

[67] Cf. in relation to fines, the case of Australia (AU-Ph1, 24).

[68] SE-Ph1, 8, 24.

[69] These statistics are, however, often unclear, and the WGB frequently calls for further refinement.

[70] FI-Ph1, 20.

[71] See our commentary on these Articles of the Convention in the corresponding chs.

all the European Members of the WGB have subscribed.[72] The terms of Article 2(1) of the instrument establishing a 'European Arrest Warrant' impose a similar threshold.[73] And WGB states not party to these European instruments apply a similar standard.[74]

The *Travaux Préparatoires* to the Convention recognised that the imprisonment penalty would have to go beyond the one year mark, if extradition were not to be limited.[75] In order to cover the eventuality of different sentencing thresholds among the contracting Parties, the Convention, however, eschewed a specific minimum and applied instead a test of 'sufficiency'. This general test is also applied to any conditions for provision of mutual legal assistance: in relation to the latter, most states do not in fact make co-operation conditional on a minimum penalty.

In each and every case, then – before it applies its general test of 'effectiveness, proportionality, and dissuasion' – the WGB will look at the particular national sanction for foreign bribery to see if it is sufficiently high to enable, first, mutual legal assistance to be effected, and second, to allow for the extradition of persons who face charges under the offence of bribery of foreign officials. Usually, if there has been a problem in any of the Parties, it has concerned extradition. The WGB has pointed out to several state Parties the need to revise their minimum penalties to meet extradition Treaty requirements.[76]

[72] Art. 2(1) COE 1957 states: 'Extradition shall be granted in respect of offences punishable under the laws of the requesting Party and of the requested Party by deprivation of liberty or under a detention order for a maximum period of at least one year or by a more severe penalty. Where a conviction and prison sentence have occurred or a detention order has been made in the territory of the requesting Party, the punishment awarded must have been for a period of at least four months.' (The European Arrest Warrant now governs extradition between EU Member States, and Art. 2(1) of this instrument applies the same condition: EU 2002c, 1.)

[73] EU 2002c.

[74] Cf. e.g. Argentina, which requires the average of the minimum and maximum penalties to be at least one year under the law of both Argentina and the requesting state (AR-Ph1, 10). Or the United States: 'generally, U.S. extradition Treaties provide for extradition for any offence that is punishable under the laws of both the requesting and request state by a maximum term of imprisonment exceeding one year' (US-Ph1, 12). For the example of Korea cf. KR-Ph1, 10: offence must be punishable for a period of 'one year or more', under Korean laws and the law of the requesting state.

[75] OECD 1999, F-1031.

[76] Recently, the WGB recommended to Chile that it amend its legislation to bring the minimum penalty for foreign bribery up to one year's imprisonment, to meet the requisite standard (CL-Ph1, 12, 30). The maximum sentence of imprisonment for foreign bribery under Norwegian law was increased from one year after the WGB found that this was not only ineffective in terms of the general test, but also risked blocking extradition from Norway for the offence, given that the Extradition Act requires offences to be punishable under Norwegian law by more than one year's imprisonment (NO-Ph1, 15).

The vast majority of Parties have complied with this parameter of the Article 3 standard. It is a basic minimum standard, however, and, even if it is met, it does not mean that the WGB will necessarily go on to find the sanctions 'effective, proportionate, and dissuasive'. As is clear from the text of Article 3, this is a broader test which involves the WGB in an independent evaluative process, in exercise of the role accorded to it by Article 12 of the Convention.

3. The OECD standard of 'effective, proportionate, and dissuasive' sanctions

3.1. Achieving a common standard: the goals of Phase 1 and Phase 2 monitoring

The EU-based standard 'effective, proportionate, and dissuasive' leaves much open. Indeed, as we have already noted, its general nature clearly commended itself to the framers of the OECD Convention. In applying the standard imported from EC law, the WGB is guided by the broad principles, parameters, and objectives of the Convention but it is not circumscribed by any binding judicial interpretation[77] or sentencing guidelines. These OECD 'specifics' may be contrasted with the EU's different orientation.[78]

Leading commentators have sought to emphasise the orientation of the Convention towards national law, partly to distinguish the method of harmonisation employed by the OECD's anti-corruption strategy from that employed by other international organisations.[79] In evaluating over thirty different national laws and sentencing practices, the WGB is confronted by considerable diversity, both as far as the sanctions themselves are concerned and with regard to their enforcement. The WGB, unlike the European

[77] It does not refer to the judgements of the European Court of Justice, which is the only judicial tribunal to have gone about interpreting the standard (albeit in the very different EU context). Nor does it elaborate upon the standard in the light of the 'explanatory reports' in which the Council of the EU offers comments on sanctions under the EU's anti-corruption instruments, under the Second Protocol or other EU anti-fraud instruments (cf., for example, EU 1999, 8).

[78] Where financial crime is concerned, the creation of a 'level playing field' for undertakings operating in a 'single' internal market gives a sharper edge to EU harmonisation efforts than we find in the OECD. Secondly, regarding criminal justice matters in general, the creation of an 'Area of Freedom, Security, and Justice' based on free movement of persons across open borders, and on intensive co-operation between police and judicial authorities, calls for direct legislative intervention in relation to certain forms of cross-border criminality, of a kind unknown to the OECD. See II.2.3. above.

[79] Pieth 2006 (see also note 7).

Commission, begins by accepting this diversity. Criminalisation of the offence of active bribery of foreign officials is the key goal and the WGB has no remit to unify national laws or sentencing practice. The principle of 'functional equivalence' occupies a different starting position than the EU's goal of 'minimum approximation' of penalties in respect of transnational crime.[80]

On the other hand, the 'peer pressure' approach to OECD monitoring of compliance with the Convention induces a very strong 'comparative ethic' which promotes a broadbased convergence to the standards of the Convention, not only where sanctions are concerned.[81] The comparative approach of the national official – as Lead Examiner and member of the WGB – to evaluation of national criminal law is, of course, strongly influenced by his or her own national system. As members of the WGB, the Lead Examiners are, however, fulfilling a collective monitoring function, and are therefore somewhat separated (if not divorced) from their national allegiances.

There are a number of procedural guidelines for the work of the WGB evaluation teams.[82] Early in 2004, the OECD Secretariat issued 'Guidelines for Phase 2 Reviews' to inform the teams of examiners in their on-site work and in reporting.[83] These indicate that the Phase 2 review process should be 'transparent, rigorous, and credible', and geared towards 'particular issues raised by the examined country's implementation of the Convention and its governmental, economic, and geographic organization'. The Secretariat has also issued a discussion paper (confidential 'non-paper') entitled 'Monitoring Issues'.[84] But these documents lack any major substantive content which might lend meaning to the standard 'effective, proportionate, and dissuasive' sanctions. The latter document does, however, stress the need to enforce the Convention: the monitoring process, meaning Phase 1 and 2 reviews, should be geared towards establishing that 'all participating countries have reached a satisfactory standard of compliance with the Convention and the 1997 Recommendation'.[85] The document concludes by saying that the Phase 2 review process can be regarded as a success 'if it has determined that countries are able and willing to enforce effectively the Convention and the 1997 Recommendation'.[86]

[80] Cf. Delmas-Marty's discussion of 'Europe as a laboratory for legal pluralism', in which she distinguishes between traditional intergovernmental mechanisms of legal integration and the new possibilities offered by the 'European space' (2002, 35).

[81] See ch. on Article 12 below. [82] For full details, see ch. on Article 12 below.

[83] DAFFE/IM/BR/WD(2003)7/final.

[84] DAF/INV/BR/WD(2004)18/REV1. This document led to the revised Guidelines on Phase 2 Monitoring of 2005: see I.5. in our ch. on Article 12.

[85] DAF/INV/BR/WD(2004)18/REV1, 5. [86] DAF/INV/BR/WD(2004)18/REV1, 9.

If Phase 1 reviews are designed to check 'paper compliance' with the criminalisation etc. requirements of the Convention, then the principal aim of the Phase 2 process is to ensure that countries apply criminal sanctions of a sufficiently dissuasive effect to deter the corruption of foreign public officials.[87]

So far there have been few prosecutions or convictions for foreign bribery, which is a new offence for almost all the contracting Parties. This means that the 'effective, proportionate, and dissuasive' standard continues to be applied, in the main, to the 'punishability', rather than the actual punishment, of the offence. As we shall see, in its Phase 1 reports the WGB has determined in several cases that national legislation falls short of the standard, because it fails to provide for sufficiently dissuasive or effective penalties. In its Phase 2 reports, the WGB is often forced to conclude that it cannot test whether such penalties, even if they exist on paper, are in fact dissuasive, because there have been too few cases. The test of application, which would lend some empirical reality to what the standard 'effective, proportionate, and dissuasive' actually means, is thus frequently left for post-Phase 2 follow-up.

In our commentary, we are also confined by the lack of empirical material to which to apply the sanctioning standard of Article 3. It is probably only when the WGB's Phase 2 reviews are completed, i.e towards the end of 2007, that the first set of cases from different countries will become available for comparison.[88]

3.2. Dismantling the 'mantra': effectiveness as the key test?

Our chapter on Article 2 of the Convention came to the conclusion that 'effectiveness' had emerged as the key element of the sanctioning standard of the Convention, as applied to legal persons.[89] It also appears as the key criterion applied to sanctions against natural persons.

Although the phrase 'effective, proportionate, and dissuasive' is, in the end, always applied to Parties' sanctions as a unified test – sometimes almost as a mantra-like refrain – we can see in the country reports that the elements 'effective' and 'dissuasive' appear to form a synonymous couple.[90]

[87] Principally criminal sanctions, though the Convention and the WGB accept that other sanctions may meet the standard.

[88] The OECD Secretariat paper indicates that the WGB's 'essential mission' of monitoring enforcement of compliance must continue after completion of the Phase 2 reviews (DAF/INV/BR/WD(2004)18/REV1, 9). See also further discussion in our ch. on Article 12 below.

[89] See III.4. in ch. on Article 2 above.

[90] Cf., for example, the Phase 2 report for Luxembourg, in which the WGB recommends that Luxembourg takes steps to enhance 'awareness among prosecuting authorities on the importance of rigorously applying the range of sanctions provided for in criminal law which may be effective and dissuasive with respect to corruption' (LU-Ph2, 45).

Effectiveness embraces dissuasion and the joining of the two concepts is manifested in the WGB's repeated references to the aim of deterrence. The connotation of the term 'proportionality' is different and will be discussed separately.

'Effective' and 'dissuasive' are used interchangeably to reflect the 'repressive' elements of the WGB's standard, centring on the WGB's endorsement of relatively high penalties for both natural and legal persons, which should serve to deter the offence of foreign bribery. The OECD standard for 'effective' and 'dissuasive' sanctions is intended to be an exacting one; this emerges already from the references in the Convention's *Travaux Préparatoires* to the need for 'significant and dissuasive penalties'.[91]

Before considering the goal of deterrence in more detail, it is necessary to say something about the 'relative' nature of effectiveness. Like all would-be harmonising concepts of the Convention, the term is to be understood against the background of 'functional equivalence', the Convention's template principle for co-ordinated legal action against bribery of foreign officials.

3.3. Effectiveness as a relative concept: allowing for divergence of national laws

3.3.1. Divergence in custodial sanctions

The main goal of the OECD's anti-bribery Convention standard is to ensure that tough monetary sanctions are available against undertakings which engage in bribery of foreign officials.[92] But sanctions imposed on natural persons must also be sufficiently threatening to promote deterrence. As we made clear in the Introduction of this commentary,[93] the objective of the Convention is not to throw as many errant company officials as possible in jail, but to encourage compliance by deterrent sanctions without the need for coercive measures. There will be further discussion of the conditions required for such effective deterrence in the next section; here we are concerned with how the WGB approaches effectiveness in the context of the wide range of penalties available under the national laws of state Parties.

As the European Commission has pointed out in its recent paper on sanctions, it is not only penalties themselves which vary considerably from one state to another, but also the way in which they are enforced.[94] Within

[91] OECD 1999, F-1031.
[92] For a detailed discussion of corporate sanctions, see ch. on Article 2 above.
[93] See part V. of Introduction. [94] EU 2004a, 22.

the more global context of the OECD, the scope for divergence is even greater. We shall see that divergence of penalties is perfectly acceptable, in principle, under the Convention, but a minimum degree of convergence is also required.

In our commentary on Article 2, we discussed how the WGB has gone about judging overall effectiveness in relation to the diversity of corporate sanctions which apply in the contracting states.[95] We saw that a 'three-step procedure' was applied. The first and second steps of that procedure – namely, testing sanctions first against domestic law and, second, testing them on an international level – are equally valid here.[96]

We will now consider how the WGB approaches divergence in relation to the custodial sentences faced by natural persons. The basic question posed by its reports (although not always made explicit) is:

- *What is the minimum standard of effectiveness?*

A failure to provide for an imprisonment sanction at all, even if it be for minor cases of bribery, will not meet the minimum standard.[97] Article 3 requires, at the very least, 'deprivation of liberty sufficient to enable effective mutual legal assistance and extradition'.

The second main issue here reaches beyond compliance with this specific parameter. It asks to what extent the Convention allows a state Party to maintain its domestic interpretation of an effective penalty, regardless of the approach of other states? Or put another way:

- *How much divergence does the Convention tolerate?*

The system of monitoring employed by the OECD certainly militates against a 'splendid isolation' approach, but the Convention standard, as interpreted by the WGB, in fact leaves state Parties substantial leeway to employ their standards. We can see this 'margin of appreciation' rather clearly in the conclusions of the WGB relating to countries with relatively low imprisonment sentences. The following evaluations should be noted:

- in the case of Austria, the WGB held that it was doubtful that Austria's maximum penalty of two years' imprisonment matched the Convention standard, and that, at least for aggravated cases, the sentence should be reviewed;[98]

[95] See III.4. of that chapter.
[96] We have dealt with the first comparison in III.2.1. above.
[97] As in the case of Turkey: TR-Ph1, 10 et seq., 26. [98] AT-Ph1, 25.

- in the case of Denmark, a maximum of three years was called into question, partly because of higher sentences for passive bribery;[99]
- Finnish law lays down maximum penalties of two and four years respectively, for ordinary and aggravated cases of bribery; this was apparently deemed acceptable, taking into account the fact that such levels were 'very normal' in the context of the Finnish system as a whole;[100]
- Norway was deemed to be in contravention of the Convention by maintaining a maximum penalty of only one year for active bribery, a situation the Norwegians quickly corrected;[101] this case is somewhat similar to that of Chile, whose penalty of 61 days to 540 days for consent to afford a bribe was regarded as not meeting the Convention standard;[102]
- Swedish law's previous maximum penalty of two years has also now been increased to six years, for aggravated cases, having previously been found to be 'comparatively weak'.[103]

These findings indicate a 'rule-of-thumb' approach to sanctions at the low level, with two years seeming to be the minimum tolerable for a maximum level sentence, and four years being regarded as a more acceptable 'minimum-maximum' limit for aggravated forms of bribery.

As we saw, the average range of custodial penalty for domestic bribery offences was referred to in the Convention's *Travaux Préparatoires* as three to five years.[104] The Nordic countries in particular, but also Austria, continue to maintain lower levels of penalty, notwithstanding certain adjustments made as a result of the above WGB evaluations. Other signatory countries to the Convention apply much higher penalties. A far higher range applies, up to ten years or more, in major OECD-exporting states including Australia, France, Germany, Ireland, Italy, Poland, and the United States, which have all put in place very high custodial penalties for aggravated cases in particular.[105]

Maximum penalties of more than ten years do not, apparently, raise any eyebrows in the WGB. With regard to the higher range of sanctions employed in OECD countries, the WGB is usually content simply to note the high level and its likely impact on enforcement,[106] rather than to draw

[99] DK-Ph1, 26. [100] FI-Ph1, 7.
[101] NO-Ph1, 6, 15; NO-Ph2, 45, indicating an increase from one to a maximum of three years for the basic offence.
[102] CL-Ph1, 9 et seq., 30. [103] SE-Ph1, 24. [104] OECD 1999, F-1030–1031.
[105] See OECD Table (Annex A).
[106] Cf. for Australia the comment that, given its ten-year maximum penalty, 'it is very unlikely that a natural person bribing a foreign public official would not be imprisoned' (AU-Ph1, 24).

any particular comparisons with other OECD countries in the lower or middle ranges. We will, however, return to the issue of possibly 'excessive' penalties in our discussion of proportionality.

A large spread of possible years of imprisonment, with a very high possible maximum of fourteen years, and a low of two years, without any indication of benchmarks or sentencing guidelines, has recently caused the WGB some concern.[107]

The WGB does not have a lot of material to go on regarding the imposition of custodial sentences for bribery of foreign officials, but it has made critical observations about the use of suspended sentences and the lack of incarceration in practice, in relation to domestic bribery convictions.[108] If it does not expect every convicted briber to be locked up, its general view clearly is that commission of the offence of foreign bribery merits a custodial sentence. This stance is linked to the WGB's goal of deterrence, which will be addressed in the next section.

3.3.2. Divergence in monetary sanctions

In addition to custodial sentences, the WGB also expects natural persons to be punishable by fines in the case of commission of the offence of foreign bribery, though the Convention does not expressly require this, as Italy pointed out in justifying its failure to provide for any monetary sanctions for natural persons.[109] The WGB, unlike Italy, is of the view that a monetary penalty applicable to natural persons is 'a useful additional deterrent'.[110]

Fines are not imposed, in practice, by some other states, such as Norway, with imprisonment being preferred.[111] The fact that states may impose a fine on a natural person found guilty of active bribery as an alternative to imprisonment, as, for example, in Germany or Hungary, is not questioned by the WGB.[112] The latter accepts, as we shall see, that it is desirable to distinguish between cases of ordinary and aggravated bribery.[113] But if a fine, not the imprisonment sanction, is deemed appropriate in the particular case, then the fine should meet the effectiveness standard.

[107] MX-Ph2, 22.

[108] Cf., for example, the Phase 2 reports for France (FR-Ph2, 56), Germany (DE-Ph2, 41) and the United States (US-Ph2, 16). Italy, on the other hand, maintains that its sentences for the offence of bribing domestic officials have been 'severe' (IT-Ph2, 47). All of these countries are criticised by the WGB for failing to keep full statistics on such cases.

[109] IT-Ph1, 14. [110] IT-Ph1, 34. [111] NO-Ph1, 6.

[112] DE-Ph1, 6; DE-Ph2, 41. The Phase 2 report for Hungary confirms that a fine of €44 000 (maximum) 'may be imposed where the Court considers imprisonment to be too severe a penalty for the offence in question' (HU-Ph2, 54).

[113] See III.4.2. below.

The effectiveness of the various methods employed by state Parties to calculate fines on natural persons is thus scrutinised principally in the light of the goal of deterrence.[114] As for legal persons, the result of the calculation should be that substantial monetary penalties should be available to punish natural persons (though the fines for legal persons should be higher).

What a 'substantial fine' might mean for natural and legal persons can be roughly gauged from the reports of the WGB.

The maximum available fines for natural persons in France (c. €150 000[115]), Germany (maximum daily fine of €5000, up to 360 rates[116]) and the United States ($100 000[117]) would appear to satisfy the WGB, though the fines actually imposed on natural persons for bribery offences, in all three jurisdictions, have been moderate.[118]

Fines applicable to natural persons in Japan are set at an even lower level than for France, Germany and the United States, i.e. a maximum of 3 million yen (c. €22 200), whereas the highest corporate fine is one hundred times that amount.[119] The WGB is concerned about the Japanese limits for both natural and legal persons and has indicated that it will follow up sanctioning practice, once cases emerge, to see if the 'effective, proportionate, and dissuasive' standard is met.[120] Italy's decision not to impose fines upon natural persons for bribery offences, only on legal persons, also raises concerns, as already mentioned.[121]

[114] See III.3.4.1. below.

[115] FR-Ph2, 55 (the maximum level for legal persons is €750 000).

[116] DE-Ph1, 6; DE-Ph2, 41 et seq. (complaining about a lack of information about the actual amount of day fines imposed in practice). There are considerable concerns in Germany, on the other hand, about the limits on 'administrative fines' for companies, notwithstanding a doubling in the maximum fine from €500 000 to €1 million (DE-Ph2, 33). See also ch. on Article 2 above.

[117] US-Ph1, 11. This is worth about €83 000 at 1 July 2005 currency rates. US-Ph2, 15 indicates that alternative maximum fines are available in certain cases of pecuniary gain or loss. Low also explains in her ch. in this commentary that U.S. law authorises alternative maximum fines equal to the greater of twice the gross gain or twice the gross loss. The FCPA charge records show charges of over $300 000 against a company president of Crawford Enterprise (US-Ph2, 42). Fines for corporate entities are set at maximum of $2 million, but Sentencing Guidelines allow for considerable increases (note the $21.8 million fine imposed on Lockheed in 1995: US-Ph2, 16, 47). Cf. further discussion of US corporate fines in Low 2005, 20 et seq., and see her ch. in this commentary.

[118] DE-Ph2, 41; FR-Ph2, 56; US-Ph2, 16. In its Phase 2 reports for these three states, the WGB calls for follow-up of penalties imposed in practice.

[119] JP-Ph2, 50. The maximum corporate fine of 300 million yen is worth c. €2 250 000 as at 1 July 2005 currency rates.

[120] JP-Ph2, 50 et seq., 61.

[121] The country has no intention of changing this practice (IT-Ph2, 47). Monetary sanctions envisaged for companies are subject to a maximum €936 000 which the WGB thinks may not be 'sufficiently high considering the size of Italian companies' (IT-Ph2, 50).

The cases of Italy and Japan, give the WGB particular concern as regards legal persons. Given the size of the companies in both countries, the imposition of maximum limits of around €1 million and €2 million, respectively, are regarded as potentially insufficient in terms of the OECD standard. Follow-up of fines actually imposed within these maximum limits will be required, in order to test effectiveness.[122] There are also concerns about German administrative fine levels for companies, notwithstanding a doubling in recent years. The WGB recommends an increase in the maximum fine beyond €1 million.[123] In the case of the United Kingdom, statutory fines are unlimited for offences like foreign bribery which are prosecuted under indictment.[124]

For poorer countries, account is taken of the economic situation of the country concerned, including the average income of the working population, so that fines for these countries may legitimately be set at a significantly lower level than for richer states.[125]

Thus, we can see that functional equivalence in the area of pecuniary penalties means that effectiveness, in the sense used by the Convention, may be achieved by different ranges and levels of fine. However, a rough alignment of maximum fine levels between the major OECD exporting countries is clearly encouraged by the WGB, notably with regard to corporate fines. The deterrent effect of the current levels of maximum corporate fines in France, Germany, Italy, and Japan for the offence of foreign bribery – set at between c. €1 million and c. €2 million – is certainly questionable.

3.3.3. Divergence in civil and administrative sanctions

We can detect a similar range of divergence in the civil and administrative penalties applied to natural and legal persons.[126]

Sanctions of a civil or administrative nature should be introduced by state Parties. Even though the Convention's Article 3(4) is not mandatory about this, the WGB is keen to endorse them, in particular for legal

[122] IT-Ph2, 53; JP-Ph2, 61. [123] DE-Ph2, 45; and see note 116.

[124] UK-Ph2, 74 et seq.: the UK Phase 2 report gives much greater attention to the new UK rules on the seizure and confiscation of assets related to crime. See also our separate ch. on Article 3(3) below.

[125] Cf., for example, the reports on Brazil (BR-Ph1, 12), Bulgaria (BG-Ph2, 24 et seq.) and Mexico (MX-Ph2, 21 et seq.). The Mexican report questions a link with income for the calculation of the number of 'fine days'.

[126] See OECD Table (Annex A).

persons: the imposition of such sanctions can in certain cases 'ameliorate' concerns about low fines for legal persons.[127] The presence of a monetary deterrent is, however, deemed essential vis-à-vis corporations.[128]

Official Commentary 24 amplifies the terms of Article 3(4) of the Convention by listing four possible types of such sanctions which should be capable of being imposed upon legal persons:

- exclusion from entitlement to public benefits or aid;
- temporary or permanent disqualification from participation in public procurement or from the practice of other commercial activities;
- placing under judicial supervision; or
- a judicial winding-up order.

The focus here is on legal persons; but nevertheless, for natural persons too, the application of civil or administrative sanctions such as restricting certain activities can clearly contribute to a finding that, overall, the sanctioning of foreign bribery by a state Party meets the Convention standard. The UK Phase 2 report refers to disqualification penalties under the Company Directors Disqualification Act 1986, but no figures are provided on the use of such sanctions in practice.[129] The recent Hungarian report confirms that the WGB sees civil and administrative sanctions as necessary for natural persons.[130] Italy would allow for a range of prohibitive sanctions upon legal persons, for example licensing and contracting prohibitions, even up to a complete ban on trading, but it is not clear if similar sanctions would be available in respect of natural persons.[131] Regarding the United States, one should also refer to the possibility of civil fines.[132]

Thus, for legal and natural persons alike, civil and administrative penalties, even if they diverge considerably, are an important element in the anti-bribery sanctions armoury.

3.4. The impact of the common standard

3.4.1. The objective of deterrence

The prevalence of corruption of foreign officials by OECD-based companies or their subsidiaries is a given assumption of the organisation's WGB, even

[127] IT-Ph2, 50.

[128] Cf. the recent discussion concerning Brazil, whose range of administrative penalties would in the view of the WGB compensate for the lack of criminal sanctions applying to corporations, provided they are applied in practice (BR-Ph1, 12).

[129] UK-Ph2, 74. [130] HU-Ph2, 54.

[131] IT-Ph2, 47 et seq. [132] See the discussion by Low in this commentary.

in the absence of an appreciable number of convictions for foreign bribery outside the United States.[133] This assumption is maintained in the face of outright denials such as those of Japan, in the context of the recent Phase 2 review.[134] The OECD and its WGB want state Parties to tackle this problem in practice by launching criminal investigations and prosecuting accused persons, under the legislation which they have adopted to implement the Convention. Criminalisation should not remain a paper exercise. It is for this reason that the WGB adopts a robust approach in its monitoring of the penalisation of foreign bribery.[135] When it evaluates Parties' sanctions for this offence, it is clearly seeking an overall result, in practice, of effective deterrence.

The appreciation of which national penalties for corruption are 'effective' is, thus, substantially driven by the goal of deterrence.[136] Deterrence is meant here not only or even primarily in the sense of individual deterrence, but in terms of *general deterrence*.[137]

The WGB supports the introduction into national law of high penalties and questions sanctions regarded by it as too low, though, as we have seen, the broad lines of national criminal law or sentencing culture are respected, even where their application results in relatively low sanctions.

The WGB gives particular emphasis to heavy monetary penalties for undertakings, as discussed in our commentary on Article 2. In relation to corporations, the WGB has repeatedly emphasised the importance of applying sanctions which are strong enough to deter. Monetary sanctions should be set at a level which does not merely reflect 'the cost of doing business'.[138] The WGB's criticism of Japan, referred to in our chapter on Article 2, suggests that the Convention requires a level of monetary sanctions commensurate

[133] Cf. US Department of Commerce 2004 for recent statistics on investigations and prosecutions: the report refers to convictions in South Korea and Sweden. The Swedish conviction is confirmed by the OECD (OECD 2005a). Regarding Korea, cf. KR-Ph2, 8, which confirms the US report. Investigations into foreign bribery offences are currently underway in several state Parties (US Department of Commerce 2004, 23 et seq.). See also ch. on Article 5.

[134] JP-Ph2, 5 et seq.

[135] Cf. its recent call to Mexico to 'increase significantly the level of sanctions' (MX-Ph2, 57).

[136] Cf. the Phase 2 report for Norway: 'economic sanctions are a fundamental deterrent for economic offences such as bribery of foreign public officials in the conduct of international business transactions' (NO-Ph2, 49). The WGB also refers clearly to the 'deterrent effect' of prohibitive sanctions in the case of Italy (IT-Ph 2, 50).

[137] The notion of 'general deterrence' has been said elsewhere to be based on the 'premise…that the general population will be dissuaded from criminal behaviour by observing that punishment will necessarily follow commission of a crime and that the pain of punishment will be greater than the benefits which may stem from the illegal act' (Cole 1995, 437).

[138] JP-Ph2, 52.

with the 'large size of. . .its undertakings'.[139] A similar line is taken in relation to Italy, whose maximum fine for legal persons is about half that of Japan's.[140]

Regarding imprisonment for natural persons, the WGB has called for higher sentences of imprisonment than merely those which would enable effective extradition to take place. It notes, with approval, the general pattern of increases in prison sentences for foreign bribery which have resulted from implementation of the Convention but is critical of the extensive use in many OECD countries of suspended sentences for white collar criminals.[141]

It is one thing to question sanctions on paper, another to question their application. The application of sanctions represents an exercise of discretion on the part of national courts, which are, clearly, in a far better position than the WGB to judge which sort of sanction might be appropriate, and which might deter future re-offending, either by the defendant or other would-be offenders. The OECD Convention does not offer grounds for the WGB to interfere with the exercise of this judicial discretion; nevertheless, in its monitoring of the application of the Convention, the WGB encourages state Parties, as a matter of general sentencing policy, to apply a relatively high range of penalties.

Whether deterrence can in reality be best achieved by the threat or imposition of criminal sanctions raises questions related to theories of punishment.[142] The WGB does not seriously question the viability of a repressive strategy where international corruption is concerned. A detailed discussion of the questions which this strategy raises, from the standpoint of criminology or penology, would fall outside the scope of this commentary, but we should at least draw attention to the fact that the OECD's criminalisation strategy begs a number of such questions.[143]

3.4.2. US experience: deterrence in practice?

The most obvious place to look for empirical evidence relating to the deterrent effect of criminal sanctions for corruption of foreign officials

[139] JP-Ph1, 28.

[140] IT-Ph2, 50 (€936 000 is the maximum fine for non-aggravated bribery).

[141] See note 108.

[142] As Cole (1995) points out, it is not really possible for social science to measure the effects of general deterrence, as this would require one 'to examine the impact of different forms of the criminal sanction on various potential lawbreakers' (437).

[143] Huber (2002) doubts the repressive strategy, suggesting that criminal law sanctions offer the prospect of only 'limited efficiency' in the combating of corruption; she endorses instead 'preventive measures. . .outside the criminal law' (149).

by corporations or natural persons is the United States, which has a much longer record of investigation and prosecution and many more convictions for bribery of foreign public officials than anyone else in the OECD.[144]

The US Phase 2 report refers extensively to the experience with the Foreign Corrupt Practices Act. One of the most important elements emerging from discussion of the FCPA experience is the commitment of law enforcement and supervisory bodies to enforcement of the legislation. A culture of 'aggressive pursuit'[145] has been established, with corporations being made acutely aware that they face a real risk of legal action if they transgress the rules. Knowledge that action is being taken by the Department of Justice and/or by the US Securities and Exchange Commission (SEC) against violators seems to encourage corporate compliance. It is clearly very important that prosecutions are regularly launched under the FCPA, as this reinforces the perception among undertakings and their staff that they will be made answerable for acts of foreign bribery.

The level of sanctions eventually imposed on natural and legal persons convicted under the FCPA may have disappointed the WGB.[146] On the other hand, it warmly welcomes the 'collateral deterrent effects' that an FCPA investigation or conviction may have on companies.[147] The latter face not only the public opprobrium generated by a critical media; damaging commercial consequences may also follow from a FCPA investigation, such as suspension of export privileges. The threat of withdrawal of the eligibility to bid for government contracts, programmes, etc. is also said to operate as a powerful incentive for companies to take the FCPA seriously.[148]

[144] Cf. US Department of Commerce 2004 (Appendix B) and Low 2005 and her ch. in this commentary for recent accounts of US FCPA practice.

[145] US-Ph2, 8. This is also borne out by Low's analysis in this commentary.

[146] US-Ph2, 16. See Low's ch. in this commentary, on the other hand, which refers to more recent practice indicating increased in penalties.

[147] In its Phase 2 report on the United States, the WGB suggests that 'adverse publicity' could be 'a more important deterrent' than fines or imprisonment, which are applied by US courts at rather moderate levels (US-Ph2, 16). Sanctions for foreign corruption are long established under US law, but offences under the FCPA continue. The report suggests that the threat of sanctions and the attendant collateral consequences of criminalisation may act as an effective deterrent to corporations (ibid.). The WGB's Lead Examiners were at pains in their conclusions to emphasise these 'collateral consequences' as much as the sanctions imposed: 'it would be misleading to look only at the level of the fines and other sanctions available on the statute book' (US-Ph2, 17).

[148] US-Ph2, 6.

3.4.3. US experience: the Federal Sentencing Guidelines and corporate compliance

In the US context, we should also refer to the impact on corporate behaviour of the formalisation of certain incentives for companies to comply with anti-bribery legislation and other legislation prohibiting corporate misdemeanours, such as fraud. The prevalence of corporate compliance programmes within companies, as reported in the US Phase 2 report,[149] geared to ensuring staff are aware of FCPA requirements and are in a position to comply with them, suggests that law enforcement strategies in the United States have achieved a measure of general effectiveness or deterrence.[150] But the compliance programmes referred to in Phase 2 are of an informal nature. A certain formalisation has since taken place in respect of sentencing of corporations under the Federal Sentencing Guidelines, which apply to a wider range of economic offences than merely bribery.

In 2004, the US Sentencing Commission revised its Sentencing Guidelines for corporations and other organisations to include a new guideline specifically entitled 'Effective Compliance and Ethics Program'.[151] By proving their adherence to the guideline, by means of endorsement and implementation of such a programme, corporations ('organisations' as defined) can obtain significant reduction in fines payable under the Sentencing Guidelines. The idea is not new, but the new version of these Guidelines specifies in much greater detail than before what would be required of a company in order to fulfil the terms of an 'effective' programme: seven 'minimum' conditions are laid out.[152] Fulfilment of these will entitle the offending company to a three-point reduction to the 'culpability score',[153] one of the principal factors used in the determination of the range of sentence, under the Guidelines.

In more general terms, the US Federal Sentencing Guidelines, like their predecessors and counterparts at state level, represent an attempt to limit the wide discretion previously enjoyed by US judges to set sentences in accordance with their personal (policy) predilections.[154] The Sentencing Guidelines do not, however, exclusively endorse the general deterrence

[149] US-Ph2, 17 et seq. The report indicates that such programmes had already been formalised, to an extent, by prosecutors making them a condition of plea agreements (17).

[150] The Phase 2 report refers to evidence from one experienced US practitioner that such programmes 'are the most important measure contributing to prevention and deterrence' (US-Ph2, 17).

[151] § 8 B2.1 Sentencing Guidelines 2004.

[152] § 8 B2.1(b) Sentencing Guidelines 2004.

[153] § 8 C2.5 Sentencing Guidelines 2004.

[154] Von Hirsch 1987, 5, who refers to the desire to bring 'purpose and order to sentencing' by introduction of the Guidelines.

school of punishment theory.[155] As pointed out in their introduction to the Guidelines, the Sentencing Commission eschews a 'clear-cut...decision' in favour of just deserts, deterrence or incapacitation or rehabilitation theories and tries to steer a middle way based on an analysis of sentencing practice.[156] The new guideline referred to above is thus to be seen as part of the 'carrot and stick' approach to corporate penalties.[157]

The impact of the US Sentencing Guidelines over the past fifteen years has recently been reviewed by the US Sentencing Commission, which is responsible for issuing and updating the Guidelines and in this sense for directing sentencing policy.[158] In terms of economic offences, the review reports a significant decline over the period in the use of simple probation for fraud offenders (reduced by about two-thirds) and for embezzlers and tax evaders (reduced by about one-half). The rate of imprisonment for fraud offenders rose from about 50% in the pre-Guidelines era to almost 70% by 2001. This is in keeping with the desire to increase sentences for 'white collar' crime, especially those of a serious character. The length of prison time actually served by fraud offenders or embezzlers has not, however, increased, even if more of them are being sent to prison. Recent further strengthening of the severity of sentence levels by the Sentencing Guidelines in the light of the corporate scandals in the United States of 2002 were not taken into account by this review.

No specific information on bribery offences is given in this review. One can, however, extrapolate from the US Phase 2 report that the general trend toward higher sentences for economic offences may not in fact yet have reached the bribery offence; the brief survey conducted for that report suggests that 'convictions under the FCPA or related charges...indicate that most of them have resulted in rather moderate fines for both corporations and individuals, and probation or confinement instead of imprisonment'.[159]

[155] As we pointed out already above in our ch. on Article 2 of the Convention, OECD state Parties differ considerably in their interpretation of the goals of corporate punishment.

[156] This is reflected in the introductory commentary to ch. 8 which states that the guidelines relating to the sentencing of organizations are supposed to ensure 'that the sanctions imposed upon organizations and their agents, taken together, will provide just punishment, adequate deterrence, and incentives for organizations to maintain internal mechanisms for preventing, detecting, and reporting criminal conduct'.

[157] Cf. the endorsement of corporate penalties, inter alia on grounds of deterrence, by R. Campos in the Financial Times, 13 April 2005, 13: 'Regulators must not abandon corporate penalties'.

[158] US Sentencing Commission 2004, 55 et seq. (cf. http://www.ussc.gov). The report can be compared with the predictions of von Hirsch, Knapp and Tonry 1987.

[159] US-Ph2, 16.

It should be pointed out, when concluding this brief review of US sentencing practice related to bribery and other economic offences, that the US Supreme Court, in its recent judgment in the case of *U.S.* v. *Booker* and *U.S.* v. *Fanfan*,[160] declared that the Sentencing Guidelines are not mandatory. This may lead judges not to base certain sentencing decisions on the criteria established by the US Sentencing Commission, but as far as corporations are concerned, it is anticipated, for a number of reasons, that compliance programmes will continue to be adopted in line with the Guidelines.[161] For example, the Department of Justice's 'Principles of Federal Prosecution of Business Organizations' point out that the existence of a company compliance programme is a factor examined by prosecutors when deciding whether to bring criminal charges.[162]

The WGB predicts that investigations and prosecutions in the United States under the FCPA will increase in the years ahead, in the light of 'increasing globalised trade'.[163] Thus, there will be more precedents, to keep up the pressure for compliance by US companies; of course, the prosecutions and precedents will themselves indicate that offending is continuing, but, as we have just pointed out, companies' adoption of compliance programmes is also likely to increase in the years ahead, inducing a significant preventive effect.

3.4.4. Contribution of repressive measures to combating corruption?

Taking the evidence gathered by the WGB at face value, we can suggest that the risk of detection in the United States is high. In these circumstances, criminologists would surmise that the risk of offending is likely to recede.[164]

No other OECD member shows a number of prosecutions of the offence of bribing foreign public officials which even approaches the US figures.[165] There are, however, examples of prosecutions and convictions for *domestic bribery* in the United States and in other OECD member countries, on the basis of which we can also try to draw some tentative conclusions about the contribution of criminal law measures to combating corruption.

[160] *U.S.* v. *Booker*, 543 U.S. 220, 125 S.Ct. 738, 160 L.Ed. 2d 621 (2005); *U.S.* v. *Fanfan*, 542 U.S. 963, 125 S.Ct. 26 (Mem), 159 L.Ed. 2d 854 (2005).
[161] Cf. the discussion by Chilton 2005 and Low 2005, 30.
[162] Department of Justice 2003. These principles of prosecution are more fully discussed in the ch. on Article 5 below.
[163] US-Ph2, 7.
[164] Ashworth 2002, 1079, and for an early statement of the theory, Beccaria 1988 (1766), 120 et seq.
[165] US Department of Commerce 2004, ch. 3.

In recent years, domestic anti-corruption strategies have increasingly targeted 'organised crime'; many of the more recent criminal law measures taken against corruption can be seen in this context. Some of the cases of systemic corruption which have affected and continue to affect certain countries' political, economic, and judicial systems have engendered rather dynamic legislative or prosecutorial intervention, in order to 'clean up' the institutions concerned.[166] Measures taken against politicians may not in all cases have been of a criminal nature, but high-profile prosecutions have been taken against well-known figures in a number of OECD countries.[167] Although resulting sentences may have been low, the investigations or convictions have served to discredit many of the individuals as well as tainting the workings of the governments in which they were involved. New institutions, laws, or practices were introduced as part of the 'cleaning up' exercise.[168]

A sustained effort by law enforcement and judiciary[169] to deter corruption by bringing offenders – particularly high-level offenders – to trial serves to create at least an 'atmosphere of deterrence' which can in turn encourage the development of compliance systems. The stigma attached to a criminal investigation and the resulting damage to reputation is enough to deter other potential wrongdoers, without paying too much attention to the precise level of penalty. This is the lesson from US experience, at least.

The deterrent effect of criminal law can be enhanced by the availability of civil or administrative sanctions. The criminal law offers an obvious coercive 'stick' with which to beat the bribers. Still, the evidence from countries which use this stick to combat corruption suggests that its use should be accompanied by a range of other non-criminal measures; together these may generate the necessary degree of public support for an anti-corruption culture which can be regarded as truly 'effective'. So, in concluding this discussion of effectiveness, it should be remembered that the Convention indeed does not put all its eggs into one basket, where the

[166] Notably in Italy: cf., for example, the comments by Forti 2000, 173 et seq. The recent Phase 2 reports for Bulgaria and Mexico are also points of reference here.

[167] One need refer here only to the investigations in Germany into party funding which resulted in the former Chancellor Helmut Kohl settling a case, though it is unclear whether the charges would have stood up in court (Walther 2004, 371 et seq.).

[168] Cf. the accounts of recent manifestations of corruption in political life in various European countries, and the responses to them, in the edited collections of Pieth and Eigen 1999 and Bernasconi 2000.

[169] The independence of prosecutors and judges from the Executive is a prerequisite for such a successful strategy. See further ch. on Article 5.

sanctioning of the foreign bribery offence is concerned. It embraces a range of possible sanctions, including those of a non-criminal nature.

4. Proportionality as a discrete element of the OECD common standard

4.1. Distinguishing proportionality from effectiveness

In EC law, the term 'proportionality' has been given its own discrete meaning; the OECD Convention, as interpreted by the WGB, fails to follow suit.

There are no discrete references to the principle of proportionality in the reports of the WGB. It is treated as part of the 'effective, proportionate, and dissuasive' mantra. In its reports asserting that the state Parties fall short of the standard expected by Convention, the emphasis of the WGB is invariably on the lack of effective and dissuasive sanctions, which usually means insufficiently high deterrent penalties. 'Proportionality' is bracketed together with the other concepts, suggesting that, if the sanction is not effective, then, equally, the proportionality standard is not met. But the proportionality element of the standard is rarely, if ever, separately tested. This may be because the WGB does not think it has ever been confronted by a 'disproportionate' penalty, but a clear meaning of proportionality, distinct from 'effectiveness' or 'dissuasion', has not emerged.

In the absence of clear analysis or definition by the WGB, it is therefore very difficult to supply readers with a clear understanding of what Article 3 of the Convention might mean by 'proportionate' sanctions. We can only surmise what it might mean, by reading between the lines and making certain assumptions about what the WGB implicitly understands to be a 'proportionate' or, for that matter 'disproportionate', sanction.

Criminological sentencing theory requires the *severity* of penalties to be determined by reference to the *seriousness* of crimes.[170] The European Court of Justice, when analysing sanctions affecting an EU interest, has opined in similar fashion that they must not be 'disproportionate to the gravity of the infringement',[171] and that 'the penalty must not exceed what is appropriate and necessary to attain the objective sought'.[172] With regard to the setting

[170] Von Hirsch and Ashworth 2005. [171] Case 157/79 *R.* v. *Pieck* [1980] ECR 2171.

[172] Made in a case concerning a non-criminal sanction (forfeiture of a security) imposed under Community law (Case 122/78 *SA Buitoni* v. *Fonds d'orientation et de régularisation des marches agricoles* [1979] ECR 677, para. 16: 'As regards the problem of proportionality, it should be examined whether the penalty laid down in [the EC Regulation] for failure to comply with the period for presentation of the proofs prescribed by that provision exceeds what is appropriate and necessary to attain the objective sought.')

of fines against companies in competition law cases, the European Court has stated that the basic principle is that 'penalties and sanctions must fit the offence'.[173]

Despite the lack of direct analysis of proportionality, we can also see the notion that 'punishment must fit the offence' at work in a general way in WGB monitoring.

The WGB views corruption as a serious economic offence, at least as serious as comparable economic offences, such as theft, fraud, and embezzlement.[174] As we have seen, it indulges in a consistent, albeit rather broad-brush, comparison of the penalties for such offences: the comparison is invariably slanted towards checking whether corruption attracts 'equally high' penalties. At this very basic assimilation level, therefore, the WGB has a certain idea of the type of sanction that would fit the crime of corruption. The thinking is that it would be disproportionate for Parties to impose penalties for the two sets of offences which diverge considerably, although there is no precise comparison of the damaging effects of these crimes, in an economic or moral sense.

The WGB believes deprivation of liberty for natural persons is, in principle, an appropriate response to the seriousness of the offence of foreign bribery, mainly because of its supposed deterrent effect. This is so even for minor cases, as we already saw.[175] The length of prison sentence should be set at broadly the same level as that applied by the national system concerned to the other economic offences, certainly not any lower.[176]

The WGB also has a certain view of the type of monetary penalties which would meet the Convention standard, particularly where undertakings are concerned; this has been discussed in our commentary concerning Article 2 of the Convention.[177]

Reviewing what we might call the WGB's 'gut approach' to an appropriate penalty for natural or legal persons, it appears to be dictated mainly by considerations of effectiveness and dissuasion. This brings us to the rather circular conclusion that a 'proportionate' penalty is one which meets the standard of effectiveness (as we have described it above). In this way, the notion of 'proportionality' is deprived of a separate meaning. But perhaps there are other dimensions of proportionality at play, at least implicitly, in the WGB's application of the Convention standard.

[173] Case T-224/00 *Archer Daniels Midland Co. and another* v. *Commission* [2003] ECR II-2597, para. 39, a case where reliance is placed by EU competition law on the criminal law principles of non-retroactivity of penalties and legal certainty.

[174] See II.2.1. above. [175] See TR-Ph1, 10 et seq., 26, and the discussion in III.3.3.1. above.

[176] See II.2.1. above. [177] See also III.3.3.2. above.

4.2. Differentiating between ordinary and serious corruption: a proportionate response by state Parties?

There is an implicit expectation that state Parties will sanction aggravated cases of foreign bribery more severely than ordinary cases. Some states may establish a specific offence of 'serious bribery' of foreign officials, whereas others may list specific aggravating circumstances which can influence the sentencing process. The WGB does not express a clear preference for one or the other approach, leaving it to national law to determine the best method, but it does call upon states actually to apply the harsher penalties in aggravated cases.

In principle, if an aggravated bribery offence exists in relation to domestic bribery, then it should be extended to bribery of foreign officials.[178]

The Swedish authorities have recently established a maximum custodial penalty of six years for the offence of serious bribery, compared to a two-year maximum applying before. Although Swedish law already provided for aggravating circumstances to be taken into account in sentencing, the WGB obviously did not believe that the maximum limit would allow for a sufficient reflection of these in the sentencing process.

Where maximum custodial penalties are comparatively low, as we saw, for example, in the cases of Austria, Chile, Denmark, Finland, Norway, and Sweden,[179] the WGB has tempered its readiness to accept these countries' comparatively low penalties by calling on them at least to penalise the aggravated cases more heavily. A two- or three-year sentence of imprisonment for aggravated bribery clearly offends the sense of justice perceived by the majority of the WGB's members.[180] This is particularly the case where commission of other similar crimes, in aggravated circumstances, would attract a higher penalty.[181] In other words, the WGB expects sentencing for economic crimes to display an 'internal coherence'. Equally, the WGB does not accept that a lower category of bribery offences should not attract imprisonment.[182]

We may ask whether the WGB should not in fact do even more to encourage state Parties to treat certain very serious forms of bribery cases more harshly, for example in relation to bribery of officials holding judicial or political office. Belgium, Italy, Luxembourg, and the Netherlands, for judicial offices, and Portugal, for political offices, provide possible models for this approach. Other countries still facing deep-seated problems of corruption in

[178] Cf. Argentina: AR-Ph1, 28. [179] See III.3.3.1. above.
[180] See III.3.3.1. above. [181] See II.2.1. above.
[182] TR-Ph1, 10 et seq., 26.

their systems of government will require to adopt similar targeted measures. It is 'proportionate' for the WGB to call for sanctioning measures targeted to the particular needs of such states. The WGB clearly links domestic institutional reform to improving the fight against foreign corruption.[183]

4.3. Comparable penalties for active and passive bribery: a proportionality requirement?

The WGB focuses on the offence of active bribery of foreign public officials. Its first priority in monitoring compliance with the Convention is to ensure that such an offence is clearly established and penalised by 'effective, proportionate, and dissuasive' penalties. But does the 'proportionate' part of the mantra mean that the offence of active bribery, once established, must be penalised in a comparable way to the passive offence? The answer would seem to be: 'not necessarily'.

The WGB's reports do draw attention to the sanctions imposed for the passive offence. Any differences in treatment will be noted: for example, it was observed in the recent report on Brazilian anti-corruption legislation that several different offences apply to passive corruption.[184] In that case, the divergence between the penalties applicable for the passive and active crimes was negligible, and no adverse conclusions were drawn. In the case of Slovenia, a bigger divergence of up to three years did not attract direct criticism from the WGB.[185] The earlier review of Denmark revealed a similar rather stark divergence of three years between the maximum penalties in question. The WGB drew critical attention to the comparatively weak penalty for the active offence in the Danish case.[186] Slovenia was probably less directly criticised because its penalty levels are in general higher than those of Denmark.

The European Commission has recently drawn attention to the fact that, in addition to Denmark, Austria,[187] Germany,[188] and Portugal,[189] albeit in

[183] Cf. the Phase 2 reports for Bulgaria (BG-Ph2, 5 et seq.) and Mexico (MX-Ph2, 4 et seq.). Tailoring the sanctioning standard to the needs of particular countries does not detract from the overall goal of harmonisation, if we recall that this is based on 'functional equivalence', and not identity, of national systems.

[184] BR-Ph2, 13. [185] SI-Ph1, 16.

[186] A maximum penalty of three years applies in the case of active bribery, whereas six years is the maximum penalty for the passive offence. Cf. DK-Ph1, 10, 26.

[187] Austria limits the penalty for active corruption to two years, whereas the passive version may attract up to three years' imprisonment (EU 2004b, 44).

[188] Germany has a higher minimum penalty of six months for passive corruption compared to three for active corruption (EU 2004b, 44).

[189] PT-Ph1, 11. In relation to Portugal, the EU report appears in fact to be incorrect: the maximum penalty for active bribery is eight years, not five (EU 2004b, 44).

different ways and to different degrees, punish active corruption less severely than passive corruption. For its part, the WGB does not take issue with the slight divergences in Austrian or German law.

We may draw the conclusion that the WGB is not unduly concerned by lower penalties for the offence of active bribery than for passive bribery, provided that in practice the sanctions imposed for the former are sufficient to meet its 'effectiveness' standard.[190] The main point of comparison for the WGB is between sanctions for active corruption of domestic officials on the one hand, and those applied to foreign officials, on the other: this indeed is the only 'official' comparison warranted by the Convention.

Can we go further and conclude that the WGB does not regard even significant differences between the active and passive offences as 'disproportionate'?[191] The answer to this is a matter of speculation. Only in the Danish case do we see the WGB expressing clear dissatisfaction with the lower penalty for active bribery, but that was in the context of a country which has generally low sanctions.

The WGB's rather reserved approach to divergences between penalties for the active and passive offences may be explained by its willingness simply to accept the approach of individual national penal policy;[192] it has no mandate to interfere in basic administrative choices of this kind.[193] The attachment of a particular 'penal value' to the offence of active bribery is, as we saw in the previous section, essentially left to the discretion of the state Party concerned (provided, of course, that it remains within the basic sanctioning parameters of the Convention). Perhaps a more robust approach would be taken, if more OECD states penalised passive bribery more severely; as it is, equal treatment of the two is the norm.

4.4. Applying proportionality to limit sanctions?

There has to date been little, if any, discussion in the OECD context of proportionality in a somewhat different sense as a means of setting *limits* to

[190] See III.3.4. above.

[191] Cf. EU 2004b, 45, in which the Commission concluded that the differences it found in the laws of Austria, Denmark, Germany, and Portugal were not disproportionate.

[192] Note the reference in its report on Slovenia to the 'overall sentencing policy of the Criminal Code', on the basis of which Slovenia justified the difference in sanctions (SI-Ph2, 16). A failure to prosecute the bribers – rather than those who accept the bribes – in the first place, cannot, on the other hand, be justified on the basis of 'efficiency of prosecution', cf. LU-Ph2, 37.

[193] In their discussion of proportionality in EU law, Craig and de Búrca (1995) argue that judicial control of sanctions as such does not entail 'undermining the entirety of the administrative policy with which it is connected' (342). In our case, were the WGB to start questioning particular aspects of national sentencing policy, it would run precisely this risk.

the severity of sanctions. Yet it is clear from national[194] and EC law[195] that proportionality, as a legal principle, does have a role to play here. It may and does serve as a limiting principle, namely by limiting the extent of legitimate intrusion by a public authority on personal liberty or economic freedom. The principle has a particular application to criminal law, whose *ultima ratio* function in regulation of social life is widely accepted by democratic societies.[196]

The WGB could apply proportionality in this sense by setting a certain 'margin of maximum intrusion', or an 'outer limit', for a sanction for bribery of foreign officials, under the Convention. Such an approach could be justified on human rights grounds, based on constitutional traditions common to the OECD as currently constituted. The leeway allowed to states would still have to be fairly wide, because the Convention accepts that different national traditions of criminal law and of sentencing exist: these should not, fundamentally, be put into question.

What, then, might the 'outer limit' be, and on what basis might it be imposed? Would a maximum twenty-year sentence of imprisonment for bribery exceed the bounds of reasonableness? Presumably the death penalty would.

We have already seen that the WGB does not raise objections in cases where the offence of bribing a foreign official is punishable by higher penalties than those applied to the bribing of domestic officials.[197] Equally, one looks in vain in the reports for a suggestion that penalties might be regarded as 'excessive'; on the other hand, we have also noted that the WGB accepts the generally lower penalties applied by a number of states, within the context of their sentencing traditions, though it recommends that aggravated bribery be singled out for higher penalties.[198]

The WGB may not yet have been confronted by a real risk of sentences being imposed in disregard of fundamental principles of criminal law, or of human rights, but future accessions to the WGB and the anti-bribery

[194] Cf. the references to the origin of the principle in Douglas-Scott 2002, 183.

[195] In EC law, as we saw in II.2.2. above, the principle of proportionality can play an important role in moderating the impact of national criminal penalties, in the Community public interest. It also has a rationale related to protection of the individual.

[196] Cf., for example, the opinion of the German Federal Constitutional Court in the famous litigation on the criminalisation of abortion to the effect that: '[d]ie Strafnorm stellt gewissermaßen die ultima ratio im Instrumentarium des Gesetzgebers dar. Nach dem das ganze öffentliche Recht einschließlich des Verfassungsrechts beherrschenden rechtsstaatlichen Prinzip der Verhätnismäßigkeit darf er von diesem Mittel nur behutsam und zurückhaltend Gebrauch machen' (BVerfGE 39, 1 et seq.).

[197] See III.2.1.1. above. [198] See III.4.2. above.

Convention may force it to address this issue. The WGB could, however, already have offered an opinion on whether it would really be reasonable for a company to be threatened with being put of business for relatively minor infringements of the Convention standard.

By taking a more explicit stance now on the limiting function of proportionality, the WGB would provide the Convention standard with the necessary content to meet this challenge. A possible source of inspiration for it may again lie in EC law. In EC competition law cases, the Community's Court of First Instance reviews the proportionality of monetary sanctions imposed on undertakings by the European Commission.[199]

It seems to be time that the term 'proportionate' in Article 3 is given a discrete meaning, in order to give the Convention standard a less imbalanced appearance.

5. 'Effective, proportionate and dissuasive': testing the totality of sanctions

For our final point in the discussion of the Convention's sanctioning standard, we should refer to the 'holistic approach' taken by the WGB to its review of Party compliance. The full range of sanctions mentioned by Article 3 should be deployed by the state Parties, to the fullest possible extent, to achieve what the WGB hopes will be effective deterrence.

This philosophy comes through strongly from any analysis of the country reports. Sanctions are viewed in the round. The sanctioning system as a whole, and not just the individual penalties, should meet the 'effective, proportionate and dissuasive' test.[200] When looking at the appended OECD Table[201] listing the sanctions applied to natural and legal persons for breach of the Convention, we should therefore be aware that they are not viewed by the WGB in isolation. Article 3 encourages such a holistic approach, but it has been left to the discretion of the WGB to develop the relative importance of each sanction and the possible links between them.

Deterrence may be achieved with the help of prohibitive sanctions of an administrative or civil nature as well as by monetary penalties.[202] Strong measures of confiscation may compensate for rather weak fines on

[199] Cf. Kerse and Khan 2005, 461, who indicate that the EC Court of First Instance has in fact been very reluctant to reduce the fines imposed by application of proportionality.
[200] Cf. the Phase 2 report on Italy, referring to the 'overall sufficiency of penalties' (IT-Ph2, 50).
[201] Annex A. [202] IT-Ph2, 50.

undertakings.[203] The WGB clearly regards confiscation as a very important modern[204] tool in the fight against corruption. The Phase 2 report on Switzerland exemplifies this.[205] The confiscation rules contained in Article 3(3) of the Convention will be considered separately in the next chapter of this commentary.

References

For documentation see the consolidated bibliography at the end of this book.

Aiolfi, G. and M. Pieth (2002), 'How to Make a Convention Work: The Organisation for Economic Co-operation and Development Recommendation and Convention on Bribery as an Example of a New Horizon in International Law' in C. Fijnaut and L. Huberts (eds.), *Corruption, Integrity and Law Enforcement*, Leiden, Boston, 349.

Arnull, A.M., A.A. Dashwood, M.G. Ross and D.A. Wyatt (2000), *Wyatt and Dashwood's European Union Laws*, 4th edn, London.

Ashworth, A. (2002), 'Sentencing' in M. Maguire, R. Morgan, and R. Reiner (eds.), *The Oxford Handbook of Criminology*, 3rd edn, Oxford, 1076.

Beccaria, C. (1988), *Über Verbrechen und Strafen* (nach der Ausgabe von 1766 übersetzt und herausgegeben von W. Alff), Frankfurt a. M.

Bernasconi, P. (ed.) (2000), *Responding to Corruption: Social Defence, Corruption, and the Protection of Public Administration and the Independence of Justice* (updated documents of the XIIIth International Congress on Social Defence, Lecce, Italy 1996), Naples.

Boch, C. (2000), *EC Law in the UK*, London.

Chilton, B. (2005), 'Supreme Court strikes down Federal Sentencing Guidelines' in *Compliance Week: Columns and Editorials*, January 2005 (available on: http://www.complianceweek.com).

Cole, G. F. (1995), *The American System of Criminal Justice*, Belmont.

Craig, P. and G. de Búrca (1995), *EC Law: Text, Cases and Materials*, Oxford.

Craufurd Smith, R. (1999), 'Remedies for Breaches of EC Law in National Courts: Legal Variation and Selection' in P. Craig and G. de Búrca (eds.), *The Evolution of EU Law*, Oxford, 287.

Delmas-Marty, M. (2002), *Towards a Truly Common Law: Europe as a Laboratory for Legal Pluralism*, Cambridge.

Delmas-Marty, M. and J. A. E. Vervaele (eds.) (2000), *The Implementation of Corpus Juris in the Member States*, Vol. 1, Antwerp, Groningen, Oxford.

Douglas-Scott, S. (2002), *Constitutional Law of the European Union*, Harlow.

Forti, G. (2000), 'Remarks on the Role of Criminal Sanction in a Sustainable Prevention of Crimes in the Public Administration. The Italian Experience of

[203] CH-Ph2, 42: 'Confiscation, hitting directly offenders' pocket books, can prove to be a powerful measure and...it can counterbalance the fact that the primary penalties imposed by the Swiss courts for economic and financial offences tend to be modest and not particularly dissuasive.'

[204] Gilmore 2004, 19 et seq. [205] CH-Ph2, 42 et seq.

Systemic Corruption' in P. Bernasconi (ed.), *Responding to Corruption: Social Defence, Corruption, and the Protection of Public Administration and the Independence of Justice* (updated documents of the XIIIth International Congress on Social Defence, Lecce, Italy 1996), Naples, 173.

Geradin, D. and D. Henry (2005), The EC Fining Policy for Violations of Competition Law: *An Empirical Review of the Commission Decisional Practice and the Community Courts' Judgments*, Global Competition Law Centre (GCLC), Working Paper 03/05.

Gilmore, W. C. (2004), *Dirty Money: The Evolution of International Measures to Counter Money Laundering and the Financing of Terrorism*, 3rd edn, Strasbourg.

Huber, B. (2002), 'Sanctions Against Bribery Offences in Criminal Law' in C. Fijnaut and L. Huberts (eds.), *Corruption, Integrity and Law Enforcement*, Leiden, Boston, 137.

Kerse, C. and N. Khan (2005), *EC Antitrust Procedures*, 5th edn, London.

Low, L. A. (2005), 'Enforcement of the FCPA in the United States: Trends and the Effects of International Standards' (presentation at the 3rd Annual Conference of the International Bar Association, International Chamber of Commerce, and Organization for Economic Co-operation and Development, *The Awakening Giant of Anti-Corruption Enforcement* in Paris, 4–6 May 2005).

Pieth, M. (2006), 'Korruption in internationalen Wirtschaftsbeziehungen' in D. Dölling (Hrsg.), *Handbuch der Korruptionseindämmung*, München.

Pieth, M. and P. Eigen (Hrsg.) (1999), *Korruption im internationalen Geschäftsverkehr: Bestandesaufnahme, Bekämpfung, Prävention*, Neuwied, Kriftel, Basel, Frankfurt a. M.

Tobler, C. (2005), *Remedies and Sanctions in EC Non-Discrimination Law: Effective, Proportionate and Dissuasive National Sanctions and Remedies, with Particular Reference to Upper Limits on Compensation to Victims of Discrimination*, Luxembourg (Office for Official Publications of the European Communities).

US Sentencing Commission (2004), *Fifteen Years of Guidelines Sentencing* (available at: http://www.ussc.gov).

Von Hirsch, A. (1987), 'The Sentencing Commission's Functions' in A. von Hirsch, K. A. Knapp, and M. Tonry, *The Sentencing Commission and its Guidelines*, Boston, 3.

Von Hirsch, A. and A. Ashworth (2005), *Proportionate Sentencing: Exploring the Principles*, Oxford.

Von Hirsch, A., K. A. Knapp, and M. Tonry (1987), *The Sentencing Commission and its Guidelines*, Boston.

Walther, S. (2004), 'Communication over Confrontation: Modern Criminal Procedure in Transformation' in A. Eser and C. Rabenstein (Hrsg.), *Strafjustiz im Spannungsfeld von Effizienz und Fairness*, Berlin, 367.

Article 3(3). Seizure and Confiscation

MARK PIETH

Article 3(3) – Seizure and Confiscation

3. Each Party shall take such measures as may be necessary to provide that the bribe and the proceeds of the bribery of a foreign public official, or property the value of which corresponds to that of such proceeds, are subject to seizure and confiscation or that monetary sanctions of comparable effect are applicable.

Official Commentary

Article 3 – Sanctions:

Re paragraph 3:

21. The 'proceeds' of bribery are the profits or other benefits derived by the briber from the transaction or other improper advantage obtained or retained through bribery.

22. The term 'confiscation' includes forfeiture where applicable and means the permanent deprivation of property by order of a court or other competent authority. This paragraph is without prejudice to rights of victims.

23. Paragraph 3 does not preclude setting appropriate limits to monetary sanctions.

Chapter contents

I. Introduction

The historical development of the rules on confiscation has taken the same peculiar twist in Common and Civil Law systems. During the period of evolution of the nation state, the Sovereign forfeited property upon conviction for high treason; other felonies could entail forfeiture of goods to the lord of the convicted felon.[1] The abolition of confiscation of property was, however, part of the rallying cry of reformers during the era of enlightenment and featured, in particular, as a demand of declarations of human rights in the eighteenth and nineteenth centuries; confiscation was increasingly considered unfair towards the families of convicted felons, who were made to suffer even though they were not party to the offence.[2]

In discussions of confiscation nowadays little attention is paid to the fact that one is seeking to revitalise an old sanction, abolished after long battles some two hundred years ago. To some extent confiscation still carries the stigma of its previous abuse by absolutist Sovereigns as a means of dispossessing the nascent moneyed class of the eighteenth century. In Continental Europe confiscation was abolished around the time of the French Revolution; in the United Kingdom it fell into disuse, until it was finally formally abolished with the Forfeiture Act 1870.[3]

Confiscation survived merely as a safety measure in respect of dangerous objects. In the context of growing unease about the rampant illicit drug-trade of the 1970s and 1980s, the wider concept of confiscation of ill-gotten or illicit gains was reintroduced. The United Nations (UN) Convention

[1] Gurulé and Guerra 1998, 10. [2] Beccaria 1988 (1766), 114 et seq.
[3] Daams 2003, 30; Pieth and Aiolfi 2004, 6.

Against Illicit Traffic in Narcotic Drugs and Psychotropic Substances of 1988 made the confiscation of proceeds a worldwide standard for effective anti-drugs law enforcement.[4] The standard gained rather rapid acceptance at a regional[5] and national level. Since 1990 the standard has been broadened to other types of economic and organised crime.[6] Article 3(3) itself is an expression of this international expansion.

Notwithstanding the prevalence of confiscation as a crime-fighting tool, its rationale varies considerably from one state Party to another. In some countries the aspect of additional deterrence (punitive effect)[7] is in the foreground, whereas others place their emphasis on restitution,[8] be it to victims or – in a more general sense – by siphoning off illicit benefits: 'crime shall not pay' is their goal. Another approach places the prevention of further (organised) crime at the centre of policy efforts: the accumulation of illegal capital is considered dangerous, because it keeps criminal organisations operational.[9]

Article 3(3) tries to bridge the gaps between the approaches by applying the principle of 'functional equivalence':[10] according to the text, state Parties have the choice either of introducing confiscation proper or of providing 'that monetary sanctions of comparable effect are applicable'.[11] The text creates the impression that fines and confiscation are interchangeable concepts. From a legal point of view this is, however, not the case. Sanctions are based on, and calibrated according to, culpability, and confiscation has its basis in the provenance of the funds derived from the crime. Furthermore, an explanation is necessary why the Convention would request the confiscation of illicit gains in addition to the 'effective, proportionate and dissuasive' sanctions already mentioned in Article 3(1) and (2) for individuals and for legal persons. If paragraph 3 is to have a discrete meaning, it must lead to additional measures beyond punishment.

The particular formula of Article 3(3) – containing these 'alternatives' – was in fact introduced in order to simplify the accession to the Convention of Japan, Korea, and the United States, which either do not use the concept of confiscation in their transnational bribery statute[12] or are unable to confiscate the proceeds of active bribery.[13] The added value of Article 3(3) is that these states must implement the phrase 'monetary sanction of comparable effect' so as to open the sanctioning bracket beyond the fines

[4] Art. 5 UN 1988; Pieth and Estermann 2002, 347.
[5] Art. 2 et seq. COE 1990, now Art. 3 et seq. COE 2005. [6] UN 2000.
[7] BG-Ph2, 25. [8] NL-Ph1, 7; SE-Ph1, 11. [9] For Switzerland: Botschaft 1993, 29.
[10] Official Commentary 2. [11] Art. 3(3) in fine. [12] US-Ph1, 12.
[13] JP-Ph1, 11; KR-Ph2, 41 (confiscation 'too severe a sanction').

foreseen under Article 3(1) and (2). Furthermore, they must follow a more objective approach than in sanctioning, the logic of confiscation being more attuned to siphoning off illicit profits than the mere expiation of culpability.[14]

II. Seizure

Article 3(3) requires state Parties to 'take such measures as may be necessary' to provide that the bribe and the proceeds of bribery are subject to seizure.

'Seizure' is here an umbrella term used for all sorts of provisional restraining orders, used in a pre-trial phase,[15] in order to secure moveable or immoveable property believed to be the instruments or products of the crime (*instrumenta* or *productas sceleris*): heritable property would be 'frozen' in the land register, bank accounts blocked upon notice, moveable objects either physically seized by police or customs officers or subjected to a prohibition of sale.[16]

Seizure may serve two different goals: 'probatory seizure' is meant to secure evidence for the court hearing;[17] 'preventive seizure' to secure ultimate confiscation.[18] Different procedures may apply according to the type of seizure: whereas probative seizure will generally be ordered by police in the first instance,[19] and later on possibly approved or rejected by a magistrate[20] or at least a prosecutor,[21] preventive seizure will typically need to be ordered by a judge.[22]

Some countries restrict seizure to 'flagrant offences'.[23] Since confiscation is also possible in certain circumstances against third parties, seizure must equally be possible against non-accused persons.[24] Similarly, seizure may anticipate the confiscation of substitutes or replacements of the original objects stemming from crime.[25]

[14] This is the reason why the US FCPA just about met the Convention standard: according to the 'alternative fine provisions of the US Code "any person may be fined no more than the greater of twice the pecuniary gain of the offence or twice the loss to a person other than the defendant"' (US-Ph1, 12).

[15] AR-Ph1, 11; BE-Ph1, 13; CA-Ph1, 11. [16] CH-Ph1, 11; NO-Ph1, 7; PL-Ph1, 18.

[17] CZ-Ph1, 10; FR-Ph1, 15; IT-Ph1, 15. [18] CA-Ph1, 11; HU-Ph1, 11; IT-Ph1, 15.

[19] IT-Ph1, 15.

[20] For United Kingdom: s. 42 Drug-Trafficking Act 1994, now: part V, ch. 3 Proceeds of Crime Act (POCA) 2002.

[21] PL-Ph1, 18. [22] BG-Ph2, 24; IT-Ph1, 15. [23] FR-Ph1, 16.

[24] DK-Ph1, 12; IS-Ph1, 8; IT-Ph1, 16. [25] Cf. also Art. 5(a) COE 2005.

III. Confiscation

1. Use of terms

States use different terms for permanent expropriation in relation to a criminal offence: in legal systems of the Anglo-Saxon world, 'forfeiture' is usually the term applied to the power of the state to take instruments of the crime (*instrumenta sceleris*), whereas 'confiscation' is reserved more particularly for the proceeds of crime.[26] Since the terms are, however, frequently used interchangeably,[27] the OECD decided to clarify the issue in Official Commentary 22: 'The term "confiscation" includes forfeiture where applicable and means the permanent deprivation of property by order of a court or a competent authority.'

2. Procedural issues

As a measure of permanent deprivation of property, confiscation typically requires to be authorised by a court order following criminal proceedings resulting in the conviction of the person concerned.[28] This is reflected in some of the international treaties.[29] However, Official Commentary 22 also refers to deprivation by any other 'competent authority' as an alternative. The OECD Convention scheme thus acknowledges that some countries have introduced procedures of '*in rem* confiscation', i.e. directing confiscation at abandoned property stemming from crime.[30] In some legal systems an investigating magistrate or even a prosecutor may declare the goods confiscated.[31]

In rem procedures may have other far-reaching consequences. The UK Proceeds of Crime Act (POCA) of 2002, even though requiring a court decision lowers the standards of proof by establishing a parallel track of 'civil forfeiture' next to 'criminal forfeiture'. Whereas criminal forfeiture must satisfy the criminal standard of proof, i.e. 'beyond reasonable doubt',

[26] United Kingdom: cf. Hodgson Committee 1984; IE-Ph1, 15; a slightly different use of the terms is made on the European Continent: cf. NL-Ph1, 17.

[27] Art. 1(d) COE 1990.

[28] AR-Ph1, 11; AU-Ph1, 11; CA-Ph2, 36; CZ-Ph1, 10; HU-Ph1, 10; IE-Ph1, 17 et seq.; MX-Ph1, 10; NL-Ph1, 17; NZ-Ph1, 15; UK-Ph1, 10.

[29] Art. 1(d) COE 1990.

[30] E.g. CN-Ph1, 11; SE-Ph1, 12 (for financial advantages obtained by entrepreneurs through economic crime); UK-Ph2, 74 et seq. and Kilchling 2002, 3.

[31] E.g. Swiss Cantonal Procedural Codes: CH-Ph2, 43; Daams 2003, 96 ('independent confiscation').

civil forfeiture is possible where the link to the crime is established on the 'balance of probabilities'.[32]

It is obviously not a matter for the OECD Convention or the Working Group on Bribery (WGB) to draw up minimal standards for the protection of the defendant or the owner of the assets. Whether the new departures from traditional criminal law concepts are acceptable or not, must, however, be discussed in the light of constitutional standards and international human rights instruments such as the European Convention on Human Rights[33] and the UN Pact II.[34]

3. The requirements for confiscation

As already mentioned, the aim of confiscation is to siphon off illicit gains and to deprive criminals of the means of committing future crimes. It is hoped that this will indirectly have strong deterrent effects.

3.1. The object of confiscation

Confiscation is directed against all sorts of economic advantages or assets, be they moveable or immoveable,[35] tangible or intangible (including rights),[36] directly or indirectly obtained.[37] Typically, confiscation extends to illicit assets intermingled with those stemming from licit sources, up to the value of the illegal influx.[38] However, some countries introduce a minimum threshold well above mere *de minimis* cases. Others restrict confiscation to serious offences entailing imprisonment[39] or a qualified fine.[40]

Since confiscation is linked to the proof of provenance from crime, it generally should not exceed the equivalent of illicit gains.[41] Official Commentary 23 makes it clear that Article 3(3) does not require state Parties to go further. On the other hand, countries which do not know confiscation of bribes and proceeds of bribery should extend the level of their fines beyond the equivalent of the gains.[42]

[32] United Kingdom: part 5 Proceeds of Crime Act 2002.

[33] Esp. Art. 6(1) and (2) COE 1950; cf. also Decision of German Constitutional Court (BVerfG 14 January 2004, 2 BvR 564/95) on the *'erweiterter Verfall'*.

[34] UN 1966.

[35] DE-Ph1, 9; in the case of Japan, however, only the confiscation of moveable property, except in cases of organised crime (JP-Ph1, 10 et seq.).

[36] AR-Ph1, 11; AU-Ph1, 11; NZ-Ph1, 15.

[37] PL-Ph1, 17.

[38] E.g. Art. 5(b) COE 2005.

[39] CZ-Ph1, 10; HU-Ph1, 10; PL-Ph1, 16.

[40] NL-Ph1, 17.

[41] AT-Ph1, 11; CZ-Ph1, 10; IT-Ph1, 17; UK-Ph1, 10.

[42] See discussion in part II. above.

Some countries have explicitly stated in their evaluations that confiscation includes assets situated abroad.[43] Obviously, this will only be the case where the country has jurisdiction and has a chance to recover the funds by means of mutual legal assistance.[44]

3.2. Confiscation of the bribe

Like the provision against money laundering contained in Article 7,[45] Article 3(3) reaches beyond the 'supply side'[46] into the 'demand side' of bribery by providing that 'the bribe be subject to seizure and confiscation'.

In so far as the funds destined for bribery are still within the control of the briber, e.g. with his bank – even though the briber may already have placed a transaction order – the laws of the state Parties present a more uneven picture: whereas some are able to forfeit such funds, at least if they are identified,[47] others are not.[48]

3.3. Confiscation of the proceeds of bribery

The scheme of the Convention is as clear on this point as it is difficult: Article 3(3) states that state Parties

> 'shall take such measures as may be necessary to provide that. . .the proceeds of the bribery of a foreign public official or property the value of which corresponds to that of such proceeds, are subject to seizure and confiscation.'

Official Commentary 21 defines what is meant by 'proceeds':

> 'The "proceeds" of bribery are the profits or other benefits derived by the briber from the transaction or other improper advantage obtained or retained through bribery.'

If the Convention and its Official Commentary leave no uncertainty that the profit for the briber is to be siphoned off, they do not tackle the difficult issues this rule raises. In fact, it is rather astonishing that the state Parties have so far not really woken up to the challenges presented by this rule.[49]

The reintroduction of sweeping confiscation rules from the 1980s to date is linked to the fight against illicit drug-trafficking and organised crime, as already mentioned. The difference between drug-dealing and

[43] BE-Ph1, 12; NZ-Ph1, 15. [44] DE-Ph1, 9; and see part VII. below.

[45] See ch. on Article 7 (V.2.2.) below. [46] See Introduction of this commentary.

[47] FI-Ph1, 9; DE-Ph1, 9; NL-Ph1, 10 ('including objects used to commit or prepare the offence').

[48] IT-Ph1, 16; SE-Ph1, 11.

[49] Cf. the inadequate treatment in BG-Ph-1, 8; DK-Ph1, 12; JP-Ph1, 11; JP-Ph2, 51; KR-Ph2, 40; NL-Ph1, 17; SE-Ph2, 49.

corruption-related contracts is, however, evident. Whereas in drug-trafficking the basic contract is illegal and the goods themselves are *extra comercium*, the underlying contract in the case of corruption will typically be a licit exchange of goods or services for remuneration. Even if, from a civil law perspective, the view is now gaining ground that the illegal corruption contract also nullifies the underlying contractual relationship or licence,[50] one has to seriously consider whether the bribe really was the determining factor behind the conclusion of the contract, decision on the licence, etc. (causality link).[51]

Furthermore, confiscation of the proceeds of bribery cannot go beyond the net profits, since the basic contract is legitimate. By contrast, most countries would demand forfeiture of the investment in the illicit drug example.

In this context, the statement of a Norwegian judge during the Phase 2 evaluation of Norway should be considered:

> 'In case of a contract obtained through the giving of a bribe, but that is otherwise legal, it may be difficult to determine the part of the benefit constituting the proceeds of bribery.'[52]

This statement echoes German prosecutors, who argued in their Phase 2 evaluation that it was very difficult to assess the 'financial benefit', the key criterion on the basis of which both the level of the fine and the amount to be forfeited are calculated.[53]

The solution offered by some countries is to allow the court discretion to determine the amount to be confiscated where the exact value of the gain cannot be established or where its establishment would require disproportionate efforts.[54] This solution may seem practical; however, it risks introducing uncertainty by eschewing the development of clear criteria.

If a bribe does not have a causal effect on the award of a contract, it should not simply lead to reduced profit forfeiture on the basis of a discretionary rebate. Establishing the causality link between the bribe and the award of the contract is a separate issue, to be decided on the basis of the available evidence. One might also consider the size of the bribe in relation to the contract. The estimation should, however, remain reserved for cases where the influence of the bribe on the contract has been established, but the benefit is uncertain or yet uncertain. To give an example:

[50] Art. 8 COE 1999b ('each Party shall provide in its internal law for the possibility for all Parties to a contract whose consent has been undermined by an act of corruption to be able to apply to the court for the contract to be declared void').

[51] CH-Ph1, 10. [52] NO-Ph2, 46. [53] DE-Ph2, 33 et seq.

[54] NO-Ph2, 46; for Switzerland: Art. 59(4) Swiss Criminal Code.

A payment of US$50 million to a Prime Minister of an emerging economy has helped win an oil exploitation concession valid for the next 10 years. It is highly likely that this sum has influenced the deal; however, it is very difficult to anticipate what the concession is worth. Here experts will have to help define the value of the contract, obviously allowing for deduction of investments and trying to account for the uncertainty of how much oil will ultimately be generated by the oil field over the exploitation period. Such a contract can be fixed with a price tag; otherwise investors would be left in total uncertainty. It will also have a market value to be considered for the purposes of confiscation.

4. Limits and exceptions

Article 3 does not prohibit the placing of certain limits on confiscation. For one thing, Official Commentary 22 expressly reserves the rights of victims.[55] Furthermore, the lapse of time can prohibit confiscation: the statute of limitations will usually apply to confiscation measures.[56] Finally, many national laws abstain from confiscation where it would place the defendant under an undue hardship.[57] Other limitations may apply in the context of international co-operation, e.g. double jeopardy.[58]

IV. Substitution

Generally, where instruments or proceeds of crime have been substituted by other assets, the confiscation order may also be directed against these assets. This is an accepted standard of national legal systems.[59] The standard is also expressed by Article 3(3) in the passage 'or property the value of which corresponds to that of such proceeds'. Of the state Parties to the Convention, however, Korea and Spain fall below the standard.[60]

Furthermore, where neither the original object nor any physical substitute can be found, confiscation is usually transformed into a mere forfeiture of assets in the possession of the convicted person or third party.[61] Equally, only a few countries depart from this established standard.[62] Where it

[55] Cf. also FR-Ph1, 16; SE-Ph1, 11; UK-Ph1, 10. The rights of other bona fide third parties will be discussed in part V. below.

[56] Art. 59(1)(III and IV) Swiss Criminal Code.

[57] AT-Ph1, 11; HU-Ph1, 11; IE-Ph1, 18; Art. 19(1)(II) Swiss Criminal Code.

[58] See the discussion of double jeopardy or *ne bis in idem* in our ch. on Articles 9–11 below.

[59] Art. 2(1) COE 1990; BE-Ph1, 12; CH-Ph1, 10; CZ-Ph1, 9; DK-Ph1, 12; HU-Ph1, 10; MX-Ph1, 10.

[60] ES-Ph1, 11; KR-Ph1, 10.

[61] BE-Ph1, 12; BE-Ph2, 45; CH-Ph1, 10; CZ-Ph1, 9; DE-Ph1, 9; FR-Ph1, 16; GR-Ph1, 9; HU-Ph1, 10; KR-Ph1, 10.

[62] ES-Ph1, 11; MX-Ph1, 10; MX-Ph2, 23.

proves difficult to calculate the exact value of assets obtained from crime, some countries allow judges to estimate this figure.[63]

V. Third party confiscation

Our treatment of third party confiscation should be prefaced by two comments. First, confiscation should not impede victims' rights. Where victims have a right to proceeds, they should be restored to them, not confiscated.[64] Second, probably the most difficult issue in the area of confiscation is how to prevent the defendant from simply evading confiscation by using third party recipients while, at the same time, protecting the rights of property of *bona fide* parties. Solutions which exclude confiscation from third parties all together invite circumvention of the rules and fall below the standard of Article 3.[65]

Rightly, most countries would confiscate property under the control of the offender,[66] even with third parties.[67] Confiscation would, at least, be permitted where the third party had knowledge of the provenance of the funds or where the third party was negligent in acquiring them.[68]

Whereas most countries would respect *bona fide* possession,[69] some make an exception and allow for confiscation against *bona fide* third parties where these have received property as a gratuity (gift, inheritance, etc.) or without adequate remuneration.[70] Following similar reasoning – that it would be unjust for a *bona fide* possessor to keep illicit gains he or she has obtained as a gift – some countries confiscate funds benefiting a legal person, even where the legal person is not responsible for the offence.[71] The legal person in such a situation has been called a 'second' instead of a 'third' party.[72]

[63] DE-Ph2, 33 et seq.; FI-Ph1, 9; Art. 59(4) Swiss Criminal Code.
[64] FR-Ph1, 16; SE-Ph1, 11; UK-Ph1, 10.
[65] CZ-Ph1, 10; GR-Ph1, 9; IE-Ph1, 18 (the reference to an exception in 'appropriate circumstance' is too vague).
[66] FR-Ph1, 16; JP-Ph1, 11; UK-Ph1, 10.
[67] AU-Ph1, 11; DK-Ph1, 12; FI-Ph1, 9; MX-Ph1, 10.
[68] BE-Ph2, 45; BG-Ph2, 25; DK-Ph1, 12; HU-Ph1, 10; NL-Ph1, 17; NO-Ph2, 46.
[69] E.g. BG-Ph2, 25; DK-Ph1, 12; ES-Ph1, 11; FI-Ph1, 9; HU-Ph1, 10; IS-Ph1, 8; IT-Ph1, 17; NL-Ph1, 17.
[70] AU-Ph1, 11; DK-Ph1, 12; NO-Ph2, 46; Art. 59(1)(II) Swiss Criminal Code.
[71] CH-Ph1, 10 (new law); ES-Ph1, 12; JP-Ph 1, 11; KR-Ph1, 10; KR-Ph2, 41; NO-Ph 2, 46; the laws in the following countries were inadequate: BG-Ph2, 25 and IT-Ph2, 49.
[72] For Switzerland: Botschaft 1999, 5544.

VI. Confiscation in practice

Given the very few cases of transnational bribery prosecuted or adjudicated under the rules of the Convention, we are obliged to refer to national experiences with domestic bribery cases in order to obtain an adequate picture of confiscation practice in state Parties.

Generally, very few states request mandatory confiscation.[73] Most countries leave it to the discretion of prosecutors or even to senior law officers,[74] whether confiscation will be requested from the court.[75] Whereas little information is available on the principles governing this discretion, New Zealand has indicated that the 'likelihood of success' is decisive.[76] With other countries the size of the sums due for forfeiture compared to the evidential difficulties of the case will be decisive. Other state Parties employ very open-textured terminology: for example Sweden, which asks whether it would be 'manifestly unreasonable' to confiscate.[77]

The WGB's Phase 2 evaluations show a rather discouraging picture. So far, confiscation has rarely been used, even in domestic corruption cases.[78] The general awareness of prosecutors is low; they are not used to applying this measure in corruption cases;[79] furthermore, they face many practical impediments, notably how to prove and calculate the benefits.[80]

VII. International co-operation

1. Obligation of co-operation

Article 9 of the Convention requires state Parties to provide each other with 'prompt and effective legal assistance'. This provision restricts co-operation, on the face of it, to 'the purpose of criminal investigations' and 'non-criminal proceedings. . .brought by a Party against a legal person'. One must question, therefore, whether the obligation to afford co-operation extends also to civil forfeiture. There should be no doubt about this in so far as civil forfeiture is based on the criminal conviction of a natural or legal person. Otherwise, the rules on co-operation in the OECD Convention are rather minimalist.[81]

[73] IT-Ph1, 13, 16; MX-Ph1, 10; PL-Ph1, 16 (for substantial benefits); Switzerland depending on cantonal procedural order.
[74] CA-Ph2, 36; NL-Ph1, 17; NZ-Ph1, 15.
[75] AR-Ph1, 11 (exception for legal entities); AU-Ph1, 11; DK-Ph1, 12; IE-Ph1, 16; IS-Ph2, 29; JP-Ph1, 11; NL-Ph1, 17; NZ-Ph1, 15; PL-Ph1, 16 (ordinary cases).
[76] NZ-Ph1, 15. [77] SE-Ph1, 11. [78] FR-Ph2, 56, 64 (table of domestic cases).
[79] IS-Ph2, 29. [80] DE-Ph2, 33. [81] See ch. on Articles 9–11 below.

Regional organisations, especially the Council of Europe (COE), have gone into far more detail with its Convention of 1990 and the new extended text of 2005.[82] There have also been a number of important developments in European Union (EU) law, to some extent in parallel to COE measures.[83] These instruments define in great detail the obligations which should be established under national law regarding the search, seizure and confiscation of proceeds of crime and elaborate on the obligations of international co-operation, in particular concerning provisional measures and confiscation.[84] The UN Convention on Corruption[85] purports to regulate asset recovery in some detail and has now been echoed in the new COE text of 2005.[86]

2. Forfeiture and confiscation upon request

In order to deal with transnational corruption cases countries will frequently ask each other for mutual legal assistance or administrative assistance. It is quite possible that their requests will go beyond seeking the securing of evidence, e.g. information on bank accounts or the extradition of persons. They may well want to confiscate illicit gains situated abroad and possibly request the return of those funds. The Convention scheme obliges state Parties to co-operate in seizing and confiscating.

3. Disposal of confiscated assets

State Parties have given themselves rules on how to dispose of assets confiscated domestically. Frequently, however, there are no clear rules for transnational co-operation. International treaties have, until recently, left it to the domestic law of the requested country to deal with international disposal.[87]

Newer treaties, especially the COE text of 2005 and the UN Treaty 2003, respectively, now suggest that countries should, to the extent permitted by domestic law and if requested to do so, 'give priority consideration to

[82] COE 1990 and COE 2005.
[83] Cf., for example, the EU Council Framework Decision of 22 July 2003 on the execution in the EU or orders freezing property or evidence (OJ 2003 No. L196, 2 August 2003, 45) and the EU Council Framework Decision of 24 February 2005 on confiscation of crime-related proceeds, instrumentalities and property (OJ 2005 No. L68, 15 March 2005, 49).
[84] Note also in this context Arts. 12 and 13 UN 2000.
[85] On the confiscation of bribes and the profits of bribery, cf. Art. 31 UN 2003, on mutual legal assistance relating to the search, seizure and confiscation, cf. Art. 46 UN 2003, and on the recovery of assets, cf. Art. 51 et seq. UN 2003.
[86] Art. 25 COE 2005. [87] Art. 15 COE 1990.

returning the confiscated property to the requesting Party, so that it can give compensation to the victims of the crime or return such property to its legitimate owners'.[88]

This rule is designed, in particular, for cases with clearly identifiable victims, e.g. case of fraud, embezzlement, and theft.[89] In the case of corruption the state of the official would primarily qualify as the 'victim state', although competitors eliminated from competition by means of corruption might also be considered as falling into this category. In so far as uncertainties persist, the additional clause on 'asset-sharing agreements' between requesting and requested states might be helpful.[90] So far, the OECD has not discussed asset recovery and sharing in its monitoring reports; the state of the art here is provided, rather, by the UN Convention Against Corruption.

VIII. 'Monetary sanctions of comparable effect'

According to the concept of 'functional equivalence' (Official Commentary 2 and Article 3(3), the Convention offers an alternative to confiscation. Countries may foresee 'monetary sanctions of comparable effect'.

Japan Korea and the United States have used this option.[91] As indicated in the introduction to this chapter,[92] the 'monetary sanction' must add something to the fine already foreseen by Article 3(1) and (2) in order to compensate for the lack of sufficient confiscation.

The US approach has been to broaden the sanctioning bracket substantially, up to twice the amount of the offender's profit or the victim's loss. This arrangement was deemed by the WGB to be acceptable, because the United States follows objective sentencing guidelines to calculate fines, and the amount of benefit and loss is an essential element in the calibration process.

The Korean approach is less convincing.[93] According to a representative of the Korean Ministry of Foreign Affairs and Trade the confiscation of the proceeds of bribery was considered too severe a sanction; punishment according to Article 3(1) and (2) suffices. The WGB was equally critical of Denmark, which is apparently unable to confiscate the profits of the active briber and is unwilling to introduce compensatory upgrading of monetary sanctions.[94]

[88] Art. 25(2) COE 2005; cf. CH-Ph2, 43. [89] Cf. also Art. 57(3)(a) and (c) UN 2003.
[90] Art. 25(3) COE 2005; Arts. 3 and 57(5) UN 2003.
[91] JP-Ph1, 11; KR-Ph1, 41; US-Ph1, 12. [92] See part I. above. [93] KR-Ph2, 40.
[94] DK-Ph1, 12.

References

For documentation see the consolidated bibliography at the end of the book.

Beccaria, C. (1988), *Über Verbrechen und Strafen* (nach der Ausgabe von 1766 übersetzt und herausgegeben von W. Alff), Frankfurt a. M.

Daams, C. (2003), *Criminal Asset Forfeiture: One of the Most Effective Weapons Against (Organised) Crime?*, Basel.

Gurulé, J. and S. Guerra (1998), *The Law of Asset Forfeiture*, Charlotteville.

Hodgson Committee (1984), *Profits of Crime and their Recovery: The Report of a Committee chaired by Sir Derek Hodgson*, London.

Kilchling, M. (Hrsg.) (2002), *Die Praxis der Gewinnabschöpfung in Europa*, Freiburg i. Br.

Pieth, M. and G. Aiolfi (eds.) (2004), *A Comparative Guide to Anti-Money Laundering: A Critical Analysis of Systems in Singapore, Switzerland, the UK and the USA* (study by the Basel Institute on Governance, commissioned by the Stiftung Finanzplatz Schweiz), Cheltenham (UK), Northhampton (USA).

Pieth, M. and J. Estermann (2002), 'Landesbericht Schweiz' in M. Kilchling (Hrsg.), *Die Praxis der Gewinnabschöpfung in Europa*, Freiburg i. Br., 371.

Article 4. Jurisdiction

MARK PIETH

Article 4 – Jurisdiction

1. Each Party shall take such measures as may be necessary to establish its jurisdiction over the bribery of a foreign public official when the offence is committed in whole or in part in its territory.

2. Each Party which has jurisdiction to prosecute its nationals for offences committed abroad shall take such measures as may be necessary to establish its jurisdiction to do so in respect of the bribery of a foreign public official, according to the same principles.

3. When more than one Party has jurisdiction over an alleged offence described in this Convention, the Parties involved shall, at the request of one of them, consult with a view to determining the most appropriate jurisdiction for prosecution.

4. Each Party shall review whether its current basis for jurisdiction is effective in the fight against the bribery of foreign public officials and, if it is not, shall take remedial steps.

Official Commentary

Article 4 – Jurisdiction

25. The territorial basis for jurisdiction should be interpreted broadly so that an extensive physical connection to the bribery act is not required.

26. Nationality jurisdiction is to be established according to the general principles and conditions in the legal system of each Party. These principles deal with such matters as dual criminality. However, the requirement of dual criminality should be deemed to be met if the act is unlawful where it occurred, even if under a different criminal statute. For countries which apply nationality jurisdiction only to certain types of offences, the reference to 'principles' includes the principles upon which such selection is based.

Chapter contents

I. Overview of the jurisdictional principles

1. 'Territoriality' and 'sovereignty'

'A state's title to exercise jurisdiction rests in its sovereignty' is one of the key sentences in the famous *Lotus* case.[1] 'Sovereignty' is the fundamental concept of the Nation State: it confers the power to enact laws (legislative jurisdiction), to apply the laws (executive jurisdiction) and to try cases (judicial jurisdiction).[2] Focusing on legislative jurisdiction, international lawyers have held that 'as a rule jurisdiction extends (and is limited) to everybody and everything within the sovereign's territory and to his nationals wherever they may be'.[3] As this principle indicates, 'territoriality' invariably contains a limiting element: a state is restricted in the exercise of its powers to its territory. For official acts on foreign territory it requires the consent of the foreign state.

Towards the end of the nineteenth century, the Nation State developed an aggressive expansionism, reflected in the literature on international law well into the first half of the twentieth century, up to the Second World War. Whereas Common Law countries tended to adhere to 'territoriality' and simply broaden its scope, Continental European states resorted to explicit 'extra-territoriality'. To a certain extent these developments may seem interchangeable; sometimes the concepts are also muddled.[4] These extensions of traditional concepts are not, however, necessarily equal in all respects, since 'territoriality' is adopted absolutely, whereas 'extra-territoriality' is frequently subject to conditions, such as 'dual criminality'.[5]

The expansion of jurisdiction shifted from 'subjective territoriality', focusing on the place where the criminal act was committed or at least commenced,[6] to include 'objective territoriality', attributing jurisdiction to the state where the crime is completed, or has its effects.[7] Most Continental European countries have adopted the 'ubiquity principle',[8] applying both 'subjective' and 'objective territoriality' concurrently, except in cases where the crime is defined by the perpetrator's conduct alone (conduct crimes as opposed to result crimes).[9]

[1] The *Lotus* case, PCIJ Ser. A, No. 10, 19. [2] Blakesley 1999, 36; Hillier 1998, 252.
[3] Hillier 1998, 251, referring to the 'Huber-Storyan-maxims'.
[4] Cf. Blakesley 1999, 82 for a critique of the US position ('objective territoriality' and 'protective extra-territoriality' are frequently mixed up).
[5] Van den Wyngaert 1996, 43; COE 1990, 10 et seq.
[6] Blakesley 1999, 47; Gilbert 1996, 117; Hillier 1998, 254 et seq.
[7] Blakesley 1999, 50; Gilbert 1996, 118; Hillier 1998, 254, 276.
[8] Conseil de l'Europe 1990, 8; Gilbert 1996, 116.
[9] Gilbert 1996, 118 et seq.; in German terminology: *'Tätigkeitsdelikt'* as opposed to *'Erfolgsdelikt'*; cf. Arzt 1990, 168 et seq. and see II.2.2.1.b. below.

Equally, in the early twentieth century, it became accepted practice to extend territorial jurisdiction to boats and aircraft (the 'flag principle', '*le principe du pavillon*').[10]

In general, international law offers states wide discretion in the definition of their jurisdictional concepts. Even if, in the *Lotus case*,[11] the Permanent Court of International Justice had maintained that a state may not exercise its power in any form in another state (executive jurisdiction), this has not prevented states from developing extra-territorial forms of legislative jurisdiction.

2. 'Extra-territoriality'

As a traditional extension to 'territoriality' 'active personality' or 'nationality' have facilitated the trial of a state's nationals at home for crimes committed anywhere in the world. This form of control over one's citizens,[12] especially when exercised without a 'dual criminality' restriction, was based on the idea that citizens owed their country allegiance.[13] Whereas Continental Europe[14] adopted this concept as a general rule, Common Law countries were initially more eclectic.[15]

The 'passive personality' or 'nationality of the victim approach' was never universally accepted.[16] In Europe it has, however, been generally adopted.[17] As part of the expansion of jurisdiction in the early twentieth century, it was meant to express distrust in foreign judiciaries.

Finally, two further concepts are not easy to distinguish. First, where the vital interests of a state are in question, the 'protective principle' or 'security principle'[18] is applied. Hillier calls the 'protective principle' 'the ugly stepchild of objective territoriality'. He goes on to say: 'this principle expresses the desire of a sovereign to punish actions committed in other places, solely because it feels threatened by those actions'.[19] Very close to this concept is the extension of 'territoriality' to encompass mere effects of offences.[20]

[10] Conseil de l'Europe 1990, 12 et seq.; Gilbert 1996, 118. [11] See note 1.
[12] Hillier 1998, 278. [13] Blakesley 1999, 61. [14] Conseil de l'Europe 1990, 10.
[15] For the United Kingdom: cf. Gilbert 1996, 110.
[16] For a critical analysis from the United States and the United Kingdom, cf. Blakesley 1999, 62, 64; Hillier 1998, 279; Gilbert 1996, 105.
[17] Gilbert 1996, 105; Hillier 1998, 258.
[18] '*Compétence de la protection*' or '*compétence réelle*'; '*Staatsschutzprinzip*': Blakesley 1999, 54; Cassani 1996, 42 et seq.; Conseil de l'Europe 1990, 13; Gilbert 1996, 106.
[19] Hillier 1998, 258. [20] Hillier 1998, 275.

Second, after the Second World War and especially towards the end of the twentieth century, when industrialisation was overtaken by an even more rapid globalisation of the economy,[21] transnational crime was more and more perceived as a serious threat.[22] 'Extensive territoriality' and 'extra-territoriality' remained an issue; however, 'international solidarity' began to replace the preoccupation with 'national security'.[23] New concepts were advanced: 'universality', developed in order to combat the most serious crimes like illegal slavery and piracy,[24] was used against drug trafficking,[25] and finally against war crimes and crimes against humanity.[26] It is now an issue whether 'universality' should also be used for serious economic crime, like corruption.

'Active personality' was redefined in a less aggressive manner: subject to 'dual criminality', it now served the purpose of ensuring that perpetrators who could not be extradited to the *'locus actus'* (*'aut dedere aut iudicare'*) could be tried in lieu by the judiciary of the place where they were held ('representational principle', *'stellvertretende Strafrechtspflege'*, *'principe de la représentation'*).[27] In general, 'nationality' now serves the purpose of protecting foreign interests (be they public interests, where transnational corruption is concerned, or private, e.g. sexual offences committed abroad). As part of the reorientation towards a more co-operative approach, the protected legal interests (*'Schutzgüter'*, *'Rechtsgüter'*) were redefined: the 'solidarity concept' is far more concerned with the foreign public good than the previously more introspective attitude of the traditional Nation State.[28]

Overlapping jurisdiction is inevitable due to the patchwork approach to regulation of jurisdiction by state Parties. Major difficulties are not necessarily thereby created, but there must be processes to deal with conflicts of competence.[29] The Council of Europe (COE) distinguishes between unilateral and multilateral instruments.[30] On the unilateral side self-restraining measures, such as the acknowledgement of the *'ne bis in idem* ('double jeopardy') *principle'* on an international level, have been identified. 'Double jeopardy' has not been accepted internationally without an explicit treaty base.[31] Measures to

[21] Beck 1998. [22] Blakesley 1999, 37; Passas 1999, 399 et seq.

[23] Conseil de l'Europe 1990, 27.

[24] Hillier 1998, 280 et seq.; Jescheck and Weigend 1996, 170; Kontorovich 2004, 188 et seq.

[25] UN 1988. [26] Hillier 1998, 281; Jescheck and Weigend 1996, 170.

[27] Conseil de l'Europe 1990, 27; Gilbert 1996, 109; see also ch. on Articles 9–11 below.

[28] Cassani 1996, 237 et seq.; Pieth 1997b, 762. [29] Hillier 1998, 250.

[30] Conseil de l'Europe 1990, 31 et seq., 33 et seq.

[31] Cf. in particular Art. 54 Schengen Implementing Agreement 1990, 19. Parts of this Convention have subsequently been incorporated in the law of the European Communities or European Union (EU). Note, for example, the provisions contained in Art. 3 EU 2000.

impede excessive foreign claims to jurisdiction have also been identified, particularly in Europe and the United States.[32]

As a minimum, the international community envisages consultations between those state Parties with competing competences. This approach is reflected in Article 4(3) of the Convention.

Specifically when targeting corruption, the international treaties all contain a minimum list of jurisdictional principles to be adopted. The more comprehensive treaties (those drafted by the COE, OAS and UN)[33] make reference to most items on the traditional list:[34]

- territoriality;
- nationality – active and occasionally passive;[35]
- the protective principle.

The OECD's anti-bribery Convention, true to its narrow goal of combating active transnational commercial bribery, has chosen to request 'territoriality' as the main principle (Article 4(1)) and 'nationality' (Article 4(2)), where countries have introduced the 'nationality principle' for other offences. In the meantime most countries, including Australia, Japan, the United Kingdom, and the United States, have adopted the 'nationality principle' in their laws implementing the OECD Convention. Only in Canada and to some extent Argentina do legal obstacles persist to such a move.

We can anticipate that the Convention's rather timid approach to jurisdiction, compared to other treaties, will become obsolete. As we shall see, the fourth paragraph of Article 4 invites each state Party to keep under continuous review the effectiveness of its current basis of jurisdiction. It is thus likely that 'nationality' will soon be part of the standard for all state Parties.

II. The requirements of the Convention

1. The compromise

In the course of lengthy discussions during the negotiations of the Convention,[36] a compromise eventually emerged, hinging largely on an extensive notion of 'territoriality' supplemented by the 'nationality' or 'active personality principle', as far as it was a concept already established in the state Parties concerned.

[32] So-called '*lois obstacles*': Conseil de l'Europe 1990, 33. [33] COE 1999a; OAS 1996; UN 2003.
[34] Harvard Research in International Law 1935, 435, 445. [35] Art. 42, s. 2(a) UN 2003.
[36] Magrini 2003, 121.

At the time, Common Law countries in particular firmly opposed the mandatory introduction of the 'nationality principle'.[37] In the meantime, the number of state Parties opposed to the idea has declined significantly.[38] In particular, the United Kingdom and the United States have introduced 'nationality'.[39] Australia made a particular issue of introducing the 'nationality principle' for the bribery of foreign public officials from the outset. The Australian Federal Parliamentary Joint Standing Committee on Treaties expressed the opinion that 'jurisdiction was central to ensuring the effectiveness of the foreign bribery offence'.[40] As mentioned in the Phase 1 report on Australia, 'it concluded that since foreign bribery is in essence international criminal activity likely to take place wholly outside Australia, the objectives and intent of the Convention would not be met without broadening the jurisdiction over the offence',[41] i.e. broadening it beyond territoriality.

The invitation to state Parties in Article 4(4) to review whether their current basis for jurisdiction is effective in the fight against bribery of foreign public officials and, if not, to take remedial steps is part of the compromise. While acknowledging that not everybody might yet be ready for the step, the Convention envisages a continuous evaluation of the situation by the state Parties, under the control of the Working Group on Bribery (WGB).

2. Territorial jurisdiction (Article 4(1))

Article 4(1) requires each state Party to 'take such measures as may be necessary to establish its jurisdiction over the bribery of foreign public officials when the offence is committed in whole or in part in its territory'. This raises two fundamental questions: how to define 'territory' and what 'committed in its territory' exactly means.

2.1. Territory

2.1.1. Definition of territory

Each state Party defines its own territory according to its 'sovereignty', subject to international recognition. Based on international treaties, the definition of

[37] AR-Ph1, 13, 28; CA-Ph1, 13 et seq.; IE-Ph1, 21, 44 and cf. also UK-Ph1, 26.
[38] Canada, however, has so far steadfastly resisted to engage in such a move (CA-Ph2, 32, 39).
[39] UK-Ph1^{bis}, 9; UK-Ph2, 67. [40] AU-Ph1, 12. [41] AU-Ph1, 12.

'territory' extends to vessels on the high seas, to aircraft, and to embassies and other diplomatically protected areas abroad ('flag principle').[42] Obviously this does not prevent competing jurisdictions, especially relating to the 'protective principle',[43] nor does it prejudge any decision on priority.[44]

2.1.2. Dependent territories

Several OECD countries still have responsibilities for dependent territories.[45] In contrast to other local or regional sub-entities, they typically enjoy a larger measure of independence, and it cannot be assumed that these areas are automatically subject to the laws of the OECD state Party. On the other hand, Dependencies frequently make a living as financial havens and may pose a considerable risk of being abused as staging posts for corruption.[46] Therefore, determining whether a territory is subject to a state Party's jurisdiction is relevant. The situation, however, differs significantly from one state Party to another, as we shall outline in the following section.

a. Denmark

Greenland and the Faroe Islands are Dependencies belonging to Denmark. The issue of the applicability of the Convention was not, however, addressed in Phase 1 of the monitoring process.[47]

b. France

France consists, beyond the mainland, of its *départements d'outre-mer* (including Corsica), its *territoires d'outre-mer* and its *collectivités territoriales.* Whereas for the *departments* the law of the motherland is applicable, this is not automatically the case for all other Dependencies.

c. The Netherlands

The Kingdom of the Netherlands includes Aruba and the Netherlands Antilles (with Curacao, Bonaire and Saba, Sint Eustatius and Sint Maarten).

[42] Geneva 1958; cf. on the details of 'extended territoriality' also Blakesley 1999, 46; Conseil de l'Europe 1990, 12; Gilbert 1996, 116 et seq.; Hillier 1998, 255. It may be mentioned as an anomaly that New Zealand extends the 'flag principle' to Commonwealth and Irish ships and aircraft landing in New Zealand (NZ-Ph1, 17).

[43] Cf. the *Lotus* case: see note 1.

[44] This discussion is becoming ever more pressing in the light of terrorist acts against means of transportation. Cf. Blakesley 1999, 46: note 68 refers to the *Lockerbie* and the *Achille Lauro* incidents.

[45] Denmark, France, Netherlands, Spain, United Kingdom, United States. [46] UK-Ph2, 73.

[47] DK-Ph1, 13.

The Dutch legislation implementing the Convention for its European mainland territory does not automatically extend to these Dependencies. The governments of the Netherlands Antilles and Aruba have the right to consider the applicability of the OECD Convention at their own discretion. Apparently, they are promising action 'in due course'.[48]

d. The United Kingdom

The situation in the United Kingdom is far more complex than in the state Parties mentioned above. First, a separate legislation must, where appropriate, be enacted by the Westminster Parliament for Scotland and Northern Ireland.[49] This is the case with the OECD Convention.[50] Furthermore, a distinction needs to be made between Crown Dependencies[51] and Overseas Territories.[52]

aa. Crown Dependencies

Historically, the Crown Dependencies – the Bailiwick of Guernse (including Alderney, Sark and Herm), the Isle of Man and the Bailiwick of Jersey – have their own elected Parliaments and systems of government. They are not part of the United Kingdom, although the United Kingdom is responsible for their international relations and for their defence, and the Crown retains ultimate responsibility for their good government.[53] As far as treaties and Conventions are concerned, the UK instrument of ratification does not normally include the Crown Dependencies, but may, however, be extended to them, following consultations between their representatives and the UK Home Office. Whereas the *Isle of Man* implemented the OECD Convention in 2001, *Guernsey* maintained that new legislation, that came into force in 2004, was in compliance with the OECD Convention, even though the United Kingdom had not formally extended the Convention to Guernsey by winter 2004. Nor had the Convention been extended to *Jersey* at the time of the Phase 2 evaluation.[54]

[48] NL-Ph1, 1.

[49] The existence, since 1999, of a Scottish Parliament and Northern Ireland Assembly with autonomous legislative powers in some areas, further muddies the waters: cf. Scotland Act 1998 and Northern Ireland Act 1998. The Northern Ireland Assembly is, however, currently suspended. There is also a National Assembly for Wales, established under the Government of Wales Act 1998, whose role is mainly to develop policy for Wales, but on basis of legislation adopted in Westminster.

[50] UK-Ph1^{bis}, 5 et seq., 9 et seq.

[51] Guernsey, Isle of Man, Jersey (incl. Sark and Alderney).

[52] 14 Overseas Territories (including Bermuda, British Virgin Islands, Turks and Caicos, the Cayman Islands, Gibraltar, Anguila, Montserrat, and the Falkland Islands).

[53] UK-Ph2, 68; and cf. for further constitutional background: Department for Constitutional Affairs 2002.

[54] UK-Ph2, 69 et seq.

bb. Overseas Territories

During the Phase 2 evaluation of the United Kingdom, concern was expressed that some of the most frequently used financial centres in the Overseas Territories, particularly in the British Virgin Islands, Bermuda, Turks, and Caicos, had not yet undertaken any steps to implement the Convention, whereas implementing laws in other Territories (Cayman Islands, Gibraltar) remained at a draft stage.[55]

2.1.3. Internationally non-recognised territories

In the chapter on Article 1 of the Convention in this commentary we discussed whether foreign public officials of a dependent territory, a free trade zone, or an area not yet internationally recognised were covered by the Convention's definition in Article 1(4). Under Article 4 a different kind of issue is at stake, a jurisdictional one, namely: is the Convention at all applicable to territories like northern Cyprus? From a Turkish point of view the northern part of the Island was first treated as a Turkish territory and therefore subject to its jurisdiction.[56] On 15 November 1983, however, a 'Turkish Republic of Northern Cyprus' (TRNC) was proclaimed.[57] Since the OECD countries do not recognise this *fait accompli*,[58] they have to insist on the fiction that the acts are committed on the territory of a unified 'Republic of Cyprus', a country now a Member of the EU, but not yet of the OECD.[59]

2.2. The territorial basis for jurisdiction

Article 4(1) states that jurisdiction is established 'when the offence is committed in whole or *in part* in its territory'. The formula follows the traditional academic doctrine and national law.[60] Official Commentary 25 adds: 'The territorial basis for jurisdiction should be interpreted broadly so that an extensive physical connection to the bribery act is not required'. These two quotes are repeated, mantra-like, in every WGB country evaluation.

[55] UK-Ph2, 70 et seq. [56] On 8 June, 1975 a 'Turkish Province Cyprus' was proclaimed.
[57] Rumpf 2004, 3; Arsava 1999 (cf. also: http://www.bmlv.gv.at>Publikationen>wissenschaftliche Publikationen>Autoren); Heinze 1997, 3.
[58] UN 1983.
[59] The EU position is that, following accession of the Republic of Cyprus, the application of EU law 'shall be suspended in those areas of the Republic of Cyprus in which the government of the Republic of Cyprus does not exercise effective control', i.e. in the Turkish-controlled northern part, until the island is reunited. Cf. EU 2003b, 955.
[60] Cf., for example, Blakesley 1999, 43, who uses the same formula, referring to the Harvard Research in International Law 1935: see note 34.

2.2.1. 'Committed'

For a long time an act-oriented ('subjective territoriality') and an effect-oriented ('objective territoriality') attachment were treated as opposites.[61] Only gradually did the 'principle of ubiquity' gain ground, both in Civil Law and Common Law systems.[62] According to this principle, the territorial basis is established, if the act was committed on or if its 'effects' occurred on the relevant territory.

a. 'By an act'

As far as acts or omissions are concerned, the Convention interpretation is clear: even the slightest of connections is sufficient. This includes all objective elements of the crime (promise, offer, giving) and any necessary intermediate actions. It includes, in particular, the use of the telephone, fax or e-mail by the offeror.[63] Virtually all countries seem to meet this standard.

Some doubts have been raised with regard to Canada, since its courts have requested that 'a significant portion of the activities constituting that offence took place in Canada'.[64] The requirement of a 'real and substantial link'[65] only deepens the concerns that too high a threshold is required. On the other hand, practice after the Canadian *Libman* case indicated that the territorial link can be quite minimal, so case law does seem to be in line with the overall standard of the Convention.[66]

In a similar way, Iceland seems to set the standard too high – at least according to a first assessment.[67]

The place of omission would be the place where the offender should have acted.[68]

b. 'By effect'

According to the now prevalent 'ubiquity principle', many countries state that they also accept a territorial attachment through 'effects' within the country.[69] Two independent historical strains have led to this concept. On the one hand, the very traditional situation that someone could have been wounded in one state and succumbed to his wounds in another often led to

[61] Blakesley 1999, 47 et seq.; Jescheck and Weigend 1996, 177.
[62] Conseil de l'Europe 1990, 8 et seq.; Cassani 1996, 246 et seq.; Gilbert 1996, 116.
[63] The WGB insists on this criterion in all its evaluative texts.
[64] CA-Ph1, 12 (reference to the *Libman* case); CA-Ph2, 32 et seq.; cf. also Gilbert 1996, 117.
[65] Also NZ-Ph1, 16. [66] CA-Ph1, 13; controversy re-emerged, however, in CA-Ph2, 32 et seq.
[67] IS-Ph1, 9 (note wording: 'a significant degree').
[68] Italy: Magrini 2003, 122; Switzerland: Federal Court Decisions BGE 82 IV 68 et seq., 99 IV 181 et seq.
[69] Denmark, Germany, Hungary, Ireland, Luxembourg, Mexico, Poland.

competing competences.[70] On the other hand, a more recent development, especially in the economic and anti-trust law of Common Law states, allows a primary territorial attachment to be maintained, while extending jurisdiction beyond the borders with the help of the 'effects doctrine'.[71]

The 'effects doctrine' raises many issues. While it might be perceived as part of the wider act to receive the bribe and to deposit it on a bank account in a bank domiciled in the territory, or to allow the funds to transit through the local banking system,[72] it seems less certain, if the Convention applies to the mere depositing of funds generated through bribery (net profits of the briber). Furthermore, it is certainly not in every country that a mere 'threat' to financial interests of competing exporters or investors would be regarded as establishing a sufficient territorial nexus under the effects doctrine.

According to most legal systems, however, bribery is a 'conduct crime' (*'Tätigkeitsdelikt'*),[73] and not a 'result crime' (*'Erfolgsdelikt'*). Therefore, the relevant elements all relate to the act or omission itself.[74] In some legal systems non-technical elements of the offence can be used as a jurisdictional basis, e.g. the place where the ultimate gain is or will be reaped.

c. Preparation, attempt, handling, and money laundering

Other issues are raised by the question of preparation and attempt. Preparatory acts are generally only regarded as relevant in as far as they are criminalised. Whereas some evaluation texts insist that only material or objective elements of the crime constitute a basis for territorial attachment,[75] it is obvious in other reports that an attempt triggers jurisdiction where commission of the crime was intended.[76] This should be considered the general standard.

Acts like money laundering, whose commission follows that of the 'predicate' offence, generate their own territorial nexus.[77]

d. Aiding or abetting and conspiracy

The accessory acting abroad, aiding the main perpetrator at home, would fall under the territorial jurisdiction of all state Parties. The reverse is true in most

[70] Blakesley 1999, 47 (with references).
[71] Cf. Gilbert 1996, 107 referring to *U.S.* v. *Layton* and other cases. [72] LU-Ph1, 16.
[73] Cf. the discussion of the Law Commission 1998, 106; Gilbert 1996, 122 et seq.
[74] Cf. for Germany: Jescheck and Weigend 1996, 178; for New Zealand: NZ-Ph1, 17; for Switzerland: Arzt 1990, 168 et seq.; Cassani 1996, 258 et seq.
[75] BE-Ph2, 32 (*un élément constitutif matériel*); NZ-Ph1, 16 (an element that forms part of the *actus reus*); cf. also Gilbert 1996, 119.
[76] For Italy: Magrini 2003, 122; for Switzerland: cf. Art. 7(2) Swiss Criminal Code.
[77] For Switzerland: Cassani 1996, 258.

countries: mere aiding or abetting is sufficient to create the territorial link.[78] Only Supreme Court practice in Switzerland has so far insisted that, since the main offender is acting abroad, the crime is considered foreign. Swiss jurisdiction therefore depends on whether other principles like the 'nationality principle' or '*aut dedere aut judicare*' take hold.[79]

e. No 'dual criminality' requirement

Under the regime of territorial jurisdiction, 'dual criminality' is not an issue. Territorial jurisdiction is a direct consequence of 'sovereignty'.

aa. Special issue: the US 'interstate nexus'

According to US law, a jurisdictional distinction is made: whereas under US territorial jurisdiction any non-national person or business is subject to the law, territorial attachment for US persons (individuals and so-called 'issuers' and 'domestic concerns') requires the 'use of mails or any means or instrumentality of interstate commerce.'[80] Whilst this special feature may be explicable historically, it does create an inequality of treatment and leaves a possible loophole in the US implementation.[81]

bb. Special issue: the Japanese 'main office exception'

The original Article 10bis, section 3 of the Japanese Unfair Competition Prevention Law provided for an exception of the offence of bribery of a foreign public official. The exception applied where a bribe was given to a foreign public official by a person whose 'main office' was located in the country in which the foreign public official was also engaged in public service. The exception also extended to cases where an agent acted for such a person.[82]

The Japanese authorities intended with this rule to limit the scope of the term 'international business' according to Article 1 and to exclude what they consider domestic bribery committed abroad.[83]

The WGB, however, was very concerned by this. This approach would mean excluding from application of the Convention those cases in which a Japanese person bribed a foreign public official on Japanese territory on

[78] E.g. FR-Ph1, 17; Germany: para. 9 Criminal Code and Jung 1979, 325 et seq.; IT-Ph1, 18 and Magrini 2003, 122; JP-Ph1, 12; UK: Gilbert 1996, 122.

[79] CH-Ph1, 12, 23; Art. 7 of the new Swiss Criminal Code will change the situation.

[80] US-Ph1, 13 et seq., 21; US-Ph2, 31 et seq.

[81] Cf. the critique of the WGB: US-Ph1, 21; US-Ph2, 31 et seq.

[82] JP-Ph1, 1.

[83] Cf. Japan's 'talking points', i.e. the informal negotiations with the OECD WGB conducted in autumn 2000.

behalf of a foreign subsidiary of a Japanese company or on behalf of any other foreign company.[84]

After the critique voiced in the Phase 1 monitoring process and following extensive negotiations with the Chair of the WGB, Japan agreed to change its law and abolished its main office exception.[85]

3. Nationality jurisdiction (Article 4(2))

3.1. The rationale

According to the 'active nationality' or 'active personality principle', nationals are liable to prosecution in their home state for offences committed abroad.[86] This concept should not be confused with the 'passive nationality' or 'passive personality approach', based on the nationality of the victim.

The 'nationality principle' goes back to two fairly different sources. The first source is the medieval pre-Nation State concept of '*iura ossibus inhaerent*' ('the laws follow the bones'): this came into disrepute under the conditions of the aggressive expansionism of the Nation State in the first half of the twentieth century.[87] A second source is far more recent: since many countries are opposed to extraditing their nationals, they have the international obligation to prosecute crimes of those nationals who seek refuge in their country ('*aut dedere aut iudicare*').[88]

For the same reason the 'nationality principle' has been extended to foreigners who cannot be extradited, because they would face political persecution in the requesting state ('*non-refoulement*' obligation).[89]

In more recent times, other states have gone beyond this narrow reading of 'nationality', pointing out that they owe each other solidarity in combating transnational crime, especially where the country in which the offence was committed does not have adequate resources available. The concept was first applied to very serious abuses of human rights (genocide, crimes against humanity, etc.) and later to sex offences committed abroad. In the meantime,

[84] JP-Ph1, 1 et seq.; letter by the Chair of the WGB of 26 October 2000 to the Japanese Ambassador at the OECD.

[85] JP-Ph1[bis], 30 (Annex 1, 25 April 2002).

[86] Blakesley 1999, 40, 61 et seq.; Hillier 1998, 257 et seq.; LaFave 2000, 144; Müller and Wildhaber 1982, 256.

[87] Jescheck and Weigend 1996, 169.

[88] This is the reason why a traditional formula for the 'nationality principle' such as contained in Art. 6 of the Swiss Criminal Code makes jurisdiction dependent on the presence of the accused in the country (Blakesley 1999, 62, 63; Conseil de l'Europe 1990, 10; Gilbert, 1996, 109 and see I.2. above).

[89] CH-Ph1, 12; IT-Ph1, 18; PL-Ph1, 19; SE-Ph1, 14.

most countries have introduced 'nationality' at least for some very serious crime, on the basis of international treaties.[90] By some countries the notion of 'nationality' has been extended to residence and occasionally (if, typically, under quite restrictive further conditions) even to non-resident foreigners. Not all state Parties, however, are ready to extend this logic to economic crime, including corruption.

3.2. Is nationality jurisdiction mandatory under Article 4(2)?

Article 4(2) gives a rather sibylline answer:

> 'Each party which has jurisdiction to prosecute its nationals for offences committed abroad shall take such measures as may be necessary to establish its jurisdiction to do so in respect of the bribery of a foreign public official, according to the same principles.'

Since all OECD countries have jurisdiction to prosecute nationals for some – at least very serious – offences committed abroad, the question remains what the normative content of Article 4(2) really is. Official Commentary 26 tries to help with the following statement in the first sentence:

> Nationality jurisdiction is to be established according to the general principles and conditions in the legal system of each party.

The reference to the 'same principles' or to 'the general principles and conditions in the legal system of each party' clearly represents another application of the concept of 'functional equivalence'.[91] As in Article 1(2) or in Article 7, the Convention refers back to the treatment of similar crimes within a given legal system. The fourth sentence of Official Commentary 26 makes it clear that:

> 'For countries which apply nationality jurisdiction only to certain types of offences, the reference to 'principles' includes the principles upon which such selection is based.'

The primary consequence of this rule is that the consistency of the decisions about jurisdiction over transnational corruption is subject to the evaluation by the WGB. And perhaps here the WGB has been a little soft in the past.[92] Common Law countries, in particular, traditionally focus on a more or less extensive reading of 'territoriality' and have discussed the principles warranting an extension of 'nationality' in some detail. As already mentioned,[93]

[90] Including AR-Ph1, 13; CA-Ph1, 13 et seq.; IE-Ph1, 21; JP-Ph1, 14.

[91] See Official Commentary 2 and the Introduction of this commentary.

[92] The WGB has been rather easily satisfied by assurances in Phase 1 in the cases of AR-Ph1, 13, 28; CA-Ph1, 13 et seq.; it demonstrated a tougher stance, however, in the case of Japan (JP-Ph1, 14, 29).

[93] See II. above.

Australia believed 'nationality' was essential for effective implementation of the Convention.[94] The United Kingdom went back to the drawing board after initially disputing the need to introduce the 'nationality principle'.[95] According to a general rule in UK law, the 'nationality principle' is the exception, only being applicable where an Act of Parliament demands it explicitly.[96] The 1996 report by an Inter-Ministerial Steering Committee already defined the criteria for the occasional introduction of the 'nationality principle'. According to the text of the Phase 1 evaluation,[97] it suggested that extra-territorial jurisdiction should be established only where 'at least one of the tests in the following list was satisfied':

- 'The offence is serious. This could be determined by the length of the sentence.
- Due to the nature of the offence, the witnesses and evidence are likely to be available in the United Kingdom.
- There is international consensus that certain conduct is reprehensible and concerted action, involving the taking of extra-territorial jurisdiction, is necessary.
- Exercising extra-territorial jurisdiction appears to be in the interests of the standing and reputation of the United Kingdom in the international community.'[98]

In the course of the evaluation, the UK authorities recognised that some of the criteria were indeed applicable. But they emphasised the difficulty in obtaining evidence from abroad. The WGB was not convinced, however, by this argument and proposed certain reforms. Since the Law Commission of England and Wales had already proposed an extended form of 'territoriality' for corruption, the government chose to introduce the 'nationality principle' in its new Act of 2001.[99]

The seriousness of the offence and the need for internationally concerted action have thus become the criteria generally accepted on an international scale: Japan, originally reserving the 'nationality principle' for the most serious offences,[100] has recently taken the step of extending it to foreign bribery.[101] So far Canada,[102] and, more half-heartedly Argentina[103] and Ireland,[104] are still opposing the step. In defence Canada refers to the need for consistency with

[94] AU-Ph1, 12. [95] UK-Ph1, 12. [96] Gilbert 1996, 110 et seq., 127.
[97] UK-Ph1, 12 et seq. [98] UK-Ph1, 13.
[99] UK-Ph1bis, 9 et seq. (s. 109 Antiterrorism, Crime and Security Act 2001); UK-Ph2, 67 et seq., criticising a lack of awareness on the part of judges.
[100] JP-Ph1, 14, 29. [101] JP-Ph2, 47. [102] CA-Ph1, 13 et seq.; CA-Ph2, 32, 39.
[103] AR-Ph1, 13, 28. [104] IE-Ph1, 21, 44.

its laws and legal history as well as its 'effective territoriality'. Both arguments are somewhat shaky: the first, in the light of the Canadian practice of establishing 'nationality' 'where there is an international consensus that a crime is of such universal concern as to justify extra-territorial jurisdiction',[105] and the second, because Canada's approach to 'territoriality' is potentially quite restrictive in comparison to other countries (requiring a 'real and substantial link').[106]

Summarising, it can be stated that a strict interpretation of Article 4(2), which takes into account the concept of 'functional equivalence', but insists on consistency within legal systems, would probably make the 'nationality principle' mandatory for all OECD states. Certainly, inconsistencies such as those presented by the Irish approach, where the 'nationality principle' is applied to domestic corruption and corruption within the EU, but not to the wider OECD-related foreign corruption, must be corrected.[107]

3.3. Additional requirements

According to the applicable rationale,[108] countries define the concept of 'nationality' relatively narrowly or broadly. The broad approach includes residents or, in some cases, even non-resident foreigners. However, all approaches make jurisdiction dependent on additional requirements,[109] i.e.:

- dual criminality;
- a request by the victim;
- action by a senior law officer;
- availability of the suspect (presence or extradition);
- non-extraditability of the suspect.

3.3.1. 'Dual criminality'

The second sentence of the Official Commentary 26 makes it clear that 'dual criminality'[110] is an acceptable condition under the 'nationality principle': 'these principles deal with such matters as dual criminality'. The Official Commentary immediately adds in the next sentence: 'However, the

[105] CA-Ph1, 14. [106] See II.2.2.1.a. above; CA-Ph1, 12 and CA-Ph2, 32.
[107] IE-Ph1, 21 (surprisingly not taken up by the WGB). [108] See II.3.1. above.
[109] Cf. in general Conseil de l'Europe 1990, 11.
[110] Van den Wyngaert 1996, 43 et seq.

requirement of dual criminality should be deemed to be met if the act is unlawful where it occurred, even if under a different criminal statute.'

This sentence has various implications: first, it reiterates the general rule that under 'dual criminality' one is neither expecting identical norms, nor even the same type of crime, but rather that it must be sufficient that the facts are unlawful under criminal law; second, the third sentence of the Official Commentary 26 makes it clear that the criminalisation of active bribery at the location of the offence is also sufficient. The reference in the law of New Zealand to 'the country in which the foreign public official's "principal office" is situated' does not, therefore, comply with the Convention standard.[111]

The notion of 'unlawful' would typically be interpreted as an abstract concept; it does not require any culpability or ability to sanction in concreto.[112]

'Unlawful', according to the third sentence of the Official Commentary 26, does not require a foreign bribery statute in the country of the offence,[113] nor is reciprocity required.[114] It is sufficient that bribery is criminalised.

On the other hand, if the bribery takes place in a third country which is neither the 'victim state' nor a state Party to the Convention, a transnational bribery statute would be required by most countries, with regard to the concept of 'dual criminality'.[115] The WGB's critique is quite unwarranted.[116] Some states claim not to require the concept of 'dual criminality' when applying the 'nationality principle' to transnational bribery.[117]

3.3.2. A complaint by the victim and the assent by a senior law officer

Some states request – in addition to 'dual criminality' – a concrete complaint by the victim.[118] Typically, another state would be considered a victim.[119] Whether private parties, such as the ousted competitor, also qualify as victims is far from clear in all state Parties.[120] In addition, the decision to prosecute could, in some countries, be reserved to (senior) prosecuting agents[121] or to the

[111] NZ-Ph1, 18, 36 (critical comments).
[112] Different: FI-Ph1, 10; FI-Ph2, 25, in concreto, whereas most other countries would apply the principle in abstracto; cf. also Conseil de l'Europe 1990, 11.
[113] DE-Ph1, 10; unclear: NZ-Ph1, 18, note 12.
[114] BE-Ph2, 32 (for universal jurisdiction).
[115] NL-Ph1, 19. [116] E.g. NL-Ph1, 35.
[117] DE-Ph1, 10 (unclear); HU-Ph1, 12; IS-Ph1, 10; LU-Ph1, 16 (not regarding serious crimes); PL-Ph1, 19.
[118] BE-Ph2, 32 et seq.; FR-Ph1, 18, 31; IT-Ph1, 18; IT-Ph2, 38.
[119] FR-Ph1, 18; IT-Ph2, 38.
[120] GR-Ph1, 11; FR-Ph1, 18. See also the discussion in ch. on Article 5 below.
[121] BE-Ph2, 33.

Minister of Justice,[122] even where private action is possible.[123] In most of these cases the discretion of the senior law officer is not limited by law.[124]

3.3.3. The presence or availability of the accused

Some laws make it an explicit condition that the accused be present in the country of the trial[125] and that he/she cannot be extradited.[126]

3.4. The application of the 'nationality principle' to corporate entities?

That delinquency by managers who possess the citizenship of the corporation's host country entails individual responsibility within the concept of the 'nationality principle' is understood.[127] The question to be discussed here is whether jurisdiction for corporate responsibility can be triggered by mere incorporation, even if the responsible employees acting abroad are foreigners.[128] Several countries state that the 'nationality principle' extends to corporations.[129] Not all of them, however, have practical experience in this area.

In accordance with the rules established under Articles 2 and 3(2) of the Convention, agents and other ancillary personnel are treated like employees of the corporation.[130] Jurisdiction also extends to foreign branches.[131] Generally a line is, however, drawn at the foreign subsidiary.[132] Especially where shell corporations or phantom companies are concerned, circumstances may well allow for the 'piercing of the corporate veil', though.[133]

Some inconsistencies have been identified regarding dependent territories. While the 'nationality principle' was introduced in the United Kingdom with the anti-terrorism legislation of 2001, a 'national' is defined as 'any individual

[122] IT-Ph2, 38.
[123] Cf. especially BE-Ph2, 38; FR-Ph2, 45 et seq.; IT-Ph2, 38.
[124] IT-Ph2, 38; NO-Ph2, 43. See the discussion of the issue concerning the law officer consent in UK law in ch. on Article 5 below.
[125] Conseil de l'Europe 1990, 11; IT-Ph1, 18; PT-Ph1, 18; SE-Ph1, 14; CH-Ph1, 12.
[126] CH-Ph1, 12 (Art. 6 Swiss Criminal Code); PL-Ph1, 19.
[127] The topics are sometimes confused in the evaluation reports, cf. JP-Ph2, 46 et seq. (applicability overall uncertain).
[128] Correct in NO-Ph2, 44.
[129] HU-Ph1, 12; KR-Ph1, 12, 22; MX-Ph1, 12; NL-Ph1, 17 et seq.; NO-Ph2, 44; PL-Ph1, 18; Switzerland: Bertossa 2003, 207 et seq.; cf. the diverging findings of the Conseil de l'Europe 1990, 11; US-Ph1, 14.
[130] See ch. on Article 2 above. [131] PT-Ph1, 18; NZ-Ph1, 17.
[132] NZ-Ph1, 17. [133] E.g. FR-Ph2, 45.

who is a British citizen, a British Overseas Territories citizen, a British National (overseas) or a British overseas citizen'.[134] Companies happen to be excluded by this definition. Since many of the British Crown Dependencies or Overseas Territories are financial centres, this loophole seemed quite unacceptable to the WGB.[135]

III. Consultation procedure (Article 4(3))

Given the different jurisdictional options endorsed by the Convention, conflicts of jurisdiction in respect of anti-bribery cases brought under legislation implementing the Convention are a real possibility. There have indeed already been several important cases where prosecutions could have occurred in a multiplicity of jurisdictions.[136] Where this situation transpires, the result may well, however, be inactivity rather than over-activity of the law enforcement agencies.[137]

Article 4(3) of the Convention foresees a consultation procedure in the case of competing competences. While most countries will allow for such consultations, a special procedure is rarely foreseen in the law.[138] Nevertheless, several state Parties have at their disposal the procedures envisaged by the COE Convention on the Transfer of Proceedings in Criminal Matters of 15 May 1972.[139] More recently, the EU's judicial co-operation body, Eurojust, has promulgated a set of suggested Guidelines for prosecuting authorities of the twenty-five EU Member States to consider when deciding on conflicts of jurisdiction.[140] Although these Guidelines are not binding, they provide certain benchmarks which may also influence the wider international law enforcement community when faced with a plurality of possible jurisdictions. The OECD Convention does not, however, foresee an international rule against 'double jeopardy'.[141]

[134] UK-Ph2, 67 et seq., 72 et seq. [135] UK-Ph2, 73.

[136] Cf., for example, the case of TSK (*Halliburton/Nigeria*) in which at least ten jurisdictions are theoretically competent, among them France (*Evening Standard*, 10 January 2005), Germany (*Le Figaro*, 13 January 2005), Italy, Netherlands, Nigeria, Portugal, Switzerland, United Kingdom (*Independent*, 25 January 2004) and United States (*Financial Times*, 2 November 2004).

[137] As outlined in the ch. on Article 5 below, there are already a number of other disincentives to effective enforcement of anti-bribery legislation.

[138] No formal procedure foreseen: FI-Ph1, 10; GR-Ph1, 11; IT-Ph1, 19; JP-Ph1, 14; MX-Ph1, 12; NZ-Ph1, 19.

[139] COE 1972. The state Parties to the OECD Convention which have both signed and ratified this COE Convention are Austria, Bulgaria, Denmark, Estonia, the Netherlands, Norway, Romania, Slovakia, Spain, Sweden, and Turkey.

[140] Eurojust Annual Report 2003, 54. [141] See also ch. on Articles 9–11 below.

IV. Review Procedure (Article 4(4))

In accordance with Article 4(4) of the Convention, 'each party shall review whether its current basis for jurisdiction is effective in the fight against bribery of foreign public officials, and, if it is not, shall take remedial steps'. This provision was accepted by the less ambitious state Parties who would not agree to the introduction of 'nationality' outright. It gives the WGB the right to monitor effectiveness on an ongoing basis. However, in its abstract formulation it also aims at additional criteria restricting the use of 'nationality'.[142] It could also address a too narrowly formulated definition of 'territoriality'.

In the course of the evaluations, most countries have, however, either indicated that they had just completed the review and were satisfied with the results,[143] that they thought such review premature,[144] or that they saw no need for it in the light of the existing broad jurisdictional regime.[145] Only Switzerland and the United Kingdom indicated a need for reform at the time of the Phase 1 evaluation.[146] It is deplorable that Canada, in particular, was unwilling to further examine its position on 'nationality'.[147]

As explained in the Introduction of this commentary, there is a follow-up procedure to the Phase 2 monitoring.[148] This allows the WGB to keep revisiting the issues as long as they have been raised in the Phase 2 evaluations.[149]

References

For documentation see the consolidated bibliography at the end of this book.

Arsava, A. F. (1999), 'Zypernkonflikt unter Berücksichtigung des Völkerrechts' in Bundesministerium für Landesverteidigung (Hrsg.), *Jahrbuch für internationale Sicherheitspolitik*, Wien (also available at: http://www.bmlv.gv.at > Publikationen > wissenschaftliche Publikationen > Autoren).

Arzt, G. (1990), 'Erfolgsdelikt und Tätigkeitsdelikt', *Schweizerische Zeitschrift für Strafrecht* **107**, 168.

Beck, U. (1998), *Was ist Globalisierung?*, Frankfurt a. M.

[142] See II.3.3.1. above (e.g. 'dual criminality').
[143] AU-Ph1, 12; MX-Ph1, 13.
[144] CZ-Ph1, 12; FR-Ph1, 19; PT-Ph1, 19.
[145] AT-Ph1, 14; DE-Ph1, 10; DK-Ph1, 15; ES-Ph1, 13; FI-Ph1, 10; GR-Ph1, 11; IT-Ph1, 19; JP-Ph1, 14; NL-Ph1, 20; NZ-Ph1, 19; SE-Ph1, 14.
[146] CH-Ph1, 13 et seq.; UK-Ph1, 13.
[147] CA-Ph1, 14; CA-Ph2, 32 et seq.
[148] Note the recent report concluded in respect of the United States: follow-up report on the implementation of the Phase 2 Recommendations on the application of the Convention: OECD WGB, 18 December 2005. See also introduction above and ch. on Article 13 below.
[149] WGB: Monitoring Issues, June 2005 (DAF/INV/BR/WD(2004)/REV3).

Bertossa, C. A. (2003), *Unternehmensstrafrecht – Strafprozess und Sanktionen*, Bern.

Blakesley, Ch. L. (1999), 'Extra-Territorial Jurisdiction' in C. M. Bassiouni, *International Criminal Law*, 2nd edn, New York, 33.

Cassani, U. (1996), 'Die Anwendung des schweizerischen Strafrechts auf internationale Wirtschaftsdelikte (Art. 3–7 StGB)', *Schweizerische Zeitschrift für Strafrecht* **114**, 237.

Conseil de l'Europe (1990), *Affaires juridiques, compétences extraterritoriales en matière pénale*, Strasbourg.

Gilbert, G. (1996), 'Crimes Sans Frontières: Jurisdictional Problems in English Law' in J. Dugard and Ch. van den Wyngaert (eds.), *International Criminal Law and Procedure*, Aldershot, Brookfield (USA), Singapore, Sydney, 101.

Heinze, C. (1997), *Zur Frage der Vereinbarkeit der Aufnahme von Zypern in die Europäische Union mit dem Völkerrecht, dem Recht der EU und den Zypern-Verträgen von 1959/60, Kurzgutachten der Republik Türkei* (available at: http://www.crh.camelot.de>Zypern>Veröffentlichungen zum Zypernkonflikt).

Hillier, T. (1998), *Sourcebook on Public International Law*, London.

Jescheck, H.-H. and T. Weigend (1996), *Lehrbuch des Strafrechts: Allgemeiner Teil*, 5th edn, Berlin.

Jung, H. (1979), 'Die Inlandsteilnahme an ausländischer strafloser Haupttat. Regelungsgehalt und Problematik des § 9 Abs. 2 Satz 2 StGB', *Juristenzeitschrift* 1979, 325.

Kontorovich, E. (2004), 'The Piracy Analogy: Modern Universal Jurisdiction's Hollow Foundation', *Harvard International Law Journal*, Vol. **45**, No. 1, 183.

LaFave, W. R. (2000), *Criminal Law*, 3rd edn, St. Paul (USA).

Magrini P. (2003), 'L'attauzione della Convenzione OCSE contro la corruzione negli Stati membri: il quadro comparato' in G. Sacerdoti, *Responsabilità d'impresa e strumenti internazionali anticorruzione*, Milano.

Müller, J. P. and L. Wildhaber (1982), *Praxis des Völkerrechts*, Bern, 256.

Passas N. (1999), 'Globalization, Criminogenic Asymmetries and Economic Crime', *European Journal of Law Reform*, Vol. **1**, No. 4, 399.

Pieth, M. (1997) [cited Pieth 1997b], 'Internationale Harmonisierung von Strafrecht als Antwort auf transnationale Wirtschaftskriminalität', *Zeitschrift für die Gesamte Strafrechtswissenschaft* **109**, 756.

Rumpf, Ch. (2004), 'Zur Rechtslage Zyperns: Grundlagen und Konfliktlinien' (available at: http://www.tuerkei-recht.de).

Van den Wyngaert, Ch. (1996), 'Double Criminality as a Requirement to Jurisdiction' in J. Dugard and Ch. Van den Wyngaert (eds.), *International Criminal Law and Procedure*, Aldershot, Brookfield USA, Singapore, Sydney, 43.

Article 5. Enforcement

PETER J. CULLEN

Article 5 – Enforcement

Investigation and prosecution of the bribery of a foreign public official shall be subject to the applicable rules and principles of each Party. They shall not be influenced by considerations of national economic interest, the potential effect upon relations with another State or the identity of the natural or legal persons involved.

Official Commentary

Article 5 – Enforcement

27. Article 5 recognises the fundamental nature of national regimes of prosecutorial discretion. It recognises as well that, in order to protect the independence of prosecution, such discretion is to be exercised on the basis of professional motives and is not to be subject to improper influence by concerns of a political nature. Article 5 is complemented by paragraph 6 of the Annex to the 1997 OECD Revised Recommendation on Combating Bribery in International Business Transactions, C(97)123/FINAL (hereinafter, ''1997 OECD Recommendation''), which recommends, inter alia, that complaints of bribery of foreign public officials should be seriously investigated by competent authorities and that adequate resources should be provided by national governments to permit effective prosecution of such bribery. Parties will have accepted this Recommendation, including its monitoring and follow-up arrangements.

Chapter contents

I. Introduction

Article 5 of the OECD's anti-bribery Convention expresses the general obligation on state Parties to 'take effective measures to deter, prevent, and combat the bribery of foreign public officials in connection with international business transactions'.[1] Article 5 complements the preceding

[1] S. I. OECD 1997a contains this text in the form of a recommendation; Art. 5 in effect transforms it from soft to hard law.

Convention provisions on the criminalisation of active foreign bribery, the responsibility of legal persons, the provision of 'effective, proportionate, and dissuasive' sanctions, and the founding of jurisdiction, by requiring that these substantive provisions be applied in practice, according to professional motives, by properly resourced investigating and prosecuting authorities who enjoy independence from political authorities.

The enforcement of the Convention is indeed substantially dependent upon the commitment, skill and resources of the authorities entrusted, at national level, with the investigation and prosecution of serious crime.[2] Their work is, in turn, dependent on the extent and adequacy of reporting of the offence, by public or private bodies of any kind or by injured parties – and the Revised Recommendation requires that 'complaints of victims should be seriously investigated by the competent authorities'.[3] (A highly developed system of private prosecutions enabling direct action by the victims of the bribery offence, such as competitors of the briber, may even compensate for prosecutorial failure to take action.[4])

Enforcement raises a whole host of issues, of a practical, policy and political nature. The country reports by the Working Group on Bribery (WGB) on the implementation of Article 5, in particular the Phase 2 reports, devote considerable space to matters such as the organisation and resourcing of the prosecution service (or services), the relations between investigators and prosecutors (especially where a number of different agencies are involved), the distribution and handling of case work, investigatory powers, training, etc. All of these factors can affect enforcement in the broad sense. We will class them in this chapter as questions pertaining to the *organisation* of anti-bribery enforcement (see part V.) Clearly, the organisation of investigation and prosecution agencies is an important factor in how well bribery of foreign officials is tackled.[5] Our primary focus of attention will, however, lie elsewhere, because the specific focus of Article 5 is in fact much narrower.

The short text of Article 5 is mainly devoted to the question of *prosecutorial discretion*, and on how to limit it. After stating that 'the applicable rules and principles of each Party' shall apply to the investigation

[2] The foreign bribery offence is generally classified as 'serious' by the state Parties. See III.4. below.

[3] Para. 6 of the Agreed Common Elements of the OECD 1997a (also referred to in Official Commentary 27).

[4] See further V.3. below. In fact, considerable scepticism was expressed on this point in the negotiations leading to the adoption of the Revised Recommendation (OECD 1997a) and the OECD Convention (OECD 1997b): see *Travaux Préparatoires* (OECD 1999, F-1032 et seq.).

[5] OECD 1999, F-1034: 'The Working Group stressed that prosecutorial discretion is linked to the problem of adequate resources, priorities, and the organisation of the law enforcement effort.'

and prosecution of the bribery of a foreign public official, the second sentence of Article 5 states that such investigation and prosecution:

> 'shall not be influenced by considerations of national economic interest, the potential effect upon relations with another State or the identity of the natural or legal persons involved.'

As Official Commentary 27 to Article 5 indicates, these limitations are precisely designed to ensure that prosecution is independent, meaning apolitical. Official Commentary 27 begins with the statement that Article 5 'recognises the fundamental nature of national regimes of prosecutorial discretion'; it immediately proceeds to require that such discretion 'be exercised on the basis of professional motives and...not...be subject to improper influence by concerns of a political nature'.

The *Travaux Préparatoires* to the Revised Recommendation and to the Convention indeed reveal the concern of the WGB about the issue of prosecutorial discretion. The intention was to introduce criteria which 'emphasise the importance of prosecutorial independence'.[6] Accordingly, the preparatory work of the WGB identified the protection of state economic interest or of good relations with other states, or having regard to the identity of 'the victim',[7] as taboo factors.

The Convention's guiding principle concerning the harmonised implementation of the Convention, namely the principle of 'functional equivalence', is again at play in the Article 5 context. As applied to the question of prosecutorial discretion, the principle expresses the acceptance of different systems of prosecution, notably the distinction between those state Parties applying a system of 'mandatory' prosecution and others which operate 'discretionary prosecution'. The former refers to a *legal obligation* on the prosecutor to commence an investigation on the basis of notice of commission of an offence, whereas the latter, also known in some systems as the 'opportunity principle',[8] implies that the prosecutor is not legally bound to act on the basis of such notice.[9] It was not so much the basic discretion available to prosecutors under the opportunity system which concerned the drafters of the Convention, but rather the possibility that

[6] OECD 1999, F-1033.

[7] We can observe, with regard to the third criterion contained in Art. 5 – 'identity of the natural or the legal persons involved' – that the text is somewhat broader than para. 6 of the Agreed Common Elements, which refers only to 'the identity of the victim'. See also V.3. below.

[8] 'Opportunity' suggests the seizing of the appropriate moment, i.e. favourable circumstances for prosecution: this can be interpreted in a number of ways, but suggests first of all the likelihood that the prosecution will lead to a conviction.

[9] Cf. Kühne 2003, 165 et seq., for the German law perspective, and Bell 2001, for a Common Law viewpoint on discretionary prosecution.

it be exercised for political, i.e. non-professional, reasons. Article 5 tries to limit only the *abuse* of prosecutorial discretion. It could hardly be otherwise, as the discretionary approach to prosecution is widely recognised as having many advantages over mandatory prosecution, particularly where the efficient use of resources is concerned.[10]

Our further discussion of Article 5 is structured as follows: part II. of this chapter looks at the approach of the Convention to the basic prosecutorial principles of discretion and independence. Part III. presents the elements of reasoned professional judgment, as applied to anti-bribery investigations/ prosecutions. The prohibited political criteria of Article 5 are then discussed in part IV. before we touch on the organisation of the fight against foreign bribery in part V.

II. Deciding to investigate/prosecute foreign bribery: basic principles of the Convention

1. Investigation and prosecution: application of similar criteria

Article 5 clearly applies both to investigation and prosecution. These different stages of the criminal process are treated separately in the Phase 2 reports. The distinction is probably less clear in practice, as the prosecuting authority may be closely involved in the carrying out of investigations, or, at least, in their supervision. Nevertheless, the decision to prosecute or bring charges represents a decisive and discrete step in the criminal process, geared towards bringing the case to trial. That decision will be based upon the evidence gathered at the investigatory stage.

The decision to bring charges affects the status of the individual concerned, who will move from being a mere witness or suspect to an accused person, with all that entails for his or her legal rights.[11] In many state Parties, decisions to bring charges are regarded as of a 'judicial' character,

[10] Cf. COE 1987, endorsing the discretionary system on the basis that it would help both in better resource allocation and in terms of the 'clearer definition of priorities for the conduct of crime policy'.

[11] Among other instruments concerning the human rights of persons subjected to criminal proceedings, we can point to the European Convention on Human Rights (COE 1950). Art. 5 of the latter protects against unlawful detention of persons; Art. 6 is designed to ensure fair treatment after charge, and in particular at trial (including a guarantee of the presumption of innocence). The rights of persons subject to arrest under Arts. 5(1)(c) and 5(3) of the European Convention on Human Rights should be compared to those pertaining to persons charged and facing court proceedings within the meaning of its Art. 6 (cf. Janis, Kay and Bradley 2000, chs. 7–8).

and the prosecutor as part of a judicial body. A prosecution, including the attendant publicity, can clearly have serious negative consequences for a natural or legal person; reputation is likely to be tarnished, even if a conviction does not follow. A mere investigation may, on the other hand, remain secret.

In our commentary upon the preceding Articles of the Convention, we already observed that prosecutions for active bribery of foreign officials have been few and far between. This is apparent from the Phase 2 reports completed so far.[12] It is not always clear at what stage of the investigation the inertia which these figures suggest occurs, or to what extent the prosecution agencies, if different from the investigators, are to blame. These factors are likely to vary from country to country, as we will see later in this chapter. It could be that formal investigations are simply not begun, or that they are discontinued half-way through, or that the prosecutor intervenes at some later stage to stop them, or that he or she decides after completion of the investigation that a prosecution is not warranted.[13]

It is clearly very important, as the WGB emphasises in its recent evaluation reports, that persons, especially legal persons, suspected of having committed the foreign bribery offence are indeed put under investigation. The necessary organisational conditions should be put into place to enable this to happen.[14] The decision to investigate, as much as any subsequent decision to prosecute, should be taken for professional reasons. The recent Phase 2 report for Japan expresses serious concerns at the apparent failure to launch formal investigations or prosecutions. Despite press allegations about criminal activity by foreign companies, no cases had led to formal investigations, let alone court proceedings.[15] With regard to the UK, at least some cases are under investigation, but the Phase 2 report notes the surprise of the lead examiners that no company or individual had been indicted or tried for the foreign bribery offence since the UK ratified the Convention.[16]

[12] Cf. also the 2004 report by the US Department of Commerce to Congress, reporting on the implementation of the OECD Convention. This reports convictions under implementing legislation only in South Korea and Sweden, but refers to investigations underway in Canada, France, Italy, and Norway (US Department of Commerce 2004, Executive Summary, vi).

[13] The speculation reflected by this statement is partly due to the failure of a surprising number of Convention signatories to keep relevant statistics, recording investigations launched and the stage they have reached, abandonment, etc.

[14] See part V. of this ch. and note the extensive comments on the non-existent, inadequate, or 'fragmented' investigatory efforts of Japan and the UK, as documented in the recent Phase 2 reports for these states.

[15] JP-Ph2, 5. [16] UK-Ph2, 8.

Such inactivity in the face of strong allegations of bribes having been given to obtain foreign contracts obviously raises heavy suspicions that cases are being hushed up for political reasons, which is exactly what Article 5 is designed to avoid.

From the point of view of the Convention, it is not so much the stage at which such inertia occurs, but the reasons for it, which are of interest. Article 5 clearly covers the activity (and inactivity) of both investigating and prosecuting authorities. Neither investigators nor prosecutors should rely on the political criteria set out in Article 5. The underlying principles and obligations of Article 5 will now be discussed.

2. Principles applicable to investigation and prosecution

2.1. The principle of prosecutorial discretion: basic approach of the Convention

The WGB is concerned to ensure that the foreign bribery offence is taken seriously by prosecutors. That it is a serious offence should already be evident on the basis of the sanctioning provisions of the Convention.[17] Article 5 seeks to further establish the offence in the minds of law enforcement and prosecutors as a serious one, compatible with similar offences of an economic nature.[18] This at least is one interpretation of the first sentence of Article 5, namely that 'Investigations and prosecution of the bribery of a foreign public official shall be subject to the applicable rules and principles of each Party'.

This first sentence of Article 5 also expresses confidence and trust in national systems, reflecting again the orientation to national law which we find expressed elsewhere, for example, in Article 3.[19]

The first sentence of Official Commentary 27 refers, in particular, to respect for 'national regimes of prosecutorial discretion', meaning the regimes of mandatory and discretionary prosecution referred to in the introduction to this chapter. The WGB's reports make clear that the Convention does not require Parties to choose between the two. Discretionary systems of prosecution exist in approximately half of the state Parties.[20] There are

[17] See our ch. on Article 3 above. [18] See further in III.4. below.

[19] See our introduction and ch. on Article 3 of this commentary.

[20] Namely (to somewhat different degrees): Australia, Belgium, Canada, Denmark, France, Ireland, Japan, Korea, Luxembourg, the Netherlands, New Zealand, Norway, United Kingdom, and the United States.

widespread tendencies, at least in Europe, to introduce discretionary elements into mandatory systems.[21] In the light of the widespread and 'fundamental'[22] nature of prosecutorial discretion, especially in practice, the approach of the Convention to the limitation of such discretion could hardly have been other than a minimalist one.

The fact that enforcement of the foreign bribery offence would have to be carried out in accordance with different systems did not therefore lead to calls for a provision *compelling* investigation and prosecution of the Article 1 offence.[23] Article 5 cannot be regarded as a means of harmonising systems of criminal procedure. What it seeks is convergence and co-ordination in the fight against active bribery of foreign officials.[24]

The WGB does, however, express certain parameters where enforcement is concerned. For example, a state Party must apply its chosen approach to prosecution (mandatory or discretionary) uniformly to natural persons and legal persons. As some of the Phase 2 reports indicate, there is a real risk that alleged foreign bribery by legal persons will not be investigated with the same diligence as alleged crimes of natural persons.[25] The risk of this will be greater if a state Party deliberately adopts a more discretionary policy vis-à-vis companies.

Our commentary on Article 2 of the Convention revealed that significantly different approaches to corporate criminality and corporate sanctions prevail among the OECD Convention signatories; *within* national criminal justice systems, the WGB looks for a consistent approach. State Parties should not therefore apply a more discretionary approach to legal persons than they do to natural persons.[26]

[21] COE 1987. The risks of taking discretion too far are pointed out by Jung (1986).
[22] Official Commentary 27.
[23] One may contrast this approach with that of the drafters of the would-be European Union (EU) Anti-Fraud Statute, the so-called 'Corpus Juris', whose Art. 19 would bind the 'European Public Prosecutor' to the principle of legality (Delmas-Marty and Vervaele 2000, 198). One of the co-authors of this text, the Cambridge professor John Spencer, has recently repeated the concerns of the Corpus Juris scholars that, without such a supranational prosecuting agency, the prosecution of cases of transnational fraud against the Community budget will fall victim to more pressing national policy concerns (Spencer 2005, 28 et seq.). The apparent lack of priority given to cases of transnational bribery, compared to the domestic bribery offence or other economic crimes, is similarly a concern of the OECD's WGB. See also IV.1.2. below.
[24] Sacerdoti 1999, 225 et seq. [25] Cf., for example, the Finnish report: FI-Ph2, 15, 19.
[26] FI-Ph2, 15, 19; cf. also the concerns voiced in relation to Germany (DE-Ph2, 36 et seq., 45). Countries like Germany, lacking a concept of corporate criminal liability, are in the view of the WGB more prone to lax enforcement (see further our discussion in the chs. on Articles 2 and 3).

2.2. The principle of prosecutorial independence: basic approach of the Convention

The *Travaux Préparatoires* to the Convention indicate that the discussions surrounding a Convention provision on enforcement centred on 'the role of prosecutorial independence and discretion'.[27] When the Convention was being drafted, the concern was to lay the ground for effective investigation and prosecution of the foreign bribery offence by removing any hindrances which might stand in the way.

Article 5 targets three possible political hindrances to investigation and prosecution. These three issues, plus one more possible criterion, will be considered in detail in part IV. below. In this section we are concerned with the general principle that investigators and prosecutors should be shielded from political influence, so that they can get on with the job of fighting foreign bribery.

Paragraph 6 of the Agreed Common Elements annexed to the Revised Recommendation of 1997 adopts a general and very direct approach to the principle of independence:

> 'In view of the seriousness of the offence of bribery of foreign public officials, public prosecutors should exercise their discretion independently, based on professional motives.'[28]

The Convention *'acquis'* (if we use that term collectively to describe the Convention, Official Commentaries and the Revised Recommendation of 1997) thus endorses the principle of independent prosecution as a principle to be applied by all signatories to the Convention. It does not take a specific position on how that principle should be secured in an institutional sense; the relationship between the prosecution services of the state Parties and their executive and judicial organs remains a matter for the respective national constitutional systems.[29] What is required is that investigators and prosecutors alike take decisions only on the basis of professional criteria.

A broad interpretation of the duty of prosecutorial independence would be consistent with other international instruments which establish common

[27] OECD 1999, F-1031. [28] See para. 6, first sentence (Annex to OECD 1997a).

[29] To take the Italian example, prosecution of crime in Italy is subject to a very strict notion of independence. There, prosecutors are said to enjoy 'total autonomy from government and other prosecutors'; this is ordained by the constitution (IT-Ph2, 26 and Perrodet 2002a, 350 et seq.). For a pan-European view of the principle of independent prosecution, cf. COE 2000a. The Recommendation eschews any attempt at synthesis of the particular national expressions of the principle. The Explanatory Memorandum recognises that the relationship between prosecution and executive power of the state in Europe 'can range from subordination to independence' (COE 2000b). See further discussion in part IV. below.

principles for public prosecutors and to which the vast majority of OECD Convention signatory state Parties have adhered. The Council of Europe (COE) Recommendation of 2000 is particularly important.[30] Although a non-binding document, the principles contained in it provide important benchmarks for the prosecution of crime in general. Of particular relevance for the current discussion is principle 11, which states:

> 'States should take appropriate measures to ensure that public prosecutors are able to perform their professional duties without unjustified interference or unjustified exposure to civil, penal or other liability.'[31]

A few years earlier, the Committee of Ministers of the Council of Europe adopted twenty 'Guiding Principles' on fighting corruption, the third of which refers to an undertaking by Ministers that: 'those in charge of the prevention, investigation, prosecution, and adjudication of corruption offences [shall] enjoy the independence and autonomy appropriate to their functions [and will be] free from improper influence'.[32]

Similar clauses can be found in the UN Guidelines on the Role of Prosecutors of 1990[33] and in the Guidelines of the International Association of Prosecutors (IAP) issued in 1999.[34]

Echoing these international standards, there is no doubt that Article 5 of the Convention, interpreted in the light of Official Commentary 27, contains a *general obligation* to exercise professional judgment when deciding whether to prosecute a case. This obligation exists over and above the particular requirements contained in the second sentence of Article 5 (exclusion of political influence under any of the specifically named grounds).[35]

We will now consider the various elements elaborated by the WGB regarding the exercise of professional judgment, in the light of its interpretation of Article 5. Collectively, these elements form the basis for what the US Principles of Federal Prosecution call the 'reasoned exercise of prosecutorial

[30] COE 2000a.

[31] The COE 2000b explains that, with regard to 'interference', the document is referring to interference by any type of authority: executive, legislative, or economic and also local public authorities. None of these bodies should intervene in prosecutorial decisions except in so far as permitted by law. The law should in any case leave prosecutors with 'such independence or autonomy as is necessary for the exercise of their duties'. Cf. COE 2000b, 11.

[32] COE 1997. [33] UN 1990.

[34] Note the 'Standards of Professional Responsibility and Statement of the Essential Duties and Rights of Prosecutors' (IAP 1999), available at: http://www.iap.nl.com.

[35] This interpretation is supported by the *Travaux Préparatoires* which refer to the principle of prosecutorial independence as a consideration in its own right: '[i]n the light of the seriousness of the offence of bribery of foreign public officials, public prosecutors should exercise their discretion independently, based on professional motives'. (OECD 1999, F-1033). The OECD Convention took over this phrase almost *verbatim*.

discretion'.[36] We group these elements here under the heading 'Exercise of Professional Motives', in line with the terminology of Official Commentary 27. In the OECD context, these elements are equally applicable to state Parties with mandatory and discretionary systems of prosecution.

III. The exercise of professional motives under the Convention

1. Source of professional motives: guidelines for prosecutors

When discretion is exercised, it should be done in a coherent way, in line with a consistent policy. If discretion is at the whim of individual prosecutors, arbitrary decisions are likely to follow.[37] There should be transparency as regards any instructions issued by political authorities, e.g. a Ministry of Justice.[38] The WGB has also emphasised that such transparency must exist within the hierarchy of the prosecution service.[39]

Furthermore, when making their decisions, prosecutors should have regard to guidelines issued by international bodies, including the 'Standards of Professional Responsibility and Statement of the Essential Duties and Rights of Prosecutors' issued by the IAP.[40]

2. A professional duty to follow up allegations of foreign bribery?

With regard to the prosecution of serious criminality, the rather banal conclusion of the two recent UN Conventions against Transnational Crime and against Corruption is that 'any discretionary legal powers' relating to the prosecution of the respective offences should be 'exercised to maximise the effectiveness of law enforcement measures'.[41] Within the OECD, the

[36] Principle 9–27.110 Department of Justice 2003.

[37] Cf. Van den Wyngaert 1993, 42, whose discussion of Belgian criminal justice system revealed that 'prosecutorial discretion is often exercised on a highly individual or local basis'. The Phase 1 report on Belgium was not particularly informative on the question of enforcement, but did state that the prosecutor's 'recognised discretionary power' is exercised in the light of guidelines issued by the Minister of Justice and the Board of Attorney Generals (BE-Ph1, 15). In its recently published Phase 2 report on Belgium, the WGB acknowledged that the combating of economic offences of a transnational character was being given greater priority following creation of an office of federal prosecutor, in 1998; discretionary decisions not to pursue cases of financial crime remain, however, very common at the local level (BE-Ph2, 21–23). Cf. also Pesquié 2002.

[38] See IV.1.1. below. [39] See previous note. [40] IAP 1999.

[41] The wording of Art. 11 of the UN 2000 and of Art. 30 of the more recent UN 2003 is in fact identical, and each Convention adds that 'due regard' should be had to the need for deterrence of the respective offences.

WGB is entrusted with monitoring the effectiveness of enforcement. In its reports, particularly the Phase 2 reports, it uses similarly banal language when it reminds the contracting parties of their obligation to ensure that all 'effective' or 'adequate' measures and mechanisms of prevention, detection, investigation, and prosecution should be taken to counteract active bribery of foreign public officials.[42]

Article 5, interpreted in the light of Official Commentary 27, requires 'that complaints of bribery of foreign public officials should be seriously investigated by competent authorities'.[43] What this language suggests is that discretion should be exercised *in favour of investigation.* This may not necessarily lead to charges being levelled, but the WGB expects that investigators should not merely adopt a 'reactive approach and wait for leads rather than engage in deterrence or active detection'.[44]

The general obligation on prosecutors under the Convention to abide only by professional motives thus also comprises an obligation to follow up allegations of commission of the Article 1 offence, as part of the possible range of serious offences which they are called upon to enforce.[45] The recent Phase 2 report on Japan again emphasised the requirement for state Parties to act upon suspicions and order a formal criminal investigation into well-founded allegations of bribery of a foreign public official.[46] It would be 'unprofessional', in the sense of the Convention, to ignore such allegations.[47]

Prosecutorial discretion may not, in other words, be used to justify the non-investigation or non-prosecution of serious offences such as foreign bribery, as a matter of policy.

[42] These terms are those used in the recommendations contained in the Phase 2 evaluation reports. It is not clear whether the term 'adequate', applied to mechanisms of investigation and prosecution, means something less than 'effective', which is applied to prevention and detection.

[43] This is part of the text of Official Commentary 27. The quote is borrowed from para. 6 of the Agreed Common Elements annexed to the OECD 1997a, which refers to 'complaints of victims'. There is no reason to suppose that complaints from other sources should be treated any less seriously. The Recommendation itself is, of course, not legally binding.

[44] BG-Ph2, 10.

[45] Recent international standards contain a similar injunction to tackle allegations of foreign bribery. Para. 15 of the UN 1990's Guidelines on the Role of Prosecutors states that '[p]rosecutors shall give due attention to the prosecution of crimes committed by public officials, particularly corruption' (UN 1990).

[46] Such a decision could in some states be a matter for the prosecutor, but the initiation of an investigation would usually lie with the police.

[47] Yet this is precisely the practice of which Japan stands accused. The WGB's recently completed Phase 2 report states: 'Japan has not demonstrated sufficient efforts to enforce the offence of bribing a foreign public official' (JP-Ph2, 57).

The Convention thus follows the US Department of Justice's 'Principles of Federal Prosecution' which assert that 'serious violations of Federal law must be prosecuted'.[48]

An apparent 'obligation to prosecute' of this kind may seem to be at odds with the 'wide latitude'[49] enjoyed by US federal prosecutors under the discretionary system which prevails there, but in fact this bald statement has to be read subject to the various conditions and caveats which these principles set out as guidance for US government attorneys. For, while it would be unprofessional and contrary to those guidelines simply to shelve allegations of foreign bribery, it is not unprofessional to apply 'reasoned exercise of prosecutorial discretion'.[50]

We now examine in detail what kind of legitimate reasons the Convention allows investigators and prosecutors to consider when weighing up whether to investigate and prosecute the foreign bribery offence.

3. Professional motives: thresholds for investigation and prosecution

3.1. Launching investigations: threshold requirements

If there is a professional duty to follow up allegations of foreign bribery, what level of suspicion is needed in order to activate such a duty?

In the first place, the allegations should be 'well-founded',[51] although this expression is in fact not used in the Convention text or in the accompanying *acquis*.

As mentioned in the last section, paragraph 6 of the Agreed Common Elements recommends that states 'seriously' investigate complaints by victims of bribery. This presupposes a certain diligence in following up allegations, but does not provide any clear guidance as to when an investigation should be commenced; it does not indicate how serious the complaint has to be, before it must be followed up.

Implementation of the Convention is dependent on the application of national principles and guidelines, which vary as to the nature or level of

[48] Principles 9–27.000, 9–27.001 Department of Justice 2002. Cf. the approach of the European Court of Justice in the so-called '*Strawberries*' case, in which the Luxembourg-based court condemned France for its failure to take effective criminal measures to tackle the violent protests against imports into France of goods from other Member States of the European Community (Case 265/95 *Commission* v. *France*, [1997] European Court Reports I-6959).

[49] Principle 9–27.110 Department of Justice 2002. [50] See previous note.

[51] 'Well-founded suspicion' is the basis for commencing investigations in Hungary (HU-Ph1, 13).

the suspicion required to warrant the opening of a criminal investigation. Unlike the European Convention on Human Rights,[52] it is not the aim of the Convention to supplant these standards with a separate harmonised standard of its own. The WGB may, however, call for an interpretation of national law in a manner favourable to starting an investigation.

In its observations in the Phase 2 report on Luxembourg, the WGB called for prosecutors not to 'appreciate too narrowly' the level of indications required to continue an enquiry.[53] The first requirement of Article 5 is, however, that enforcement be carried out in accordance with applicable national law and practice. If the standard for commencing criminal investigations is 'reasonable suspicion'[54] that an offence has been committed, at least no higher standard should be applied to infringements of the Convention.

The WGB is clearly anxious to see as many investigations as possible launched into allegations of bribery of foreign public officials. Phase 2 reviews encourage action to be initiated on the basis of a rather low threshold of suspicion, for both natural and legal persons. Fundamental rights considerations must be borne in mind.[55]

Both Japan and the United Kingdom have been criticised in recent Phase 2 reports for the lack of effective enforcement. There was a lack of investigations in the Japanese case and an absence of prosecutions in the case of UK. In both countries, there had been reports of cases in the media or apparently linked cases in other jurisdictions, which in the view of the WGB would have warranted investigative action. This situation contrasts with recent investigations into contravention of the Convention in other countries, for example, in Italy[56] and in Korea,[57] and with the increasingly proactive approach of Swiss prosecutors to investigations of bribery.[58]

[52] Cf. the comments of Feldman 1993, 195 et seq. [53] LU-Ph 2, 23.

[54] In England and Wales this is the standard required for arrest of a suspect. As Feldman (1993) explains, with reference to case law, the standard is not a rigorous one: arresting officers 'need only have as much material as a reasonable person would need in the circumstances to hold the relevant suspicion' (194). This standard is clearly different from the standard of evidence which would be needed to lay charges against a person. On the other hand, the suspicion should be a real one: persons should not be arrested 'simply to make it easier to obtain information' (195 et seq.).

[55] The lack of reasonable suspicion would risk breaching the rights of individuals, particularly where they face arrest leading to detention by the investigating authorities. In the EC context, a set of rules and principles exists to protect legal persons against excessively intrusive anti-trust investigations (cf. Kerse and Khan 2005, esp. ch. 4).

[56] IT-Ph2, 25 et seq., referring to the proceedings against *Enelpower SpA*.

[57] For Korea cf. the reference in the WGB report to the *Aulson and Sky* cases and the *Seo* case (KR-Ph2, 7 et seq.).

[58] CH-Ph2, 23 et seq.

It will always be difficult for the WGB to judge whether the failure to investigate an alleged instance of the bribery of a foreign official has been due to a lack of genuine suspicion or of evidence, or owing to some other factor. But it must insist that at least the normal national standard for commencing investigations be applied.

In the case of Japan, what particularly astonished and disturbed the WGB was the complete lack of official filing of any cases of foreign bribery, even though several cases were being discussed in public.[59] In fact, no statistics could even be provided by Japan on the number of complaints made or whether these had been followed up. It was not even clear to the WGB whether filing had been considered in certain cases.

In the UK Phase 2 report, there is a very explicit critique by the WGB of the application of 'an extremely high level of proof'[60] regarding the evidence necessary to open an investigation. This observation was made against the background of the failure by UK investigating authorities to look properly into details presented to them regarding bribes allegedly paid as part of defence deals done by UK defence contractors in the Middle East. In the WGB's view, this failure was inexplicable because of the 'availability of substantial documentary evidence and witnesses who allegedly had first-hand knowledge of suspicious transactions'.[61]

Going beyond compliance with national law, a second step for the WGB would be to look more carefully at the 'functional equivalence' of the thresholds applied in the state Parties for commencing investigation of the foreign bribery offence. A more direct comparison of these thresholds would be needed before any judgement could be made whether to recommend to a country that it review its approach. The critical finding vis-à-vis the UK might now be regarded as a basic point of reference for future Phase 2 evaluations of this matter.

A comparative approach of this kind should, however, rest on a more explicitly stated standard. The 'reasonable suspicion' standard should be recommended.[62] This is not only the test used in many national systems,

[59] Such as the *Halliburton* case related to alleged bribery of Nigerian officials by, inter alia, the Japanese Gasoline Corporation, as part of a consortium involving a subsidiary of Halliburton: cf. Le Figaro, 6 February 2004. Investigations by the US Department of Justice and the Securities and Exchange Commission (SEC) into Halliburton's role in this consortium are said to be continuing: http://www.fcpaenforcement.com. This case is also referred to in the Introduction and in Low's chapter of this commentary.

[60] UK-Ph2, 48. [61] See previous note.

[62] This appears to be what the framers of the OECD Convention had in mind. The Convention's *Travaux Préparatoires* refer to the expectation that 'reasonable efforts' will be made to find evidence (OECD 1999, F-1032).

but has been adopted both by the European Convention on Human Rights,[63] and by EU instruments in the context of anti-trust investigations.[64]

3.2. Bringing cases to trial: the threshold for prosecution

In 2003, the US Department of Justice promulgated a set of 'Principles of Federal Prosecution of Business Organisations'.[65] In addition to 'the sufficiency of evidence; the likelihood of success at trial; the probable deterrent, rehabilitative, and other consequences of conviction; and the adequacy of non-criminal approaches' – being 'the factors normally considered in the sound exercise of prosecutorial judgment' – this document lists nine additional factors to be taken into account by prosecutors when deciding whether to investigate or prosecute a corporation or other legal entity, or whether to negotiate plea agreements.[66]

In comparison, neither Article 5 of the OECD Convention nor the accompanying *acquis* provides clarity on what reasons may legitimately be given by prosecutors for a professional decision not to prosecute. Some indications are, however, given by the WGB's evaluation reports.

The raison d'être of the prosecutor being prosecution, the most important consideration is to gather sufficient evidence to bring the case to trial. With regard to anti-bribery prosecutions, the sufficiency of evidence is therefore also a key factor, and the WGB is interested first of all in the standard set by the Parties.[67] Sufficiency of evidence is a hurdle to be overcome by all systems of prosecution, discretionary and mandatory alike. The *Travaux Préparatoires* drew attention to the dangers of prosecutors

[63] Cf. the case law of the European Court of Human Rights concerning Art. 5 of the COE 1950 (Janis, Kay, and Bradley 2000, ch. 7).

[64] Arts. 20 and 21 EU 2003d. These provisions allow the European Commission to inspect private or company property on the basis of reasonable suspicion of the existence of incriminating evidence on those premises.

[65] Department of Justice 2003.

[66] Department of Justice 2003, part II ('Charging a Corporation: Factors to be Considered'): first (and foremost) comes 'nature and seriousness of the offence'; second, 'the pervasiveness of wrongdoing within the corporation'; third, 'the corporation's history of similar conduct'; fourth, 'the corporation's timely and voluntary disclosure of wrongdoing and its willingness to cooperate in the investigation of its agents'; fifthly, 'the existence and adequacy of the corporation's compliance program'; sixth, 'the corporation's remedial actions'; seventh, 'collateral consequences'; eighth, 'the adequacy of the prosecution of individuals responsible for the corporation's malfeasance' and finally 'the adequacy of remedies such as civil or regulatory enforcement actions'.

[67] The Crown Prosecution Service of England and Wales calls this the 'evidential test' (CPS 2004). This is an 'objective test' to discover whether there is a 'realistic prospect of conviction', which in turn depends on whether the evidence can be used in court (admissibility test) and whether it is reliable (reliability test).

in countries with mandatory systems 'hiding behind' a sufficiency threshold in order to excuse failure to investigate thoroughly for other reasons.[68]

During the US Phase 2 evaluation, the Department of Justice interviewees indicated that 'the only reason for the US to decline a prosecution is lack of sufficient or available evidence'.[69] The Phase 1 and Phase 2 reviews of other state Parties also refer to the state of evidence as the fundamental issue in the decision whether to proceed.[70] The evidential test may, however, be coupled with a 'public interest' test in those state Parties with discretionary systems.[71] This can make it difficult to distinguish evidential issues from other discretionary questions. The WGB does, however, go behind any argument that evidence was insufficient to go ahead with a prosecution.

As mentioned in the previous section, the UK report identified shortcomings in the investigation of certain bribery allegations, before the stage of prosecution was reached. There was a suggestion that the standard was too high. The WGB does not, by contrast, challenge the sufficiency test as applied to prosecution, i.e. the 'realistic prospect of conviction' standard.

The UK standard appears very similar to the US one, i.e. 'probable cause'.[72] Other state Parties apply broadly similar standards. There is no doubt that the standard of evidence required to justify bringing a case to trial should be set higher than that required for police investigations. We should, however, note that, according to the legal system concerned, the powers of the judge will vary. In Civil Law systems, the role of the intermediate judge or judge of preliminary enquiry may be important and will influence how a case proceeds.[73]

The Convention does not put these specialities of national criminal procedure into question, so long as they do not render enforcement impossible, or excessively difficult. The Convention respects national methods, trusting

[68] OECD 1999, F-1032. [69] US-Ph2, 25.

[70] For example, Denmark (DK-Ph1, 16): 'prosecutors virtually always take action when so warranted by the evidence'. The Code for Crown Prosecutors in England and Wales states: 'Crown Prosecutors must be satisfied that there is enough evidence to provide 'a realistic prospect of conviction' against each defendant on each charge' (para. 5.1. CPS 2004).

[71] Cf., for example, Australia (AU-Ph1, 13), referring to the guidelines document 'Prosecution Policy of the Commonwealth'. The Code for Crown Prosecutors in England and Wales lists the two tests quite distinctly, but, on the other hand, indicates that they are part of a continuum: 'two stages in the decision to prosecute' (para. 4.1. CPS 2004).

[72] Principle 9–27.220 Department of Justice 2003 defines this requirement to mean that 'the admissible evidence will probably be sufficient to obtain and sustain a conviction'.

[73] Cf. the discussion by Salas 2002 of 'Judges and the Power of Investigation' (506 et seq.), in which he refers, for example, to the power of the Italian judge at a preliminary hearing to declare a prosecution unfounded under Art. 422 Code of Criminal Procedure.

that they will be more effective tools than any imposed supranational system of prosecution.[74]

The core concern for the WGB is to see prosecutions occurring. Given the similarity of evidential standards and legal systems in the UK and in the US, and given US experience, a number of prosecutions could now have been expected in the UK (all other things being equal). That this has not been the case is what troubles the OECD.

This lack of prosecutions is not, of course, peculiar to the UK, nor one confined to legal systems which apply the discretionary principle. The UK report should, however, serve as a warning to all state Parties to ensure that, both as regards investigation and prosecution, the threshold of evidence required does not become an obstacle to effective implementation.

4. Prosecuting bribery of foreign public officials as a 'serious' offence

In terms of general criminal justice policy, one of the main applications of the discretionary principle is to allow offences of a minor nature to escape prosecution, and to be remedied where appropriate by alternative, non-criminal, means.[75] Moreover, prosecutorial codes and other guidelines take great pains to stress that the seriousness of the offence should be considered as one of the most important factors in deciding whether to pursue the prosecution of a case.[76]

Is there a risk that bribery cases would not be treated as serious enough to warrant prosecution? The risk would appear to be quite limited, if we take the comments of the countries examined in the monitoring reports at face value. There are suggestions in a few reports that minor instances of bribery would

[74] We may again contrast this approach with that favoured by the Corpus Juris group, who would have the EU introduce a 'judge of freedoms', with powers in respect of bringing cases of EU fraud to trial. Art. 25[bis] of these proposals and the implementing provisions refer to the role of the judge in deciding 'whether there is sufficient evidence giving serious grounds to believe that the accused person has committed each of the offences he is alleged to have committed' (Delmas-Marty and Vervaele 2000, 204). Cf. also note 23 above.

[75] Cf. Kühne 2003, 168.

[76] Cf. FR-Ph2, 20 referring to the specification of the French authorities that 'the principle of prosecutorial discretion necessarily entails an evaluation of the disturbance to public order caused by the facts at issue, taking into account their seriousness, as measured in particular by the amount of the bribe'. A similar line is taken by Luxembourg, which indicates that the amount of the bribe is the most important factor in determining seriousness (LU-Ph1, 17). Guidelines to prosecutors in Common Law states, such as Australia, Canada, Ireland, New Zealand, the United Kingdom, and the United States, suggest that 'public interest' considerations which might tend towards not pursuing a prosecution should carry less weight in serious cases (cf. e.g. AU-Ph1, 13; CA-Ph1, 15; in Ireland, all except very minor foreign bribery cases would be prosecuted under indictment: IE-Ph1, 24). As for 'honest Iceland' (only one case of bribery in the last century?), cf. IS-Ph1, 11.

not receive criminal punishment,[77] but in general the Parties regard the foreign bribery offence as meriting the full force of the criminal law.

The position taken by the WGB is that state Parties should classify bribery as a serious offence, attracting strong rather than weak enforcement.[78] Powers which may exist in national law to allow for waiver, suspension or abandonment of prosecution for offences of a minor character, or for the application of non-criminal enforcement, should not apply to foreign bribery cases.[79]

This approach to Article 5 mirrors that followed in relation to Article 3. The WGB rarely, if ever, questions the merits of a criminal law approach to combating bribery. It pursues the logic of criminalisation.[80] A state Party's choice to sanction bribery by non-criminal means is reluctantly accepted in the case of legal persons, where there is no corporate criminal liability.[81] Where enforcement is concerned, the WGB expects legal persons to be subject to criminal prosecution, wherever possible, but it accepts that deterrence of wrongful conduct by legal persons may also be achieved by the adoption of preventive measures by the companies concerned.[82]

[77] In Germany 'informal fines' can be imposed in order to avoid formal legal proceedings: the WGB expressed certain concerns about these fines (DE-Ph2, 38). The 'transaction' procedures under Dutch law are subjected to similar critical scrutiny by the WGB (NL-Ph1, 21 et seq.). Compare also the Austrian reassurance that proceedings for termination of prosecution could not be applied to foreign bribery cases, as they imply 'grave' guilt to which the limiting provisions do not apply (AT-Ph1, 15). The WGB is obviously anxious that the foreign bribery offence is sanctioned by the full weight of national criminal law.

[78] The most plaudits accorded by the WGB in terms of recent Phase 2 reports have gone to Switzerland, whose legislative and organisational reforms of recent years have successfully targeted 'the urgent need to prosecute economic crime more effectively' (CH-Ph2, 24). But one still has to wait for the cases of prosecution of foreign bribery to come, even if there has been a significant increase in investigations. The Swiss starting point was probably a very low one, compared to the United States, for example. The WGB's approach to enforcement is very much linked to its desire to see serious sanctions imposed, as is evident, for example, from a reading of the Phase 2 report for Germany (DE-Ph 2, 33 et seq. and recommendation at para. 162).

[79] Note the concerns voiced by the WGB regarding Chilean legislation, whose low minimum penalties for foreign bribery suggest that conditional suspension of prosecutions or termination may be possible (CL-Ph1, 17, 30). On the other hand, in Portugal suspension provisions cannot apply to foreign bribery cases (PT-Ph1, 20). Enforcement against legal persons may, however, be subject to separate non-criminal measures.

[80] See our ch. on Article 3 above. [81] See our chs. on Articles 2 and 3 above.

[82] Finnish legislation makes the prosecution of legal, as opposed to natural, persons discretionary and allows for the waiver of prosecution in relation to corporate offences of a 'minor character' (FI-Ph1, 6). In the Phase 2 report the WGB recommends that Finland offers clearer guidance to prosecutors regarding the application of the penal provisions on bribery to legal persons, fearing that the discretion given at present is too broad (FI-Ph2, 19, 29). Concerns have also been expressed about prosecutorial discretion in Germany, as related to the administrative liability of legal persons (DE-Ph2, 32 et seq.). The WGB recommended that the German authorities issue guidelines to clarify that such liability is possible. The WGB has concerns that legal persons are not effectively sanctioned under German law.

The US Principles of Federal Prosecution of Business Organisations (hereafter 'the Principles') start from the proposition that corporations should not receive more lenient treatment just because of their 'artificial nature'.[83] The Principles refer to the importance of 'corporate self-policing'[84] and set out the conditions to be considered by prosecutors when assessing whether a corporation has an effective compliance programme. We saw in our commentary on Article 3 that having such a programme can be important in terms of obtaining a reduced sentence; the Principles, however, make clear that 'the existence of a compliance program is not sufficient, in and of itself, to justify not charging a corporation for criminal conduct undertaken by its officers, directors, employees, or agents'.[85]

The US approach to prevention of company wrongdoing finds parallels in Europe, for example in Germany and in Finland. They would both allow prosecution to be waived in minor cases, where the company can show that it has since strengthened its internal control measures to a level sufficient to prevent further offending.[86]

5. Professional motives: charging and plea-bargaining

Plea-bargaining can take different forms. It may mean agreeing to plead guilty in exchange for a reduced sentence for the offence in question, or it may be that certain charges will be dropped in favour of less serious ones, as part of the bargain. Plea-bargaining in one form or another is a feature of many Common Law systems of criminal justice, but is not confined to them, as Civil Law countries are also coming under pressure to introduce it for administrative reasons.[87]

WGB scrutiny of plea-bargaining practice sometimes focuses on the sanctioning aspect, owing to the concern that the practice may lead to reductions in the sentence for foreign bribery, thereby reducing the intended deterrent effect of sentence. For example, the Italian legal system's concept of plea

[83] Principle I.A. Department of Justice 2003. [84] Principle VII. Department of Justice 2003.

[85] Principle VII. Department of Justice 2003. Cf. Low 2005, 30 et seq. and in this commentary for an up-to-date discussion of compliance programmes in the specific context of FCPA prosecutions.

[86] DE-Ph2, 33; FI-Ph1, 6. The WGB is, however, sceptical about such an approach.

[87] Walther 2004 writes of the transformation of the German civilian system from a classical criminal process to a more consensual one, oriented to negotiated disposals. Other systems outside Europe are also coming under the influence of plea-bargaining practices (CL-Ph1, 17). Apart from the German and Chilean examples, cf. the discussion in France, which has now introduced guilty pleas, though not without some legal difficulties (note *Cour de Cassation* decision of 18 April 2005, reported in *Le Monde*, 19 April 2005, requiring particular procedures to be observed, when the judge accepts the plea).

bargaining, the *patteggiamento*, was put under the microscope by the WGB in the recent Phase 2 report from the point of view of the reduced penalties which may result from the procedure.[88]

One can also see plea-bargaining as a professional method of dealing with a large caseload, i.e. the practice can be viewed in more systemic terms related to the operation of the criminal justice system as a whole. In so far as it forms part of the established fabric of the national legal system in question, the WGB will not question the practice as such; its concern is to ensure that it does not operate to the obvious detriment of effective enforcement.[89]

The US Phase 2 report gives surprisingly little attention to plea agreements, mentioning only the recent practice of some prosecutors to require defendant companies to submit to a compliance programme as a condition of such an agreement.[90] This practice is encouraged by the Principles.[91] The WGB would doubtless approve of the additional statement that 'prosecutors generally should not agree to accept a guilty plea in exchange for non-prosecution or dismissal of charges against individual officers and employees'.[92]

The WGB's recent discussion of UK plea-bargaining practice indicates sympathy for a more systemic interpretation. Evidence was presented to the lead examiners by the Serious Fraud Office that plea-bargaining and other forms of co-operation by defendants would greatly assist disposal of cases of serious organised crime.[93]

Methods of disposal of cases in Germany and the Netherlands without criminal accusation should also be noted under this rubric. In those systems, formal criminal charges can be dropped in return for compliance with orders.[94] The WGB remains sceptical about diversion of foreign bribery offenders from formal criminal measures.[95]

There is a certain lack of clarity in WGB reports as to the desirability of plea-bargaining. It is regarded, on the one hand, as risky, because

[88] IT-Ph2, 48, 50, 53. The UK Phase 2 report discusses plea bargaining under the heading 'Witnesses and Special Investigative Powers' (UK-Ph2, 43).

[89] IT-Ph2, 53: regarding the need for the WGB to follow up the use of the *patteggiamento* procedure.

[90] US-Ph2, 17. [91] Principle XII. Department of Justice 2003.

[92] See previous note. [93] UK-Ph2, 43.

[94] Walther 2004, 369 et seq. provides a critical account of the Art. 153a proceedings under the German Code of Criminal Procedure. She points out the risks of these procedures for defendants and victims alike.

[95] Cf. DE-Ph2, 38 et seq. for Germany; the Dutch situation is discussed in the Phase 1 report (NL-Ph1, 21 et seq.). In both countries these procedures would seem to apply, in principle, to serious as well as minor cases. The question whether the German procedures would actually be used in cases of foreign bribery was answered differently by the Ministry of Justice and the prosecutors (cf. DE-Ph2, 38).

enforcement and punishment might be weakened in the individual case; on the other hand, it can help more cases to be resolved by encouraging defendants to co-operate with the system. What the WGB seems not to notice (or to ignore) is the widespread academic critique of plea bargaining, from the point of view of fair trial rights.[96]

6. Evidence-gathering: implications of Article 5

The Convention also requires that the usual investigative techniques applied under national law be applied to the gathering of evidence required to support an investigation.

The WGB (rather anxiously) recommends the most sophisticated and modern methods to detect and investigate foreign bribery. It has commented adversely on perceived shortcomings in certain legal systems, for example in Finland, with regard to the lack of legislation enabling interception of communications or undercover operations, or in Luxembourg, regarding constraints on search and seizure powers.[97]

It is doubtless correct to assume that certain special investigative techniques may be required to assist in the investigation of foreign bribery, for example in order to infiltrate a criminal gang. Interception of telecommunications may be required (a complicated matter, particularly in a cross-border setting). Witness protection schemes are clearly also helpful in facilitating the appearance in court of threatened witnesses.[98]

Convention cases will, by definition, have a cross-border element. Mutual legal assistance will therefore be required, or extradition proceedings. These procedures can still be laborious and subject to political interference.[99] Many state Parties have, however, updated their laws in recent years, partly as a result of international initiatives.[100]

The involvement of high-ranking public officials, including politicians, is also likely to cause problems for investigators. In addition to state secrets arguments,[101] police and prosecutors might be confronted with immunity

[96] Walther 2004; and note the further critique by Baker 2004 in the same collection. These issues are also taken up by Tulkens 2002, 641 et seq. under the broader heading of 'negotiated justice'.

[97] FI-Ph2, 14; LU-Ph2, 29.

[98] Cf., for example, the measures introduced by the UK (UK-Ph2, 43). Such measures are also under consideration elsewhere (LU-Ph2, 28 et seq.). See generally Crowe 2005.

[99] The domestic law of some state Parties allows mutual legal assistance to be refused on the basis of essential interests of the state.

[100] Notably, instruments have been introduced at EU level to harmonise procedures. EU measures have played an important role, for example, in the reform of UK law (UK-Ph2, 45 et seq.). The same can be said of Ireland: cf. Hamilton 2005. Cf. also ch. on Arts. 9–11.

[101] See IV.2.4. below.

claims, making access to items of evidence difficult if not impossible.[102] These legal obstacles may be difficult to overcome.

In its discussion of cross-border evidence-gathering and judicial co-operation, little or no emphasis is given by the WGB to the requirements of due process and the protection of fundamental rights.[103] There is next to no discussion of judicial control of investigations, except as a possible 'obstacle' to effective investigations.[104] This is a serious weakness of the reports, reflecting a bias towards the interests of the prosecution. On the other hand, the reports do show an awareness of the need to have laws in place protecting whistleblowers from adverse consequences, if they report suspected bribery offences.[105]

IV. Excluding politics from foreign bribery investigations: Article 5 requirements

1. General duties of state Parties

1.1. Obligation of state Parties not to block prosecutions for political reasons

Is political pressure of all kinds to desist from investigation or prosecution into allegations of the foreign bribery offence prohibited by the OECD Convention?

The question arises particularly in relation to the decision to prosecute but can also be applied to the opening of investigations.

With regard to the structure of the public prosecution service in national legal systems, it is necessary to distinguish between two basic sets of relationships: first, the external relationship with the political authorities; second, the

[102] In the case of Bulgaria, the WGB argues that judicial immunity needs to be reviewed, owing to suspected corruption among judges (BG-Ph2, 35 et seq.). See more generally ch. by Low in this commentary.

[103] Cf. the growing body of literature relating to the need to protect the fundamental rights of natural and legal persons in the context of anti-money laundering or anti-trust investigations, for example Mitsilegas 2003 and Kerse and Khan 2005. Parallels are drawn by the WGB between such investigations and the investigation and prosecution of transnational corruption but only from the prosecution standpoint, not from a defence rights perspective. See also our ch. on Articles 9–11.

[104] This lack of balance is apparent, for example, in the negative perception by the WGB of appeal procedures initiated by defendants (cf. the comments in the Swiss report relating to appeals in the context of mutual assistance proceedings: CH-Ph2, 29). The role of defence lawyers is also rather bluntly criticised in the Luxembourg Phase 2 report (LU-Ph2, 25).

[105] Note the recommendation to Italy, for example, that it should consider strengthening the protection of employees in this regard (IT-Ph2, 17, 51). There is further discussion of whistleblower protection in our ch. on Article 8.

internal relationship within the Public Prosecutor's office.[106] The WGB's evaluations have given attention to both issues.

First, regarding the relationship with political authorities, the WGB has expressed concern about the dangers of too subordinate or dependent a relationship. This concern surfaced most clearly in respect of France, which the WGB described as being characterised by 'statutory subordination of the Public Prosecutor's office to the executive by virtue of the very hierarchical internal organisation presided over by the Ministry of Justice'.[107] Subordination within the French system also results from the second relationship, the internal one, which in France, and in other systems based on the Napoleonic Code, results in a strongly hierarchical functioning of the Public Prosecutor's office or *parquet*.[108]

Such a structure is clearly not, as such, contrary to the Convention, but it creates risks of political interference contrary to Article 5.

The concern of political influence expressed in relation to France was exacerbated by two additional factors. First, the centralisation of anti-corruption prosecutors in Paris suggested an extra risk of political influence, owing to the proximity to the Ministry of Justice. Second, concern was expressed regarding the limitation of the victim complaint procedure, meaning that the *partie civile* option of private petition does not apply to Convention-based anti-bribery proceedings (except in the case of bribery of EU officials).[109]

There is a wider relevance to the WGB's findings in the evaluation of France. First and foremost, the political authorities of a contracting state should not issue instructions to the prosecution to desist from a prosecution, or to terminate one already begun, for non-professional reasons.[110] This obligation is couched in general terms, i.e. it exists as an obligation independent of the specific duties of non-intervention contained in the second sentence of Article 5. This general obligation would be in keeping with the stance taken by international instruments, such as the Council of Europe's Recommendation of 2000.[111] Secondly, the relations between ministry and prosecution must be transparent. There should be no grounds for suspicion of political influence behind the scenes. This means, ideally,

[106] Cf. the use of similar terminology by Manacorda 2004, 147 et seq. [107] FR-Ph2, 30.
[108] Cf. Van den Wyngaert 1993, 7 et seq. for Belgium.
[109] FR-Ph2, 29 et seq.; see V.3. below for a more detailed discussion of this point.
[110] 'The lead examiners noted the assurances given by the Ministry of Justice that, in accordance with the law, no instruction not to prosecute is given in specific cases' (FR-Ph2, 31). Note also the discussion in the Phase 1 reports in respect of Denmark and the Netherlands, where there is scope for influence by the Minister of Justice on prosecutions, though it is maintained that in practice this is not exercised (DK-Ph1,17; NL-Ph1, 22).
[111] Rec. 13f. COE 2000a urges states to prohibit the giving of instructions not to prosecute in a particular case.

that policy guidelines should be provided, and that these should be public. This standard is particularly clearly stated in the evaluation reports relating to those countries with discretionary systems of prosecution.[112] Again, this obligation corresponds to international standards.[113]

Political consent requirements are particularly problematic. In New Zealand, as in the UK, the question of potential political interference in prosecutions is raised by the requirement of consent by the Attorney General for prosecution. The WGB report for New Zealand criticises the lack of legislative guidelines relating to the exercise of consent.[114] With regard to Ireland, a decision on whether to prosecute or not is taken in accordance with the 'General Guidelines for Prosecutions' issued by the Director of Public Prosecutions; the Phase 1 report states that no allowance is made for political interference in the decision-making process by prosecutors, but this will have to be followed up in the Phase 2 report.[115] The WGB's Phase 2 report for the UK expresses concerns about the Attorney General consent requirement for prosecutions of the foreign bribery offence in England and Wales; this will be discussed in more detail below in the context of the prohibition of interference on grounds of national economic interest.[116]

Thus, in the external sense of political control by the Ministry of Justice or similar executive body, the bottom line of the Convention is that countries should not allow political interference in the decision to prosecute. Policy guidelines issued by a Ministry or contained in codes approved for prosecutors should exclude such a possibility.

Prosecutorial priorities may be set as a result of guidelines; this is not contrary to the Convention. Indeed, such policy guidance can be helpful in making the prosecution of the foreign bribery offence a priority. This is what we might call 'affirmative guidance'. Policy guidelines should not apply negatively ('negative guidance'). They should not encourage the executive to block a prosecution for the foreign bribery offence for political reasons. The only exception may be on fundamental grounds of national security.[117]

[112] Cf., for example, the Phase 2 report for Canada which is particularly explicit in its call for clarity in the guidelines issued to federal prosecutors on whether a prosecution is in the public interest: political interests should not be brought to bear on the decision whether to prosecute (CA-Ph2, 33 et seq., 39). The absence of guidelines for the exercise of prosecutorial discretion has been criticised, inter alia, in the evaluation report on Luxembourg (LU-Ph1, 26). During the Phase 1 investigation into the Netherlands, the Dutch authorities indicated that they would issue guidelines on the settlement of bribery cases, as for other felonies, being of the opinion that such guidelines 'reduce the risk of a lack of uniformity in the application of prosecutorial discretion in different parts of the country' (NL-Ph1, 22).

[113] Apart from the COE 2000a, there are the UN standards and other developing international professional standards referred to above: see UN 1990 and IAP 1999.

[114] NZ-Ph1, 20 et seq., 37. [115] IE-Ph1, 23, 25. [116] See IV.2.1. below.

[117] See IV.2.4. below.

With regard to the internal controls operating within the prosecution system, hierarchical structures as such are not necessarily problematic, provided the possible interference by superior prosecutors in the work of their subordinates is based on professional reasons and not politically biased. Should a prosecutor drop a bribery case, a review of this decision by a higher authority should indeed be envisaged. The recent development in French law to require reasons to be given by prosecutors for dropping cases is welcomed by the WGB, not least because this can assist victims or other affected persons.[118]

Some state Parties, notably Italy, entirely reject the application of institutional hierarchy to the prosecution service, with the result that individual prosecutors enjoy more or less full autonomy.[119] Their independence has been weakened somewhat in recent years owing to the need to centralise the prosecution of mafia-type crime.[120] Similar centralisation may be desirable for bribery offences, but it has not come about.

1.2. Setting criminal policy priorities: a duty to 'assimilate' foreign bribery with other serious crime?

Setting policy priorities for combating serious organised crime is intimately connected with the allocation of resources, a matter we will consider further in part V. of this chapter. Before the allocation of resources, however, comes substantive criminal policy.

The Convention requires states to recognise the foreign bribery offence as a serious offence, which should be taken seriously by investigators and prosecutors.[121] Such recognition should, in the view of the WGB, be promoted by the appropriate use of guidelines, issued either by the political authorities or internally, in accordance with the institutional structure of the system concerned. The US Phase 2 report, for example, refers to the priorities of prosecution, calling for greater clarity on the criteria currently employed by the US Department of Justice.[122] Norway refers to corruption being given 'high priority' by prosecutors.[123]

The OECD Convention's *Travaux Préparatoires* state that 'prosecutors must fairly consider the full range of crimes, and they should not be asked

[118] FR-Ph2, 31. [119] IT-Ph2, 26 and see note 29 above.
[120] Cf. Perrodet 2002b, 438 et seq.; she contrasts this approach with the 'single and indivisible' nature of public prosecution (as an institution) in France and Belgium (436 et seq.).
[121] See III.4. above.
[122] The WGB recommended that the US government make a public statement identifying the priorities for prosecution of particular cases under the FCPA (US-Ph2, 39).
[123] NO-Ph1, 9.

to do more regarding corruption than, for example, crimes against persons or against children'.[124] Does this imply that, under the Convention, equal priority must be given to the investigation and prosecution of bribery offences compared to other offences of a comparable nature?[125] The answer is clear neither from the text of the Convention nor from WGB evaluations.

It would be consistent with its approach to sanctions under Article 3 of the Convention for the WGB to insist that investigation and prosecution of crimes against the Convention be carried out with the same rigour as in respect of crimes such as theft, embezzlement, and fraud.[126] But such a comparative test is not in fact undertaken in respect of Article 5 compliance. We are therefore left with the obligation of state Parties to devote resources to the combating of foreign bribery, sufficient to enable serious allegations to be followed up.[127] This entails a certain prioritisation in policy terms, but is less than the assimilation requirement which applies under Article 3.

2. The prohibited grounds of state interference in foreign bribery cases

2.1. National economic interest

2.1.1. General

The fundamental objective of the Convention is to prevent trade advantages being unfairly gained by bribery. Where such bribery does occur, the offence should be investigated and a prosecution brought, if the evidence is sufficient. Article 5 is thus very much part of the raison d'être of the Convention.

The implementation of the Convention requires states to commit to use only legitimate means to advance national economic interest or other public interests. Article 5 is a logical expression of the desire stated in the very first clause of the preamble which recognises that bribery 'distorts international competitive conditions'.

The preamble to the OECD Convention also refers to the reality that 'bribery is a widespread phenomenon in international business transactions'. It was then, in 1997, and the evidence available today suggests that, notwithstanding

[124] OECD 1999, F-1033.

[125] Such an obligation would hardly correspond to current practice, as the UK's and other recent Phase 2 reports have shown.

[126] See III.2.1.2. in the ch. on Article 3.

[127] Cf. Official Commentary 27 and para. 6 of the Agreed Common Elements of OECD 1997a. The resources issue is further discussed in V.2. below.

the adoption and ratification of the Convention and of other international and national standards against foreign bribery,[128] the situation is little different today. A main reason for this is that the new laws are not yet being effectively enforced.[129]

Virtually in unison, state Parties subject to Phase 1 monitoring by the WGB sing their reassurance to the OECD that investigations and prosecutions have never been, and never will be, influenced by considerations of national economic interest. This is difficult to reconcile with the existence of discretionary systems which precisely call upon the prosecution to take account of the 'public interest' in their decisions about investigation and prosecution.

There would be no contradiction between a public interest requirement for prosecution and Article 5, if that requirement were always interpreted in a positive sense in favour of investigation and prosecution. This is the approach which the WGB recommends. State Parties should identify it as 'in the public interest' to tackle bribes paid in breach of the Convention, just as they should regard it as in the public interest to pursue money launderers.[130]

2.1.2. Defining 'national economic interest'

When contemplating the adoption of policy guidelines or instructions relating to prosecution of the bribery offence, state Parties face the difficulty that 'national economic interest' is not defined by the Convention.

The *Travaux Préparatoires* do not provide an answer, but the reports of the WGB provide indications, perhaps the most important of which is that there are no 'permissible degrees' of national economic interest which would justify influencing a prosecutorial decision. There are no national economic considerations which could justify a decision not to go ahead with an investigation or prosecution.[131]

The term 'interest' is sufficiently vague to capture all manner of economic concerns, and reflects the very broad approach of the Convention's Article 5 to the exclusion of political considerations from the exercise of discretionary powers.

The term 'national' refers to the domestic interests of the state Party concerned, where the state Party itself is involved in the transaction, for

[128] Low 2004.
[129] This is the general picture presented by the WGB's Phase 2 reports; cf. Department of Commerce 2004, ch. 3.
[130] Bell 2001. [131] Note Phase 2 report on Canada: CA-Ph2, 33 et seq., 39.

example, as a seller or exporter. It clearly also encompasses the economic activities of private undertakings and corporations incorporated under that state Party's laws and operating from its territory. Multinational corporations are also covered by this definition, in so far as their closest association is with a particular state Party. They are a major target of the OECD Convention, as their activities are likely to be global and export-oriented.[132]

The term 'economic' is not qualified in any way by the Convention, so that neither a fundamental interest, nor a far less pressing interest of the state Party concerned, may be taken into account. The reality is that state Parties may certainly be tempted to protect leading export companies by condoning bribes paid to secure contracts which may have significant repercussions at home, particularly where employment is concerned. In today's global economy, the fight to win prestigious international contracts, be it in sectors of defence, construction, utilities, etc., is intense. The OECD's criminalisation of bribes paid to secure such contracts may still not act as a sufficient deterrent to companies. Possible sanctions are still low.[133] The chances of investigation and prosecution remain rather remote.

Nor does the term 'economic' distinguish between different sectors of the economy of state Parties. Particular sectors of the economy, i.e. particular industries,[134] may be more or less prone to indulge in the type of behaviour prohibited by the Convention, but all sectors are equally covered. The WGB does, however, recognise the susceptibility of particular sectors and will analyse the risks of involvement of those sectors in foreign bribery.[135]

Contracting Parties must police high-risk sectors, in particular, with vigilance and will in turn face detailed scrutiny of any suggestion that such policing is open to political interference.[136] This is particularly the case where a specific role is accorded to a member of the government.

In foreign bribery prosecutions conducted in England and Wales, the Attorney General's consent is required for prosecution.[137] Although the

[132] OECD 2000b. [133] See III.3.3.2. in our ch. on Article 3 above.

[134] Cf. the sectors represented by member companies of the World Economic Forum (WEF) initiative PACI 2005. Major engineering, construction and petroleum industries have subscribed to these principles of corporate self-policing, which endorse company compliance strategies against bribery.

[135] Note its statement in the recent UK Phase 2 report that 'the international defence industry is widely perceived as being at high risk for foreign bribery' (UK-Ph2, 37).

[136] The UK's policing of contracts, entered into by domestic defence contractors, is regarded by the OECD's WGB as lacking in transparency. While the independence of the Ministry of Defence Police (MDP) from the Ministry of Defence was understood and accepted by the WGB after some discussion, the extent of the MDP's jurisdiction over defence contracts was not clear (UK-Ph2, 36 et seq.).

[137] Though not for the Common Law offence, only for the statutory foreign bribery offence – an anomaly which occasioned much head-scratching in the WGB (UK-Ph 2, 53 et seq.).

UK government protested that the Attorney General's advice is always independent and not coloured by political considerations, the WGB report states:

> 'The examiners are...concerned that the consent process involves the possible consideration of UK interests that the Convention expressly prohibits in the context of decisions about foreign bribery cases.'[138]

The Phase 2 report on the United Kingdom refers to the inadequate handling of a case concerning defence contracts concluded by a UK defence contractor in the Middle East. The WGB was not satisfied that the case had been investigated with sufficient diligence by the UK authorities. No investigation was launched despite the existence of considerable evidence. This raised the concern that economic interests had played a role in the decision not to pursue the case (the UK Ministry of Defence was involved in at least one of the contracts). The Phase 2 report concludes that the UK authorities may therefore have breached Article 5 of the Convention.[139]

The only convincing way to counter the WGB's suspicions that political influence is being brought to bear on investigation and prosecutions is to show that companies with an important role in these sectors are properly investigated, where well-founded suspicions surface.[140] The lack of investigations is bound only to heighten the WGB's suspicions.

2.2. Relations with other states

Article 5 also refers to the 'potential effect upon relations with other states' as a factor which may not be considered in relation to investigation or prosecution.

Proof of the existence of corruption in dealings with another state's administration will cause acute embarrassment both to the state of the public official concerned and to the home state of the bribery; more importantly, it is likely to damage economic and political relations between the two countries.

[138] UK-Ph 2, 54. The political independence of the Attorney General was again put into question when the current Attorney General, Lord Goldsmith, gave his opinion to the UK government concerning the legality of declaring war on Iraq without a second UN resolution. It was widely reported that Lord Goldsmith was pressured by the government into changing his initial opinion that a second resolution would be needed, though he strenuously denied this was the case (cf. *The Independent*, 25 April 2005, 1 et seq.; *The Guardian*, 26 April 2005, 17, referring to the Attorney General's 'combined political and legal roles').

[139] UK-Ph2, 48 et seq. (especially at para. 151). The UK response was basically to argue that, after the adoption of the OECD Convention in national law, this could not happen. A similar line is taken by Sweden in the Phase 1 report: Sweden argued that the OECD Convention would now take precedence over any competing public interest considerations (SE-Ph1, 23).

[140] Note France's rebuffal of WGB suggestions that political influence may be brought to bear on prosecutions with the observation that 'several preliminary investigations involving major French exporting companies or foreign entities had been opened on the orders of the prosecutors, and that it was thus obvious from French judicial practice that the decision whether to prosecute was not influenced by improper considerations' (FR-Ph2, 31).

The opening of an investigation into a case of foreign bribery can thus be a highly sensitive matter, in diplomatic terms.[141] The Convention was, however, ratified by all the signatories in a very short space of time, so, as far as combating supply-side corruption is concerned, their relations are now governed by it, or at least should be.

There can be no question of an 'opt-out' from enforcement on the grounds of friendly diplomatic relations. In any case, the general requirement of independent prosecution would prevent governments from doing deals with each other to avoid investigations or prosecutions.

Foreign bribery investigations, especially in high-profile cases, can clearly have negative implications in terms of foreign relations but they should not prevent criminal proceedings being taken. It is in reality quite likely that Foreign Ministries will become involved in reviewing the impact of domestic criminal investigations commenced on the basis of Article 5 obligations, especially if important trading interests and economic relations are at stake. The UK Phase 2 evaluation raised questions about notification by the Serious Fraud Office or other investigating authorities to the Foreign and Commonwealth Office and to the Ministry of Defence of the state of investigations into foreign bribery cases. The WGB recommended that this notification requirement be reconsidered.[142] The general point here is that the involvement of a non-investigative agency, for example, a Ministry for Foreign Affairs or Ministry of Defence, in the investigative process, should be clearly circumscribed. The purpose of disclosure of information to such agencies should be made transparent.

After completion of all Phase 1 reports and a number of major Phase 2 reports, it is clear that public interest considerations do enter into the assessments of investigators and prosecutors whether to proceed with their foreign bribery cases, particularly in discretionary systems. 'Public interest' as such, may be a legitimate consideration. What the Convention requires is that it must not be given a political slant contrary to Article 5. Guidelines for prosecutors must not include the criteria prohibited by that provision. The Code for Crown Prosecutors applicable in England and Wales transgressed this rule.[143] Understandably, the WGB report reflected its

[141] Cf. Hawley 2003: 'Western governments are often reluctant for investigations into bribery to go ahead for fear of upsetting trade or diplomatic relations with the country in which a foreign official is alleged to have taken a bribe' (9).

[142] UK-Ph2, 44 et seq., 81.

[143] This document refers to the risk that 'details may be made public that could harm sources of information, international relations, or national security' (para. 6.5(i) Crown Prosecution Service 2004). A similar clause can be found in Canada's Crown Counsel Policy Manual (CA-Ph1, 15).

disquiet on this point.[144] Its concerns were not entirely appeased by reassurances from the UK that the code is not intended to be 'case specific'.[145] The WGB recommended that it and other related documents be amended to ensure that the Article 5 prohibitions are excluded from consideration.[146]

It is quite obvious that the UK will be unable to convince anyone of the apolitical nature of anti-bribery investigations, if it does not limit its notion of public interest, which should also involve removal of the involvement of the Attorney General in prosecutions (subject, perhaps, to fundamental security concerns[147]).

The UK report serves as a strong indicator to other state Parties applying public interest criteria that these must be based solely on professional or organisational considerations. The concerns voiced in the UK report have been echoed in other recent evaluations, for example in the review of Japan. Article 248 of the Japanese Code of Criminal Procedure refers to a number of factors relating to the offender and the offence which may justify not going ahead with a case; these include the 'character' of the offender.[148] The Phase 2 report for Japan suggests that this criterion is broad enough to allow public officials to escape prosecution for bribery.[149] This brings us to the third ground set out in Article 5, relating to the identity of persons involved in the case.

2.3. Identity of natural or legal persons involved

This ground of non-intervention is broader than the terms of the Revised Recommendation of 1997, which refers only to non-consideration of factors related to 'the identity of the victim'.

Perhaps the term 'victim' was used in the Recommendation in order to ensure that the interests of all victims are respected so far as possible, regardless of their relative economic importance or their importance as public or private figures. There is also a link here with the question of victims' access to justice, raised by paragraph 6 of the Annex to the Revised Recommendation: '[c]omplaints of victims should be seriously investigated by the competent authorities'.[150]

[144] UK-Ph2, 52. [145] See note 144. [146] UK-Ph2, 81.
[147] See further discussion in IV.2.4. below.
[148] Discretion is conferred on prosecutors not to prosecute where it is unnecessary in the light of 'the character, age, and environment of an offender, the weight and conditions of an offence as well as the circumstances of an offence' (JP-Ph2, 49).
[149] JP-Ph 2, 49.
[150] Cf. Agreed Common Elements of Criminal Legislation and Related Action.

The broader wording is nevertheless to be preferred. First, it will not always be entirely clear who the 'victim' of foreign bribery is; it may comprise a wide group of competitors of the bribing company or business person; it could also be a state body, for example in a tender procedure where public funds are lost as a result of illicit practices.[151] Second, the word 'victim' connotes a direct relationship to the offence, whereas there may be other figures or companies involved in the surrounding circumstances whom the state might be inclined to protect. For example, the leader of a government or other important figure in the public gaze may be implicated in the illicit transaction, either as a stakeholder in the bribing companies or in companies which accepted the bribe.[152] In the recent Phase 2 evaluation of Japan, a Japanese lawyer suggested that the potentially negative effects for the economy of prosecuting a well-known Japanese company might be a 'substantial' consideration for prosecutors.[153] Here we see the third ground mentioned in Article 5 overlapping with the first ground of 'economic interest'.

The Swiss authorities are praised for their refusal to consider the importance of the persons involved in arms deals, with particular reference being made to 'Indian and African leaders'.[154] Switzerland may in principle refuse to execute a request for mutual legal assistance, should that request endanger the country's national interests. France is in a similar position.[155] The discussion in the Swiss and French reports makes clear that political reasons of this kind should not be used to justify not providing mutual legal assistance. Otherwise, Article 5 could be easily undermined.[156] Mutual legal assistance should also not be influenced by economic interests.[157]

2.4. National security?

Does Article 5 also exclude national security from the public interest criteria to which a prosecutor may resort in deciding not to pursue a case?[158]

One could envisage cases where an anti-bribery investigation or prosecution might reveal facts about an importing state's defence capabilities or aspects of its national defence strategy, which that state would rather not see released for public consumption.[159]

[151] See further discussion of the notion of victim in V.3. below.

[152] The Phase 2 report for Canada gives the hypothetical example of a senior political figure suspected of bribing a foreign public official; a prosecution of that person could prove highly embarrassing for the country (CA-Ph2, 33).

[153] JP-Ph2, 50. [154] CH-Ph2, 29. [155] FR-Ph2, 37. [156] See ch. on Articles 9–11 below.

[157] FR-Ph2, 37. [158] The term appears, for example, in CPS 2004.

[159] UK CPS 2004; and see also the equivalent Canadian Code (CA-Ph2, 33).

The usual connotation of the term 'security', when referring to 'national security', is to military or police security, meaning the external or internal defence of the nation or of public order. The term is also used in a wider sense to denote not only military security but also the general social and economic conditions for the well-being of the state.[160] In the context of Article 5, there is obviously scope for overlap between the definition of national economic interests and national security interests. States may hide behind the latter to protect the former. This entanglement can be found in particular in defence industry contracts.

Bribes paid to promote or protect defence production in a state, by securing exports, are squarely covered by the prohibition of the Convention. In the view of leading commentators, the application of the Convention to the defence sector is indeed of vital importance. It offers the prospect, if fully implemented, of 'cleaning up' this sector, in which bribery by major OECD exporting countries is prevalent.[161] Such bribes are covered by the Convention precisely because they are intended to advance economic interests; there will indeed always be an economic interest in sale of weapons, so it is almost impossible to separate defence interests from economic interests (except perhaps in time of war).

There is certainly no defence exception to the Convention. National security arguments based on considerations of international relations would also, clearly, fall foul of the Article 5 prohibition.[162] The central question which arises, however, is whether a discrete notion of national security can be used as a ground *legitimately* to influence any aspect of an investigation or prosecution. Such influence may take different forms. It might take the form of direct pressure to stop or delay the investigation, or it might amount to less direct obstruction, by denial of information to the judicial or police authorities.

[160] Cf. Glaessner 2003, esp. ch. 1.

[161] Cf. Courtney 2002, 26 et seq. State connivance in such bribery, notably through the provision of export credit insurance in circumstances where corruption is suspected, was alleged in a major study by Hawley 2003. Her critical findings, which focus on the UK's Export Credit Guarantee Department (ECGD), are based on nine case studies (cf. especially her conclusions: 55 et seq.). For its part, the UK Phase 2 report welcomes improvements in the ECGD's screening procedures introduced in 2004, but regrets that there has since been some watering down of the obligations on companies, apparently as a result of pressure on the government from major UK companies: UK-Ph2, 78 et seq. and cf. House of Commons 2004, 24–26, 29. With regard to France, Courtney 2002 refers to sources suggesting that the *Compagnie Française d'Assurance pour le Commerce Extérieure*, the French equivalent of the ECGD, 'funded around £2 billion in bribes in the armaments industry' (15) in the 1990s. Hawley 2003, 11 provides statistics on all the major export credit agencies. See also the discussion by Low in this commentary.

[162] See IV.2.3. above.

There is a general duty on the state Parties to respect the independence of prosecution.[163] Moreover, Official Commentary 27 refers to 'concerns of a political nature' in a general way which would also extend to national security concerns.[164] Thus, in principle, the Convention may be interpreted as prohibiting interference on national security grounds. The WGB has, however, not (yet) interpreted Article 5 to this effect. Nor has it read Article 5 literally to apply only to those considerations specifically excluded.

The WGB's Phase 1 evaluation report on German compliance with the Convention may suggest that it would accept a limited national security exception.[165] The WGB's Phase 2 evaluation does not question the possibility of a national security exception, but in the course of this later review the German authorities themselves underplayed the possible application of national security reasoning to prosecution of the offence of foreign bribery.[166]

Two controversial cases involving the sale of naval frigates by France to Taiwan and the sale of arms by the UK to Saudi Arabia should be mentioned in this context. In the former case, commissions were alleged to have been paid by a major French industrial group as part of the sale, in 1991, of French frigates to Taiwan.[167] The French authorities invoked the '*secret de la Défense nationale*' exception provided for in national law to obstruct national judicial investigations.[168] They denied access to a dossier regarding payment of commissions.[169] In the latter case, the UK government refused to publish a 1992 National Audit Office report into corruption allegations concerning the sales, apparently because of national security interests.[170] Close entanglement of economic interests with national security concerns is revealed by such cases.

Some commentators would leave narrow room for national security to intervene in investigations of foreign corruption in such cases.[171] But to be

[163] See IV.1.1. above.

[164] The counter-argument that it refers only to the political concerns specifically mentioned in Art. 5 is also tenable but leaves the difficult question of the precise delimitation of national economic interests from national security interests.

[165] DE-Ph 1, 11, 19. The reference is to national security in the context of discontinuation of proceedings under the Code of Criminal Procedure.

[166] DE-Ph2, 37.

[167] Although mentioned at the beginning of the French Phase 2 report, the Taiwan case is not discussed further, perhaps because proceedings in some jurisdictions are continuing (cf. FR-Ph2, 6).

[168] Cf. Jean-Pierre 2003, esp. chs. 25 et seq.

[169] Jean-Pierre 2003, 224 et seq. (reproduction of letter from investigating magistrates to the then French Finance Minister, M. Fabius, asking him to apply the procedure laid out in law 98–567 of 8 July 1998 and declassify the documents concerned; the Minister refused.)

[170] Courtney 2002, 35.

[171] Cf. Courtney 2002, 19: '[w]hile the genuine security concerns of allies cannot be dismissed lightly'.

capable of trumping a clear international law obligation to facilitate the investigation of transnational bribery, an *ordre public* exception on the ground of national security would have to be very compelling in nature and have a clear basis in national law. Even if such a legal basis were found to exist, it should be interpreted and applied so far as possible in accordance with the obligations of the Convention.[172]

The main problem with allowing such an exception is the likelihood of its being abused. State Parties would almost certainly tend to employ it for precisely the reasons which the Convention seeks to exclude. The most likely grounds for concealment of information from police or judicial authorities are not genuine national security concerns but a desire to protect economic interests, shield national politicians or not to damage relations with another state (i.e. considerations expressly banned by Article 5).[173]

Often what is being concealed in such cases is in fact the corruption itself, not real state secrets. The risks of concealment of corruption are very evident from the large number of allegations which surface every year concerning corruption in the export of weaponry by leading OECD exporting countries,[174] and if we consider how past allegations of this nature have been swept under the carpet by governments, claiming national security reasons.[175]

The notion of state secrets certainly exists as a recognised legal concept in some state Parties to the Convention, in order to protect national security. It is not confined to French or UK law.[176] It is clear, however, that an extensive and undifferentiated interpretation of state secrecy can

[172] The resolution of a conflict between national law and international law will, however, ultimately depend on how the constitution of the state concerned regulates the relationship: cf. Dixon and McCorquodale 1991, ch. 4.

[173] Courtney 2002, 20 et seq. refers to the main 'structural factors' behind the tendencies of governments to turn a blind eye to corruption in defence contracts. These include: strategic considerations; the perceived imperative of promoting sales to shore up domestic arms capacity; competition in the industry. The shroud of secrecy thrown over trading in weapons is often justified by reference to the need for commercial confidentiality (18 et seq.), but the secrecy is more often than not used to hide the corrupt payments, which she asserts are 'an accepted and integral part of arms contracts' (11).

[174] Courtney 2002, 10 refers to US Department of Commerce statistics attributing half of all allegations of foreign bribery to defence contracts.

[175] The conclusion by Courtney 2002 is that corruption in the official arms trade 'has been allowed to fester and increase, fuelled by secrecy' (40). Will criminalisation pursuant to the OECD Convention or other international instruments really help halt bribery in this sensitive sector? Hawley 2003 is sceptical about the results so far, asserting 'business as usual' (8 et seq.).

[176] Cf. the Crown Counsel Policy Manual for Canada, which refers to the risk of 'disclosure of information that would be injurious to international relations, national defence, national security or that should not be disclosed in the public interest' (CA-Ph1, 15). In the Phase 2 report further consideration is given to these guidelines, which in the view of the WGB lack clarity, as they fail categorically to rule out the use of economic or other political grounds to influence prosecutions (CA-Ph2, 39).

fundamentally undermine the operation of Article 5. A 'culture of secrecy' surrounding the investigation of foreign bribery allegations only serves to fuel suspicion that some contracting parties are not serious about their obligations to bring offenders to book.[177]

In conclusion, Article 5 may not prevent a very limited national security exception which would allow investigators or prosecutors to seek clarification whether there are fundamental and compelling reasons related to national security why an investigation or prosecution should not proceed, or why certain details of the matter should not be revealed. It should, however, be possible to limit or focus the investigations in such a way that national security interests are protected, while the bribers are prosecuted. The security interests of the state would not then prevent the prosecution as such.

The state concerned would in any case have to demonstrate a clear legal basis for invoking national security. It would have to provide reasons and not just refuse to co-operate with the criminal justice authorities.[178] Ideally, the relevant procedures should take place with judicial or parliamentary oversight. The French procedure for lifting defence secrets does not give the appearance of being independent; the oversight committee is too close to government.[179]

V. Organisation of enforcement

1. Effectiveness of national systems of investigation and prosecution

How the state Parties organise the fight against corruption, be it domestic or foreign, is basically up to them. The Convention does not contain any specific obligations in this respect, although it does require respect for the role of the victim as complainant.

There is an implicit basic requirement that the national systems themselves and specifically the agencies of enforcement (notably, police,

[177] For example, in their recent Phase 2 investigation the Japanese argued that details of investigations could not be revealed owing to the need to protect the privacy of persons who may be implicated in bribery allegations and to preserve confidentiality (JP-Ph2, 5 et seq.). But this only prompted the WGB to condemn Japan for their lack of serious efforts in detecting and prosecuting corruption cases (JP-Ph2, 57).

[178] Cf. Courtney 2002, 24, who refers to the tendency of states to put forward 'the blanket justification of national security'.

[179] Jean-Pierre 2003, 225 et seq. Compare also the discussion in the UK Phase 2 report (UK-Ph2, 53 et seq.). Courtney 2002, 32 et seq. argues for more effective parliamentary scrutiny of export licensing procedures and of defence procurement decisions by the Parliaments of importing countries.

prosecutors and judiciary) be free of corruption. The WGB has identified certain OECD state Parties which it feels still need to come to terms with corruption within their institutions.[180]

Measuring the effectiveness of national systems in relation to investigation and prosecution of crime has led the WGB to make a number of proposals or recommendations, mostly related to the specifics of organisation in individual countries. It has also drawn some general conclusions, as follows:

- first, that investigation and prosecution of the foreign bribery offence should preferably be centralised;[181]
- second, that specialist investigative and prosecution teams should, where possible, be given responsibility for cases;[182]
- third, that training should be provided in the application of the Convention and implementing legislation by the responsible national training institutions;[183]
- fourth, that communications between different national agencies should be such as to facilitate well-managed investigations, including the necessary exchange of information;[184]
- fifth, that conflicts of competence and overlapping responsibilities should be avoided.[185]

Most of these general parameters should be capable of being observed without fundamental reform of existing institutional arrangements, though some countries, such as Switzerland,[186] have chosen to alter the competences

[180] Cf. the Phase 2 reports for Bulgaria and Mexico. The WGB's evaluations of both countries praise efforts already undertaken, but call for further measures to address continuing corruption in political and judicial circles.

[181] In the United States, enforcement has been concentrated in the hands of the Federal Department of Justice; the Swiss federal system now seems to be moving in the same direction, whereas in Germany cases continue to be handled at the *Länder* level. Excessive fragmentation of efforts, as in the case of the UK, should be avoided (UK-Ph2, 32, 37).

[182] The development of a core of experts and dedicated prosecutors contributes to the US' relatively robust enforcement efforts (US-Ph2, 24 et seq.). Cf. also France (FR-Ph2, 32 et seq.) and Finland (FI-Ph2, 8 et seq.).

[183] This is emphasised in the Phase 2 reports, which all contain sections on 'awareness and training'.

[184] Obviously, the more agencies are involved, the greater is the risk that information will not be passed on (UK-Ph2, 33).

[185] The nature of the Italian system is said to make it particularly susceptible to such conflicts because of the territorial jurisdiction of prosecutors (IT-Ph2, 26 et seq.).

[186] The Swiss Phase 2 report discusses the impact of new laws giving the Confederation competence over economic (organised) crime, including bribery. The reforms place the Office of the Attorney General, as a central authority, at the heart of the new system (CH-Ph2, 23 et seq.).

for dealing with serious economic crime (including bribery), and others, such as the UK,[187] are in the process of doing so.

As the Swiss and German cases show, the organisation of prosecution of foreign bribery cases can be complicated by the division of competences between the federal and provincial levels of government. Within some German *Länder*, specialised teams have been set up to deal with corruption cases; the location of these teams reflects the growth of corruption cases in Germany from the 1980s.[188] The Phase 2 report for Germany continues to express concern about lack of specialisation in other *Länder*, and a general lack of training, as well as a shortage of resources.[189]

2. Resources

Paragraph 6 of the Agreed Common Elements of the Revised Recommendation of 1997 (as referred to in Official Commentary 27) states as follows:

> 'National governments should provide adequate resources to prosecuting authorities so as to permit effective prosecution of bribery of foreign public officials.'

The problem of resources is a key issue for enforcement of the Convention, perhaps the major factor influencing the choice of those who would be in a position to investigate and prosecute bribery of foreign officials.

The consequences of not resourcing the various systems devised by state Parties to meet the challenge of tacking foreign bribery are addressed at some length by the WGB in its reports. Gaps in policing and in judicial staffing are bound to frustrate even the best organisational efforts made to streamline investigations and prosecutions.[190]

The main thrust of the WGB's reviews is to put political pressure on state Parties to fund their criminal justice systems sufficiently to enable the obligations of the Convention to be met.[191] The reports recognise that

[187] The UK report refers to and welcomes the policy decision to confer on the Serious Fraud Office (SFO) the primary responsibility for anti-bribery investigations and prosecutions (UK-Ph2, 32 et seq., 49 et seq.). The UK is also in the process of setting up a 'Serious Organised Crime Agency' (SOCA) under the Serious Organised Crime and Police Act 2005. Evidence given to the WGB suggests that SOCA will not, however, take away from the SFO the latter's responsibilities for investigating and prosecuting foreign bribery cases.

[188] Cf. Schaupensteiner 1999 on scandals in Frankfurt, *Land* Hessen.

[189] DE-Ph2, 11 et seq.

[190] The success of Swiss centralisation efforts, for example, is said to be endangered by resources not being made available to the federal authorities (CH-Ph2, 26). A shortage of qualified personnel is identified as a problem in other countries, such as (admittedly tiny) Luxembourg (LU-Ph2, 24 et seq.).

[191] Italian prosecutors pointed out to the WGB's examiners that resourcing anti-bribery investigations can be disproportionately expensive, because bribery investigations 'often lead to discovery of additional offences' (IT-Ph2, 28).

bribing of foreign public officials is hardly likely to be the first priority in resource allocation.[192] The WGB nevertheless calls for appropriate investments to be made.[193]

It would not be realistic for the WGB to recommend the allocation of particular amounts; the recommendations tend rather to concentrate on the need for pooling or concentration of resources,[194] particularly at the central level, and on their efficient use.[195]

We fear that, without a change of political will, a relative lack of funding in this area will continue. Lack of resources is likely to continue to be a major reason why foreign bribery cases are not thoroughly investigated or brought to trial.[196]

3. Role of the victim and of private action

There is considerable divergence among the legal systems applying the Convention regarding the role of the victim in criminal proceedings. Of those state Parties which do envisage a role for the victim, the following possibilities of intervention can be noted:

- a right of complaint to the prosecutor, required as a precondition for commencing a prosecution;[197]
- an independent right of action as a civil party (*partie civile*) to the proceedings;[198]
- a right of appeal, either to the prosecutor or a judicial body, for review of a decision not to prosecute.[199]

[192] The Swiss Attorney General is quoted as referring to anti-terrorist investigations as the first priority (CH-Ph2, 26).

[193] The UK Phase 2 report also highlights the lack of resources for foreign bribery investigations. It suggests that resources are not earmarked for foreign bribery cases because so few investigations are conducted, suggesting a vicious circle (UK-Ph2, 40 et seq.).

[194] See our remarks in V.1. above, concerning centralisation and specialisation in investigations.

[195] Cf. the inordinate amount of money spent by Italy in 2003 on wiretapping in criminal investigations: cutting back on spending of this kind may help in better targeting certain criminal activities (IT-Ph2, 28).

[196] UK-Ph2, 40.

[197] The general principle at stake here is that, for some offences, fairness requires that proceedings should not be started without the victim's wishes being taken into account (Chiavario 2002, 542). This is not such a cogent argument, however, for bribery offences, as the victim is less well defined than for other offences.

[198] Cf. the Phase 2 reports for France and Luxembourg and, regarding Belgium, Perrodet 2002b, 453 et seq.

[199] In Germany, for example, 'aggrieved persons' may complain in such circumstances to the Prosecutor General (DE-Ph1, 11).

These procedures are all recognised by the WGB as legitimate ways of enforcing the Convention. They can also be interpreted as a form of external control of the prosecution.

Private action by victims is even held out – perhaps somewhat hopefully[200] – as a possible compensation for the apparent inertia of public prosecution agencies in some countries regarding prosecution of the offence of foreign bribery.[201] The Convention requires that the complaints of victims be seriously investigated,[202] but does not define what a 'victim' is. The evaluation reports of the WGB discuss this point but reveal a lack of clarity in several major countries. For example in France,[203] Germany[204] and several other countries,[205] it is not clear whether you can regard a competitor of the briber as a victim and thus entitled to avail of the procedures of complaint, intervention etc. This lack of clarity is also a drawback in terms of any civil claim which could be lodged.[206]

France decided by law of 30 June 2000 to rule out any possibility for a company excluded from a contract by virtue of a competitor's bribery to initiate *partie civile* proceedings, except with regard to bribery of officials of an EU Member State. This exception to the usual rule for criminal proceedings breaches the requirement of Article 5 of the Convention that the 'applicable rules and principles' of each state Party shall apply. The WGB did not accept the explanations offered by the French government for this law, which include a fear that companies would abuse this procedure as a weapon in their economic conflicts.[207] It has recommended that France repeal the law.[208]

Article 35 of the UN Convention against Corruption requires signatory states to ensure that persons who have suffered damage as a result of an act

[200] Spencer 2002, 36 et seq. is generally sceptical about the ability of victims to achieve much under any system: monetary claims must be enforced separately in civilian systems, and English law places many obstacles in the way of the victim.

[201] This thinking can, for example, be found in the Phase 2 report for Luxembourg (LU-Ph2, 23).

[202] Cf. Official Commentary 27, referring to para. 6 of the Agreed Common Elements of the OECD 1997a.

[203] FR-Ph1, 21. Note also the discussion in FR-Ph2 in relation to the founding of personal jurisdiction: the effectiveness of this form of jurisdiction is conditional on the prior lodging of a complaint by the victim or by an official denunciation. Where victims are concerned, the problem is that French law appears to regard only the foreign state as the victim of the offence of foreign bribery (FR-Ph2, 45 et seq.).

[204] DE-Ph2, 38.

[205] See, for example, DK-Ph1, 16, concerning the right to complain to a superior prosecutor against a decision not to prosecute. Luxembourg, on the other hand, believes that persons cheated out of contracts would have a claim as a *partie civile*, in principle (LU-Ph2, 23).

[206] FR-Ph1, 21. [207] FR-Ph2, 29. [208] FR-Ph2, 31, 59.

of corruption have the right to initiate legal proceedings for compensation against those responsible for that damage. Low argues that the Convention may be pointing the way towards more effective enforcement of private claims.[209]

References

For documentation see the consolidated bibliography at the end of this book.

Baker, E. (2004), 'Guilty Pleas, Diversion and Consensual Disposition: England and Wales' in A. Eser and C. Rabenstein (Hrsg.), *Strafjustiz im Spannungsfeld von Effizienz und Fairness*, Berlin, 381.

Bell, R. E. (2001), 'Discretion and Decision Making in Money Laundering Prosecutions', *Journal of Money Laundering Control*, Vol. **5**, No. 1, 42.

Chiavario, M. (2002), 'Private Parties: the Rights of the Defendant and the Victim' in M. Delmas-Marty and J. R. Spencer (eds.), *European Criminal Procedures*, Cambridge, 541.

Courtney, C. (2002), 'Corruption in the Official Arms Trade' in Transparency International (ed.), *Policy Research Paper* 001, Sutton (available at: http://www.transparency.org.uk > TI (UK) Papers and Newletters).

Crowe, R. (2005), 'The Schengen Acquis in Police Cooperation: Implementation in an Enlarged Europe', *ERA-Forum*, No. **3**, Trier, 415.

Delmas-Marty, M. and J. A. E. Vervaele (eds.) (2000), *The Implementation of Corpus Juris in the Member States*, Vol. **1**, Antwerp, Groningen, Oxford.

Dixon, M. and R. McCorquodale (1991), *Cases and Materials on International Law*, London.

Feldman, D. (1993), *Civil Liberties and Human Rights in England and Wales*, Oxford.

Glaessner, G.-J. (2003), *Sicherheit in Freiheit: Die Schutzfunktion des demokratischen Staates und die Freiheit der Bürger*, Opladen.

Hamilton, J. (2005), 'Mutual Assistance in Criminal Matters in Ireland and the Proposed European Evidence Warrant', *ERA-Forum Special Issue*, Trier, 53.

Hawley, S. (2003), *Turning a Blind Eye: Corruption and the UK Export Credits Guarantee Department*, Sturminster Newton.

Janis, M., R. Kay, and A. Bradley (2000), *European Human Rights Law: Text and Materials*, 2nd edn, Oxford.

Jean-Pierre, T. (2003), *Taiwan Connection: Scandales et meurtres au Coeur de la République*, Paris.

Jung, H. (1986), 'Legalität oder Opportunität im Strafverfahren?' in H. Prütting (Hrsg.), *Recht und Gesetz im Dialog III*, Köln, 55.

Kerse, C. and N. Khan (2005), *EC Antitrust Procedures*, 5th edn, London.

Kühne, H.-H. (2003), *Strafprozeßrecht*, 6th edn, Heidelberg.

Low, L. A. (2004), 'Towards Universal International Anticorruption Standards: The United Nations Convention Against Corruption and other International Anticorruption Treaties: Too Much of a Good Thing?' (presentation at the 2nd Annual Conference of the International Bar Association, International Chamber of

[209] Low 2004, 15 et seq. and see her ch. in this commentary.

Commerce, and Organization for Economic Co-operation and Development, *The Awakening Giant of Anti-Corruption Enforcement* in Paris, 22–23 April 2004).

Low, L. A. (2005), 'Enforcement of the FCPA in the United States: Trends and the Effects of International Standards' (presentation at the 3rd Annual Conference of the International Bar Association, International Chamber of Commerce, and Organization for Economic Co-operation and Development, *The Awakening Giant of Anti-Corruption Enforcement* in Paris, 4–6 May 2005).

Manacorda, S. (2004), 'Investigation and Prosecution: Prosecution Authorities' in P. J. Cullen (ed.), *Enlarging the Fight Against Fraud in the European Union* (Academy of European Law Trier Series of Publications, Vol. **36**), Cologne, 139.

Mitsilegas, V. (2003), *Money Laundering Counter-Measures in the European Union: A New Paradigm of Security Governance versus Fundamental Legal Principles*, The Hague, London, New York.

Perrodet, A. (2002) [cited Perrodet 2002a], 'The Italian System' in M. Delmas-Marty and J. R. Spencer (eds.), *European Criminal Procedures*, Cambridge, 348.

Perrodet, A. (2002) [cited Perrodet 2002b], 'The Public Prosecutor' in M. Delmas-Marty and J. R. Spencer (eds.), *European Criminal Procedures*, Cambridge, 415.

Pesquié, B. (2002), 'The Belgian System' in M. Delmas-Marty and J. R. Spencer (eds.), *European Criminal Procedures*, Cambridge, 81.

Sacerdoti, G. (1999), 'Das OECD-Übereinkommen 1997 über die Bekämpfung der Bestechung ausländischer Amtsträger im internationalen Geschäftsverkehr' in M. Pieth and P. Eigen (Hrsg.), *Korruption im internationalen Geschäftsverkehr: Bestandesaufnahme: Bekämpfung, Prävention*, Neuwied, Kriftel, Basel, Frankfurt a. M., 212.

Salas, D. (2002), 'The Role of the Judge' in M. Delmas-Marty and J. R. Spencer (eds.), *European Criminal Procedures*, Cambridge, 488.

Schaupensteiner, W. J. (1999), 'Korruption in Deutschland – Das Ende der Tabuisierung' in M. Pieth and P. Eigen (Hrsg.), *Korruption im internationalen Geschäftsverkehr: Bestandesaufnahme, Bekämpfung, Prävention*, Neuwied, Kriftel, Basel, Frankfurt a. M., 131.

Spencer, J. R. (2002), 'Introduction' in M. Delmas-Marty and J. R. Spencer (eds.), *European Criminal Procedures*, Cambridge, 1.

Spencer, J. R. (2005), 'An Academic Critique of the EU Acquis in Relation to Trans-Border Evidence Gathering', *ERA-Forum Special Issue*, Trier, 28.

Tulkens, F. (2002), 'Negotiated Justice' in M. Delmas-Marty and J. R. Spencer (eds.), *European Criminal Procedures*, Cambridge, 641.

Van den Wyngaert, Ch. (1993), 'Belgium' in Ch. van den Wyngaert (ed.), *Criminal Procedure Systems in the European Community*, London, 1.

Walther, S. (2004), 'Communication over Confrontation: Modern Criminal Procedure in Transformation' in A. Eser and C. Rabenstein (Hrsg.), *Strafjustiz im Spannungsfeld von Effizienz und Fairness*, Berlin, 367.

Article 6. Statute of Limitations

PETER J. CULLEN

Article 6 – Statute of Limitations

Any statute of limitations applicable to the offence of bribery of a foreign public official shall allow an adequate period of time for the investigation and prosecution of this offence.

Chapter contents

I. Introduction

The *Travaux Préparatoires* of the OECD Convention deal with the limitation period for bribery cases under the rubric of enforcement, placing Article 6 squarely in the context of investigation and prosecution of the active bribery of foreign public officials. The clear aim of Article 6 is to facilitate effective enforcement by allowing sufficient time for the police to follow up bribery allegations and for the prosecution to bring the case to trial. Article 6 does not aim to be protective of the defendant so much as understanding of police and prosecution needs, reflecting the overriding Convention aim of criminalisation.

There is indeed a closer connection between Articles 5 and 6 than the express terms of each Article would suggest. Article 5 does not deal explicitly with how enforcement is organised, e.g. in terms of the powers of the investigative agencies, their co-operation with the prosecution, the degree of centralisation and specialisation in enforcement, questions of resources, etc.[1] In practice, the evaluation reports of the Working Group on Bribery (WGB) do give considerable attention to these highly practical matters and many of its recommendations focus on such questions. Article 6 is more directly enforcement-oriented and can be seen as a logical extension of the organisational concerns voiced in the *Travaux Préparatoires.*[2]

It is not possible to extrapolate a great deal from the very concise wording of Article 6 itself, nor is there any accompanying Official Commentary which might throw further light upon its meaning. The *Travaux Préparatoires* state only as follows:

> 'In view of the complexity of the offence of bribery of foreign public officials and the potential difficulties of obtaining evidence from several jurisdictions, the statute of limitations for the offence should allow adequate time for investigation and prosecution.'[3]

We can see from the text of Article 6 and from this passage that the Article does not call upon state Parties to introduce a common limitation period. It is not, directly, a harmonising provision. The use of the term 'adequate', referring to the period of time within which investigation and prosecution should be conducted, nevertheless opens the door to a comparative analysis of countries' limitation periods, within the framework of peer review conducted by the WGB.

[1] See ch. on Article 5 above. [2] OECD 1999, F-1033–F-1034.
[3] OECD 1999, F-1034.

In part II. of this chapter we will look at the underlying philosophies and general features of the limitation models of OECD countries. In part III we will review the analysis conducted by the WGB of national limitation periods: this will reveal the general Convention standard which has emerged on the basis of Article 6. The criteria used by the WGB and their application in the evaluation reports form the core of part III.

II. Limitation models and their underlying philosophies

1. An emerging international standard for economic crime?

There is wide recognition of the inapplicability of limitation periods to certain crimes under international law. These are, however, only the most heinous crimes such as genocide, crimes against humanity and war crimes, not those of a purely or mainly economic nature.

Article 29 of the Rome Statute for an International Criminal Court of 17 July 1998 stipulates that '[t]he crimes within the jurisdiction of the Court shall not be subject to any statute of limitations.'[4] In the Council of Europe context, the Convention of 25 January 1974 on the Non-Applicability of Statutory Limitations to Crimes against Humanity and War Crimes contains similar terms.[5]

These instruments do not apply to economic crime such as corruption, the effects of which may be extremely deleterious for a country and its people but which is less morally reprehensible, because it does not pose a direct threat to life and limb. In the Final Communiqué issued on 27 November 2005 to conclude their summit meeting in Malta, Commonwealth Heads of State and Government declared that combating corruption was one of their major priorities, stressing inter alia the need for 'effective enforcement'.[6] They, nevertheless, distinguished corruption from morally more repugnant offences against the person, stating: '[c]orruption, reprehensible as it is, should not, however, be equated with war crimes or genocide'.[7]

Of the international instruments which do deal with economic crime, the first and most important in this context is the United Nations Convention against Corruption of 9 December 2003. Like the OECD anti-bribery

[4] These crimes are: genocide, crimes against humanity, war crimes, and the crime of aggression. Cf. earlier UN documents, e.g. UN 1968.

[5] ETS no. 82. This Convention has remained something of a dead letter, however, only entering into force in 2003 following ratification by the minimum of three states.

[6] Cf. http://www.thecommonwealth.org. [7] See previous note 6.

Convention, this Convention contains a specific provision dealing with a limitations period, namely Article 29:

> 'Each State Party shall, where appropriate, establish under its domestic law a long statute of limitations period in which to commence proceedings for any offence established in accordance with this Convention and establish a longer statute of limitations period or provide for the suspension of the statute of limitations where the alleged offender has evaded the administration of justice.'

Almost identical wording is contained in the United Nations Convention against Transnational Organised Crime which is of somewhat earlier vintage.[8] Like Article 29, Article 11(5), the relevant clause of the latter Convention, refers to the need for a 'long period' which should be extended when the alleged offender evades justice (the possibility of suspension is not mentioned).

There are therefore two principal differences from the OECD Convention: first, the reference to a 'long' period, not just an 'adequate' one. Though 'long' is, of course, a relative concept, requiring a comparative analysis, the intention appears to be to go further than the OECD, mandating a generous approach to time limits for investigation and prosecution. Admittedly, the UN Convention Against Corruption aims at a wider range of corruption offences than the OECD Convention but its scope clearly encompasses active bribery of public officials.[9] Its stronger approach is buttressed by the addition of the second clause, concerning either extension or suspension of the basic limitations period concerned, in the case of fugitives from justice. We will see in the next section that suspension and interruption of the periods of limitation are important features of national limitation models.

These international instruments refer to the limitation of the period for *prosecution* of the offence (i.e. time to 'commence proceedings'), not to extinction of the time limit for *execution of sentence*. Some national laws explicitly make this distinction.[10]

Regarding developments in European Union law, the EU lacks any formal competence in matters of criminal procedure, with the consequence that its proposals or instruments in criminal matters do not purport to harmonise the Member States' approach to issues such as the statute of limitations. For example, the recent EU proposal made in relation to the

[8] It dates from December 2000.

[9] In relation to the Convention on Transnational Crime, this can perhaps be explained by the very serious nature of the offences coming within its ambit.

[10] See II.2.2.2.a. below.

fight against organised crime does not mention the subject.[11] Moreover, neither the EU Convention on the fight against corruption, nor its COE counterpart, contains a statute of limitations, leaving this to national law to determine.[12]

We should, however, note at least one important initiative by the European Community (EC) which does address the subject. We refer to the proposals of the 'Corpus Juris' group. In the 1990s, the EC mandated a group of criminal law experts to draft proposals (in essence policy recommendations) relating to the more effective combating of fraud against the Community budget.[13] The group devised a draft anti-fraud Code, which they entitled 'Corpus Juris'. Article 22(2) of the Code specifies a limitations period of five years. This was deemed by the group to be a sufficient period for the investigation. It appears to have been taken as the average period applying in the then fifteen Member States of the EU to fraud prosecutions. The commentary to the Code indicates that the limitation periods for fraud offences vary considerably from system to system and '[i]t might be difficult to reach an agreement on duration through a synthesis'.[14]

The Corpus Juris experts also discussed setting an upper limit for the limitation period. Their deliberations resulted in 2000 in the insertion into the proposed Code of a note ('implementing provision') to the effect that in any event, 'suspensions and interruptions should not prolong the limitation period beyond ten years'.[15] The question how to determine the commencement of the limitation period – 'the day when the offence was committed' – was not dealt with.

The Corpus Juris experts were clearly aware of the complexity of EC anti-fraud investigations but their proposals sought to balance the interests of investigators and the prosecution in having sufficient time with the competing interests of the defence and of legal certainty. The defence, of course, has an interest in as short a time limit as possible, one which is likely to expire before the case can be brought to trial. Its tactics may often be to play for time. There are also considerations of legal certainty, especially the certainty of evidence, behind the idea of time limits for prosecution. From a policy point of view, the more distant the offence, the

[11] EU 2005b. [12] EU 1997a, COE 1999a.

[13] Delmas-Marty 1997; Delmas-Marty and Vervaele 2000.

[14] Delmas-Marty and Vervaele 2000, 336; cf. also the commentary in Delmas-Marty 1997, 96–98.

[15] Delmas-Marty and Vervaele 2000, 201 (note to Art. 22(2)).

less pressing becomes the public need or justification for action. Clearly, more recent crimes have a stronger claim on public resources because of the more immediate desire for retribution or prevention.

With regard to economic crime, the prevailing approach seems to be that most states do apply limitation periods for economic or white collar crimes such as corruption and money laundering and that the average period lies around the five-year mark.[16] Recent international instruments, notably the UN Convention Against Corruption, indicate a trend towards longer periods.

In the next section, we will look at national law concerning limitation periods in terms of its most general features. First, there is the question whether limitation applies or not. Second, we must distinguish different types of limitation period and look at the details of national classification.

National models are by no means uniform. There is no common approach to the length of the limitation period. Again here it is important to emphasise that the OECD Convention does not seek to harmonise national laws. It aims rather to ensure the 'functional equivalence' of national provisions. This means that the periods allowed under national law may vary but must be sufficiently long to guarantee effective enforcement under the general conditions of each state's criminal justice system. An approximate or rough degree of equivalence is implied.

2. National models: general features

2.1. A limitation period or not?

'To limit or not to limit, that is the question'. In fact, this is not the question for the vast majority of state Parties to the Convention who do impose limitation periods for the offence of active bribery of foreign public officials. The question for most state Parties is not *whether* there should be a limitation period, but *how long* it should be.

Continental European states have all opted to limit the time given to investigate and prosecute and also distinguish in some cases between limitation of prosecution and of execution of sentence.[17] Japan, Korea, the United States, and South American states all impose limitation periods in respect of prosecution.

[16] More details will be provided in II.2. below. [17] See II.2.2.2.a. below.

The English Common Law approach is different, eschewing a limitation period altogether.[18] The English approach is followed by Australia, Canada, and New Zealand. Apart from this small group of countries whose laws are modelled on the English system, limitation periods are *de rigueur.*

For those who favour limitation periods, their choice may be motivated by one or more factors. These may be of a legal-theoretical character or based on more pragmatic considerations related to the organisation and efficiency of prosecution.

Various theories are presented to justify limitation periods. There is first the theory that the offender's personal culpability may diminish with time or at least that he may develop a sense of remorse and turn away from crime, making his prosecution on grounds of individual deterrence less compelling.

The state's objective interest in prosecution may also diminish with time: society's desire to punish wrongdoing is at its most urgent in the immediate aftermath of crime. The failure to take measures within an 'adequate' period of time may indicate that the state's interest in exacting retribution, or in general deterrence, is not so pressing in the particular case.

Given that the effectiveness of the criminal process is substantially based on the reliability of evidence, it is logical that a time limit be set. The value of evidence will dissipate as time passes, both in terms of physical evidence and also as regards the evidence of witnesses to the crime. It would be unfair to the accused person to convict him or her on the basis of unsound evidence; limitation periods are in this sense part of the 'fair trial' concept.[19]

Viewed from a human rights standpoint, a limitation period can be seen as encouraging the speedy resolution of cases called for by European and other international law instruments. The right to prompt adjudication of one's case is well established in case law of the European Court of Human Rights.[20]

[18] In English law the doctrine of 'abuse of process' can be invoked to allow a prosecution to be stopped, if the judge is of the opinion that continuation would be oppressive (cf. Zander 1999, 308). New Zealand has a similar rule (NZ-Ph1, 21). But these are highly exceptional discretionary procedures; they are only very rarely, if ever, applied to cases of delay.

[19] For some legal systems the idea that you could bring a case against a person 62 years after the facts occurred, as in the case of the former Head of the East German *Stasi*, Erich Mielke, convicted in 1993 of murders committed in 1931, would be aberrant (cf. mention of the case in McAdams 2001, 37; McAdams' book focuses in fact on the 'regime crimes' committed under the auspices of the German Democratic Republic, of whose government Mielke was a member).

[20] Janis, Kay, and Bradley 2000, 454 et seq. And note the observation on Article 6 of the European Convention on Human Rights in the Phase 1 report for Luxembourg (LU-Ph1, 18).

A more pragmatic justification for imposing a limitation period concerns the resources of investigative and prosecuting agencies. Their resources to tackle bribery are very limited, as we saw in our discussion of Article 5. It is logical therefore to prioritise cases of recent vintage, which are easier to pursue. The older a case file, the lower priority it is likely to have within an under-resourced prosecutor's office.[21] Limitation periods are of particular assistance to states applying the principle of mandatory prosecution ('legality principle'), which would otherwise face the daunting prospect of following up even minor cases over unlimited periods.

There are, of course, counter-theories and arguments which may be used to support the approach of England and Wales and other like-minded Common Law states. Where the (serious) damage caused by crime is not remedied or at least addressed, the passage of time may be as likely to increase resentment and promote lingering suffering as to diminish it. The victim's perspective is particularly important here. This counter-argument is probably less compelling in relation to economic crime such as bribery than as regards offences against the person. There is, however, increasing awareness of the dangers of white-collar crime such as bribery. In many states, the public has recent experience of major financial scandals which have damaged political as well as financial institutions. Prevention of corruption of this kind is at the heart of the Convention and its criminalisation strategy. A sufficient number of prosecutions must be brought, if the Convention's deterrent effect is to be realised; limitation periods should not stand in their way.[22]

The argument that shorter limitation periods are more appropriate for economic crimes than for serious crimes against the person such as murder has thus become less sustainable as knowledge about the prevalence and effects of these crimes has become more widespread. While they may still not generate moral outrage, the damage they cause to welfare or economy and political reputation arguably justifies a new perspective on limitation. This thinking can be seen in the international instruments recently adopted at global level; arguably, the OECD approach is too timid.

The evidence argument can be put another way. It can be argued that the collection and sifting of evidence in cases of corruption and other economic offences *requires* a long period of time and that the setting of limits hinders

[21] Cf., for example, the discussion in the Phase 2 report for Belgium: BE-Ph2, 26.

[22] See our discussion in the ch. on Article 3 above and note Müller 2003: '*Gesichtspunkte der positiven und negativen Generalprävention [sprechen] eher gegen eine Verjährung*' (vor Art. 70, Rn. 37).

these complex investigations or may even prevent them from being tackled seriously in the first place.

The *Rechtsfrieden* concept presented by certain German law-based systems does not have an exact counterpart in countries of the Common Law. If the idea behind it is to prevent the legal system from being blocked or overloaded by late claims, then this is, of course, a valid concern for the latter too, especially in civil matters. In criminal cases, the *Rechtsfrieden* argument appears to be that criminal law should restore legal order after the 'peace' has been breached. It can be interpreted as an argument against too short a limitation period.[23]

Finally, it is obvious that limitation periods can be abused, with consequences for high-level as well as low-level examples of corruption. Regrettably, reliable information about the actual effects of limitation periods on preventing prosecutions of suspected offenders is not really provided by most criminal statistics, as the WGB's evaluation reports are forced to admit.

2.2. Classifications of national law

2.2.1. A special limitation period for bribery and other economic offences?

Bribery cases, especially foreign bribery cases, arguably demand a particularly generous approach to limitation, given their complex nature. This would justify special regulation. They could, for example, be placed in a special category of economic offences singling them out from other general criminal law offences. In contrast to its approach to sanctions under Article 3, the WGB has not, however, explicitly taken this line. The foreign bribery offence is not assimilated to other forms of economic crime such as theft, fraud, and embezzlement, where limitation periods are concerned.

The standard approach of most systems of national law is to classify the bribery offence in terms of the level of sanction imposed, bringing it within the general classification systems of 'serious' or 'ordinary' offences. There is a simple link to the length of sanction. The Brazilian system provides an example: 'the longer the term of imprisonment available,

[23] Cf. Müller 2003, who argues that the disturbance to legal order recedes with time: '*[d]ie durch die Straftat verursachte Störung des Rechtsfriedens nimmt mit zunehmendem Zeitablauf ab*' (vor Art. 70, Rn. 34).

the longer the limitations period'.[24] Increases in the sanction for foreign bribery to meet the standard of the Convention may accordingly bring about a lengthening of the limitation period, as in the case of Norway.[25]

French criminal law treats the foreign bribery offence pursuant to the Convention as a *délit* subject to *prescription* of three years under Article 8 of the Code of Criminal Procedure. In German and Swiss law, the crime is classified as a *Verbrechen*, in Austria as a *Vergehen*. The Swiss classification was introduced directly to comply with the Convention. It placed the foreign bribery offence in a higher sanctions category and accordingly increased the limitation period.[26]

English law makes an exception to its rule of no limitation periods in the case of 'summary' offences, i.e. offences of a minor character tried in Magistrates' Courts. A six-month limitation period applies to them.[27] Bribery is, however, subject to higher penalties, so this category cannot apply to Convention cases.

Even where states have adopted special statutes for the foreign bribery offence, a specific limitation period is not often imposed: for example, the Foreign Corrupt Practices Act (FCPA) is silent on the issue.

The conclusion that most states apply the limitation periods laid down in general criminal law is important, because it indicates that the limitation period for bribery is regarded as very much part of the fabric of such law. In general, the Convention respects national criminal traditions. It does not insist on a particular form of adaptation to Convention requirements. Moreover, Article 6 is a particularly 'open' provision, not requiring a specific form of compliance.

2.2.2. Types of limitation periods: distinctions in national law

a. Limitation at different stages of criminal procedure: investigation, prosecution, and sentence

The main concern of Article 6 is with the limitation period applied to the *action public*, i.e. the state's right to commence proceedings with a view to bringing a case to trial. We call this the 'prosecution limitation period' or simply the 'statute of limitations'.

National law may also apply a limitation period to particular aspects of an *investigation* and also to the *execution of sentence*.

[24] BR-Ph1, 21. [25] NO-Ph2, 41 et seq. [26] CH-Ph2, 27, 40.
[27] S. 127 Magistrates Court Act 1980.

In German-speaking jurisdictions, the distinction is made between *Verfolgungsverjährung* and *Vollstreckungsverjährung.*[28] The Austrian Criminal Code refers to *Verjährung der Strafbarkeit* and *Verjährung der Vollstreckbarkeit.*[29] Here, the terms *Verfolgungsverjährung* and *Verjährung der Strafbarkeit* refer to prescription of the standard limitation period for commencing proceedings (prosecution limitation period), whereas *Vollstreckungsverjährung* and *Verjährung der Vollstreckbarkeit* refer to prescription of the execution of sentence.

As regards *investigation*, the period set may well be a relatively short one, to encourage charges to be brought as swiftly as possible or to allow the case to be dropped, if there is no prospect of successful prosecution.[30] Apart from the state interest at stake here, there is a strong defence interest that a case should be swiftly investigated, especially where the suspect is in custody.[31] Where national law superimposes a limitation period for investigations on the statute of limitations, the relationship between the two will be regulated. Argentine law, for example, allows the very short investigations period of four months to be extended without upper limit until the expiry of the six-year-long statute of limitations.[32]

Regarding the *execution of sentence*, here we are concerned with the time limit within which the sanction imposed may be executed. Where such periods are imposed, they are commonly longer than the limitation period and are calculated as a factor of the sentence imposed.

b. Relative and absolute limitation periods

The setting of an absolute time limit may be deemed appropriate where the prosecution limitation period is capable of interruption, in order not to allow the successive periods to run without an upper limit.[33]

[28] Cf., for example, Arts. 78 and 79 German Criminal Code and Arts. 70 and 73 Swiss Criminal Code, respectively.

[29] Arts. 57 and 59 Austrian Criminal Code, respectively.

[30] Compare for example, the Phase 1 reports on Poland, Portugal, and Slovenia and note the concerns expressed in the recent Phase 2 report in respect of Hungary, in which the WGB called for longer suspensions of a two-year time limit for investigations (HU-Ph2, 36 et seq., 61).

[31] Cf. Zander 1999, 306 et seq. on the introduction of certain time limits for prosecution in England and Wales. These limits were to some extent modelled on the Scottish '110-day rule', i.e. that the defendant must be brought to trial within 110 days of his committal for trial. Such a rule reflects the right to have one's case dealt with promptly.

[32] AR-Ph1, 16.

[33] Cf. the French system, which is noted for the possibility of repeated interruptions, but where no absolute limit exists. The Austrian, German, and Italian systems, on the other hand, apply absolute limits.

Swiss law formerly used the absolute limitation period to restrict repeated interruption.[34] Under Italian law, the limitation period for the base offence can be extended by one-half again, meaning up to seven-and-a-half years maximum ('ultimate limitation period').[35]

The basic concept here is of a composite period, including the periods of time in respect of which interruption occurs. After expiry of this period, the case may no longer be brought to trial.

c. Special period for aggravated bribery?

As we noted in our chapter concerning Article 3 of the Convention, state Parties may choose to impose a higher sanction for aggravated cases of bribery: this would be in keeping with the notion of 'proportionality'. Given the categorisation of offences in national systems, this may move the offence into a different, i.e. higher, limitation period. The WGB noted in the Phase 2 report for Norway that significant divergences in the limitation periods for the basic and aggravated offence can create anomalies.[36]

d. Different periods for natural and legal persons?

The law in Denmark[37] and Iceland[38] resulted in different statutes of limitations for natural and legal persons. This approach failed to meet Convention standards.

2.3. Suspension, interruption, and extension

An important general feature of national statutes of limitations is the provision for suspension and interruption of the limitation period owing to the occurrence of certain events. It may also be possible to extend the statute of limitations.

Suspension may, for example, occur where an offender is serving a sentence abroad or where a suspected offender has sought refuge abroad.[39] There may also be an impediment of a legal or factual nature, such as an immunity or illness of the charged person, to continuing with the prosecution, which causes time to stop running.[40] The suspension does

[34] Cf. the discussion in Schubarth 2002, 323 et seq. [35] IT-Ph2, 37.
[36] NO-Ph2, 42. [37] DK-Ph1, 17 et seq. [38] IS-Ph1, 12.
[39] For Japanese law on this point cf. JP-Ph1, 16. Note also the UN instruments referred to in II.1. above.
[40] Cf. the examples given in Jescheck and Weigend 1996, 914.

not affect the time which has already passed; the latter is aggregated with the period which recommences after the suspension has lapsed.[41]

A limitations period may be *interrupted* by the commencement of proceedings (prosecution) or by the preliminary enquiry by the *juge d'instruction*. The precise circumstances are laid down by statute or Code; for example, Article 78c of the German Criminal Code lays down no fewer than eleven possible steps in the criminal procedure having the effect of *Unterbrechung* of the limitation period. After each interruption, a new limitations period will begin to run.[42] Article 160 of the Italian Criminal Code contains similar provisions indicating interruption when various acts are taken in the pre-trial stage and also when the judgment or decree of conviction is made.[43]

French law appears to offer the most extensive possibilities for interruption. This has engendered criticism that the principle of *prescription* contained in the Code of Criminal Procedure is being undermined in practice.[44] Swiss law, on the other hand, has recently abandoned completely the concepts of suspension and interruption, preferring to lengthen the overall statute of limitations. The Swiss reform seeks to rid the system of the many complexities associated with absolute and relative limitation periods.[45]

The third concept to be discussed is *extension*. Extensions would appear to be granted by all the state Parties concerned in respect of their investigation limitation periods, though it involves the exercise of judicial discretion.[46] To extend the statute of limitations is on the other hand more difficult, in principle, so states tend to 'extend' by suspension. On the other hand, some state Parties, including Chile and Mexico, provide extensions of time for certain maximum periods, rather than suspension, to cover the case of wanted persons being absent abroad.[47]

In the United States, extension of the statute of limitations is well known, being justified by the particular complexities of foreign bribery cases.

[41] Cf. for the discussion of French law Larguier 1999, 83.

[42] Cf. Tröndle and Fischer 2004: '*Unterbrechung der Verjährung bedeutet im Gegensatz zum bloßen Ruhen...die Beseitigung des schon abgelaufenen Teils einer noch laufenden Verjährungsfrist durch bestimmte Prozesshandlungen...mit der Wirkung, daß die Frist von neuem voll zu laufen beginnt*' (§ 78c, Rn. 2).

[43] IT-Ph1, 21.

[44] Cf. the discussion of case law giving the grounds of interruption an extensive interpretation in Stefani, Levasseur, and Bouloc 2000, 160 et seq.

[45] They had to be continually recalculated in the light of the many suspension or interruption possibilities (cf. Schubarth 2002, 338).

[46] Poland (PL-Ph1, 22). [47] CL-Ph1, 18 and MX-Ph1, 14.

The standard five-year period can be extended for up to three years on request by the prosecution, where there is a finding by a court that more time is needed to gather foreign evidence.[48] In the Phase 2 report for the United States and in the recent follow-up report, this 'regular' extension is used as an argument to counter the WGB's suspicion that the limitation period is too short. The US authorities claim that the prosecutor's request for an extension, which is automatic for FCPA cases involving foreign evidence, will invariably be approved by the judge.[49]

2.4. The beginning and end of the limitation period

Limitation begins in most systems with the date of commission of the offence.[50] This may be defined somewhat differently from system to system.

There seems, currently, to be some doubt in the French system concerning when exactly the statute of limitations for certain economic offences begins. For bribery cases, however, the courts have ruled that the offence of corruption is renewed each time the 'bribe pact' is repeated.[51]

German legislative provisions refer to the 'ending' of the offence but the High Court (*Bundesgerichtshof*) has explained that this means the point when the offender 'has finally completed his illegal behaviour'.[52] Bribery is therefore completed when the promise, offer, or act of giving the bribe is done.[53]

Luxembourg law provides for three possible triggering events.[54]

Regarding the end of limitation, most national systems provide that it is concluded with a binding judgment of the court, with the specification that this means the date on which the judgment actually takes legal effect.[55]

[48] US-Ph1, 16. But note the recent decision of the US Court of Appeals for the Third Circuit that the Government application must be made before the foreign evidence is received; an extension may not be granted simply to give the authorities more time to sift that evidence: *U.S.* v. *Atiyeh*, 402 F.3d 354 (3rd Cir. 2005).

[49] US-Ph2, 29 and note US-Ph2 follow-up report, 13.

[50] Italian law is typical in this respect: cf. IT-Ph1, 13.

[51] The Phase 1 report for France explains that 'the triggering of the statute of limitation is moved forward from the day the bribery agreement was concluded to the day of the final payment or the day of the last receipt of the advantage that was promised' (FR-Ph1, 22). Cf. also FR-Ph2, 38.

[52] BGH 5 StR 489/02, judgment of 18 June 2003.

[53] Cf. again from the German law perspective Stree and Sternberg-Lieben 2001: '*Hingabe des Vorteils*' (§ 78a, Rn. 2).

[54] The dates when the corruption pact is concluded; when the last bribe is given; when the act is performed by the foreign public official (LU-Ph1, 18).

[55] Cf., for example, Jescheck and Weigend 1996, 914: limitation ceases on the issuing of a judgment by a court of first instance.

The danger of abuse of limitation periods was evident in the former version of Swiss law, under which it was possible for the defendant or his lawyer to spin out appeal proceedings in the hope of exhausting the absolute limitation period during the appeal. This is no longer possible; the new law stipulates that the period ends with the decision of the first instance court.[56]

III. The Article 6 standard: limitation in foreign bribery cases

1. Comparative analysis: developing the Convention criteria

Given the specificity and diversity of national rules, it would have been futile for the drafters of the Convention to insist on a single common statute of limitations. The overriding consideration of Article 6 is to ensure that, whatever means they choose, state Parties give their investigative and prosecuting authorities sufficient – 'adequate' – time to prove commission of the offence. The WGB is guided in its work of evaluation of national laws by this overriding consideration.

The WGB, of course, applies the principle of 'functional equivalence' so central to the Convention. This means that it does not itself apply a single standard of 'adequacy' but looks at national law in context, taking into account in particular the general conditions of enforcement of national criminal law and the overall coherence of national systems.

In its Phase 1 reports on state Parties' legislative compliance with Article 6, the WGB generally limited itself to noting the length of limitation periods. Where it had doubts as to their adequacy, for example in the case of France, it usually observed only that 'this matter [i.e. the shortness of the statute of limitations] constitutes a *general problem* calling for a comparative analysis of the legal situation in Member countries with a view to ensuring *the coherent and effective implementation of the Convention.*'[57]

Apart from France, Denmark, Hungary, Iceland, Japan, Norway, and Slovakia also found their statute of limitations questioned in Phase 1 evaluations, albeit to different degrees.

Danish law's two-year period for legal persons was criticised outright by the WGB as being 'too short'.[58]

[56] Pieth 1996, 57 et seq.; Schubarth 2002, 327.
[57] The emphasis in italics has been added. [58] DK-Ph1, 27.

In the Hungarian case, the view was taken that 'the three-year limitation period could be short'.[59] By the time of the Phase 1bis evaluation, it was extended to five years for the offence of inducement to breach duties; a three-year period remains for the offence of promising or giving an undue favour to a foreign official person in connection with his/her functions.[60]

The Phase 1 investigation of Iceland established that the limitation period for legal persons was only two years: the WGB 'expressed concern' about this and the period was subsequently increased to five years.[61]

Regarding Japan's three-year period, the WGB expressed only the view that the matter merited further consideration, again in the light of the need to ensure 'the consistent and effective application of the Convention'.[62]

In the case of Norway, the WGB made very clear that the two-year limitation period was not adequate.[63]

Most recently, in the case of the Phase 1 evaluation of the Slovak Republic, a three-year limitation period (applicable to non-aggravated bribery cases) caused the WGB concern; it recommended to Slovakia that it consider extending it – this was duly done.[64]

In the case of the Phase 1 evaluation of Germany, a five-year statute of limitations allied to a ten-year absolute limitation was regarded as adequate but still raised 'a general issue for a comparative analysis of the legal situation in member states'.[65] In its Phase 1 evaluation of Italy, the WGB did not comment adversely on the country's basic limitation period of five years but the Phase 2 evaluation found the country's overall scheme wanting, as we shall see in the next section.[66]

As for the United States, the five-year period was called into question in a general way, referring to the need to take the matter up again 'at a later stage'.[67]

Thus we see that in the Phase 1 evaluations the WGB was reluctant to take a clear or final position on a Convention standard, except in the case of the very short two-year periods. It lacked the full information at that stage to reach a decision on a standard. It is only in the Phase 2 investigations that the WGB enters into a fuller analysis of the working of state Parties' anti-bribery legislation in practice. In Phase 2 it is concerned

[59] HU-Ph1, 22.

[60] HU-$Ph1^{bis}$, 13 et seq. We will see in III.2. below that a stronger line was taken by the WGB in the Phase 2 evaluation.

[61] IS-Ph1, 20. [62] JP-Ph1, 29. [63] NO-Ph1, 9, 15.

[64] SK-Ph1, 24 [65] DE-Ph1, 19. [66] IT-Ph1, 21. [67] US-Ph1, 22.

not only with the particular rules on bribery crimes but also with the general operation of their criminal justice systems. The next section will review the WGB's Phase 2 evaluation reports, in order to determine whether a clearer standard has now emerged.

2. Limitation periods in practice: applying a Convention standard

2.1. An 'adequate' statute of limitations: holistic approach

The WGB has used the Phase 2 evaluation process to elaborate a reasonably clear standard relating to the statute of limitations.[68] Its approach is based upon its conviction that the Article 6 'adequacy' criterion must be applied in the light of the particular circumstances of enforcement and criminal proceedings in each jurisdiction but also according to the demands of the principle of functional equivalence.

The WGB's starting point is that tackling and proving foreign bribery is very complex, frequently involving the obtaining of evidence located abroad. The complexity of the investigations calls for a longer rather than a shorter period, both to investigate and to try the case. Moreover, 'due to the secretive nature of acts of corruption, they are often not detected until several years after having been committed'.[69]

A particular limitation period deemed to be satisfactory for one state Party may not necessarily satisfy the Convention standard when applied by another state, depending how efficiently and effectively the overall system of criminal proceedings functions in the latter.

The position taken by the WGB on equivalence between systems is well illustrated by the case of Italy, whose five-year limitation period for the basic offence (ten years for aggravated cases) was looked at in conjunction with the much more limited deadline of six months to complete an investigation (this could, however, be extended to twenty-four months maximum). As we have seen, the limitation period for the base offence can be extended by one-half again, meaning up to seven-and-a-half years

[68] Our concern in this section is not with the limitation period in respect of investigations or execution of sentence. Recent Phase 2 reports have, however, also emphasised the importance of providing for sufficiently long limitation periods in respect of investigations, where state Parties distinguish between the two sets of rules (HU-Ph2, 36 et seq., 61). Regarding limitation periods in respect of execution of sentence, the WGB requires that the sentence or sanction should take account of absences of the sentenced person from the jurisdiction: suspension would be appropriate in such a case (IS-Ph2, 30).

[69] DK-Ph1, 27.

maximum. Taking an overall view, the WGB finds that, while the length of these periods 'are *prima facie* unremarkable when compared to those in other jurisdictions', the 'lengthy delays in Italian criminal proceedings' mean that the limitation periods may expire before proceedings can be commenced.

The WGB formally recommended to Italy that it increase its ultimate limitation period.[70] As justification for this approach, it pointed to substantial and well-documented evidence of delays in the Italian system of justice which have their roots in 'complex investigations, lengthy trials, an overburdened judiciary and prosecutor's office, and too many cases in the system'.[71] The difficulties of gathering evidence in foreign bribery investigations only exacerbated these endemic problems. Similar deficits were identified in the recent Phase 2 report concerning Greece, which also applies a five-year limit. The Greek authorities were duly urged to ensure that lengthy delays do not result in expiry of limitation periods.[72]

A more nuanced critique of a five-year limitation period is evident in the 2005 Phase 2 report on Belgian law and practice. This merely calls upon the Belgian authorities to set criminal policy priorities and ensure sufficient means are available to stop the time-bar from intervening in cases.[73] Other countries applying the five-year period include Korea[74] and the United States.[75] In both cases, the WGB politely raises the question of adequacy – in the United States, the extension period of up to three years comes automatically into play in foreign bribery cases.[76]

Given its questioning of the five-year statute of limitations, it is not surprising that the WGB takes countries applying lower limitation periods more squarely to task. The French three-year limit is deemed inadequate. French law does not, in the view of the WGB, meet the standard required by the Convention: the three-year statute of limitations does 'not allow a reasonable period of time for investigation and prosecution, and may therefore prejudice the effective implementation of the law'.[77] The French authorities have come in for strong criticism from the WGB for sticking to their three-year limit, in the face of many calls from within the country for reform.[78]

[70] IT-Ph2, 36 et seq., 52. [71] IT-Ph2, 37. [72] GR-Ph1, 33 et seq., 45. [73] BE-Ph2, 26.

[74] KR-Ph2, 34, 46, where the WGB throws doubt on its adequacy and calls for follow-up.

[75] Cf. most recently US-Ph2 follow-up, 4, 13.

[76] See discussion in II.2.3. above. [77] FR-Ph2, 39.

[78] Most of the French prosecutors, magistrates, and other non-governmental representatives interviewed by the WGB's members concluded that the current statute of limitations was a 'serious obstacle' to prosecutions: FR-Ph2, 38.

In its recommendation to France to amend its law by extending the period for *prescription*, the WGB was, however, careful not itself to specify what the new period should be.[79] It mentions some earlier proposals for extension which would have raised the period to five, six, or even ten years.[80] The WGB has also condemned the three-year limitation periods applying in Hungary[81] and Japan.[82] As in the French case, the WGB indicates that a three-year statute of limitation is inadequate.

The continuing Phase 2 evaluation process thus signals that a three-year period is highly problematic and falls below the Convention standard. The WGB had already decided in its Phase 1 evaluations that a two-year statute of limitations was inadequate.[83] Moreover, a five-year period will not be sufficient, if the legal system is hamstrung by delays.

The recent US Phase 2 follow-up suggests that a five-year period, with provision for automatic extension for up to three years, will be sufficient.[84] The US case may, however, be a special one. Given its highly-trained and motivated corps of prosecutors, and extensive FCPA practice, the US legal system is equipped to work within these time limits in a way other countries applying a similar time-bar but with less experience of foreign bribery cases are probably not.

The Convention's *minimum standard* therefore seems to have been set at around five years. The clear preference of the WGB would be for a substantially longer period. One may note in this context the praise recently heaped on Switzerland for its adoption of a fifteen-year period.[85]

The WGB's analysis in both Phase 1 and Phase 2 reports is handicapped by insufficient statistical information concerning the effect of limitation periods on the handling and resolution of cases.[86] The WGB often lacks the information necessary for a fully reasoned interpretation. How does it really know whether a three-year or five-year period is going to be sufficient to allow a foreign bribery case to be properly investigated and brought to trial? In the case of Germany, the WGB concluded that it was unable, in the absence of sufficient statistical information, to say whether five years would be sufficient.[87] It pledged to follow up German practice to eke out the truth

[79] Rec. 9 refers only to the 'need to extend to an *appropriate* period the statute of limitations so as to ensure the effective prosecution of the offence and to facilitate responses to requests for extradition' (emphasis added): cf. FR-Ph2, 59.
[80] FR-Ph2, 38.
[81] HU-Ph2, 35 et seq. and note recommendation for an extension: 61.
[82] JP-Ph2, 55 et seq., 60 (recommendation).
[83] As applied by Denmark and Iceland (for legal persons) and by Norway (across the board).
[84] US-Ph2 follow-up, 4, 13. [85] CH-Ph2, 27. [86] Cf., for example, DE-Ph2, 43.
[87] DE-Ph2, 43.

and will have to do the same for all those countries about which it has expressed doubts during their Phase 2 evaluation.

The WGB does, however, make major efforts to garner evidence from those directly concerned 'at the coal face' of investigation and prosecution of the foreign bribery offence. They are often the best source of information and can convince the WGB that the period in question represents a real and serious obstacle to enforcement of the Convention and therefore falls short of the Convention standard. The WGB also seems to have developed its own 'gut feeling' for what is adequate, having now reviewed application of the Convention over a very wide range of countries and jurisdictions (including all the major OECD exporting countries). The gut feeling is that five years is the minimum time needed but will frequently not be enough to bring a case successfully to trial.

2.2. Assessing the coherence of national rules

In addition to its emphasis upon the need for effective rules on the statute of limitations and investigative periods, the WGB also refers to the requirement of 'coherence' or 'consistency'.[88] The evaluation reports do not make it terribly clear what this is supposed to mean but we may draw a few conclusions, partly by reading between the lines.

It is implicit in a consistent approach to economic crime in general that foreign bribery offences should not be treated radically differently from other types of economic crime, where limitation periods are concerned. In the case of France, the WGB noted critically that it had become common for prosecutors to charge what is really a bribery case as a different crime, namely 'misuse of corporate assets', in order to take advantage of the fact that the limitation period for that offence does not begin until actual discovery of the offence.[89] A wider debate is taking place in France on the question of limitation periods for financial offences. This debate has been prompted by the lack of legal clarity concerning commencement of limitation periods, following certain developments in the case law.[90]

The recent reform of Swiss law shows a common approach to limitation periods in respect of bribery and money laundering offences.[91] It is clear that this type of development is welcomed by the WGB. The Working Group is wont to emphasise the complexity of investigating economic crime

[88] FR-Ph1, 31; JP-Ph1, 29. [89] FR-Ph1, 22, 31; FR-Ph2, 7, 38.
[90] See the WGB reports on France (see previous note 89) and II.2.4. above.
[91] CH-Ph2, 27.

in general; foreign bribery investigations are clearly part of this general context. Although, therefore, it has not drawn a clear line between the foreign bribery offence and other economic offences with regard to limitation periods, in the way it has done for sanctions, the WGB would obviously favour a common approach in this respect – at a higher rather than lower level. A Convention standard of rough equivalence between bribery and fraud, or bribery and money laundering would, moreover, be consistent with national trends.[92]

More clearly, the Convention requires limitation to apply in an equal way to natural and legal persons. The divergences found in the laws of Denmark[93] and Iceland[94] were roundly criticised by the Working Group. Iceland has since equalised the periods.[95]

In the case of Finland, the WGB criticised the five-year difference between the limitation periods for ordinary or basic bribery (five years) and the aggravated form (ten years).[96] It called for follow-up on this matter. Similar concerns were voiced in respect of Norway.[97]

2.3. Provision for suspension, interruption, and extension

There is considerable diversity among national rules relating to suspension, interruption, and extension.[98] The Convention does not demand a harmonised approach. The comments and recommendations of the WGB focus on the need to ensure that, whatever rules are adopted, they serve the goals of effectiveness and consistency.

States are clearly free to choose not to apply rules on suspension and interruption at all, as under Swiss law,[99] if they wish. If rules of this kind *are* adopted, they should take into account the difficulty the prosecution often faces in obtaining evidence located abroad. Where the statute of limitations is rather short, it should be capable of suspension or extension, in order to overcome this difficulty. The WGB made this point in its reports on Italy[100] (which does not provide for such extension) and the United States (which does).[101]

Another matter which should be taken into account by national rules is the possibility that the suspect or defendant may abscond to or simply

[92] See previous note 91.
[93] DK-Ph1, 27 (two-year statute for legal persons: five years for natural persons).
[94] Iceland applied similar rules to Denmark: IS-Ph2, 20.
[95] IS-Ph2, 20 (it increased the period for legal persons to five years following the Phase 1 report).
[96] FI-Ph2, 16. [97] NO-Ph2, 42. [98] See II.2.3. above.
[99] Schubarth 2002, 330 et seq.; CH-Ph2, 27. [100] IT-Ph2, 36. [101] US-Ph2, 29.

be located in another country. Article 29 of the UN Convention Against Corruption calls for suspension or extension in such circumstances; one can assume that this is also part of the OECD Convention standard.[102]

Regarding periods of interruption, some concern has been expressed about Norwegian law which may contain a loophole resulting in a time bar in respect of undertakings when individual responsibility cannot be determined.[103]

Finally, the Working Group is sceptical about the argument that generous provision for suspension, interruption, and extension can compensate for the lack of a sufficiently long basic statute of limitations. The French argument to this effect has fallen on deaf ears. A three-year period such as the French one is so short that it acts as a deterrent even to commencing criminal proceedings in the first place.[104]

3. Limitation periods as a real obstacle in foreign bribery cases?

Article 6 of the Convention addresses only one of the many hindrances to effective enforcement of anti-bribery legislation. It may not be the most important. The shortness of the limitation period in some jurisdictions is nevertheless regarded as a 'serious obstacle' to prosecutions.[105] Several state Parties have lengthened and/or simplified their statute of limitations on the heels of the WGB's evaluation reports. These legislative steps should be followed up by more practical measures. Article 6, if implemented correctly, can ensure that time is not their implacable enemy, but what over-stretched police and prosecutors need most to combat foreign bribery effectively is better organisation and more resources.[106]

References

For documentation see the consolidated bibliography at the end of this book.

Delmas-Marty, M. (ed.) (1997), *Corpus Juris: Introducing Penal Provisions for the Purpose of the Financial Interests of the European Union*, Paris.

[102] Cf. IS-Ph2, 30. [103] NO-Ph2, 42 et seq.

[104] Cf. FR-Ph1, 22 for a statement of the argument; in FR-Ph2, 38 et seq., 59 the WGB emphasises that only an extension of the basic period will do.

[105] Notably France (FR-Ph2, 38).

[106] Cf. the recent Phase 2 report in respect of Belgium: there, a lack of resources is said to combine with a five-year limitation period to jeopardise prosecutions (BE-Ph2, 26).

Delmas-Marty, M. and J. A. E. Vervaele (eds.) (2000), *The Implementation of Corpus Juris in the Member States*, Vol. **1**, Antwerp, Groningen, Oxford.

Janis, M., R. Kay, and A. Bradley (2000), *European Human Rights Law: Text and Materials*, 2nd edn, Oxford.

Jescheck, H.-H. and T. Weigend (1996), *Lehrbuch des Strafrechts: Allgemeiner Teil*, 5th edn, Berlin.

Larguier, J. (1999), *Procédure pénale*, 17th edn, Paris.

McAdams, A. J. (2001), *Judging the Past in Unified Germany*, Cambridge.

Müller, P. (2003), commentary *vor Art.* 70 in M. A. Niggli and H. Wiprächtiger (Hrsg.), *Basler Kommentar zum Strafgesetzbuch I, Art. 1–110 StGB*, Basel, Genf, München, 1021.

Pieth, M. (1996), 'Die verjährungsrechtliche Einheit gemäss Art. 71 Abs. 2 StGB bei Bestechungsdelikten', *Basler Juristische Mitteilungen*, 57.

Schubarth, M. (2002), 'Das neue Recht der strafrechtlichen Verjährung', *Schweizerische Zeitschrift für Strafrecht* **120**, 321.

Stefani, G., G. Levasseur and B. Bouloc (2000), *Procédure pénale*, 17th edn, Paris.

Stree, W. and D. Sternberg-Lieben (2001), commentary of §§ 78–79 in A. Schönke and H. Schröder (Hrsg.), *Strafgesetzbuch Kommentar*, 26th edn, Munich.

Tröndle, H. and T. Fischer (2004), *Strafgesetzbuch und Nebengesetze*, 52nd edn, Munich.

Zander, M. (1999), *Cases and Materials on the English Legal System*, 8th edn, London.

Article 7. Money Laundering

MARK PIETH

Article 7 – Money Laundering

Each Party which has made bribery of its own public official a predicate offence for the purpose of the application of its money laundering legislation shall do so on the same terms for the bribery of a foreign public official, without regard to the place where the bribery occurred.

Official Commentary

28. In Article 7, 'bribery of its own public official' is intended broadly, so that bribery of a foreign public official is to be made a predicate offence for money laundering legislation on the same terms, when a Party has made either active or passive bribery of its own public official such an offence. When a Party has made only passive bribery of its own public officials a predicate offence for money laundering purposes, this article requires that the laundering of the bribe payment be subject to money laundering legislation.

Chapter contents

I. Introduction

Over the last fifteen years the international community has made considerable progress in developing instruments to reduce corruption. The policy changes by the large multilateral money lenders,[1] the new Recommendations, Resolutions, and Conventions of International Organisations[2] as well as the codes of conduct of the private sector[3] and the work done by Non Government Organisations (NGOs),[4] the media and other representatives of the civil society have raised the issue of corruption to the top of the political agenda around the world.[5]

[1] Cf. the new Anti-Corruption Policies of the World Bank and amongst the regional development banks, especially the Asian Development Bank (ADB).
[2] Organisation of American States (OAS) 1996; European Union (EU) 1995b; EU 1996b; EU 1997b; EU 1997a; EU 1998b; Council of Europe (COE) 1997; COE 1999a; COE 1999b; Organisation for Economic Co-operation and Development (OECD) 1997a; OECD 1997b; United Nations (UN) 2003.
[3] International Chamber of Commerce (ICC) 2005.
[4] In particular the specialised NGO Transparency International (TI).
[5] Cf. the G-7 meeting on 22 January 2000, focusing on international financial reform as one of its topics. Under the heading of international efforts to fight financial crime the work of the Financial Action Task Force (FATF) to identify 'non-cooperative jurisdictions' and the OECD initiatives on bribery have received special attention.

So far, the focus has primarily been on the actual acts of bribery, be it the offering or the receiving end. Little attention has been given, however, to the financial flows relating to corruption.

In matters of 'petty-corruption' the bribes are paid in cash. This is still the most common form of bribery and its endemic character in some regions of the world is particularly dangerous to the social fabric. However, 'grand corruption',[6] the specific area of interest of the OECD instruments against transnational commercial bribery, frequently depends upon wire transfer and the use of financial institutions in general. In many instances, such institutions will not be based in the country of the recipient, nor even in the home country of the briber. Focusing on the money management in bribery shifts attention away from the supply- and demand-side of bribery to a third dimension, the intermediaries and financial centres, especially the so-called 'Off-Shore Financial Centres' (OFCs) and the specific services they have to offer, i.e. the rapid and cheap incorporation of domiciliary companies ('International Business Corporations' (IBCs)).

The role of OFCs and IBCs in money laundering has been addressed in a multitude of international fora and in a variety of contexts, along with related issues such as bank secrecy. We will discuss these issues in part II. of this chapter.

In part III. we will provide a brief overview of the most recent initiatives of the UN, the FATF, the OECD, the COE, and the EU as well as private sector initiatives.

Part IV. will examine how the OECD is adding its voice to this international chorus. At the time of adoption of the Convention in December 1997 some issues requiring further study were deliberately left open. The Council[7] decided to give the Working Group on Bribery (WGB) the mandate to examine further action on five specific issues: the bribery of party officials, parties, and candidates, the use of foreign subsidiaries and of Off-Shore Centres for bribery and the topic of money-laundering.

The WGB debated the issue of corruption-related money laundering (hereafter 'corruption-money laundering') in two seminars held briefly after the adoption of the Convention.[8] It acknowledged that the money management of corruption could become crucial for the success or failure of the OECD initiative. Private sector actors have repeatedly warned that rogue market participants would be induced by the tougher standards applying on the territory of the state Parties to the Convention to go 'off-shore' and bribe

[6] Moody-Stuart 1997, 2. [7] OECD 1997c.

[8] On 11 February 1999 (prosecutors' meeting) and on 29 February 2000 (cf. DAFFE/IME/BR/WD(2000)4).

from financial centres outside the reach of OECD instruments, as long as these places were not subject to similar standards.

II. Money flows related to corruption

The OECD has always addressed the management of corruption related to money flows under the headings of money laundering, book-keeping offences, and the misuse of OFCs. In the OECD's evaluation hearings prosecutors repeat over and over again that 'grand corruption' should be analysed in its typical chronological stages:

Grand corruption typically requires the creation of 'slush funds' (invariably held outside the briber's and the bribee's country of domicile). In a second stage the actual bribe payment is effected and in a third the bribe and possibly also the profits of bribery are laundered. If this is merely a model, it is based on experience.[9]

It has been recognised that OFCs play a key role when seeking to obscure transactions. It should, however, be noted that many of the techniques applied are also available in the large financial centres of the OECD area. In order to prevent financial institutions being used to prepare and execute corrupt payments, it would, therefore, be more efficient to concentrate on the specific measures needed to impede access to regulated financial centres rather than to focus exclusively on OFCs and on the sanctioning of the non-cooperative countries and territories.

1. The creation of 'slush funds'

The term 'slush fund' (*fondi neri, caisses noires, schwarze Kassen*) is used in different contexts: in taxation law it is used for undeclared funds, and in book-keeping law it is used for 'off the books' assets or at least for funds eluding consolidated book-keeping. The word 'slush fund' does not automatically connote illegal activities, even if in many cases criminal techniques will be applied to obscure these 'informal reserves' (false book-keeping, forged documentation or even fraud and embezzlement).[10]

In practice, the size and the structure of such funds will diverge substantially. In an Italian case courts heard evidence of a *caisse de guerre* of several hundreds of billions of Lire.[11] And this is certainly not the only known case of

[9] Note the oral comments of Messrs. Colombo and Greco at the OECD hearing in February 1996; cf. also Bernasconi 1995, 5.

[10] See ch. on Article 8 below.

[11] *SEC* v. *Montedison, S.p.A.* Civil Action No. 1: 96CV02631 (RWR) (D.D.C.), Litigation Release No. 16948/March 30, 2001; Trepp 1996, 201.

such dimensions. These funds usually serve multiple purposes. They allow the management to act outside the company controls, since they can effectively disguise the financial performance of a company. They could also be used to exert illegal political influence or to bribe for the purpose of obtaining business deals.

Some methods for creating 'slush funds' have been described by Jermyn Brooks in his expert opinion to the OECD WGB in 1996:

> 'Members of the senior management team of a company establish a bank account, usually outside the jurisdiction in which the company operates. The bank account is maintained in the name of an off-shore company which is beneficially owned by the members of the management team in question. . .Arrangements are made for the company to make payments to the bank account of the off-shore company and documentation is prepared to 'support' the payments made, usually in the form of invoices for consultancy or similar services, the purported nature of which usually enables the amounts involved to be deducted for tax purposes.'
>
> 'Arrangements are made by the senior management of a company for one of its customers to remit moneys to an off-shore bank account which is controlled by senior management and from which corrupt payments are made.'
>
> 'Company moneys are deposited overtly in an off-shore bank account maintained in the company's name supposedly for reasons of tax efficiency. The amount of the deposit is included among the company's assets as reported on its balance sheet which makes this method attractive to managements seeking artificially to maintain earning and net assets. Covertly, the asset is used to secure borrowings, usually from another bank, the proceeds of which are used to make corrupt payments.'[12]

These methods to create 'slush funds' are quite well known.[13]

Another classical approach would involve transfer-pricing. This would function as follows:

> A company belonging to the 'slush fund'-structure overcharges its 'mother' or a 'legitimate sister' for goods or services delivered, possibly including the raw materials of a product sold with the help of bribes.[14] Current practice is to bill the legitimate company for fictitious services like advertising campaigns, market studies, expert opinions, consulting[15] or the notorious commissions to fictitious intermediaries.

A more 'elegant' method would involve imagined or pre-arranged financial operations without ulterior economic reason between captive corporations, leading to a loss for the legitimate company and a gain for the underground partner.[16] A further variation observed has been to request payments for goods

[12] Pieth and Eigen 1999, 393 et seq.

[13] Service Central de Prévention de la Corruption, Rapport Annuel 1995, 44 et seq. and 1996, 99 et seq.

[14] Cf. Trepp 1996, 53 et seq. on the *Cronassial* case.

[15] *U.S.* v. *Goodyear International Corp.*, (Cr. No. 89-0156), D.D.C., May 11, 1989.

[16] See note 11.

and services to an off-shore account and to book a loss or a fictitious rebate on the official books of the parent company.

2. Laundering structures

Whereas in the creation of 'slush-funds' legally obtained funds are usually diverted from the regular books, the laundering of bribes and proceeds pursues a dual goal:

The initial objective is to interrupt the link with the illegal origin of the funds. This part of the operation implies the creation of a smoke screen by using financial services. In the classic terminology of law enforcement authorities dealing with drug-money laundering these are the so-called 'placement' and 'layering' stages.[17]

In the next phase the funds receive a credible 'legend' as seemingly legally obtained in order to allow them to surface into the visible economy. Careful money launderers would, of course, declare these funds to tax authorities when integrated into the legal economy ('integration phase'). They might, alternatively, be recycled into hidden structures, to be used for further bribery, or – in the case of the bribee – to pay off accomplices or other officials, party members, etc.

Until recently, relatively little was known about the micro-mechanisms of corruption-money laundering.[18] On the basis of some investigated cases we may now assume that large-scale corruption follows the established methods of structuring financial operations applied to tax fraud or drug-based money laundering.

A classic structure requires a professional 'organiser'. Frequently, he will be a fiduciary, a banker,[19] or ideally an attorney[20] operating from a large financial centre of an OFC. Although the client – attorney privilege would in most countries not withstand criminal investigation, if the attorney acted merely as financial intermediary, the legal difficulties created in clarifying the situation would suffice to impede law enforcement substantially. Organisers would regularly use IBCs and open bank accounts for them, preferably in under-regulated banking centres with little inclination to accord mutual legal assistance. Sometimes launderers also resort to the use of 'stooges' or even

[17] Department of the Treasury, US Custom Service, Typology of Money Laundering, Washington D.C., 6–8 October 1989 (FATF I, Sub-Group Money Laundering Techniques); cf. also Pieth 1992, 13.
[18] Stanley Morris at the Limassol Conference of the COE, October 1999.
[19] Cf. the *S. Holding* case in: Trepp 1996, 142 et seq.
[20] *U.S.* v. *Steindler*, Dotan, King (Cr. No. 1: 94-29), S.D. Ohio (Indictment of) March 17, 1994.

non-existent 'ghost companies', even though this method can add to the risks of detection.

IBCs belong to the typical services offered by an OFC. Non-residents are allowed to incorporate companies not conducting business where they are registered rapidly and cheaply. Registration requirements are light; registers rarely – if at all – indicate the genuine beneficial owner of the company. Under the internationally agreed standards to prevent money laundering the beneficial owners of funds, including IBCs, have to be identified when entering into a business relation with financial institutions ('know your customers' policy).[21]

Opening an account for an IBC or a series of IBCs with a banking institute in an under-regulated OFC offers additional discretion.[22] Bank secrecy is not necessarily an impediment to law enforcement.[23] Bank secrecy may, however, contribute considerably to fending off access to information and assets, where it is not accompanied by strict identification and due diligence procedure; it may be invoked to block a mutual legal assistance request.

These observations bring us back to the conclusions of the OECD WGB's ad-hoc meeting of February 1999: at that time these conclusions suggested three areas which required further examination, both in law and practice:

- the level of regulation of financial centres, in particular regarding customer due diligence;
- the adequacy of company law requirements; and
- the efficiency of administrative and judicial international co-operation.

III. International instruments against money laundering

1. Inventing a new paradigm

The opening of markets and the increasing pace of economic globalisation in the late 1980s offered new opportunities to 'crime entrepreneurs'. The burgeoning drug trade allowed for a massive accumulation of illegally obtained capital, threatening, in the eyes of many, to destabilise legitimate economies. Strenuous efforts were undertaken by the world community to further restrict illicit trafficking in drugs. Building on the UN Convention Against Illicit Traffic in Narcotic Drugs and Psychotropic Substances,[24]

[21] OECD 2001a. [22] See the case mentioned in note 11.
[23] Cf. the *Pemex* case, Swiss Federal Court Decisions BGE 110 Ib 173 et seq., 115 Ib 517 et seq.; cf. also Pieth and Aiolfi 2004, 424.
[24] Art. 3 UN 1988.

the G-7 created a task force with the objective of developing a new strategy against organised crime. Its focus was on identifying the paper trail of money flows in order to seize and confiscate ill-gotten gains systematically. Those helping to conceal the funds were also to face criminal penalties.

The advent of this criminal law concept of money laundering was paralleled on the regulatory side by new standards relating to 'customer due diligence'. These standards were rooted in traditional risk concerns such as the prevention of cumulative risks and other forms of exposure.

The fear of rampant organised crime was used, in particular, to upgrade the 'know your customer' rules. Introduced internationally by the Cooke Committee of the Bank for International Settlements (BIS) in the 1989 'Basel Statement of Principles',[25] together with the Vienna Convention on Drugs, they formed the basis for the so-called '40 Recommendations' with which the FATF set the tune for the following decade and more. The FATF deliberately made use of 'soft law' in order to develop its standards as quickly as possible. As early as 1990 the text was translated into binding law by regional organisations[26] and FATF member states. Then the FATF rapidly further intensified political pressure by developing a peer evaluation process.

2. Broadening the scope

Shortly after the first standards were enacted, suggestions were made by various fora to extend the predicate offence beyond drug trafficking to other activities typically associated with organised crime. Later they extended the reach to still other forms of serious crime, including 'graft' (the abuse of power, embezzlement of public funds and corruption). In 1996, when the FATF revised its Recommendations for the first time, the predicate offence was extended to 'serious offences'. It was, however, left to FATF member governments to define what they considered 'serious'.[27] Only in 2003, in the aftermath of 9/11, when the FATF Recommendations were overhauled once more, did the FATF demand unambiguously that 'countries should apply the crime of money laundering to all serious offences, with a view to including the widest range of predicate offences'.[28] The FATF Glossary, appended to the Recommendations, adds the additional qualification that 'designated categories of offences' include 'corruption and bribery'.[29]

Concurrently, the FATF and other organisations developing anti-money laundering rules, such as the COE and the EU, gradually extended the reach of

[25] Basel Statement of Principles, 12 December 1988. [26] COE 1990.
[27] Rec. 4 FATF 40/1996. [28] Rec. 1 FATF 40/2003. [29] FATF 2003: Glossary, 12.

the regulatory rules beyond banks to other financial institutions and further so-called 'gate keepers': first, fiduciaries, foreign exchange dealers, casinos and insurers were included.[30] At a later stage the FATF went so far as to include some non-financial businesses considered at risk, including real estate agents, dealers in precious metals and stones, lawyers and notaries.[31]

3. 'Spreading the Gospel'

In a next step the anti-money laundering community began to spread its geographic reach by, first, embracing all OECD countries, the Gulf Cooperation Council and Singapore and, later, by creating regional satellites (e.g. CFATF, MENAFATF).[32] Finally, the countries unwilling to adopt corresponding rules were coerced by a blacklisting system, which bracketed them as 'non-cooperative territories and countries'.[33]

4. Attempts to redefine the topic

A closer examination of the materials reveals that from the outset anti-money laundering initiatives were not exclusively directed at combating criminal behaviour. Historical evidence shows that the US administration attempted, from the first FATF negotiation round of 1989 onwards, to enhance the ability of the central bankers worldwide to produce meaningful aggregate data on financial flows (in cash and electronically). As a consequence of the liberalisation of financial markets and the increasing pace of globalisation there were fears that national control over financial markets was diminishing. As the FATF was not necessarily the right institution to promote macro-economic policy instruments, the issue was picked up by the International Monetary Fund (IMF) in its 'Data Dissemination Standards' of 1996 and 1997 and in its 'Code of Good Practices on Transparency in Monetary and Financial Policies' of July 1999.[34]

[30] Rec. 8 FAFT 40/1996 and Interpretative Note, 10 et seq.

[31] FATF 2003: Glossary, 12 et seq.: 'Designated non-financial businesses and professions'; EU 2005a.

[32] Asia/Pacific Group on Money Laundering (APG): cf. http://www.oecd.org; Eastern and Southern African Anti-Money Laundering Group (ESAAMLG); Caribbean Financial Action Task Force (CFATF); Middle East and North Africa Financial Action Task Force (MENAFATF); South American Financial Action Task Force (GAFISUD); cf. also para. 84 FATF Annual Report 2002/3.

[33] Cf. the FATF criteria for defining non-cooperative countries or territories in: FATF XI, Report, 18 et seq.

[34] IMF, Special Data Dissemination Standard (SDDS), March 1996; General Data Dissemination System (GDDS), December 1997; cf. also http://dsbb.imf.org.

Whilst concerns about the stability of financial markets in macroeconomic terms may have been a hidden sub-text to the FATF discourse from the early days, the issue was placed firmly and prominently on the international agenda following the establishment of the Financial Stability Forum (FSF) in February 1999. This G7-initiated body was created to 'promote international financial stability, to improve the functioning of markets, and to reduce systemic risks through enhanced information exchange and international co-operation in financial market supervision and surveillance'.[35] On 25 May 2000 the FSF published a list of 'jurisdictions considered having significant financial off-shore activities'. The list distinguishes between three categories of jurisdictions, reflecting their perceived quality of supervision and degree of co-operation.[36]

Shifting from the narrow focus of money laundering to the control of OFCs implied that a definition of OFCs was required. Earlier neutral definitions of 'off-shore banking' referred to 'banking abroad', meaning outside the territory of commercial activity. These definitions were superseded and the notion of 'Off-Shore Centre' rapidly became morally tainted given its use as an equivalent to a 'regulatory' or 'tax haven'.[37] When relating to 'Off-Shore Financial Centres', reference was typically made to the services they offered, specifically the rapid and cheap incorporation of domiciliary companies or IBCs, a minimal regulatory and supervisory structure and a combination of strong customer confidentiality laws with weak mutual legal assistance.[38]

An integral part of the drive to control OFCs is the work on corporate vehicles used to obscure the provenance of funds. Within the FATF such efforts started in 1993 with the discussion on 'shell corporations'.[39] The work was followed up consistently over several years but only brought to greater public prominence by the publication of the OECD report 'Behind

[35] FSF, International Standards and Codes to Strengthen Financial Systems, April 2001, 19 (available at: http://www.fsforum.org); cf. also Sansonetti 2001, 40.

[36] Financial Stability Forum Releases Grouping of Offshore Financial Centres (OFCs) to Assist in Setting Priorities for Assessment (available at: http://www.fsforum.org and http://www.bis.org).

[37] UN Office for Drug Control and Crime Prevention (ODCCP), Paradis financiers: sécret bancaire et blanchiment d'argent, Vienne, 19 Mai 1998.

[38] IVth European Conference of Specialised Services in the Fight Against Corruption, *International Co-operation in the Fight Against Corruption and Off-Shore Financial Centres: Obstacles and Solutions*, in Limassol, 20–22 October 1998; Meeting of the Inter-governmental Expert Group of the UN for the Prevention of Crime and Criminal Justice, *The Corruption and the International Financial Circuits: Elements of a Global Strategy in the Fight Against Corruption*, in Paris, 30 March–1 April 1999; a similar definition is used by the OECD WGB: cf. DAFFE/IME/BR/WD 2000(4), 6.

[39] US Department of Justice (DoJ) (1993), Shell Corporation Typology.

the Corporate Veil'.[40] The discussion of trusts and corporate entities is a sub-topic of a wider issue, namely the identification of the beneficial owner. Finally, the Basel Committee on Banking Supervision launched further initiatives related to customer due diligence, culminating in the publication of its 'Customer Due Diligence for Banks' in October 2001.

5. Sharpening the focus: towards a 'risk-based approach'

Initially, the main task of the international standard setters on anti-money laundering was seen as defining and enforcing equal application of basic obligations throughout the financial sector.

The standards first focused on account-opening procedures, concentrating on 'know your customer' rules including detailed rules on how to identify the immediate client (varying according to whether an individual or a corporation is concerned). Additionally, the institutions included rules on the identification of beneficial owners. Furthermore, obligations on record-keeping were defined in the early standards.

'Increased diligence' was prescribed for so-called 'unusual circumstances'. As the concepts developed, this approach proved to be the nucleus of an entire risk categorisation.[41] Finally, the financial operators were obliged to notify 'suspicious' or, depending upon the system, 'unusual' circumstances to a Financial Intelligence Unit (FIU).[42] The FIU could be an independent body, specialised police unit or a unit within the ministry of finance.[43]

As the standards developed, more emphasis was placed on ongoing monitoring throughout the client relationship.

Whereas originally the main tool to enforce the standards was the sanctioning power of regulators ('rule-based approach'), it was soon accepted that there was a far greater role for self-regulation of the industry and the individual institution. There are many sub-sectors of the business, and financial institutions know their clients' segment and the specific risks they pose best. On the one hand, the standards expected of financial institutions rose: they were placed under an obligation to understand the business of their clients. On the other hand, self-regulation enabled them to focus their efforts better on those high-risk activities and sustain them on a day-to-day basis for simple retail transactions.

Regulators helped financial institutions by suggesting a series of criteria to screen their clients, especially geographic, personal, sector specific and

[40] OECD 2001a; cf. also the study by Wymeersch 2001; Savona 2002.
[41] Rec. 15 FATF 40/1990. [42] Rec. 15 FATF 40/1996. [43] See VI.2. below.

product-related criteria. A particular focus was placed on so-called 'particularly exposed persons' (PEPs),[44] who should be screened with great attention, especially with regard to the source of their funds. Another area of particular concern is 'correspondent banks', especially when based in under-regulated areas. Specific rules apply to the screening of their anti-money laundering structures.[45]

6. The involvement of the private sector

As the rules of money laundering were gradually refined by regulators,[46] it became obvious that the know-how of the industry needed to be tapped. Various forms of public-private sector co-operation emerged. Clearly this approach goes beyond mere self-regulation,[47] because the fundamental concepts are mandatory. The regulating process did not, however, stop with public sector rules: as 'multi-stakeholder' groups emerged, hybrid regulations became more and more important,[48] building on the empowerment of the private sector.[49] The evolution is not without contradictions, however, since the expectations of regulators are very high. Moreover, regulators are not always ready to accept that even the best of compliance systems can fail, even where risk management has been delegated to the private sector.

IV. International instruments and fora addressing corruption – money laundering

Most of the anti-corruption conventions written during the 1990s addressed the issue of money laundering as an ancillary topic.[50] Article 23 of the UN Convention Against Corruption[51] requires criminalisation of money laundering offences, whereas Article 14 specifies the required preventive measures.

The overlaps between money laundering and corruption have been addressed at several major international gatherings and notably at a COE Conference in Limassol[52] and a Paris Conference organised by the French

[44] Pieth and Aiolfi 2003b, 16, 39, 45; Pieth and Aiolfi 2004, 32.
[45] US Patriot Act: Low, Tillen, and Abendschein 2003, 346 et seq.; Wolfsberg 2002b.
[46] Cf. especially the Basel Committee on Banking Supervision (BCBS) and its Customer Due Diligence for Banks (CDD) paper 2001.
[47] Critical of pure self-regulation: Black 2001, 4 et seq.; Brütsch and Lehmkuhl 2005, 12 et seq.; Haufler 2001, 7 et seq., esp. 10; Jenkins 2001; Knill and Lehmkuhl 2002.
[48] Wolfsberg 2000; Aiolfi and Pieth 2002.
[49] Black 2001, 6 et seq.; Brütsch and Lehmkuhl 2005, 17.
[50] Art. 13 COE 1999a; Art. 2 EU 1997b; Art. 7 OECD 1997b.
[51] UN 2003. [52] See note 38.

Ministry of Finance on behalf of the UN.[53] Both events, which took place in the late 1990s, produced concrete proposals. More recently, the FATF has shown interest in closer co-operation with the OECD's WGB on the topic.[54] Finally, the Wolfsberg group, a group of leading banks operating in private sector, is expected to adopt a text relating to the interconnection between corruption and money laundering in summer of 2006. The goal is, on the one hand, to raise awareness in the sector and to demonstrate leadership; on the other hand, it clearly also wants to warn against exaggerated expectations.[55]

The recommendations and conclusions of these initiatives can be grouped under three headings:

- regulatory standards (customer due diligence and notification requirements);[56]
- criminal law, including mutual legal assistance;[57]
- company law requirements.[58]

V. The criminal law standard of the Convention (Article 7)

1. Defining money laundering

The definition of the offence of money laundering in the 1988 UN Convention Against the Illicit Traffic in Narcotic Drugs and Psychotropic Substances and in all the main international instruments in this field, adopted since then, is virtually identical.[59]

Put in somewhat simplified fashion, the texts all define money laundering as:

- the conversion or transfer;
- the concealment;
- the acquisition of property, knowing that it is proceeds of crime (as well as related ancillary offences).

[53] Groupe d'expert de la commission des Nations-Unis pour la prévention du crime et la justice pénale, *La corruption et ses circuits financiers internationaux: éléments d'une strategie globale de lutte contre la corruption*, Réunion à Paris les 30, 31 mars et 1er avril 1999.

[54] Thanks in particular to the intervention of the Chairman of the FATF: cf. letter by Professor Kader Asmal of 1 November 2005 addressed to the WGB.

[55] Wolfsberg 2006b.

[56] Rec. 5 et seq. FATF 40/2003; BCBS CDD 2001; Wolfsberg 2000.

[57] COE 1990; Rec. 1 et seq. FATF 40/2003; Paris Conclusions 4 (see reference in note 53).

[58] OECD 2001a; Limassol Conclusions III. 5 (see reference in note 38).

[59] Art. 3 UN 1988; Art. 6 COE 1990; Art. 23 UN 2003; Art. 6 COE 1990; Art. 9 COE 2005.

We will now discuss whether the OECD Convention defines a minimum standard for its own constituency.

2. Objective elements of the offence

2.1. Bribery as a predicate offence to money laundering?

Already during the negotiations of the Convention one of the key issues was whether bribery, according to Article 1, could not simply be made a mandatory predicate offence in all state Parties. At the time, Japan[60] and Korea[61] saw this as a major impediment to accede to the Convention, since both countries restricted their money laundering concept to bribes and to passive bribery. The compromise reached was once more based on the principle of 'assimilation'. Article 7 reads:

> 'Each Party which has made bribery of its own public official a predicate offence for the purpose of the application of its money laundering legislation shall do so on the same terms for the bribery of a foreign public official.'

'Assimilation' clearly applies to the issue whether bribery is a predicate offence and on what terms it needs to be assimilated. Official Commentary 28, however, is more confusing than helpful: Its first sentence –

> 'in Article 7, "bribery of its own public official" is intended broadly, so that bribery of a foreign public official is to be made a predicate offence for money laundering legislation on the same terms, when a Party has made either active or passive bribery of its own public official such an offence' –

does not really address the Japanese and Korean problem. On the contrary, the second sentence of Official Commentary 28 only makes the contradiction even more apparent:

> 'When a Party has made only passive bribery of its own public officials a predicate offence for money laundering purposes, this article requires that the laundering of the bribe payment be subject to money laundering legislation.'

The only state Parties escaping the requirements of Article 7 seem to be those who do not have an anti-money laundering statute altogether,[62] or those with a restriction in domestic law.[63]

This debate has, however, for the current state Parties to the Convention become far less relevant, following the FATF's upgrading of its requirements

[60] JP-Ph1, 16 et seq. [61] KR-Ph1, 14.

[62] E.g. Chile at the time of the Phase 1 evaluation: CL-Ph1, 19.

[63] E.g. Germany, where the laundering of bribes of a Member of Parliament would escape capture, since domestic Members of Parliament are not covered by anti-bribery laws in general (DE-Ph2, 23).

on predicate offences between 1996 and 2003. The 40 Recommendations of 2003 now leave no doubt that the FATF expects all its members (including all OECD WGB members) to consider 'corruption and bribery' a predicate to money laundering.[64] It is acknowledged that the FATF Recommendations remain 'soft law'. Over the last 15 years they have, however, developed into a politically binding standard, in particular given the regular evaluation of implementation by members and non-members.

Article 7 of the Convention could therefore probably now be easily adapted to read 'bribery as defined in Article 1 shall be considered a predicate offence to money laundering'. This approach would be supported by developments in Japanese and Korean legislation.[65] The UN Convention Against Corruption of 2003 shows that this would be a move in the right direction: Its Article 23(2) states:

> '(a) Each State Party shall seek to apply paragraph 1 of this article to the widest range of predicate offences;
> (b) Each State Party shall include as predicate offences at a minimum a comprehensive range of criminal offences established in accordance with this Convention.'

2.2. Laundering of the bribe?

Even though the OECD Convention primarily addresses the supply side of bribery, it is understandable that the anti-money laundering provisions focus in the first instance on the bribe itself: the larger financial centres are based in the state Parties of the OECD Convention. Preventing financial centres from acting as 'relay stations' for the world of bribery follows the same logic as forcing companies based in the northern hemisphere to abstain from active bribery.

Some uncertainty has been voiced in country evaluations whether funds set aside by the briber to be handed over or transferred are already forfeitable and whether they could become the object of money laundering.[66]

Setting aside cases in which these assets are part of a 'slush fund' (embezzlement, falsified books) and therefore independently the object of money laundering as ill-gotten gains from an offence against property, such funds may be forfeitable as instruments of the crime (*instrumenta sceleris*). They do not, however, at least in the context of bribery, yet stem from crime (they are not *producta sceleris*). As they are not 'proceeds of crime' in the sense

[64] Rec. 1 FATF 40/2003, and Glossary: 'Designated Categories of Offences', 12.
[65] J-Ph2, 27 et seq.; K-Ph2, 18 et seq.
[66] AU-Ph1, 15; IT-Ph1, 22; NZ-Ph1, 22; PL-Ph1, 24.

of the general definition of money laundering mentioned in V.1. above, they are not the object of money laundering in the sense of Article 7.

2.3. Laundering of the proceeds of bribery?

As indicated in our chapter on Article 3(3),[67] the latter provision obliges state Parties to provide for confiscation of the bribe 'and the proceeds of the bribery'. Official Commentary 21 states by way of clarification that:

> '"proceeds" of bribery are the profits or other benefits derived by the briber from the transaction or other improper advantage obtained or retained through bribery.'

Many WGB evaluation reports discuss the issue whether the proceeds of bribery in the sense of Article 3(3) could also be the object of the money laundering provision. We must make a few distinctions here.

First, the countries who have chosen to define money laundering as the 'impeding of confiscation' would quite naturally extend their money laundering provisions to the proceeds of bribery.[68] Several other countries claim to do likewise without being obliged to do so by their internal law or the Convention,[69] whereas other countries find this option more problematic.[70]

For the purposes of this commentary, the second and central question is, however, whether the OECD Convention requires that the profit derived by the briber should be made an object of money laundering.

As indicated in our chapter on Article 3(3) above, the concept of forfeiture of proceeds of bribery poses a series of formidable practical challenges. Which requirements must be fulfilled in order to establish that a bribe was really instrumental in order to obtain a contract, permit, or licence? This is the question concerning the causal link between the bribe and the obtaining of the contract. How is the net benefit of the bribe profit to be calculated? How much may be deducted for legitimate efforts? In many countries judges are permitted to estimate the value of the benefits reaped by the briber. Article 3(3) allows state Parties to sidestep these difficulties by using other monetary sanctions.

Even if these questions can be answered satisfactorily,[71] the question remains whether the additional step beyond confiscation should be taken

[67] See III.3.3. in ch. on Article 3(3) above. [68] E.g. Germany, Switzerland.

[69] AR-Ph1, 16 et seq.; AU-Ph1, 15; BE-Ph1, 16; BG-Ph1, 11; BR-Ph1, 23; CH-Ph1, 16; CA-Ph1, 16; IT-Ph1, 22; IT-Ph2, 23; NL-Ph1, 24; NZ-Ph1, 22; PT-Ph1, 22; SE-Ph1, 17; TR-Ph1, 17; US-Ph1, 17 (even if other means appear to be favoured in practice).

[70] FI-Ph1, 12; HU-Ph1, 15; IS-Ph1, 13; JP-Ph1, 16; SI-Ph1, 27. [71] See note 67.

and the recipient of the funds criminalised (be it the banker of the bribing company, its creditors or even its employees)? There is nothing in the *Travaux Préparatoires* to the Convention which would compel such a conclusion. If countries decide to go beyond the Convention on this point, it is up to them.

2.4. Proof of provenance from crime

One of the most difficult practical issues in controlling money laundering is proving the illegal origin of the funds, especially when a previous conviction for the predicate offence[72] or clear evidence of a criminal background is required. It is sufficient for the court to establish the provenance of the funds on the basis of objective indicators (circumstantial evidence), provided the necessary type and gravity of offence are proved. According to this approach, details of the perpetrator, the exact factual circumstances of the predicate offence or the concrete sums involved, need not to be proven.[73]

2.5. Predicate offence committed abroad

Article 7 applies 'without regard to the place where the bribery occurred'. This concept again conforms to the overall definitions of bribery. Article 23(2)(c) of the UN Convention Against Corruption is more explicit when stating 'predicate offences shall include offences committed both within and outside the jurisdiction of the State Party in question.'[74]

The UN Convention continues:

> 'offences committed outside the jurisdiction of a State Party shall constitute predicate offences only when the relevant conduct is a criminal offence under the domestic law of the state where it is committed and would be a criminal offence under the domestic law of the State Party implementing or applying this Article had it been permitted there.'

This extensive requirement of 'dual criminality' relating to the predicate offence is common practice in many state Parties[75] and acceptable

[72] IC-Ph2, 34.

[73] For Switzerland: Federal Court Decisions BGE 120 IV 232 E.3d; and BGE 8 September 2003, 6, S. 22/2003, S.2.; BGE 31 July 2000, 6 P. 23/2000, E.9c; cf. also Trechsel 1997: Art. 305bis, Rn. 11.

[74] AR-Ph1, 18; AU-Ph1, 16; BE-Ph1, 16; CH-Ph1, 16; DE-Ph1, 12; DK-Ph1, 18; FR-Ph1, 23; HU-Ph1, 16; IS-Ph1, 13; IT-Ph1, 22; LU-Ph1, 19; PL-Ph1, 24; PT-Ph1, 23; SE-Ph1, 17; SL-Ph1, 28.

[75] AR-Ph1, 18; DE-Ph1, 12; IE-Ph1, 26; NZ-Ph1, 23; SL-Ph1, 28; Switzerland: Art. 305bis(3) Swiss Criminal Code.

according to the logic of the Convention for extraterritorial acts of bribery.[76] Other countries do not require 'dual criminality' in this context.[77]

3. Subjective elements of the offence

According to Article 1, the minimum standard for the bribery offence is 'intent', including '*dolus eventualis*' and 'turning a blind eye'.[78] This standard also extends to the laundering of the proceeds of bribery.[79] State Parties may, however, go beyond this standard and introduce the offence of money laundering in the case of recklessness[80] or even of negligence.[81] On the other hand, requesting 'direct intent' would amount to making convictions next to impossible, especially in international cases. Therefore, Finnish law may well be in conflict with the requirements of effectiveness expressed in Article 3 of the Convention.[82]

4. Applicability to legal persons

It is in the logic of the Convention that Articles 2 and 3 extend to the ancillary criminal provision of the Convention (Articles 7 and 8), even though the text of Article 2 refers only to the offence of bribery of foreign public officials. Article 18(1) of the COE Criminal Law Convention on Corruption[83] and Article 26(1) of the UN Convention Against Corruption[84] explicitly extend corporate liability to money laundering. Nevertheless, it may be assumed that the prohibition of corruption money laundering according to Article 7 of the OECD Convention also applies to corporations.[85]

VI. The regulatory standard of the Revised Recommendation

In its Phase 2 evaluations the WGB regularly goes beyond the examination of the criminal law aspects of bribery-related money laundering. It assesses the regulatory standards of evaluated countries and reports on their

[76] See II.3.3.1. in ch. on Article 4 above. [77] ES-Ph1, 16; IT-Ph1, 22; PT-Ph1, 23.
[78] See part III. in ch. on Article 1 above.
[79] Art. 9(1) and (2) COE 2005; Art. 23(1) UN 2003.
[80] IE-Ph1, 26 ('recklessness'); NL-Ph1, 23 ('should have suspected'); PL-Ph1, 24 ('justifiable suspicion').
[81] ES-Ph1, 15 ('serious negligence'); SE-Ph1, 16; SL-Ph1, 28 ('negligence').
[82] FI-Ph1, 12; FI-Ph2, 26. [83] COE 1999a. [84] UN 2003.
[85] Insufficient therefore: IT-Ph2, 23.

application. There is, however, potential for overlap and friction with other evaluation bodies covering the same ground (FATF, IMF, COE). The legal basis for the WGB's analysis is provided by the Revised Recommendation of May 1997 (either section I. or II.).

1. Obligations of financial operators

Financial operators have traditionally been subjected to five basic obligations to:

- identify their clients;
- apply increased diligence in unusual circumstances;
- keep records of these activities;
- notify suspicious circumstances;
- introduce internal compliance systems.

Over time these obligations have been refined. Application has been extended to non-banking financial institutions and increasingly also to some key non-financial institutions potentially attractive to money launderers or to so-called 'gatekeepers'. The Second and Third EC Anti-Money Laundering Directives[86] have led to rapid changes in EU Member States.[87] In several OECD countries subjecting lawyers to anti-money laundering controls remains controversial.[88]

1.1. Customer identification and increased diligence

Customer identification began with detailed rules for individual and corporate clients and for beneficial owners, including special rules for e-banking and correspondence banking. Identification gradually moved towards verification.[89]

Verified identification was in turn intended to be the stepping stone towards 'increased diligence in unusual circumstances'.[90] According to the now prevailing 'risk-based approach',[91] financial institutions are expected to categorise their customer database according to risk criteria.[92] Particular care

[86] EU 2001b; EU 2005a. [87] E.g.: DE-Ph2, 20; FI-Ph2, 12; FR-Ph2, 23; LU-Ph1, 19.
[88] E.g.: Canada and the United States.
[89] Para. 23, 32 et seq. BCBS CDD 2001; Rec. 5 FATF 40/2003; Art. 1 Wolfsberg 2000.
[90] Rec. 15 FATF 40/1990; Rec. 14 FATF 40/1996; Rec. 11 FATF 40/2003.
[91] Wolfsberg 2005.
[92] Para. 20 BCBS CDD 2001; Rec. 5 FATF 40/2003; no. 4 Wolfsberg 2000.

needs to be given to the profiling of so-called 'particularly exposed persons' (PEPs).[93]

1.2. Monitoring

Whereas these rules apply to the client acceptance in the first place, an ongoing monitoring programme should also be put in place to allow the financial operator to pick up unusual or suspicious circumstances during the client relationship.[94]

2. Notification and FIUs

Suspicious circumstances should be notified to the appropriate authorities. The national notification systems are, however, built in many different ways. First, the threshold for monitoring diverges. Some countries have introduced an early warning system,[95] reacting already to mere 'unusual transactions': they would not, however, expect financial operators to block transactions routinely, unless requested by the Financial Intelligence Unit or a law enforcement agency. Other systems demand concrete evidence and automatic internal blocking for several days.[96] Even when notification must be based on evidence there may be special rules for certain risks (e.g. financing of terrorism).[97]

Second, the body receiving notification can be a specialised police unit[98] or part of the supervisory authority.[99] In some cases it may be an independent body.[100]

VII. Implementation

As a result of the intense pressure applied by the FATF and other anti-money laundering agencies, the overall legal standard applying both to criminal and regulatory law on money laundering in the state Parties to the OECD anti-bribery Convention is high.

[93] Rec. 6 FATF 40/2003; and see note 44. [94] No. 5 Wolfsberg 2000.

[95] France, The Netherlands, United Kingdom, United States; cf. Pieth and Aiolfi 2004, 428 et seq.; Pieth and Aiolfi 2003b, 22 et seq.

[96] E.g. Switzerland: Pieth and Aiolfi 2004, 424 et seq.; Pieth and Aiolfi 2003b, 20 et seq.

[97] Special rules in Switzerland oblige operators to notify early in the case of pre-suspicion of financing terrorism.

[98] BG-Ph2, 17 et seq.; DE-Ph2, 19 (*Bundeskriminalamt* (BKA)); IS-Ph2, 19.

[99] E.g. France (Traitement du renseignement et action contre les circuits financiers clandestins (TRACFIN)).

[100] E.g. Canada (Financial Transactions Reports Analysis Centre of Canada (FINTRAC)).

Obviously, clearly sub-standard are those countries lacking applicable money laundering rules altogether.[101] Specific legal deficits are to be found in the following areas:

- Germany's lack of coverage of the laundering of bribery of Members of Parliament;[102]
- Italy's lack of coverage of legal persons;[103]
- the high subjective requirements of 'direct intent' in Finland.[104]

The WGB was rightly far more critical of practical implementation. Overall, awareness of the phenomenon of transnational bribery is not high where it should be high. Although, as we said at the beginning of this chapter, transnational bribery is receiving far greater political prominence these days; it is not even near the top of the agenda for financial institutions, which consider themselves far removed from the actual problems.[105]

References

For documentation see the consolidated bibliography at the end of this book.

Aiolfi, G. and M. Pieth (2002), 'How to Make a Convention Work: The Organisation for Economic Co-operation and Development Recommendation and Convention on Bribery as an Example of a New Horizon in International Law' in C. Fijnaut and L. Huberts (eds.), *Corruption, Integrity and Law Enforcement*, Leiden, Boston, 349.

Bernasconi, P. (1995), 'New Criminal Law Provisions Against the Corruption of Public Officials', Multidisciplinary Group on Corruption (GMC), Council of Europe, 5.

Black, J. (2001), 'Decentring Regulation: Understanding the Role of Regulation and Self Regulation in a "Post-Regulatory" World', *Current Legal Problems* **54**, 4.

Brütsch, C. and D. Lehmkuhl (2005), *Hard, Soft and Private Legalities: The Increase, Variation and Differentation of Law-Like Arrangements in International Relations* (unpublished manuscript).

Haufler, V. (2001), *A Public Role for the Private Sector: Industry Self-Regulation in a Global Economy*, Washington.

Jenkins, R. (2001), 'Corporate Codes of Conduct, Self-Regulation in a Global Economy', *UN Research Institute for Social Development*, **21**.

Knill, C. and D. Lehmkuhl (2002), 'Private Actors and the State: Internationalization and Changing Patterns of Governance', *Governance: An International Journal of Policy, Administration, and Institutions*. Vol. **15**, No. 1, 41.

Low, L. A., G. Tillen and K. Abendschein (2003), 'Country Report: The US Anti-Money Laundering System' in M. Pieth and G. Aiolfi (eds.), *A Comparative Guide to Anti-Money Laundering: A Critical Analysis of Systems in Singapore, Switzerland, the UK and the USA* (study by the Basel Institute on Governance,

[101] CL-Ph1, 19. [102] DE-Ph2, 23. [103] IT-Ph2, 23. [104] FI-Ph1, 12; FI-Ph2, 26.
[105] E.g. LU-Ph2, 19 et seq., 40.

commissioned by the Stiftung Finanzplatz Schweiz), Cheltenham (UK), Northhampton (USA), 346.

Moody-Stuart, G. (1997), *Grand Corruption*, 3rd edn, Oxford.

OECD (2001) [cited OECD 2001a], *Behind the Corporate Veil – Using Corporate Entities for Illicit Purposes*, Paris.

Pieth, M. (1992), *Bekämpfung der Geldwäscherei – Modellfall Schweiz?*, Basel, Frankfurt.

Pieth, M. and G. Aiolfi (2003) [cited Pieth and Aiolfi 2003b], *Anti-Money Laundering: Levelling the Playing Field* (study by the Basel Institute on Governance, commissioned by the Stiftung Finanzplatz Schweiz), Basel.

Pieth, M. and G. Aiolfi (eds.) (2004), *A Comparative Guide to Anti-Money Laundering: A Critical Analysis of Systems in Singapore, Switzerland, the UK and the USA* (study by the Basel Institute on Governance, commissioned by the Stiftung Finanzplatz Schweiz), Cheltenham (UK), Northhampton (USA).

Pieth, M. and P. Eigen (Hrsg.) (1999), *Korruption im internationalen Geschäftsverkehr: Bestandesaufnahme, Bekämpfung, Prävention*, Neuwied, Kriftel, Basel, Frankfurt a. M.

Sansonetti, R. (2001), 'Die Problematik der Offshore-Finanzzentren und die Position der Schweiz', *Die Volkswirtschaft – Das Magazin für Wirtschaftspolitik* **2**, 40.

Savona, E. (2002), 'Obstacles in Company Law to Anti-Money Laundering: International Cooperation in European Union Member States' in M. Pieth (ed.), *Financing Terrorism*, Dordrecht.

Trechsel, S. (1997), *Geldwäscherei: Prävention und Massnahmen zur Bekämpfung*, Zürich.

Trepp, G. (1996), *Swiss Connection*, Zürich.

Wymeersch, E. (2001), *Study of the Regulation and its Implementation in the EU Member States, that Obstruct Anti-Money Laundering International Co-operation*, Trento.

Article 8. Accounting

GREGORY S. BRUCH AND AKITA N. ADKINS

Article 8 – Accounting

1. In order to combat bribery of foreign public officials effectively, each Party shall take such measures as may be necessary, within the framework of its laws and regulations regarding the maintenance of books and records, financial statement disclosures, and accounting and auditing standards, to prohibit the establishment of off-the-books accounts, the making of off-the-books or inadequately identified transactions, the recording of non-existent expenditures, the entry of liabilities with incorrect identification of their object, as well as the use of false documents, by companies subject to those laws and regulations, for the purpose of bribing foreign public officials or of hiding such bribery.

2. Each Party shall provide effective, proportionate and dissuasive civil, administrative or criminal penalties for such omissions and falsifications in respect of the books, records, accounts, and financial statements of such companies.

Official Commentary

Article 8 – Accounting

29. Article 8 is related to section V of the 1997 OECD Recommendation, which all Parties will have accepted and which is subject to follow-up in the OECD Working Group on Bribery in International Business Transactions. This paragraph contains a series of recommendations concerning accounting requirements, independent external audit and internal company controls the implementation of which will be important to the overall effectiveness of the fight against bribery in international business. However, one immediate consequence of the implementation of this Convention by the Parties will be that companies which are required to issue financial statements disclosing their material contingent liabilities will need to take into account the full potential liabilities under this Convention, in particular its Articles 3 and 8, as well as other losses which might flow from conviction of the company or its agents for bribery. This also has implications for the execution of professional responsibilities of auditors regarding indications of bribery of foreign public officials. In addition, the accounting offences referred to in Article 8 will generally occur in the company's home country, when the bribery offence itself may have been committed in another country, and this can fill gaps in the effective reach of the Convention.

Revised Recommendation

Section V.: Accounting Requirements, External Audit and Internal Company Controls

[THE COUNCIL] RECOMMENDS that Member countries take the steps necessary so that laws, rules and practices with respect to accounting requirements, external audit and internal company controls are in line with the following principles and are fully used in order to prevent and detect bribery of foreign public officials in international business.

A. Adequate accounting requirements

- *i) Member countries should require companies to maintain adequate records of the sums of money received and expended by the company, identifying the matters in respect of which the receipt and expenditure takes place. Companies should be prohibited from making off-the-books transactions or keeping off-the-books accounts.*
- *ii) Member countries should require companies to disclose in their financial statements the full range of material contingent liabilities.*
- *iii) Member countries should adequately sanction accounting omissions, falsifications and fraud.*

B. Independent External Audit

- *i) Member countries should consider whether requirements to submit to external audit are adequate.*
- *ii) Member countries and professional associations should maintain adequate standards to ensure the independence of external auditors which permits them to provide an objective assessment of company accounts, financial statements and internal controls.*
- *iii) Member countries should require the auditor who discovers indications of a possible illegal act of bribery to report this discovery to management and, as appropriate, to corporate monitoring bodies.*
- *iv) Member countries should consider requiring the auditor to report indications of a possible illegal act of bribery to competent authorities.*

C. Internal company controls

i) Member countries should encourage the development and adoption of adequate internal company controls, including standards of conduct.
ii) Member countries should encourage company management to make statements in their annual reports about their internal control mechanisms, including those which contribute to preventing bribery.
iii) Member countries should encourage the creation of monitoring bodies, independent of management, such as audit committees of boards of directors or of supervisory boards.
iv) Member countries should encourage companies to provide channels for communication by, and protection for, persons not willing to violate professional standards or ethics under instructions or pressure from hierarchical superiors.

Chapter contents

I. Introduction: the role of accounting in combating bribery of foreign public officials

Article 8 of the OECD Convention on Combating Bribery of Foreign Public Officials in International Business Transactions (the 'Convention') requires each state Party to adopt Accounting standards prohibiting 'the establishment of off-the-books accounts [and] the making of off-the-books or inadequately identified transactions. . .for the purpose of bribing foreign public officials or of hiding such bribery'.[1]

The accounting[2] standards required by Article 8 can facilitate the identification and prosecution of individuals and entities involved in the bribery of foreign public officials. Accounting standards, and sanctions for violating those standards, can be important tools in combating bribery, because they do not usually include a *scienter* requirement. Prosecutions for bribing foreign public officials on the other hand often require a showing that payment of the bribe was undertaken with the necessary mental state or *mens rea*,[3] namely intent.[4]

Accounting standards can also be valuable in combating the bribery of foreign public officials, because there is truth in numbers. Implicit in the use of numbers generally, and accounting specifically, is the belief that it is difficult to hide or obscure in numbers what is easily concealed, or made less quantifiable, by words. Accounting acts as an information system which provides transparency, which in turn allows for the detection and reduction of corrupt activities. The existence of a system designed to elicit reliable financial data is imperative in combating 'supply-side bribery' – bribery focused on the bribe payer as opposed to the bribe recipient.[5] Deficiencies in accounting controls can be the breeding ground for under-the-table and off-the-books payment of bribes, allowing such payments to go unnoticed and unaccounted for.

[1] Cf. Art. 8 OECD Convention (OECD 1997b) – Accounting. Art. 8 resembles other provisions of the Convention, for example, Art. 8(1), like Art. 5, requires a specific action under the Convention's general mandate that Parties 'take effective measures to deter, prevent and combat the bribery of foreign public officials in connection with international business transactions'; and Art. 8(2), like Art. 3, provides sanctions for violating the related substantive provisions. Art. 5 OECD 1997b – Enforcement; Art. 3(1) OECD 1997b.

[2] This chapter uses the term 'accounting' to refer to all laws and regulations relating to 'the maintenance of books and records, financial statement disclosures, and accounting and auditing standards' (cf. Art. 8 OECD 1997b) rather than to the substantive financial statement presentation standards found in US Generally Accepted Accounting Principles (US GAAP) or other International Accounting Standards (IAS).

[3] See part III. in our ch. on Article 1 above.

[4] Art. 1(1) OECD 1997b.

[5] 'Supply-side bribery' is also referred to as 'active bribery'. Cf., for example, Official Commentary 1.

This chapter examines legislation Parties would be required to implement under Convention Article 8. It observes the gaps created by Article 8 and the practical challenges and open issues faced by member countries in efforts to implement legislation that accomplishes the Convention's goals. Section II. examines the standards imposed by the Convention and the associated practical issues; Section III. discusses sanctions for violating Article 8; Section IV. concludes with a discussion of the future of the Convention and the Working Group on Bribery (WGB) as it relates to accounting, internal controls, and independent audits.

II. OECD rules and standards on accounting and internal controls

Article 8 presents a broad accounting directive with which member countries must comply – 'prohibit the establishment of off-the-books accounts, the making of off-the-books or inadequately identified transactions, the recording of non-existent expenditures, the entry of liabilities with incorrect identification of their objects, [and] the use of false documents'.

However, article 8 does not detail substantive requirements that must be present in Party legislation implementing Article 8. This lack of specificity is in line with the Convention's attempt to achieve 'functional equivalence'.[6] Providing broad rather than narrow directives allows Convention goals to be achieved in the context of Parties' existing laws and cultural norms. Nonetheless, additional interpretative guidance on issues Parties should consider in adopting accounting laws would be useful.

The Revised Recommendation of the OECD Council on Combating Bribery in International Business Transactions provides guidance on issues state Parties implementing the Convention should consider.[7]

[6] Official Commentary 2; cf., for example, Art. 2 of the Convention (looking to the law of Parties to provide the definition of 'legal person'). See also part III. of this ch. (noting the same harmonization efforts with respect to Art. 3).

[7] Cf. OECD 1997a. Reference to other international treaties aimed at combating bribery of foreign public officials are also instructive in interpreting Art. 8's accounting standards. The UN Declaration Against Corruption and Bribery in International Commercial Transactions asks Member States to 'develop or maintain accounting standards and practices that improve the transparency of international commercial transactions, and that encourage private and public corporations, including transnational corporations, and individuals engaged in international commercial transactions to avoid and combat corruption, bribery, and related illicit practices' (UN 1996).

Section V. of the Revised Recommendation delineates three areas legislation of Parties implementing Article 8 should address:

- adequate accounting requirements;
- internal company controls; and
- independent external audit.[8]

The following discussion examines what is likely expected of member countries in each of the areas outlined in the Revised Recommendation.[9]

1. Accounting laws

In accordance with the Convention's guiding principle of obtaining functional equivalence, Article 8 defers to Parties' domestic laws regarding the maintenance of books and records, financial statement disclosures, and accounting and auditing standards to provide the framework for prohibiting the establishment of off-the-books accounts and other documentation deficiencies and omissions prohibited by Article 8. However, Parties' accounting laws and regimes vary considerably. Consequently, as examined below, the Convention's deference to local accounting laws and frameworks as the basis for implementing Article 8 creates multiple issues.

One potential issue created by Article 8's reliance on Parties' accounting laws is that the entities subject to domestic accounting law can vary significantly among Parties.[10] These differences can create two potential issues. First, certain entities involved in international transactions may not be subject to domestic accounting laws.[11] Second, certain types of entities may be subject to

[8] See the text of S. V. OECD 1997a in the Documentary Appendix of this commentary.

[9] S. V. OECD 1997a relates back to Art. 8. As indicated by its title the Revised Recommendation (OECD 1997a) is voluntary, not compulsory, in nature. Nonetheless, the procedures adopted by the OECD's WGB in its examinations, specifically its 'Phase 2' monitoring examinations, illustrate that Parties' compliance with the OECD 1997a is a factor in assessing their compliance with the Convention. Cf. FR-Ph2, 17, 58.

[10] For example, in Argentina, entities subject to Accounting obligations include: general partnerships, statutory limited partnerships, limited liability companies, corporations, and companies registered abroad that establish branch offices in Argentina (AR-Ph1, 18 et seq.). In addition, Argentina's Code of Commerce provides Accounting requirements applicable to 'traders' and co-operative associates. 'Traders' are defined as 'all natural persons, who, having legal capacity to enter into contracts, exercise on their own acts of commerce, in a manner that becomes a usual profession' (AR-Ph1, 18).

[11] Because these entities do not have to comply with domestic Accounting laws, they will not be subject to provisions created within the framework of those laws aimed at prohibiting falsified or fraudulent accounts and records for the purpose of bribing foreign public officials or hiding such bribes – despite their interaction in international business and commensurate increases in opportunities and incentives to bribe foreign public officials.

the accounting laws of some state Parties but not others, thus creating a gap in the regulatory schemes and oversight.[12]

Transparency International suggests a solution to the first dilemma.[13] Transparency International recommends amending the Convention to include a requirement that Parties extend their accounting provisions to 'all companies engaged in significant international business transactions and to affiliates outside the country over which the company has significant influence'.[14] Such a requirement could be a substantial step toward addressing gaps created by local accounting laws that do not require certain entities, such as small or closed companies, to maintain books and records. A further refinement might include an OECD Recommendation that Parties pass legislation requiring companies engaged in international transactions to segregate bribery and facilitation payments in a separate line item entry in their books and records or provide a separate narrative discussion regarding the payment of bribes.

Differences in accounting laws can also present difficulties in attaining another Convention goal – facilitating comparison and dialogue on the subject of corruption. Variations in the substantive requirements of Parties' accounting laws can make ensuring comparison of like elements complicated. Although altering Parties' accounting regimes would facilitate cross-country comparisons, such a broad change is impractical. Accounting systems often reflect a country's political, economic, social, and moral judgments. Efforts to dictate Parties' substantive accounting provisions might be met with substantial resistance.

2. Internal company controls

2.1. Overview

Section V.C. of the Revised Recommendation suggests that Parties encourage the development and adoption of 'adequate internal controls,

[12] This creates a gap that might allow a covered entity, subject to domestic Accounting laws, to use a non-covered entity, not subject to its country's Accounting laws, as a conduit for paying bribes to foreign public officials.

[13] Transparency International 2000. The paper was composed by a Transparency International-commissioned task force chaired by Thomas L. Milan and assisted by Steven E. Morehart, both of Ernst & Young. Other members of the task force included individuals from General Electric, Arthur Andersen, KPMG, PricewaterhouseCoopers, Deloitte & Touche, as well as sixteen others located in the countries reviewed. The study was conducted under the overall direction of a steering committee co-chaired by Charles Bowsher, former US Comptroller General of the United States, and Alan Levenson, former Director of Corporate Finance of the US Securities and Exchange Commission.

[14] Transparency International 2000.

including standards of conduct'.[15] This recommendation likely stems from the fact that a number of Parties do not have a legal requirement that companies maintain an adequate system of internal controls.[16]

It is unclear whether the reference in the Revised Recommendation is to internal Accounting controls, controls related to financial documentation and the maintenance of books and records, or a broader category of internal controls encompassing all control mechanisms used by an entity, including those to prevent bribery – in particular, bribery of foreign public officials.[17] The WGB's reports are a possible source for discerning whether the Revised Recommendation refers to internal Accounting controls or broader internal controls. However, few country report sections on Article 8 mention internal controls.[18]

Another source for discerning the type of internal control contemplated is the Revised Recommendation itself. The Revised Recommendation suggest that internal controls include 'standards of conduct'. This implies that the Revised Recommendation referes to general internal controls, not solely internal Accounting controls.[19]

[15] S. V.C.i) OECD 1997a.

[16] Transparency International 2000. The task force, authors of the Overall Observations, call for an OECD requirement that member countries adopt an adequate system of internal controls. However, the task force does not believe the requirements pursuant to such an obligation should be overly prescriptive. Rather, they believe a mandatory system of internal controls should rely on judgement in the light of the 'comprehensive frameworks' provided in resources such as the International Chamber of Commerce's Manual on Corporate Practices, the Combined Code of the Committee on Corporate Governance (The London Stock Exchange), Appendix B (see reference in Bibliography).

[17] S. V. OECD 1997a refers back to Art. 8 of the Convention. However, Art. 8 does not mention internal controls.

[18] Discussions of internal controls in country reports can be divided into one of three categories: (1) country reports limiting discussion of internal controls to internal Accounting controls; (2) country reports discussing internal controls only as they apply to internal audits; and (3) country reports examining all internal controls aimed at detecting and preventing bribery. Cf. CA-Ph2, 19; DK-Phl, 20; GR-Ph2, 17 et seq.; IS-Phl, 15; IT-Phl, 25; JP-Ph2, 35 et seq.; TR-Phl, 19 et seq.; UK-Ph2, 22 et seq. (discussing internal controls).

[19] This reading is also supported by the Official Commentary 29 to the OECD Convention, which states that '[Art. 8] contains a series of recommendations concerning accounting requirements, independent external audit and internal company controls *the implementation of which will be important to the overall effectiveness of the fight against bribery in international business*' (italics added). However, given that there is no separating grammar (such as a comma) after the words 'internal controls', an alternative reading of the section is also possible, namely that the clause 'the implementation of which will be important to the overall effectiveness of the fight against bribery in international business' applies to modify the preceding clause 'accounting requirements, independent external audit and internal company controls', and not just 'internal company controls'.

The following examines what might be included in Party legislation related to internal Accounting controls and general internal controls.[20]

2.1.1. Internal Accounting controls

Assuming the Revised Recommendation refers solely to internal *Accounting* controls, it is helpful to examine what internal Accounting controls might include. According to the Committee of Sponsoring Organizations of the Treadway Committee (COSO),[21] a company's internal Accounting controls consist of: (1) the company's Accounting system and (2) specific controls.[22]

(1) Accounting systems consist of:

- adequate physical documents and records; and
- adequate procedures.[23] Maintaining adequate physical documents and records, requires that organisations create and maintain documents supporting amounts and goods outlayed or received.[24]

Following the COSO framework, the second component of a company's internal Accounting controls is specific controls. Specific Accounting controls refer to a company's 'individual policies and procedures for processing transactions'.[26] These policies and procedures are established by company management to provide assurance that its objectives will be achieved.[27]

[20] The term 'internal controls' is used in this ch. to refer to an entity's entire programme of internal controls. Controls relating to an entity's programme for tracking funds, goods, and services outlaid and received are referred to as 'internal Accounting controls'.

[21] Treadway Report 1987, Appendix F. COSO was formed in 1985 in the United States to sponsor the National Commission on Fraudulent Reporting, an independent private sector initiative that studied causal factors that can lead to fraudulent financial reporting. COSO then issued a report in October 1987, which included recommendations.

[22] Treadway Report 1987, Appendix F.

[23] Adequate procedures under an Accounting system might include procedures to: identify and record all valid transactions; describe the transactions in sufficient detail to permit them to be properly classified; measure the value of the transactions accurately; ensure the transactions are recorded in the proper period; and present and disclose the transactions properly in the financial statements.[25] See note 24.

[24] Such documents might include: purchase orders, cheque requests, bank drafts, petty cash authorisations, vendor invoices, cheque registers etc.

[25] Treadway Report 1987, Appendix F

[26] See previous note 25. [27] See note 25.

(2) Specific accounting controls include those related to:

- segregation of duties – such that no financial transactions is handled by one person from beginning to end;
- authorisation and processing of disbursements – detailing who in the organisation can authorise payments;
- cheque signing – stating the number of signatures required on cheques and those authorised to sign cheques;
- reconciliations;
- reviews of data used to prepare management reports; and
- control access to and use of computer programmes.[28]

The above list is a non-exhaustive sampling of the physical documents, procedures, and specific controls an organisation might utilise in implementing effective internal Accounting controls. Internal Accounting controls can be important in tracking an entity's use of funds and allowing entities to exercise proper oversight of expenditures.[29]

Neither the Convention nor the Revised Recommendation specify what level or type(s) of internal Accounting controls are considered 'adequate.' This may be explained by the fact that suitability of internal Accounting controls depends on a number of factors unique to each entity including: organisation size, complexity, ownership characteristics, business nature, number of employees, etc.[30] This is one reason monitoring bodies within an organisation are essential. Monitoring bodies, such as audit committees of

[28] Cf. Treadway Report, Appendix F; and also Price Waterhouse 1988 (see reference in Bibliography).

[29] Turnbull Report 1999: '[e]ffective financial controls, including the maintenance of proper accounting records, are an important element of internal control. They help ensure that the company is not unnecessarily exposed to avoidable financial risks and that financial information used within the business and for publication is reliable. They also contribute to the safeguarding of assets, including the prevention and detection of fraud'. The Turnbull Report was published by the Internal Control Working Party of the Institute of Chartered Accountants in England & Wales. It was designed to provide guidance consistent with the requirements of the Combined Code and related Listing Rules regarding disclosure requirements and what is expected of boards of directors of listed companies.

[30] Treadway Report 1987. The Foreign Corrupt Practices Act (FCPA) provides limited guidance as to the level and type of internal Accounting controls considered adequate. Under the FCPA, covered companies are required to devise and maintain a system of internal Accounting controls sufficient to provide reasonable assurances that: transactions are executed in accordance with management's general or specific authorisation; transactions are recorded as necessary (1) to permit preparation of financial statements in conformity with generally accepted Accounting principles or any other criteria applicable to such statements, and (2) to maintain accountability for assets; access to assets is permitted only in accordance with management's general or specific authorisation; and the recorded accountability for assets is compared with the existing assets at reasonable intervals and appropriate action is taken with respect to any differences. Cf. s. 13(b)(2) Securities and Exchange Act 1934 [15 U.S.C. § 78m(b)(2)].

the board of directors, serve as a check on an entity's internal Accounting controls. By reviewing the internal Accounting controls used by an entity on a periodic basis monitoring bodies ensure the controls being used are appropriate for the organisation given its business and risks.[31]

2.1.2. General internal controls

Assuming the Revised Recommendation refers to general internal controls, the number and types of controls Parties could encourage pursuant to the Recommendation are limitless. The range of general internal controls can be limited by concentrating on specific areas where developing internal controls is particularly effective in combating bribery of foreign public officials.[32]

Internal controls in the form of written policies and procedures in key areas are critical to preventing bribes to foreign public officials. However, written internal controls alone are insufficient. An effective system of internal controls focuses on both written policies and procedures and broader controls, some of which cannot be reduced to writing.

Controls begin with the overall atmosphere at the company.[33] The compliance atmosphere at a company is generated from the top down. Setting the compliance atmosphere at a company begins with top company management. Top management's attitude toward bribery, which creates the environment or culture at a company, is often referred to as the 'tone at the top'. Tone at the top includes:

- making top management of the organisation responsible for establishing, implementing, and maintaining an effective internal controls system with appropriate oversight by corporate monitoring bodies;
- adopting a code of conduct which provides information and guidance to those within an organisation about the organisation's

[31] See II.2.3. below (discussing the role of monitoring bodies, such as audit committees).

[32] State Party legislation requiring companies to implement internal controls would likely be more effective if they included measures designed to sanction failures to adopt and implement such controls as well as incentives to do so. For example, § 8C2.5 Sentencing Guidelines 2005, ch. 8, entitled 'Culpability Score', provide for a downward departure in the applicable sanctions where, at the time of the offense, the organisation had in place an effective compliance and ethics programme: 69 Fed. Reg. 28994 (May 10, 2004). See also the discussion in ch. on Article 3 above.

[33] People engage in corrupt behavior for a variety of reasons. The popular 'fraud triangle' illustrates the three factors that typically contribute to a person's decision to engage in fraud for or against the company. The three factors are: opportunity, motive, and rationalization. Focusing on the overall atmosphere of compliance at a company encourages entities to develop a system of internal controls that extends beyond written procedures. This creates a greater likelihood that the controls will address factors contributing to decisions to pay bribes.

philosophy toward ethical business conduct and the basic principles governing that conduct; and

- establishing processes to monitor compliance with policies and procedures that are implemented to prevent and/or detect illegal acts including bribery.[34]

Tone at the top operates on the premise that one, if not the, most effective way to send the message about the importance of ethical behaviour is by example.[35] Tone at the top requires senior management to consider the effects of business pressures on compliance. Management must not create an environment in which the pressure on employees to achieve results is so excessive as to create compliance issues.

Another broad control against bribery is a code of conduct.[36] A code of conduct provides company employees guidance in handling questionable or difficult situations not covered by a specific written policy or procedure.[37] A code of conduct should:

- provide employee guidance on giving and receiving gifts;
- outline what constitutes a conflict of interest;
- remind employees that the company will compete in the marketplace honestly, directly, fairly, and in compliance with all applicable laws; and
- instruct an employee as to what they should do, if offered or solicited to give a 'gift' to a supplier, vendor or government official.[38]

Once established, organisations should distribute copies of the code of conduct to all employees including newly hired staff.[39] Once the code of

[34] Transparency International 2000 (see note 13).

[35] Stephen Cutler, former Director of the Division of Enforcement of the US Securities and Exchange Commission, noted the connection between some of the largest cases settled against companies and company executives in the preceding two years and the tone at the top at the companies implicated. He also emphasised that the tone at the top must come from all of senior management, not just the legal department, the compliance professionals, or human resource experts (cf. Cutler 2004).

[36] Sometimes referred to as an ethics policy, a code or standard of conduct is a 'management tool for establishing and articulating the corporate values, responsibilities, obligations, and ethical ambitions of an organization' (see reference in Bibliography for Institute of Business Ethics).

[37] A code of conduct is important to a company's atmosphere of compliance in much the same way as tone at the top. Also, as noted by DeGeorge 1987: '[t]he very exercise of developing a code is in itself worthwhile; it forces a large number of people…to think through in a fresh way their mission and the important obligations they as a group and as individuals have with respect to society as a whole'.

[38] J. T. Wells 1999.

[39] Some companies use orientation training, booklets, and the company intranet as the means of disseminating their code of conduct to employees.

conduct has been implemented, the company must take active steps to ensure that the rules and aspirations contained in the code are practised at the company and embedded at all levels. This necessitates having an open dialogue about challenges employees encounter in applying the code and questions employees may have about the code.

Outside the broad measures discussed above, Parties might encourage or require entities to develop and implement specific written internal controls to guard against bribes to foreign public officials.

Internal controls particularly effective in guarding against bribes to foreign public officials can be identified by looking at business areas where issues or 'red flags' related to bribery of foreign public officials are more likely to arise.[40] For example, opportunities for bribes to foreign public officials are amplified where there is increased access to foreign officials.[41] This would include areas such as customs and visas. Other business areas where internal controls would be particularly helpful in guarding against bribes to foreign public officials include:

- mergers/acquisitions;[42]
- joint ventures or other partnerships with other parties;
- interactions with and hiring of foreign agents;
- facilitation payments;
- charitable contributions;[43]
- taxes;[44]
- customs; licensing; bids/contracts involving government owned/controls entities; relationships with third parties, including contractors, vendors, suppliers, etc.;[45] high-risk countries or distant operations, etc.

[40] Further, these generalisations provide a wealth of information as to the types of internal controls that should be developed as well as the breadth of areas in which internal controls should be implemented with an eye toward combating bribery of foreign officials. See also the discussion of 'red flags' in ch. on Article 1 above.

[41] Other pressure areas can be identified using anecdotal evidence from prosecutions involving bribes to foreign public officials.

[42] Rapidly taking on new assets, liabilities, lines of business, and employees can drastically alter the compliance balance at a company. Mergers, acquisitions, and other business combinations also present issues regarding the surviving entity's liability for illicit payments by its predecessor or merger target.

[43] Charitable organizations can be used as a proxy for foreign government officials.

[44] The payment of taxes in excess of amounts actually due can be used as a method concealing bribes to foreign public officials.

[45] Internal controls should be risk-based and take into consideration an entity's relationship with, and scrutiny of, its outside vendors, suppliers, agents, and contractors to guard against the payment of bribes to foreign public officials.

Once an organisation has created a written system of internal controls tailored to its needs, it should continually monitor and asses the effectiveness of the controls. This is in part the role of internal audit departments.

An internal audit department should provide management with reasonable assurances that management is meeting its governance responsibilities. Internal audit should also provide management with guidance on opportunities to enhance governance, including anti-bribery internal controls.[46] While responsibility for conducting internal audits and related special investigations often falls to members of the audit department, it is the company's responsibility to ensure the internal audit department has the expertise and funding needed to perform its functions.

2.2. Annual statements and reports on internal controls

The Revised Recommendation also encourage Parties to adopt legislation requiring company management to make statements in annual reports about internal control mechanisms.[47] A review of Party legislation annual statements on internal controls is instructive as to what such statements might include.

The Turnbull Report, interpreting the requirements under the Combined Code applicable in England and Wales, calls for a 'narrative statement' on how the company has applied sections of the Combined Code relating to internal controls.[48]

> The board should, as a minimum, disclose that there is an ongoing process for identifying, evaluating, and managing the significant risks faced by the company, that it has been in place for the year under review and up to the date of approval of the annual report and accounts, that it is regularly reviewed by the board and accords with the guidance in [the Report]. . .The disclosures relating to the application of [internal control provisions] should include an acknowledgement by the board that it is responsible for the company's system of internal control and for reviewing its effectiveness. It should also explain that such a system is designed to manage rather than eliminate the risk of failure to achieve business objectives, and

[46] One of the first tasks in setting up an internal audit department is to hire a head of internal audit who is knowledgeable, qualified, and competent. Once the director of internal audit is chosen, the department should then be staffed with competent employees possessing the same characteristics. Internal audit should then compose a written audit plan detailing the audit scope and create audit work papers. Internal audits should result in written audit findings, which should be provided to heads within the organization as well as to senior management and the audit committee of the board of directors. In instances where special circumstances arise, internal audit should, as necessary, conduct special investigations. Cf., for example, Bill 2004, 5.

[47] OECD 1997a. [48] Turnbull Report 1999 (see note 29).

can only provide reasonable and not absolute assurance against material misstatement or loss.[49]

Similar provisions requiring statements regarding internal controls have been enacted under US law. Section 404 of the Sarbanes-Oxley Act of 2002 directed the US Securities and Exchange Commission to adopt rules requiring certain companies to include in annual reports a statement of management's responsibility for establishing and maintaining adequate internal control over financial reporting, as well as an assessment of the effectiveness of those internal controls.[50] While US law limits management's required statement of Accounting controls[51] the required statement is similar. The internal control report must include:

- a statement of management's responsibility for establishing and maintaining adequate internal control over financial reporting for the company; management's assessment of the effectiveness of the company's internal control over financial reporting as of the end of the company's most recent fiscal year;
- a statement identifying the framework used by management to evaluate the effectiveness of the company's internal control over financial reporting; and
- a statement that the registered public Accounting firm that audited the company's financial statements included in the annual report has issued an attestation report on management's assessment of the company's internal control over financial reporting.[52]

[49] The Turnbull Report 1999 also states that '[i]n relation to Code provision…the board should summarise the process it (where applicable, through its committees) has applied in reviewing the effectiveness of the system of internal control. It should also disclose the process it has applied to deal with material internal control aspects of any significant problems disclosed in the annual report and accounts. Where a board cannot make one or more of the disclosures [including the narrative statement and the processes applied in reviewing the effectiveness of systems of internal controls], it should state this fact and provide an explanation. The Listing Rules require the board to disclose, if it has failed to conduct a review of the effectiveness of the company's system of internal control. The board should ensure that its disclosures provide meaningful, high-level information and do not give a misleading impression. Where material joint ventures and associates have not been dealt with as part of the group for the purposes of applying this guidance, this should be disclosed'.

[50] Sarbanes-Oxley Act 2002, 15 U.S.C. § 7262.

[51] Rules 13a-14(d) and 15d-14(d) Amended Securities and Exchange Act 1934: 'Internal control over financial reporting is defined as 'a process designed by, or under the supervision of, the registrant's principal executive and principal financial officers, or persons performing similar functions, and effected by the registrant's board of directors, management, and other personnel, to provide reasonable assurance regarding the reliability of financial reporting and the preparation of financial statements for external purposes in accordance with generally accepted accounting principles.'

[52] Sarbanes-Oxley Act 2002, 15 U.S.C. § 7262.

Management is also required to evaluate any change in the company's internal control over financial reporting that occurred during a fiscal quarter that has materially affected, or is reasonably likely to materially affect, the company's internal control over financial reporting.[53]

2.3. Monitoring bodies

The Revised Recommendation also encourages state Parties to adopt legislation requiring entities to use monitoring bodies independent of management, such as audit committees. An audit committee is typically a standing committee of a company's board of directors. The audit committee is usually composed of directors not part of senior management and guided by an audit committee chair.

Audit committees are responsible for overseeing the company's accounting and financial reporting, and monitoring and evaluating its independent internal audit processes.[54] The audit committee depends on information sought and received from company management, internal audit, outside auditors, and its own advisor.[55] Where necessary, audit committees conduct special internal investigations.[56] Where payments to foreign public officials are concerned special internal investigations may be warranted.

Audit committees and other comparable monitoring bodies can be valuable in a company's effort to combat bribery of foreign public officials. They can provide oversight and a disinterested review of company actions. This is particularly important where company management is implicated in the payment of bribes.

2.4. Reporting bribery

The final internal control provision in the Revised Recommendation asks Parties to 'encourage companies to provide channels for communications by, and protection for, persons not willing to violate professional standards or ethics under instructions or pressure from hierarchical superiors'.[57] This Recommendation is actually two-pronged. Parties are advised

[53] See previous note 52. [54] Bill 2004, 1.
[55] See previous note 54. [56] See note 54.
[57] S. V.C.iv) OECD 1997a. State Parties seem to have been more responsive in implementing legislation encouraging these types of internal controls than the other recommended internal controls discussed above. This enhanced willingness may be attributable, at least in part, to the fact that interpreting this Recommendation and creating a framework under which it is widely applicable to many entities is easier and more clear cut than interpreting and applying the other recommended internal controls.

to: (1) encourage companies to provide channels for communication by persons unwilling to violate professional standards or ethics under instruction or pressure from hierarchical superiors; and (2) provide protection for persons who engage in such communications.[58]

2.4.1. Channels for communication

The initial step in providing channels for communication is establishing procedures for receipt of complaints. Party legislation can be effective by outlining general requirements of any such procedures.[59] Company procedures for the receipt of complaints might include, among other things:

- an explanation of the types of complaints to which procedures apply;[60]
- identification of the individual to whom employees should report complaints/concerns;
- identification of an alternative person to whom concerns/ complaints should be directed where the initial designee appears to have a conflict of interest or is otherwise unresponsive;

[58] Protection for persons not willing to violate professional standards or ethics under instructions or pressure from hierarchical superiors is often referred to as 'whistleblower protection'. Whistleblowing refers to the act of 'disclosing information that you reasonably believe is evidence of a violation of any law, rule, or regulation, or gross mismanagement, a gross waste of funds, an abuse of authority, or a substantial and specific danger to public health or safety' (FATF 40/2003).

[59] See, for example, US law: s. 301 Sarbanes-Oxley Act 2002. Under this section, audit committees are mandated to establish procedures for receipt of complaints by employees (301.4.A) and for the confidential submission of the complaint by employees (301.4.B). The exact language states: '(4) COMPLAINTS – Each audit committee shall establish procedures for: (A) the receipt, retention, and treatment of complaints received by the issuer regarding accounting, internal accounting controls, or auditing matters; and (B) the confidential, anonymous submission by employees of the issuer of concerns regarding questionable accounting or auditing matters.'

[60] For example, the company policy may state that complaints may refer to any possible breach by a company employee (or a third party affiliated with the company) of any external or internal regulation or any procedure, including any corrupt activity involving foreign public officials. How a company characterises reportable complaints is important. The description must be narrow enough so as to preclude frivolous complaints but broad enough so as not to chill employees in reporting where they have a reasonable belief that misconduct has occurred but no solid evidence in support of that belief. The task of locating and developing concrete evidence should not be delegated to the whistleblower employee, rather that is a function of the company's corollary investigation of the complaint. Additionally, in the foreign corruption context descriptions of complaints that should be reported should emphasise the importance of reporting suspicious activity involving foreign government officials. This could be accomplished by distributing circulars or other materials to employees.

- identification of the person(s) responsible for preliminary investigation of complaints;[61]
- identification of the methods by which complaints may be made;
- descriptions of how complaints will be handled;
- descriptions of the level of information the whistleblower should expect to receive regarding the progress of the investigation and its outcome;
- descriptions of circumstances under which the decision must be taken to report the suspicion to the law enforcement authorities.[62]

Once procedures for receiving complaints have been identified, the next step is establishing the means by which to report suspected activity. Possible reporting methods include verbal reports to the individual responsible, typed/written reports, and reports sent via mail. In many member countries hotlines have become the preferred communication method for reporting suspected bribes.[63]

It is important to note that even once procedures and mechanisms for reporting complaints have been established impediments to reporting known

[61] It is important that this individual be selected with forethought and caution and be made known to employees. Employee knowledge of who is responsible for investigating complaints will probably influence an employee's willingness to report known or suspected misconduct. Additionally, the rank of the person responsible for investigating complaints, as well as the resources dedicated to investigating complaints, indicates the level of seriousness with which the company views such complaints.

[62] SE-Ph2, 26 et seq.: '[The] Swedish International Development Cooperation Agency's [SIDA] Anticorruption Regulation of May 4, 2001, which was issued in the form of a manual in December 2004, contains background information about corruption and instructions on the actions to be taken when corruption is suspected. The guide does not identify at what level or in what circumstances the decision must be taken to report the suspicion to the law enforcement authorities in Sweden and/or abroad. SIDA states that there is no mandatory obligation for the agency to report any suspicion on development partners or consultants to the police for investigation in national or international law.'

[63] The OECD WGB has recommended that certain Parties establish 'hotlines'. Hotlines enable individuals to file complaints or provide information about known or suspected offences, including bribery of foreign public officials. Advantages of hotline reporting include 24-hour access and anonymity. Although many public institutions and private entities within member countries have set up hotlines, in many instances the actual value of these hotlines remains to be seen. For example, during on-site visits in Bulgaria in connection with the Phase 2 Country Report, OECD lead examiners noted that the hotlines, though in place, did not appear to be an important source of information about bribery offences. In fact, 'in some ministries, the hotlines were answered once a week and the representatives from one ministry were not aware of how the hotline was being used. Information was not provided about how many reports made to hotlines have led to prosecutions, or for what offences reports had been made' (BG-Ph2, 15). Cf. also GR-Ph2, 22.

or suspected incidents of bribes to public officials still exist – including cultural barriers.[64] These intrinsic cultural differences might be overcome by concentrated government and private sector initiatives within member countries to alter the perception of reporting offences.

2.4.2. Whistleblower protection

The second prong of the Revised Recommendation on anonymous reporting encourages Parties to adopt legislation protecting persons not willing to violate professional standards or ethics under instructions or pressure from hierarchical supervisors – whistleblowers.

Whistleblower protections are necessary, because any form of retaliation can deter public and private sector employees from reporting known or suspected incidents of bribes to foreign public officials and result in a failure of communication channels.[65]

OECD Phase 2 Country Reports indicate that quite a few state Parties have yet to adopt legislation providing for whistleblower protection; further, where enacted, such legislation may fail to provide sufficient protections to whistleblowers.[66]

Whistleblower policies are, however, important in that they emphasise a company's commitment to integrity and ethical behaviour by helping to foster and maintain an environment where employees can act appropriately, without fear of retaliation. Effective whistleblower protections should provide for the security of both civil servants and private employees.

[64] For example, as noted in the OECD's Phase 2 report for France, FR-Ph2, 15: 'in practice, it is unusual in France for employees to report business-related offences or instances of bribery. Spontaneously reporting financial misconduct to the competent authorities is not easy for an employee, because, in the French historical context, it tends to be regarded as *de□lation* (laying information with malicious intent against a person)'; cf. also IT-Ph2, 17: 'Foreign bribery committed by companies may also be reported by the company's employees who discover the crime. However, several police officers, academics, and representatives of trade unions at the on-site visit believed that Italian employees are unlikely to become whistleblowers. First, whistleblowing is not ingrained in the Italian culture, because it is linked to the historical concept of *delazione* [informers].'

[65] Cf., for example, BG-Ph2, 13: '[o]ne disincentive to the reporting of alleged cases of corruption is the absence of whistleblower protection legislation in Bulgaria. Representatives of the trade unions who met with the lead examiners at the on-site visit cited the lack of whistleblower protection as the main obstacle to the reporting of bribery by employees, particularly in companies where the union organs are weak. Employees most often fear retaliation in the form of dismissal by their employers as well as prosecution for insult and defamation'; GR-Ph2, 22–23: 'Another reason for the lack of reporting may be inadequate protection for whistleblowers from reprisals by their employers. There are no laws which specifically deal with this issue.'

[66] Cf., for example, HU-Ph2, 17 et seq.; IT-Ph2, 17; DE-Ph2, 25.

Consequently, an effective whistleblower protection regime includes both government legislation and company polices.[67]

Most whistleblower legislation provides for confidential or anonymous reporting. Confidential reporting allows employees to disclose the violation to certain people while assuring they are not publicly disclosed as the source of the complaint. Anonymous reporting, on the other hand, allows employees to disclose the violation such that no one, including those responsible for investigating the allegation, knows the employee's identity. Anonymous reporting, while possible, cannot always be guaranteed.[68] Many of the goals sought by anonymous reporting can be achieved using confidential reporting.[69] Confidential reporting is also advisable, because guarantees of confidentiality can be made subject to disclosure of the whistleblower under certain exigent circumstances, such as where required by law enforcement authorities.

In some countries whistleblower protection is considered strong absent formal legislation protecting whistleblowers. In other countries, in the absence of specific legislation, protection of whistleblowers derives from collective agreements and corporate codes of conduct.[70]

3. Independent external audit

The Revised Recommendation encourages Parties to take certain actions related to independent external audit. According to the OECD, '[f]inancial audits conducted by independent auditors provide external and objective assurance on the way in which financial statements have been prepared and presented'.[71]

[67] Cf., for example, IT-Ph2, 16 et seq., 51 (acknowledging that even where a private company provides whistleblower protections, those protections alone are insufficient because, if the company fails to abide by those protections, there is no overriding protection available to employees under Italian labour law, which does not sufficiently protect whistleblowers).

[68] In many instances guaranteeing a whistleblower's anonymity may not be possible. After receipt of the initial complaint, it may be necessary to speak with the whistleblower further to determine where and how corroborating information may be obtained. Also, complete anonymity may encourage the filing of false or malicious reports that use the company's whistleblower procedures to further personal intra-company vendettas. In addition, guarantees of anonymity may be usurped where investigating personnel must reveal the whistleblower's identity to law enforcement authorities: cf., for example, BG-Ph2, 13.

[69] Confidential reporting ensures that the employee is not widely known as the source of the complaint thus further insulating them from possible retaliatory actions.

[70] Cf., for example, GR-Ph2, 22. [71] OECD 2001b.

3.1. Requirement to submit to external audit

The Revised Recommendation asks Parties to consider whether their requirements for submitting to external audit are adequate. Entities subject to auditing requirements differ in each member country. In many instances, only entities with certain characteristics are subject to external audits, and/or government supervision.[72] This might create difficulties or thwart transparency as entities where there is a heightened risk of improper payments to foreign public officials may not be subject to external audit requirements.[73]

3.2. Auditor independence

The Revised Recommendation states that state Parties and professional associations should maintain adequate standards to ensure the independence of external auditors.[74] OECD Country Reports affirm that the rules of auditor independence vary considerably among state Parties.[75] The auditor independence rules of most member countries focus on the degree of sanguinity between the auditor (and the auditor's business partners, spouse, and immediate family members) and the audited entity.[76] However, even where there is initially little or no connection between the entity and the auditor this can change over time and the auditor and entity can become more interrelated by providing services for each other outside of the audit relationship. In recognition of this, some state Parties go one step further

[72] Cf., for example, AR-Ph1, 18 et seq.; CA-Ph2, 18 et seq. ('Pursuant to the CBCA and pursuant to securities legislation, all public companies in Canada are required to submit to an independent external audit. On the other hand, privately owned corporations can exempt themselves from an independent external audit with the unanimous consent of the shareholders. Representatives of the major accounting firms indicated that in practice privately owned Canadian companies are generally not independently audited unless specifically requested by a lender or investor, which rarely occurs. As a result, some of the largest companies in Canada are not subject to such an audit. Moreover, a privately owned corporation can obtain an exemption from consolidating accounts with the unanimous consent of the shareholders. Thus it is possible that some very large corporations (including foreign subsidiaries located in Canada) could exempt themselves from an independent audit and have no accounting records kept in Canada, which could create an accounting/auditing loophole.')

[73] Cf. again CA-Ph2, 18 et seq. An alternative suggestion is an OECD Recommendation that state Parties require all entities to subject their books and records to annual or bi-annual external review. These reviews could be limited targeting only business lines and areas where there is an increased likelihood of bribes.

[74] S. V.B.ii) OECD 1997a.

[75] Cf., for example, BR-Ph1, 27 et seq.; CA-Ph2, 19; PT-Ph1, 24 et seq.

[76] See previous note 75.

and impose mandatory auditor rotation.[77] Other Parties guarantee auditor independence by requiring that companies are audited by public officials that have no relation to the audited entity.[78] However, this situation also presents potential issues in the bribery context as the company's external auditors are government officials.

In the light of the varying standards of auditor independence, OECD guidance on certain minimum criteria necessary for ensuring auditor independence is advisable. Another option is a revised OECD Recommendation that Parties adopt, at a minimum, the auditor independence standards articulated by a specified international agency, such as the International Auditing & Assurance Standards Board (formerly the International Auditing Practices Committee (IAPAC)) of the International Federation of Accountants.[79] This would provide Parties with a benchmark by which to gauge the appropriateness of their existing auditor independence laws and provide guidance in formulating new laws.

3.3. Auditor reporting obligations

The third and fourth Revised Recommendation related to independent external audit suggests that Parties consider requiring the auditor who discovers indications of a possible illegal act of bribery to report this discovery to management and, as appropriate, to corporate monitoring bodies and ultimately, where necessary, to competent authorities.[80] OECD country reports indicate that Parties' adoption of this Recommendation vary. In some countries, auditors are required to report suspicions of foreign bribery to management and prosecutorial authorities.[81] In others, conflicting professional secrecy obligations would prohibit external auditors from revealing information about an audited company to an 'outsider'.[82] More perplexing are countries where external auditors have both the duty to report suspected illegal bribes to competent authorities and a professional

[77] BR-Ph1, 27 et seq. Under Brazilian law, rotation is mandatory for external independent auditors of listed companies, based on the belief that providing audit services to the same client for a long length of time may damage the quality of auditing or the independence of auditors. Brazilian law bans the provision of services to the same client for more than five consecutive years, and requires an interval of three years before being rehired.
[78] Cf., for example, AR-Ph1, 20.
[79] International Federation of Accountants 2005 (see reference in Bibliography).
[80] V.B.iii)–iv) OECD 1997a. [81] Cf., for example, SE-Ph1, 17 et seq.
[82] Cf., for example, FI-Ph2, 11; MX-Ph1, 18 et seq.

obligation to maintain the secrecy of the audited company – requirements that seem to be directly at odds.[83]

These differences and conflicts in the duty of external independent auditors to report suspicions of illegal activity often stem from cultural differences in the perceived role of auditors. For example, in Sweden auditors have an obligation to report suspicions of illegal acts by board members 'without undue delay' to the Board of Directors or the Managing Director.[84] Then, within two weeks of notifying the Board of Directors or Managing Director the auditor is expected to resign and report to the prosecutor.[85] While this might seem a robust system for reporting suspicions of illegal bribes, it is weakened by the fact that Swedish auditors do not perceive themselves as having an important role in detecting foreign bribery.[86] To fully realise the value of independent external auditors a shift is necessary such that the public and auditors view the external audit function as instrumental in combating bribery of foreign public officials.

III. Sanctions

1. Overview

The Convention calls for 'effective proportionate and dissuasive' sanctions for accounting offences. Despite this three-prong requirement some scholars believe compliance with the Convention's sanction provisions is measured by effectiveness alone.[87]

Further, the term 'effective' is often used synonymously with the term 'dissuasive', which is also referred to as deterence.[88] Hence, the objective of article 8's sanction requirements might be described as: the imposition of sanctions that sufficiently deters the activity in question, namely accounting offences. Having established effectiveness and deterrence as the goals of

[83] Cf., for example, CA-Ph2, 17 et seq.

[84] SE-Ph1, 17. [85] See previous note 84. [86] See note 84.

[87] See part III. in our ch. on Article 3 above ('it is clear that the effectiveness standard is always the final measure of compliance with [Art. 3] of the Convention. The evaluations and recommendations of the WGB contained in the monitoring reports (especially in the 'Phase 2' reports), invariably cite the [effectiveness] standard as their final framework'). The assertion in our ch. on Article 3 above relies on the WGB reports to corroborate effectiveness as the final measure of compliance with the sanction requirements of Art. 3. By correlation, effectiveness is also the likely final measure of compliance with the sanction requirements of Art. 8(2). This is also corroborated by the monitoring reports of the WGB. Cf., for example, FI-Ph2, 23.

[88] 'Dissuasive' means to deter. The Oxford English Dictionary defines 'dissuasive' as a verb meaning 'to persuade not to do'.

the sanctions, the question then becomes how does one measure success? According to chapter 3 of this commentary, the basic questions implicit in the WGB's reports are:

- What is the minimum standard of effectiveness?
- How much divergence does the Convention tolerate?[89]

In the context of Article 8 sanctions, these questions vary slightly. Review of the WGB country reports indicates that the basic questions posed regarding Article 8 sanctions are:

- Under Convention standards, what persons/entities must be subject to sanctions?
- What is the minimum standard of effectiveness?
- How much divergence does the Convention tolerate?

2. Parties subject to Accounting sanctions

Article 8 does not list the individuals, groups or entities that must be subject to sanctions for violation of Party accounting rules, enacted pursuant to Article 8. Unlike Article 3, which explicitly requires sanctions applicable to legal and natural persons, Article 8 leaves it to state Parties to determine which persons or entities will be subject to sanctions for accounting offences.

Notwithstanding this leeway, the Convention and reports of the WGB clearly envisage accounting sanctions applicable to both legal and natural persons.[90] In its Phase 2 monitoring reports, the WGB has scrutinised state Parties which do not provide sanctions against legal entities for Accounting violations. The WGB has expressed concern that, in the absence of 'liability of legal persons for Accounting offences it may not be possible to effectively address Accounting offences connected with the concealment of foreign bribery'.[91] However, despite the WGB's position, many Parties do not impose

[89] See part III. in our ch. on Article 3 above (discussing the implicit questions of the WGB with regard to the sanction provisions of Art. 3).

[90] Cf., for example, FI-Ph2, 22. This is further bolstered by Art. 3, which explicitly requires that state Party sanctions for active bribery apply to both legal and natural persons. It is unlikely that the Convention would repeatedly acknowledge the significance of corporate liability in combating active bribery but disregard the importance of corporate liability in combating accounting offences.

[91] FI-Ph2, 23. Despite this stance, the WGB appears to waiver in some instances, finding a state Party's Accounting sanctions effective despite the fact that legal entities are not held liable for Accounting offences. Cf., for example, BR-Ph1, 26 et seq. Based on the report by the WGB, it appears that Brazil only imposes sanctions for violations of Accounting provisions

liability on legal persons for Accounting offences.[92] Some Parties take the WGB position further and in addition to holding individuals and companies liable for accounting offences also hold auditors and audit firms liable for accounting offences. Australia, Brazil, Canada and the United States are among countries that impose some form of auditor liability. This is notable as there is no Convention requirement or Recommendation that accounting sanctions apply to auditors or audit firms.

Auditor liability may be premised on active involvement in the accounting offence or failure or malfeasance in the performance of audit duties.[93] Auditor penalties may include:

- civil damages where the performance of the auditor's audit functions causes a loss to other parties;
- deprivation of liberty where criminal charges are involved;
- administrative sanctions, e.g. warnings, disciplinary proceedings etc.

Countries unwilling to hold auditors or auditing firms civilly or criminally liable for accounting violations might consider alternative sanctions from civil organisations or professional societies. In some countries such sanctions already exist.

Sanctions imposed by these organisations might include internal disciplinary actions, bars, suspensions, and narrowing the offending party's audit rights.

on natural persons. Despite this shortcoming, the WGB found Brazil's system of rules and regulations regarding the maintenance of books and records, and financial statement disclosures, and Accounting and auditing standards, sufficient to provide effective, proportionate, and dissuasive penalties in relation to omissions and falsifications and in compliance with the requirements of the Convention.

[92] BR-Ph1, 26 et seq. Even where legislation exists sanctioning legal persons for Accounting offences, there are practical issues associated with prosecutions under such laws, many of which mirror difficulties in prosecuting legal persons for active bribery. One issue is how senior the offending party must be to impute liability to the company. Conditions under which a legal person can be held liable where no individual perpetrator has been identified also present problems. Additionally, there are difficulties with imposing liability for Accounting offences where the legal person alleged to have engaged in the bribe has been absorbed by or merged with another company. One view, in the context of active bribery prosecutions, is that the remaining company cannot be prosecuted because no-one can be responsible for acts other than their own: cf. FR-Ph2, 49. An alternative view is that prosecuting the acquiring legal entity is possible where that entity received the product of the principal bribery offence committed by the merged or acquired company.

[93] Malfeasance in the performance of audit duties might include violation of auditor independence rules, failure to report a material error, or misstatement in financial statements where there is an obligation to do so, etc. (cf. CA-Ph2, 19).

3. Minimum effectiveness and divergence in sanctions

Adhering to its goal of 'functional equivalence', the Convention does not enumerate specific sanctions for accounting violations which every Party must adopt. The Convention merely requires that 'each party shall provide…civil, administrative *or* criminal penalties' (italics added). Based on this standard, in order to be deemed effective, sanctions implemented by member countries must, at a minimum, provide civil, criminal, or administrative penalties. Failure to provide any sanctions for accounting offences would not meet the minimum standard.

There are also corresponding minimum standards for each category of sanctions – civil, criminal and administrative. Examination of the minimum standard for effectiveness in each category answers the second question posed in Chapter 3: how much divergence does the Convention tolerate?

The short answer to this question is that the Convention allows wide diversion in sanctions imposed for accounting offences. This is in accord with the Convention's recurring theme of functional equivalence. Parties can adopt criminal, civil, or administrative sanctions or some assortment of the three and still realise the Convention's minimum effectiveness standard or its deterrence objective.

3.1. Divergence in criminal sanctions

As noted, the Convention does not require state Parties to authorise any criminal sanctions for Accounting violations. On this basis it is possible for a country with no criminal sanctions for Accounting violations to obtain effectiveness under the Convention.[94]

At this juncture the question returns again to what level of criminal sanctions for Accounting violations are effective – or provide adequate deterrence. Although the Convention does not require criminal sanctions, criminalisation is clearly a priority of the WGB. In its report on Canada, the WGB noted that Canada's criminal sanction of six months imprisonment seemed 'relatively low'.[95] Nonetheless, the WGB ultimately found Canada's sanctions for accounting offences 'effective, proportionate, and dissuasive'

[94] See, for example, DE-Ph1, 13 and FR-Ph1, 24. Although both Germany and France impose criminal sanctions for Accounting violations, it appears that criminal punishment is an alternative to civil fines.

[95] CA-Ph2, 18.

after noting there were potentially much higher penalties under other provincial securities legislation.[96]

The WGB generally found acceptable Party legislation providing for imprisonment ranging from a low of one year[97] to a high of ten years. On average, Parties impose three to five years' imprisonment for accounting violations.[98] The range is comparable to the average imprisonment for active bribery. This is an important fact as it indicates that Parties and the WGB are equally concerned with penalising accounting violations as active bribery.

3.2. Divergence in civil sanctions

In addition to criminal sanctions, the Convention and the WGB also permit punishment for accounting offences in the form of civil penalties. Again, Parties are not required to impose any civil penalties for accounting violation and, based on country reports, the WGB does not seem particularly concerned where a Party does not impose civil liability for accounting offences but instead opts only to impose criminal sanctions.[99] The WGB also seems nonplussed by Parties that impose fines as an alternative to imprisonment.[100]

Civil sanctions for accounting violations may include: monetary fines;[101] orders prohibiting offending natural persons from managing a corporation;[102] and joint and several liability of company administrators and managers where the accounting offences cause damage to third parties.[103] Monetary fines seem to be the civil penalty most widely used by Parties. In its country reports, the WGB reviews the amount of the monetary penalty to which individuals and entities may be subject under the Parties' sanctioning regime, in order to determine if the potential penalty amount satisfies the Convention's effectiveness/deterrence objective. Reviewing the amounts of monetary fines the WGB has found acceptable and in accord with the Convention it is clear that a wide range of monetary penalties are viewed as acceptable in providing the desired deterrence effect.

[96] See previous note 95.

[97] BR-Ph1, 25 et seq. Brazil does impose a lesser imprisonment term of six months to two years, and a fine, for falsification of books and records, but only where the intent is tax evasion.

[98] DE-Ph1, 21; FI-Ph1, 13; KR-Ph1, 16.

[99] BG-Ph1, 16 et seq.

[100] Cf., for example, FR-Ph1, 24 et seq.

[101] Cf., for example, CA-Ph1, 17; CH-Ph1, 16 et seq.; CL-Ph1, 18 et seq.; FI-Ph1, 13; FR-Ph1, 24 et seq.; KR-Ph1, 16.

[102] AU-Ph1, 18 et seq.

[103] BE-Ph1, 16 et seq.

3.3. Divergence in administrative sanctions

The Convention also allows Parties to impose administrative penalties for accounting violations. Administrative penalties are imposed by entities and agencies of the executive branch, as opposed to civil penalties which are imposed by the legislative or judicial branch. Administrative penalties imposed by Parties include: fines, 'loss of rights',[104] and in the case of corporations, revocation of corporate existence.[105]

Based on a strict reading of the Convention, Parties could opt to only impose administrative penalties for accounting violations and forego any civil or criminal penalties. However, the WGB has not had the opportunity to address whether administrative sanctions alone would satisfy the 'effective, proportionate, and dissuasive' standard, as no Party has opted to only impose enacted administrative penalties for accounting offences. On the contrary, most state Parties do not use administrative penalties.

IV. Conclusion

Reports of the WGB demonstrate that most Parties have successfully adopted legislation giving effect to the goals of Article 8 – prohibiting the establishment of off-the-books accounts, the making of off-the-books or inadequately identified transactions, the recording of non-existent expenditures, and the entry of liabilities with incorrect identification of their object, as well as the use of false documents for the purpose of bribing foreign public officials or of hiding such bribery. Nonetheless, 'gaps' and differences in Parties' domestic accounting laws, such as differences in the types of entities covered by those laws, threaten to jeopardise comprehensive application and enforcement of the Convention's standards.

As to the Revised Recommendations relating to Article 8, Parties' acceptance of the Recommendations vary greatly; and even where Parties have implemented one or more of the Revised Recommendations the manner and extent to which a particular Recommendation has been implemented varies significantly. On some level, this variation is completely acceptable, if not desired, as it is in line with the Convention goal of

[104] BE-Ph1, 13, 17. 'Loss of Rights' is provided for under the Belgian Criminal Code; however, during its review Belgium described the sanction to the WGB as administrative in nature. Loss of rights 'allow[s], or require[s], depending on the case, the courts to forbid those found guilty of certain offences to exercise [sic] various rights, such as holding public functions, employment or office, acting as an administrator of an estate, etc. The courts have latitude to deprive the convicted person of all or part of the rights listed'.

[105] CL-Ph1, 21.

functional equivalence. However, the variations also highlight the need for more lucid guidance on precisely what a Recommendation calls for and how Parties should implement the Recommendation.

As to sanctions under Article 8, review of the WGB country reports indicates that, by Convention standards, most Parties have implemented sanctions capable of attaining the Convention's goal of effective deterrence, and much of the remaining work in this area will be waiting to see if these sanctions will in fact serve as effective deterrence to accounting offences.

References

For documentation see the consolidated bibliography at the end of this book.

Bill, A. (2004), *Audit Committee Guide: A Source of Information for Audit Committees of Public Company Boards of Directors*, 2nd edn, New York.

Cutler, S. (2004), 'Tone at the Top: Getting it Right' (speech by SEC Staff at the *Second Annual General Counsel Roundtable*, 3 December 2004, available at: http://www.sec.gov > Speeches and Publications > 2004/fourth quarter).

DeGeorge, R. T. (1987), *Military Ethics: A Code of Ethics for Officers*, Washington.

Institute of Business Ethics, *Codes of Conduct* (available at: http://www.ibe.org.uk > Site Map > Codes of Conduct).

International Chamber of Commerce (2000), *Fighting Bribery: A Corporate Practices Manual*, London.

International Federation of Accountants (2005), *Handbook of International Auditing, Assurance, and Ethics Pronouncements* (available at: http://www.ifac.org).

Price Waterhouse (1988), *Effective Internal Accounting Controls for Non-Profit Organizations: A Guide for Directors and Management.*

Transparency International (ed.) (2000), *Overall Observations, Financial Transparency and Accounting Initiative: OECD Convention on Combating Bribery of Foreign Public Officials* (available at: http://www.transparency-usa.org > Publications).

Wells, J. T. (1999), *Fraud Prevention: A Fistful of Dollars* (available at: http://www.securitymanagement.com > Library > search by title).

Articles 9, 10, and 11. International Co-operation

MAURICE HARARI AND
ANNE VALÉRIE JULEN BERTHOD

Article 9 – Mutual Legal Assistance

1. Each Party shall, to the fullest extent possible under its laws and relevant treaties and arrangements, provide prompt and effective legal assistance to another Party for the purpose of criminal investigations and proceedings brought by a Party concerning offences within the scope of this Convention and for non-criminal proceedings within the scope of this Convention brought by a Party against a legal person. The requested Party shall inform the requesting Party, without delay, of any additional information or documents needed to support the request for assistance and, where requested, of the status and outcome of the request for assistance.

2. Where a Party makes mutual legal assistance conditional upon the existence of dual criminality, dual criminality shall be deemed to exist if the offence for which the assistance is sought is within the scope of this Convention.

3. A Party shall not decline to render mutual legal assistance for criminal matters within the scope of this Convention on the ground of bank secrecy.

Official Commentary

Article 9 – Mutual Legal Assistance

30. Parties will have also accepted, through paragraph 8 of the Agreed Common Elements annexed to the 1997 OECD Recommendation, to explore and undertake means to improve the efficiency of mutual legal assistance.

Re paragraph 1:

31. Within the framework of paragraph 1 of Article 9, Parties should, upon request, facilitate or encourage the presence or availability of persons, including persons in custody, who consent to assist in investigations or participate in proceedings. Parties should take measures to be able, in appropriate cases, to transfer temporarily such a person in custody to a Party requesting it and to credit time in custody in the requesting Party to the transferred person's sentence in the requested Party. The Parties wishing to use this mechanism should also take measures to be able, as a requesting Party, to keep a transferred person in custody and return this person without necessity of extradition proceedings.

Re paragraph 2:

32. Paragraph 2 addresses the issue of identity of norms in the concept of dual criminality. Parties with statutes as diverse as a statute prohibiting the bribery of agents generally and a statute directed specifically at bribery of foreign public officials should be able to co-operate fully regarding cases whose facts fall within the scope of the offences described in this Convention.

Article 10 – Extradition

1. Bribery of a foreign public official shall be deemed to be included as an extraditable offence under the laws of the Parties and the extradition treaties between them.

2. If a Party which makes extradition conditional on the existence of an extradition treaty receives a request for extradition from another Party with which it has no extradition treaty, it may consider this Convention to be the legal basis for extradition in respect of the offence of bribery of a foreign public official.

3. Each Party shall take any measures necessary to assure either that it can extradite its nationals or that it can prosecute its nationals for the offence of bribery of a foreign public official. A Party which declines a request to extradite a person for bribery of a foreign public official solely on the ground that the person is its national shall submit the case to its competent authorities for the purpose of prosecution.

4. Extradition for bribery of a foreign public official is subject to the conditions set out in the domestic law and applicable treaties and arrangements of each Party. Where a Party makes extradition conditional upon the existence of dual criminality, that condition shall be deemed to be fulfilled if the offence for which extradition is sought is within the scope of Article 1 of this Convention.

Official Commentary

Article 10 – Extradition

Re paragraph 2:

33. A Party may consider this Convention to be a legal basis for extradition if, for one or more categories of cases falling within this Convention, it requires an extradition treaty. For example, a country may consider it a basis for extradition of its nationals if it requires an extradition treaty for that category but does not require one for extradition of non-nationals.

Article 11 – Responsible Authorities

For the purposes of Article 4, paragraph 3, on consultation, Article 9, on mutual legal assistance and Article 10, on extradition, each Party shall notify to the Secretary-General of the OECD an authority or authorities responsible for making and receiving requests, which shall serve as channel of communication for these matters for that Party, without prejudice to other arrangements between Parties.

Chapter contents

I. Introduction

1. General background

For a long time, 'issues of criminal justice policy were thought of in almost exclusively national terms',[1] with the notable exception of extradition law. Criminal offences were indeed mostly local in their commission or their effects and criminal statutes reflected this situation through their territorial application. Moreover, states considered that there was no legal duty upon them to render assistance in criminal matters absent a specific binding agreement to that effect. The circumstances changed as a result of technological advances, important migrations, the growth of international travel and the sophistication of modern communications. Today, the assertion that one state need not pay attention to the penal law of another can no longer be upheld. The transnational elements of modern crimes, their magnitude and complexity, the organisation of criminals acting simultaneously in several states, require new or more efficient instruments of co-operation capable of overcoming the barriers of sovereignty and the differences between legal systems. Indeed, national frontiers no longer constitute obstacles for criminals. They only render their prosecution more difficult.[2] Accordingly, states began

[1] Gilmore 2004, 13. [2] Hafiez 2004, 159.

at the end of the nineteenth century and through the twentieth century to provide each other with both formal and informal assistance so that criminals do not escape detection or prosecution by crossing national boundaries.

The expanded effort to tackle transnational corruption, among other crimes of great concern on the international scale,[3] exemplifies that shift in policy. It reflects a growing awareness of the urgent need to improve the mechanisms of assistance to combat more effectively those criminal activities in which persons from various countries are implicated. The gathering of evidence, the freezing of assets, the location and surrender of an accused across borders are indeed cumbersome proceedings. They contrast dramatically with the ease of capital movements or global travel, of which criminals take great advantage to hide and conceal the proceeds of their crimes.[4] One of the goals of the Convention was precisely to improve judicial co-operation specifically in relation to the offence of bribery of a foreign official. Mutual legal assistance and extradition are among the core instruments of the judicial authorities in the framework of international co-operation, while a significantly wide range of assistance is also handled through informal police-to-police channels, provided that no coercive measures are envisaged.[5] Here, however, only prosecutorial and judicial forms of assistance will be considered.

2. Some definitions

2.1. Mutual legal assistance in criminal matters

Mutual legal assistance in criminal matters can be defined as a process by which the requested state executes on its territory an official act to gather evidence on a specific criminal case which is under investigation or is being prosecuted in the requesting state. It covers an ever-expanding range of measures including interviewing witnesses, transfer of evidence, search of private or business premises, including bank account enquiries. It can also cover the confiscation of assets, the service of a summons to appear in court or intimation of other court decisions or court documents.[6]

[3] Such as drug trafficking, money laundering, or terrorism. [4] Dommel 1999.

[5] 'The principal types of such police level co-operation are: (1) obtaining and providing public record information; (2) locating persons; (3) serving documents; (4) executing investigative requests; (5) conducting joint investigations; and (6) directly assisting investigations in the requested country' (Abbell 2004, 1 et seq.).

[6] Hafiez 2004, 159; Spinellis 1999, 373 et seq.

2.2. Extradition

Extradition involves, by contrast, the surrender by one state, at the request of another, of an individual who is accused or has been convicted of an offence committed within the jurisdiction of the requesting state for the purpose of (a) prosecution or (b) serving of the sentence passed on the offender.[7] 'Although many of the legal principles underlying mutual legal assistance derive from extradition law and practice',[8] there are important differences between these two forms of judicial co-operation. Extradition directly affects the liberty of a person. As such, it logically enables less flexibility in the granting of a request for assistance. Moreover, to achieve extradition, some level of agreement has to be reached between the states involved. Without this 'contract', there is no obligation to surrender a fugitive.[9] There are several ways to reach such an arrangement, whether formal or informal, based on a treaty, bilateral or multilateral, or by application of the national legislation of the requested state. In fact, regardless of the type of assistance sought in criminal matters, the presence of coercive measures means that states must fulfil certain prerequisites. In the light of the inherent cross-border aspects of bribery of a foreign official, international co-operation is of the essence in order to ensure an efficient prosecution.

3. Contents of this chapter

This chapter will be structured as follows. In part II. we will first look at the existing framework and scope of international agreements. Part III. will describe, in broad terms, the commonly accepted requirements and conditions for granting assistance. Then, in part IV., we will briefly state the main features of Articles 9, 10, and 11, and will attempt to reveal the standard which has emerged on the basis of OECD monitoring. Part V. will address selected issues which the Convention left open but which from the

[7] Cf. Gilbert 1998, 15 referring to 'Extradition and Interstate Rendition', Vol. 1, 3, (1891) translating Billot (1874), *Traité de l'extradition*, 1.

[8] Aiolfi and Ledergerber 2005, 54.

[9] The principle that no obligation to extradite exists in the absence of a specific binding agreement has been laid down by many states, in particular those of a Common Law tradition. The Civil Law countries are less restricted to treaty-based extradition. They also seek and provide extradition as a matter of comity or reciprocity, despite the lack of a specific treaty: this is, for instance, the case in Switzerland (Art. 8 IMAC). Nevertheless, some Civil Law jurisdictions have also entered into such arrangements, particularly with the states whose domestic law mandated such a relationship (Bassiouni 1974, 7 et seq.).

practitioner's standpoint are very important. There will be some final words of conclusion regarding the impact of the Convention on international co-operation.

II. An overview of international instruments for co-operation in criminal matters

1. Legal framework

1.1. The universal approach

At global level, efforts to agree binding general instruments achieving the widest international co-operation in mutual legal assistance and extradition have largely foundered. One has, however, seen adoption of model treaties, prepared under the auspices of the United Nations (UN).[10] In the absence of a deeper global consensus, these texts are simple and provide 'a mere framework' to serve as a reference point for future negotiations between states or as a basis for domestic legislation.[11] Nevertheless, they have over 130 signatories.

Other global efforts have been more successful in approaching co-operation from the standpoint of the repression of some specific offences. One can point to several major international Conventions dealing with the repression of specific offences which also embrace the concept of judicial co-operation at an international level.[12] These instruments, although mostly framed in general terms, have made 'a major contribution towards increasing' the availability of mutual assistance 'in areas of the world, where it was underdeveloped or unknown'.[13] They also brought recognition of the role international co-operation can play in combating transnational organised crime.[14] The UN Convention Against Corruption of 2003, signed by 140 countries and ratified by seventy up to October 2006,[15] is particularly worthy of mention. The extent to which it embraces and articulates in detail a strategy to prevent and redress the effects of

[10] Model Treaty on Extradition (UN MTE 1990); Model Treaty on Mutual Assistance in Criminal Matters (UN MTMA 1990); Model Treaty on the Transfer of Proceedings in Criminal Matters (UN MTTP 1990); Model Treaty on the Transfer of Supervision of Offenders Conditionally Sentenced or Conditionally Released (UN MTTS 1990).
[11] McClean 2002, 214.
[12] Specifically the UN Conventions against terrorism (UN 1973; UN 1997; UN 1999a), illicit drug trafficking (UN 1988) and transnational organized crime (UN 2000).
[13] Gilmore 2004, 63. [14] Prost 1998.
[15] UN 2003. It entered into force on December 14, 2005.

corruption through mutual legal and technical assistance distinguishes it from earlier multilateral treaty initiatives at the global level.

1.2. The multilateral regional approach

1.2.1. The Council of Europe

At the regional level and not only in Europe, multilateral arrangements abound.[16] States sometimes limit themselves to a set of recommendations intended to foster national implementation according to an agreed pattern;[17] they may also undertake to lay down minimum rules designed to create general binding obligations. In Europe,[18] the leading role for the promotion of co-operation in criminal law matters has traditionally been played by the COE, whose membership, since the end of the Cold War, has embraced numerous countries from Central and Eastern Europe.[19] Beginning with the Conventions on Extradition,[20] Mutual Assistance in Criminal Matters [21] and their Additional Protocols,[22] the COE has made great advances in judicial co-operation by developing commonly used instruments that reflect principles recognised as general concepts and adhered to by most European states.[23]

[16] Among the non-European instruments in the area of extradition, cf., for example, the Arab League Extradition Agreement of 1952; the Inter-American Convention on Extradition of 1981; the Economic Community of West African States Convention on Extradition of 1994. Among the vehicles of mutual legal assistance, cf. the Arab League's Convention on Mutual Assistance in Criminal Matters of 1983; the Inter-American Convention on Mutual Assistance in Criminal Matters of 1992 (ratified to date by eighteen countries); the Economic Community of West African States Convention on Mutual Assistance in Criminal Matters of 1992 and the Declaration on Law Enforcement Co-operation adopted by the South Pacific Forum in July 1992.

[17] For a discussion of the Commonwealth Scheme for Mutual Assistance, cf. Gilmore 2004, 230.

[18] The most extensive multilateral developments in transnational co-operation are more frequent in jurisdictions drawn from the Civil Law tradition. Common Law countries prefer bilateral treaties as a consequence of their concept of the 'territorial nature of prescriptive jurisdiction' (Gilmore 1995, xv). The United Kingdom eventually ratified both the COE Convention on Extradition (COE 1957) and the COE Convention on Mutual Assistance in Criminal Matters (COE 1959) in 1991.

[19] Albania, Armenia, Azerbaijan, Bosnia and Herzegovina, Bulgaria, Croatia, the Czech Republic, Estonia, Georgia, Hungary, Latvia, Lithuania, Moldova, Poland, Romania, the Russian Federation, Serbia and Montenegro, Slovak Republic, Slovenia, 'The former Yugoslav Republic of Macedonia', and Ukraine.

[20] COE 1957, signed on 13 December 1957, in force since 18 April 1960. By the end of 2006, it had been ratified by forty-seven states including all the new Members from Central and Eastern Europe.

[21] COE 1959, entered into on 20 April 1959, in force since 12 June 1962. It has since been ratified by forty-six states.

[22] COE 1975; COE 1978b; COE 1978a; COE 2001.

[23] The COE 1983 is particularly worthy of mention. Several non-Member States of the COE have adhered to it: inter alia Australia, Canada, Panama, the United States.

Sufficiently flexible to be adapted to a variety of legal systems throughout Europe and further afield, these Conventions nonetheless leave room for different interpretations, as the execution of a request is still formally governed by the law of the requested state.[24] Reservations are permissible in respect of any provision of the Conventions and ample use has been made of this possibility, creating impediments to extradition and mutual legal assistance. Nevertheless, recent Protocols have expanded the role of the Conventions by eliminating some of these procedural impediments. In the 1990s, COE action in this field has been built upon in the narrower geographic context of the European Union (EU); some of these EU developments have in turn influenced COE developments.[25]

1.2.2. The European Union

Actively engaged in judicial co-operation in criminal matters since the entry into force in 1993 of the Maastricht Treaty,[26] the EU has since concluded a number of important Conventions and more recently Framework Decisions relating to mutual legal assistance and extradition (now known in the EU context as 'surrender' of persons). Regarding mutual legal assistance, the Convention on Mutual Assistance in Criminal Matters of 29 May 2000 and its Protocol of 2001 deserve particular mention.[27] Regarding extradition and

[24] McClean 2002, 173.

[25] Many Arts. of the COE 2001a are, for example, derived from the EU 2000 and its Additional Protocol (EU 2001). The EU 2000 Convention entered into force on 23 August 2005.

[26] Title VI of the Maastricht Treaty (EU 1992) created the 'Third Pillar' dealing with co-operation in the fields of Justice and Home Affairs, to which the Treaty of Amsterdam (EU 1997d), reformulating the policy goal to be the creation of an 'Area of Freedom, Security and Justice' which would require some harmonisation of criminal laws as well as much closer co-operation in criminal justice matters. The Schengen Agreements should also be mentioned. They are now in force in the fifteen Member States of the EU pre-enlargement of 1 May 2004 as part of EU law (except in the United Kingdom and Ireland, though they have opted in to part of the provisions). Two non-Member States, Norway and Iceland, also apply the Schengen provisions, in intergovernmental relations with the EU. The newly acceded EU Member States (Cyprus, Czech Republic, Estonia, Hungary, Latvia, Lithuania, Malta, Poland, Slovakia and Slovenia) are expected to fully implement the Schengen acquis for the end of 2007. Switzerland is expected to do so in 2008. Designed as a means of gradually abolishing controls at frontiers, the Schengen Agreement of 1985 and the Schengen Implementing Agreement of 1990 contain mutual assistance provisions, establishing a computerised database (Schengen Information System). They also contain visa and asylum provisions, some of which have now been superseded by EU measures (McClean 2002, 169; Swart 1999, 180 et seq.). The Schengen Agreements now function within the EU's institutional system.

[27] The range of available co-operation is expanded to administrative criminal offences and cases involving corporate liability. The EU 2000 and its Protocol also foster new developments such as the interception of telecommunications, the application of controlled deliveries, infiltration or undercover operations, joint investigative teams, hearings by video or telephone conference, personal data protection, and assistance relating to banking information.

surrender of persons, the Convention on Simplified Extradition Procedure of 10 March 1995 and the Convention on Extradition of 27 September 1996 should be mentioned, though these have now been superseded, as far as the twenty-five EU Member States are concerned, by the Framework Decision on the European Arrest Warrant. The main obstacles to speedy extradition have in fact been lifted. The old procedures of extradition have been replaced by the mutual acceptance of the validity of an Arrest Warrant emanating from a competent judicial authority of a Member State.[28] The European Arrest Warrant lends procedural and substantive cohesion to extradition law and practice in the EU.

1.2.3. Other relevant agreements

Aside from agreements dealing specifically with international co-operation, some regional agreements related to the prosecution of specific offences are also relevant as they echo previous work on mutual legal assistance and extradition and introduce some innovative elements. In its Convention on Money Laundering of 1990, the COE outlined for the first time a reference to spontaneous communication of information (Article 10), execution of provisional measures (Article 11) and confiscation (Articles 13–17).[29] Non-European States were involved in its elaboration.[30]

Regional Conventions dealing specifically with corruption should also be mentioned, since they in effect bind the parties to co-operate in prosecuting with the offences described: the Inter-American Convention Against Corruption of 1996 (Articles 13–20), the African Union Convention on Preventing and Combating Corruption of 2003, the EU Convention Against Corruption of 1997 (Articles 8–9), the COE Criminal Law Convention on Corruption of 1999 (Articles 21, 23, 25–31)[31] and, of course, Articles 9–11 of the OECD anti-bribery Convention[32] all provide for such co-operation.

[28] Art. 2 EU 2002c. The system that prevails now is one of free movement of judicial decisions in criminal matters. Member States should execute any European Arrest Warrant on the basis of the principle of mutual recognition, without enforcement of the dual criminality requirement (at least for thirty-two generic types of offences, including drug trafficking, terrorism, corruption, and laundering of the proceeds of a crime). This instrument has been widely accepted. All Member States had transposed the Framework Decision in national law by 1 November 2004. The first experiences have also been conclusive, with the exception of the surrender of nationals. For a discussion, cf. Huet and Koering-Joulin 2005, 471 et seq.

[29] This Convention will be superseded by the COE 2005, which is open to signature and has to date been signed by twenty-three countries. It has not yet entered into force.

[30] Australia, Canada, Colombia, and the United States, but only Australia ratified it so far.

[31] Entered into force in July 2002. An Additional Protocol was adopted on 15 May 2003 and entered into force in February 2005.

[32] Six non-OECD states (Argentina, Brazil, Bulgaria, Chile, Estonia, and Slovenia) are among the thirty-six signatories of the anti-bribery Convention (as at 30 October 2006).

1.3. The bilateral approach

Alongside these global and multilateral treaties there exists a vast network of bilateral treaties, in particular in the area of extradition. Since extradition is not an absolute international obligation in the absence of a binding agreement, the domestic laws of most states do not contemplate granting extradition in such a situation. To overcome this hurdle, states have resorted to the negotiation of extradition treaties, often on a bilateral basis.[33] In the United States, as in most Commonwealth countries, the restriction to treaty-based extradition was quasi-absolute. It led to a major undertaking of treaty-making to cover all parts of the world and then to keep the instruments up to date.[34] As already mentioned, in states with a Civil Law tradition, international co-operation, including extradition, is also possible in the absence of a treaty, relying on the principle of reciprocity.[35] Historically, bilateral treaties were the first means to ground extradition relationships. States have since developed regional and international instruments because of the practical problems of negotiating and renegotiating individual instruments[36] in a world community in which closer co-operation in criminal matters is essential, given worldwide concern over global threats to peace and security.[37]

Originally, provisions on international legal assistance were thought of as an accessory to extradition; they were embodied in extradition treaties. Only a few articles would deal with this aspect. But the development of international co-operation led to the negotiation of numerous mutual assistance agreements which also take a bilateral form, often supplementing existing multilateral agreements.[38]

This need to establish bilateral treaties was felt to be particularly acute in order to accommodate differences between Civil Law and Common Law jurisdictions. The United States had a pioneering role in negotiating the first breakthrough instrument. The mutual legal assistance treaty with Switzerland, which came into force in January 1977, was indeed the first ever concluded for co-operation in criminal matters between a Common Law and a Civil Law nation. Since then, the United States has been a

[33] Bassiouni 1974, 13. See also Art. 10(2) of the Convention, analysed in IV.3. below, that refers to the state Parties making extradition conditional on the existence of an extradition treaty.
[34] Bassiouni 1974, 25 et seq. [35] See note 9. [36] Prost 1998.
[37] For example, drug trafficking, international hijacking, and hostage-taking, terrorism, and child pornography.
[38] For instance, Switzerland adopted a specific agreement with all neighbouring countries (Austria, Germany, France, and Italy) to supplement the Convention on Mutual Assistance in Criminal Matters (COE 1959).

leading force in the growth of the bilateral assistance network.[39] The positive first experience acted as a powerful inducement for others to follow. Australia and Canada have, in recent years, undertaken an ambitious programme of bilateral negotiations.[40] Today, the rapidly expanding network of bilateral mutual assistance treaties rivals the network of extradition treaties.

1.4. National legislation on international co-operation

Finally, in some states, mutual assistance as well as extradition can be provided on the sole basis of domestic national legislation. It must be noted that such legislation cannot prevail over the provisions contained in the bilateral treaties or the multilateral Conventions to which a state has adhered.[41] Therefore, internal legislation can only complete existing agreements and allow for a larger scope of co-operation. This internal legislation is applicable without genuine reservation when the request for assistance originated in a state to which the requested country is not 'contractually' bound.[42] In those circumstances, assistance may be granted either generally to all states[43] or to specific states so indicated.

III. The accepted standards of international judicial co-operation

We shall now briefly describe the requirements and governing principles of, and the obstacles to, international co-operation. As stated above, these principles and obstacles derive from extradition practice; in fact the most important of them were later on integrated in mutual assistance arrangements and agreements.

[39] By 2004, the United States had fifty-four mutual legal assistance Treaties (or MLAT) in force and eight others at various stages of implementation with China, Colombia, Germany, India, Ireland, Japan, Sweden, and Venezuela. The United States are particularly concerned to work more closely with the major 'bank secrecy jurisdictions' in order to investigate and prosecute drug trafficking and money laundering crimes: cf., for example, the Treaty of 1986 with the United Kingdom concerning the Cayman Islands or the Treaty of 1987 concerning the Bahamas (Abbell 2004, A-45, 46).

[40] Australia has concluded more than 20 mutual legal assistance Treaties and Canada more than 35.

[41] Poncet and Gully-Hart 1999, 283. [42] Bertossa 2004, 176.

[43] As provided inter alia in Belgium, Finland, Luxemburg, Sweden, and Switzerland. It should be noted that, in general, such domestic legislation will allow for co-operation in the absence of a treaty but not create an obligation to grant it. It will, however, usually be given on a reciprocal basis. Cf. Gilbert 1991, 26 et seq.

1. Requirements and governing principles

1.1. Pacta sunt servanda

It is a fundamental principle of international public law that treaties are binding on the parties and must be performed in good faith.[44] Agreements in the field of co-operation in criminal matters are thus subject to this principle, the effects of which are important since they allow the requested state to rely fully on the assertions of the requesting state. Therefore, the facts alleged in a request will not have to be verified, since the corollary of this principle is that it will be presumed that the requesting state is acting bona fide.

It follows that, even in states where a request, including the underlying facts, are very closely scrutinised, the *authenticity* of the facts alleged by the requesting state may not be subject to challenge. Equally, questions related to the competence or jurisdiction of the requesting authorities, or the relevance of the documentation asked for in mutual assistance cases, will not be challenged. Finally, in situations where the evidence requested could also be used for other purposes (including of a non-criminal nature), the assertion that the requesting state will not abide by the speciality principle[45] will not be an admissible argument.[46]

1.2. The dual criminality test

International co-operation in criminal matters is to be granted, by definition, when *criminal proceedings* are conducted in the requesting state. The prerequisite for co-operation is therefore the existence of a foreign criminal proceeding. But the existence of such a proceeding is not in itself always sufficient to obtain the co-operation requested. Many states, when asked to proceed with coercive measures, also require that the facts under investigation in the requesting state be qualified as a criminal offence

[44] This principle was codified by Art. 26 Vienna Convention 1969, entered into force on 27 January 1980.

[45] See III.1.3. below.

[46] In mutual assistance cases, one of the defences raised to prevent the transmission of evidence related to business secrets or bank documents is very often that the evidence will be also used for investigation of purely fiscal matters. This is particularly true in states such as Switzerland where the mere existence of 'tax evasion' in the requesting state does not allow for international co-operation. However, the Swiss Supreme Court has consistently asserted that the obligation of the requesting state to respect the speciality rule was to be construed as a presumption of good faith, which could only be rebutted upon clear evidence of violation of this obligation.

in their own law.[47] In other words, they require that 'both Parties criminalise the conduct underlying the offence'.[48]

This test of dual criminality is embodied in several international instruments.[49] It requires that the conduct charged in the requesting state could also be prosecuted under the jurisdiction of the requested state.[50] In extradition matters,[51] the dual criminality test also encompasses a minimum penalty for the offence, in order to avoid extradition for minor offences (*cas bagatelle*).[52] Usually, the dual criminality test is applied *in abstracto*: the requested state does not have the obligation to ascertain the guilt or innocence of the offender or the existence of extenuating circumstances but only to verify whether the behaviour is punishable under its own law. This test does not require parties to have the same definition of the criminalised conduct, nor do they need to have comparable sanctions. What is essential is that the conduct constitutes an offence in both states. The test of dual criminality can also encompass jurisdictional issues: the jurisdictional principle on which the requesting state asserts its right to prosecution should be recognised by the law of the requested state.[53]

[47] As will be discussed below, Art. 9 OECD 1997b specifically provides for mutual assistance, even if non-criminal proceedings are brought, when the offender is a legal person. This provision stems from the fact that the liability of corporations is not always embodied in national law in a criminal statute and the proceedings brought against a corporation are sometimes qualified as non-criminal.

[48] Cf., for example, the wording of Art. 28(1)(g) COE 2005; cf. in general Van den Wyngaert 1989, 131 et seq.; Huet and Koering-Joulin 2005, 402.

[49] Cf., for instance, Art. 5(a) COE 1959; Art. 2(1) COE 1957; Art. 18(1)(f) COE 1990.

[50] See also IV.2.2. below.

[51] The definition of extraditable offences has always been a delicate question; for long, a 'positive' list of extraditable offences was set forth in the extradition treaty or in domestic legislation. However, considering the major drawbacks of this method in terms of flexibility, an eliminative method has been widely adopted instead (Gilbert 1998, 85).

[52] Art. 3(1) of the Convention is a reflection of this requirement in asking for 'a range of penalties. . .sufficient to enable effective MLA and extradition' (see ch. on Article 3 above).

[53] At least in extradition matters: cf., for instance, Art. 7 COE 1957. It allows for refusal of extradition, if the jurisdictional ground asserted by the requesting state is not recognised in the domestic law of the requested state, for instance, if the conduct occurred outside the territory of the requesting state and did not involve a national of the latter, either as offender or victim. This test is particularly relevant to the application of the OECD Convention since, by definition, more than one state has jurisdiction to prosecute. It is, therefore, a real issue in situations where a state contemplates only the territoriality principle as its ground of jurisdiction. Note, however, Gilbert 1998: '[s]uch problems do not arise so much for civil law states which operate wide extraterritorial jurisdiction, nor, for that matter, for the USA now that it has adopted several of those principles, too, but rather for other common law states with merely territorial jurisdiction' (113). Cf. also Blakesley 1992, 234.

1.3. The speciality principle

Extradition practice has given rise to the so-called 'principle of speciality'. This was originally designed to protect the sovereignty of the requested state but is now viewed as a key protection for the individual. It entails, in extradition cases, that the prosecution of the extradited person for conduct other than that in respect of which extradition was granted is not admissible without the consent of the requested state. In other words, prosecution for different facts is not permissible, if those facts have not been included in the extradition request, even if the requesting state would have had jurisdiction to prosecute. This principle has been embodied in most treaties, whether bilateral or multilateral.[54] By extension, this principle is also applied in mutual assistance cases to prevent the requesting state from using the evidence collected for a purpose other than that for which co-operation was granted.[55] The speciality protection is not absolute, since the person concerned can waive his or her right.[56]

1.4. The reciprocity rule

Under the rule of reciprocity, states may grant assistance to a requesting state with which it has no specific agreement. The underlying condition is that, if the situation were to be reversed, the requesting state could also provide judicial assistance.[57] The reciprocity rule may for example apply in extradition cases, where a state refuses to extradite its nationals. This prohibition may be mitigated by allowing extradition on the condition that reciprocity is observed by the requesting state.[58] In the absence of a treaty, the rule of reciprocity is usually embodied in domestic law; this is the case in Europe, in particular.[59]

[54] Cf., for example, Art. 14 COE 1957. [55] Moreillon 2004, 112.

[56] This is valid both in extradition and in mutual assistance cases. The extradited person can waive his or her right by remaining in the requesting state either after completion of the sentence, if guilty or if acquitted for the offence for which extradition was granted. In mutual assistance cases, however, the consent of the individual to the use of information for non-criminal proceedings, and, in particular for fiscal matters, cannot prevent the requested state from asserting that the speciality rule has been violated.

[57] Poncet and Gully-Hart 1999, 285.

[58] This is quite common in the Common Law countries.

[59] This reciprocity rule has been incorporated into various national legislation, for example., in s. 5 German Law on International Mutual Assistance Law in Criminal Matters; Art. 8 Swiss IMAC.

2. Exclusion of and objections to international co-operation

2.1. Exclusion of offences or offenders

2.1.1. Excluded offences

Traditionally, political[60] and military offences are excluded from those crimes which are extraditable or for which mutual legal assistance can be granted; the exclusion of military offences concerns offences of a purely military nature such as desertion.[61]

Similarly, fiscal offences are regularly excluded from international agreements. A distinction must be made with regard to the nature of the tax offence. *Tax evasion* offences are usually excluded from extradition or mutual assistance agreements, unless otherwise specifically provided for. Concerning *tax fraud*, however, both extradition and mutual legal assistance are available.[62] In *minor cases*, extradition is not available; however, mutual legal assistance can be granted.[63]

2.1.2. Excluded offenders

In many Civil Law states, the extradition of nationals is prohibited.[64] Instead, the case is referred to the competent authorities for prosecution in the requested state, as those countries usually have domestic jurisdiction over their nationals even for offences committed outside their territory. Nevertheless, the nationality principle of jurisdiction[65] is barely an alternative to extradition because of 'the difficulty and costs of obtaining evidence' from abroad and 'the serious burdens imposed by such trials on

[60] The refusal to extradite for political offences or other offences connected with such political offences stems from considerations related to the possibility that the extradition request aims at prosecuting or punishing a person on account of his political opinions. The same exception usually applies with respect to prosecutions conducted on account of race, religion, or nationality. Cf. Art. 3 COE 1957. A distinction is to be made between 'pure' and 'relative' political offences (considerations of space prevent a further development of this point).

[61] During the Vietnam War, deserters from the US Army took refuge in Nordic countries, from which they were not extradited by reason of the purely military aspects of the offence.

[62] For instance, in Switzerland, where domestic legislation specifically provides for mutual assistance (Art. 3(3) IMAC). It is questionable whether extradition can be granted under this provision. By contrast, Art. 5 COE 1957 does not forbid extradition for fiscal offences, provided that a specific – separate – agreement has been reached between the respective states.

[63] Minor cases are defined by their maximal punishment. In Art. 2(1) COE 1957 an 'extraditable' offence is defined by a maximum penalty of at least one year of imprisonment.

[64] Oehler 1983, 175 et seq.; Wise 1999, 15. [65] See ch. on Article 4 above.

the victims and witnesses'.[66] This being said, the principle is so deeply entrenched in most European states that it has been a steady fixture of international Conventions.[67] However, most Member States of the EU have, with the implementation of the European Arrest Warrant, accepted the surrender of nationals, subject in some cases to the condition that the sentence should be executed on their territory.[68]

Diplomatic immunity will not constitute an affirmative defence or impediment to extradition when persons benefiting from the immunity pursue private economic activities which typically give rise to corruption.[69]

2.2. Statute of limitations

The lapse of time is a bar to extradition in most treaties and domestic laws.[70] In mutual assistance, the lapse of time does not usually constitute an obstacle to the grant of assistance by the requested state.[71]

2.3. Ne bis in idem

Most, if not all states – either in their penal law or their Constitution –, recognise the principle that an offender should not be prosecuted or judged twice for the same offence.[72] The availability of *ne bis in idem* on an international level is not, however, universal. In some cases, domestic law permits recognition of the effects of a foreign penal decision: a conviction, acquittal, or a reasoned dismissal of the proceedings may in those countries bar a new prosecution. Where the fundamental interests of a state have been endangered, however, even the most progressive national or international texts do not contemplate a complete bar to prosecution.[73]

[66] Cf. Prost 1998, citing the Report of the UN Expert Working Group on Extradition for the Convention on the Prevention and Punishment of the Crime of Genocide, December 9, 1948 8 UNTS 277.

[67] Cf., for example, Art. 6 COE 1957. The Convention has ratified this principle in its Art. 10(3).

[68] Arts. 4(6) and 5(3) EU 2002c. [69] Bertossa 2004, 177.

[70] Cf., for example, Art. 10 COE 1957. It is immaterial whether the lapse of time has occurred in the requesting state or the requested state when the dual criminality requirement is necessary. In both cases extradition cannot occur.

[71] Popp 2001, 170 et seq. [72] Vervaele 2005, 100 et seq.

[73] Art. 54 of the Convention on application of the Schengen *acquis* (Schengen Implementing Agreement 1990) embodies for the first time in an international agreement a general bar to prosecution under the *ne bis in idem* principle. However, reservations are allowed, if a state has a territorial jurisdiction over the offence, or if such an offence endangered the essential interests of that state. In this context, cf. Case C-187/01 and C-385/01 *Gözütok* and *Brügge*, judgement of 11 February 2003, published in [2003] European Court Reports I-1345.

International agreements on judicial co-operation recognise that *ne bis in idem* may be a valid defence to extradition or to the grant of mutual assistance.[74] There is, however, no clear rule of international law preventing a state from prosecuting a case already tried in another state. This means that the individual is not sufficiently protected in the international context.[75] The Convention fails to address this problem since Article 4(3) merely refers to the possibility of consultation when more than one Party asserts its jurisdiction.[76]

2.4. Minimum procedural standards

The proceedings conducted in the requesting state should conform to the standards embodied in Articles 5 and 6 ECHR, where those provisions apply to the state concerned. In some agreements on co-operation, specific reservations can be made in respect of these minimum standards, reflecting deference to conflicting fundamental interests of the requested state.[77]

IV. Setting the Co-operation Standard of the Convention

1. Overview of Articles 9, 10, and 11

The states Parties to the Convention emanate from very different legal systems.[78] The Convention basically seeks to co-ordinate the different approaches to (criminal) liability for bribery of foreign public officials in order to arrive at a minimum standard. Thus, although the substantive norms of the Convention are not self-executing and require reformulation before their implementation into the national legal systems, no reservations may be entered in respect of its provisions.

Although the Convention formally addresses mutual legal assistance and extradition aspects of co-operation in the battle against foreign bribery, and demands that proper channels of communications be established to

[74] Cf., for instance, Art. 9 COE 1957. The MLA equivalent, COE 1959, does not contain any comparable provisions but has come to embrace the principle indirectly following its affirmation by state signatories in reservations made pursuant to Art. 2. Belgium, Bulgaria, Finland, Georgia, Norway, and Sweden are cases in point.

[75] Vervaele 2005; Van den Wyngaert and Stessens 1999, 785; Henzelin 2005, 345 et seq.

[76] See ch. on Article 4 above.

[77] Cf. the reservations made pursuant to Art. 2 COE 1959 by several COE Member States.

[78] If South African accession is to proceed, there will be state Parties from all five Continents (though, of course, membership is in practice limited to significant world economies or established democracies). See further discussion in ch. on Article 13 below.

facilitate implementation of Articles 9 and 10 and of Article 4(3), it does not establish new standards nor break new ground; it mainly refers to existing agreements.

Before undertaking a detailed analysis of the relevant provisions, we will highlight their main features:

- Article 9(1) states that the Parties are requested to make use 'to the fullest extent possible' of existing national laws or treaties. It follows that conclusion of a specific treaty is not a prerequisite for enforcing the Convention and co-operating in prosecuting the bribery of a foreign official.
- Procedurally, Article 9(1) formalises the notion of 'speedy treatment' which entails expeditious and efficient execution of rogatory letters.[79] This provision asks and allows for free and intensive communication between the state Parties on the status and the execution of the request.
- Substantively, Article 9(1) is in line with Article 2 of the Convention in treating identically the 'criminal' prosecution of the natural person and the possibly 'non-criminal' prosecution of the legal person. It opens the door to granting judicial assistance to administrative bodies and not only penal authorities, in systems which do not accept corporate criminal liability.
- Article 9(2) addresses the dual criminality requirement, confirming the *in abstracto* approach and allowing for a general description of the offence. It softens the test in stating that in the absence of similar norms it is sufficient that 'the description of the offence is within the scope of the Convention'.
- Article 9(3) constitutes an incentive for states to reject bank secrecy as a valid obstacle to applying mutual assistance in criminal matters subject to the Convention. Although the legislation of most financial centres no longer admits the bank secrecy objection in criminal proceedings, this provision provides a valid basis for passing new legislation if needed.
- Article 10(1) states that bribery of a foreign public official is an extraditable offence whether or not on the list of offences or in the categories described in a specific extradition treaty or in domestic law.

[79] Several international instruments now embody this notion. Cf., in particular, Art. 1 COE 2001. The explanatory report for this provision states that 'by adding the adverb "promptly", it introduces a requirement of swiftness in responding to requests'.

In order to comply with this provision, the state Parties may have to amend their laws; at any rate they must accept that international co-operation may be granted even in the absence of such national legislation.

- Article 10(2) recognises and endorses the application of the reciprocity principle. Based on this provision, extradition may be granted to another Party to the Convention even in the absence of a formal agreement between them to this end.
- Article 10(3) is a direct application of the *aut dedere aut prosequi* principle.[80] The state Parties are not obliged to extradite their nationals but, if they do not, they must forward the case to their competent authorities for the purpose of prosecution.
- Article 10(4) refers the extradition process to existing national law or treaties, and softens the dual criminality test as stated in Article 9(2).
- Article 11 obliges the state Parties to determine the authorities responsible for receiving and sending communications relating to judicial co-operation under the Convention. Many countries will have central authorities responsible for dealing with mutual legal assistance requests or with extradition but responsibilities may also be shared among different agencies, depending on the structure of the administration and the organisation of the judicial system in the country concerned. The obligation here is to notify the list of the authorities responsible in respect of the Convention to the OECD Secretary-General and to accept that requests made and received via this channel are competent. The state Parties are, however, free to use more direct channels of communication such as those already provided for in bilateral or multilateral arrangements, in order to speed up the process. This Article also applies to Article 4(3) regarding determination of the most appropriate forum for prosecution when more than one state has jurisdiction.

A detailed analysis of Articles 9 to 11 now follows, bearing in mind that the Convention does not seek to achieve uniformity at the national level. The standards provided under the Convention are, of course, binding on the state Parties, meaning that lower national standards will be in breach of the Convention.

[80] Discussed in IV.3.2. below.

2. The mutual legal assistance standard: Article 9

2.1. The scope of mutual legal assistance

Article 9 links the criminalisation of the bribery offence under the Convention with the provision of effective mutual legal assistance. According to paragraph 8 of the Agreed Common Elements, mutual legal assistance is indeed 'critical to be able to investigate and obtain evidence in order to prosecute cases of bribery of foreign public officials'.[81]

By virtue of this Article, mutual legal assistance should be accorded as follows: each state Party should co-operate with each other in the gathering of evidence not only after the requesting state Party has brought charges in a bribery prosecution but also during the investigative stage of the criminal case. The provision contains the additional requirement of processing the request promptly.

The length of co-operation proceedings can indeed significantly reduce the effectiveness of international co-operation. Some countries, like Luxembourg, have adapted their law on international mutual legal assistance to establish the principle that international requests for assistance in criminal matters are to be treated as 'urgent priority cases'; this has had an impact on the number of appeals allowed against the decisions of the investigating magistrate who processes the foreign requests.[82] The suspensive effect of an appeal is indeed often used as a tactic for delaying the handling of a request.[83] The requested state must also inform the requesting country if there are flaws in the request in order to have it supplemented without delay. The issue of delay is a crucial one; it will be discussed in more detail below when dealing with the lifting of bank secrecy and the nomination of central authorities.[84]

Law enforcement co-operation under Article 9(1) is addressed in a general manner. The Convention therefore makes possible a wide range of measures for the gathering of evidence, including, according to Official Commentary 31,

[81] The Agreed Common Elements are appended to the Revised Recommendation (OECD 1997a): see Documentary Appendix of this commentary.

[82] The Luxembourg Law on International Mutual Legal Assistance in Criminal Matters of 2000 forbids any delay in the execution of the international requests for assistance on grounds of lodging of several appeals. They are now limited to two and must be resolved at the same time (LU-Ph2, 30).

[83] In Switzerland, even defendants residing abroad can lodge appeals. This state of affairs has been criticised for substantially increasing the workload of the Swiss justice system and delaying proceedings – and this in a country where 97% appeals are ultimately rejected (CH-Ph2, 29).

[84] See IV.2.3. and IV.4. below.

the obtaining of information from persons in custody if they agree to be transferred to the requesting country 'to assist in investigations or to temporarily participate in proceedings without the necessity of extradition proceedings'.[85] The spontaneous transmission (i.e. without prior request) to the foreign judge of any information that could be useful is not expressly provided for, unlike in other Conventions.[86] Nevertheless, one can surmise that the Convention aims at promoting this active form of co-operation as well as the use of direct channels of information, given that the Revised Recommendation of 1997 indeed encourages international co-operation 'through such means as sharing of information (spontaneously or upon request)'.[87] Switzerland, along with other countries, has been consistent in implementing the Recommendation to this effect.[88]

Article 9(1) is also the basis for mutual legal assistance concerning the prosecution of legal persons. This provision requires that mutual legal assistance be granted in order to facilitate criminal as well as non-criminal investigations and proceedings against legal persons regarding offences within the scope of the Convention. The OECD Convention and the COE Criminal Law Convention on Corruption of 1999 approach corporate liability in a similar way.

While the concept of the responsibility of companies is expressed in several international treaties, these treaties do not, however, impose on their contracting parties an obligation to introduce corporate criminal liability. In the absence of the latter, legal persons must, however, be subject to equivalent non-criminal sanctions – these can be administrative or civil in nature, as long as they are 'effective, proportionate and dissuasive'.[89] A requested Party must therefore be able to provide mutual legal assistance in cases where the requesting state is taking measures against a company for the offence of bribing a foreign public official, liable under administrative or civil law proceedings.

[85] Dietrich 1998, 168. Similar provisions can be found in Art. 9 EU 2000; Art. 3 COE 2001 and Art. 46(10) UN 2003.

[86] For example, Art. 10 COE 1990; Art. 28 COE 1999a; Art. 46(4) UN 2003; Art. 20 COE 2005.

[87] S. VII.i) OECD 1997a (see Documentary Appendix of this commentary).

[88] Indeed, 'judges are even authorised to transmit information which is normally covered by secrecy if it is of such a nature as to enable their foreign colleagues to make a request for mutual legal assistance to Switzerland' (CH-Ph2, 28).

[89] Art. 19(2) COE 1999a and Art. 3(2) OECD 1997b explicitly allow for non-penal sanctions. They could consist of monetary penalties or confiscation of benefits, exclusion from entitlement to public benefits, temporary or permanent disqualification from participation in public procurement, placing under judicial supervision, or even of dissolution (OECD 1999, F-1031; and see also ch. on Article 3 above). The fact that co-operation must also be granted when the conduct is sanctioned by non-criminal means in the requested Party represents a further attenuation of dual criminality.

Where corporate criminal liability is not recognised in a legal system,[90] assistance is often provided on the basis of the pertinent Hague Conventions,[91] the Lugano Convention on Jurisdiction and the Enforcement of Judgements in Civil and Commercial Matters of 1988, or on the basis of domestic legislation.[92] Within the EU, mutual assistance in non-criminal proceedings against legal persons can be based on Article 3 of the EU Convention on Mutual Assistance of 2000.[93]

Several countries fail so far to comply with the requirements of Article 9(1) on this very specific issue. One in particular has not yet established the criminal liability of legal persons and cannot provide mutual legal assistance in relation to non-criminal proceedings; the authorities of this contravening country nevertheless claim that criminal charges can in practice always be brought against the individual who stands behind the acts of the legal person.[94] The OECD's Working Group on Bribery (WGB) disapproves of this approach: mutual legal assistance should not be conditional upon the proceedings against a natural person. Indeed, it can be difficult to identify one individual decision-maker within a management chain that may comprise several levels. Such an approach enables complex corporate structures to act as an obstacle to prosecutions. Similarly, the WGB has on several occasions condemned the concept of 'identification' of a natural person which is used by certain state Parties to ground their theory of criminal or administrative liability.[95]

[90] Corporate criminal liability has been established in Belgium, Canada, Finland, France, Iceland, Japan, Korea, Mexico, Norway, Portugal, Slovenia, Sweden, Switzerland, and in the United States. The implementation of this concept remains, however, problematic in some other countries, and others continue to reject it (see ch. on Article 2 above). The Swiss requirement of additional negligence (CH-Ph2, 36) and the principle of discretion used at prosecutorial and court levels in Norway (NO-Ph2, 32) should also be mentioned in this context.

[91] Hague Convention on Civil Procedure of 1954 (HCCH 1954); Hague Convention on the Service Abroad of Judicial and Extra-Judicial Documents in Civil and Commercial Matters of 1965 (HCCH 1965); Hague Convention on the Taking of Evidence Abroad in Civil and Commercial Matters of 1970 (HCCH 1970).

[92] For example, AR-Ph1, 22; CL-Ph1, 25; CZ-Ph1, 18; IE-Ph1, 35; SK-Ph1, 19; UK-Ph1, 19.

[93] EU 2000; cf. also HU-Ph2, 29; NL-Ph1, 29.

[94] BG-Ph2, 26.

[95] In Canada, the criminal liability of legal persons is based on the principle of the prior identification of the natural persons who committed the offence on their behalf (CA-Ph2, 30–31). As for Hungary, Japan, and Mexico, corporate criminal liability can apply only where the natural person who committed the bribery offence was previously convicted and sanctioned (HU-Ph2, 29; JP-Ph2, 45; MX-Ph2, 21). Many countries also base their theory of administrative liability upon the fault of senior management (DE-Ph2, 32; ES-Ph1, 25; GR-Ph2, 35). Sometimes, the administrative liability of a legal person is conditional upon the existence of a legal proceeding against some natural person, even if unidentified (LU-Ph2, 31) or, more strictly, upon the prior conviction of a natural person (PL-Ph1, 32).

2.2. The requirement of dual criminality

Article 9(2) tackles the obstacles to international co-operation created by dual criminality. The *Travaux Préparatoires* reveal that the drafters of the Convention wanted to avoid the strict forms of dual criminality which are required by some countries in respect of judicial co-operation. This strict form applies in particular in almost all countries when extradition and the provision of coercive measures are concerned.[96] Coercive measures usually entail such actions as taking the deposition of a witness, searches, seizures, restraint orders, and freezing of assets, telecommunications monitoring, and interceptions. In states with bank secrecy laws, coercive measures may also include the disclosure of bank account details (often crucial evidence in international bribery cases).[97]

The Convention addresses this issue by encouraging the establishment by all state Parties of the same offence of bribery of a foreign official in their criminal laws. The Convention does not, however, require full uniformity.[98] Thus, a generous interpretation of the dual criminality requirement is required if effective mutual legal assistance is to be ensured. National legislation should be tailored in line with Official Commentary 32 so as to allow co-operation between 'Parties with statutes as diverse as a statute prohibiting the bribery of agents generally and a statute directed specifically at bribery of foreign public officials'.[99]

Some state Parties even consider the dual criminality requirement to be fulfilled where the act of foreign bribery was committed before the entry into force of the amended legislation in the requesting country.[100] Others, however, strictly monitor the implementation by the requesting country of Article 1 of the Convention before evaluating the dual criminality requirement.[101]

In addition, paragraph 8 of the Agreed Common Elements encourages a broad recognition by the requested state of the principles of jurisdiction asserted by the requesting state. This again aims to permit extensive co-operation; the goal is 'to permit co-operation with countries investigating cases of bribery of foreign public officials, even including third countries (country of the offeror; country where the act occurred)'.[102] Despite the

[96] OECD 1999, F-1036–37. [97] See previous note 96.
[98] See, for a more comprehensive discussion, ch. on Article 1 above.
[99] Cf. the report of Brazil on the application of dual criminality in the case of different national classifications (BR-Ph1, 29).
[100] PT-Ph1, 27. Generally the condition of dual criminality is required at the time of the commission of the alleged act of foreign bribery.
[101] For example, DK-Ph1, 22 and UK-Ph2, 46.
[102] A broad interpretation of the territorial jurisdiction principle extends the scope of mutual legal assistance. The country through which bribes paid to banks are laundered will, for example, be able to establish jurisdiction over the foreign bribery offence and can therefore grant assistance.

impression which may be created by this approach, Article 9 is not, however, applicable to relations between a state Party and a non-state Party.[103]

The Agreed Common Elements envisage the co-existence of the territorial and nationality principles of jurisdiction in order to cover every situation. The operation of a single principle of jurisdiction can be replete with limitations. Chile, for example, has restricted its territorial jurisdiction over the offences initiated within its territory, whereas in New Zealand nationality jurisdiction can be established over a foreign bribery offence only if the conduct is also an offence under the law of the country where the foreign public official's 'principal office' is situated.[104] The *Travaux Préparatoires* underline that 'the effectiveness of jurisdiction based on the nationality principle may be limited when, to carry out the offence, a company acts through persons or intermediaries who are nationals of other countries' or when 'no element of the offence occurred in the territory' of the requesting state.[105]

WGB monitoring shows that some state Parties now adopt a more generous approach to dual criminality along the path opened to them by the UN Convention Against Corruption of 2003.[106]

2.3. Bank secrecy

Article 9(3) includes a statement prohibiting the use of so-called 'bank secrecy' provisions in order to deny a request for mutual assistance in criminal matters. Even where professional secrecy is strongly protected, the Convention requires it to be lifted whenever major public interests so demand. The UN Drug Convention of 1988 and the COE Convention on Money Laundering of 1990 were the first Treaties to take this stand. Since then, the provision has become a recognised standard of international judicial co-operation.[107]

[103] Aiolfi and Ledergerber 2005, 55.
[104] CL-Ph1, 30 et seq.; NZ-Ph1, 36.
[105] OECD 1999, F-1030.
[106] BG-Ph2, 39; CA-Ph1, 19; GR-Ph1, 15; SK-Ph1, 19. In these states Parties, dual criminality is not a requirement for granting a request for mutual legal assistance, even when coercive measures are involved. Under Art. 46(9) UN 2003, Parties cannot decline to render assistance for lack of dual criminality, if the request does not involve any coercive action. If it does, the requested Party shall take into account the purposes of the Convention before responding to the request.
[107] Art. 7(5) UN 1988; Art. 18(7) COE 1990; Art. 26(3) COE 1999a; Art. 7 EU 2001a and Art. 46(8) UN 2003.

Nevertheless, in order to waive secrecy, most countries still require well-grounded elements of suspicion of the commission of a criminal offence and frequently also a connection between the offence and the required information. 'Fishing expeditions', aimed at ascertaining the existence of foreign bank accounts, are usually prohibited.[108] Sometimes access to confidential banking accounts is even more restricted, if not impossible.[109] Questions of bank secrecy may also arise in the context of non-criminal proceedings brought against legal persons in those countries which do not have a concept of corporate criminal liability, but Parties may frequently be unwilling to lift bank secrecy in such cases because of the absence of criminal proceedings.[110]

Finally, several Parties have mentioned the long delays that occur when they request search warrants or legal authorisations for the lifting of bank secrecy. These delays can constitute major obstacles to financial investigations and prosecutions. The requesting country should be in a position to provide banking information without undue delay or else the efficiency of mutual legal assistance will be undermined. Frequently, the lifting of bank confidentiality requires the ruling of a judge; the WGB therefore encourages state Parties to provide efficient legal mechanisms and to impose deadlines on courts to provide their decisions, streamline the process of appeal or take provisional measures to block bank accounts, subject to judicial confirmation.[111] Ideally, a general obligation should be imposed on all financial intermediaries and bank officials to disclose banking information spontaneously where it can be proved that the assets may be of criminal origin.[112]

[108] Cf., in particular, AT-Ph1, 20. By contrast, the production of banking records is not deemed to be a coercive measure in Finland, and the dual criminality requirement does not therefore apply (FI-Ph1, 14). In Italy, requests for the lifting of bank secrecy can even be made at an early stage of the proceeding without any supporting evidence, and it is also possible to request information through fishing expeditions (IT-Ph1, 30).

[109] Chile, for example, cannot order the disclosure of banking information pursuant to a request for mutual legal assistance in the absence of a specific treaty. Chile has not yet entered into any such treaty and does not consider the OECD Convention to be a sufficient legal basis for the lifting of bank secrecy (CL-Ph1, 25).

[110] In Brazil, for example, there would need to be at least an investigatory procedure in order to justify the lifting of banking secrecy (BR-Ph1, 31). Cf. also IS-Ph1, 17 and PT-Ph1, 27 et seq.

[111] BG-Ph2, 34; MX-Ph2, 52 et seq.

[112] The obligation could be modelled on Swiss legislation, which, contrary to what is often believed, is one of the most advanced in relation to bank secrecy. Cf. Art. 305ter Swiss Criminal Code and Art. 9 Law on Money Laundering (CH-Ph1, 18).

3. The extradition standard: Article 10

3.1. The legal basis for extradition

Where extradition is concerned, the Convention is in line with the traditional approach adopted by most instruments dealing with international criminality.[113] First, Article 10(1) seeks to provide a broad legal basis for extradition between the state Parties by requiring that the Article 1 offence be deemed an extraditable offence under their laws and the extradition treaties between them.

The method of designation specifies as extraditable those offences subject to a certain term of imprisonment under the laws of the respective states.[114] Most state Parties already applied the minimum sentencing threshold of one year of imprisonment for extradition purposes.[115] This standard was adopted by the WGB when monitoring the implementation of the 'effective, proportionate and dissuasive' test for sanctions laid down by Article 3 of the Convention. The penalty must be of a severity sufficient to facilitate extradition.[116]

Under Article 10(2) the Convention may be considered to form the legal basis for extradition where the extradition relations of the requested country are conditional on the existence of an extradition treaty and where no such treaty exists between the state Parties involved. The use of permissive language in Article 10(2) repeats pre-existing extradition practice.[117] In certain countries, extradition can be allowed without a treaty on the sole basis of domestic legislation, which basically imposes a condition of reciprocity.[118] In others, notably the United States,[119] it can only take place where an extradition treaty applies. Thus, in the absence of any treaty, the Convention should be regarded as the legal basis for extradition between the state Parties in respect of the offence of bribing a foreign public official.

The WGB has identified problems in the provision of extradition pursuant to Article 10(2) only in relation to Finland. Finland does not

[113] Cf., for instance, Art. 6(2), (3) and (9) UN 1988; Art. 13(2), (3) and (6) OAS 1996; also Art. 16(3), (4) and (10) UN 2000.

[114] See note 51.

[115] This is the standard required by Art. 2(1) COE 1957. Other states not party to the COE Convention have adopted a similar approach (AR-Ph1, 23; AU-Ph1, 19; KR-Ph1, 18; NZ-Ph1, 30).

[116] See generally the discussion in ch. on Article 3 above.

[117] Cf., for example, Art. 6(3) UN 1988.

[118] Cf. FR-Ph1, 27; JP-Ph1, 23; KR-Ph1, 18.

[119] US-Ph1, 19.

consider the Convention as a legal basis for extradition when there is no applicable treaty, because, in those circumstances, the competent Finnish authorities must investigate the adequacy of the foreign sentence or the prosecution initiated abroad and the Convention does not comply with this requirement.[120]

3.2. *Aut dedere aut prosequi*

Article 10(3) requires the state Parties either to take appropriate measures for extradition of their nationals[121] or to prosecute them in respect of conduct contrary to Article 1. The inclusion of a provision imposing an obligation on the state Parties to extradite their nationals would face the overwhelming opposition of most Civil Law countries, who are deeply attached to jurisdiction based on nationality.[122] Therefore, the Article embodies the *aut dedere aut prosequi* principle, according to which the case is referred to the competent prosecutorial authority of the requested state for initiation of domestic proceedings if extradition is refused on the sole basis of nationality.[123]

As mentioned above, it is, however, often very difficult in practice to try a person for an offence committed outside the territorial jurisdiction of the court.[124] Additional procedural requirements, like the prior lodging of a complaint by the victim or an official denunciation, can make it even

[120] Thus, the Finnish authorities become involved in the weighing of evidence, in order to verify that the enforceable foreign sentence or the warrant for detention is adequate. The WGB is concerned that such investigation may impede effective extradition (FI-Ph2, 27).

[121] The following state Parties may extradite their nationals for the offence of bribery of a foreign public official: Argentina (the Argentinean citizen can choose either to be extradited or tried in Argentina unless a treaty provides otherwise: AR-Ph1, 24), Australia, Canada, Hungary (only, however, if the Hungarian national is also a national and a permanent resident of the requesting state: HU-Ph1, 19), Ireland, Italy, Japan, Korea, Mexico, New Zealand, Portugal (the offence in question should relate to terrorism or to international organised crime: PT-Ph1, 29), Slovenia (but only to another Member State of the EU: SI-Ph1, 36), the United Kingdom and the United States. Most of them extradite their nationals on a reciprocal basis only. In accordance with Official Commentary 33, the Convention may be considered as a basis for the extradition of nationals where there is no applicable treaty (ES-Ph1, 22).

[122] Often the principle of non-extradition of nationals may be enshrined in the national constitution (AT-Ph1, 21; BG-Ph1, 16; DE-Ph1, 17; PL-Ph1, 30; TR-Ph1, 22).

[123] Literally '*extradite or prosecute*', as in the English version of recent international agreements. It is the 'modern' application of the Grotius maxim *aut dedere aut punire*. On account of the presumption of innocence, it had evolved to the *aut dedere aut judicare* maxim. Nowadays, it is admitted that the obligation of the requested state is to prosecute and not always to refer the case for judgment, for instance, when there is no sufficient supporting evidence: hence the evolution of the wording from *punire* to *judicare* and finally to *prosequi*.

[124] See III.2.1.2. above.

more problematic.[125] Some countries have for this reason developed alternative practices in respect of their nationals.

Under the Nordic Extradition Act of 1975, Denmark, Finland, Iceland, Norway, and Sweden have agreed to the extradition of a national to another Nordic country provided that this national was a resident in the requesting state for at least two years prior to the commission of the offence.[126] In the Netherlands, extradition of nationals is possible provided that they will be allowed to return to their home country to serve any sentence that may be imposed abroad.[127] Article 7 of the 1996 Convention relating to Extradition between the Member States of the EU also provided that extradition may not be refused on the sole ground of nationality; Member States were, however, entitled to make a reservation concerning this Article. The European Arrest Warrant now stipulates that nationals of EU countries may and must be surrendered to other EU jurisdictions, subject only to the grounds specifically laid out in the EU instrument concerned.[128]

3.3. The requirement of dual criminality

The dual criminality principle is deeply rooted and very technically applied in extradition practice. It frequently operates to frustrate the rendering of assistance.[129] Article 10(4), like its counterpart Article 9(2), therefore endorses a relatively light application of the principle in the context of the Convention: dual criminality is deemed fulfilled if the offence for which extradition is sought is within the scope of the OECD Convention. Implementation alone of the Convention by the requesting state Party could therefore provide a basis for extradition to be granted.[130] Some countries also consider the requirement to be fulfilled if the act is unlawful where it

[125] BE-Ph2, 33; DE-Ph2, 29; FR-Ph2, 46.

[126] DK-Ph1, 23; FI-Ph1, 15; SE-Ph1, 21. [127] NL-Ph1, 31. [128] See note 28 above.

[129] Art. 2(1) COE 1957.

[130] A thorny problem could have arisen for those countries which implemented the Convention last of all and whose laws required the condition of dual criminality to be fulfilled at the time of commission of the offence. If the offence was committed before the implementation of the Convention in the requested state, the dual criminality requirement could have blocked extradition. New Zealand and Polish legislation presented a potential problem in this respect, but both countries interpreted dual criminality flexibly so that it was deemed to be fulfilled even in these circumstances; this flexibility was possible, because the domestic bribery offence was already punishable in both states (NZ-Ph1, 33 and PT-Ph1, 30). Note also that in some states Parties, such as Switzerland, co-operation may be granted, if dual criminality is satisfied *at the time of the examination of the request*: cf. Zimmermann 2004, 397.

occurred even if under a different criminal law provision.[131] Moreover, the twenty-five EU Member States have passed new laws to give effect to the EU Framework Decision on the European Arrest Warrant. This instrument rules out enquiry by the requested state ('executing state') as to dual criminality in respect of the offences listed (among which feature corruption offences), provided that the Warrant is competently issued by a judicial authority of one of the other Member States.[132]

4. Channels of communications: Article 11

Success in international co-operation is almost entirely dependent 'on the knowledge and most critically the flexibility of the authorities providing the assistance'.[133] The designation, in each Member State, of a central co-ordinating office responsible for making the requests for mutual legal assistance and extradition, and for receiving and responding to foreign requests, should greatly facilitate co-operation among state Parties.

A central authority, usually the Ministry of Justice or Office of the Attorney General,[134] may play a particularly active role in advising the competent foreign authorities. Discussions between central authorities can often provide the answers to practical questions, e.g. regarding the information which should be included in a request for mutual assistance. This central authority will manage foreign requests by carefully reviewing each of them, advising the requesting state how to meet the basic formal requirements, before if necessary returning the request for modification. If the request appears to be in order, the central office may either execute it independently or send it to the authority entrusted with execution. In the latter case, it must ensure that the competent authority follows through with execution and transmits the relevant information to the requesting state without undue delay. Clauses similar to Article 11 are found in numerous other treaties pertaining to judicial co-operation in criminal matters.[135]

[131] AR-Ph1, 24; BG-Ph1, 16; BR-Ph1, 33; CL-Ph1, 27; DK-Ph1, 23; ES-Ph1, 22; FI-Ph1, 16; MX-Ph1, 21.

[132] See note 28 above. [133] Prost 1998.

[134] Or sometimes both, acting within the framework of their respective duties: the Attorney General may, for example, intervene for mutual legal assistance purposes and the Ministry of Justice in extradition (LU-Ph1, 23). Responsibility for mutual legal assistance may also be divided between the Prosecutor-General and the Ministry of Justice (CZ-Ph1, 19; SK-Ph1, 20).

[135] Cf., for example, Art. 7(8) UN 1988; Art. 29 COE 1999a; Art. 46(13) UN 2003.

5. Global assessment: how do the co-operation provisions of the Convention fare when compared to other treaties?

The greatest achievements in the area of extradition have been accomplished between states which already enjoy very close relations of a political and judicial character, for example COE Member States but, in particular, the Member States of the EU.[136]

European initiatives have been at the forefront of developments at the international level to abolish the dual criminality requirement.[137] Other traditional obstacles to co-operation such as the political offence exception and the non-extradition of nationals have also come under strong challenge in recent years in the light of the vastly increased pressure on States to put sovereignty concerns to one side and co-operate better with each other in cases of cross-border criminality. Already some time before adoption of the European Arrest Warrant, the EU, in its Convention relating to Extradition of 1996, limited 'the scope of the political offence exemption, the rules on the non-extradition of nationals and the exclusion of fiscal offences from the definition of extraditable crimes'.[138] The speciality rule was also relaxed and time bars lifted.[139]

Beside these rather revolutionary developments, the OECD anti-bribery Convention addresses extradition in a somewhat limited, even tentative, manner. Its basic contribution is to require the state Parties to establish the bribery of foreign public officials as an extraditable offence.

With regard to mutual legal assistance, the regional instruments of co-operation have also been in the forefront of recent trends. Already in 1978, the Additional Protocol to the COE Mutual Assistance Convention expanded the application of the COE Convention to fiscal matters. Much more recently, the Second Additional Protocol of 2001 extends the provision of mutual assistance to 'administrative criminal law' and introduces several innovative co-operation measures which were in turn largely inspired by the EU Convention on Mutual Assistance of 2000.[140]

[136] European forerunners of EU developments were, for example, the Nordic Passport Union of 1954 (details of current co-operation among Nordic countries are available at: http://www.norden.org) and cf. Benelux Treaty 1962. Other simplified schemes have been adopted in bilateral treaties (Gilbert 1998, 45 et seq.).

[137] Notably now the European Arrest Warrant: for more details, see II.1.2.2. and IV.3.3. above; and also note 28.

[138] Gilbert 1998, 38 et seq.

[139] Arts. 5–8 and Art. 10 EU 1996a; Zimmermann 2004, 647.

[140] The EU 2000, supplemented by its EU 2001a Protocol, enhances and modernises the provisions of mutual assistance by taking into account advances in technology. It also reflects the growing concern of facilitating access to bank information. In particular, banks may no longer disclose to their customers the fact that information has been transmitted to the requesting state or that an investigation is being carried out (Arts. 1 and 4 EU 2001a).

The Commonwealth Scheme for Mutual Assistance of 1986 does not create binding obligations but does pave the way for signatory states to remove traditional obstacles to co-operation. It also incorporates some innovative provision, for example relating to jurisdiction: the Scheme eschews reference to the exercise of jurisdiction by the requesting country, because it is deemed sufficient, in intra-Commonwealth relations, if the requesting state is able 'to take jurisdiction under its own legal principles'.[141] The scheme also introduces cross-border freezing and confiscation of the proceeds of the crime.[142]

The features of the OECD Convention are less innovative, being mostly attuned to existing agreements dealing with international co-operation. It should be pointed out, however, that the Convention leaves scope for improvement and innovation. The state Parties are indeed exhorted to undertake steps which would enhance the efficiency of mutual legal assistance by adopting national legislation or concluding new international agreements.[143] Thus, the ambitious EU developments could eventually be reflected in state Parties' application of the Convention in practice.

V. Some additional issues of interest

This commentary is obviously geared towards an analysis of existing law and practice under the Convention but in this last part we would like to extend the analysis to three issues which are not specifically addressed by the Convention or are only addressed in a rather unsatisfactory manner. In ignoring these issues, the Convention fortifies or at least prolongs difficulties in certain areas of co-operation and individual protection. When analysing these issues, we adopt the standpoint of the legal practitioner. We hope that our discussion of these issues will stimulate further debate concerning possible shortcomings of the Convention.

1. International co-operation practised by 'victim' states

If the state of the bribed foreign official is a state Party to the Convention, Article 9(1) provides a sufficient basis for asking for, and receiving, judicial

[141] McClean 2002, 199 et seq.; cf. also Gilmore 2004, 230.
[142] See Art. 1 of the Commonwealth Scheme for Mutual Assistance.
[143] Cf. Official Commentary 30 and para. 8 Agreed Common Elements annexed to the OECD 1997a (also reproduced in the Documentary Appendix of this commentary).

assistance. It is not uncommon, however, to see prosecutions being launched first in the state where the *active bribery* took place, or where the *laundering* of the bribe occurred. Requests for co-operation from the state of the bribed official are unfortunately much less common. This reluctance stems from political and other internal reasons.

States in which prosecutions are underway on the basis of active bribery by one of their nationals or by a company based in their territory are bound to ask for assistance from the state of the bribed foreign official ('victim state'). They often receive the dispiriting reply that no offence has occurred and no irregularity has been found. This state of affairs is particularly damaging in money laundering cases, in which the absence of evidence of the existence of the predicate offence can completely prejudice a possible conviction for money laundering. Such deficiencies of co-operation should not be feared from state Parties to the Convention since by definition they have shown a particular interest in the prosecution of international bribery and will obviously have enacted statutes criminalising it. The limits of efficiency of the Convention will, however, be reached when state Parties to the Convention are in the process of prosecuting active bribery of a foreign official but fail to receive adequate co-operation from the victim state. Experience has shown that judicial and prosecutorial efforts to obtain co-operation in these cases and trigger a local investigation are likely to be less productive than media attention and the pressure of public opinion.

2. The unsolved consequences of confiscation

In the application of Article 3(3) of the Convention, the rights of victims should be preserved.[144] No mention is made either by the Convention itself or the Official Commentaries of the foreign state where the bribe was paid, i.e. the victim state, as described in the last section. No indication is given concerning the 'destination' of the confiscated assets as it is taken for granted that the confiscating state will dispose of them. This approach is extremely short sighted, concentrating only on the 'deprivation' aspect of confiscation. Once the illicit owner of the assets has been deprived of their use, justice is deemed to have been rendered. But this can and does lead to unfair, if not even immoral, situations.

[144] Official Commentary 22; and see ch. on Article 3(3) above.

Confiscated funds will benefit countries in which this type of money traditionally flows.[145] It is not moral that the confiscating state should benefit from the mere presence of the assets on its soil, without any consideration of the place where the offence occurred. The situation is also unfair, because it ignores the fact that the foreign state is at least a potential, if not also a real, victim of the bribery.

Application of the Convention should therefore take into consideration the evolution of the appropriate instruments of the COE.[146]

Confiscation pertains very directly to issues of international co-operation, solidarity and to the notion of sharing. In some states, domestic law has been passed to this effect, recognising that corruption is not a victimless crime.[147] When enacting its domestic statute on the sharing of the proceeds of confiscation,[148] Switzerland recognised that corruption money should be returned to the state where the corruption occurred, reasoning that the legal or the natural person who paid the bribe is not entitled to restitution. In effect, the price paid to the company has often been increased in order to include the amount of the bribe. Switzerland has followed this line consistently, in particular in the *Roldan* and *Abacha* cases.[149].

If the deprivation of the illicitly earned assets is of the essence, so should be the restitution to the country of the bribed official. Instruments to this effect now exist both on the domestic and international levels.[150]

One can also find other instruments of global reach that aim to maximise the effectiveness of international co-operation to address more effectively crimes with an international dimension. Whilst some of their provisions are mandatory, most of them are usually softened through the use of permissive language. By way of illustration, Article 5 of the UN Drug Convention of 1988 refers to assistance in confiscation and uses the phrase 'shall adopt'

[145] States with a banking system which works efficiently are more likely to be the recipients of such funds. One can draw a parallel here with the provisions contained in the UN 1961. The obligation to confiscate assets was imposed upon the countries where they were located, not in the states where the drug offences occurred: cf., for example, Austria, Luxembourg, or Switzerland.

[146] Compare, for instance, Art. 15 COE 1990 and Art. 25(2) COE 2005. The destination of the confiscated funds is not only left to the goodwill of the confiscating state.

[147] The notion of 'victimless crime' has been consistently invoked when discussing the confiscation of the proceeds of drug trafficking.

[148] The Swiss Federal Law on the Sharing of Confiscated Assets has been in force since 1 August 2004. It mostly envisages 50–50 sharing schemes between the states concerned (Art. 13(3)).

[149] The assets have been returned to Spain and Nigeria, respectively.

[150] Cf., for example, Art. 74(a) Swiss International Mutual Assistance Code (IMAC); Art. 28 COE 2005.

but qualifies this by stating 'as may be necessary'. Similar language enables the Parties to the UN Convention Against Corruption of 2003 to limit their obligations related to asset recovery.[151] In comparison, the OECD Convention does not have adequate provisions for co-operation in the area of confiscation.[152]

3. The multiple prosecutions issue

With the extension of grounds of jurisdiction to prosecute bribery,[153] it is to be expected that more than one state Party to the Convention will have such jurisdiction and therefore also the obligation or possibility to prosecute (depending on the system or prosecution in place).[154] In practice, multiple prosecutions are, for example, possible when companies originating from different state Parties act through a joint venture which is involved in the bribery of a foreign official. Several states may also claim jurisdiction when proceeds of bribery have been laundered in a third state. In some instances prosecution for money laundering can indeed run in parallel to prosecution for active bribery.

The Convention recognises that multiple prosecutions can arise and in Article 4(3) state Parties are therefore invited to use the channels provided for in Article 11 to consult with one another, *if one of the states* deems it useful. The objective here is precisely to pool or concentrate resources and not to duplicate efforts in investigations and in evidence gathering.

Conspicuous by its absence from the Convention, however, is any mention of the plight of the natural or legal person under investigation. How will the *ne bis in idem* principle be applied? Can it operate in order to avoid multiple prosecution? This aspect seems to be deliberately ignored. Neither the Official Commentaries nor the Agreed Common Elements shed any light on this question.

[151] States shall 'as may be necessary' impose on financial institutions the obligation to verify the identities of customers and owners of high-value accounts and to closely scrutinise accounts of persons who hold or have held prominent public functions, as well as accounts held by their family members and close associates. Furthermore, they are encouraged to establish financial disclosure systems for public officials, including disclosure of an interest in financial accounts in a foreign country. The UN 2003 also prescribes 'to the greatest extent possible' areas of international co-operation regarding the tracing and freezing proceeds of a Convention offence and, more ambitiously, the return of confiscated property to the requesting country (Arts. 52(1), 52(6), 55, and 57 UN 2003).

[152] Thus, in countries which are not Parties to the UN 2003 or COE 1990 foreign confiscation orders cannot be enforced. Cf. BG-Ph2, 40.

[153] See ch. on Article 4 above. [154] See ch. on Article 5 above.

As stated above, multiple prosecutions and even multiple judgements for the same offence are not legally barred in transnational cases, except to a certain extent between EU countries.[155] The *ne bis in idem* prohibition has obtained international currency only in selected international instruments or domestic laws.[156] Experience shows that it is not, in practice, uncommon for parallel investigations to be launched in several states at the same time, resulting in multiple grief for the individual or company concerned.

The demands of effectiveness and efficiency of prosecution notwithstanding, one could expect greater attention to the rights of the natural or legal person under prosecution. Although the Convention is currently silent on this point,[157] we would suggest the following step-by-step approach:

- recognition that only one prosecution should be tolerated for active bribery of a foreign official, and for the laundering of the bribe (when both offences are committed by the same natural or legal person);
- provision to enable the natural or legal person to 'trigger' the consultation mechanism provided for by Article 4(3) in order to favour one jurisdiction and therefore one prosecution only;
- acceptance of the need for mutual recognition of judicial decisions, be they convictions, acquittals, or reasoned dismissals of charges.

4. Concluding remarks

Judicial co-operation in criminal matters is governed by a large number of international treaties, including the frequently mentioned COE and EU Conventions and Protocols and most recently by EU instruments such as the Framework Decision on the European Arrest Warrant. For the Parties to these instruments, the Convention only supplements their substantive legislation, which already guarantees a certain standard of assistance. Considering that more than two-thirds of the OECD Members are located in Europe, the OECD Convention is therefore not in the forefront of practical innovation, except for the relations with state Parties who have not subscribed to the European instruments concerned.[158]

[155] See III.2.3. above.
[156] Cf., for example, Art. 9 COE 1957 and Art. 54 Schengen Implementing Convention 1990.
[157] As are other Conventions dealing with corruption, e.g., COE 1999a; UN 2003.
[158] The Convention is therefore of greater interest for its European Members in terms of co-operation with Argentina, Australia, Brazil, Canada, Chile, Japan, Korea, Mexico, New Zealand, and the United States. But the Convention is not, as such, applicable to relationships with a state which is not a Party to the Convention.

The Convention's appeal also depends on the new members the OECD may attract in order to spread its standards in areas of the world where effective international co-operation is still thin on the ground. Under Article 13(2) of the Convention, any non-OECD Member that has joined the WGB may accede to the Convention.[159]

Prosecution of bribery cases was expected to be relatively frequent in EU countries, where all states concerned 'have a strong interest in seeing that the single market flourishes'.[160] While EU Member States generate a substantial flow of mutual assistance in criminal matters, this is not true in respect of anti-bribery prosecutions as other chapters of this commentary also serve to illustrate. Only a few cases of alleged bribery of foreign public officials were being investigated or prosecuted, as at the beginning of 2005.[161] In most states outside the United States, no convictions have been obtained. This is particularly surprising in the EU context, given the size of the EU's economy. Japan is another case in point.[162] Beside the United States, only in Korea and Sweden would convictions appear to have been obtained.[163]

Minor deficiencies apart, the mechanisms set up by the state Parties in compliance with the requirements of the Convention are fundamentally sound, rooted as they are in existing and evolving provisions for relatively effective and swift judicial assistance in criminal cases. But the continuing paucity of concrete law enforcement or judicial actions to pursue or adjudicate active bribery cases under the Convention puts its credibility as a multilateral anti-corruption instrument at stake and puts in question any supposed contribution it can make to improving judicial co-operation in

[159] See ch. on Article 13 below. Criteria have been established for the participation of non-Member countries in the WGB. They should be major market participants whose inclusion would provide significant mutual benefit (Official Commentary 37). The WGB is advocating further enlargement.

[160] Cockcroft 1999.

[161] Parties to the COE Conventions of the Schengen area represent about 90% of the mutual assistance files dealt with, for example, by Belgium, France and Luxembourg (BE-Ph2, 28; FR-Ph2, 36; LU-Ph2, 30). However, only four foreign bribery cases were under investigation or preliminary inquiry in Belgium at the time of the on-site visit (January 2005), and none has been handled by the Belgian criminal justice system yet (BE-Ph2, 4, 41). France and Italy have also initiated investigations, but only Sweden has obtained a conviction (SE-Ph2, 41 et seq.). Cf. Department of Commerce 2004, 23 and further discussion in ch. on Article 5 above.

[162] When questioned about whether any cases had been filed, formally investigated, or led to court proceedings, the Japanese authorities refused to answer, stating that they were bound by a secrecy rule that prohibits the release of information concerning any investigations that had not resulted in an official filing with the prosecutors (JP-Ph2, 5). See again further discussion in ch. on Article 5 above.

[163] Department of Commerce 2004, 23.

this field. Its true effectiveness will only be capable of measurement after a sustained increase in the number of investigations and prosecutions of international bribery cases. Such cases will in turn demonstrate the importance of enhanced international co-operation.

References

For documentation see the consolidated bibliography at the end of this book.

Abbell, M. (2004), *Obtaining Evidence Abroad in Criminal Cases*, New York.

Aiolfi, G. and Z. Ledergerber (2005), 'Glossary of International Anti-Corruption Standards with Examples of National Legal Practice' (paper prepared for the 6th General Meeting *Anti-Corruption Network for Transitional Economies* in Instanbul, 30–31 May 2005, available at: http://www.anticorruptionnet.org).

Bassiouni, M. Ch. (1974), *International Extradition and World Public Order*, Leiden.

Bertossa, B. L. (2004), 'Mechanisms for Gathering Evidence Abroad' in Asian Development Bank (ed.), *Controlling Corruption in Asia and the Pacific* (key papers by speakers at the 4th Regional Conference of the ADB/OECD Anti-Corruption Initiative for Asia and the Pacific in Kuala Lumpur, 3–5 December 2003, online edn available at: http://www.adb.org/ > Publications > Controlling Corruption > Chapter7).

Blakesley, L. Ch. (1992), *Terrorism, Drugs, International Law, and the Protection of Human Liberty: A Comparative Study of International Law, its Nature, Role, and Impact in Matters of Terrorism, Drug Trafficking, War, and Extradition*, New York (Transnational Publishers).

Cockcroft, L. (1999), *Implementation of the OECD Convention: The Conditions for Success* (available at: http://www.transparency.org.uk > Papers by TI (UK) Members).

Dietrich, O. (1998), 'OECD Convention on Combating Bribery of Foreign Officials in International Business Transactions', *Austrian Review of International & European Law* **3**, 159.

Dommel, D. (1999), 'Les défis de la corruption' (working paper, available at: http://www.transparency.org/ > Research and Publications > Country Papers).

Gilbert, G. (1991), *Aspects of Extradition Law*, Dordrecht, Boston, London.

Gilbert, G. (1998), *Transnational Fugitive Offenders in International Law, Extradition and Other Mechanisms*, The Hague, Boston, London.

Gilmore, W. C. (ed.) (1995), *Mutual Assistance in Criminal and Business Regulatory Matters*, Cambridge.

Gilmore, W. C. (2004), *Dirty Money: The Evolution of International Measures to Counter Money Laundering and the Financing of Terrorism*, 3rd edn, Strasbourg.

Hafiez, M. (2004), 'Mutual Legal Assistance and Repatriation of Proceeds – Pakistan's Experience' in Asian Development Bank (ed.), *Controlling Corruption in Asia and the Pacific* (key papers by speakers at the 4th Regional Conference of the ADB/OECD Anti-Corruption Initiative for Asia and the Pacific in Kuala Lumpur, 3–5 December 2003, online edn available at: http://www.adb.org/ > Publications > Controlling Corruption > Chapter7).

Henzelin, M. (2005), '"Ne bis in idem": un principe à géométrie variable', *Revue Pénale Suisse*, Tome 123, 345.

Huet, A. and R. Koering-Joulin (2005), *Droit pénal international*, 3rd edn, Paris.

McClean, D. (2002), *International Co-operation in Civil and Criminal Matters*, New York.

Moreillon, L. (ed.) (2004), *Entraide internationale en matière pénale, Commentaire romand*, Bâle, Genève, Munich.

Oehler, D. (1983), *Internationales Strafrecht*, 2nd edn, Köln, Berlin, Bonn, München.

Poncet, D. and P. Gully-Hart (1999), 'Legal Framework of Extradition in Europe' in M. Ch. Bassiouni (ed.), *International Criminal Law, Procedural and Enforcement Mechanisms*, Vol. **2**, 2nd edn, New York, 277.

Popp, P. (2001), *Grundzüge der internationalen Rechtshilfe in Strafsachen*, Basel.

Prost, K. (1998), *Breaking Down the Barriers: International Co-operation in Combating Transnational Crime* (available at: http://www.oas.org/ > Documents > Search by Title > MLA Resources).

Spinellis, D. D. (1999), 'Securing Evidence Abroad: A European Perspective' in M. Ch. Bassiouni (ed.), *International Criminal Law, Procedural and Enforcement Mechanisms*, Vol. **2**, 2nd edn, New York, 359.

Swart, B. (1999), 'The European Union and the Schengen Agreement' in M. Ch. Bassiouni (ed.), *International Criminal Law, Procedural and Enforcement Mechanisms*, Vol. **2**, 2nd edn, New York, 177.

Van den Wyngaert, Ch. (1989), 'Double Criminality as a Requirement to Jurisdiction' in J. Dugard, and Ch. van den Wyngaert (eds.) (1996), *International Criminal Law and Procedure*, Aldershot, Brookfield (USA), Singapore, Sydney, 131.

Van den Wyngaert, Ch. and G. Stessens (1999), 'The International Ne Bis In Idem Principle: Resolving Some of the Unanswered Questions', *International and Comparative Law Quarterly* **48**, 779.

Vervaele, J. A. E. (2005), 'The Transnational Ne Bis In Idem Principle in the EU: Mutual Recognition and Equivalent Protection of Human Rights', *Utrecht Law Review*, Vol. **1**, No. 2, 100–118 (online version available at: http://www.utrechtlawreview.org > Archive).

Wise, E. M. (1999), '*Aut Dedere Aut Judicare*: The Duty to Prosecute or Extradite' in M. Ch. Bassiouni (ed.), *International Criminal Law, Procedural and Enforcement Mechanisms*, Vol. **2**, 2nd edn, New York, 15.

Zimmermann, R. (2004), *La coopération judiciaire internationale en matière pénale*, 2nd edn, Berne.

Article 12. Monitoring and Follow-up

NICOLA BONUCCI[1]

Article 12 – Monitoring and Follow-up

The Parties shall co-operate in carrying out a programme of systematic follow-up to monitor and promote the full implementation of this Convention. Unless otherwise decided by consensus of the Parties, this shall be done in the framework of the OECD Working Group on Bribery in International Business Transactions and according to its terms of reference, or within the framework and terms of reference of any successor to its functions, and Parties shall bear the costs of the programme in accordance with the rules applicable to that body.

Official Commentary

Article 12 – Monitoring and Follow-up

34. The current terms of reference of the OECD Working Group on Bribery which are relevant to monitoring and follow-up are set out in Section VIII of the 1997 OECD Recommendation. They provide for:

i) receipt of notifications and other information submitted to it by the [participating] countries;

ii) regular reviews of steps taken by [participating] countries to implement the Recommendation and to make proposals, as appropriate, to assist [participating] countries in its implementation; these reviews will be based on the following complementary systems:

a system of self evaluation, where [participating] countries' responses on the basis of a questionnaire will provide a basis for assessing the implementation of the Recommendation;

a system of mutual evaluation, where each [participating] country will be examined in turn by the Working Group on Bribery, on the basis of a report which

[1] The views and opinions expressed in this chapter are personal and do not necessarily represent those of the OECD or of the state Parties to the Convention.

will provide an objective assessment of the progress of the [participating] country in implementing the Recommendation.

iii) examination of specific issues relating to bribery in international business transactions;

...

v) provision of regular information to the public on its work and activities and on implementation of the Recommendation.

35. The costs of monitoring and follow-up will, for OECD Members, be handled through the normal OECD budget process. For non-members of the OECD, the current rules create an equivalent system of cost sharing, which is described in the Resolution of the Council Concerning Fees for Regular Observer Countries and Non-Member Full Participants in OECD Subsidiary Bodies, C(96)223/FINAL.

36. The follow-up of any aspect of the Convention which is not also follow-up of the 1997 OECD Recommendation or any other instrument accepted by all the participants in the OECD Working Group on Bribery will be carried out by the Parties to the Convention and, as appropriate, the participants party to another, corresponding instrument.

Revised Recommendation

Section VIII.: Follow-up and institutional arrangements

[THE COUNCIL] INSTRUCTS the Committee on International Investment and Multinational Enterprises, through its Working Group on Bribery in International Business Transactions, to carry out a programme of systematic follow-up to monitor and promote the full implementation of this Recommendation, in co-operation with the Committee for Fiscal Affairs, the Development Assistance Committee and other OECD bodies, as appropriate. This follow-up will include, in particular:

i) receipt of notifications and other information submitted to it by the Member countries;

ii) regular reviews of steps taken by Member countries to implement the Recommendation and to make proposals, as appropriate, to assist Member countries in its implementation; these reviews will be based on the following complementary systems:

– a system of self-evaluation, where Member countries? responses on the basis of a questionnaire will provide a basis for assessing the implementation of the Recommendation;

– a system of mutual evaluation, where each Member country will be examined in turn by the Working Group on Bribery, on the basis of a

report which will provide an objective assessment of the progress of the Member country in implementing the Recommendation.

iii) examination of specific issues relating to bribery in international business transactions;
iv) examination of the feasibility of broadening the scope of the work of the OECD to combat international bribery to include private sector bribery and bribery of foreign officials for reasons other than to obtain or retain business;
v) provision of regular information to the public on its work and activities and on implementation of the Recommendation.

Chapter contents

I. Monitoring procedures

1. The general issue of monitoring of the Convention

'If not complied with, any legal norm becomes meaningless. This simple statement is of special importance in international law, where no central enforcement agency exists as in the domestic area, which has the state itself.'[2]

The lack of monitoring of international conventions has always been viewed as one of the main weaknesses of international law. In a book dedicated to the issue of effective supervision by international organisations, the authors indicated that 'for most international organizations, the member states themselves are the most important source of information. Traditionally, there are two methods for organizations to obtain such information: periodic reports from states about their own conduct in view of the rules of the organization, and complaints by states about alleged non-compliance by other states'.[3] This is not the model followed so far by the Convention, which heavily relies on a specific method of monitoring very well known within the OECD, namely 'peer review' and its political consequence the 'peer pressure'.[4]

There is little literature on the negotiations leading to the text of the Convention and the Official Commentaries and even what has been published does not really address the issue of monitoring and how the language of Article 12 of the Convention and its related Official Commentaries (34–36) was crafted and agreed. However, there seems to be a consensus amongst those who had been involved in the negotiation on two points:

- all recognised the importance of having in place a rigorous monitoring mechanism;

[2] Ehrmann 2002, 1. [3] Blokker and Muller 1994, 281.
[4] For a broader presentation of these mechanisms, cf. OECD 2003a and Guilmette 2004b.

- none had any precise idea on how such a mechanism could or should work.

This apparent contradiction is reflected in Article 12 of the Convention and its related Official Commentaries which present a certain number of interesting characteristics.

First, Article 12 provides that there shall be 'a programme of systematic follow-up to monitor and promote the full implementation of this Convention'. It is interesting to note that such obligation, enshrined in the Convention, has no time limit and, henceforth, Parties to the Convention remain bound until and unless they decide to amend this provision.

Second, while the Convention is a 'free-standing agreement' – in the sense that it is not strictly speaking an OECD Convention but a Convention negotiated within the OECD framework and opened to countries which are not OECD Members – its monitoring is entrusted to a full-fledged OECD body, i.e. the Working Group on Bribery in International Business Transactions (WGB). Such an unusual institutional setting entails that, since entry into force of the Convention, the WGB performs a dual function. On the one hand, it is an OECD body fully integrated in the OECD hierarchy: this means, inter alia, that it works under the supervision of the OECD Council acting as the supreme governing body.[5] On the other hand, the WGB also acts as a Conference of the Parties, in line with what provided for in a number of international treaties.[6] A more detailed analysis of the peculiarities entailed by the 'hybrid' nature of the WGB is presented by our commentary on Article 13 of the Convention.

While Article 12 merely sets the basis under which the monitoring will be carried out, Official Commentary 34 enters into some more details. The main elements of a 'systematic follow-up' as provided for in Official Commentary 34 can be summarised as follows:

- a regular process of exchange of information;
- a system of self-evaluation based on a questionnaire sent to all WGB participants;
- a system of mutual evaluation in which each WGB participant will be examined by the WGB on the basis of a report;
- provision of regular information to the public;

[5] According to Art. 7 of the Convention establishing the OECD (OECD 1960), the Council is 'the body from which all acts of the organisation derive'.

[6] Cf., for example, the Conferences of the Parties established by a number of multilateral environmental agreements; and also Sands 2004.

- examination of bribery-related issues common to a number of countries or at least not specifically related to a country, the so-called 'horizontal issues'.

It must be recognised that even Official Commentary 34 does not really help those who want to understand the mechanics of the monitoring of the Convention, even though such monitoring is widely recognised as being an essential tool for ensuring the effectiveness of the Convention. In its report published in December 2004, Transparency International stated that 'the OECD Working Group on Bribery deserves great credit for its follow-up monitoring of government enforcement. Continuation of the monitoring program is essential in order to ensure that enforcement will progress to a level where substantial reductions in foreign bribery will be achieved'.[7]

The specific monitoring procedures of the Convention were already briefly presented in the Introduction of this commentary which also contains the references to the related OECD documents that are publicly available.[8]

It is interesting to observe that, in fact, most of the technical, but vital, details of the monitoring mechanism were agreed by the WGB after the negotiation of the Convention and are regularly reviewed and modified by it. Moreover, not all the technical guidelines related to monitoring are publicly available. While one could criticise this course of action as not transparent and favouring a possible 'mutual back-scratching', the reality proves the contrary.

We will argue that the evolutionary character of the procedures and the confidentiality of the mutual evaluation process are key to the success of the monitoring.

2. The so-called '*Tour de Table*'

The first monitoring procedure, in line with Official Commentary 34, is the exchange information amongst participating countries on developments undertaken in each of them. This is done at each WGB meeting[9] during what is called a '*Tour de Table*'. The information formally shared on this occasion is made publicly available on the OECD website.[10] Since its

[7] Heimann, Dell, Sng-Sachsenroeder, and Whittier 2005, 2.
[8] See also Documentary Appendix of this commentary.
[9] The WGB usually meets four or five times per year.
[10] For the last document produced within the time period analysed by this commentary, cf. OECD 2005a.

inception, the *Tour de Table* has retained the same format but has evolved considerably in content.

2.1. Format

During this session, each WGB participant takes the floor in order to inform all other participants of new developments in their country with respect to implementation of the Convention. The order of the interventions follows the alphabetical order in which countries are seated in the room, which explains the name of the exercise. Interventions are supposed to be clear and concise. After each intervention, other participants may ask questions to the country which intervened, in order to seek either clarification or further explanation of the intervention or to raise issues not addressed during the intervention.

2.2. Content

The dynamic and evolutionary nature of the monitoring process is perfectly illustrated by the evolution of the *Tour de Table.*

In the earlier days of WGB monitoring, the *Tour de Table* focussed on the legislative developments occurring in each country, in particular with respect to the ratification process and the adoption of the necessary domestic legislation.[11] This exercise has now lost a lot of relevance given that a satisfactory legal framework is in place in almost all the Parties to the Convention. It may still happen that legislative changes which may have an impact on the implementation of the Convention are brought to the attention of the Group, but this has become more the exception than the rule.

The *Tour de Table* has gradually evolved towards a much more practical session of questions and answers on alleged cases of transnational bribery. While an earlier attempt to introduce this dimension, based on press clippings collected by the Secretariat, was dismissed by the WGB, it is now accepted that participating countries can ask questions to other participants on on-going cases or allegations which have come to their attention or even that have been reported publicly; recently, the WGB discussed a methodology for selecting such cases. It is important to note that this part of the *Tour de Table* is informal and confidential and thus it is not fully reflected in the document that is made available on-line. The choice of a closed door process has been contested in some quarters, in particular by NGOs; however, it appears to be an effective

[11] For the 'Table of Ratifications' see Introduction of this commentary.

way of stimulating a frank and open dialogue. It is also a means of maintaining and increasing, as appropriate, the peer pressure on selected countries. Finally, it responds to earlier criticisms regretting the absence of such tool.[12]

As we can see, the content of the *Tour de Table* is not rigidly defined. The WGB can, at any stage, decide to improve it so as to remain close to evolving international priorities. For example, the WGB recently agreed that state Parties should provide information on their intention concerning the ratification of the United Nations (UN) Convention Against Corruption and on any new development concerning actions undertaken in response to the information contained in the reports recently published by the Volcker Commission with respect to the 'Oil for Food' programme.[13]

3. 'Phase 1 monitoring'

The procedure for Phase 1 monitoring was agreed by the WGB at its meeting on 29 June–1 July 1998, i.e. after the adoption of the Convention but before its entry into force. In that context one can say that the WGB was acting as a pre-Conference of the Parties group. According to the procedural document adopted by the WGB, 'the principal objective of Phase 1 is to evaluate whether the legal texts through which participants implement the Convention meet the standard set by the Convention as well as initial actions to implement the Recommendation'.[14] In plain words this means that 'Phase 1' is devoted to the assessment of the text of the relevant laws and regulations in order to see if such text accurately translates the obligations of the Convention and the commitments of the Revised Recommendation. Indeed, it must be recalled that the Convention is not self-executing and that its implementation is left to each Party with due respect to the concept of 'functional equivalence'.[15] As such, Parties do not have to implement the Convention through identical provisions. For instance, some Parties have implemented Article 1 of the Convention by establishing the foreign bribery offence in their Penal Codes, while others

[12] Thus, according to Tarullo 2004 'the most obvious shortcoming of current institutional arrangements under the OECD Convention is the absence of information flows about specific instances of bribery. Without such information it is difficult for signatories to determine whether other governments are, in fact, complying by prosecuting overseas bribery in appropriate cases' (695).

[13] Cf. the various articles published in the media. For example, note the article 'Panel Pushes Probe of Oil-for-Food Program', which was released on the website of CBS on 16 December 2005.

[14] OECD 1998.

[15] The concept of 'functional equivalence' is defined in Official Commentary 2 and illustrated in Official Commentary 3. Further discussion can be found in Aiolfi and Pieth 2002, 351.

have established stand-alone legislation, and one Party has used the unfair competition legislation. In addition, the Phase 1 also includes a review of the implementation of the 1996 Recommendation of the Council on the Tax Deductibility of Bribes to Foreign Public Officials.

In April 1999, the WGB began Phase 1 with the examination of the United States and, as of 31 December 2005, all state Parties to the Convention – with the exception of Estonia which was examined in January 2006 – had been assessed by the WGB under Phase 1 procedures.

3.1. Self- and mutual evaluation provided for in Phase 1

3.1.1. The questionnaire

The first task of the WGB was to agree on a standard questionnaire to be transmitted to all signatories and future acceding countries.[16] This twelve-page questionnaire follows the order of the Articles of the Convention. All countries had to reply to the questionnaire in such a way as to ensure a serious assessment of conformity of their laws with the Convention. Thus the related procedural document indicates that replies should:

- be precise and provide sufficient detail;
- reflect all relevant elements of the legal system (including, for example, other relevant laws, regulations, judicial precedent, other treaties, the constitution);
- take into account the Official Commentaries to the Convention which are part of its context.

In order to ensure consistency of the replies to the questionnaire, the WGB also mandated the OECD Secretariat to 'examine if the replies are complete and, if necessary, request additional information from the participant'. Finally, it was agreed that all the replies to the questionnaire would be circulated to all participants in the WGB.

3.1.2. The preparation of a preliminary report

This stage is particularly interesting as it recognises an important role for the OECD Secretariat.[17] Indeed, the procedural document explicitly states

[16] The questionnaire is available at: http://www.oecd.org.

[17] In view of the fact that the WGB is an OECD body, it is served by a Secretariat which is fully integrated in the OECD Secretariat and more specifically in the Directorate for Financial and Enterprises Affairs (DAF). The independence, the high quality, and the credibility of the Secretariat is a very important factor for the success of the monitoring but cannot be fully analysed in the context of this book.

that 'the report would be drafted principally by the Secretariat'.[18] Two 'lead examiners' nominated by two different participating countries should 'assist the Secretariat'. In selecting the lead examiners, the Secretariat should seek to ensure that one of them comes from a country with a legal system close to that of the reviewed country whilst the other should be from a country with a different legal tradition.

The procedural document also interestingly points out that, while the report 'should have a standard format...the format could be elaborated further'.[19] Again this shows the evolutionary and dynamic character of the monitoring process.

The draft report is foreseen as short with a descriptive part, an evaluation section and recommendations for further measures. The country being reviewed has an opportunity to 'review the report and comment on it prior to its submission to the Working Group'.

The specific wording used in the procedural document is most interesting. It indicates that the country reviewed cannot oblige the drafters of the report to incorporate any drafting suggestion that it may make nor it can veto the submission of the report to the WGB. This next stage is, naturally, the more important one.

3.1.3. WGB consultation and adoption of results

Again the choice of words here is not neutral. The procedural document refers to 'consultation' rather than 'evaluation' or 'examination', probably in order to take into account the sensitivities of countries towards any suggestion that they would be subject to an exam which they could pass but also could fail.

The so-called 'consultation' is, however, in fact an evaluation by the WGB, as explicitly recognised by the procedural document which specifies that 'the lead examiners could help initiate the discussion, but all delegates would be invited to participate in the evaluation'.[20]

Furthermore, while using diplomatic language, the procedural document clearly states that the reviewed country will not be able to block the adoption of the conclusions of the WGB. Indeed the document stresses that 'this

[18] OECD 1998. [19] OECD 1998. [20] OECD 1998.

assessment could be adopted by consensus or reflect differences in opinion among participants in the Working Group'.[21]

In concrete terms, this crucial step operates as follows:

- the draft report is presented to the WGB and is discussed in plenary (around one hour of discussions on average);
- the report is then re-examined by the lead examiners and the Secretariat together with the reviewed country during an informal meeting. In that meeting the reviewed country is also presented with draft conclusions prepared by the Secretariat and the lead examiners. The reviewed country can comment on the draft conclusions, including by disagreeing to some or all of them but cannot block the submission of the draft conclusions to the WGB;
- the draft conclusions are submitted to the WGB for adoption. The reviewed country is given a last opportunity to make its own views known, but, if necessary, the report, including the conclusions and recommendations, may be adopted on the basis of the 'consensus minus one' principle. The 'minus one' is, obviously, the reviewed country.

In practice, there have been only a very few instances in which the reports voice the dissenting opinion of the reviewed country.[22]

3.1.4. The results of 'Phase 1 monitoring'

Phase 1 reports are all available on the OECD website.[23] Even a cursory reading of them – and in particular of their conclusions – demonstrates that any 'mutual back scratching' has been avoided.

The language used by the WGB clearly distinguishes those countries which 'overall' met the standards of the Convention and the Revised Recommendation from those which only partially met those standards and those which, at the time of the Phase 1 examination, did not appear to have adequately translated the obligations of the Convention in their national legislation.

[21] See previous note 19. This particular wording is typical 'OECD language'. The reference to 'consensus' reflects the decision-making process generally applied within the OECD. Contrary to unanimity, consensus does not require an affirmative vote of all participating countries but leaves a right of veto to each of them. The wording 'reflect differences in opinion' is a clear reference to Rule 23c) of the OECD Rules of Procedure, which indicate that 'reports or proposals submitted by a Committee or a Sub-Committee shall call attention to the different attitudes adopted by the members'.

[22] Cf., for example, UK-Ph1, 24 et seq. [23] Cf. http://www.oecd.org.

The deficiencies identified by the WGB can be broadly divided in three categories:[24]

- major issues requiring immediate action (often legislative);
- issues of concern to be followed up during the so-called 'Phase 2';
- minor issues to be addressed as appropriate by the reviewed country.

It is remarkable to note that most if not all the observations and criticisms expressed by the WGB have been taken on board by the reviewed countries. As a result, a number of them had to go back to their executive or legislative authorities in order to modify and amend national laws and regulations. Even more remarkable is the fact that, in a number of cases, this was done rather swiftly.

4. 'Phase 1 plus' or 'Phase 1bis' monitoring

This is yet another illustration of the flexibility of the monitoring procedures elaborated by the WGB as 'Phase 1bis' was not originally contemplated in the procedural document setting out the procedure for the 'Phase 1 monitoring'.

In fact the need for this additional step stemmed from practical considerations. Indeed, the WGB had been confronted with a variety of situations that required it to reassess the national legislation of some reviewed countries:[25]

- some Phase 1 reports required that the reviewed country undertake immediate legislative action to meet the standards of the Convention;[26]
- in other cases, the reviewed country modified its relevant legislation after the Phase 1 evaluation had been carried out and the WGB considered that had to be reassessed in light of these developments in the situation.[27]

The procedure followed for the 'Phase 1bis' is, *mutatis mutandis*, the one followed for Phase 1. The Phase 1bis report is adopted under the same conditions as the Phase 1 report. Originally, it was appended to the latter and made publicly available. Practice here has again evolved over time.

[24] See Introduction of this commentary.
[25] So far the following countries have gone through Phase 1bis monitoring: Bulgaria, Czech Republic, Hungary, Iceland, Italy, Japan, United Kingdom.
[26] This is the case, inter alia, of BG-Ph1, 18; JP-Ph1, 27; UK-Ph1, 24.
[27] This was the case for Italy.

Now legislative or other changes that potentially affect Phase 1 findings normally undergo a Phase 1-like analysis in Phase 2.

5. 'Phase 2 monitoring'

Whilst Phase 1 focuses on the laws and regulations as they stand in the books of the reviewed countries, the main objective of Phase 2 is quite different. The basic procedural document outlining the procedures for the Phase 2 indicates that 'the purpose of Phase 2 is to study the structures put in place to enforce the laws and rules implementing the Convention and to assess their application in practice. Phase 2 should broaden the focus of monitoring to encompass more fully the non-criminal aspects of the 1997 Revised Recommendation. Phase 2 would also serve an educational function as participants discuss problems and different approaches'.[28]

The procedural document for Phase 2 was adopted only in early 2001, even if its main outline was already contained in the procedural document concerning Phase 1 monitoring. It is interesting to note that in addition to the basic procedural document, the WGB felt the need to adopt more detailed guidelines in October 2003 on the basis of its experience in conducting Phase 2 examinations.[29] The Phase 2 Guidelines were further revised in June 2005 and in January 2006 to include newly agreed steps: the latter will be analysed below. The Phase 2 Guidelines are informal; they are designed to cover practical matters of interest to the parties involved in the examination process, i.e. the various logistical steps to be taken by the lead examiners, Secretariat, and country under examination during the different stages of the examination process.

By virtue of the adoption and the regular revision of the Phase 2 Guidelines, the WGB has repeatedly demonstrated its desire to preserve the dynamic character of the monitoring and its flexibility.

The WGB began Phase 2 with its examination of Finland at its meeting of June 2002. As of 31 December 2004, all G7 countries had been reviewed by the WGB. As of 31 December 2005, twenty-one Parties to the Convention had been assessed by the WGB under the Phase 2 procedures. All Parties to the Convention are to be reviewed in the framework of the on-going Phase 2 cycle due for completion by the end of 2007. The timetable of all scheduled examinations until the end of the cycle is publicly available on the OECD website.[30]

[28] OECD 2001c.

[29] Hereafter the 'Phase 2 Guidelines'. These Guidelines are published at: http://www.oecd.org and in paper version (OECD 2006a).

[30] Cf. http://www.oecd.org.

To summarise and differentiate Phase 2 from Phase 1, one could say that while Phase 1 looks at compliance of domestic legislation with the standards of the Convention, Phase 2 examines how the domestic framework works in practice. Phase 1's main objective is to assess formal compliance with the Convention. Phase 2's main objective is to evaluate the substantive degree of implementation of the 'essential object and purpose of the treaty': which is to achieve 'equivalence among the measures to be taken by the Parties'.[31]

5.1. Self- and mutual evaluation provided for in Phase 2

The procedure for the Phase 2 monitoring comprises four main elements.

5.2. The questionnaire

As for Phase 1, a Phase 2 monitoring starts with a questionnaire. However, while the WGB adopted a standard questionnaire for Phase 2,[32] this is not the only questionnaire a reviewed country will receive.

5.2.1. The standard questionnaire

The standard questionnaire was adopted by the WGB in December 2000. The questionnaire is much more practice-oriented than the one adopted for Phase 1, given that the focus of Phase 2 is to make sure that the legislation in place works effectively. Therefore the information required from the reviewed countries concerns a variety of different areas, including the following:

- the level of human and financial resources available for the implementation of the Convention;
- the level of coordination amongst the various law enforcement agencies and ministries concerned;
- efforts undertaken by the Government to raise awareness not only within the governmental structure but also towards the legal profession, the companies, the civil society and the public opinion at large;
- any relevant jurisprudence not only in relation to foreign bribery but also on domestic bribery and on any other relevant offence (in particular other economic crimes);
- application of corporate liability to the foreign bribery offence;
- application of the foreign bribery offence to cases that take place outside a Party's territory (e.g. in the foreign public official's country);

[31] 8th recital of the preamble to the OECD Convention.
[32] Available at the OECD website: http://www.oecd.org.

- practical information on the difficulties experienced concerning investigation and prosecution of offences of bribery of foreign public officials;
- information about how the authorities have dealt with concrete cases of foreign bribery;
- role of public agencies like export credit agencies and development aid agencies in detecting and deterring foreign bribery;
- reporting requirements and procedure both for public officials and for private individuals;
- whistleblowing and witness protection;
- information on tax inspection requirements the tax treatment of bribe payments, and the reporting obligations of tax inspectors who detect foreign bribery in the course of tax audits;
- accounting and auditing rules and practices for the purpose of detecting and reporting foreign bribery.

5.2.2. The supplementary questionnaire

In addition to the standard questionnaire, a supplementary questionnaire specific to the country concerned is prepared for each reviewed country. The supplementary questionnaire draws on independent research performed by the examination team and on the evaluation of that country in Phase 1. In practice, the supplementary questionnaire, being tailor-made, can enter into specific problem areas raised in the Phase 1 evaluation, as well as important practical areas regarding compliance with the Convention and related instruments, such as the level of priority that a Party's law enforcement apparatus places on foreign bribery cases. While usually shorter than the main questionnaire, it could include as many if not more questions than the standard questionnaire.[33]

The supplementary questionnaire is drafted by the Secretariat in collaboration with the lead examiners.

5.3. On-site visits by the lead examiners and the Secretariat

This is the major element of all Phase 2 examinations and is where the main difference between the Phase 1 and Phase 2 monitoring lies.

On-site visits were already envisaged in 1998, at the time of the adoption of the basic procedural document concerning the Phase 1 monitoring.

[33] A few weeks before the on-site visit in March 2002, the United States received a list of seventy-two additional questions. This was rather exceptional. It reflected the need to take account of longstanding FCPA enforcement practice.

It should be noted that the 1998 procedural document establishes a presumption that all participants would be evaluated in a follow-up to Phase 2: 'following the first cycle of country reviews in Phase 2, the Working Group could decide to undertake a more focused or selective round of country reviews or a more horizontal approach to evaluation'.[34]

Neither the 1998 procedural document nor the Phase 2 Guidelines provide much detail concerning the on-site visits.

In any case, some of the information contained in the 1998 document has been superseded by practice. Thus, it is indicated that on-site visits would be 'approximately 2–3 days long' but this proved very quickly to be impossible and the current practice, recognised by the Phase 2 Guidelines, is to provide for a four- to five-day visit.

If there is an element of monitoring which has been greatly developed and refined by dint of practice, then it is the on-site visit. This is also why the informal Phase 2 Guidelines devote several pages to the issue and go into a level of detail which reflects the variety of points and questions raised. To name but a few:

- Who sets the dates and the agenda of the on-site visit?
- Who organises and/or decides the composition of the panels?
- How should an examining team be composed?
- How should civil society be involved?
- Who leads the discussions?
- At what level of detail should discussion take place?

In order to provide answers to these and other questions, the WGB elaborated and recently amended the Phase 2 Guidelines.

Typically a Phase 2 on-site visit will take the following format:

- The examination team is composed of representatives from the Secretariat and experts from two countries designated as 'lead examiners'. The selection of the lead examiners is based, in principle, on the same geographical balance as in Phase 1, except that it was agreed from the outset that G7 countries would act as lead examiners to other G7 countries. The Secretariat is headed by a senior analyst. In principle, each lead examiner country must provide at least one law enforcement expert, e.g. prosecutor, investigating magistrate, or police officer) with experience of domestic or foreign bribery investigations and prosecutions or of

[34] OECD 1998. See part II. of this ch. for more details on post-Phase 2.

complex international investigations and prosecutions.[35] The examining team should also include other experts relevant to specific issues raised by the reviewed country, e.g. accounting and auditing or tax experts. The size of the team is variable and depends on the complexity of the review. A team could go from a minimum of six people to a maximum of ten–twelve persons.[36]

- Before the on-site visit, the Secretariat, in consultation with the lead examiners, prepares a summary of the preliminary issues which should be addressed during the on-site visit. This informal document, which has developed on the basis of practical experience, serves a dual purpose: first, it helps or should help the reviewed country to better prepare itself for the on-site visit; second, it assists the lead examiners in focussing the discussions.
- A preliminary agenda is prepared by the Secretariat and the lead examiners in accordance with a format agreed by the WGB. Each on-site visit must include one more panel covering the following issues: the criminal enforcement of anti-bribery laws; accounting-securities regulations; book and records and auditing; tax-auditing and deductibility; the role of the private sector, in-house and external legal counsel, auditors and accountants; also included should be a panel dealing with the role of official development assistance and export credit support systems in detecting and deterring foreign bribery. Finally, each on-site visit should include a panel which will allow the 'civil society' to express its views on implementation and enforcement. In addition to these panels, others may be set up based upon the outstanding issues identified by the lead examiners and the Secretariat. The agenda is then finalised in collaboration with examined country.
- The exact composition of the panels is one of the most important issues in practice. The Phase 2 Guidelines provide that the panels shall be assembled by the examined country in accordance with the

[35] According to Tarullo 2004 'there is some doubt that those conducting the reviews have the incentives and expertise to monitor the implementation of the Convention effectively. To a considerable extent the reviews are being conducted by officials from countries that themselves have yet to prosecute anyone for overseas bribery' (686). This argument is highly questionable, for two reasons. First, following Tarullo's logic, it would mean we would have had to wait for years before starting the Phase 2 cycle; second, how can it be said that a prosecutor with extensive experience of cases of domestic bribery or money laundering or other economic crimes like anti-trust violations would lack the requisite level of expertise?

[36] The higher figure is typical of the examination of a G7 country. For example, the examination team for the United States was composed of eleven persons, the one for Italy of twelve persons, the one for Germany of ten people.

agenda and in consultation with the Secretariat and the lead examiners. The Guidelines further specify that the examined country should do its outmost to ensure that the composition of the panels reflects the proposals of the examination team. At the end of the day, the decision on whom to meet with and where to meet rests, de facto, with the examined country but if the final outcome is not to the satisfaction of the WGB it would, in all likelihood, be reflected in the Phase 2 report. While, generally speaking, the composition of the panels has not raised any major difficulties, there have been some instances in which this point became a real issue.[37] On average, during a five-day working visit, the examination team will meet with eighty to one hundred different individuals.

- At the end of the on-site visit, a 'wrap-up' session with the examined country and the examination team is usually organised. This session may revisit some of the issues addressed during the week but it also an opportunity for the examination team, if it so wishes, to communicate its preliminary reflections.

5.4. Preliminary report assessing performance

This is another element of Phase 2 which has evolved considerably through practice. While, according to the procedural document adopted for Phase 1, the drafting of the Phase 1 report was mainly in the hands of the Secretariat, the 2001 procedural document concerning Phase 2 is more ambiguous and merely indicates that the 'preliminary report would be drafted by the Secretariat with the lead examiners' and that 'the country undergoing evaluation would have an opportunity to comment on it'.[38]

The Phase 2 Guidelines were developed in order to be more specific on the role and responsibilities of all parties involved in monitoring and to clarify the emerging practice so that such practice was consistent across the board for all Phase 2 examinations.

On the one hand, it is now accepted that while the Secretariat holds the pen and drafts the preliminary report, the lead examiners should vet such report. In the unlikely event that the lead examiners disagree amongst

[37] For example, during the on-site visit of Italy, the examination team was not able to meet with law enforcement officials in Milan: cf. IT-Ph 2, 5, 6. In other cases in which the examined country resisted the idea of meeting with certain categories of people or specific individuals, a satisfactory solution could be found, albeit often at the very last moment and only after pressure had been exerted on the examined country.

[38] OECD 2001c.

themselves or with the Secretariat on any proposed recommendation or comment, such disagreement shall be noted in the draft report. So far this has never formally happened.

On the other hand, the Phase 2 Guidelines indicate that the examined country may offer comments to the lead examiners but that such comments should be limited to corrections and clarifications and should be indexed to specific paragraphs in the draft report. Moreover, the Phase 2 Guidelines state this should not be viewed as an opportunity to rewrite the report. This last idea is particularly important in order to preserve the discussions in the reports concerning weaknesses in countries' anti-foreign bribery systems and to avoid instances in which the examined country would seek ample revisions to the draft report. At the same time, it is also important that the examined countries have an opportunity to correct factual errors and present their opinions regarding the weaknesses identified by the lead examiners. It is also interesting to note that it is for the lead examiners and not for the Secretariat to accept or refuse comments made by the examined country. Far from undermining the role of the Secretariat, such a provision is intended to protect it from political and other pressures emanating from the examined country. The Secretariat does, however, have an important role in ensuring that the WGB is informed about all problem areas in a country's implementation of the Convention. For instance, lead examiners may be reluctant to point out a weakness in the examined country's anti-foreign bribery system if the same weakness applies to their own system.

5.5. WGB consultation and adoption of the report

As in Phase 1, consideration by the WGB of the report is an essential part of the process and one which has led to tensions on several instances. Equality of treatment and fairness are keys to the success of the monitoring procedure; it is equally vital to ensure the smooth and efficient running of the WGB meetings in which draft reports are reviewed. It is with these various parameters in mind that the WGB has recently adopted a full Guidance Note on the subject, which is now annexed to the Phase 2 Guidelines.

5.5.1 Preparation of the WGB discussion

Prior to the WGB discussion, two preliminary meetings are organised in Paris, usually the day preceding the formal WGB session. The first meeting, which groups only the Secretariat and the lead examiners, is mainly devoted to discuss the commentaries that the lead examiners intend to make before the WGB on actions to be undertaken by the examined country and WGB follow-up. The second one, which also includes the examined country, focuses on the outstanding issues contained in the preliminary Phase 2 report and on the main point(s) of disagreement, if any, between the lead examiners and the examined country. At this stage, the draft report is examined paragraph-by-paragraph to ensure that there are no factual errors.

5.5.2. Consideration of the report by the WGB

The WGB devotes its first meeting, scheduled to last between two to three hours, to a review and debate of the preliminary Phase 2 report, including the commentaries of the lead examiners. After an introduction by the lead examiners followed by the initial responses of the examined country all delegations have an opportunity to react to the report and to the points raised by the lead examiners. The difficulty of the exercise resides in the need to give everybody, in particular the examined country, an opportunity to make their views known while not losing too much time on details and addressing the core issues. In this context, the role of the Chairman is vital.[39]

5.5.3. The break-away sessions

After the first reading, the Secretariat meets with the lead examiners to formulate the draft recommendations and the draft executive summary to be presented the next day to the WGB.[40] The examined country is then provided with these documents and is given an opportunity to react; at this stage, however, the full responsibility of the text to be produced for the WGB is in the hands of the lead examiners. These break-away sessions are scheduled to last around two-and-a-half hours but can last much longer. The ultimate length depends on the number and extent of outstanding issues but also on more practical considerations like the degree of resistance of the examined country and the level of patience of the lead examiners.

[39] Guilmette 2004b distinguishes between three types of OECD chairs: the 'persistent diplomat', the 'maverick', and the 'passive diplomat'. Later on, Guilmette describes the current Chair of the WGB as corresponding to the 'maverick' profile. It may be useful to reproduce, verbatim, Guilmette's description of the 'maverick profile': 'the maverick must possess a high independence of view, even be financially independent; he rides a group very hard, at times cutting a discussion short to refocus the participants on the real agenda. The maverick 'has an attitude' but also intellectual leadership, and coupled with recognised ethics the maverick is acceptable to trained bureaucrats...This archetype may be best used when the agenda is protracted and requires risk-taking to overcome embedded resistance'.

[40] The WGB has recently decided to introduce in each Phase 2 report an executive summary which has also to be adopted by the WGB.

5.5.4. Adoption of the report by the WGB

The second reading of the report focuses on the draft recommendations. The WGB is responsible for adopting a comprehensive set of recommendations identifying areas for action by the examined country and follow-up by the WGB. In addition, the WGB will need to discuss and agree on the executive summary to be included in the report. With respect to the decision-making process, the procedural document for Phase 2 states that 'the examined country will not block the Group's decision to adopt the evaluation. The examined country does, however, have the right to have its views, comments, and explanations fully reflected in the report and the evaluation'.[41] The Phase 2 Guidelines confirm therefore the 'consensus minus one' principle.

Typically, the evaluation section of a Phase 2 report will contain three kinds of issues:

- those which require action to be taken;
- those which the country is invited 'to consider' or where it is recommended that it 'should' undertake certain actions; and
- those for follow-up by the WGB.

6. Analysis of Phase 2 outcomes

While it is too early to fully evaluate the effectiveness of Phase 2 monitoring, there are good reasons to be relatively optimistic.[42] By and large, countries appear to take the Phase 2 recommendations very seriously. The WGB agreed to follow-up mechanisms to ensure a uniform approach to its recommendations.[43] One important indicator about the effectiveness of the process is the number and nature of amendments that have been made by state Parties to implementing legislation in response to recommendations of the WGB. Another measure is the level of participation of the examined country at the

[41] OECD 2001c.

[42] The seriousness of the Phase 2 monitoring has been underlined by various authors, including Low 2003b. Even, Tarullo 2004, while critical of the process, recognises that 'the OECD Phase 2 report on US implementation of the Convention, tactfully but clearly identified the limits of U.S. law enforcement organization, in seeking out evidence of bribery' (707).

[43] These mechanisms are described in part II. of this ch. A good example of how seriously countries are addressing the Phase 2 recommendations can be seen in the reaction of the French authorities. Following the release of the Phase 2 report in February 2004, the Ministry of Justice issued a six-page circular to all French prosecutors and magistrates highlighting the recommendations and inviting them to actively pursue the offence with a focus on the liability of legal persons. Cf. Circulaire 2004.

on-site visits. A further piece of evidence is the excellent participation and involvement of the lead examiners.

The WGB recently concluded and published a 'Mid-Term Study' of the substantive findings of Phase 2 evaluation reports approved up until end of 2005. This study provides further detailed analysis which can be used in the framework of future WGB monitoring.

With respect to process, three interrelated issues are worth mentioning because they raised a certain level of concern at the time of the adoption of the monitoring procedures.

6.1. Disclosure and confidentiality

From the outset the WGB has had to strike a fine balance between the need to protect and respect the confidentiality of the information provided to the Secretariat and the lead examiners and the importance given to the transparency of the monitoring process. The basic procedural document for Phase 2 emphasises that 'the mutual review itself needed confidentiality if it were to be frank and efficient'. The document further recognises that 'if the examined country makes available to the examiners information is considers confidential, confidentiality of this information will be respected'.[44] Confidentiality is the rule not only during the formal sessions of the WGB but also in the panels organised during the on-site visit, and more generally throughout the monitoring process.

The corollary of this respect for confidentiality entails that the examination team and the WGB can legitimately expect disclosure to the fullest possible extent from government officials as well as an attitude of good faith from all the other individuals interviewed during the on-site visit. Failure to disclose what would be considered necessary information for carrying out a meaningful Phase 2 examination would give rise to strong criticism from the WGB as illustrated by the Phase 2 evaluation of Japan.[45]

6.2. The role of civil society

One of the main criticisms of the existing monitoring process is the lack of participation by civil society, in particular NGOs in the peer review.[46] For both Phase 1 and Phase 2, the WGB decided that 'because peer review is an

[44] OECD 2001c.
[45] JP-Ph2: para. 2 of the section entitled 'Recommendations of the Working Group and Follow-up'.
[46] On this point cf. in particular Tronnes 2000; but also Tarullo 2004.

intergovernmental process, business and civil society groups would not be invited to participate in the formal evaluation process, in particular, in the consultation in the Working Group'.[47]

This is not to say, however, that civil society is not in a position to make a contribution to the Phase 2 monitoring process; the WGB indeed explicitly agreed that there should be an opportunity for the views of civil society 'to be expressed and reflected in Phase 2'. This opportunity exists before, during, and after the on-site visit.

6.3. Prior to the on-site visit

The schedule of the on-site visits is published in advance and is publicly available on the OECD website.[48] The WGB has noted that 'providing information on the schedule of the country examinations would permit such groups (NGOs) to provide information or opinion in a timely way'.[49] Indeed, any NGO can provide the Secretariat and/or the lead examiners with its written opinion on the state of implementation in the country to be reviewed. This possibility has been used on several occasions in the past.[50] Similarly, the media can focus its attention on the future on-site visit in the country concerned.

6.4. During the on-site visit

All on-site visits include a specific panel in which civil society can present its views.[51] According to the Phase 2 Guidelines, such a panel should ideally include relevant NGOs as well as academics and the media. With respect to representatives of media, however, their presence is allowed for the purpose of providing information to the examiners and not for reporting on the examination. It should also be noted that the Phase 2 Guidelines indicate that government representatives should not, in principle, participate actively in the civil society and the private sector panels.

6.5. After the on-site visit

One other way in which civil society can assist the monitoring process is naturally to publicise the WGB evaluation reports. In this respect, as in many

[47] OECD 2001c. [48] Cf. http://www.oecd.org. [49] OECD 2001c.
[50] In particular by Transparency International and by a grouping of NGOs based in the United Kingdom called UNICORN.
[51] See I.5.3. above.

others, the position of the WGB has evolved. It was decided recently that all published reports should be announced by OECD press release. NGOs and media alike can then make use of the reports for their own purposes. One cannot fail to observe that the media attention concerning OECD reports has steadily increased in recent years.[52] NGOs can also build on the Phase 2 reports to push for appropriate domestic action.[53] Consideration could be given, however, to increase the dissemination of the report by for example by sending copies of the report to selected Parliamentarians of the Parties to the Convention or even to other international organisations.

6.6. Fair and equitable treatment

Fairness and equal treatment has always been a great concern of the WGB. In establishing the monitoring procedure, the WGB stressed that 'monitoring must be fair and this means an equal treatment for all participants'.[54]

Naturally this requirement applies both to the substance of the monitoring exercise and to the process. The WGB considers that 'the Secretariat has an important role in ensuring uniform application of the procedures'.[55]

Fairness and equal treatment do not, however, mean identical treatment. While the position of state Parties with respect to the enactment of appropriate legislation is identical, the issues raised by the implementation of the legislation cannot, *prima facie*, be compared. Accordingly, the WGB does not view as comparable the situation of two Parties, both of which have failed to record an investigation or prosecution of foreign bribery, where the first Party has few companies involved in international business transactions in high-risk countries and faces no credible allegations of foreign bribery by its companies, and the second Party has many companies involved in substantial international business transactions and several credible foreign bribery allegations have been made against them. In the

[52] Cf. the following examples of media reporting of Phase 2 reports. With respect to IT-Ph2: 'Giudici off limits', L'Espresso, 26 December 2004; concerning CH-Ph2: 'Corruption: l'OCDE cherche un pou à la Suisse, La Tribune de Genève, 2 February 2005; following UH-Ph2 several articles were published in the press: cf. in particular 'OECD hits at failure to crack down on corrupt business', *The Times*, 19 March 2005, 'Embarassement for Blair as UK faulted on bribery drive', *Financial Times*, 19 March 2005, 'OECD criticises UK bribery fight', BBC News, 18 March 2005. The recent release of the Phase 2 report of Australia also raised a lot of attention from the Australian media.

[53] Cf., for example, the seminar organised on 12 December 2005 by UNICORN in collaboration with the Crown Prosecution Service of England and Wales concerning the follow-up to the UK-Ph2 recommendations with respect to liability of legal persons.

[54] See note 20. This language appears in identical terms in both basic procedural documents.

[55] See previous note 53.

drafting of the Phase 2 reports, care has always been taken to analyse the legal situations in identical terms and to reach uniform conclusions. As these examples show, equal treatment cannot, however, be interpreted as meaning that strictly identical consequences should be drawn from identical factual situations.

With respect to process equal treatment is, on the other hand, an absolute criterion. The WGB has been very scrupulous in seeking that all countries, large or small, be examined with the same level of scrutiny. So far, the WGB has always resisted any suggestion that the monitoring process could follow a dual-track approach, with some countries submitted to a stricter examination than others, even if there could be objective reasons for that. Similarly, deadlines and procedural obligations are the same for all countries; the WGB does not hesitate to appropriately communicate its concerns with respect to any deviation from the agreed procedures.[56]

II. The Post-Phase 2 Process

Article 12 of the Convention sets out the basic principle that there should be a 'systematic follow-up to monitor and promote the full implementation of this Convention'. Official Commentary 34 further specifies what elements such monitoring shall contain. For its part, the WGB has agreed a certain number of procedures and technical guidance, specifying in detail the forms, purpose, and content of the monitoring procedures.

Taking into account the general principles of international law on the law of treaties as codified by the Vienna Convention on the Law of Treaties of 1969, the following propositions can be made:

- the basic principle set out in the first sentence of Article 12 cannot be set aside without a formal amendment to the Convention even though subsequent practice of the Parties to the treaty can offer some scope for change;[57]

[56] The latest example is the unilateral postponement by the Czech authorities of the Phase 2 on-site visit just a few days before the visit scheduled for October 2005. This unprecedented step, which was taken in contradiction with the Phase 2 Guidelines, led the OECD to publish a press release which itself sparked a political debate in the Czech Republic: cf. 'Klaus disagrees with Paroubek's postponement of OECD visit', Czech News Agency, 2 December 2005. One could see in this mode of operation another expression of peer pressure as well as a subtle way to use the 'name and shame' concept.

[57] On the various ways in which the subsequent practice of the Parties may modify a treaty, cf. Distefano 1994, 42 et seq.

- the elements of the monitoring contained in Official Commentary 34 can be modified by the OECD Council in view of the fact that they are contained in the terms of reference of the WGB which are approved by Council;
- if there is a consensus of the Parties, monitoring can also be carried by a body other than the WGB and outside the current framework;
- irrespective of any other step, the WGB can agree on any kind of monitoring in accordance with the text and spirit of Article 12 and Official Commentary 34.

With this in mind, we will now examine what kind of follow-up to Phase 2 reports has already been agreed and how monitoring could be pursued at the end of the on-going Phase 2 cycle.

1. Follow-up to Phase 2 reports

The basic procedural document did not contain any indication of a possible follow-up to Phase 2 reports. This weakness was noticed and criticised by some.[58] It was also noticed by some countries in the WGB which therefore pushed hard for establishing a follow-up mechanism. The latter has now been inserted in the Phase 2 Guidelines and strengthened in their recent revision.

1.1. The regular follow-up procedure

Such procedure comprises two reporting mechanisms: (1) an oral report and (2) a written report.

1.1.1. The oral report

The oral report is due one year after WGB approval of the Phase 2 report. The country concerned must indicate what steps it has taken or is planning to take to implement the WGB recommendations. The system is one of self-reporting, followed by a question and answer session. While the report can be made orally, the Phase 2 Guidelines indicate that the information provided by the reporting country will be reflected in the summary record of the meeting.

[58] Tarullo 2004 notes that Phase 2 contained 'no mechanisms for assessing or encouraging compliance in the period after a review of a country is completed' (685).

1.1.2. The written report

The written report is due two years after the adoption of the Phase 2 report by the WGB and should be submitted in accordance with the standard format agreed by the WGB. The written report should address each and every recommendation of the Phase 2 report. Where no action has been taken to implement a recommendation which required action, reasons should be given. The written report is mainly – but not entirely – a self-reporting procedure. The lead examiners are invited to intervene after the presentation by the country and before a discussion in the plenary. Moreover, the discussion is a separate item on the agenda. Finally, while the written report as provided by the reporting country will be appended to the Phase 2 report and made publicly available, the Secretariat is requested to prepare a summary of the discussion of the follow-up written report as a cover note. This document must be approved by the WGB.[59]

The Phase 2 Guidelines further specify that if a reporting country failed to implement a recommendation for action on one of the 'core matters' under the Convention, it will be required to provide additional reports on its progress in implementing this recommendation within a fixed timeframe. The Phase 2 Guidelines do not specify what is intended by 'core matters'. There are some obvious examples one could easily imagine, like non-effective implementation of Article 2 of the Convention. It is not clear whether such 'core matters' could cover not only failures to implement specific Articles of the Convention but also a more general non-willingness to comply with the object and purpose of the treaty. It therefore remains to be seen how the WGB would deal with a persistent, long-term failure of a Party to the Convention to investigate or prosecute obvious cases of foreign bribery.

This mechanism leads to the follow-up mechanism envisaged in case of inadequate implementation of the Convention.

1.2. Follow-up in case of inadequate implementation of the Convention

In revising the Phase 2 Guidelines, in 2005, the WGB tackled a very sensitive and difficult issue, i.e. what to do in the event of inadequate implementation of the Convention by a state Party.

The WGB agreed that, in such case, a 'Phase 2bis Review' could be envisaged. Such procedure would take the form of a second on-site evaluation of the

[59] Reports on Bulgaria, Germany, and the United States are available at: http://www.oecd.org.

country concerned. A decision to conduct such a review could be made by the WGB on the occasion of the discussion of the Phase 2 report or after it has considered the oral and written follow-up reports. The Phase 2 Guidelines do not explicitly state that such decision shall be taken under the same 'consensus minus one' procedure which is used for the adoption of the Phase 1 and Phase 2 reports. However, the principle of *parallelisme des formes* and simple common sense suggest that this shall be the case. The Phase 2bis reports should be made available on the OECD website.

The procedure described above is being used vis-à-vis Japan. The examination team visited Japan in February 2006 and issued a report available on the OECD website.[60]

Furthermore the WGB has envisaged a series of informal and formal steps to deal with the continued failure to implement adequately the Convention after a Phase 2bis review. In so doing, the WGB could make use of the whole spectrum of peer pressure tools, including a public 'naming and shaming' of the country in question.

2. Horizontal issues

A number of Phase 1 and Phase 2 reports have highlighted certain bribery-related issues common to a number of countries or at least not specifically related to a country, the so-called 'horizontal issues'.

The WGB has recently published a 'Mid-Term Study' which is designed to present an analysis of the main issues raised so far in the Phase 2 reports.[61] Such an analytical document is not only a very useful stock-taking exercise, but it also constitutes a valuable instrument in preparation of the further revision of the 1997 Recommendation scheduled to take place in 2007.

The Phase 2 reports have certainly enabled the WGB to highlight the importance of some issues which are either not mentioned in the Convention or are only implicitly referred to. One good example is the need to ensure effective co-ordination and communication between law enforcement authorities in foreign bribery cases.

The possibility of introducing more 'horizontal' monitoring in the future has always been there for the WGB. The way in which these new issues could become part of the monitoring of the WGB is naturally dependent on how they will be incorporated in the *corpus* of the Convention or the

[60] This was contemplated in JP-Ph2, para. of the section entitled 'Recommendations of the Working Group and Follow-up'.

[61] See I.6. above, available on the OECD website.

Revised Recommendation.[62] However, the WGB has a certain *marge de manoeuvre* in interpreting the exact scope and content of the monitoring required by the Convention and the related commentaries.

Therefore, in principle, nothing in the existing texts would prevent the WGB from deciding to initiate some form of horizontal monitoring. In practice, however, the resources of the OECD Secretariat are already stretched to a maximum in order to fulfil the WGB mandate to carry out seven Phase 2 reviews per year by the end of 2007.[63] It is therefore unlikely that any meaningful horizontal monitoring will take place before the end of the on-going Phase 2 cycle. One could, however, envisage that in the context of a future 'Phase 3', the WGB would establish an 'issue-by-issue' monitoring of selected important areas instead of or in conjunction with a 'country-by-country' monitoring.

3. What kind of monitoring after Phase 2?

The basic parameters of the monitoring procedure established in Article 12 and Official Commentary 34 remain in place even after the conclusion of the on-going Phase 2 cycle. The need of a 'systematic follow-up to monitor and promote the full implementation of the Convention' is enshrined in Article 12 and as such it is an international obligation binding on all Parties to the Convention.

Monitoring of the OECD Convention undoubtedly represents its added value compared to all other similar international instruments, including the UN Convention Against Corruption. So what is the way ahead after Phase 2?

Even if we put aside, for obvious political and legal reasons, the option of stopping monitoring, a certain degree of flexibility exists on how to interpret the obligations set out in Article 12. After all, we have seen that the detailed procedures of Phases 1 and 2 and their follows-up have been decided by the WGB, acting effectively as a Conference of the Parties

Already in 1998, the WGB indicated that 'following the first cycle of country reviews in Phase 2, the Working Group could decide to undertake

[62] On the various options available to the Parties to the Convention, see our commentary on Article 16 below.

[63] It should be pointed out that according to the OECD Secretariat, a Phase 2 review requires almost the equivalent of one year's time of an OECD staff. The average cost for the OECD of a Phase 2 review has been established at EUR 140 000. To these figures one must add the time and money spent by the lead examiners by the examined countries and by all the delegations coming to a WGB meeting. This simple calculation illustrates that the monitoring process is not only technically difficult for the examined country but also requires a real human and financial commitment by all the state Parties to the Convention.

a more focused or selective round of country reviews or a more horizontal approach to evaluation'.[64]

The WGB has always demonstrated flexibility in adapting and expanding its procedures to the challenges brought about by practice. The options highlighted in 1998 should be seriously considered but this should not be to the detriment of more innovative mechanisms. For example, the idea of 'establishing a sub-group of prosecutors within or alongside the OECD Working Group' put forward by Tarullo is worth considering.[65] Another complementary option could be to initiate mutual on-site visit with other international organisations in charge of the monitoring of a Convention: the first and most obvious candidate would be the Council of Europe but one could also think of the UN, once a monitoring mechanism has been agreed. A third avenue worth exploring would be to strengthen the formal relationship of the WGB and the OECD Secretariat with institutions like the World Bank, the International Monetary Fund (IMF), other International Financial Institutions, and possibly other bodies like the Financial Action Task Force (FATF). Such co-operation would enable the results of WGB monitoring to be incorporated in the internal policies and guidelines of such institutions.

The objective of the Convention is clear. In adopting Article 12, the Parties to the Convention committed themselves to ensuring uniformity in the implementation of the Convention. While the tools to ensure such uniformity may differ and evolve, the objective shall remain the same.

References

For documentation see the consolidated bibliography at the end of the book.

Aiolfi, G. and M. Pieth (2002), 'How to Make a Convention Work: The Organisation for Economic Co-operation and Development Recommendation and Convention on Bribery as an Example of a New Horizon in International Law' in C. Fijnaut and L. Huberts (eds.), *Corruption, Integrity and Law Enforcement*, Leiden, Boston, 349.

Blokker, N. and S. Muller (1994), 'Towards More Effective Supervision by International Organizations: Some Concluding Observations' in N. Blokker and S. Muller (eds.), *Towards More Effective Supervision by International Organizations. Essays in Honour of Henry G. Schermers*, Vol. **1**, Dordrecht.

Distefano, G. (1994), 'La pratique subséquente des états parties à un traité', *Annuaire français de droit international* XL, 41.

Ehrmann, M. (2002), 'Procedures of Compliance Control in International Environmental Treaties', *Colorado Journal of International Law and Policy* **13**, 377.

Guilmette J.-H. (2004) [cited 2004b], *Peer Pressure Power: Development Cooperation and Networks – Making Use of Methods and Know-How from the Organisation for*

[64] OECD 1998. [65] Tarullo 2004, 701.

Economic Co-operation and Development (OECD) and the International Development Research Centre (IDRC) (available at: http://www.idrc.ca > search by full title).

Heimann, F., G. Dell, A. Sng-Sachsenroeder, and N. Whittier (2005), *Transparency International Progress Report: Enforcement of the OECD Convention on Combating Bribery of Foreign Public Official, 21. January 2005* (available at: http://www.ipocafrica.org > search by 'TI Progress Report').

Low, L. A. (2003) [cited 2003b], 'Milestones in Mutual Evaluation: The Phase 2 Review of the United States under the OECD Anti Bribery Convention', *International Law Forum*, Vol. **5**, No. 2, 101.

OECD (2003) [cited OECD 2003a], *Peer Review: A Tool for Co-operation and Change*, Paris.

Sands, P. (2004), *Principles of International Environmental Law*, 2nd edn, Cambridge.

Tarullo, D. K. (2004), 'The Limits of Institutional Design: Implementing the OECD Anti-Bribery Convention', *Vanderbilt Journal of International Law* **44**, 665.

Tronnes, R. D. (2000), 'Ensuring Uniformity in the Implementation of the 1997 OECD Convention on Combating Bribery of Foreign Public Officials in International Business Transactions', *George Washington International Law Review*, Vol. **33**, 100.

Articles 13–17. Final Provisions

NICOLA BONUCCI[1]

Article 13 – Signature and Accession

1. Until its entry into force, this Convention shall be open for signature by OECD members and by non-members which have been invited to become full participants in its Working Group on Bribery in International Business Transactions.

2. Subsequent to its entry into force, this Convention shall be open to accession by any non-signatory which is a member of the OECD or has become a full participant in the Working Group on Bribery in International Business Transactions or any successor to its functions. For each such non-signatory, the Convention shall enter into force on the sixtieth day following the date of deposit of its instrument of accession.

Official Commentary 37

The Convention will be open to non-members which become full participants in the OECD Working Group on Bribery in International Business Transactions. Full participation by non-members in this Working Group is encouraged and arranged under simple procedures. Accordingly, the requirement of full participation in the Working Group, which follows from the relationship of the Convention to other aspects of the fight against bribery in international business, should not be seen as an obstacle by countries wishing to participate in that fight. The Council of the OECD has appealed to non-members to adhere to the 1997 OECD Recommendation and to participate in any institutional follow-up or implementation mechanism, i.e., in the Working Group. The current procedures regarding full participation by non-members in the Working Group may be found in the Resolution of the Council concerning the Participation of Non-Member Economies in the Work of Subsidiary Bodies of the Organisation, C(96)64/REV1/FINAL. In

[1] The views and opinions expressed in this chapter are personal and do not necessarily represent those of the OECD or of the state Parties to the Convention.

addition to accepting the Revised Recommendation of the Council on Combating Bribery, a full participant also accepts the Recommendation on the Tax Deductibility of Bribes of Foreign Public Officials, adopted on 11 April 1996, C(96)27/FINAL.

Article 14 – Ratification and Depositary

1. This Convention is subject to acceptance, approval or ratification by the Signatories, in accordance with their respective laws.

2. Instruments of acceptance, approval, ratification or accession shall be deposited with the Secretary-General of the OECD, who shall serve as Depositary of this Convention.

Article 15 – Entry into Force

1. This Convention shall enter into force on the sixtieth day following the date upon which five of the ten countries which have the ten largest export shares (see annex), and which represent by themselves at least sixty per cent of the combined total exports of those ten countries, have deposited their instruments of acceptance, approval, or ratification. For each signatory depositing its instrument after such entry into force, the Convention shall enter into force on the sixtieth day after deposit of its instrument.

2. If, after 31 December 1998, the Convention has not entered into force under paragraph 1 above, any signatory which has deposited its instrument of acceptance, approval or ratification may declare in writing to the Depositary its readiness to accept entry into force of this Convention under this paragraph 2. The Convention shall enter into force for such a signatory on the sixtieth day following the date upon which such declarations have been deposited by at least two signatories. For each signatory depositing its declaration after such entry into force, the Convention shall enter into force on the sixtieth day following the date of deposit.

Article 16 – Amendment

Any Party may propose the amendment of this Convention. A proposed amendment shall be submitted to the Depositary which shall communicate it to the other Parties at least sixty days before convening a meeting of the Parties to consider the proposed amendment. An amendment adopted by consensus of the Parties, or by such other means as the Parties may determine by consensus, shall enter into force sixty days after the deposit of an instrument of ratification, acceptance or approval by all of the Parties, or in such other circumstances as may be specified by the Parties at the time of adoption of the amendment.

Article 17 – Withdrawal

A Party may withdraw from this Convention by submitting written notification to the Depositary. Such withdrawal shall be effective one year after the date of the receipt of the notification. After withdrawal, co-operation shall continue between the Parties and the Party which has withdrawn on all requests for assistance or extradition made before the effective date of withdrawal which remain pending.

Chapter contents

I. The Rules of Article 13

Article 13 on 'Signature and Accession' is one of the most interesting Articles of the Convention as, in conjunction with Official Commentary 37, it sets out a mechanism pretty unique in international law.

The two paragraphs of Article 13 deal with two different factual situations but in an identical manner. Paragraph 1 indicates how a country can become a signatory of the Convention prior to its entry into force, while paragraph 2 concerns accession to the Convention after it enters into force.

The criteria set out by both paragraphs are identical: in order to become a state Party to the Convention you either have to be an OECD member or a 'full participant' to the Working Group on Bribery (WGB).[2]

In a way, this Article is the perfect illustration of the hybrid character of the Convention: formally detached from the OECD but in fact intrinsically linked to it. Article 13 and the related Official Commentary 37 also make clear the 'semi-open' nature of the Convention. While in principle any country can become a Party to the Convention, this is not in reality the case.

1. The Convention and OECD members

The Convention on Combating Bribery of Foreign Public Officials in International Business Transactions was negotiated within the framework of the OECD and with the support of the OECD Secretariat but is a free standing agreement, i.e. an international agreement independent of the Convention establishing the OECD.

It would have been possible to negotiate a legally binding agreement by means of a Decision, in accordance with Article 5 of the Convention

[2] Art. 12(c) of the Convention establishing the OECD (OECD 1960) indicates that the organisation may 'invite non-member Governments or organisations to participate in activities of the Organisation'.

establishing the OECD. In principle, OECD Acts are addressed only to OECD members; there are, however, several precedents for non-OECD members' adherence to an OECD Act, including a legally binding Decision.[3]

While such an avenue was, therefore, legally possible and might in some respects have presented some advantages, in particular with regard to future amendment of the text, it was not pursued. The negotiators preferred to remain within the more traditional scheme of a fully fledged international treaty.

The close link to the OECD is, nevertheless, acknowledged by the Convention, which provides that any OECD member can become party to it. Naturally, in recognition of the principle of sovereignty of states, no OECD member is bound to become a state Party. Article 13 confers a right upon OECD members but does not, and could not, per se impose any obligation. We will now examine the effects of Article 13 on OECD members, both current members and possible future ones.

1.1. Article 13 and existing OECD members

All current OECD members, with the exception of Slovakia – which was nevertheless a full participant in the WGB – were already members at the time of the entry into force of the Convention. They were, therefore, all entitled to become signatories to the Convention, which they did. This was a logical step, given that a few months before the adoption of the Convention the same countries had adopted the Revised Recommendation of the Council on Combating Bribery in International Transactions, which included a decision to 'open negotiations promptly on an international convention to criminalise bribery'.[4]

While there was no legal obligation to do so, all OECD members felt compelled to become state Parties to the Convention; this concerted behaviour is a further illustration of peer pressure which is referred to in other parts of this commentary.[5] We should also note that Article 13 does not make any distinction among OECD members; all current OECD members, irrespective of economic size or share of world exports, are entitled to be a state Party to the Convention.

[3] Art. 5 OECD 1960 provides that: '[i]n order to achieve its aims, the Organisation may: (a) take decisions which, except as otherwise provided, shall be binding on all the Members; (b) make recommendations to Members'. All the OECD Decisions and Recommendations are available at: http://www.oecd.org.

[4] See full text of the Revised Recommendation (OECD 1997a) in the Documentary Appendix.

[5] See part IV. in the Introduction of this commentary.

One hypothetical situation is, however, worth mentioning. In accordance with Article 17, any current OECD member could withdraw from the Convention while remaining an OECD member. In that scenario, the withdrawing member, in its capacity of OECD member, would also maintain the political commitments undertaken in the Revised Recommendation[6] and in the Recommendation on the Tax Deductibility of Bribes of Foreign Public Officials.[7] Furthermore, the withdrawing member would still be entitled to fully participate in the WGB, by virtue of its status as OECD Member. Such an implausible but legally possible scenario would undoubtedly raise a number of intricate institutional and legal issues.

1.2. Article 13 and future OECD members

Since the entry into force of the Convention only one country has joined the OECD. This is Slovakia. Slovakia cannot, however, really be considered a precedent given that it was already participating in the WGB and negotiations for its OECD membership were at an advanced stage.[8]

Article 13 does not distinguish between current and future members of the OECD. Any country which joins the OECD can, irrespective of its size or share of world export, also adhere to the Convention.

There could be, however, a substantial difference in treatment between current and future OECD members as a result of OECD Council policy regarding future accession to the OECD.

Contrary to most other international organisations, accession to the OECD is not automatic upon request. Accession to the OECD requires, in accordance with Article 16 of the Convention establishing the OECD, the unanimous agreement of all OECD members. Furthermore, negotiations for accession may begin only if and when the OECD Council issues an invitation to this effect and take place upon the terms and conditions set out by the Council.[9]

This last point is crucial. The OECD Council enjoys total discretion in deciding on the substantive commitments a candidate country must make in order to become an OECD member. If and when future negotiations are launched, the OECD Council could, therefore, decide that accession to the Convention is part of the 'OECD *acquis*' and that, in order

[6] OECD 1997a. [7] OECD 1996.

[8] Slovakia finally joined the OECD in December 2000.

[9] For a brief description of the accession process to the OECD cf. the document 'Becoming a Member to the OECD: The Accession Process', available at: http://www.oecd.org.

to become an OECD member, a country must also adhere to the Convention. If the Council were to follow this course of action, future members would, therefore, not have the option of not acceding to the Convention.

Discussions on the enlargement of the OECD are ongoing and very much in a state of flux. While there seems to be a general agreement that, in the future, the OECD should reach a number close to 40 to 45 members compared to the current thirty members, there are still profound divergences amongst OECD members on the target countries for such an enlargement and on the possible timing of accession. It is obvious, however, that any enlargement of the OECD will have an impact on the Convention, in particular, if participation in the Convention is established as a condition of OECD membership.

2. The Convention and non-OECD members

'The Convention will be open to non-members which become full participants in the OECD Working Group on Bribery in International Business Transactions.' This wording, provided in the first sentence of Official Commentary 37, sets the basic condition for how a non-OECD member may become a state Party to the Convention. This is where the relationship between the Convention and the OECD as an international institution becomes fairly unique and complex. The concept of full participation is indeed not contained in the Convention but is a concept developed by the OECD as a form of possible participation of non-OECD members in OECD bodies and activities. It is not even explicitly focused on the Convention and, as implicitly indicated in Official Commentary 37, procedures for full participation may evolve and have indeed evolved.

We are in fact faced with a system which recalls the 'Matrioska', i.e. the Russian dolls which are inserted one into each other.

In the final analysis, the system put in place has two consequences: first, unlike OECD members, a non-member is not entitled to become a state Party to the Convention upon request; second, the terms and conditions for a non-member to become a state Party to the Convention, may go beyond its acceptance of the obligations under the Convention, as the non-member also has to satisfy the criteria for becoming a full participant in the WGB.

In this context, we should note that Official Commentary 37 makes the acceptance of other OECD legal instruments a condition of accession to the

Convention. This is done *en passant*, i.e. in a quite incidental manner. This very important requirement is, indeed, not mentioned in the Convention but is contained in the final part of Official Commentary 37, which states that, 'in addition to accepting the Revised Recommendation of the Council on Combating Bribery, a full participant also accepts the Recommendation on the Tax Deductibility of Bribes of Foreign Public Officials.[10]

II. Full participation: the rules set out by the OECD council and WGB practice

The Convention entered into force in February 1999. Argentina, Bulgaria, Brazil, Chile and Slovakia, which were already observers in the WGB and participated actively in the negotiations, were invited to become full participants and signed the Convention at the time of its adoption in November 1997. Slovenia acceded to the Convention in 2001 and Estonia in 2004. South Africa was recently invited to become a state Party and is in the process of ratifying the Convention. Furthermore, a few years ago, Israel was invited to become state Party to the Convention; no official reply was ever received by the OECD.

Official Commentary 37 states that 'full participation by non-members in this Working Group is encouraged and arranged under simple procedures. Accordingly, the requirement of full participation in the Working Group, which follows from the relationship of the Convention to other aspects of the fight against bribery in international business, should not be seen as an obstacle by countries wishing to participate in the fight'.

There are several possible explanations for the apparent contradiction between the very open and welcoming phraseology of Official Commentary 37 and the very limited number of new state Parties which have acceded so far.

1. Framework established by the Council

It was in 1992 that, for the first time, the OECD Council established a general framework for the participation in OECD subsidiary bodies and activities. This framework was amended first in 1996 and more recently in 2004.[11]

[10] OECD 1996.

[11] The relevant Resolutions of the Council concerning the participation of non-Member economies in the work of subsidiary bodies of the organisations are: OECD 1992, OECD 2000c (revised twice) and OECD 2004a.

While not entering into a detailed presentation of this framework and of the general policy of the OECD vis-à-vis non-members, the basic principles ought to be illustrated here in so far as they affected and still affect accession to the Convention.

The 1996 Resolution established the following framework:

- The process was a reactive one; it was initiated by the non-member which would ask to participate in one or several bodies. Such a request was then examined by the OECD Council which would decide whether or not to refer it to the body or bodies concerned for a technical opinion. The technical opinion was then transmitted to the OECD Council which retained the final decision-making power. It is interesting to note that the Resolution used the terminology 'technical opinion' in order to stress that it was not for the subsidiary body to enter into a political assessment: that remained the prerogative of the Council.
- The technical opinion had to be based on a number of criteria. The two most important were, first, the assessment whether the non-member was a 'major player' in the field of activity covered by the OECD body, and, second, whether there was a 'mutual benefit' in the participation of the non-member in question.
- The normal status for the participation of a non-member in OECD bodies was that of 'regular observer'. The status of 'full participant' was reserved for a non-member 'willing and able 'to adhere to any OECD rule applicable in the area covered by the OECD body in question. The main differences between the two types of status are that the observer has limited rights of intervention but no obligations, whereas a full participant participates 'on an equal footing' with OECD members. Moreover, the observer status is of a fixed term duration, albeit renewable, while the full participant status is granted for an undefined duration.

In 2004, the Resolution was considerably revisited and re-issued with a new number.[12] Several important changes have been introduced by this Resolution, including two of particular interest for the WGB and for future accessions to the Convention:

First, OECD bodies have been requested to devise a proactive strategy so that the process for participation of non-members would be undertaken on the initiative of the OECD and not upon request of the non-member.

[12] OECD 2004a.

Second, the 'major player' and 'mutual benefit' criteria no longer appear explicitly. The focus of the 2004 Resolution is on the need to assess participation of non-members pursuant to a proactive strategy to be developed by each OECD body. According to the Council Resolution, 'the strategy should consider the following elements in order to identify the non-Members to be invited and the appropriate form of participation:

- whether non-Member participation would facilitate appreciably the achievement of the mandate and the programme of work of the subsidiary body concerned;
- whether and in what ways association of non-Members with its work would be of benefit to the Organisation including in fulfilling its mandate of contributing to the development of non-Members;
- whether economic growth and/or the welfare of Members, considered on a national, regional or global basis,[13] within the substantive area covered by the subsidiary body concerned, are influenced to a significant degree by the policy orientations of non-Members;
- in relation to the substantive area covered by the mandate of the subsidiary body concerned, the degree to which non-Members' institutional and policy know-how contributes significantly to OECD peer learning/influencing and rule-making processes;
- the appropriate number of non-Member participants, focusing both on the non-Members and the time period of the invitations in the light of the requirements of the mandate of the subsidiary body concerned, its programme of work and its methods of work;
- the consequences that non-Members' participation might have on the working methods, programme of work and Secretariat resources devoted to the subsidiary body concerned;
- in the case of full participants, the non-Member has been found to be willing and able to commit to the relevant OECD *acquis*, as appropriate.'[14]

As we can see, the framework put in place by the OECD is a general one, not specifically tailored to accession to the Convention; it is also very much an evolving framework.

[13] The impact of a non-Member's policies on an individual OECD Member state, or indeed on a region, should not be of itself sufficient justification for that non-Member's participation in an OECD body. National or regional impact should be merely one element in the analysis behind the drawing up of a strategy.

[14] This Council Resolution (OECD 2004a) is publicly available.

2. WGB practice

It is in the context described above that the WGB has struggled to develop its own thinking on accession to the Convention.

We have already seen that there was a prima facie contradiction between the openness encouraged by Official Commentary 37 and the 'major player' criteria enshrined in the applicable Resolution of the Council Concerning Participation of Non-Member Economies in the Work of Subsidiary Bodies of the Organisation.[15]

The position taken publicly by some important stakeholders, at least in the early stage of the Convention, did not help to clarify the situation.[16]

During the period when its Article 12 monitoring mechanism was being put into place, the WGB was also confronted with a number of requests for accession to the Convention, coming from a variety of different countries such as Cyprus and Russia.

Discussions from 1999 to 2001 proved particularly difficult, illustrating the hybrid nature of the WGB. While several members of the WGB stressed that, first and foremost, the WGB was a conference of the state Parties and as such could and should determine its own views on the accession of new Parties to the Convention, others insisted on the fact that, like any other OECD body, the WGB had to comply with the rules and procedures set out by the OECD Council.

The difficulty faced by the WGB in assessing these requests was how to reconcile the 'major player' criteria applicable by virtue of the OECD procedure and strongly defended by a number of OECD countries with the policy directions offered by Official Commentary 37 and supported by several state Parties to the Convention.

[15] [C(96)64/REV1/FINAL].

[16] Thus, in a speech made at the WTO Ministerial Conference in 1998, President Clinton indicated that: 'a trading system for the 21st century must be comprised of governments that are open, honest, and fair in their practices: by next year, all members of the WTO should agree that government purchases should be made through open and fair bidding and every nation should adopt the anti-bribery Convention developed by the OECD' (cf. http://www.ukabc.org). Similarly, and as recently than 2005, the European Commission was encouraging all EU Member States (including non-OECD countries) to become state Parties to the Convention. Thus, the EU's Anti-Corruption Policy document of April 2005 states that: 'the Commission is also in favour of accession to a number of instruments originating with other international bodies. The aim is to take account of the activities that already exist, in order to avoid duplication, and to ensure that measures already existing in the EU have the same mandatory character in other international organisations. The Organisation for Economic Co-operation and Development (OECD), the Council of Europe and the United Nations have already produced their own conventions on corruption' (cf. http://www.europa.eu.int > Gateway to the European Union > Information Sources and Contacts > Bibliographic and Documentary References > Scadplus > Fraud > Corruption > A Comprehensive EU Anti-Corruption Policy).

Debate within the WGB was complicated by the fact that the Convention is focused on the 'supply-side' of bribery, i.e. the active bribery of the foreign public official. Several state Parties, therefore, failed to see a strong interest in accepting the membership of small countries with few enterprises, if any, capable of operating in the world market.

In the course of 2003, the debate became focused around the request for accession of Estonia, which gave rise to strong exchange of views amongst the participants to the WGB and in the OECD Council. Ultimately, a pragmatic compromise was achieved. In order to reinforce the principle of openness in line with Article 13 of the Convention, the WGB favourably explored the approach whereby new requests for accession would be measured and thoroughly examined against two criteria: 'willing and able' and 'mutual benefit'. Under this approach, the 'major player' criterion would not be retained as an independent measure; the WGB would then incorporate under 'mutual benefit' certain elements considered relevant as new candidates were evaluated.

As a prerequisite for the new approach, the WGB undertook to reach a more accurate common definition of the 'willing and able' and 'mutual benefit' criteria in order to ensure that the principle of openness would be consistent with the effectiveness of the Convention and the retention of its current standards. This means that a request from a country applying for participation in the WGB is examined against a number of different elements. The acceding country must demonstrate:

- that its existing legal framework for combating bribery on a *domestic* level, including legislation relating to the criminalisation of passive bribery, is satisfactory;
- that it can meet the standards laid down in the Revised Recommendation of 1997, including criminalisation of bribery of foreign public officials (section III. of the Recommendation); that it already disallows the tax deductibility of bribes (section IV.), that it has accounting requirements, external audit and internal company controls compatible with the Recommendation (section V.); and that it is able to cooperate with other state Parties to the Convention as concerns mutual legal assistance (section VII.);
- that it has adequate enforcement capacity, particularly for investigation and prosecution of bribery cases;
- that it is ready and able to submit to the same rigorous monitoring mechanism as the other state Parties to the Convention and that it

is prepared and able to participate as a lead examiner in peer reviews of other state Parties to the Convention;
- whether its companies engaged in international business are involved in transactions where solicitation of bribes by/for foreign public officials could occur;
- that it is a significant economic actor in its geographic region or sub-region, or in particularly important or sensitive economic sectors;
- the extent of its GDP derived from international trade and investment activities.

In fact, the pragmatic solution found by the WGB and endorsed by the OECD Council in early 2004 appears to be a precursor to the new Resolution, which was adopted a few months later by the same OECD Council and is of general application.[17]

As a consequence of these developments, the inherent tension between the general framework applicable within the OECD and the openness encouraged by Official Commentary 37 is certainly mitigated somewhat. It remains, however, to be seen whether the state Parties to a Convention focused on the supply-side of international bribery and which contains a sophisticated and time-consuming monitoring mechanism have a real interest in expanding its membership.

In this context the fact that Article 16(1) of the UN Convention Against Corruption[18] requests that Members of the UN Convention criminalise the bribing of foreign public officials is an important development. Indeed, any Member of the UN Convention Against Corruption is now obliged to criminalise the bribing of a foreign public officials and this might reduce the incentive for joining the OECD Convention.

III. Possible future developments

As indicated earlier, the WGB and the OECD will in the near future face two main questions.

For the WGB, the issue will be to decide on a clear and sustainable strategy concerning future accession to the Convention, in particular after the completion of the ongoing Phase 2 cycle, scheduled to finish at the end of 2007. This important question was relaunched in mid-2005, and it is currently under discussion in the WGB. The WGB agreed that outreach

[17] OECD 2004a. [18] UN 2003.

towards non-members should be proactive and should distinguish between potential accession countries and non-members which would not be on the accession path. It remains to be seen, if the WGB will be able to agree on a list of possible candidates for eventual accession and how to approach these candidates.

For the OECD Council, the same question will have to be addressed, but in the context of the more general discussion on future enlargement of the OECD. Should accession to the Convention be enshrined in the 'OECD *acquis*' or not and, if not, can the OECD accept that in the future that one OECD member might not be state Party to the Convention?

It is regrettable that conflicting and contradictory signals have in the past been given to the international community and, in particular, to possible candidates. However, one must recognise the difficulties involved in arriving at a consensus on these highly political issues. One also has to take into account a number of different parameters, including the evolution of the UN Convention Against Bribery. Having said that, it is submitted that neither the OECD nor the state Parties to the Convention have an interest in freezing the Convention at its current membership.

IV. The rule of Article 14

The text of Article 14 is very laconic and consistent with general international law as codified by the Vienna Convention on the Law of Treaties of 1969.[19]

The only specific feature of this provision is the designation of the Secretary-General of the OECD's Depositary of the Convention. Apart from the Treaty of 1962 establishing an international agricultural institute,[20] and a Convention on Administration assistance in fiscal matters the OECD's anti-bribery Convention is the only multilateral Treaty for which the Secretary-General of the OECD acts as Depositary. However, such possibility is explicitly provided for in the Vienna Convention.[21]

If the text of Article 14 per se does not present much substantive interest, it is interesting by the fact that it does not make any explicit reference to

[19] Hereafter 'Vienna Convention'. Art. 11 Vienna Convention 1969 states that 'the consent of a State to be bound by a treaty may be expressed by signature, exchange of instruments constituting a treaty, ratification, acceptance, approval or accession, or by any other means if so agreed'.

[20] This was the CIHEAM, created on 21 May 1962. More information is available at: http://www.ciheam.org.

[21] Art. 76 Vienna Convention 1969 provides that 'the depositary may be one or more States, an international organisation or the chief administrative officer of the organisation'.

the possibility or not to enter a reservation. Moreover, no other Article of the Convention covers this issue.

V. The treatment of reservations in the Convention

The Vienna Convention, which applies to treaties 'adopted within an international organisation',[22] contains a number of provisions on reservations.[23] Those provisions have been the object of a number of criticisms and of some doctrinal controversy, as it cannot be said that they were a codification of existing general international law at the time of their adoption.[24]

A reservation is defined in Article 2(d) of the Vienna Convention as: 'a unilateral statement, however phrased or named, made by a State, when signing, ratifying, accepting, approving or acceding to a treaty, whereby it purports to exclude or to modify the legal effect of certain provisions of the treaty in their application to that State'.

In accordance with Article 19 of the Vienna Convention a State may, when signing, ratifying, accepting, approving, or acceding to a treaty, formulate a reservation *unless*:

- the reservation is prohibited by the treaty;
- the treaty provides that only specified reservations, which do not include the reservation in question, may be made; or
- the reservation is incompatible with the object and purpose of the treaty.

Of these three hypotheses, the second one is clearly inapplicable with respect to the Convention as there are no explicit provisions in it dealing with reservations – but what about the other two?

1. Are reservations permitted?

The Convention does not contain any Article on reservations, nor is there any explicit reference to reservations in its text. However, an accurate

[22] Cf. Art. 5 Vienna Convention 1969.
[23] The whole of s. 2 Vienna Convention 1969 (Arts. 19–24) is devoted to the subject.
[24] The international debate stemmed from the opinion of the International Court of Justice (ICJ) in its Report of 28 May 1951, 15 on 'Reservations to the Convention on Genocide'. There is an ample literature on the general subject of reservations; for a brief and clear presentation of the main issues cf. Aust 2000. The difficulty of interpreting the provisions of the Vienna Convention 1969 led the International Law Commission (ILC) to work on possible guidelines. The ILC work on the subject is ongoing and available at: http://untreaty.un.org.

reading of the Convention shows that it is not totally silent on the issue. The last recital of the preamble to the Convention reads as follows:

> 'Recognising that achieving equivalence among the measures to be taken by the Parties is an essential object and purpose of the Convention, which requires that the Convention be ratified without derogations affecting this equivalence.'

This text was introduced at a very late stage of the negotiations as a compromise between those who wanted the inclusion in the Convention of an Article expressly prohibiting reservations and those who were afraid that the inclusion of such an Article could be criticised domestically and could jeopardise the ratification process.[25]

The ordinary meaning of this recital is not crystal clear. There is no mention of the matter in the *Travaux Préparatoires*, which might assist interpretation. Several remarks can, however, be made with respect to the scope of this recital.

First, the fact that this text appears in the preamble and not in an Article of the Convention is not in itself of great significance, given that, irrespective of the value attributed to the preamble, it certainly forms part of the context for the purpose of the interpretation of the Convention, in accordance with Article 31(2) of the Vienna Convention.

Second, while the word 'reservation' does not itself appear in the recital, the scope and purpose of the wording would appear to prohibit any 'derogation' affecting an equivalent (though not identical) application of the Convention. It is difficult to imagine how a reservation to any of the Articles of the Convention would not affect such equivalence.

Third, the fact that the recital expressly states that 'achieving equivalence among the measures to be taken by the Parties is an essential object and purpose of the Convention' is a clear signal of the intentions of the negotiators not to admit reservations to the Convention.

2. Are reservations compatible with the object and purpose of the Convention?

Even if reservations are not expressly prohibited by the OECD Convention, in order to be accepted a reservation must be compatible with the object

[25] This was in particular the position of the US negotiators. Their concern may be illustrated by this extract from a document on US practice contributed by Robert E. Dalton of the US Department of State, which is available on the website of the American Society of International Law (ASIL): 'the Senate frequently makes reservations to multilateral treaties and has on several occasions in recent years emphasized its opposition to the conclusion of multilateral treaties that prohibit reservations' (cf. Dalton 1999).

and purpose of the Convention. The recital of the Preamble provides very useful guidance in this respect: any reservation which would have the legal consequence of modifying the 'equivalence among the measures taken by the Parties' must be regarded as contrary to the object and purpose of the Convention.

It can, therefore, be argued that any reservation, i.e. any statement aiming at excluding or modifying the legal effect of any of the substantive Articles of the Convention (Articles 1–12) would be incompatible with the object and purpose of the Convention.

Naturally, in this somewhat unclear situation, the question whether a statement is a reservation or not and, if so, whether it is compatible with the object and purpose of the Treaty, becomes quite crucial. Accordingly, the role of the depositary of the Convention assumes greater objective significance.

VI. The role of the OECD Secretariat as depositary

Article 14(2) assigns the role of Depositary to the 'Secretary-General of the OECD'. In practical terms, the role is performed by the Directorate for Legal Affairs of the OECD.

In the absence of further specification in the Convention, the main functions are those outlined in Article 77 of the Vienna Convention. Three are of particular interest with regard to reservations:

- the function of receiving and keeping in custody any instruments, notifications and communications relating to the treaty;
- the function of examining whether the signature or any instrument, notification or communication relating to the treaty is in due and proper form and, if need be, bringing the matter to the attention of the State in question;
- the function of informing the parties and the States entitled to become parties to the treaty of acts, notifications and communications relating to the treaty.

A number of state Parties to the Convention have accompanied the deposit of their instrument of ratification with statements or declarations on various issues, including the territorial application of the Convention and the interpretation of some Articles, in particular those concerning mutual legal assistance and extradition. These statements have then been circulated to all state Parties as well as to states entitled to become Parties to the Convention.

In one case, a country presented the OECD Secretariat with a written statement cast as a reservation by the relevant authorities of that country. Confronted with this unexpected scenario, the reaction of the Secretariat was fully in line with the practice of the Secretary-General of the United Nations, as described by Horn 1988:

> 'The Secretary-General does not consider himself competent to receive an instrument of ratification or accession with a reservation that is not permitted under the treaty. If the contents of the statement are not clear he will have to clarify the matter in close consultation with the declaring state. He will ask the declaring state if the statement really intends to modify the application of the treaty. He is however free to explore the substance of the matter and is not necessarily bound to accept the view of the declarant. In doing this he will strive towards a solution which offers the greatest safeguards to all parties. Frequently he has preferred to construe such statements as declarations of policy or interpretation.'[26]

The OECD Secretariat, after having analysed the content of the so-called reservation, came to the conclusion that the statement did not intend to exclude or modify any Article of the Convention but only to specify how a particular Article, namely Article 2 on the liability of legal persons, would be implemented in the future. The Secretariat brought its conclusion to the attention of the country in question, which eventually withdrew its original 'reservation' and submitted instead a 'declaration', which was received by the depositary and circulated to all other signatories.

VII. Ratification and implementing legislation

One further issue related to Article 14 is worth mentioning, namely the relationship between the ratification of the Convention and the adoption of implementing legislation.

The question is whether the Convention can be ratified without having implementing legislation in place. While the Convention is silent on the matter, the vast majority of the Parties to the Convention have deposited their instrument of ratification only after having introduced appropriate implementing legislation; this practice has been encouraged by the OECD Secretariat, in the light of the importance of the monitoring and the necessity to put legislation in place as early as possible.

In some instances, however, countries deposited their instrument of ratification before adoption of the implementing legislation. This was the case, in particular, with Turkey and with some Latin American countries.

[26] Horn 1988, 351.

In one single case, a state Party adopted domestic legislation giving effect to the provisions of the Convention well before ratification of the Convention. That was the case of Ireland, which adopted the Prevention of Corruption (Amendment) Act in late 2001 but only deposited its instrument of ratification with the Secretary-General of the OECD in November 2003.

VIII. Article 15: introduction

While mainly of historical interest, Article 15 is a perfect example of the spirit of the Convention and of the creativity of its drafters. It was also considered to be very important by the negotiators of the Convention.[27]

The Convention foresaw two possible ways for it to enter into force: Article 15(1) prescribed what one could call 'the ideal scenario', whereas Article 15(2) represented the 'fallback scenario'. Overall the Convention came up with a fairly original mechanism.

IX. The 'ideal scenario'

Article 15(1) was built on two premises: first, the need to push the large countries to quickly ratify, second, the need to maintain the political momentum. This dual objective is illustrated by two specific points set out in the first paragraph of Article 15.

1. A strong push for large countries to ratify first

The primary mechanism for the date of entry into force of the Convention, as set out in Article 15(1), is 'the sixtieth day following the date upon which five of the ten countries which have the ten largest export shares set out in an annex to the Convention,[28] and which represent by themselves at least sixty per cent of the combined total exports of those ten countries, have deposited their instruments of acceptance, approval, or ratification'.

This provision therefore triggers a dual economic threshold which requires that the Convention be ratified by five out of the ten largest

[27] According to Metcalfe 2000, 147, the negotiators considered the entry into force provision as the most important issue (28%), even before the discussion of political parties (21%) and of sanctions (17%).

[28] Cf. statistical annex to the Convention (OECD 1997b) reproduced in the Documentary Appendix of this commentary.

exporter economies *and* that these five shall represent at least 60% of the total combined exports of the ten.

The figures to be used have been annexed to the Convention and represent data calculated by the OECD in relation to the exports over the seven-year period preceding the negotiation of the Convention. By inserting the 60% threshold the negotiators made it impossible for the Convention to enter into force, in accordance with the requirements of Article 15(1), without at least one of the three main exporters (Germany, Japan and the United States). On the other hand, the requirement that at least five of the ten main exporters had to ratify also made it impossible for the Convention to enter into force, even if ratified by the four main exporters representing more than 60% of the total combined exports of the ten largest exporters.

This procedure differs radically from the traditional mechanism used both in the United Nations (UN) Convention Against Corruption[29] and in the Criminal Law Convention on Corruption of the Council of Europe (COE),[30] which are based merely on ratification by a certain number of states.[31]

The peculiar character of Article 15(1) is enhanced by the paramount importance it gives to economic considerations; the Convention, of course, formally aims at harmonising the domestic criminal laws of the state Parties to the Convention, but Article 15(1) reveals rather this economic dimension.

Obviously, the economic angle can be explained by the fact that this is an OECD Convention. Article 15 also reflects the need for the Convention to ensure a 'level playing field' in order to be credible and equitable and therefore 'politically enforceable'. The Article was, therefore, clearly designed to confer an undisputed legitimacy to the Convention as soon as it entered into force.

A little more than one year after its adoption, the Convention was ready to enter into force following the deposit of the instrument of ratification

[29] Art. 68(1) UN 2003 provides that the Convention will enter into force simply upon ratification by thirty countries or regional economic integration organisations (effectively the European Community).

[30] Art. 32(3) COE 1999a provides that it 'shall enter into force on the first day of the month following the expiration of a period of three months after the date on which fourteen States have expressed their consent to be bound by the Convention'.

[31] Thus, UN 2003 entered into force on 14 December 2005 and, as of 20 January 2006, forty-four countries are Parties to it. Amongst the ten largest exporters mentioned in the Annex to the OECD Convention, only France had, however, ratified the UN 2003 as of the time of writing.

by Canada on 17 December 1998.[32] In accordance with Article 15(1), the Convention entered into force sixty days after that ratification, i.e. on 15 February 1999.

2. The wish to maintain political momentum

This wish is reflected by the brief time span given to the signatories of the Convention, and in particular to the 'group of ten', to ratify the Convention. Indeed, as implicitly reflected by the first sentence of Article 15(2), the conditions for the entry into force of the Convention under Article 15(1) were expected to be fulfilled in little more than a year, i.e. before 31 December 1998.

This date was more a political commitment than a legal one, as demonstrated by the language used in the G7 summit in May 1998. On this occasion the G7 Heads of State agreed 'to provide effective support for the efforts of these countries to build democracy and good governance, stronger civil society and greater transparency, and to take action against corruption, for example, by making every effort to ratify the OECD Anti-Bribery Convention by the end of 1998'.[33]

Even though not legally binding, the political pressure was, therefore, great on the G7 countries to speed their process of ratification.[34] The pressure proved to be effective and the ratification by Canada in late December 1998 allowed the signatories of the Convention to have virtually fulfilled their objective, i.e. to have a new multilateral criminal convention entering into force one year after its adoption and with the participation of the major players.

X. A pragmatic 'fall back scenario'

If the entry into force of the Convention was certainly a 'success story', we can also observe that, as prudent negotiators, the drafters of the Convention had inserted a 'fall back scenario', in case the Convention could not enter

[32] Before Canada ratified, Germany, Japan, the United Kingdom and the United States (amongst the ten largest exporters) had deposited their instruments of ratification. The Table of Ratifications is available at: http://www.oecd.org. See also the Introduction of this commentary.

[33] Text available at: http://www.g8.utoronto.ca.

[34] In this context, the NGO Transparency International played a very active role. Cf., for example, its press release of 12 May 1998 requesting the G7 countries to ratify before the end of that year: http://www.transparency.org.

into force as provided for under Article 15(1). This was the object and purpose of Article 15(2) of the Convention.

While Article 15(2) was not used and never will be used, it is worth briefly describing the special mechanism it envisaged.

While there is no mention in the *Travaux Préparatoires* of how the language of Article 15(2) was agreed on, the basic assumption underlying Article 15(2) was that the Convention might not enter into force by 31 December 1998 owing to the fact that the process of ratification was facing difficulties in one or more G7 countries. In such a scenario, those countries which had already ratified the Convention, and more specifically companies situated in those countries, could have been put in a competitive disadvantage. On the other hand, not to provide an alternative mechanism for the entering into force of the Convention would have meant that six countries out of the 'group of ten' or even only a few of them representing more than 40% of exports could have prevented the Convention from ever entering into force.

Article 15(2), therefore, provided a pragmatic solution to this dilemma by basically leaving the choice to the countries which had ratified by the Convention by 31 December 1998 (this could also have been another incentive for speedy ratification). Article 15(2) leaves to each signatory of the Convention having deposited its instrument of acceptance, approval, or ratification to declare its readiness to accept the entry into force of the Convention. The Convention would then enter into force after two declarations but only between the countries which had made such a declaration and not amongst all ratifying countries.

This very original mechanism could have led to the situation in which the Convention would have applied only amongst a sub-group of countries which had ratified the Convention and not to all the countries having done so.

In conclusion, Article 15(2) could have created a new category of countries besides the signatories and the Parties, whom we might have called the 'ratifying non-Parties'.

XI. The amendment procedure contained in Article 16

Article 39 of the Vienna Convention on the Law of Treaties of 1969[35] stipulates the basic principle that 'a treaty may be amended by agreement

[35] Hereafter called Vienna Convention.

between the parties'.[36] Thus, the Vienna Convention recognises the freedom of the parties to agree on any specific procedure for amending a treaty.

Article 16 of the OECD Convention is therefore the primary rule for amendment of the Anti-Bribery Convention. Article 40 of the Vienna Convention specifies general rules for amendment of treaties.[37] These are, however, of a residual or fall-back nature: they are superseded by express provision such as in Article 16 of the OECD Convention. Article 40 of the Vienna Convention would, therefore, apply to the OECD Convention, only if and in so far as the latter failed to regulate the amendment procedure.[38]

In this context, we will now focus on the four substantive elements introduced by the text of Article 16 with respect to adoption and entry into force of an amendment.

1. Adoption of amendments by consensus

In accordance with Article 16, any amendment shall, in principle, be adopted 'by consensus of the Parties'. Consensus of all the state Parties in this sense is something different from unanimity. It does not require an affirmative vote from all state Parties but merely requires that none of the state Parties would object to the adoption of the amendment.

The provisions of Article 16 look more stringent than the residual rule of Article 40(2) of the Vienna Convention, which gives ample flexibility to each Party to 'participate in the negotiation and conclusion of any agreement for the amendment of the treaty'.

By simply not participating in the negotiation of an amendment to the OECD anti-bribery Convention and objecting to the conclusion of any

[36] First sentence of Art. 39 Vienna Convention 1969.

[37] The full text of Art. 40 Vienna Convention 1969 (amendment of multilateral treaties) provides as follows: '1. Unless the treaty otherwise provides, the amendment of multilateral treaties shall be governed by the following paragraphs.; 2. Any proposal to amend a multilateral treaty as between all the parties must be notified to all the contracting States, each one of which shall have the right to take part in: (a) the decision as to the action to be taken in regard to such proposal; (b) the negotiation and conclusion of any agreement for the amendment of the treaty.; 3. Every State entitled to become a party to the treaty shall also be entitled to become a party to the treaty as amended.; 4. The amending agreement does not bind any State already a party to the treaty which does not become a party to the amending agreement; Article 30, paragraph 4(b), applies in relation to such State.; 5. Any State which becomes a party to the treaty after the entry into force of the amending agreement shall, failing an expression of a different intention by that State: (a) be considered as a party to the treaty as amended; and (b) be considered as a party to the unamended treaty in relation to any party to the treaty not bound by the amending agreement.'

[38] First sentence of Art. 40(1) Vienna Convention 1969.

amendment to it, any state Party would be able to block the adoption of such amendment.

2. Adoption of amendments by other mechanism

It was probably with the above-mentioned 'blockage scenario' in mind that the drafters of the Convention introduced the possibility of agreeing, by consensus, to a different type of amendment procedure. This can be inferred by the reference, in Article 16, to the possibility of an amendment being adopted 'by such other means as the Parties may determine by consensus'. It is, therefore, conceivable that an amendment can be adopted by means of a qualified majority or even a simple majority.

The introduction of any more flexible means of amendment would, however, itself require consensus, meaning that, as indicated above, any state Party to the Convention could block a new mechanism simply by refusing to join the consensus.

3. Entry into force of amendments by consensus

This principle set out in Article 16 differs greatly from the residual rule of Article 40(4) of the Vienna Convention as it requires that all state Parties to the Convention must become state Parties to an amendment for that amendment to come into force. The requirement of Article 16 is by no means exceptional.[39] It is consistent with the strong Convention rationale of ensuring a 'level playing field' for all state Parties.[40]

Article 16 may, however, be said to 'raise the stakes' compared to Article 15 (on entry into force of the Convention) by effectively requiring that all state Parties, irrespective of their size and economic importance, become state Parties to an amendment. One single refusal can block the adoption of an amendment. This is not only a hypothetical issue, as recently illustrated by the difficulties surrounding ratification of the so-called 'European Constitution'.[41]

[39] Thus, Art. 39(5) COE 1999a provides that 'any amendment adopted in accordance with paragraph 3 of this Article shall come into force on the thirtieth day after all Parties have informed the Secretary-General of their acceptance thereof'.

[40] It should be recalled that the final recital of the preamble of the Convention (OECD 1997b) recognises that 'achieving equivalence among the measures to be taken by the Parties is an essential object and purpose of the Convention'.

[41] The text in question is the EU Constitutional Treaty (EU 2004c), which required ratification by all EU Member States to enter into force. In the course of 2005, both France and the Netherlands rejected the draft by referendum.

4. Entry into force of amendments by other mechanism

The drafters of the Convention, having opted for this very stringent principle relating to entry into force of Convention amendments, then relaxed the principle by leaving state Parties the possibility of agreeing on a different mechanism by consensus, just as they did in relation to the procedure for adoption of an amendment.

The language used in Article 16 refers to 'such other circumstances as may be specified by the Parties at the time of adoption of the amendment'. This rather loose drafting leaves matters somewhat unclear. Does it imply that state Parties may specify the procedure for entry into force by means other than providing an explicit text on this question in the amendment to be adopted by consensus? This is maybe what the drafters of the Convention had in mind; but legally and for all practical purposes it is difficult to see how a different procedure may be specified other than by setting it out in the amendment to the Convention.

What kind of different procedure might be specified? One could, for example, apply the same mechanism as provided by Article 15 of the Convention for entry into force of the Convention itself.

5. Concluding remarks

The provisions of Article 16 are based on the postulate that any amendment of the Convention will be based on a real consensus amongst the state Parties to the Convention. This is in line not only with the historical tradition of the OECD but also with the negotiating history of the Convention. The procedure in place, coupled with the fact that the Convention is of an indefinite duration, can also be seen as introducing a sort of 'stand-still' or status quo. It would be very difficult to adopt any amendment backtracking on the obligations of the Convention. On the other hand, Article 16 means that, failing a consensus among the state Parties to the Convention, it will be impossible, formally, to amend the Convention.

XII. Other options available to state parties to complement the convention

The Convention does not provide for any other possibility for modifying or reinforcing its provisions than amendment. Both general international law and the institutional setting of the OECD do, however, offer other options that state Parties to the Convention may consider if and when they would wish to revisit the Convention.

1. Negotiation of Protocol or additional Convention

While not explicitly provided for in the Convention, nothing would prevent the state Parties from negotiating another Convention complementing the original one or from negotiating a Protocol to the Convention. In both cases the general principles of international law as reflected in the Vienna Convention would apply.

Indeed, whatever the formal title of the new text might be – Protocol, Agreement, or Convention – it would be considered a treaty, if it fits the definition of a treaty under Article 2(a) of the Vienna Convention. The latter provides that a treaty 'means an international agreement concluded between States in written form and governed by international law, whether embodied in a single instrument or in two or more related instruments and whatever its particular designation'.[42]

The relevant Article would then be Article 30 of the Vienna Convention on the 'application of successive treaties relating to the same subject-matter'.[43]

The relationship between successive treaties relating to the same subject matter is a question which has provoked considerable controversy and much doctrinal argument.

In any case the concrete advantages of the making use of this possibility are not self-evident. One could perhaps see a sub-group of state Parties to the Convention agreeing to strengthen or expand the provisions of the original Convention. This scenario could occur as a response to the failure

[42] Vienna Convention 1969.

[43] Art. 30 Vienna Convention 1969 (application of successive treaties relating to the same subject-matter), provides as follows: '1. Subject to Article 103 of the Charter of the United Nations, the rights and obligations of States parties to successive treaties relating to the same subject-matter shall be determined in accordance with the following paragraphs.; 2. When a treaty specifies that it is subject to, or that it is not to be considered as incompatible with, an earlier or later treaty, the provisions of that other treaty prevail.; 3. When all the parties to the earlier treaty are parties also to the later treaty but the earlier treaty is not terminated or suspended in operation under Article 59, the earlier treaty applies only to the extent that its provisions are compatible with those of the latter treaty.; 4. When the parties to the later treaty do not include all the parties to the earlier one: (a) as between States parties to both treaties the same rule applies as in paragraph 3; (b) as between a State party to both treaties and a State party to only one of the treaties, the treaty to which both States are parties governs their mutual rights and obligations.; 5. Paragraph 4 is without prejudice to Article 41, or to any question of the termination or suspension of the operation of a treaty under Article 60 or to any question of responsibility which may arise for a State from the conclusion or application of a treaty the provisions of which are incompatible with its obligations towards another State under another treaty.'

to achieve consensus for the amendment procedure set out in Article 16. In this scenario it would be, however, difficult to ascertain how the two legal instruments would co-exist in practice and the general rule of Article 30(4) of the Vienna Convention does not in fact offer much guidance.

2. Modification of Convention among a limited number of state Parties

This procedure is explicitly provided for in Article 41 of the Vienna Convention which provides that 'two or more of the parties to a multilateral treaty may conclude an agreement to modify the treaty as between themselves'.[44] It is virtually never used in practice.

It is true that this possibility is, in fact, quite restricted as, according to Article 41, it shall 'not affect the enjoyment by the other parties of their rights under the treaty or the performance of their obligations' and it shall not 'not relate to a provision, derogation from which is incompatible with the effective execution of the object and purpose of the treaty as a whole'. It is interesting to note that this last provision is very close to the language used in the last recital of the preamble to the Convention.

The combination of the various requirements of Article 41 and of the text of the Convention strongly suggests that the only way in which two or more of the state Parties to the Convention may conclude an agreement to modify the Convention as between them, would be by agreeing to additional obligations under the Convention. However, this immediately raises the question of how and by whom these additional obligations would be monitored.

3. Agreement on interpretative notes

Amending the Convention, negotiating a new text or agreeing to modify some of its provisions all entail a certain number of formal procedures

[44] The full text of Art. 41 Vienna Convention 1969 (agreements to modify multilateral treaties between certain of the parties only) provides as follows: '1. Two or more of the parties to a multilateral treaty may conclude an agreement to modify the treaty as between themselves alone if: (a) the possibility of such a modification is provided for by the treaty; or (b) the modification in question is not prohibited by the treaty and: (i) does not affect the enjoyment by the other parties of their rights under the treaty or the performance of their obligations; (ii) does not relate to a provision, derogation from which is incompatible with the effective execution of the object and purpose of the treaty as a whole.; 2. Unless in a case falling under paragraph 1(a) the treaty otherwise provides, the parties in question shall notify the other parties of their intention to conclude the agreement and of the modification to the treaty for which it provides.'

and may be considered to be too cumbersome by the state Parties to the Convention.

Making use of the flexibility offered by the rules of interpretation set out in Article 31 of the Vienna Convention may then be seen as an option, at least with respect to the existing text of the Convention. Article 31(1) of the Vienna Convention provides that 'a treaty shall be interpreted in good faith in accordance with the ordinary meaning to be given to the terms of the treaty in their context and in the light of its object and purpose'.

In the general framework set out by Article 31, the Vienna Convention places much emphasis on any subsequent agreement among the Parties to the Convention concerning the interpretation or application of the provisions of a treaty.

Thus, Article 31(3) provides that 'there shall be taken into account, together with the context: (a) any subsequent agreement between the parties regarding the interpretation of the treaty or the application of its provisions; (b) any subsequent practice in the application of the treaty which establishes the agreement of the parties regarding its interpretation', whereas Article 31(4) indicates that a 'special meaning shall be given to a term if it is established that the parties so intended'.

A possible option would, therefore, be, for the state Parties to the Convention, to agree on one or several interpretative notes on some provisions or terms used in the Convention. This could be done either by expanding the existing Official Commentaries or by adding new Official Commentaries to the Convention. For all practical purposes, however, such interpretative notes should be adopted by consensus of all the Parties to the Convention.

4. Revision of existing OECD Acts or adoption of new Acts

Under this option, the state Parties to the Convention would use the OECD legal and institutional framework, in order to adopt new binding or non-binding norms.[45] This option was used in 1994 and 1997 to adopt the Recommendation and Revised Recommendation and in 1996 to adopt the OECD Recommendation on the non tax deductibility of bribes.[46]

[45] According to Art. 5 of the Convention establishing the OECD (OECD 1960) 'the Organisation may: (a) take decisions which, except as otherwise provided, shall be binding on all the Members; (b) make recommendations to Members'. Decisions and Recommendations adopted under Art. 5 are known 'OECD acts'.

[46] The evolution of these acts is discussed in the Introduction of this commentary.

Further revision of the Revised Recommendation of 1997 or adoption of a new OECD Act, be it a legally binding Decision or a non-binding Recommendation, can certainly be envisaged. The fact that a certain number of countries are state Parties to the Convention but not OECD members is a complicating factor but not an insurmountable one. Such non-members could be invited to adhere unilaterally to the Acts in question; this invitation could be issued by the OECD Council as a condition for retaining their full participant status in the Working Group on Bribery (WGB).

Were one or more OECD members to abstain at the time of the adoption of the revised or new Act, the matter would be more difficult to settle.[47] In these circumstances, the revised Act would bind all the other OECD members and the non-OECD member to the Convention but not the abstaining OECD member(s). In institutional terms, this scenario is possible; practically speaking, it is difficult to imagine that any Act would be presented to the OECD Council without full consensus of all the state Parties to the Convention.

XIII. Withdrawal according to Article 17

The text of Article 17 is a classic. It does not, prima facie, raise any particular difficulty of interpretation, which may also explain why no Official Commentary is attached to this Article.

Indeed, the right of withdrawal provided for in the Convention is fully in line with the relevant provisions of the Vienna Convention on the Law of Treaties, in particular Articles 54 and 56 thereof.[48]

The Convention does, however, explicitly provide that, in case of withdrawal, the withdrawing state Party remains subject to some obligations. In particular, Article 17 provides that the state Party concerned shall continue to co-operate with all remaining state Parties 'on all requests for assistance or extradition made before the effective date of withdrawal which remain pending'.

This provision is interesting but its precise content is not easy to define. In particular, doubts may be cast on the exact scope and meaning of the phrase 'shall continue to co-operate'.

[47] Art. 6(2) OECD 1960 provides that 'each Member shall have one vote. If a Member abstains from voting on a decision or recommendation, such abstention shall not invalidate the decision or recommendation, which shall be applicable to the other Members but not to the abstaining Member'.

[48] The twelve-month period is the residual rule in case a treaty does not contain any provision on withdrawal (Art. 56(2) Vienna Convention 1969).

One possible reading is that, even after withdrawal has become effective, a withdrawing state Party remains bound by the provisions of Articles 9 and 10 of the Convention vis-à-vis requests made before the withdrawal became effective. Such a reading would probably be in conformity with the spirit of the Convention and may also be consistent with the drafters' intentions. It would, however, give to the duty of co-operation a very specific content which is not reflected by the 'ordinary meaning' of Article 17.[49] Indeed, the negotiating countries could have either explicitly referred to Articles 9 and 10 of the Convention in the text of Article 17 or specified in a related Official Commentary that the expression 'shall continue to co-operate' was to be understood as an obligation to give continuing effect to those provisions in respect of requests made before withdrawal. Neither step was in fact taken.

A more reliable interpretation of the expression 'shall continue to co-operate' would therefore be that this expression does not entail any specific obligation but only a general duty of co-operation in good faith. This would be in line with the ordinary meaning of the text and supported by the fact that Article 17 requires the withdrawing state Party to continue to co-operate on 'all requests for assistance' and not only with the requests for 'mutual legal assistance' covered by Article 9. If the withdrawing state Party is indeed asked to co-operate on requests for other forms of assistance than mutual legal assistance, the configuration clearly becomes one not explicitly contemplated by the current text of the Convention as far as state Parties to the Convention are concerned. It would seem odd to consider that a withdrawing state Party had not only a general duty of co-operation but also the duty to fully comply with the specific obligations contemplated in Articles 9 and 10 of the Convention, even if only for pending requests.

References

For documentation see the consolidated bibliography at the end of the book.

Aust, A. (2000), *Modern Treaty Law and Practice*, Cambridge.

Dalton, R. E. (1999), 'National Treaty Law and Practice: United States' in M. Leigh, M. R. Blakeslee and L. B. Ederington (eds.), *National Treaty Law and Practice (Austria, Chile, Japan, Netherlands and the US)*, Washington DC (available at: http://www.asil.org).

Horn, F. (1988), *Reservations and Interpretative Declarations to Multilateral Treaties*, Amsterdam, Oxford, North-Holland.

Metcalfe, D. (2000), 'The OECD Agreement to Criminalize Bribery: A Negotiation Analytic Perspective', *International Negotiation* **5**, 129.

[49] Art. 31 Vienna Convention 1969 makes the 'ordinary meaning' the primary method of interpretation.

PART III

The Convention in Practice

The OECD Convention: A US Perspective on Combating Bribery in International Business

LUCINDA A. LOW

Chapter contents

I. Introduction

Previous chapters of this book have focused on specific articles of the OECD Convention, analyzing both the Convention's requirements and approach, and how those articles have been implemented by parties to the Convention to date. This chapter will comment on the Convention from a different perspective. After briefly reviewing the comparative advantages of the OECD Convention and the challenges to its effectiveness, it will examine the impact of the Convention on pre-existing transnational bribery laws, specifically the United States Foreign Corrupt Practices Act (FCPA) and other related laws, including money laundering laws.

Subsequently, it will examine developments in areas outside the Convention's purview of criminalisation but which are nonetheless relevant to the overall effectiveness of any effort to curb corrupt practices in international business. These will include (1) the complementary initiatives of the OECD to eliminate the tax deductibility of bribes in OECD Member States, and to curb bribery in officially supported export credits; (2) preventive measures, particularly in the arena of corporate compliance programmes; (3) the sanctions programmes of other public financing institutions, such as the World Bank; and (4) controls over corruption in private international business transactions. The final part of this chapter will discuss emerging trends in international standards and their enforcement, at the governmental and private levels, and their implications for international businesses, as well as gaps in the international system.

II. The OECD Convention – comparative advantages and challenges

1. The Convention in the context of other initiatives to criminalise transnational bribery

As previous chapters have shown, the OECD Convention was designed to be, and is, a highly targeted instrument. Rather than trying to address corruption in a multifaceted way, it focuses on criminalisation of the supply, or active, side of public sector corruption in international business transactions. This supply side focus is an outgrowth of the composition of the membership of the OECD, whose member states include the principal capital exporting states worldwide, and its institutional capacity.

Prior to the Convention's adoption, only the United States, through the FCPA, had criminalised the supply side of transnational bribery. By requiring criminalisation of the supply side of transnational official bribery throughout the OECD membership, and inviting other qualifying non-OECD Member States to accede to the Convention, the OECD Convention drafters attempted to level the playing field among capital exporters, making competition for business opportunities fairer.[1]

At the time the OECD Convention was adopted, there was only one other international treaty focused on the issue of corruption – the Inter-American Convention against Corruption, negotiated under the auspices of the Organization of American States (OAS).[2] Today, the picture is very different.

[1] See the more detailed discussion of the background to the OECD Convention (OECD 1997b) in the Introduction of this commentary.

[2] OAS 1996.

In addition to a number of other regional conventions, including the Council of Europe Criminal and Civil Law Conventions Against Corruption,[3] an African Union Convention (which is not yet in force),[4] and an EU Convention,[5] a global United Nations anticorruption Convention has just come into force.[6]

All of these Conventions overlap in part with the OECD Convention. All except the African Union Convention require criminalisation of transnational official bribery in international business, although in somewhat different terms than the OECD Convention.[7] All require cooperation of states Parties in the areas of mutual legal assistance and extradition.[8] All have some overlap with the OECD Convention membership,[9] and the potential, with the UN Convention, for complete overlap.

But here the major similarities stop. Each of these Conventions is significantly broader in scope than the OECD Convention. Not only do they take a broader approach to criminalisation, going beyond the area of transnational bribery, but many pursue a more holistic approach to combating corruption, focusing on preventive measures and regulatory approaches as well as criminalisation. Some in addition deal with issues of civil liability, revocation of contracts, and other topics.[10] The importance of these topics to the fight against corruption in international business will be discussed in parts III. and IV. of this chapter.

2. Challenges to the OECD Convention's effectiveness in a crowded international landscape

Especially in light of the entry into force of the UN Convention and its potential for a global architecture for cooperation, the question arises as to

[3] COE 1999a: as of the end of 2005, thirty-two parties had ratified this Convention. COE 1999b: at the end of 2005, twenty-five countries had ratified or acceded to this Convention. Cf. also COE 2003: fifteen countries have ratified this Additional Protocol.

[4] African Union Convention on Preventing and Combating Corruption (African Union 2003).

[5] EU 1997a.

[6] UN 2003. As of February 19, 2006, the Convention had hundred-and-forty signatories and forty-seven parties. For signatories, cf. http://www.unodc.org.

[7] Art. VIII OAS 1996; Arts. 5–6 COE 1999a; Art. **16**(1) UN 2003.

[8] Arts. XIII-XVI OAS 1996; Arts. 25–31 COE 1999a; Arts. 15–19 African Union 2003; Arts. 43–50 UN°2003.

[9] Six countries are parties to both the OAS 1996 and OECD Conventions. For the COE 1999a, the number is seventeen, while for the UN 2003, the current number is seven.

[10] For a more detailed analysis of the Convention, cf. Lucinda A. Low (2004), 'Towards Universal Anti-Corruption Standards: The United Nations Convention Against Corruption and Other International Anticorruption Treaties: Too Much of a Good Thing?' (presentation at the 2nd Annual Conference of the International Bar Association, International Chamber of Commerce and Organization for Economic Co-operation and Development, *The Awakening Giant of Anti-Corruption Enforcement*, Paris, 22–23 April 2004).

the future importance of the OECD Convention in combating transnational bribery. But while a global approach has potentially unique benefits, the key question for any international anticorruption instrument is effectiveness.

The OECD Convention's more limited scope may give it a comparative advantage in that regard. It allows monitoring resources to be targeted on a single cluster of issues rather than dispersed and diffused in pursuit of a broader agenda. It also eliminates or reduces the need to choose among competing priorities. The WGB's greater homogeneity of membership may also permit progress to be made more quickly, in part due to the benefits of peer pressure,[11] and in part due to the more uniform capacities of countries to implement the Convention.

However, a narrow focus sometimes brings its own challenges, particularly when international instruments and bodies are concerned. The competitive nature of the state Parties for business opportunities may cause them to be concerned about moving too quickly towards aggressive implementation and enforcement, for fear of disadvantaging their businesses vis-à-vis foreign competitors. And the narrow focus means that there are fewer opportunities for negotiating trade-offs that might be used to induce a recalcitrant country to act. Nor has funding for the WGB been an easy or certain proposition to date, and the competing demands of other anticorruption monitoring bodies may mean that funding will only become more difficult going forward.

Moreover, while the state Parties in the WGB represent a very substantial percentage of international capital flows, some key capital exporting states (such as the People's Republic of China) are currently not parties to the OECD Convention, while other states of less significance in such terms, primarily in Central and Eastern Europe, are Parties. Especially in a competitive Convention landscape, the OECD Convention will be unable to fulfil its targeted role to full effectiveness if it does not attract all of the major capital exporting countries.

Further, the limited scope of the OECD Convention even within its targeted area, i.e. transnational bribery, may pose a disadvantage as other more expansive Convention regimes attract adherence. The Convention does not, for example, deal currently with payments to political parties, party officials, and candidates for political office. Covering the full array of supply-side bribery issues in international business may over time become more critical to maintaining the OECD Convention's position as the leading instrument in disciplining the supply side of the bribery problem internationally.

[11] On the impact of peer pressure on compliance, see the discussion in ch. on Article 12 above.

Notwithstanding these issues, the OECD Convention remains the key instrument for progress on the supply side of transnational official bribery. The WGB has shown some success in ensuring that countries' implementing legislation meets the Convention's standards. Its reviews have also served as a spur to enforcement. Although enforcement is still in the early stages in countries other than the United States, the forum offered by the WGB undoubtedly has enhanced the possibilities for cooperation between Member States in cases where evidence is located in multiple jurisdictions.

As other chapters of this commentary also demonstrate, the key test over the next five to ten years for the OECD Convention will be the extent to which its members besides the United States actually bring enforcement actions. These countries are in the first generation of enforcement efforts with respect to transnational bribery. As such, they face all the issues that first generation efforts confront when dealing with a complex offence that transcends national borders, from the internal expertise and capacity to successfully prosecute cases, to political will, to whatever limitations arise from their internal legal systems.

Of particular interest from a US perspective will be the extent to which other OECD Convention parties successfully establish responsibility for the actions of third parties, such as agents and consultants, pursue corporate criminal liability, impose serious fines, and take an expansive approach to jurisdiction, as have US authorities.

III. The OECD Convention's impact on US law and enforcement

1. Introduction

Although the OECD Convention has been in force for only a short period of time, it has had a discernible effect on US law and enforcement. US ratification of the OECD Convention provided the opportunity for expansion of the reach of the FCPA's anti-bribery provisions, in jurisdictional, substantive, and penalty terms. The OECD Convention has also had both tangible and intangible impacts on FCPA enforcement, which are likely only to continue to grow over time. Having said that, the recent explosion in FCPA cases in the United States must fairly be ascribed only in part to the OECD Convention; domestic factors accounted for a larger part of the increase in enforcement activity in recent years than the Convention.

2. Impact on the terms of the Foreign Corrupt Practices Act

2.1. Background to the Foreign Corrupt Practices Act

For many years prior to the FCPA's enactment, the United States, like most other countries, had legislation prohibiting domestic official bribery.[12] The United States's first efforts to address the issue of foreign bribery came in 1958, when the federal income tax laws were amended to deny any tax deduction for bribes paid to foreign officials.[13] The revelations in the early to mid-1970s, under a voluntary disclosure programme of the US Securities and Exchange Commission (SEC), that many major US companies had secured foreign contracts through the payment of bribes, often using slush funds and off-book accounts to disguise their practices, led to a public outcry. Congress responded with the passage of the FCPA in 1977.[14] The law has been amended only twice since its enactment, the first time in 1988, as part of the Omnibus Trade and Competitiveness Act of 1988,[15] and the second time in 1998, by the International Anti-Bribery and Fair Competition Act of 1998, the implementing legislation for the OECD Convention.[16]

The FCPA consists of two distinct sets of provisions: the anti-bribery provisions; and the accounting provisions. The 1998 Amendments made significant changes to the anti-bribery provisions, while leaving the accounting provisions unchanged.

2.2. The anti-bribery provisions[17]

2.2.1. Basic prohibitions

Implementation of the OECD Convention in the United States did not produce any fundamental alteration in the basic concept of the FCPA's anti-bribery prohibitions. Stated differently, the FCPA's basic offence already met most of the requirements of Article 1 of the OECD Convention. In fact, the FCPA's offence swept (and sweeps) more broadly than the OECD Convention, since it is not limited to payments to 'foreign public officials' and officials of public international organisations.

[12] 18 U.S.C. § 201 (1994). [13] I.R.C. § 162(c).
[14] Pub. L. No. 95–213, 91 Stat. 1494 (FCPA 1977).
[15] Pub. L. No. 100–148, 102 Stat. 1107 (FCPA 1988) [hereinafter 1988 Amendments].
[16] Pub. L. No. 105–366, 112 Stat. 3302 (FCPA 1998) [hereinafter 1998 Amendments].
[17] The arguments in this section partially go over ground covered in our ch. on Article 1 above, to which readers are referred for further detail.

The Amendments did, however, result in expansion of the substantive reach of the provisions in one respect, and a variety of other noteworthy changes in the areas of jurisdiction and penalties that had the cumulative effect of significantly expanding the scope of the statute.

In general terms, the anti-bribery provisions of the FCPA prohibit US companies and individuals from paying bribes to foreign officials and certain other categories of covered recipients[18] for the purpose of obtaining a business benefit. Specifically, the FCPA prohibits subject persons from:

- acting with the required territorial nexus (if any) in furtherance of
- a payment, offer, promise to pay, or authorisation of a payment, promise, or offer
- of money or anything of value
- directly or indirectly to any foreign official, to any foreign political party or party official, or to any candidate for foreign political office
- corruptly
- for the purpose of (i) influencing any act or decision of that person in his or her official capacity; (ii) inducing that person to do or omit to do any act in violation of his or her lawful duty; (iii) inducing that person to influence any government act or decision; or (iv) obtaining any improper advantage
- for the purpose of obtaining or retaining business, or directing business to any person.

The penultimate element, sometimes referred to as the *quid pro quo* requirement, had only three prongs prior to the 1998 Amendments. Those Amendments added the fourth, the 'any improper advantage' language. This addition was a direct result of US ratification of the OECD Convention. However, the United States added this language not to the last element, which deals with obtaining or retaining business, where it appears in the OECD Convention, but to the *quid pro quo* element.

This drafting choice may have been motivated by a prosecutorial desire not to take action that could undercut the enforcement agencies' historically broad interpretation of the 'business' element.[19] Although the scope of this element, like many aspects of the statute, had never been fully litigated prior to US ratification of the OECD Convention, enforcement agencies had

[18] In addition to proscribing payments to 'foreign officials', the FCPA prohibits payments to political parties, party officials, and candidates for political office. See III.2.2.2. below.
[19] US-Ph1, 22.

consistently taken the position that this element encompassed much more than the award of government contracts.

Ironically, the decision not to amend the 'business' element in 1998 almost threatened US compliance with the Convention. In *U.S.* v. *Kay*, a United States district court in Houston held that this element did not include payments to customs officials,[20] while in *Mattson & Harris*, a different judge in the same district in Houston found it did not include payments to tax officials.[21] On appeal in February 2004, the Fifth Circuit rejected this limited view, holding that such payments could satisfy the 'business' element where there was a nexus between the payment and obtaining or retaining business.[22]

In its decision, the Fifth Circuit Court of Appeals cited Official Commentaries to the OECD Convention and made the following observations:

> 'Unlawfully reducing the taxes and customs duties at issue here to a level substantially below that which ARI was legally obligated to pay surely constitutes 'something [ARI] was not clearly entitled to', and was thus potentially an 'improper advantage' under the Convention...[T]he 1977 and 1988 legislative history already make clear that the business nexus requirement is not to be interpreted unduly narrowly...there really was no need for Congress to add 'or other improper advantage' to the [business nexus] requirement [in 1998]...That the Convention...also appear to prohibit the types of payments at issue in this case only bolsters our conclusion that the kind of conduct allegedly engaged in by defendants can be violative of the statute.'[23]

It is possible, of course, that the court would have construed the 'obtain or retain business' element of the FCPA as broadly as it did even in the absence of the 'improper advantage' language of the Convention. The quoted language from the Fifth Circuit's opinion makes it clear, however, that the Convention was a significant factor in the Court's decision.

2.2.2. Prohibited payees

The FCPA defines 'foreign official' to include 'any officer or employee of a foreign government or any department, agency, or instrumentality thereof,

[20] *U.S.* v. *Kay*, 200 F. Supp. 681 (S.D. Tex. 2002).
[21] *SEC* v. *Mattson*, Civil Action 01-CVH-01–3106 (S.D. Tex. 2001).
[22] *U.S.* v. *Kay*, 359 F.3d 738 (5th Cir. Feb. 4, 2004). The case was remanded to the District Court for further proceedings consistent with the opinion.
[23] *U.S.* v. *Kay*, 359 F.3d 754–55 (5th Cir. Feb. 4, 2004): stating in a footnote, that otherwise, it would likely create a conflict with our international treaty obligations, with which we presume Congress meant to comply fully.

or any person acting in an official capacity for or on behalf of any such' entities, and any official of a public international organisation.[24] 'Foreign officials' has always been an autonomous definition, and its scope and approach are consistent with the requirements of the OECD Convention. Although the Convention did not affect this basic term, the inclusion in the group of prohibited payees of officials of public international organisations was another 1998 amendment to the statute taken by the United States to implement the Convention.[25]

Adoption of the Convention did not result in any change with respect to the FCPA's coverage of officials of state 'instrumentalities', nor any definitive resolution of what that term may mean. The term is generally viewed as covering state-owned or -controlled enterprises, but the absence of a statutory definition in the FCPA has opened the door for enforcement officials to take a broader view of what the term means. In addition, there are many unanswered questions regarding the statute's coverage, including its applicability to second- or third-tier enterprises, 50/50 joint ventures, 'golden' shares, and other arrangements conferring less than affirmative control over an enterprise on the part of a government but still substantial influence.

No US court has addressed these issues prior to or since US ratification of the Convention. The Official Commentary 14 defines state ownership to include those 'public enterprise[s],' regardless of legal form, over which a government may, directly or indirectly, 'exercise a dominant influence.'[26] The Commentaries provide further, 'This is deemed to be the case, inter alia, when the government or governments hold the majority of the enterprise's subscribed capital, control the majority of votes attaching to shares issued by the enterprise or can appoint a majority of the members of the enterprise's administrative or managerial body or supervisory board.'[27]

The Official Commentaries thus look not only to ownership, but to functional control. Applying their definition to the privatisation scenario, they appear to treat an entity as a public enterprise until the moment when the government gives up control. Although the Commentaries do not address explicitly the issue of negative control – veto power – the 'dominant influence' language appears to suggest affirmative rather than negative control. If correct, this interpretation would mean, for example, that 50/50 joint ventures, or 'golden share' arrangements, would not confer public enterprise status under the OECD Convention.

[24] 15 U.S.C. §§ 78dd-1(f)(1), 78dd-2, and 78dd-3.
[25] Pub. L. No. 105–366, 112 Stat. 3302 (§§ 2(b), 3(c), 4).
[26] Official Commentary 14. [27] See previous note 26.

The OECD Commentaries also look to another factor to determine whether officials or employees of 'public enterprises' fall within the scope of the OECD Convention's prohibitions: whether officials of such enterprises should be deemed to perform a 'public function'. This analysis reflects the common sense notion that, when governments become involved in private commercial activity, not all of that activity should be deemed to be 'public functions.' Sometimes these state-owned enterprises are just commercial actors and the prohibitions on corruption of public officials should not extend to such actors just because some countries choose, unlike the United States, to be commercial actors. The Official Commentaries state that

> '[a]n official of a public enterprise shall be deemed to perform a public function unless the enterprise operates on a normal commercial basis in the relevant market, i.e., on a basis which is substantially equivalent to that of a private enterprise, without preferential subsidies or other privileges.'[28]

Whether US courts will look to the OECD Convention for guidance on this topic in interpreting the FCPA remains to be seen. The fact that the Official Commentaries focus on facts regarding the enterprise at issue that may not be easily ascertained (e.g. whether an entity operates on a regular commercial basis) may discourage reliance on the Commentaries' standard in compliance practice.

The OECD Convention currently does not explicitly apply to payments to officials of political parties, candidates for political office, or the political parties themselves. All of these categories of recipients have been covered by the FCPA since its enactment, and were unaltered in 1998. These provisions have been important in several FCPA prosecutions over the years.[29] The OECD Working Group has included these items on a list of unresolved issues for further study.[30] Even in the years since the OECD Convention's enactment, public disclosures of payments to political parties transnationally have revealed the need to cover these categories.[31]

[28] Official Commentary 15.

[29] Cf., for example, *U.S.* v. *Halford*, (01-00221-01-CR-W-1) (W.D. Mo. 2001) and *U.S.* v. *King and Barquero* (W.D. Mo. 2001) (officers of Owl Securities and Investments prosecuted for payments made to Costa Rican political parties, party officials, and candidates for public office to obtain a land concession); *U.S.* v. *Titan Corp.*, S.D. Ca., Case No. 05CR0314-BEN (filed March 1, 2005) (Plea Agreement); *SEC* v. *Titan Corp.*, D.D.C., Civil Action No. 05-0411 (JR), March 1, 2005 (Complaint); SEC Litigation Release No. 19107 (March 1, 2005).

[30] Cf. Questionnaires on Bribery Acts in Relation to Foreign Political Parties, Party Officers and Candidates, and on the Role of Foreign Subsidiaries (September 20, 2001), available at: http://www.oecd.org.

[31] For example, disclosures revealed questionable contributions to former German Chancellor Helmut Kohl's political party, the Christian Democratic Union (CDU). Cf. 'Q&A Germany's Party Funding Scandal', BBC News Online, June 29, 2000 (available at: http://news.bbc.co.uk).

2.2.3. Third party liability

In addition to liability for direct payments to foreign officials, persons subject to the FCPA may also be liable for indirect payments to such officials, that is, payments, promises or offers made to a third party such as a foreign agent, representative, consultant, or other third party while 'knowing' that the third party will make improper payments, promises, or offers of the type described above to a foreign official. 'Knowing' is a defined term which includes wilful ignorance as well as actual knowledge. Even if the first party did not specifically authorise the payment, under certain circumstances, it may be deemed to have knowledge of the third party's action.[32]

This third party liability standard – in place since 1988 in its current form[33] and left unaltered when the United States ratified the OECD Convention – is not only compliant with the standards of the OECD Convention, but arguably goes beyond it in terms of its specificity. The OECD Convention prohibits indirect as well as direct bribery, but establishes no standard for vicarious liability for the acts of a third party.

Historically, this provision of the FCPA has had tremendous compliance implications for companies subject to the FCPA, perhaps surpassing all others. Preventing wilful ignorance implies a need for companies to conduct due diligence in advance of engaging third parties such as agents and consultants, and to develop safeguards that the due diligence suggests are necessary. Given the challenges of law enforcement, it is critical to encourage companies engaged in international business to take steps to prevent violations.[34]

How effective the OECD Convention (and/or other international Conventions) will be in spurring Member states to adopt standards for

[32] Under the FCPA as amended in 1988, a person's state of mind is 'knowing with respect to conduct, a circumstance, or a result' if the person has actual knowledge of the conduct, circumstance, or result, or 'has a firm belief' that the conduct, circumstance, or result exists or is 'substantially certain' to occur (15 U.S.C. § 78dd-2(h)(3)). The statute explains further that when knowledge of a circumstance is a required element of the offence, that knowledge is established 'if a person is aware of a high probability of the existence of such circumstance, unless the person actually believes that such circumstance does not exist' (15 U.S.C. § 78dd-2(h)(3)). Prior to the 1988 Amendments, the FCPA imposed a 'reason to know' standard, which many were concerned set a simple negligence standard of liability. Although the 1988 Amendments eliminated that standard as an inappropriate basis for criminal liability, they made clear that the definition of 'knowledge' continues to extend beyond actual knowledge to include a 'conscious disregard' of the truth. Cf. H.R. Conf. Rep. No. 100-576, at 920 (1988).

[33] See previous note 32.

[34] This point is explored more fully in part IV. below.

vicarious liability that will have a similar prophylactic effect similar to that achieved in the United States remains to be seen.

2.2.4. Exceptions and affirmative defences

The FCPA contains no express exceptions or defences for payments of small monetary value, for payments which are usual or customary, or for gifts and entertainment. There is one statutory exception to the FCPA's anti-bribery provisions – for gratuities given to government officials performing 'routine governmental action'. These so-called 'facilitating' or 'grease' payments, used to expedite the processing, typically by a low-level official, of non-discretionary permits or licences or other routine documentation, are not prohibited by the FCPA's anti-bribery provisions.[35]

The OECD Convention permits but does not require such an exception; thus, US adoption of the Convention resulted in no change to this provision.[36] However, as noted in the chapter on Article 1, this exception is not contained in many other OECD Convention parties' transnational bribery laws. Nor is it typically an exception to local anti-bribery laws. The result has been a growing trend of multinational companies to prohibit or at least strongly discourage facilitating payments, which in any event must be properly booked.

In addition to the exception for facilitating payments, since 1988 the FCPA has featured two affirmative defences for certain types of payments. First, an affirmative defence exists where the payment at issue 'was lawful under the *written* laws and regulations of the foreign official's. . .country'.[37] The 'written laws' requirement was chosen to ensure that only the law in a country, not its customary practices, could be the basis for this defence.

[35] 15 U.S.C. §§ 78dd-1(b), 78dd-2(b). This exception (which is not mirrored on the accounting side of the statute) was added in the 1988 Amendments. A similar exception existed in the original Act by virtue of the original definition of 'foreign official'. Prior to the 1988 Amendments, government employees whose duties were primarily 'ministerial or clerical' were excluded from the definition of 'foreign official'. Cf. H.R. Conf. Rep. No. 95-831, at 12 (1977); S. Rep. No. 100-85, at 52 (1987). Thus, payments to those employees were not payments to 'foreign officials' and, accordingly, fell outside the scope of the Act's prohibitions. The original exception hinged on the duties of the recipient, rather than the purpose of the payment. As a practical matter, however, it was often difficult to determine whether an employee's duties were ministerial or discretionary. S. Rep. No. 100-85, at 52–53; H.R. Rep. No. 100-40, at 77 (1987). Therefore, the 1988 Amendments changed the exception to focus on the purpose of the payment, to allow only those payments that secure or expedite performance of duties that an official is required to perform in the normal course of business and that do not involve the exercise of the official's discretion. S. Rep. No. 100-85, at 52–53; H.R. Rep. No. 100-40, at 77.

[36] Official Commentary 9.

[37] 15 U.S.C. §§ 78dd-1(c)(1), 78dd-2(c)(1) (emphasis added).

Second, an affirmative defence may be asserted where a payment was a 'reasonable and bona fide expenditure, such as travel and lodging expenses', incurred by or on behalf of a foreign official and 'directly related' to the 'promotion, demonstration, or explanation of products or services' or 'the execution or performance of a contract with a foreign government or government agency'.[38]

The OECD Convention has no counterpart to these affirmative defences. The WGB Phase 1 and Phase 2 reviews of the United States have questioned these defences, especially the local law affirmative defence.[39] Recognising that the scope of the latter in particular is unclear, the defence nevertheless reflects a larger role that local law plays in the analysis of legal risk and compliance measures. It is obviously important for transnational businesses to focus attention not just on laws in their home country or other significant countries of operations, but also on host country law. While neither the FCPA nor the OECD Convention provide an exception for local culture, practice, or tradition, paying heed to local law is consistent with comity and providing some deference to the policy judgments of host countries that are reflected in their legislation.

2.2.5. Persons subject to the law and jurisdictional reach

Besides its effects on the substantive terms of the anti-bribery provisions, the OECD Convention has had a significant impact on the FCPA's jurisdictional reach, both over US persons and over foreign persons. Prior to the 1998 Amendments, the statute featured two separate but parallel anti-bribery provisions – one for 'issuers', and the second for 'domestic concerns'. 'Issuers' are essentially public companies – any entity (US or foreign) which has a class of securities registered pursuant to section 12 of the Securities and Exchange Act of 1934[40] or which is required to file reports under section 15(d) of the 1934 Act.[41] 'Domestic concerns' include any US citizen, national, or resident, as well as any corporation, partnership, association, joint-stock company, business trust, unincorporated organisation, or sole proprietorship that has its principal place of business in the United States, or that is organised under the laws of a state of the United States, or a territory, possession, or commonwealth of the United States.

[38] 15 U.S.C. §§ 78dd-1(c)(2), 78dd-2(c)(2). [39] US-Ph1, 21 et seq.; US-Ph2, 35 et seq.

[40] 15 U.S.C. § 781.

[41] 15 U.S.C. § 78o(d). This would include, for example, foreign companies that list American Depository Receipts (ADRs) on a US stock exchange.

Prior to the 1998 Amendments, the FCPA required that both 'issuers' and 'domestic concerns' make use of the mails or other instrumentality of US interstate or foreign commerce in furtherance of an improper payment for the law to be triggered.[42] Although that provision remains, the 1998 Amendments added alternative jurisdictional bases to both dd-1 (for issuers) and dd-2 (for domestic concerns), which permit the elimination of any territorial nexus requirement for 'US persons' – US issuers and domestic concerns.[43] Thus, US persons are now effectively subject to nationality jurisdiction.[44] The change was prompted by the OECD Convention's provision on jurisdiction, which requires states that use nationality-based jurisdiction for other offences to do so for the Convention's transnational bribery offence.[45]

In addition, the 1998 Amendments expanded the FCPA to 'any person', by adding a new provision covering actions of such persons in furtherance of a bribe while in US territory.[46] 'Any person' encompasses non-US nationals and legal entities organised under foreign laws.[47] This new provision establishes a different, and slightly higher, standard than the 'instrumentality of interstate commerce' standard described above. It effectively extended the FCPA to cover foreign persons not subject to the statute as issuers, provided there is a territorial link to the United States (and, of course, subject to being able to obtain personal jurisdiction over the foreign party).[48]

It is relatively rare for the United States to establish jurisdiction over US persons on a nationality basis.[49] There is no question, however, that this alternative provision materially expands the statute's effective reach, since it obviates the need for prosecutors to look for a US nexus to the actions of a US person. Thus, US nationals working for foreign companies may be

[42] 15 U.S.C. §§ 78dd-1(a), 78dd-2(a). [43] 15 U.S.C. §§ 78dd-1(g), 78dd-2(g).

[44] Given the disparity that would have been created between the jurisdictional scope of US law and the jurisdictional scope of other countries' laws, the compromise reached was for the United States' implementing legislation to 'mirror' the anticipated scope of other OECD countries' laws. This meant the assertion of nationality jurisdiction over US persons, and territorial jurisdiction over 'any person', including foreign persons (and, therefore, foreign subsidiaries of US companies as well), acting within US territory.

[45] Art. 4(2) OECD 1997b. [46] 15 U.S.C. § 78dd-3(a). [47] 15 U.S.C. § 78dd-3(f)(1).

[48] The penalty provisions of the Act (see note 16) also effectively expand the FCPA's application to non-US persons by making any officer, director, shareholder, employee, or agent of a domestic concern or issuer subject to penalties. See III.2.2.6. below.

[49] The Economic Espionage Act of 1996 (EEA 1996), 18 U.S.C. §§ 1831 et seq., has a similar nationality-based jurisdictional reach. It includes in its coverage, conduct occurring outside the United States by US citizens, permanent resident aliens, and organisations organised under the laws of the United States, or a State or political subdivision thereof.

personally covered by the FCPA when acting abroad, even if their employer is not. And US companies acting abroad will not have a jurisdictional shield to assert as a defence.

Where do foreign subsidiaries fare in all this? Unlike some US laws and regulations,[50] the FCPA does not seek to treat foreign subsidiaries of US companies as US persons, and does not seek to reach their activities which are wholly extra-territorial.[51] Nor does it make parent companies automatically criminally liable for their foreign subsidiaries' improper payments. The OECD Convention did not require any change to these features.

The fact that the FCPA does not provide for such liability or coverage to be automatic does not mean that US law exempts foreign subsidiaries from the anti-bribery provisions. Foreign subsidiaries have potentially liability under the 'any person' prohibition adopted in 1998. Moreover, their subsidiary status may create a higher risk that their actions will satisfy the territorial nexus requirement and personal jurisdiction standards than a foreign-owned foreign company's would. In addition, US parents may have exposure in certain situations under the anti-bribery provisions for the acts of their foreign subsidiaries under theories such as alter ego, or agency law, and are effectively strictly responsible for the accounting and internal controls of their majority-owned and controlled foreign subsidiaries.

Several recent US enforcement actions have involved foreign subsidiaries of US companies.[52] However, most of these cases have come to the attention of enforcement officials as the result of voluntary disclosures.

[50] Cf., for example, Cuban Assets Control Regulations, Title 31 of the U.S. Code of Federal Regulation Part 515 (1999).

[51] By contrast, the Iran and Libya Sanctions Act of 1996 penalises those persons engaging in certain prohibited transactions with Iran and Libya, regardless of whether those persons are US nationals or whether the transactions have connections with US commerce. Cf. Iran and Libya Sanctions Act of 1996, Pub. L. No. 104-72, §§ 5(a), 5(b), 14(14), 110 Stat. 1541, 1543, 1550 (1996). Title III of the controversial Cuban Liberty and Democratic Solidarity (LIBERTAD) Act of 1996 (popularly known as the Helms-Burton Act) authorises US nationals claiming an interest in Cuban property confiscated by the Castro regime to sue foreign nationals who are currently 'trafficking' in such property. Cf. The Cuban Liberty and Democratic Solidarity (LIBERTAD) Act of 1996, Pub. L. No. 104–114, Title III, 110 Stat. 785, 814–822 (1996). Enforcement of Title III has been suspended by US Presidents since its enactment in response to strong diplomatic pressure from US allies. The Cuban Assets Control Regulations, which predate the Helms-Burton Act and which codify the US embargo against Cuba, subject 'any person within the United States' to US jurisdiction, but do not require the person to be a US resident, national, or citizen. 31 C.F.R. §§ 515.329, 515.330 (2002).

[52] For example, based on several foreign subsidiaries' illicit payments to doctors employed by hospitals controlled by foreign authorities, the Department of Justice prosecuted the Taiwanese subsidiary of Syncor International Corporation. *U.S.* v. *Syncor Taiwan, Inc.*,

Thus, the full scope of the FCPA's jurisdictional reach since the 1998 Amendments has not been tested.

In short, the OECD Convention's adoption has resulted in significantly expanded jurisdiction under the FCPA, legally and practically, over both US and foreign persons.

2.2.6. Penalties and enforcement

The FCPA's anti-bribery provisions are enforced by two federal government agencies – the Department of Justice and the SEC. US courts have held that private persons do not have direct rights of action to enforce the law.[53] The SEC's enforcement authority only extends to 'issuers'. The Department of Justice has enforcement authority over all subject persons.

A criminal violation of the anti-bribery provisions by enterprises may result in fines of up to $2 million per violation. Officers, directors, shareholders, employees or agents may also face fines of up to $100 000, and/or five years' imprisonment.[54] Those fines may not be reimbursed by their employers. Furthermore, if the criminal offence causes a pecuniary gain or loss, US law authorises alternative maximum fines equal to the greater of twice the gross gain or twice the gross loss.[55] Individuals may be fined on this basis, or in the alternative up to $250 000, and/or may be imprisoned for up to five years.[56] The amount of the fines and/or prison terms will generally be determined according to the Federal Sentencing Guidelines, which take into account factors such as the size of the bribe, the number of counts, and prior convictions, as well as any mitigating factors such as corporate compliance programmes and cooperation with the government's investigation.[57] In the second *Lockheed* case in the mid-1990s, the application of these provisions resulted in a combined civil and criminal

No. 02-CR-1244-ALL (C.D. Ca.). The SEC also charged the parent, Syncor International Corporation, with violation of the anti-bribery, books-and-records and internal accounting controls provisions of the FCPA (cf. Order, Securities Exchange Act 1934, Release No. 46979, December 10, 2002, available at: http://www.sec.gov). More recently, the Chinese subsidiary of Diagnostic Products Corporation was similarly charged by the Department of Justice, and the parent was also charged by the SEC for payments made by its Chinese subsidiary (cf. Order, Securities Exchange Act 1934 Release No. 51724, May 20, 2005, available at: http://www.sec.gov).

[53] Cf., for example, *Lamb* v. *Phillip Morris, Inc.*, 915 F.2d 1024 (6th Cir. 1990), cert. denied, 498 U.S. 1086 (1991); *McLean* v. *International Harvester Co.*, 817 F.2d 1214 (5th Cir. 1987).

[54] 15 U.S.C. §§ 78dd-2(g)(1)(A), 78ff(c)(1)(A).

[55] 15 U.S.C. §§ 78dd-2(g)(2)(a)-(b), 78ff(c)(2)(a)-(b).

[56] See previous note 55. [57] Sentencing Guidelines 2004, 69 Fed. Reg. 28994.

fine totaling US $24.8 million and the first time individuals were sentenced to serve jail terms for FCPA violations.[58] More recently, a fine of $28 million was imposed in the *Titan* case.[59]

In addition to criminal penalties, the FCPA authorises civil penalties of up to $10 000 against enterprises and individuals for violations of the anti-bribery provisions.[60] By application of the Securities Enforcement Remedies and Penny Stock Reform Act of 1990, these civil penalties can be increased up to $100 000 for individuals or $500 000 for business organisations per violation, or the gross amount of pecuniary gain resulting from the violation, in cases involving acts such as fraud, deceit, or substantial loss to other persons.[61] The SEC or the Department of Justice (depending on whether the violation is committed by an issuer) may also seek injunctive relief to enjoin any act of an enterprise or individuals acting on behalf of an enterprise which violates or may violate the FCPA. These statutory fine levels were not affected by the OECD Convention.

The 1998 Amendments to the FCPA, occasioned by the Convention, did, however, significantly expand the application of the statute's penalty provisions to foreign persons. The Act imposes penalties against '[a]ny natural person that is an officer, director, employee, or agent of a domestic concern, or stockholder acting on behalf of such domestic concern' for wilful violations of the Act.[62] Prior to the 1998 Amendments, the FCPA subjected employees and agents (as distinguished from officers, directors and stockholders) to criminal liability only if they were 'otherwise subject to the jurisdiction of the United States'.[63] The 1998 Amendments eliminated this disparity, so that today, employees, agents, officers, directors, and stockholders are all subject to criminal liability.

2.2.7. Statute of limitations

The statute of limitations for a criminal violation of the FCPA is five years from the date that the potential offence was committed; this derives from the general federal criminal statute of limitations.[64] This period can be

[58] *U.S.* v. *Lockheed*, No. 1:94-CR-226–01 (Plea Agreement) (N.D. Ca. 1995), reprinted in 3 FCPA 1977 Rep. 699.175 (January 27, 1995).

[59] *U.S.* v. *Titan Corp.*, S.D. Ca., Case No. 05CR0314-BEN (filed March 1, 2005) (Plea Agreement); *SEC* v. *Titan Corp.*, D.D.C., Civil Action No. 05–0411 (JR), March 1, 2005 (Complaint); SEC Litigation Release No. 19107 (March 1, 2005).

[60] 15 U.S.C. §§ 78dd-2(g)(1)(B) and (g)(2)(B), 78dd-3(e)(1)(b) and (e)(2)(B), 78ff(c)(1)(B) and (c)(2)(B).

[61] 15 U.S.C. § 80b-9(e)(2)(C). [62] 15 U.S.C. § 78g(2)(A).

[63] 15 U.S.C. § 78g(2)(B). [64] 18 U.S.C. § 3282.

extended for up to three years, upon a request by a prosecutor and a finding by a court that additional time is needed to gather evidence located abroad.[65] The length of time granted for an extension will depend on how long it takes a foreign authority to act on a request for evidence and when the statute would run in the absence of any extension. However, that request can be made only after the commencement of a formal inquiry within the general five-year limitation period.[66] These provisions have not changed as a result of the OECD Convention.

3. Impact on the FCPA's accounting standards

3.1. Introduction

As noted earlier, the FCPA's accounting standards were not affected by the OECD Convention. Although Article 8 of the Convention requires states Parties to take measures in this regard, the United States took the position that existing law already satisfied these requirements.[67]

The FPCA's accounting standards, although applicable only to issuers of listed securities, and not all companies subject to US jurisdiction, have had a significant deterrent effect on corruption in international business activity and serve as an important complement to the criminalisation of transnational bribery. That is largely because their requirements for systems of internal accounting controls and accurate books and records approach strict liability in how they are interpreted by enforcement officials. Moreover, these provisions extend throughout a multinational enterprise, requiring parent companies to take far-reaching steps to control the activities of their foreign subsidiaries. They have no standards of financial materiality, and affect qualitative as well as quantitative recording of transactions. Corporate governance reforms embodied in the Sarbanes-Oxley legislation of 2002 have made these provisions even more significant.

Most of the international anti-corruption conventions, including the OECD Convention, include provisions regarding accounting standards.[68] The requirements of these Conventions are very general, and their effectiveness will ultimately depend on a unified set of international accounting standards or a common international baseline, and, most importantly, active national regulatory agencies.

[65] 18 U.S.C. § 3292(a)-(c). [66] See previous note 65.
[67] See further discussion in ch. on Article 8 above. [68] See previous note 67.

3.2. Requirements

In general terms, the accounting standards and internal control provisions of the FCPA require 'issuers' to keep accurate books and records and to establish and maintain a system of internal accounting controls adequate to ensure accountability for assets. These provisions were designed to ensure the integrity of the financial information presented by 'issuers' to shareholders and potential investors, and to prevent the use of 'slush funds' and off-book accounts to finance improper activities, including but not limited to foreign bribery.

In particular, the accounting provisions require issuers to:

- make and keep books, records, and accounts which in reasonable detail accurately and fairly reflect the transactions and dispositions of the assets of the issuer; and
- devise and maintain a system of internal accounting controls sufficient to provide reasonable assurances that:
  - transactions are executed in accordance with management's general or specific authorisation;
  - transactions are recorded as necessary to permit preparation of financial statements in conformity with generally accepted accounting principles and to maintain accountability of such assets;
  - access to assets is permitted only in accordance with management's general or specific authorisation; and
  - the recorded accountability for assets is compared with the existing assets at reasonable levels and appropriate action is taken with respect to any differences.[69]

The accounting provisions require issuers to reflect accurately all transactions and dispositions of assets 'in reasonable detail.' This requirement applies to all expenditures, rather than just those that would qualify as 'material' in an accounting or disclosure context. Although the provisions thus require reporting in greater detail than a 'materiality' standard, the FCPA requires 'reasonable' rather than absolute assurance that accounting controls are adequate. The records must be kept in 'such level of detail and degree of assurance as would satisfy prudent officials in the conduct of their own affairs.'[70] The Senate Report accompanying the original Act recognises that 'standards of reasonableness must apply' and that 'management must

[69] 15 U.S.C. § 78m(b)(2). [70] 15 U.S.C. § 78m(b)(7).

necessarily estimate and evaluate the cost/benefit relationships' in establishing a system of controls.[71]

3.3. Subject persons

Unlike the anti-bribery provisions, the accounting provisions apply only to 'issuers.'[72] 'Issuers' in this context has the same definition as the anti-bribery context. Thus, not only US public companies but also foreign companies with publicly-traded stock in the United States, may be 'issuers.'[73] This limited scope of application of the accounting provisions has been questioned in the OECD review of the United States.[74]

The accounting rules apply to *all* operations of issuers, domestic and overseas. Moreover, issuers are required to ensure that their majority-owned domestic and foreign subsidiaries comply with the accounting requirements of the FCPA. Where an issuer holds 50% or less of the voting power of a foreign subsidiary, however, a 1988 amendment to the accounting provisions requires only that the issuer make a 'good faith attempt' to cause the affiliated company to maintain the internal accounting controls.[75] Where a parent has a minority interest but effectively controls the subsidiary, it will be expected to cause the subsidiary to comply. Thus, the greater the control, the higher the expectation of the parent's compliance efforts.

3.4. Penalties and enforcement

Like the anti-bribery provisions, the accounting and internal control requirements of the FCPA are enforced by the Department of Justice and

[71] S. Rep. No. 95–114, at 8 1977, reprinted in 1977 U.S.C.C.A.N. 4098, 4106.

[72] 15 U.S.C. § 78m(b). However, a civil suit by the Department of Justice in the late 1990s against a non-issuer alleged books and records violations, and the Consent Agreement settling the case required the company, as part of its compliance programme, to adhere to books and records and internal control standards. *U.S.* v. *Metcalf & Eddy*, Civ. No. 1:00cv 12566 (D. Mass. Dec. 14, 1999) (Complaint for Permanent Injunction and Ancillary Relief; Consent and Undertaking of *Metcalf & Eddy*, Inc.).

[73] Thus, under these provisions foreign issuers will be held to the same standards of financial reporting and fair dealing as domestic issuers. This policy has most recently been exhibited in the SEC enforcement actions against *ABB and Montedison*, S.p.A., an Italian company that traded American Depositary Receipts (ADRs) on the New York Stock Exchange and for several years falsified its reports to disguise an estimated $400 million in bribes. Cf. *SEC* v. *ABB Ltd.*, 1:04CV1141 (RBW) (D.D.C.), Lit. Rel. No. 18775, July 6, 2004, and *SEC* v. *Montedison, S.p.A.*, SEC Lit. Rel. No. 16948 (2001).

[74] US-Ph2, 19–20, 38. [75] 15 U.S.C. § 78m(b)(6).

the SEC. Generally, the SEC polices inadvertent or negligent violations, and refers wilful violations to the Department of Justice for prosecution.

Article 8(2) of the Convention, like Article 3, requires the state Parties impose 'effective, proportionate, and dissuasive penalties' for violations of the accounting requirements. These provisions have not resulted in any changes in penalties under US law, although in practice penalty levels have been increasing. The SEC may impose civil penalties under its general enforcement authority over all reporting companies.[76] Under this authority, the SEC may impose civil fines, bring an injunctive action or enter a cease-and-desist order against a person who violates, or is about to violate, the anti-bribery provisions, and/or order disgorgement of ill-gotten gains.

The Department of Justice has enforcement authority over criminal violations of the accounting rules. Under the 1988 Amendments to the FCPA, persons may be criminally liable under the accounting rules only if they 'knowingly circumvent or knowingly fail to implement a system of internal accounting controls or knowingly falsify any book, record, or account' required to be maintained under the FCPA.[77]

The penalties for such violations are the same penalties applicable to other criminal violations of the securities laws. Under those laws, individuals found to have committed a 'wilful' violation may be fined up to $1 million and/or imprisoned up to ten years; enterprises found to have 'wilfully' violated the accounting requirements may be fined up to $2.5 million.[78]

4. Impact of the OECD Convention on FCPA enforcement

Since the passage of the 1998 Amendments to the FCPA, enforcement of the statute by the Department of Justice and SEC has increased dramatically. More cases were brought in the five years following the Amendments than in the previous twenty. Moreover, penalty levels have increased as well.

The OECD Convention has contributed to this upsurge in enforcement activity, but is not by any means the sole cause of the increase.

[76] 15 U.S.C. § 78u-1(9)(1)(A).

[77] 15 U.S.C. § 78m(b)(5). 'Knowledge' in this context parallels the general US criminal law definition and is thus narrower than that used in the third party provisions of the anti-bribery prohibitions. The 'knowledge' standard in the accounting rules is merely intended to align the FCPA's standard for liability with the SEC's general enforcement policy that inadvertent conduct not be subject to criminal penalties. The legislative history explains that this standard is meant to criminalise the 'deliberate falsification of books and records and other conduct calculated to evade the internal accounting controls requirements'. S. Rep. No. 100-85 at 50.

[78] 15 U.S.C. § 78ff(a).

Other domestic and international developments must also be credited. The OECD Convention has encouraged greater US enforcement in several ways, through its international co-operation provisions, through its expansion of the statute, and possibly in less tangible ways as well, through the impetus that the monitoring process may have given to enforcement efforts.

4.1. The effects of international co-operation on US enforcement

In addition to its criminalisation requirements, the OECD Convention requires state Parties to co-operate in investigations and enforcement of bribery cases. It builds on networks of mutual legal assistance and extradition treaties, making them tools in corruption investigations and prosecutions.[79] These provisions require no implementing legislation, and in some countries will provide the legal basis for co-operation even in the absence of a separate bilateral treaty on those topics. As such, the co-operation provisions are of substantial practical significance to enforcement.

Prior to the OECD Convention, US prosecutors often encountered difficulties obtaining evidence abroad, due to the lack of dual criminality (often a requirement for mutual legal assistance or extradition) or other reasons. In just a few years, the OECD Convention has already demonstrated the changed dynamic in international co-operation in evidence-gathering in transnational bribery cases. The *Bodmer* and *Giffen* cases illustrate this point. Such co-operation – likely the direct result of international standards – is significant given the difficulty of prosecuting transnational bribery due to the complexity of the offence and the fact that evidence is often scattered in more than one country.[80]

Bodmer, a lawyer and Swiss citizen, acted as an agent on behalf of a group of investors formed to attempt to acquire interests in SOCAR, the Azerbaijan national oil company, which was due to be privatised. Several of the members of the consortium were US persons. The US government alleged that Bodmer facilitated the payment of millions of dollars in cash and wire transfers to acquire privatisation instruments issued by the government of Azerbaijan, as well as to fund payments to senior officials of Azerbaijan, the oil company, and the State Property Committee. For this conduct, Bodmer was charged with one count of conspiracy to violate

[79] See the detailed discussion in ch. on Articles 9–11 above.
[80] See further discussion in ch. on Article 5 above.

the FCPA's anti-bribery prohibition and one count of conspiracy to launder money. (The indictment also sought $150 million in restitution, among other claims.)[81]

Although Swiss authorities will not extradite their nationals to other countries for criminal prosecution, Mr. Bodmer was apprehended by the Korean authorities at the request of the United States and brought to the United States for trial. Korea being a party to the OECD Convention, such co-operation should be seen as a direct result of the Convention's provisions.

In July 2004, a New York federal district court dismissed the conspiracy to violate the FCPA charge against Bodmer, based on its finding that, as a foreign national, he lacked fair notice that the criminal sanctions of the FCPA applied to him prior to the 1998 Amendments. His motion to dismiss the money laundering conspiracy charge, however, was denied. The court held that the case could go forward, even though the alleged corrupt practices were entirely extra-territorial, and even though the FCPA conspiracy count had been dismissed on jurisdictional grounds.[82]

The *Giffen* case also reflects the fruits of international cooperation, in this case both spontaneous and formal legal assistance provided by the Swiss Government to the US authorities. Mr. Giffen, chairman of a New York-based merchant bank, allegedly made payments to senior Kazakh officials through the accounts of foreign shell organisations. He was charged in 2003 with sixty-two criminal counts, including violations of the anti-bribery provision of the FCPA, money laundering and wire fraud. The case is currently pending in the District Court for the Southern District of New York.[83] The Swiss government's information came from money laundering investigations it had underway of certain officials of Kazakhstan.

Press reports also suggest there may be cooperation between the French and US authorities in the pending *Halliburton* case, which is still at the investigative stage.[84] Other cases that feature co-operation between the United States and other OECD Convention state Parties are believed to be in the pipeline.

[81] *U.S.* v. *Bodmer*, No. 03-Crim. 947, 2004 U.S. Dist. LEXIS 959 (S.D.N.Y. Jan. 28, 2004). For other related prosecutions, cf. *U.S.* v. *Kozeny, Bourke and Pinkerton*, 05 Crim. 518 (Indictment filed May 12, 2005).

[82] *U.S.* v. *Bodmer*, 342 F. Supp. 2d 176 (S.D.N.Y. 2004).

[83] *U.S.* v. *Giffen*, Cr. No. 03–663 (S.D.N.Y., March 2003).

[84] Newsweek (web version), February 4, 2004; cf. also *Halliburton* 10-Q filings (May and August 2004).

4.2. Prosecutions under the expanded statute

4.2.1. Increased prosecutions of foreign persons

Since the amendment of the FCPA in 1998 pursuant to the OECD Convention, numerous prosecutions have relied on the new statutory authority provided by those Amendments, particularly with respect to foreign persons.

The first joint prosecution of the SEC and Department of Justice, *U.S.* v. *KPMG Siddharta Siddharta & Harsono*, was also the first case to rely on the new authority of the government under 15 U.S.C § 78dd-3 to bring bribery cases against foreign persons for acts in furtherance of an improper payment while in US territory.[85] Other prosecutions based on this authority have followed, including the *Syncor* case against Syncor's Taiwanese representative, the DPC case cited earlier.[86]

No bribery cases against US persons to date have been based on the alternative nationality jurisdiction established by the 1998 Amendments. That is probably because the territorial jurisdiction requirements for US persons – requiring only the use of the mails or other instrumentality of interstate or foreign commerce – are readily met in most cases. Moreover, as discussed in III.4.5. below, the prevalence of voluntary disclosures in recent years has made jurisdictional issues less critical.

4.2.2. Wider sweep of substantive conduct

FCPA prosecutions in recent years have also involved a wider range of conduct than had been the case in the past. As discussed in subsection III.2.2.1. above, in the only fully litigated case involving issues of the scope of the statute's reach since the 1998 Amendments to the FCPA, the *Kay* case, the Court of Appeals for the Fifth Circuit cited the Official Commentaries in holding that the FCPA was not limited to payments to secure government contracts, but applied to a much wider range of improper payments.

Several settled prosecutions have involved a scope of activity that reaches beyond the traditional realm of FCPA prosecutions, including the *Schering-Plough* case, involving a charitable contribution,[87] two cases

[85] *U.S. & SEC* v. *KPMG Siddharta, Siddharta & Harsono (SSH) and Sonny Harsono* (Civil Action No. H-01–3105) S.D. Tex., September 2001; SEC Litigation Release No. 17127 (September 12, 2001).

[86] See note 52.

[87] In the matter of *Schering-Plough Corp.*, SEC Administrative Proceeding Filing No. 3-11517 (June 9, 2004).

involving distributors,[88] the *Monsanto* case involving an environmental permit,[89] and cases involving gifts and entertainment.[90] There have also been a host of cases involving successor liability in the mergers and acquisitions context.[91]

These cases suggest a concerted effort on the part of US enforcement authorities to bring cases that arise not only at the procurement stage, but at any stage of overseas operations.

4.3. The intangible effect of the OECD Convention

Although difficult to quantify, it also seems likely the Convention has had a significant intangible effect on US prosecutions. The monitoring of the WGB, and particularly the Phase 2 enforcement monitoring, created an incentive for US prosecutors to bring cases in order to demonstrate active enforcement and to seek substantial penalties. A number of cases were in fact brought prior to the Phase 2 review of the United States in 2002. Moreover, the mere existence of the WGB, and the relationships that it fosters, may facilitate more informal co-operation.

4.4. The use of money laundering laws in combating corruption

The OECD Convention has also contributed to the increased use of money laundering laws as a tool to combat corruption. Recognising the potency of those laws, Article 7 of the OECD Convention requires that transnational bribery be made a predicate offence for money laundering laws to the same extent as domestic bribery. In this regard, the OECD Convention was groundbreaking. The Inter-American Convention, which preceded it, did not make that linkage, although it does require that states Parties criminalise the fraudulent use or concealment of property derived from acts of corruption.[92]

[88] For example, *GE/Invision*, SEC Exchange Act 1934 Release No. 51199 and Acctg. Release No. 2186; Litigation Release No. 19078 and Acctg. Release No. 2187 (all February 14, 2005).

[89] *U.S.* v. *Monsanto Company* (Docket No. 1:05cr8) D.D.C., Jan. 2005; *SEC* v. *Monsanto Company*, Case No. 1:05CV00014 (D.D.C. January 6, 2005), Lit. Rel. No. 19023 (2005).

[90] E.g., *SEC* v. *ABB Ltd.*, 1:04CV1141 (RBW) (D.D.C.), Lit. Rel. No. 18775, July 6, 2004; *U.S.* v. *ABB Vetco Gray, Inc. and ABB Vetco Gray UK, Ltd.*, Case No. 04-CR-279–01 (S.D. Tex. July 6, 2004).

[91] For example, *SEC* v. *ABB* (see note 73), *GE/Invision*, above note 88.

[92] Art. VI(d) OAS 1996; Art. 13 Council of Europe Criminal Law Convention (COE 1999a), which followed the OECD Convention (OECD 1997b), requires States Parties to make all of the corruption-related offences to which it applies predicate offences for criminal violations of their money-laundering laws. The UN Convention (UN 2003) goes even further with

4.4.1. Of means and proceeds

The effect of making transnational bribery a predicate offence for money laundering laws will depend on the scope of such laws at the national level.

As discussed in our chapter on Article 7 above, money laundering is most frequently defined in relation to the proceeds of criminal activity.[93] Specifically, classic money laundering is the placement of the proceeds of a serious crime into the financial system, and the subsequent engagement in transactions designed to obscure the origin of the proceeds and, in many cases, render them able to be used in subsequent, legitimate, transactions. One early study in the United States succinctly defined it as 'the process by which one conceals the existence, illegal source, or illegal application of incomes, and disguises that income to make it appear legitimate'.[94]

In addition, however, some jurisdictions' criminal money laundering legislation allow for the prosecution of corruption-related activities at an earlier stage before there are proceeds of crime. The United States is one such example.

4.4.2. The US approach

The United States has criminalised money laundering in the Money Laundering Control Act of 1986 (MLCA), codified principally at 18 U.S.C. §§ 1956–1957. This Act creates potential liability for any person who conducts a monetary transaction or certain other activity knowing, or with reason to know, that the funds involved were derived from unlawful activity. Section 1956 covers the knowing and international transportation or transfer of monetary funds derived from 'specified unlawful activities.' It is further subdivided into three subsections: subsection (a)(1), dealing with money laundering involving 'financial transactions'; subsection (a)(2) addressing cross-border funds transfers; and (a)(3), which permits the use of government sting operations to expose criminal activity. Section 1956(a)(2), the money transfer section, applies not just to transactions involving the proceeds of crime, but also transfers intended to *promote* specified unlawful activities. Section 1957 prohibits the knowing engagement in transactions using or involving property valued over $10 000 which is derived from specific unlawful activities.

respect to the linkages between corruption and money laundering, including both criminalisation and preventive provisions: Arts. 23 (mandatory criminalisation of laundering of the proceeds of corruption), 14 and 52 (preventive measures).

[93] See chs. on Article 3(3) and 7 above. [94] President's Commission 1984.

'Specific unlawful activity' is defined in the MLCA to encompass a wide range of predicate offences. Besides RICO-related offences, and acts that constitute a continuing criminal enterprise under the Controlled Substances Act, the Act contains a long list of US law violations. Literally hundreds of such offences are specified, from various types of serious violent crime, to white collar financial crimes, including several corruption-related expenses. Among the domestic predicate offences are domestic official bribery under 18 U.S.C. § 201, and felony convictions of the FCPA.[95] The Act also contains a much shorter list of offences against a foreign nation which can serve as predicate offences.[96] Prior to the adoption of the PATRIOT Act in 2001, only seven foreign offences were specified, and only one of these focused on fraud. The PATRIOT Act, however, added foreign official bribery and the misappropriation of public funds as predicate offences.[97] These changes were not required by the OECD Convention; transnational bribery was already a predicate act. By allowing US money laundering cases to be based on foreign bribery that is not an FCPA violation, they greatly expand the scope of corrupt activities that can serve as predicate offences under the US money laundering laws.

These laws, especially 18 U.S.C. § 1956(a)(2) (monetary transfers to promote a specified unlawful activity) have played a central role in recent FCPA prosecutions. The largest FCPA case brought to date, *Giffen*, concerned the prosecution of the Swiss lawyer Hans Bodmer. The more recent prosecution of other alleged co-conspirators of Mr. Bodmer, have relied on this provision.[98]

With respect to jurisdiction, Section 1956 takes essentially a property- or activity-based, rather than a person-based, focus, defining 'financial transaction' (a term used in both subsections (a)(1) and (a)(3), as transactions involving US interstate or foreign commerce,[99] while subsection (a)(2) focuses on the import or export of funds or monetary instruments to or from the United States, essentially using a territorial jurisdiction test.[100] In contrast, the provisions of Section 1957 appear to permit the assertion of nationality jurisdiction as to US persons, similar to the FCPA as amended in 1998.[101] As to foreign persons, the PATRIOT Act has

[95] 18 U.S.C. § 1956 (c)(7)(D). [96] 18 U.S.C. § 1956 (c)(7)(B).
[97] § 315 Patriot Act 2001. [98] See III.4.1. above. [99] 18 U.S.C. § 1956 (c)(4).
[100] It should also be noted that 'crimes against a foreign nation' elucidated in 18 U.S.C. § 1956 (c)(7)(b) requires that the crime occur in whole or in part in the United States: cf. 18 U.S.C. § 1956 (c)(4).
[101] 18 U.S.C. § 1956 (d) requires that the monetary transaction take place either in the United States or outside the United States but involving a US person.

broadened the jurisdictional scope of these US laws. Section 317 of that Act gives federal district courts jurisdiction over properly served foreign persons not only where they commit an offence involving a financial transaction that occurs in whole or in part in the United States, but also where the foreign person 'converts, to his or her own use, property in which the United States has an ownership interest by virtue of the entry of an order of forfeiture by a court of the United States', and where the foreign person is a financial institution that maintains an account at a financial institution in the United States. The *Bodmer* case held that a cause of action based on an alleged conspiracy to violate section 1956(a)(2) based on the predicate offence of corruption could go forward, even though the alleged corrupt practices were entirely extraterritorial, and even though the FCPA conspiracy count was dismissed on jurisdictional grounds.

4.5. Other factors affecting the level of US enforcement

The upsurge in US enforcement of the FCPA and related laws since the adoption of the OECD Convention cannot fairly be subscribed to the Convention alone, or even to the emergence of international standards. Many of the FCPA cases in the last several years have arisen as the result of voluntary disclosures by companies, particularly issuers subject to both the anti-bribery provisions and the accounting provisions of the statute by virtue of having securities listed on a public exchange. Although the FCPA itself does not mandate disclosure of violations, US enforcement authorities have made it clear in recent years that they view disclosure as part of corporate responsibility. Moreover, the Sarbanes-Oxley legislation in the United States,[102] and the corporate accounting scandals that gave birth to it, have had a prophylactic effect on disclosures by issuers. Sarbanes-Oxley has required assessments of internal controls, and certifications by senior management with respect to the effectiveness of controls. Boards of directors of such companies, when confronted with an FCPA issue, may opt for disclosure for fear of being accused later of having improperly covered up problems in the company. The impact of these events on FCPA enforcement in the last several years cannot be overstated.

Whether the recent trend towards increased disclosure will continue is debatable. Because the benefits of disclosure in terms of reduced penalties are not guaranteed, there is increasing resistance to disclosure that is not

[102] Pub. L. No. 107–204, 116 Stat. 745 (2002).

legally required, but is merely thought to be a reflection of the enforcement agencies' view of corporate responsibility. Companies may choose not to disclose but nonetheless correct and remedy a problem to demonstrate corporate responsibility; or more cynical companies may simply choose not to disclose and hope that any risks will be eliminated through the passage of time.

In addition to voluntary disclosures, there are other reasons for increased enforcement that also have an impact on FCPA enforcement. These reasons stem from domestic law and the domestic environment, as well as the broader international landscape. Whistleblowing, for instance, a protected activity under the Sarbanes-Oxley legislation, may continue to bring potential violations to the fore.[103] An increase in civil litigation may also bring forward evidence that can be used to prosecute corrupt practices.[104] An increase by developing countries or other OECD countries in prosecution for violations of domestic anticorruption laws may also trigger cases.[105] An activist press and NGO community may engender cases. Referrals from international financial institutions such as the World Bank[106] have also produced cases.

Although the OECD Convention is thus only one of various factors that contributes to the level of US enforcement, it is an important one. Particularly if other WBG members engage in active enforcement themselves, and continue through the WGB to exchange information in the 'tour de table' and less formally through prosecutor contacts, the prospects for cross-referrals seem high. And, it must be remembered that just as the OECD countries are capital exporters, so many of them are financial centres as well. Being a financial centre means that money is constantly flowing in and out; active enforcement of AML laws as well as anticorruption laws in those jurisdictions should give rise to a stream of cases that will inevitably have international dimensions that could affect US enforcement. In this regard, too, the growing trend in the United States to bring cases involving non-US persons should be emphasised. Although some of these cases involve the affiliates of US companies, others

[103] See the more detailed discussion of whistleblowing in ch. on Article 8 above.

[104] For example, the reported investigation of *Lucent* with respect to its activities in Saudi Arabia (cf. *Lucent 8-K* filing, August 8, 2003) followed its having been sued in the United States by a former subcontractor, and the investigations against *DaimlerChrysler* may have arisen from a wrongful termination suit brought by a whistleblower. Cf. 'Daimler Fires Workers Following Its Bribery Probe', *Wall Street Journal*, March 7, 2006, A3.

[105] For example, the *Halliburton* case began as a French investigation of a co-party to its consortium, and has since spread to several jurisdictions. See note 84.

[106] See IV.2. below.

involve foreign persons taking advantage of US capital markets or facilities.[107]

IV. Other initiatives to combat transnational bribery – beyond the OECD Convention

1. Other anti-corruption initiatives of the OECD

So far we have focused on the OECD Convention's role compared to other international anti-corruption Conventions and on the OECD Convention's impact on prosecutions under the FCPA. Because the OECD Convention's approach is criminalisation, we have focused primarily on criminal prosecutions. Criminalisation serves, or is intended to serve, a deterrent function. But it is not the only approach to reducing bribery in international business. Preventive measures, regulatory approaches, targeted programmatic and sectoral measures, and others may also be relevant. This section describes the complementary work of the OECD in eliminating tax deductibility of bribe payments and in combating corruption in government-supported export financing.

1.1. Eliminating tax deductibility

Permitting bribes to be tax-deductible creates a clear corporate incentive to make improper payments. For that reason, the OECD targeted the elimination of tax deductibility early on. The 1996 OECD Council Recommendation on the Tax Deductibility of Bribes to Foreign Public Officials, an initiative of the OECD whose adoption paralleled the Anti-bribery Convention,[108] has had significant success in causing OECD Member States to eliminate tax deductibility. At the time the Recommendation was adopted, an astonishing number of OECD Member States permitted deductibility.[109] But in the years since, it has been effectively eliminated in those countries.[110]

[107] Compare the *DPC* and *Syncor* cases, cited at note 52 with the *ABB* case, note 90.

[108] OECD 1996.

[109] Not all countries eliminated deductibility in response to the OECD Recommendation (OECD 1996). The United States's action in this regard preceded its enactment of the FCPA by a number of years. See III.2.1. above.

[110] Examples of countries that allowed tax deductibility at the time of the 1996 Recommendation (OECD 1996): Australia, Austria, Belgium, Denmark, France, Germany, Luxembourg, Netherlands, New Zealand, Norway, Netherlands, Sweden, Switzerland, United Kingdom. Cf. OECD update (OECD 2002).

1.2. Combating corruption in government-supported export financing

Governments support international business transactions through official export credit and credit guarantee programmes. These programmes provide financing in the form of loans, loan guarantees, and insurance, among others. The OECD, building on its work on tax deductibility and criminalisation, has endeavoured to ensure that anti-corruption standards are applied by OECD member states in such financing activities by officially supported export credit agencies. This work has been done through the OECD Working Party on Export Credits and Credit Guarantees, which began work in 1998. Towards the end of the year 2000, the Working Party agreed on an 'Action Statement on Bribery and Officially Supported Export Credits'.[111] This Action Statement called on OECD Member States to take appropriate measures to deter bribery in transactions where export credit support is granted.

The Action Statement requires as follows: that all applicants for official export credit support be informed of the consequences of bribery in international business transactions; that applicants be invited to submit a declaration that neither they, nor anyone acting on their behalf, have been engaged in bribery in the transaction; that credit support be denied, if there is sufficient evidence that bribery was involved in the award of the contract; and if bribery is proven after credit is given, that appropriate action be taken, such as denial of payment, refund of sums and/or referral of evidence of bribery to appropriate national authorities.

The Working Party periodically surveys the practice of the State Parties to determine what steps are being taken by its official agencies in furtherance of the Action Statement. These surveys indicate that most OECD countries have implemented the action statement, although the number of reported enforcement cases is limited.[112]

Since adoption of the Action Statement, further efforts have been underway to enhance its effectiveness. In September 2005, the United States put forward a proposal to enhance the Action Statement. Among other things, this proposal calls for the applicant or exporter to provide a declaration/undertaking that appropriate due diligence was exercised in selecting persons acting on their behalf in connection with the transaction, and possibly also to disclose the identity of persons acting on their behalf in connection with the transaction as well as commissions and fees paid in connection with the transaction. It also calls on the applicant or exporter

[111] OECD 2003b. [112] OECD 2005b.

to disclose any debarment of it or its affiliates by the World Bank or other international financial institution, as well as any national enforcement actions against it or its affiliates, within the last seven years, and for enhanced due diligence by the export credit agency if such enforcement actions by international financial institutions or national agencies have occurred. Finally, it requires export credit agencies to report any evidence of bribery in the transaction to national authorities, as well as to take action, depending on the timing of the discovery, either to prevent or cancel its support of the transaction, and to take other corrective and remedial action.[113]

This action came in the wake of resistance by some companies to the efforts of national export credit agencies to adopt stronger rules. A 2004 initiative in the United Kingdom that would have required disclosure of agents' identities, for example, met with significant resistance from a number of companies and was watered down as a consequence.[114] Deliberations by the Working Party on steps to enhance the Action Statement are scheduled to continue in 2006.

What is the importance of strong action in the area of official export credits? While export credit agencies may or may not finance the activities of a large number of companies (the U.S. Eximbank, for instance, has been criticised for concentrating its financing on a limited number of beneficiaries), the standards set by these government bodies are significant for several reasons. First, they help prevent the use of public monies for improper purposes. Second, export credit agencies' policies and standards are likely to have a multiplier effect on the policies and standards of other financing institutions. Co-financing in transactions or projects, and simply the perception of a best practices standard, are both likely to influence the behavior of other institutions.

2. The role of the international financial institutions in enforcement

While progress in the export credit agency arena is halting, there have been significant developments in the anti-corruption programmes of international financial institutions such as the World Bank. These institutions play a potentially key role in preventing and sanctioning corrupt practices in projects they finance. These actions can have an effect extending

[113] Proposal from the United States to Enhance the Action Statement, September 2, 2005 (available at: http://www.eca-watch.org).

[114] Cf. 'Firms Can Keep Secret Agents, The Guardian, 25 January 2005 (available at: http://www.guardian.co.uk). See also the discussion in ch. on Article 5 above.

substantially beyond the monetary amount of their financing, because of the central role they play in development projects.

After many years of ignoring corruption in their projects, international financial institutions have recently taken new initiatives to avoid financing corrupt activity. The OECD Convention and the emergence of international standards more generally have provided an important impetus for these initiatives. If enforced and supported by various civil service reform efforts encouraged by the banks in borrower countries, these international financial institution anti-corruption efforts may have a substantial long-term impact on corruption on both the supply and demand sides in the developing and developed world.

Within the World Bank Group, the International Development Association (IDA) and the International Bank for Reconstruction and Development (IBRD) have issued revised guidelines for procurement under IBRD loans and IDA credits and for the use of consultants by borrowers that included anti-corruption provisions.[115]

The procurement guidelines delineate immediate and specific consequences for violations. Upon discovery of fraudulent or corrupt conduct by a bidder or, once financing has been granted, by a borrower, the guidelines state that the Bank will reject the bidder's proposals for awards, cancel the remaining portions of loans already granted to the borrower, and debar the borrower from future World Bank financing, either for a specified time period or indefinitely. To help Bank officials in policing possible corrupt activities, the guidelines give the Bank the right to inspect the books and records of any suppliers and contractors involved in the performance of a bank-financed contract, and to submit the records to outside auditors appointed by the Bank. Similar requirements are created by the consultant guidelines, which include provisions for cancelling financing to borrowers if it is determined that their consultants engaged in corrupt or fraudulent behaviour.

The International Finance Corporation and other international financial institutions involved in project lending have also adopted, or are adopting in this area, new rules and contractual standards to enforce these rules. And in early 2004, the Bank determined to require that bidders on Bank-financed projects certify that they have a compliance programme in place.

As noted in the introduction to this chapter, these rules are being enforced, even as the World Bank is subject to continuing criticism about not doing enough to stem corruption in donee countries. To date,

[115] §§ 1.14, 1.15 World Bank 2004b; §§ 1.22, 1.23 World Bank 2004a.

hundreds of firms and individuals have been sanctioned, including major multinational companies. These sanctions are made public on the Bank's website.[116] The Asian Development Bank recently reported that it had sanctioned forty companies in 2005.[117] To the extent investments involve international financial institution financing or funding, the risks of running afoul of the international financial institution's new anti-corruption standards must be taken into account.

The World Bank and other international financial institutions have recently agreed to increase coordination of their anti-corruption programmes.[118] The World Bank has also been conducting a pilot voluntary disclosure programme in an effort to better leverage its enforcement resources. Disclosures made through this programme will not lead to referrals of the disclosing company to the host government for prosecution.[119] However, information that the Bank obtains through means other than a protected disclosure may result in such referrals. Moreover, the voluntarily disclosed information may lead to the prosecution of other corrupt actions, on both the supply and the demand sides.

To date, the World Bank has made at least two criminal referrals to US authorities which resulted in prosecutions and guilty pleas. Both involved Bank personnel based in the United States involved in questionable activities.[120]

Whether through the imposition of sanctions including debarment, requiring compliance programmes, or referrals to national prosecuting authorities, the international financial institutions stand in a position to significantly affect the activities of enterprises that participate in projects financed by these institutions. Unlike the OECD, they may also have

[116] Cf., for example, List of Debarred Firms: Fraud and Corruption (available on: http://web.worldbank.org/website/external/projects/procurement/debarred.html).

[117] 'ADB Bars 40 Firms, 33 People due to Corruption in 2005', release dated February 14, 2006 (available at: http://www.adb.org/media).

[118] Cf. News and Broadcast, Multilateral Development Banks Agree on a Common Approach to Fight Corruption, World Bank News Release No. 2006/275/S, February 18, 2006 (available at: http://www.worldbank.org).

[119] Cf. http://www.worldbank.org > click on 'About us' > Organization > Organizational Units > Department of Institutional Integrity > Proactive tools.

[120] *U.S.* v. *Sengupta* (Cr. No. 02-40) D.D.C., January 2002; Africa News (February 6, 2004); and *U.S.* v. *Basu* (Cr. No. 02-475) D.D.C., November 2002. Mr. Sengupta allegedly entered into an agreement to cause World Bank-funded business to be awarded to a Swedish consultant in return for a kickback. He also allegedly received a related request for money from a Kenyan official, which he relayed to the Swedish consultant, which paid the Kenyan official. Mr. Basu admitted to facilitating the payment of a \$50 000 bribe to a Kenyan government official via an American and a Swedish consultant. Both were charged with conspiracy to commit wire fraud and violation of the FCPA's anti-bribery prohibitions.

a material impact on the demand side, including both prevention and increasing the likelihood of prosecution.

3. The role of corporate preventive measures, including internal compliance programmes

Another important area in combating bribery in international business transactions is the area of preventive measures. This area is addressed by an array of non-governmental initiatives, along with governmental initiatives and treaty provisions.

3.1. Compliance programme initiatives

While the threat of criminal prosecution and other sanctions may serve as an important deterrent to corrupt practices, such prosecution will never be able to reach all of the activities it may aspire to control. Internal compliance efforts are critical to bridging this gap.

A number of initiatives encourage companies to adopt internal compliance programmes – in effect, to police themselves, by voluntarily developing policies, procedures, and other control mechanisms to prevent, detect and punish corrupt practices. These programmes go beyond internal accounting controls.[121]

On the private sector side, such compliance initiatives can be found in the Rules of Conduct and Recommendations of the International Chamber of Commerce,[122] the Partnering Against Corruption Initiative of the World Economic Forum, Transparency International, the Basel Institute on Governance, and a task force of companies,[123] and the Business Principles for Countering Bribery of Transparency International and Social Accountability International.[124]

These initiatives are roughly parallel in calling for companies to develop anti-corruption programmes that deal with the following risk areas:

- third party relationships;
- political contributions;
- charitable contributions and sponsorships;
- facilitation payments; and
- gifts hospitality and expenses.

[121] For more details see ch. on Article 8 above.
[122] Combating Extortion and Bribery: ICC 2005.
[123] Cf. http://www.weforum.org. [124] TI and SAI 2002.

In addition, an increasing number of international financial institutions and export credit agencies require that companies have a programme as a condition to doing business with the entity.[125] Among international conventions, the UN Convention calls for countries to encourage companies to establish compliance programmes.[126]

Such initiatives are wholly complementary to the OECD Convention.

3.2. Industry-specific initiatives

Recent years have seen the emergence of a number of industry-specific anticorruption initiatives, which attempt to address particular sectoral risks. For instance, 'Publish What You Pay', a coalition of NGOs, was founded around 2002 to press oil, gas, and mining companies to disclose all payments to host governments in consideration for the right to extract natural resources.[127] A complementary initiative of the UK government and others in 2003 founded the Extractive Industries Transparency Initiative, which is designed to secure the commitment of the host governments where such resources are located to make publicly available and subject to audit information about their revenues from resources companies.[128]

4. Preventive measures in the public sector

Preventive measures in the public sector also play a role in preventing bribery, particularly on the demand side. Although the OECD Convention does not address preventive measures, all of the other anticorruption conventions or their affiliated bodies do.[129] The provisions run from mandatory to hortatory and aspirational. Some of the most frequently used tools are financial declarations for public officials, the establishment of anticorruption watchdog bodies, civil service reforms, including whistleblower protection mechanisms and codes of conduct, procurement reforms, and others.[130] These are important to controlling the demand side of the corruption problem.

[125] OECD 2005b. [126] Art. **12**(2)(b) UN 2003.
[127] Cf. http://www.publishwhatyoupay.org. [128] Cf. http://www.eitransparency.org.
[129] For the Council of Europe, this activity is promoted by its monitoring body, GRECO. Cf. COE 1998 (announcing adoption of Resolution (98) 7 creating the GRECO). GRECO was activated in the summer of 1999; at the end of 2005, it had forty members, plus observers from the EU and several other international organisations.
[130] Cf., for example, ch. 2, Arts. 5–14 UN 2003; Art. III OAS 1996.

5. Private sector bribery

Finally, a variety of initiatives seek to apply the same standards to companies' dealings with other private bodies as apply to their dealings with public officials. In some cases, the impetus to do so has stemmed from the consequences of privatisation programmes which have moved assets from public to private ownership but without changing standards of conduct. In other cases, the impetus appears to stem from a view that corrupt practices are harmful regardless of the context in which they occur. At the convention level, the Council of Europe Criminal Law Convention, the African Union Convention, and the UN Convention contemplate criminalisation of private sector bribery.[131] Private sector initiatives such as those described in Section 3.1. tend to cover both the public and private sector activities of companies on an undifferentiated basis. And many companies' internal programmes apply to both. Having said that, there should be little doubt that public sector corruption has a broader set of harmful effects than private sector corruption; for that reason, the OECD Convention focuses on official corruption. However, it is unlikely an expanded focus on private as well as public sector bribery will dilute the effectiveness of instruments focused on public sector bribery. The two are complementary.

V. The outlook for the OECD Convention and other initiatives – issues for the next decade

1. A need for greater harmonisation?

With the proliferation of enforcement actors and standards of conduct, the harmonisation of standards of conduct becomes increasingly important. That this is an issue at all is testament to the success of the last decade in the establishment of international standards, a point that should not be overlooked. But the mere establishment of standards is no longer the challenge – the challenge is effectiveness. In that regard, the harmonisation question arises on two levels – within the OECD Convention membership, and as between the OECD Convention and other international instruments.

The OECD Convention and other conventions, while promoting harmony on a general level (e.g. by requiring the adoption of transnational

[131] Arts. 7, 8 COE 1999a (mandatory for active and passive actions); Art. 4(e) African Union 2003; Art. 21 UN 2003.

bribery statutes), have also promoted proliferation of standards and disharmony by leaving many questions to national implementation through its core concept of 'functional equivalence'. The application of this concept in specific contexts of the Convention is amply illustrated in previous chapters, but particularly in the discussions of standards of corporate criminal liability, sanctions, and jurisdiction.[132] Divergence can also be seen in the implementation of the basic offence specified in Article 1, for example with respect to the issue of facilitating payments.[133]

At the international level, these differences are compounded. While the OECD Convention, for example, takes an autonomous approach to the definition of a 'foreign official', other Conventions, such as the Council of Europe Criminal Law Convention, do not.[134] Transnational bribery offences show other significant scope differences as well.[135]

Such differences complicate both enforcement challenges and the compliance challenges faced by multinational companies. Neither one is desirable. On the enforcement side, such differences can create additional barriers to international cooperation and delay or frustrate enforcement efforts. On the compliance side, some of the challenges may be addressed by a company's adopting the most stringent national standard as its internal compliance standard. However, internal compliance standards only provide a part of the answer. They do not obviate the need for a company doing business in a particular country to know the law. When there is a proliferation of laws, compliance costs go up significantly since those differences must be investigated and reconciled. Moreover, it is often difficult, especially when dealing with new laws whose enforcement history may be limited, to gain a clear understanding of their scope and application. Accordingly, the OECD WGB and other bodies need to be attentive to the possible need for greater harmonisation of national and international standards in the next decade.

2. The risk of multiple parallel proceedings[136]

Inevitably the proliferation of Conventions and the expansion of enforcement will lead to multiple proceedings. Where transnational bribery is concerned, there are by definition at least two jurisdictions with likely competence to prosecute a bribery case – the home country of the supply-side party and the

[132] See chs. on Articles 2, 3 and 4 above. [133] See III.2.2.2. above. [134] Art. 1(a) COE 1999a.
[135] Art. 7 COE 1999a (limited scope of *quid pro quo*).
[136] See the discussion in ch. on Articles 9–11 above.

home country of the demand side. The latter will typically have legislation that will permit it to prosecute parties on both sides of the transaction, while the former will likely only be focused on the supply side.[137]

Third countries will increasingly be involved in these proceedings as well. Their interest may arise from jurisdiction over other parties to the transaction-partners, for example co-venturers, agents, etc., from jurisdiction over activities occurring in their territory in connection with the transaction-funds transfers, for example, or, more rarely, from the implication of other state interests that are sufficient to create jurisdiction. The result may be multiple simultaneous prosecutions by different jurisdictions – the 'three-ring circus'.[138]

The OECD Convention addresses this possibility only in very general and non-outcome-prescriptive terms. The OECD Convention, in Article 4 (3), sets forth that '[w]hen more than one Party has jurisdiction over an alleged offence. . .the Parties involved shall, at the request of one of them, consult with a view to determining the most appropriate jurisdiction for prosecution'. Whether this solution will be sufficient as the incidence of multiple simultaneous proceedings grows, as predicted here, or not, remains to be seen. If not, some more definitive elaboration of the factors that may give primacy of enforcement jurisdiction and will govern the exercise of comity may become necessary. Factors that may be key will be the ability of one jurisdiction to develop an evidentiary record that would be helpful to the resolution of other cases.[139]

3. Revocation of contracts and concessions

The OECD Convention does not address the collateral consequences of corruption. This will, however, be an increasingly important topic in the

[137] There may be incidental demand-side implications, for example, if a corrupt official attempts to come to the United States, or to transfer funds or acquire assets in the United States that are the proceeds of crime.

[138] An example is the *Halliburton* case, discussed in III.4.1. above. Allegations relating to participants and persons involved in a consortium of multinational companies operating in the natural gas sector in Nigeria, which includes a subsidiary of Halliburton Corp., continue to be investigated by a French magistrate judge, the Nigerian legislature, Nigerian enforcement authorities, and US enforcement authorities. Cf., for example, 'UK lawyer named in bribery inquiry', The Guardian, February 6, 2005 (available at: http://www.guardian.co.uk); 'Halliburton Venture in Nigeria investigated by SEC (update 5)', June 11, 2004 (available at: http://www.quote.bloomberg.com); see on the absence of an international rule on 'double jeopardy' our chs. on Articles 3(3) and 9–11 above.

[139] Other proposals are made in our ch. on Articles 9–11 above.

coming years. The UN Convention, through Article 34, obliges states to take measures to address the consequences of corruption, including through the annulment or rescission of contracts, withdrawal of concessions, or other similar instruments that may have been tainted by corrupt practices. Although written in mandatory terms, the provisions direct states to give due regard to the rights of third parties acquired in good faith, as well as to fundamental principles of the host state's domestic law.[140]

Such actions will almost certainly provoke disputes between foreign investors and host governments under contracts or bilateral investment treaties. The latter make host governments directly responsible to foreign investors from treaty countries, typically giving them a right to seek damages through arbitration, for breaches of specified obligations owed to foreign investors. These obligations may include payment of compensation for expropriation, the obligation to accord national and most-favored-nation treatment to foreign investors, remittability of profits and capital, fair and equitable treatment, freedom from trade and investment-distorting performance requirements, and others depending on the specific treaty. Already, corruption issues have emerged as factors in a number of investment disputes to date, and this number can be expected to increase.[141]

4. The role of civil liability

Civil liability, another area that is beyond the scope of the OECD Convention, is also likely to be a major focus of activity in coming years. The Council of Europe Civil Law Convention Against Corruption is devoted entirely to this topic. The UN Convention Against Corruption also contains mandatory provisions in this regard.[142]

Civil suits can generate evidence that is useful to prosecutors. They can also serve as an adjunct to government enforcement. The risk of civil liability may act as a deterrent, especially if there is a significant risk of

[140] This Article is not limited by its terms to offenders, i.e. those convicted of violations of the offences prescribed by the UN Convention (UN 2003). The absence of such a limitation may enable this Article to be applied in a wider variety of situations than has traditionally been the case in enforcement actions, potentially even to third party investors. Thus, companies that do business abroad or at home through government contracts, concessions, licences, and permits (upon which substantial investments are often predicated) should be aware that this provision may prompt more widespread efforts by host countries to revoke acquired rights than has historically been the case.

[141] Cf., for example, *Empresas Lucchetti, S.A. and Lucchetti Peru, S.A.* v. *Republic of Peru*, 19 ICSID Review-Foreign Law Journal, No. **2** Issue (2005).

[142] Art. 35 UN 2003.

monetary damages. In the United States, several recent investigations or prosecutions have roots in civil litigation.[143]

Given its potentially global reach, the UN Convention is of particular interest in regard to its provisions on private rights of action. Article 35 of the UN Convention requires states to take such measures as may be necessary, in accordance with their domestic law principles, 'to ensure that entities or persons who have suffered damage as a result of an act of corruption have the right to initiate legal proceedings against those responsible for that damage in order to obtain compensation'. The mandatory language of this article appears to require states to establish private rights of action in civil proceedings for damages. Although corruption issues have represented increasingly fertile ground for private civil litigation in recent years, recognizing private rights of action from criminal anti-corruption statutes such as the FCPA[144] or based on other statutes would almost certainly expand the scope of such actions.

5. Barriers and challenges on the demand side

While supply side risks and corporate compliance responsibilities are growing, the importance of dealing with the demand side of corruption cannot be ignored. Most countries' domestic anticorruption laws apply to the demand side, and often have provisions that affect only the demand side of the equation. Transnational laws have historically focused on the supply side because of the jurisdictional and comity issues that would flow from prosecution foreign officials outside their host country. It should be noted, however, that the UN Convention permits but does not require countries to pass transnational bribery legislation focusing on the demand side.[145] Whether this authority is invoked by many countries will be interesting to see.

The UN Convention and other international instruments have not tackled the sensitive issues of official immunities in any significant way. But abuse of immunities is a significant barrier to prosecution in many countries.[146] Development of an instrument dealing with the abuse of

[143] See III.4.5. above.

[144] The FCPA has been traditionally held not to confer such rights. Cf. *Lamb* v. *Phillip Morris, Inc.*, 915 F.2d 1024 (6th Cir. 1990), *cert. denied* 111 S. Ct. 961 (1991); *J.S. Serv. Ctr.* v. *GE Tech. Servs. Co.*, 937 F. Supp. 216 (S.D.N.Y. 1996). US ratification of the UN Convention 2003 will not change the result in all likelihood.

[145] Art. 16(2) UN 2003.

[146] Cf. A. Barreto and J. Kessler, 'Latin Leaders' Escape Hatch', The Washington Post, May 23, 2004, B02.

immunities, although a challenging task, is likely to become necessary in the near future for anti-corruption efforts to reach their full potential.

Extortion is also a topic that bears further examination in this context. Although a defence to criminal responsibility in many national systems, the standard of proof is typically high and often not capable of being met unless a threat of physical harm is present. While this may arise in some contexts (e.g. extortion by a host country's military or police authorities), in most contexts it is economic extortion – demands by an official who controls a procurement or permitting process. What the scope should be for an extortion defence in the corruption context is a question that requires careful consideration. On the one hand, such a defence could swallow supply side measures if too broadly cast. On the other hand, where extortion or compulsion can be proven to be the precipitating cause of a bribe, there is a legitimate question whether such circumstances should affect the assessment of culpability. Put this way, extortion becomes a supply side issue that the international community needs to address.

VI. Conclusions

Combating corruption in international business transactions requires a multi-pronged strategy to change behavior both on the supply and the demand side of the problem. Criminalisation of transnational bribery, the strengthening of accounting and money laundering laws, accounting standards, and the development of an infrastructure for international cooperation, are important elements of this strategy. In this arena, the OECD Convention plays a key role, since it focuses on the activities of the capital-exporting countries whose companies account for a significant amount of international trade and investment flows.

For the OECD Convention to maintain its position as a premier instrument in the next decade will require demonstrable success in enforcement by WBG members in addition to the United States of their new transnational bribery statutes, attraction of key capital exporters not currently a party to the Convention, and broadening of the scope of the OECD Convention to deal with the full range of supply side issues.

Other anti-corruption conventions play an important role in combating transnational bribery as well, and their role can be expected to increase over time, particularly as the UN Convention garners additional adherents. Not only do these other Conventions contain complementary criminalisation measures on both the supply and demand side, and broaden the network of international cooperation provisions – a network which needs to be as universal as possible to avoid capital flowing to the most permissive jurisdiction – but they also address a number of other important issues that go beyond the scope of the OECD Convention. These include preventive measures in the public and private sectors, measures for private civil liability, contract revocation, and civil liability.

The OECD has done important complementary work in its initiative to eliminate the tax deductibility of bribes in its Member States; its ongoing work on export credits has the potential to be significant as well. It has spurred initiatives in international financial institutions, which play an important role in disciplining corruption in international development projects. Companies are increasingly being pressed to strengthen their internal compliance programmes.

That all this has happened in a relatively short time is impressive. Much remains to be done, however. The proliferation of Conventions has left a cluttered landscape, characterised by the possibility of multiple and not entirely consistent obligations. Harmonisation has become necessary as a result. The political will to oversee enforcement, as evidenced by the difficulties the WGB has had with funding at times, can be variable. Enforcement, a key tool if a system is to be credible, is difficult. However, while enforcement in many countries remains weak, where it does occur, it often leaves multinational companies facing multiple proceedings in different jurisdictions.

Rationalising and prioritising an allocation of authority among authorities in a multiple proceedings context, addressing extortion and the abuse of official immunities, aiming for greater harmonisation instead of a common floor, and ensuring that as the collateral consequences of corrupt practices grow, innocent parties are not penalised, are all goals that should be pursued in the name of improvement of the systems that have evolved in recent years.

ANNEX A

Table of applicable sanctions in the twenty-one PARTIES reviewed in the mid-term study

	Prison (maximum penalty)	Fines for natural persons (NPs) and legal persons (LPs)[*], [**] (maximum penalty)	Other Sanctions upon Criminal Conviction[***]	Confiscation	Sanctions for other economic crimes
Australia	2 years (summary)	**NPs**: AUD 13 200 on summary offence (EUR 8137); AUD 66 000 on indictment (EUR 40 684)	– Disqualification from managing corporations	Bribe and proceeds. Possible if in possession of non bona fide third parties.	Cartel offences: maximum penalty of AUD 10 million (EUR 6 164 278) for LPs
	10 years (indictment)	**LPs**: AUD 330 000 (EUR 203 421)	– Suspension of financial services licence	Monetary equivalent possible	
Belgium	1 to 15 years (depending on rank of foreign public official)	**NPs:** EUR 55 000 to EUR 1.1 million	– Loss of rights (to hold a public function, act as estate administrator, etc.)	Mandatory for bribe	Not addressed in Phase 2 Report
		LPs: EUR 10 million	– Disqualification from public procurement	Discretionary for proceeds Monetary equivalent possible	

Continued

	Prison (maximum penalty)	Fines for natural persons (NPs) and legal persons (LPs)*, ** (maximum penalty)	Other Sanctions upon Criminal Conviction***	Confiscation	Sanctions for other economic crimes
Bulgaria[1]	3 years	**NPs:** BGN 5000 (EUR 2554) (introduced after Ph.1) **LPs:** EUR 500 000	– Disqualification from public procurement (2004 Law on Public Procurement)	Bribe and proceeds Not for legal persons Possible if in possession of non bona fide third parties	Not addressed in Phase 2 Report
Canada	5 years	No upper limit	Not directly on foreign bribery offence conviction	Bribe and proceeds	Not addressed in Phase 2 Report
Finland	4 months to 4 years	**NPs:** 120 day/fines (1/60th personal income) **LPs:** EUR 850 000	Not directly on foreign bribery offence conviction	Bribe and proceeds Possible if in possession of non bona fide third parties No monetary sanctions of comparable effect	Comparable
France	10 years	**NPs:** EUR 150 000	– Deprivation of civic and civil rights (NPs)	Bribe and proceeds	Not addressed in Phase 2 Report

		LPs: EUR 750 000	– Professional restrictions (NPs and LPs) – Closure of establishment (LPs) – Exclusion from PP (LPs) – Ban on public appeals for funds (LPs) – Ban on use of checks and/or credit cards (LPs)		
Germany	2 to 10 years, depending on seriousness of the offence (or fine)	**NPs:** 360 daily rates (1 daily rate = EUR 1 to 5000)(or prison) **LPs:** EUR 1 million, or higher if the economic profit of the offender exceeds 1 million.	Exclusion from public contracts (for LPs) – Project to create a federal corruption register	Bribes and proceeds only if person receiving in Germany	Comparable
Greece	5 years	**NPs:** available (no indication of amount) **LPs:** up to 3 times the value of the benefit	Exclusion from PP and privatisation	Proceeds Unclear whether "undue advantage" may be confiscated	Not addressed in Phase 2 Report

Continued

	Prison (maximum penalty)	Fines for natural persons (NPs) and legal persons (LPs)*, ** (maximum penalty)	Other Sanctions upon Criminal Conviction***	Confiscation	Sanctions for other economic crimes
Hungary	5 years	**NPs:** HUF 10 million (EUR 39 700) (not applicable if confiscation) **LPs:** up to 3 times the value of the advantage gained or intended to be gained	Only for LPs: – Winding-up – Limitation of activity, incl. exclusion from PP, concession contracts, public funding (but not export credit, ODA, privatisation)	Bribe and proceeds Mandatory Possible if in possession of non bona fide third parties	Not addressed in Phase 2 Report
Iceland	3 years	**NPs:** ISK 4 million (EUR 53 195) **LPs:** no upper limit	Not directly on foreign bribery offence conviction	Bribe if still in possession of briber Proceeds	Not addressed in Phase 2 Report
Italy	5 years	Not for **NPs** **LPs:** between max. EUR 312 000 and max. EUR 1.248 million, depending on seriousness of the bribery	– Disqualification from public office or management positions (NPs and LPs) – Loss of capacity to enter into contracts with the public administration (LPs)	Obligatory for proceeds Discretionary for the bribe (for non EU officials)	Fines available for economic and financial offences

			– Suspension or revocation of authorisations and licenses (LPs) – Denial of facilitations, funding, subsidies (LPs) – Prohibition from conduct of business activities (LPs)		
Japan	3 years	**NPs:** JPY 3 million (EUR 21 495) **LPs:** JPY 300 million (EUR 2 149 488)	Not directly on foreign bribery offence conviction	Bribe (or monetary equivalent)[3] Not proceeds (too difficult to quantify)	Not addressed in Phase 2 Report
Korea[4]	5 years	**NPs:** KRW 20 million (EUR 16 966) or twice the amount of profit if profit > KRW 10 million (EUR 8 483) **LPs:** KRW 1 billion or twice the amount of profit if profit > KRW 500 million (EUR 424 147)	Not directly on foreign bribery offence conviction to date, but under consideration (disbarment from PP)	Mandatory if bribe if in possession of offender Discretionary for monetary equivalent Not proceeds	Not addressed in Phase 2 Report

Continued

	Prison (maximum penalty)	Fines for natural persons (NPs) and legal persons (LPs)*, ** (maximum penalty)	Other Sanctions upon Criminal Conviction***	Confiscation	Sanctions for other economic crimes
Luxembourg	10 years	**NPs:** EUR 187 500 **LPs:** no liability	Not directly on foreign bribery offence conviction	Bribe, if still in possession of offender Proceeds or monetary equivalent Mandatory for crimes[5]	Not addressed in Phase 2 Report
Mexico	2 to 14 years (concern of LEs over wide range)	1000 fine days (fine day = net daily wage for the NP and declared income for the LP)[6]	– Dismissal and disablement from holding a public job, post or commission (NPs) – Declared null and void (LPs)	Bribe and proceeds Mandatory Monetary equivalent in draft bill (following Ph1 Recs)	Comparable
Norway[7]	3 years (simple bribery) 10 years (aggravated)	No upper limit	– Loss of public office – Prohibition from exercising certain activities linked to the offence (no explicit exclusion from PP or other public subsidies)	Mandatory for "gains accrued from a criminal act" Discretionary for bribe Monetary equivalent possible	Not addressed in Phase 2 Report

Slovak Republic[8]	5 years (non-aggravated foreign bribery) 12 years (aggravated)	SKK 10 million (EUR 264 101) for both aggravated and non-aggravated	– Disqualification from public procurement	Mandatory for bribe and proceeds, but only if in possession of the offender Discretionary for property held by a non bona fide third party	Lower than for other economic offences (see footnote 116 of Phase 2 Report)
Sweden[9]	2 years (non-aggravated bribery) 6 years (aggravated) NB: Imprisonment or fine	**NPs:** SEK 150 000 (EUR 15 941 (non aggravated)) NB: Fine or imprisonment **LPs:** SEK 3 million (EUR 318 820)	Exclusion from public procurement	Bribe only in possession of briber Proceeds, only under certain circumstances[10]	Not addressed in Phase 2 Report
Switzerland[11]	5 years	None for **NPs**. **LPs:** CHF 5 million (EUR 3 208 810)	– Expulsion for foreigners (NPs) – Disqualification from a profession, industry or business (NPs) – Exclusion from public procurement, export credit support, ODA and others (NPs and LPs)	Bribe and proceeds Mandatory Assets that are proceeds from a foreign bribery offence may also be confiscated Monetary equivalent possible	Not addressed in Phase 2 Report
United Kingdom	6 months (summary 7 years (indictment)	GBP 5000 (EUR 7265) (summary) No upper limit (indictment)	– Disqualification of directors from certain functions (NPs) – Not directly on foreign bribery offence conviction for LPs	Bribe and proceeds (benefit derived from criminal conduct) Monetary equivalent possible	Not addressed in Phase 2 Report

Continued

	Prison (maximum penalty)	Fines for natural persons (NPs) and legal persons (LPs)*, ** (maximum penalty)	Other Sanctions upon Criminal Conviction***	Confiscation	Sanctions for other economic crimes
United States[12,13]	5 years (*Since corrected to 15 years*)	**NPs:** USD 100 000 (EUR 84 441) **LPs:** USD 2 million (EUR. 1 688 818) + twice gross gain sought (NPs and LPs) (Fines may not be paid by employer or principal for NPs)	– Civil penalties up to USD 10 000 (for NPs as well as LPs) – Debarment from US government contracting – Ineligibility for government benefits and/or suspension of export licensing for defence goods and services – Additional fine not to exceed the greater of (i) the gross amount of the pecuniary gain to the defendant as a result of the violation, or (ii) a specified dollar limitation, ranging from	Bribe Not proceeds[14]	15 years for domestic bribery (*foreign bribery offence brought to same level after Ph.2 in November 2002*)

USD 50 000 to USD 100 000 for a NP and 50 000 to 500 000 for any other person
– The Attorney-General or SEC, as appropriate, may bring a civil action to enjoin any act or practice of a firm whenever it appears that the firm (or an officer, director, employee, agent, or stockholder acting on behalf of the firm) is in violation (or about to be) of the anti-bribery provisions.

---

* Fines are indicated in the local currency, as well as in their euro equivalent, as of 31 December 2005.

** NPs = natural persons; LPs = legal persons.

*** This column shows civil and administrative penalties which may be pronounced by the courts upon sanctioning a foreign bribery offence. It does not include decisions to exclude natural or legal persons from publicly funded schemes, which may be taken independently by public agencies such as those involved in official export credit support, official development assistance, public procurement or privatisation.

[1] According to information provided in the Oral Follow-Up Report, there has been one foreign bribery conviction in a relatively minor case. No information was provided on the nature of sanctions pronounced by the court.

[2] The administrative liability of legal persons was introduced under Bulgarian law following the Phase 2 Recommendations, as indicated by Bulgaria in its Written Follow-Up Report.

[3] According to information provided by Japan after the Phase 2 Report, the monetary equivalent to the bribe can be confiscated under the Japanese Law for Punishment of Organized Crimes, Control of Crime Proceeds and Other Matters.

[4] A total of four cases have been investigated in Korea resulting in convictions for 7 natural persons and 2 legal persons.

[5] Foreign bribery is a crime under Luxembourg law, but bribery is often "downgraded" to a lesser offence for reasons of efficiency. For lesser offences, confiscation is only discretionary.

[6] These penalties were increased following recommendations made to Mexico in Phase 1 (previous maximum fines amounted to 500 times the minimum daily wage). Mexico's Oral Follow-Up report indicates that these monetary sanctions entered into force in August 2005 with the Decree amending the Federal Criminal Code.

[7] The Norwegian authorities indicate in their Oral Follow-Up Report that a number of courts have handed down severe sanctions, and cites as an example a court decision for a gross breach of trust offence (equivalent to the foreign bribery offence, but under the former legislation) where the natural person was sentenced to 6 years imprisonment and a fine of NOK 16 million (EUR 2 million).

[8] The sanctions indicated are as of 1 January 2006, when the new Penal Code came into force.

[9] One conviction in a case of bribery of a foreign public official, in the "World Bank" case: two natural persons have been sentenced by the first instance court to 18 months and one year imprisonment. Appeals are underway: the prosecution has appealed the dismissal of certain charges, and the defendants have cross-appealed their convictions.

A number of proceedings concerning possible instances of foreign bribery were also underway at the time of the Phase 2 Review.

[10] It would appear that the rules on forfeiture would be applicable in cases where there is a direct link between the active corruption and the profit, and where, consequently, the perpetrator could commit a crime also when he receives or handles the profit.

[11] In the one Swiss foreign bribery trial (petty bribery of an Italian customs officials for a passport stamp), the sentence was a 30-day suspended prison term + expulsion from Switzerland for three years.

[12] Statistics from 1977 to 2001 indicate that fines imposed on natural persons have ranged from USD 2500 to 309 000 (EUR 2021 to 250 000), and only four prison sentences ranging from four to 84 months.

[13] Further information provided in the Phase 2 Oral and Written Follow-up Report indicates that 12 cases have been prosecuted under the FCPA since the Phase 2 Report. Statistics on the amount of fines imposed were only provided in aggregate form for the totality of the cases, with no breakdown for each case or individual sanctioned.

[14] The US contends that the possibility to impose a fine equivalent to twice the gain amounts to confiscation. The Working Group did not fully accept this approach.

CONSOLIDATED BIBLIOGRAPHY

Books and Articles

Abbell, M. (2004), *Obtaining Evidence Abroad in Criminal Cases*, New York.

Acquaviva, G. (2003), 'Il Foreign Corrupt Practices Act statunitense e il dilemma della lotta alla corruzione internazionale: azione unilaterale o cooperazione multilaterale?' in G. Sacerdoti (ed.), *Responsabilità d'impresa e strumenti internazionali anticorruzione*, Milano, 167.

Aiolfi, G. and Z. Ledergerber (2005), 'Glossary of International Anti-Corruption Standards with Examples of National Legal Practice' (paper prepared for the 6th General Meeting *Anti-Corruption Network for Transitional Economies* in Instanbul, 30–31 May 2005, available at: http://www.anticorruptionnet.org).

Aiolfi, G. and M. Pieth (2002), 'How to Make a Convention Work: The Organisation for Economic Co-operation and Development Recommendation and Convention on Bribery as an Example of a New Horizon in International Law' in C. Fijnaut and L. Huberts (eds.), *Corruption, Integrity and Law Enforcement*, Leiden, Boston, 349.

Aiolfi, G. and M. Pieth (2005), 'International Aspects of Corporate Liability and Corruption' in S. Tully (ed.), *Research Handbook on Corporate Legal Responsibility*, Cheltenham (UK), Northhampton (USA), 689.

Arlen, J. and R. Kraakman (1997), 'Controlling Corporate Misconduct: An Analysis of Corporate Liability Regimes', *New York University Law Review* **72**, 687.

Arnull, A. M., A. A. Dashwood, M. G. Ross and D. A. Wyatt (2000), *Wyatt and Dashwood's European Union Law*, 4th edn, London.

Arsava, A. F. (1999), 'Zypernkonflikt unter Berücksichtigung des Völkerrechts' in Bundesministerium für Landesverteidigung (Hrsg.), *Jahrbuch für internationale Sicherheitspolitik* 1999, Wien (also available at: http://www.bmlv.gv.at > Publikationen > wissenschaftliche Publikationen > Autoren).

Arzt, G. (1990), 'Erfolgsdelikt und Tätigkeitsdelikt', *Schweizerische Zeitschrift für Strafrecht* **107**, 168.

Ashworth, A. (2002), 'Sentencing' in M. Maguire, R. Morgan and R. Reiner (eds.), *The Oxford Handbook of Criminology*, 3rd edn, Oxford, 1076.

Aust, A. (2000), *The Modern Treaty Law and Practice*, Cambridge.

Baker, E. (2004), 'Guilty Pleas, Diversion and Consensual Disposition: England and Wales' in A. Eser and C. Rabenstein (Hrsg.), *Strafjustiz im Spannungsfeld von Effizienz und Fairness*, Berlin, 381.

Balmelli, M. (1996), *Die Bestechungstatbestände des schweizerischen Strafgesetzbuches*, Bern.

Bassiouni, M. Ch. (1974), *International Extradition and World Public Order*, Leiden.

Beccaria, M. C. (1988), *Über Verbrechen und Strafe*n (nach der Ausgabe von 1766 übersetzt und herausgegeben von W. Alff), Frankfurt a. M.

Beck, U. (1998), *Was ist Globalisierung?*, Frankfurt a. M.

Bell, R. E. (2001), 'Discretion and Decision Making in Money Laundering Prosecutions', *Journal of Money Laundering Control*, Vol. **5**, No. 1, 42.

Bernasconi, P. (1995), 'New Criminal Law Provisions Against the Corruption of Public Officials', Multidisciplinary Group on Corruption (GMC), Council of Europe, 5.

Bernasconi, P. (ed.) (2000), *Responding to Corruption: Social Defence, Corruption, and the Protection of Public Administration and the Independence of Justice* (updated documents of the XIIIth International Congress on Social Defence, Lecce, Italy 1996), Naples.

Bertossa, C. A. (2003), *Unternehmensstrafrecht - Strafprozess und Sanktionen*, Bern.

Bertossa, B. L. (2004), 'Mechanisms for Gathering Evidence Abroad' in Asian Development Bank (ed.), *Controlling Corruption in Asia and the Pacific* (key papers by speakers at the 4th Regional Conference of the ADB/OECD Anti-Corruption Initiative for Asia and the Pacific in Kuala Lumpur, 3–5 December 2003, online edn available at: http:/www.adb.org/ > Publications > Controlling Corruption > Chapter 7).

Bill, A. (2004), *Audit Committee Guide: A Source of Information for Audit Committees of Public Company Boards of Directors*, 2nd edn, New York.

Bindschedler, R. L. (1996), 'International Organisations, General Aspects' in R. Bernhardt (ed.), *Encyclopedia of Public International Law*, Vol. **2**, Amsterdam, 1289.

Black, J. (2001), 'Decentring Regulation: Understanding the Role of Regulation and Self-Regulation in a "Post-Regulatory" World', *Current Legal Problems* **54**, 4.

Blakesley, Ch. L. (1992), *Terrorism, Drugs, International Law, and the Protection of Human Liberty: A Comparative Study of International Law, its Nature, Role, and Impact in Matters of Terrorism, Drug Trafficking, War, and Extradition*, New York.

Blakesley, Ch. L. (1999), 'Extra-Territorial Jurisdiction' in M. Ch. Bassiouni, *International Criminal Law*, 2nd edn, New York, 33.

Bliss, J. C. and G. J. Spak (1989), 'The Foreign Corrupt Practices Act of 1988: Clarification or Evisceration?', *Law & Policy in International Business* **20**, 441.

Blokker, N. and S. Muller (1994), 'Towards More Effective Supervision by International Organizations: Some Concluding Observations' in N. Blokker and S. Muller (eds.), *Towards More Effective Supervision by International Organizations. Essays in Honour of Henry G. Schermers*, Vol. **1**, Dordrecht.

Boch, C. (2000), *EC Law in the UK*, London.

Bonvin, J. and C. Morrisson (1998), *L' organisation de coopération et de développement économiques (OCDE)*, Paris.

Brown, H. L. (1999), 'Parent-Subsidiary Liability under the Foreign Corrupt Practices Act' in American Bar Association (ed.), *The Foreign Corrupt Practices Act: How to Comply under the New Amendments and the OECD Convention*, Chicago, F 1–51.

Brownlie, I. (2003), *Principles of Public International Law*, 6th edn, Oxford.

Brütsch, C. and D. Lehmkuhl (2005), *Hard, Soft and Private Legalities: The Increase, Variation and Differentiation of Law-Like Arrangements in International Relations* (unpublished manuscript).

Cadwalader, Wickersham and Taft (2005), FCPA Newsletter, March, June and July edns (available at: www.cadwalader.com).

Cartier-Bresson, J. (2000), 'The Causes and Consequences of Corruption: Economic Analyses and Lessons Learnt' in OECD (ed.), *No Longer Business as Usual*, Paris, 11.

Cassani, U. (1996), 'Die Anwendung des schweizerischen Strafrechts auf internationale Wirtschaftsdelikte (Art. 3–7 StGB)', *Schweizerische Zeitschrift für Strafrecht* **114**, 237.

Chavranski, H. (1997), *L'OCDE au coeur des grands débats économiques*, Paris.

Chiavario, M. (2002), 'Private Parties: the Rights of the Defendant and the Victim' in M. Delmas-Marty and J. R. Spencer (eds.), *European Criminal Procedures*, Cambridge, 541.

Chilton, B. (2005), 'Supreme Court strikes down Federal Sentencing Guidelines' in *Compliance Week: Columns and Editorials*, January 2005 (available at: http://www.complianceweek.com).

Clough, J. (2002), 'Sentencing the Corporate Offender: The Neglected Dimension of Corporate Criminal Liability' in J. Clough and C. Mulhern (eds.), *The Prosecution of Corporations*, Melbourne.

Cockcroft, L. (1999), *Implementation of the OECD Convention: The Conditions for Success* (available at: http://www.transparency.org.uk > Papers by TI (UK) Members).

Coeurdray, M. (2003), *Du dévoilement médiatique de la 'corruption' à la gestion déontologique des affaires* (dissertation/thesis), Paris.

Coffee, J. C. (1981), 'No Soul To Damn: No Body To Kick: An Unscandalised Inquiry into the Problem of Corporate Punishment', *Michigan Law Review* **79**, 386.

Coffee, J. C. (1999), 'Corporate Criminal Liability: An Introduction and Comparative Survey' in A. Eser, G. Heine and B. Huber (eds.), *Criminal Responsibility of Legal and Collective Entities*, Freiburg i. Br., 9.

Cohen, M. A. (1996), 'Theories of Punishment and Empirical Trends in Corporate Criminal Sanctions', *Managerial and Decision Economics* **17**, 399.

Cole, G. F. (1995), *The American System of Criminal Justice*, 7th edn, Belmont.

Conseil de l'Europe (1990), *Affaires juridiques, compétences extraterritoriales en matière pénale*, Strasbourg.

Corr, C. F. and J. Lawler (1999), 'Damned If You Do, Damned If You Don't? The OECD Convention and the Globalization of Anti-Bribery Measures', *Vanderbilt Journal of Transnational Law* **32**, 1252.

Courtney, C. (2002), 'Corruption in the Official Arms Trade' in Transparency International (ed.), *Policy Research Paper 001*, Sutton (available at: http://www.transparency.org.uk > TI (UK) Papers and Newsletters).

Craig, P. and G. de Búrca (1995), *EC Law: Text, Cases and Materials*, Oxford.

Cramer, P. (2001), commentary of § 311 in A. Schönke and H. Schröder (Hrsg.), *Strafgesetzbuch*, 26th edn, Munich, 2570.

Craufurd Smith, R. (1999), 'Remedies for Breaches of EC Law in National Courts: Legal Variation and Selection' in P. Craig and G. de Búrca (eds.), *The Evolution of EU Law*, Oxford, 287.

Crowe, R. (2005), 'The Schengen Acquis in Police Cooperation: Implementation in an Enlarged Europe', *ERA-Forum*, No. 3, Trier, 415.

Crutchfield George, B., K. A. Lacey and J. Birmele (1999), 'On the Threshold of the Adoption of Global Anti-Bribery Legislation: A Critical Analysis of Current Domestic and International Efforts Toward the Reduction of Business Corruption', *Vanderbilt Journal of Transnational Law* **32**, 1.

Cutler, S. (2004), 'Tone at the Top: Getting it Right', Speech by SEC Staff at the Second *Annual General Counsel Roundtable*, 3 December 2004 (available at: http://www.sec.gov > Speeches and Publications > 2004/fourth quarter).

Daams, C. (2003), *Criminal Asset Forfeiture: One of the Most Effective Weapons Against (Organised) Crime?*, Basel.

Dahm, G., J. Delbrück and R. Wolfrum (1989), *Völkerrecht*, 2nd edn, Berlin, New York.

Dalton, R. E. (1999), 'National Treaty Law and Practice: United States' in M. Leigh, M. R. Blakeslee and L. B. Ederington (eds.), *National Treaty Law and Practice (Austria, Chile, Japan, Netherlands and the US)*, Washington DC (available at: http://www.asil.org).

Davies, M. N. (2003), 'The Role of Agents and Sales Representatives' in F. Vincke and F. Heimann (eds.), *Fighting Corruption*, Paris, 57.

DeGeorge, R. T. (1987), *Military Ethics: A Code of Ethics for Officers*, Washington.

Delmas-Marty, M. (1994), 'Die Strafbarkeit juristischer Personen nach dem neuen französischen Code Pénal' in B. Schünemann and C. S. González (Hrsg.), *Bausteine des europäischen Wirtschaftsstrafrechts, Madrid-Symposium für Klaus Tiedemann*, Köln, Berlin, Bonn, München, 305.

Delmas-Marty, M. (1997), *Corpus Juris: Introducing Penal Provisions for the Purpose of the Financial Interests of the European Union*, Paris.

Delmas-Marty, M. (1998), *Trois défis pour un droit mondial*, Paris.

Delmas-Marty, M. (2002), *Towards a Truly Common Law: Europe as a Laboratory for Legal Pluralism*, Cambridge.

Delmas-Marty, M. and J. A. E. Vervaele (eds.) (2000), *The Implementation of Corpus Juris in the Member States*, Vol. **1**, Antwerp, Groningen, Oxford.

Deming, S. H. (2005), *The Foreign Corrupt Practices Act and the New International Norms*, Chicago.

Dietrich, O. (1998), 'OECD Convention on Combating Bribery of Foreign Officials in International Business Transactions', *Austrian Review of International & European Law* **3**, 159.

Distefano, G. (1994), 'La pratique subséquente des états parties à un traité', *Annuaire français de droit international* **XL**, 41.

DiMento, J. F. C. and G. Geis (2005), 'Corporate Criminal Liability in the United States' in S. Tully (ed.), *Research Handbook on Corporate Legal Responsibility*, Cheltenham (UK), Northhampton (USA), 159.

Dixon, M. and R. McCorquodale (1991), *Cases and Materials on International Law*, London.

Doering, K. (2004), *Völkerrecht*, 2nd edn, Heidelberg.

Dommel, D. (1999), 'Les défis de la corruption' (working paper, available at: http://www.transparency.org > Research and Publications > Country Papers).

Douglas-Scott, S. (2002), *Constitutional Law of the European Union*, Harlow.

Ehrmann, M. (2002), 'Procedures of Compliance Control in International Environmental Treaties', *Colorado Journal of International Law and Policy* **13**, 377.

Epping, V. (2004), 'Völkerrechtssubjekte' in K. Ipsen ed., *Völkerrecht*, 4th edn, München.

Eser, A., G. Heine and B. Huber (eds.) (1999), *Criminal Responsibility of Legal and Collective Entities*, Freiburg i. Br.

Feldman, D. (1993), *Civil Liberties and Human Rights in England and Wales*, Oxford.

Ferguson, J. (1999), 'The Basis for Criminal Responsibility of Collective Entities in Canada' in A. Eser, G. Heine and B. Huber (eds.), *Criminal Responsibility of Legal and Collective Entities*, Freiburg i. Br., 153.

Fisse, B. (1991), 'The Attribution of Criminal Liability to Corporations: A Statutory Model', *Sydney Law Review* **13**, 277.

Fisse, B. (1993), 'Rethinking Criminal Responsibility in a Corporate Society: An Accountability Model' in P. Grabosky and J. Braithwaite (eds.), *Business Regulation and Australia's Future*, Canberra, ch. 18.

Fisse, B. and J. Braithwaite (1988), 'The Allocation of Responsibility for Corporate Crime: Individualism, Collectivism and Accountability', *Sydney Law Review* **11**, 468.

Forti, G. (2000), 'Remarks on the Role of Criminal Sanction in a Sustainable Prevention of Crimes in the Public Administration. The Italian Experience of Systemic Corruption' in P. Bernasconi (ed.), *Responding to Corruption: Social Defence, Corruption, and the Protection of Public Administration and the Independence of Justice* (updated documents of the XIIIth International Congress on Social Defence, Lecce, Italy 1996), Naples, 173.

Frowein, J. A. (1968), *Das de facto Regime im Völkerrecht*, Köln, Berlin.

Gareis, R. J. (1999), 'The 1998 Amendments to the US Foreign Corrupt Practices Act: A Comparative and Pragmatic Analysis of, and with, the OECD Convention on Combating Bribery of Foreign Officials', *International Trade Corruption Monitor (ITCM)*, A-1013.

Geradin, D. and D. Henry (2005), *The EC Fining Policy for Violations of Competition Law: An Empirical Review of the Commission Decisional Practice and the Community Courts' Judgments*, Global Competition Law Centre (GCLC), Working Paper 03/05.

Gilbert, G. (1991), *Aspects of Extradition Law*, Dordrecht, Boston, London.

Gilbert, G. (1996), 'Crimes sans Frontières: Jurisdictional Problems in English law' in J. Dugard and C. Van den Wyngaert (eds.), *International Criminal Law and Procedure*, Aldershot, Brookfield (USA), Singapore, Sydney, 101.

Gilbert, G. (1998), *Transnational Fugitive Offenders in International Law, Extradition and Other Mechanisms*, The Hague, Boston, London.

Gilmore, W. C. (ed.) (1995), *Mutual Assistance in Criminal and Business Regulatory Matters*, Cambridge.

Gilmore, W. C. (2004), *Dirty Money: The Evolution of International Measures to Counter Money Laundering and the Financing of Terrorism*, 3rd edn, Strasbourg.

Glaessner, G.-J. (2003), *Sicherheit in Freiheit: Die Schutzfunktion des demokratischen Staates und die Freiheit der Bürger*, Opladen.

Global Witness (2004), *Time for Transparency: Coming Clean on Oil, Mining and Gas Revenues*, Washington.

Gobert, J. (1998), 'Controlling Corporate Criminality: Penal Sanctions and Beyond', *Webjournal of Current Legal Issues* 2.

Gordon, G. (2000), *The Criminal Law of Scotland*, 3rd edn, Edinburgh.

Guilmette, J.-H. (2004) [cited Guilmette 2004a], *The Power of Peer Pressure – Development Co-operation Among Nations Using OECD and IDRC Network Approach* (unpublished manuscript).

Guilmette, J. H. (2004) [cited Guilmette 2004b], *Peer Pressure Power: Development cooperation and networks - Making use of methods and know-how from the Organisation for Economic Co-operation and Development (OECD) and the International Development Research Centre (IDRC)* (available at: http://www.idrc.ca > search by full title).

Gurulé, J. and S. Guerra (1998), *The Law of Asset Forfeiture*, Charlotteville.

Hafiez, M. (2004), 'Mutual Legal Assistance and Repatriation of Proceeds – Pakistan's Experience' in Asian Development Bank (ed.), *Controlling Corruption in Asia and the Pacific* (key papers by speakers at the 4th Regional Conference of the ADB/OECD

Anti-Corruption Initiative for Asia and the Pacific in Kuala Lumpur 3–5 December 2003, online edition available at: http://www.adb.org/ > Publications > Controlling Corruption > Chapter7).

Hailbronner, K. (2004), 'Der Staat und der Einzelne als Völkerrechtssubjekte' in W. Vitzthum (ed.), *Völkerrecht*, 3rd edn, Berlin, New York, 149.

Hamilton, J. (2005), 'Mutual Assistance in Criminal Matters in Ireland and the Proposed European Evidence Warrant', *ERA-Forum Special Issue*, Trier, 53.

Haufler, V. (2001), *A Public Role for the Private Sector: Industry Self-Regulation in a Global Economy*, Washington.

Hawley, S. (2003), *Turning a Blind Eye: Corruption and the UK Export Credits Guarantee Department*, Sturminster Newton.

Heimann, F. (2004), 'The ICC Rules of Conduct and the OECD Convention' in F. Vincke and F. Heimann (eds.), *Fighting Corruption*, Paris, 13.

Heimann, F. and C. Mohn (1999), 'Die Rolle der Privatwirtschaft bei der Bekämpfung der Korruption' in M. Pieth and P. Eigen (ed.), *Korruption im internationalen Geschäftsverkehr: Bestandesaufnahme, Bekämpfung, Prävention*, Neuwied, Kriftel, Basel, Frankfurt a. M.

Heimann, F., G. Dell, A. Sng-Sachsenroeder and N. Whittier (2005), *Transparency International Progress Report: Enforcement of the OECD Convention on Combating Bribery of Foreign Public Officials, 21 January 2005* (available at: http://www.ipocafrica.org > Search by 'TI Progress Report').

Heine, G. (1995), *Die strafrechtliche Verantwortlichkeit von Unternehmen*, Baden-Baden.

Heine, G. (1999), 'Sanctions in the Field of Corporate Criminal Liability' in A. Eser, G. Heine and B. Huber (eds.), *Criminal Responsibility of Legal and Collective Entities*, Freiburg i. Br., 237.

Heine, G. (2000), *Corporate Liability Rules in Civil Law Jurisdictions*, (OECD Room Document [DAFFE/IME/BR (2000) 23], Paris).

Heine, G. (2001), 'Europäische Entwicklungen bei der strafrechtlichen Verantwortlichkeit von Wirtschaftsunternehmen und deren Führungskräften', *Schweizerische Zeitschrift für Strafrecht* **119**, 22.

Heine, G. (2003), 'Das kommende Unternehmensstrafrecht (Art. 100^{quater} et seq.)', *Schweizerische Zeitschrift für Strafrecht* **121**, 24.

Heine, G., B. Huber and T. O. Rose (2003), *Private Commercial Bribery – A Comparison of National and Supranational Legal Structures*, Freiburg i. Br.

Heinze, C. (1997), *Zur Frage der Vereinbarkeit der Aufnahme von Zypern in die Europäische Union mit dem Völkerrecht, dem Recht der EU und den Zypern-Verträgen von 1959/60, Kurzgutachten der Republik Türkei* (available at: http://www.crh.camelot.de > Zypern > Veröffentlichungen zum Zypernkonflikt).

Henzelin, M. (2005), '"Ne bis in idem": un principe à géométrie variable', *Revue Pénale Suisse*, Tome **123**, 345.

Hillier, T. (1998), *Sourcebook on Public International Law*, London.

Hines, J. R. (1995), *Forbidden Payment: Foreign Bribery and American Business After 1977* (National Bureau of Economic Research Working Paper 5266, available at: http://www.nber.org > Publications > Working Papers).

Hodgson Committee (1984), *Profits of Crime and their Recovery: The Report of a Committee chaired by Sir Derek Hodgson*, London.

Horn, F. (1988), *Reservations and Interpretative Declarations to Multilateral Treaties*, Amsterdam, Oxford, North-Holland.

Huber, B. (2002), 'Sanctions Against Bribery Offences in Criminal Law' in C. Fijnaut and L. Huberts (eds.), *Corruption, Integrity and Law Enforcement*, Leiden, Boston, 137.

Huet, A. and R. Koering-Joulin (2005), *Droit pénal international*, 3rd edn, Paris.

Institute of Business Ethics, Codes of Conduct (available at: http://www.ibe.org.uk> Site Map>Codes of Conduct).

International Chamber of Commerce (2000), *Fighting Bribery: A Corporate Practices Manual*, London.

International Federation of Accountants (2005), *Handbook of International Auditing, Assurance, and Ethics Pronouncements* (available at: http://www.ifac.org).

Janis, M., R. Kay and A. Bradley (2000), *European Human Rights Law: Text and Materials*, 2nd edn, Oxford.

Jean-Pierre, T. (2003), *Taiwan Connection: Scandales et meurtres au coeur de la République*, Paris.

Jenkins, R. (2001), 'Corporate Codes of Conduct, Self-Regulation in a Global Economy', *UN Research Institute for Social Development*, 21.

Jescheck, H.H. and T. Weigend (1996), *Lehrbuch des Strafrechts: Allgemeiner Teil*, 5th edn, Berlin.

Jung, H. (1979), 'Die Inlandsteilnahme an ausländischer strafloser Haupttat. Regelungsgehalt und Problematik des § 9 Abs. 2 Satz 2 StGB', *Juristenzeitschrift* 1979, 325.

Jung, H. (1986), 'Legalität oder Opportunität im Strafverfahren?' in H. Prütting (Hrsg.), *Recht und Gesetz im Dialog* III, Köln, 55.

Kerse, C. and N. Khan (2005), *EC Antitrust Procedures*, 5th edn, London.

Kilchling, M. (Hrsg.) (2002), *Die Praxis der Gewinnabschöpfung in Europa*, Freiburg i. Br.

Knill, C. and D. Lehmkuhl (2002), 'Private Actors and the State: Internationalization and Changing Patterns of Governance', *Governance: An International Journal of Policy, Administration, and Institutions* **15**, No. 1, 41.

Kontorovich, E. (2004), 'The Piracy Analogy: Modern Universal Jurisdiction's Hollow Foundation', *Harvard International Law Journal*, Vol. **45**, No. 1, 183.

Kühne, H.-H. (2003), *Strafprozeßrecht*, 6th edn, Heidelberg.

LaFave, W.R. (2000), *Criminal Law*, 3rd edn, St. Paul (USA).

Langer, S.H. and J. Pelzman (2001), 'An Analysis of the OECD Convention on Combating Bribery of Foreign Officials' in K. Fatemi (ed.), *International Public Policy and Regionalism at the Turn of the Century*, Amsterdam, New York, 60.

Larguier, J. (1999), *Procédure pénale*, 17th edn, Paris.

Low, L.A. (2003) [cited Low 2003a], 'The Global Legal Framework: The OECD, OAS and Council of Europe Antibribery Conventions: New International Standards and National Anti-Corruption Laws: Challenges for Effective Implementation and Enforcement' (unpublished paper prepared for a Conference in Paris, April 2003).

Low, L.A. (2003) [cited 2003b], 'Milestones in Mutual Evaluation: The Phase 2 Review of the United States under the OECD Anti Bribery Convention', *International Law Forum*, Vol. **5**, No. 2, 101.

Low, L.A. (2004), 'Towards Universal International Anticorruption Standards: The United Nations Convention Against Corruption and other International Anticorruption Treaties: Too Much of a Good Thing?' (presentation at the 2nd Annual Conference of the International Bar Association, International Chamber of Commerce, and Organization for Economic Co-operation and Development, *The Awakening Giant of Anti-Corruption Enforcement* in Paris, 22-23 April 2004).

Low, L. A. (2005), 'Enforcement of the FCPA in the United States: Trends and the Effects of International Standard' (presentation at the 3rd Annual Conference of the International Bar Association, International Chamber of Commerce, and Organization for Economic Co-operation and Development, *The Awakening Giant of Anti-Corruption Enforcement* in Paris, 4-6 May 2005).

Low, L. A. and M. L. Burton (2000), 'The OECD, OAS and Council of Europe Antibribery Conventions – A Comparison with the Corrupt Practices Act: New International Standards and their Implications', *The California International Practitioner*, Vol. **10**, No. 2, 1.

Low, L. A., G. Tillen and K. Abendschein (2003), 'Country Report: The US Anti-Money Laundering System' in M. Pieth and G. Aiolfi (eds.), *A Comparative Guide to Anti-Money Laundering: A Critical Analysis of Systems in Singapore, Switzerland, the UK and the USA*, (study by the Basel Institute on Goveranance, commissioned by the Stiftung Finanzplatz Schweiz), Cheltenham (UK), Northhampton (USA), 346.

Magrini, P. (2003), 'L'attuazione della Convenzione OCSE contro la corruzione negli Stati membri: il quadro comparato' in G. Sacerdoti (ed.), *Responsabilità d'impresa e strumenti internazionali anticorruzione*, Milano, 95.

Manacorda, S. (2004), 'Investigation and Prosecution: Prosecution Authorities' in P. J. Cullen (ed.), *Enlarging the Fight Against Fraud in the European Union* (Academy of European Law Trier Series of Publication, Vol. **36**), Cologne, 139.

Mauro, P. (1995), 'Corruption and Growth', *Quarterly Journal of Economics* **110**, 681.

McAdams, A. J. (2001), *Judging the Past in Unified Germany*, Cambridge.

McClean, D. (2002), *International Co-operation in Civil and Criminal Matters*, New York.

Metcalfe, D. (2000), 'The OECD Agreement to Criminalize Bribery: A Negotiation Analytic Perspective', *International Negotiation* **5**, 129.

Miller, S. K. (1998), 'Piercing the Corporate Veil Among Affiliated Companies in the European Community and in the U.S.: A Comparative Analysis of U.S., German and U.K. Veil-piercing Approaches', *American Business Law Journal* **36**, 73.

Mitsilegas, V. (2003), *Money Laundering Counter-Measures in the European Union: A New Paradigm of Security Governance versus Fundamental Legal Principles*, The Hague, London, New York.

Möhrenschlager, M. (1999), 'Developments on the International Level' in A. Eser, G. Heine and B. Huber (eds.), *Criminal Responsibility of Legal and Collective Entities*, Freiburg i. Br., 89.

Moody-Stuart, G. (1997), *Grand Corruption*, 3rd edn, Oxford.

Moreillon, L. (ed.) (2004), *Entraide internationale en matière pénale, Commentaire romand*, Bâle, Genève, Munich.

Müller, P. (2003), commentary *vor Art. 70* in M. A. Niggli and H. Wiprächtiger (Hrsg.), *Basler Kommentar zum Strafgesetzbuch I, Art. 1–110 StGB*, Basel, Genf, München, 1021.

Müller, J. P. and L. Wildhaber (Hrsg.) (1982), *Praxis des Völkerrechts*, Bern.

OECD (ed.) (2000) [cited OECD 2000a], *No Longer Business as Usual: Fighting Bribery and Corruption*, Paris.

OECD (2001) [cited OECD 2001a], *Behind the Corporate Veil - Using Corporate Entities for Illicit Purposes*, Paris.

OECD (2003) [cited OECD 2003a], *Peer Review, A Tool for Co-operation and Change*, Paris.

Oehler, D. (1983), *Internationales Strafrecht*, 2nd edn, Köln, Berlin, Bonn, München.

Parker, J. S. (1996), 'Doctrine for Destruction: The Case of Corporate Criminal Liability', *Managerial and Decision Economics* **17**, 381.

Passas, N. (1999), 'Globalization, Criminogenic Asymmetries and Economic Crime', *European Journal of Law Reform*, Vol. **1**, No. 4, 399.

Perrodet, A. (2002) [cited Perrodet 2002a], 'The Italian System' in M. Delmas-Marty and J. R. Spencer (eds.), *European Criminal Procedures*, Cambridge, 348.

Perrodet, A. (2002) [cited Perrodet 2002b], 'The Public Prosecutor' in M. Delmas-Marty and J. R. Spencer (eds.), *European Criminal Procedures*, Cambridge, 415.

Pesquié, B. (2002), 'The Belgian System' in M. Delmas-Marty and J. R. Spencer (eds.), *European Criminal Procedures*, Cambridge, 81.

Pieth, M. (1992), *Bekämpfung der Geldwäscherei – Modellfall Schweiz?*, Basel, Frankfurt.

Pieth, M. (1996), 'Die verjährungsrechtliche Einheit gemäss Art. 71 Abs. 2 StGB bei Bestechungsdelikten', *Basler Juristische Mitteilungen*, 57.

Pieth, M. (1997) [cited Pieth 1997a], 'International Cooperation to Combat Corruption' in K. A. Elliott (ed.), *Corruption and the Global Economy*, Washington, 119.

Pieth, M. (1997) [cited Pieth 1997b], 'Internationale Harmonisierung von Strafrecht als Antwort auf transnationale Wirtschaftskriminalität', *Zeitschrift für die Gesamte Strafrechtswissenschaft* **109**, 756.

Pieth, M. (1999) [cited Pieth 1999a], 'Die Strafbarkeit der aktiven Bestechung ausländischer Beamter' in M. Pieth and P. Eigen (Hrsg.), *Korruption im internationalen Geschäftsverkehr: Bestandesaufnahme, Bekämpfung, Prävention*, Neuwied, Kriftel, Basel, Frankfurt a. M., 341.

Pieth, M. (1999) [cited Pieth 1999b], 'International Efforts to Combat Corruption' in American Bar Association (ed.), *The Foreign Corrupt Practices Act: How to Comply under the New Amendments and the OECD Convention*, Chicago, E-1.

Pieth, M. (1999) [cited Pieth 1999c], 'International Efforts to Combat Corruption', *International Trade Corruption Monitor (ITCM)*, A-1038.

Pieth, M. (2000) [cited Pieth 2000a], 'From Ideal to Reality: Making the New Global Standard Stick' in OECD (ed.), *No Longer Business as Usual*, Paris, 51.

Pieth, M. (2000) [cited Pieth 2000b], '"Funktionale Äquivalenz": Praktische Rechtsvergleichung und internationale Harmonisierung von Wirtschaftsstrafrecht', *Zeitschrift für Schweizerisches Recht* **119**, 447.

Pieth, M. (2001), 'Internationale Anstösse zur Einführung einer strafrechtlichen Unternehmenshaftung in der Schweiz', *Schweizerische Zeitschrift für Strafrecht* **119**, 1.

Pieth, M. (2003), 'Die strafrechtliche Verantwortung des Unternehmens', *Schweizerische Zeitschrift für Strafrecht* **121**, 353.

Pieth, M. (2004), 'Risikomanagement und Strafrecht: Organisationsversagen als Voraussetzung der Unternehmenshaftung, Risiko und Recht' in *Festgabe zum Schweizerischen Juristentag 2004*, Basel, Bern, 597.

Pieth, M. (2006), 'Korruption in internationalen Wirtschaftsbeziehungen' in D. Dölling (Hrsg.), *Handbuch der Korruptionseindämmung*, München.

Pieth, M. and G. Aiolfi (2003) [cited Pieth and Aiolfi 2003a], 'The Private Sector Becomes Active: The Wolfsberg Process' in A. Clark and P. Burell (eds.), *A Practitioner's Guide to International Money Laundering Law and Regulation*, Surrey, 267.

Pieth, M. and G. Aiolfi (2003) [cited Pieth and Aiolfi 2003b], *Anti-Money Laundering: Levelling the Playing Field* (study by the Basel Institute on Governance, commissioned by the Stiftung Finanzplatz Schweiz), Basel.

Pieth, M. and G. Aiolfi (eds.) (2004), *A Comparative Guide to Anti-Money Laundering: A Critical Analysis of Systems in Singapore, Switzerland, the UK and the USA* (study by the Basel Institute on Governance, commissioned by the Stiftung Finanzplatz Schweiz), Cheltenham (UK), Northhampton (USA).

Pieth, M. and P. Eigen (1999) (Hrsg.), *Korruption im internationalen Geschäftsverkehr: Bestandesaufnahme, Bekämpfung, Prävention*, Neuwied, Kriftel, Basel, Frankfurt a. M.

Pieth, M. and J. Estermann, J. (2002), 'Landesbericht Schweiz' in M. Kilchling (Hrsg.), *Die Praxis der Gewinnabschöpfung in Europa*, Freiburg i. Br., 371.

Pletscher, T. (1999), 'Wie halten wir uns sauber? – Bekämpfung der Korruption aus Sicht der Wirtschaft' in M. Pieth and P. Eigen (Hrsg.), *Korruption im internationalen Geschäftsverkehr: Bestandesaufnahme, Bekämpfung, Prävention*, Neuwied, Kriftel, Basel, Frankfurt a. M., 275.

Poncet, D. and P. Gully-Hart (1999), 'Legal Framework of Extradition in Europe' in M. Ch. Bassiouni (ed.), *International Criminal Law, Procedural and Enforcement Mechanisms*, Vol. **2**, 2nd edn, New York, 277.

Popp, P. (2001), *Grundzüge der internationalen Rechtshilfe in Strafsachen*, Basel.

Posner, R. A. (1994), *The Economics of Justice*, Cambridge (USA).

Préfontaine, D. (1999), 'Effective Criminal Sanctions Against Corporate Entities: Canada' in A. Eser, G. Heine and B. Huber (eds.), *Criminal Responsibility of Legal and Collective Entities*, Freiburg i. Br., 277.

Price Waterhouse (1988), *Effective Internal Accounting Controls for Non-Profit Organizations: A Guide for Directors and Management.*

Prost, K. (1998), *Breaking Down the Barriers: International Co-operation in Combating Transnational Crime* (available at: http://www.oas.org/ > Documents > Search by Title > MLA Resources).

Reuter, P. (1995), *Introduction au droit des traités*, 3rd edn, Geneva.

Rose-Ackermann, S. (1999), 'Globale Wirtschaft und Korruption' in M. Pieth and P. Eigen (Hrsg.), *Korruption im internationalen Geschäftsverkehr: Bestandesaufnahme, Bekämpfung, Prävention*, Neuwied, Kriftel, Basel, Frankfurt a. M., 40.

Rumpf, Ch. (2004), 'Zur Rechtslage Zyperns: Grundlagen und Konfliktlinien' (available at: http://www.tuerkei-recht.de).

Sacerdoti, G. (1999), 'Das OECD-Überkommen 1997 über die Bekämpfung der Bestechung ausländischer Amtsträger im internationalen Geschäftsverkehr' in M. Pieth and P. Eigen (Hrsg.), *Korruption im internationalen Geschäftsverkehr: Bestandesaufnahme, Bekämpfung, Prävention*, Neuwied, Kriftel, Basel, Frankfurt a. M., 212.

Sacerdoti, G. (2000), 'To Bribe or not to Bribe?' in OECD (ed.), *No Longer Business as Usual*, Paris, 29.

Sacerdoti, G. (ed.) (2003), *Responsabilità d'impresa e strumenti internazionali anticorruzione*, Milano.

Salas, D. (2002), 'The Role of the Judge' in M. Delmas-Marty and J. R. Spencer (eds.), *European Criminal Procedures*, Cambridge, 488.

Sands, P. (2004), *Principles of International Environmental Law*, 2nd edn, Cambridge.

Sansonetti, R. (2001), 'Die Problematik der Offshore-Finanzzentren und die Position der Schweiz', *Die Volkswirtschaft – Das Magazin für Wirtschaftspolitik* **2**, 40.

Savona, E. (2002), 'Obstacles in Company Law to Anti-Money Laundering International Cooperation in European Union Member States' in M. Pieth (ed.), *Financing Terrorism*, Dordrecht.

Schaupensteiner, W. J. (1999), 'Korruption in Deutschland: Das Ende der Tabuisierung' in M. Pieth and P. Eigen (Hrsg.), *Korruption im internationalen Geschäftsverkehr: Bestandesaufnahme, Bekämpfung, Prävention*, Neuwied, Kriftel, Basel, Frankfurt a. M., 131.

Schoenlaub, F. E. (1999), 'International Bribery, Corruption and Fair Competition: Part 1', *International Trade Corruption Monitor (ITCM)*, A-1056.

Schubarth, M. (2002), 'Das neue Recht der strafrechtlichen Verjährung' in *Schweizerische Zeitschrift für Strafrecht* **120**, 321.

Seidl-Hohenveldern, I. and W. Hummer (2004), 'Die Staaten' in H. Neuhold, W. Hummer and Ch. Schreuer (Hrsg.), *Österreichisches Handbuch des Völkerrechts*, Vol. **1**, 4th edn, Wien, 135.

Shaw, M. (2003), *International Law*, 5th edn, Cambridge.

Shibahara, K. (1999), 'Le droit japonais de la responsabilité pénale, en particulier la responsabilité pénale de la personne morale' in A. Eser, G. Heine and B. Huber (eds.), *Criminal Responsibility of Legal and Collective Entities*, Freiburg i. Br., 39.

Sinclair, I. M. (1973), *The Vienna Convention on the Law of Treaties*, Manchester.

Spencer, J. R. (2002), 'Introduction' in M. Delmas-Marty and J. R. Spencer (eds.), *European Criminal Procedures*, Cambridge, 1.

Spencer, J. R. (2005), 'An Academic Critique of the EU Acquis in Relation to Trans-Border Evidence Gathering', *ERA-Forum Special Issue*, Trier, 28.

Spinellis, D. D. (1999), 'Securing Evidence Abroad: A European Perspective' in M. Ch. Bassiouni (ed.), *International Criminal Law, Procedural and Enforcement Mechanisms*, Vol. **2**, 2nd edn, New York, 359.

Stefani, G., G. Levasseur and B. Bouloc (2000), *Procédure pénale*, 17th edn, Paris.

Stree, W. and D. Sternberg-Lieben (2001), commentary of §§ 78-79 in A. Schönke and H. Schröder (Hrsg.), *Strafgesetzbuch Kommentar*, 26th edn, Munich.

Swart, B. (1999), 'The European Union and the Schengen Agreement' in M. Ch. Bassiouni (ed.), *International Criminal Law, Procedural and Enforcement Mechanisms*, Vol. **2**, 2nd edn, New York, 177.

Tarullo, D. K. (2004), 'The Limits of Institutional Design: Implementing the OECD Anti-Bribery Convention', *Vanderbilt Journal of International Law* **44**, 665.

Tobler, C. (2005), *Remedies and Sanctions in EC Non-Discrimination Law: Effective, Proportionate and Dissuasive National Sanctions and Remedies, with Particular Reference to Upper Limits on Compensation to Victims of Discrimination*, Luxembourg (Office for Official Publications of the European Communities).

Transparency International (ed.) (2000), *Overall Observations, Financial Transparency and Accounting Initiative: OECD Convention on Combating Bribery of Foreign Public Officials* (available at: http://www.transparency-usa.org > Publications).

Trechsel, S. (1997), *Geldwäscherei: Prävention und Massnahmen zur Bekämpfung*, Zürich.

Trepp, G. (1996), *Swiss Connection*, Zürich.

Tröndle, H. and T. Fischer (2004), *Strafgesetzbuch und Nebengesetze*, 52nd edn, Munich.

Tronnes, R. D. (2000), 'Ensuring Uniformity in the Implementation of the 1997 OECD Convention on Combating Bribery of Foreign Public Officials in International Business Transactions', *George Washington International Law Review* Vol. **33**, 100.

Tulkens, F. (2002), 'Negotiated Justice' in M. Delmas-Marty and J. R. Spencer (eds.), *European Criminal Procedures*, Cambridge, 641.

Tully, S. (ed.) (2005), *Research Handbook on Corporate Legal Responsibility*, Cheltenham (UK), Northhampton (USA).

US Sentencing Commission (2004), *Fifteen Years of Guidelines Sentencing* (available at: http://www.ussc.gov).

US Department of Commerce International Trade Administration (2004), *Addressing the Challenges of International Bribery and Fair Competition* (available at: http://www.tcc.mac.doc.gov > Bribery Complaints and Reports > 2004 Anti-Bribery Report).

Van den Wyngaert, Ch. (1993), 'Belgium' in Ch. Van den Wyngaert (ed.), *Criminal Procedure Systems in the European Community*, London, 1.

Van den Wyngaert, Ch. (1996), 'Double Criminality as a Requirement to Jurisdiction' in J. Dugard and Ch. Van den Wyngaert (eds.), *International Criminal Law and Procedure*, Aldershot, 43.

Van den Wyngaert, Ch. and G. Stessens (1999), 'The International Ne Bis In Idem Principle: Resolving Some of the Unanswered Questions', *International and Comparative Law Quarterly* **48**, 779.

Van den Wyngaert, Ch. (ed.) (2005), *International Criminal Law, A Collection of International and European Instruments*, 3rd edn, Leiden, Boston.

Vervaele, J. A. E. (2005), 'The Transnational Ne Bis In Idem Principle in the EU: Mutual Recognition and Equivalent Protection of Human Rights', *Utrecht Law Review*, Vol. 1, No. 2, 100-118 (online edn available at: http://www.utrechtlawreview.org > Archive).

Vincke, F. and F. Heimann (2003), *Fighting Corruption*, Paris.

Von Hirsch, A. (1987), 'The Sentencing Commission's Functions' in A. von Hirsch, K. A. Knapp and M. Tonry, *The Sentencing Commission and its Guidelines*, Boston, 3.

Von Hirsch, A. and A. Ashworth (2005), *Proportionate Sentencing: Exploring the Principles*, Oxford.

Von Hirsch, A., K. A. Knapp and M. Tonry (1987), *The Sentencing Commission and its Guidelines*, Boston.

Walther, S. (2004), 'Communication over Confrontation: Modern Criminal Procedure in Transformation' in A. Eser and C. Rabenstein (Hrsg.), *Strafjustiz im Spannungsfeld von Effizienz und Fairness*, Berlin, 367.

Warbrick, C. (2003), 'States and Recognition in International Law' in M. D. Evans (ed.), *International Law*, Oxford, 205.

Weinstein, M. J. and C. A. Trambley (2003), 'Obtaining or Retaining Business under the Foreign Corrupt Practices Act: The Implications of U.S. v. Kay and SEC v. Mattson' (presentation at the 2ndAnnual Conference of the International Bar Association, International Chamber of Commerce, and Organization for Economic Co-operation and Development, *The Awakening Giant of Anti-corruption Enforcement in Paris*, 24–25 April 2003).

Wells, C. (1999), 'Developments in Corporate Liability in England and Wales and a New Offence of Corporate Killing – the English Law Commission's Proposals' in A. Eser, G. Heine and B. Huber (eds.), *Criminal Responsibility of Legal and Collective Entities*, Freiburg i. Br., 119.

Wells, C. (2000), *Criminal Responsibility of Legal Persons in Common Law Jurisdictions*, (OECD Room Document [DAFFE/IME/BR (2000) 22], Paris).

Wells, C. (2001), *Corporations and Criminal Responsibility*, 2nd edn, Oxford.

Wells, C. (2005), 'Corporate Criminal Responsibility' in S. Tully (ed.), *Research Handbook on Corporate Legal Responsibility*, Cheltenham (UK), Northhampton (USA), 147.

Wells, J. T. (1999), *Fraud Prevention: A Fistful of Dollars* (available at: http://www.securitymanagement.com > Library > search by title).

Wise, E. M. (1999), 'Aut Dedere Aut Judicare: The Duty to Prosecute or Extradite' in M. Ch. Bassiouni (ed.), *International Criminal Law, Procedural and Enforcement Mechanisms*, Vol. **2**, 2nd edn, New York, 15.

Wymeersch, E. (2001), *Study of the Regulation and its Implementation in the EU Member States that Obstruct Anti-Money Laundering International Co-operation*, Trento.

Zander, M. (1999), *Cases and Materials on the English Legal System*, 8th edn, London.

Zimmermann, R. (2004), *La coopération judiciaire internationale en matière pénale*, 2nd edn, Berne.

Selected Documentation

African Union 2003, African Union Convention on Preventing and Combating Corruption, 11 July 2003, available at: http://www.africa-union.org.

American Law Institute 1987, Restatement of the law, third, foreign relations law of United States.

BCBS CDD 2001, Bank for International Settlements, Basel Committee on Banking Supervision, Customer due diligence for banks, October 2001.

Benelux Treaty 1962, Benelux Treaty on Extradition and Mutual Assistance in Criminal Matters of 27 June 1962.

Botschaft 1993, Botschaft (Switzerland) 1993 über die Änderung des Schweizerischen Strafgesetzbuches und des Militärstrafgesetzes (Revision des Einziehungsrechts, Strafbarkeit der kriminellen Organisation, Melderecht des Financiers) vom 30. Juni 1993, BBl. 1993 III 277 (93.058).

Botschaft 1998, Botschaft (Switzerland) 1998 über die Änderung des Schweizerischen Strafgesetzbuches (Allgemeine Bestimmungen, Einführung und Anwendung des Gesetzes) und des Militärstrafgesetzes sowie zu einem Bundesgesetz über das Jugendstrafrecht vom 21. September 1998 (98.038).

Botschaft 1999, Botschaft (Switzerland) 1999 über die Änderung des Schweizerischen Strafgesetzbuches und des Militärstrafgesetzes (Revision des Korruptionsstrafrechts) sowie über den Beitritt der Schweiz zum Übereinkommen über die Bekämpfung der Bestechung ausländischer Amtsträger im internationalen Geschäftsverkehr vom 19. April 1999 (99.026).

Bundesministerium für Justiz (Austria) 2004, Entwurf eines Bundesgesetzes über die Verantwortung von Verbänden für mit gerichtlicher Strafe bedrohte Handlungen (Verbandsverantwortlichkeitsgesetz [VbVG]), JMZ 318.017/0001-II2/2004.

Business Principles 2003 for Countering Bribery, An Initiative of Transparency International and Social Accountability International, June 2003, available at: http://www.transparency.org.

Circulaire 2004, Bulletin Officiel du Ministère de la Justice, No. 94, Circulaire de présentation des évaluations de la France par l'OCDE et le GRECO et fixant des orientations de politique pénale (CRIM 2004–06 G3/21-06-2004, NOR: JUSD0430119C, 21 juin 2004).

Conseil de L' Europe (1990), *see reference in Books and Articles.*

COE 1950, Council of Europe, European Convention for the Protection of Human Rights and Fundamental Freedoms (ETS No. 5, 4 November 1950).

COE 1957, Council of Europe, European Convention on Extradition (ETS No. 24, 13 December 1957).

COE 1959, Council of Europe, European Convention on Mutual Assistance in Criminal Matters (ETS No. 30, 20 September 1959).

COE 1972, Council of Europe, European Convention on the Transfer of Proceedings in Criminal Matters (ETS No. 73, 15 May 1972).

COE 1974, Council of Europe, European Convention on the Non-Applicability of Statutory Limitations to Crimes against Humanity and War Crimes (ETS No. 82, 25 January 1974).

COE 1975, Council of Europe, Additional Protocol to the European Convention on Extradition (ETS No. 86, 15 December 1975).

COE 1978a, Council of Europe, Additional Protocol to the European Convention on Mutual Assistance in Criminal Matters (ETS No. 99, 17 March 1978).

COE 1978b, Council of Europe, Second Additional Protocol to the European Convention on Extradition (ETS No. 98, 17 March 1978).

COE 1983, Council of Europe, Convention on the Transfer of Sentenced Persons (ETS No. 122, 21 March 1983).

COE 1987, Council of Europe, Committee of Ministers, Recommendation No. R(87)18 concerning the Simplification of Criminal Justice (adopted 17 September 1987).

COE 1988, Council of Europe, Committee of Ministers, Recommendation No. R(88)18 concerning Liability of Enterprises having Legal Personality for Offences committed in the Exercise of their Activities (adopted 20 October 1988).

COE 1990, Council of Europe, Convention on Laundering, Search, Seizure and Confiscation of the Proceeds from Crime (ETS No. 141, 8 November 1990).

COE 1997, Council of Europe, Resolution (97)24 on the Twenty Guiding Principles for the Fight against Corruption (adopted by the Committee of Ministers on 6 November 1997).

COE 1998, Council of Europe, Final Communiqué of the 102nd Session of the Comittee of Ministers (Strasbourg, 4–5 May 1998), available at: http://press.coe.int.

COE 1999a, Council of Europe, Criminal Law Convention on Corruption (ETS No. 173, 27 January 1999).

COE 1999b, Council of Europe, Civil Law Convention on Corruption (ETS No. 174, 4 November 1999).

COE 2000a, Council of Europe, Committee of Ministers, Recommendation Rec(2000)19 on the Role of Public Prosecution in the Criminal Justice System (adopted 6 October 2000).

COE 2000b, Council of Europe, Explanatory Memorandum to Recommendation Rec(2000)19 (adopted 6 October 2000).

COE 2001, Council of Europe, Second Additional Protocol to the European Convention on Mutual Assistance in Criminal Matters (ETS No. 182, 8 November 2001).

COE 2003, Council of Europe, Additional Protocol to the Criminal Law Convention on Corruption (ETS No. 191, 15 May 2003).

COE 2005, Council of Europe, Convention on Laundering, Search, Seizure and Confiscation of the Proceeds from Crime and the Financing of Terrorism (ETS No. 198, 16 May 2005).

Conseil de L' Europe (1990), *see reference in Books and Articles.*

CPS 2004, The Code for Crown Prosecutors (England and Wales), published November 2004, also available at: http://www.cps.gov.uk.

Cuban Liberty and Democratic Solidarity Act 1996, Cuban Liberty and Democratic Solidarity (Libertad) Act of 1996, Pub.L.No. 104–114, 110 Stat. 785, 814-822.

Department of Commerce 2004, US Department of Commerce, International Trade Administration, Adressing the Challenges of International Bribery and Fair Competition, the sixth Annual Report under Section 6 of the International Anti-Bribery and Fair Competition Act of 1998, July 2004.

Department of Justice 1999, US Principles of Federal Prosecution of Corporations, Washington, available at: http://www.usdoj.gov.

Department of Justice 2002, US Principles of Federal Prosecution, Washington, available at: http://www.usdoj.gov.

Department of Justice 2003, US Principles of Federal Prosecution of Business Organisations, Washington, available at: http://www.usdoj.gov.

Drug Trafficking Act 1994, United Kingdom Drug Trafficking Act 1994, chapter c. 37, 3 November 1994.

EEA 1996, The Economic Espionage Act of 1996, 18 U.S.C. 90, chapter 19, Sec. 1831 et seq., 11 October 1996.

EU 1991, First Directive on Prevention of the Use of the Financial System for the Purpose of Money Laundering (OJ L166, 28 June 1991, 77–83).

EU 1992, Treaty on European Union, *Maastricht Treaty* (OJ C191, 29 July 1992, 1).

EU 1995a, Convention on Simplified Extradition Procedure (OJ C078, 3 March 1995, 2–10).

EU 1995b, Convention drawn up on the basis of Article K.3 of the Treaty on European Union, on the Protection of the European Communities' Financial Interests (OJ C316, 27 November 1995, 49–57).

EU 1996a, Council Act of 27 September 1996, adopted on the basis of Article K.3 of the Treaty on European Union, drawing up the Convention relating to Extradition between the Member States of the European Union (OJ C313, 23 October 1996, 11).

EU 1996b, Protocol drawn up on the basis of Article K.3 of the Treaty on European Union to the Convention on the protection of the European Communities' Financial Interests (OJ C313, 23 October 1996, 1–10).

EU 1997a, Convention drawn on the basis of Article K.3(2)(c) of the Treaty on European Union on the fight against Corruption involving Officials of the European Communities or Officials of Member States of the European Union (OJ C195, 25 June 1997, 2–11).

EU 1997b, Protocol drawn on the basis of Article K.3 of the Treaty on European Union, on the Interpretation, by way of Preliminary Rulings, by the Court of Justice of the European Communities of the Convention on the Protection of the European Communities' Financial Interests (OJ C151, 20 May 1997, 2–14).

EU 1997c, Explanatory Report on the Second Protocol drawn on the basis of Article K.3 of the Treaty on European Union, to the Convention on the Protection of the European Communities' Financial Interests, text approved by the Council on 19 December 1997 (OJ C11, 15 January 1998, 8).

EU 1997d, Treaty of Amsterdam amending the Treaty on European Union, the Treaties establishing the European Communities and related Acts (OJ C340, 10 November 1997).

EU 1998a, Guidelines on the Method of Setting Fines Imposed pursuant to Article 15(2) of Regulation No. 17 and Article 65(5) of the ECSC Treaty (OJ C9, 14 January 1998, 3).

EU 1998b, Joint Action of 22 December 1998, adopted by the Council on the basis of Article K.3 of the Treaty on European Union, on Corruption in the Private Sector (OJ L358, 31 December 1998, 2–4).

EU 1999, European Commission Report of the European Antifraud Office (OJ C91, 31 March 1999, 8).

EU 2000, Convention on Mutual Assistance in Criminal Matters between the Member States of the European Union (OJ C197, 12 July 2000, 3).

EU 2001a, Council Act of 16 October 2001 establishing, in accordance with Article 34 of the Treaty on European Union, the Protocol to the Convention on Mutual Assistance in Criminal Matters between the Member States of the European Union (OJ C326, 21 November 2001, 1).

EU 2001b, Second Directive on Prevention of the Use of the Financial System for the Purpose of Money Laundering (OJ L344, 28 December 2001, 76–82).

EU 2002a, Consolidated Version of the Treaty establishing the European Community (OJ C325, 24 December 2002, 33).

EU 2002b, Council Framework Decision on Combating Terrorism (OJ L164, 13 June 2002, 3).

EU 2002c, Council Framework Decision of 13 June 2002 on the European Arrest Warrant and the Surrender Procedures between Member States (OJ L190, 18 July 2002, 1).

EU 2002d, Council Regulation of 16 December 2002 on the Implementation of the Rules on Competition laid down in Articles 82 and 83 of the Treaty (OJ L1, 4 January 2003, 1).

EU 2003a, Council Framework Decision on Combating Corruption in the Private Sector (OJ L192, 31 July 2003, 54).

EU 2003b, Protocol No. 10 on Cyprus (OJ L236, 23 September 2003, 955).

EU 2003c, Proposal for a Council Framework Decision to strengthen the Criminal-Law Framework for the Enforcement of the Law against Ship-Source Pollution, 2 May 2003 (COM (2003) 227 final).

EU 2003d, Council Regulation on the Implementation of the Rules on Competition laid down in Articles 81 and 82 of the Treaty (OJ L001, 16 December 2002, 1).

EU 2004a, Commission of the European Communities, Green Paper on the Approximation, Mutual Recognition and Enforcement of Criminal Sanctions in the European Union, 30 April 2004 (COM (2004) 334 final).

EU 2004b, Commission of the European Communities, Staff Working Paper: Annex to the Report from the Commission 'Implementation of the Convention on the Protection of the European Communities' Financial Interests and its Protocols: Article 10 of the Convention', 25 October 2004 (COM (2004) 709 final).

EU 2004c, Treaty Establishing a Constitution for Europe (OJ C310, 16 December 2004).

EU 2005a, Third Directive on Prevention of the Use of the Financial System for the Purpose of Money Laundering or Terrorist Financing (Ref. IP/05/682, 26 May 2005).

EU 2005b, Commission of the European Communities, Proposal for a Council Framework Decision on the Fight against Organised Crime, 19 January 2005 (COM (2005) 6 final).

Eurojust Annual Report 2003 (The Hague, February 2004), 60 et seq.

FATF 40/1990, The Forty Recommendations of the Financial Action Task Force on Money Laundering (29 July 1990).

FATF 40/1996, The Forty Recommendations of the Financial Action Task Force on Money Laundering 1990 (revised 28 June 1996).

FATF 40/2003, The Forty Recommendations of the Financial Action Task Force on Money Laundering 1990 (revised 20 June 2003).

FCPA 1977, Foreign Corrupt Practices Act (Pub.L.No. 95-213, 91 Stat. 1494).

FCPA 1988, The Omnibus Trade and Competitiveness Act 1988, Pub.L.No. 100-418, 102 Stat. 1107 (3 August 1988).

FCPA 1998, International Anti-Bribery and Fair Competition Act of 1998, Pub.L.No. 105-366, 112 Stat. 3302 (10 November 1998).

Geneva Convention 1958, Geneva Convention on the High Seas of 29 April 1958, adopted 30 September 1962.

Geneva Protocol 1977, Protocol Additional to the Geneva Conventions of 12 August 1949, and relating to the Protection of Victims of International Armed Conflicts (Protocol 1), (adopted 8 June 1977).

GRECO 1999, Resolution (99)5 establishing the Group of States against Corruption (GRECO) (adopted 1 May 1999).

Harvard Research International Law 1935, Draft Convention on Jurisdiction with Respect to Crime, *American Journal of International Law* **29**, 435 (supp. 1935).

HCCH 1954, Hague Convention on Civil Procedure (concluded 1 March 1954, entered into force 12 April 1957).

HCCH 1965, Hague Convention on the Service abroad of Judical and Extrajudical Documents in Civil or Commercial Matters (concluded 15 November 1965, entered into force 10 February 1969).

HCCH 1970, Hague Convention on the Taking of Evidence Abroad in Civil or Commercial Matters (concluded 18 March 1970).

House of Commons 2004, House of Commons Trade and Industry Committee, The Work of the Export Credits Guarantee Department, Sixth Report of Session 2003–2004, Vol. **1**, HC 506-I.

IAP 1999, International Association of Prosecutors, Standards of Professional Responsibility and Statement of the Essential Duties and Rights of Prosecutors (adopted 23 April 1999).

ICC 2005, International Chamber of Commerce, Rules of Conduct and Recommendations on Combating Extortion and Bribery in International Business Transactions (first adopted 1977, revised 2005).

Iran and Libya Sanctions Act 1996, Iran and Libya Sanctions Act of 1996, Pub.L.No. 104-72, 110 Stat. 1541, 1543, 1550.

Law Commission (England and Wales) 1996, Legislating the Criminal Code: Involuntary Manslaughter, Report No. 237, London (HMSO).

Law Commission (England and Wales) 1998, Legislating the Criminal Code: Corruption, Report No. 248, London (HMSO), 106.

Law Reform Commission (Australia) 2003, Report 102 - Sentencing: Corporate Offenders.

OAS 1996, Inter-American Convention against Corruption (G.A/RES/1398(XXVI-O/96, 29 March 1996).

OECD 1960, Convention on the Organisation for Economic Co-operation and Development (14 December 1960).

OECD 1992, Resolution of the Council concerning the participation of Non-Member Economies in the Work of Subsidiary Bodies of the Organisation (C(92)65/FINAL).

OECD 1994, Recommendation of the Council of the OECD on Bribery in International Business Transactions (adopted by the Council 27 May 1994).

OECD 1996, Recommendation on the Tax Deductibility of Bribes of Foreign Public Officials (adopted 11 April 1996, C(96)27/FINAL).

OECD 1997a, Revised Recommendation of the Council of the OECD on Combating Bribery in International Business Transactions (adopted by the Council 23 May 1997).

OECD 1997b, Convention on Combating Bribery of Foreign Public Officials in International Business Transactions (adopted 21 November 1997, signed 17 December 1997).

OECD 1997c, Council Decision of 19 December 1997, (C(97)240/FINAL).

OECD 1998, Procedure for Self- and Mutual Evaluation of Implementation of the Convention and the Revised Recommendation, Phase1 (DAFFE/IME(98)17).

OECD 1999, *Travaux Préparatoires* of the OECD Convention on Combating Bribery of Foreign Officials, International Trade Corruption Monitor (ITCM), 1001 et seq., also (DAFFE/IME/BR(97)14).

OECD 2000a, *see reference in Books and Articles.*

OECD 2000b, Guidelines for Multinational Enterprises (first adopted 1976, revised 2000).

OECD 2000c, Resolution of the Council concerning the Participation of Non-Member Economies in the Work of Subsidiary Bodies of the Organisation, 25 September 2000 (C(96)64/REV2/FINAL).

OECD 2001a, *see reference in Books and Articles.*

OECD 2001b, Guidelines for Multinational Enterprises: Text, Commentary and Clarifications, 31 October 2001 (DAFFE/IME/WPG(2000)15/FINAL).

OECD 2001c, Procedure for Self- and Mutual Evaluation of Implementation of the Convention and the Revised Recommendation, Phase 2 (DAFFE/IME(2001)3).

OECD 2001d, Notes by the Secretariat, The Liability of Legal Persons for Bribery Acts (DAFFE/IME/BR(2001)12).

OECD 2002, Update on the Implementation of the OECD Recommendation on the Tax Deductibility of Bribes to Foreign Public Officials in Countries Party to the Bribery Convention, (information as of January 2002).

OECD 2003a, *see reference in Books and Articles.*

OECD 2003b, Trade Directorate, Trade Commission, Action Statement on Bribery and Officially supported Export Credits, 20 February 2003 (TD/ECG(2000)15).

OECD 2004a, Resolution of the Council concerning the Participation of Non-Members in the Work of Subsidiary Bodies of the Organisation, 5 August 2004 (C(2004)132/FINAL).

OECD 2004b, Principles of Corporate Governance, endorsed by OECD Ministers in 1999 (reviewed in 2004).

OECD 2004c, Steps taken and planned Future Actions by Participating Countries to Ratify and Implement the Convention on Combating Bribery of Foreign Public Officials in International Business Transactions, 12 November 2004 (DAFFE/IME/BR(2004)9/REV2).

OECD 2005a, Steps taken by State Parties to Implement and Enforce the Convention on Combating Bribery of Foreign Public Officials in International Business Transactions, Submissions as of December 2005, available at: http://www.oecd.org.

OECD 2005b, Trade Directorate, Trade Commission, Working Party on Export Credits and Credit Guarantees, Export Credits and Bribery: Review of Responses to the 2004 Revised Survey on Measures taken to Combat Bribery in

Officially supported Export Credits, Situation as of 30 September 2005 (TD/ECG(2005)4/REV).
OECD 2006a, OECD Anti-Bribery Convention, Phase 2 Monitoring Information Resources, Paris.
OECD 2006b, OECD WGB, The Mid-Term Study (forthcoming) (DAF/INV/BR/WD(2005)19/FINAL).
PACI 2005, Partnering against Corruption, Principles for Countering Bribery, An Initiative of the World Economic Forum in Partnership with Transparency International and the Basel Institute on Governance.
Patriot Act 2001, United States Uniting and Strengthening America by Providing Appropriate Tools Required to Intercept and Obstruct Terrorism, USA Patriot Act of 2001, 24 October 2001.
POCA 2002, United Kingdom Proceeds of Crime Act 2002 (ch. 29, adopted 24 March 2003).
President's Commission 1984, President's Commission on Organized Crime, Interim Report to the President and the Attorney General, The Cash Connection: Organized Crime, Financial Institutions and Money Laundering 1984.
Sarbanes-Oxley Act 2002, United States Sarbanes-Oxley Act 2002, Pub.L.No. 107-204, 116 Stat. 745 (30 July 2002).
Schengen Agreement 1985, Agreement between the Governments of the Benelux Economic Union, the Federal Republic of Germany and the French Republic on the Gradual Abolition of Checks at their Common Borders (OJ 2000 L239 22 September 2000, 13).
Schengen Implementing Agreement 1990, Convention applying the Schengen Agreement of 14 June 1985 (OJ 2000 L239, 29 June 1990).
Securities and Exchange Act 1934, United States Securities and Exchange Act of 1934, 48 Stat. 881 (6 June 1934).
Securities and Exchange Commission 2003, United States Securities and Exchange Commission 2003, Final Rule: Management's Reports on Internal Control over Financial Reporting and Certification of Disclosure in Exchange Act Periodic Reports, SEC Release No. 33-8238; 34-47986 (14 August 2003).
Securities and Exchange Commission 2005, United States Staff Statement on Management's Report on Internal Control over Financial Reporting, Division of Corporation Finance, Office of the Chief Accountant, 16 May 2005.
Sentencing Guidelines 1991, United States Sentencing Commission 1991, Guidelines Manual, available at: http://www.ussc.gov.
Sentencing Guidelines 2004, United States Sentencing Commission 2004, Revised Guidelines Manual, available at: http://www.ussc.gov.
Sentencing Guidelines 2005, United States Sentencing Commission 2005, Revised Guidelines Manual incorporated with new amendments, 1 November 2005, available at: http://www.ussc.gov.
The Civil Asset Forfeiture Reform Act 2000, Pub.L.No. 106-185, 114 Stat. 202 (25 April 2000).
TI and SAI 2002, Transparency International (TI) and Social Accountability International (SAI), Business Principles for Countering Bribery, 9 December 2002, available at: http://www.sa-intl.org.
Treadway Report 1987, United States Report of the National Commission on Fraudulent Financial Reporting, October 1987.

Turnbull Report 1999, Internal Control, Guidance for Directors on the Combined Code, England and Wales, September 1999.

UN MTE 1990, United Nations Model Treaty on Extradition (A/RES/45/116, 14 December 1990).

UN MTMA 1990, United Nations Model Treaty on Mutual Assistance in Criminal Matters, (G.A/RES/45/117, 14 December 1990).

UN MTTP 1990, United Nations Model Treaty on the Transfer of Proceedings in Criminal Matters (A/RES/45/118, annex, 45 U.N. GAOR Supp. (No. 49A) at 215, U.N. Doc. A/45/49, 14 December 1990).

UN MTTS 1990, United Nations Model Treaty on the Transfer of Supervision of Offenders Who Have Been Conditionally Sentenced or Conditionally Released (A/RES/45/119, 14 December 1990).

UN 1961, United Nations Single Convention on Narcotic Drugs, as amended by the 1972 Protocol amending the Single Convention on Narcotic Drugs 1961 (adopted 30 March 1961).

UN 1966, United Nations International Covenant on Civil and Political Rights, (G.A/Res/2200A(XXI), 21 U.N. GAOR Supp. (No. 16) at 52, U.N. Doc. A/6316, 16 December 1966, 999 U.N.T.S. 171).

UN 1968, United Nations Convention on the Non-Applicability of Statutory Limitations to War Crimes and Crimes against Humanity, (G.A/RES/2391(XXIII), annex, 23 U.N. GAOR Supp. (No. 18) at 40, U.N. Doc. A/7218, 26 November 1968).

UN 1973, United Nations Convention on the Prevention and Punishment of Crimes against Internationally Protected Persons, including Diplomatic Agents, (G.A/RES/3166(XXVIII), 14 December 1973).

UN 1974, United Nations General Assembly Resolution 3237 (A/RES/3237(XXIX), 22 November 1974).

UN 1983, United Nations Security Council Resolution 541 (S/RES/541(1983), 18 November 1983).

UN 1988, United Nations Convention Against Illicit Traffic in Narcotic Drugs and Psychotropic Substances (adopted on 19 December 1988).

UN 1990, United Nations Guidelines on the Role of Prosecutors, adopted by the Eighth United Nations Congress on the Prevention of Crime and the Treatment of Offenders, Havana, Cuba, 27 August–7 September 1990.

UN 1996, United Nations Declaration against Corruption and Bribery in International Commercial Transactions (A/RES/51/191, 16 December 1996).

UN 1997, United Nations International Convention for the Suppression of Terrorist Bombings, adopted by the General Assembly of the United Nations (A/RES/52/164, 15 December 1997).

UN 1999a, United Nations International Convention for the Suppression of the Financing of Terrorism (A/RES/54/109, 9 December 1999).

UN 1999b, United Nations Security Council Resolution 1244 (S/RES/1244(1999), 10 June 1999).

UN 2000, United Nations Convention against Transnational Organised Crime (G.A/RES/55/25, 15 November 2000).

UN 2002, United Nation Security Council Resolution 1410 (S/RES/1410(2002), 17 May 2002).

UN 2003, General Assembly Resolution (A/RES/58/422, 31 October 2003), Annex United Nations Convention Against Corruption.

United States Sentencing Commission 2004, *see reference in Books and Articles.*

Vienna Convention 1969, Vienna Convention on the Law of Treaties of 1969 (UKTS No. 58 (1980), Cmnd 7964).

Wolfsberg 2000, Global Anti-Money-Laundering Guidelines for Private Banking (30 October 2000, updated in 2002).

Wolfsberg 2002a, The Suppression of the Financing of Terrorism Wolfsberg Statement (11 January 2002).

Wolfsberg 2002b, The Wolfsberg Anti-Money Laundering Principles for Correspondent Banking (21 October 2002).

Wolfsberg 2002c, Anti-Money Laundering Principles on Private Banking (revised version May 2002).

Wolfsberg 2006a, Wolfsberg Statement, Guidance on a Risk-Based Approach for Managing Money Laundering Risks (forthcoming 2006).

Wolfsberg 2006b, Wolfsberg Guidance on Public Corruption (forthcoming 2006).

World Bank 2004a, Guidelines: Selection and Employment of Consultants by World Bank Borrowers, May 2004, available at: http://www.worldbank.org.

World Bank 2004b, Guidelines: Procurement under IBRD Loans and IDA Credits, May 2004, available at: http://www.worldbank.org.

Subject Index